THE

LIFE AND WRITINGS

OF

JOHN ALBERT BENGEL,

PRELATE IN WÜRTEMBERG.

A

MEMOIR

OF THE

LIFE AND WRITINGS

OF

JOHN ALBERT BENGEL,

Prelate in Würtemberg;

COMPILED PRINCIPALLY

FROM ORIGINAL MANUSCRIPTS

NEVER BEFORE PUBLISHED.

BY THE REV.

JOHN CHRISTIAN FREDERIC BURK, A.M. D.Ph.

RECTOR OF GREAT BOTTWAR, IN WÜRTEMBERG.

Translated from the German

BY ROBERT FRANCIS WALKER, M.A.

CURATE OF PURLEIGH, ESSEX,

AND FORMERLY CHAPLAIN OF NEW COLLEGE, OXFORD.

Wipf and Stock Publishers
199 W 8th Ave, Suite 3
Eugene, OR 97401

A Memoir of the Life and Writings of John Albert Bengel,
Prelate in Wuertemberg
Compiled Principally from Original Manuscripts Never Before Published
By Burk, John C. F.
ISBN: 1-59752-199-X
Publication date 5/17/2005
Previously published by William Hall, 1837

TO THE

REV. C. F. A. STEINKOPFF, D.D.

MINISTER OF THE GERMAN LUTHERAN CHURCH,

SAVOY, LONDON, &c.

My Dear Friend,

It is now some years since you offered and rendered me very timely assistances towards securing the correctness of the present translation; it was a kindness not to be forgotten, and I take this opportunity of publicly and gratefully acknowledging it. To "paint a diamond" I shall not attempt; either by here saying more of yourself, or by praising the real jewelry of this book. Neither the one nor the other has any need of the kind. My thoughts will be better directed to whatever failures are attributable to my work or to myself, who have such bright examples before me.

Yet as I have often said how much reason I have to be thankful that I ever became acquainted with Bengel, so allow me to add, that the benefit I have thus alluded to will, I am confident, ever be increased by my remaining, what I now subscribe myself,

Most gratefully and affectionately

Yours,

R. F. WALKER.

PURLEIGH PARSONAGE,
26th June, 1837.

PREFACE

TO THE FIRST GERMAN EDITION.

In undertaking the present work, the author was fully sensible that Bengel deserved a far better biographer; but the solicitation of friends with whose wishes he has always felt it his delightful duty to comply, made him the readier to set about it; especially as among Bengel's numerous descendants he possessed the largest portion of requisite materials, with greater facilities than most of his respected relatives for collecting what remained in other hands. And through the kindness of such relatives and friends, he has been successful in doing it beyond what might have been expected for the memoir of one who died nearly eighty years ago, and who flourished not in the great theatre of the world, but in the more retired walks of literature and social excellence. Besides the published works of Bengel, and those earlier printed notices of his life, which are specified in the margin below,* the author has availed himself of the following unprinted documents:

I. Valuable Memoranda, contained in about 150 quarto leaves, (somewhat injured by a fire, which happened at Tübingen in 1789,) entitled "Bengeliana," or "Remains of Bengel," committed to writing immediately from his conversations; and partly transcribed from his papers during the years 1738—1752, by Ph. D. Burk, a familiar friend, curate, and son-in-law of the deceased.

* 1. J. J. Moser's "Account of Würtemberg," vol. i. p. 211. Tübing. 1729.
2. Ernst Ludwig Rathlef's "Memoirs of Learned Persons now living," vol. v. p. 426. Printed in 1742.
3. J. J. Moser's "Contributions for a Biographical Dictionary of living Divines," pp. 56, 789, 992.
4. Jacob Brucker's "Picture Gallery of Learned Men now living." Seventh Decade. No. 3. 1748.
5. John Philip Fresenius's "Authentic Memoir of the Life, Death, and Writings of John Albert Bengel."
6. Dr. William Gottlieb Tafinger's "Funeral Discouse at the Interment of J. A. Bengel, with Notices of his Life." 1752.
7. A variety of later memoirs of Bengel.

II. A quarto MS. half as large, containing many transcribed letters of Bengel and his correspondents; with memoranda of him by others of his curates.

III. A folio Memorandum, in which are found notices respecting the Church of the United Brethren, which he made use of in drawing up the "Sketch" of that Church, referred to in Part III. chapter xv. of the present work.

IV. Several fasciculi of his letters in his own hand, with replies to many of them, some in autograph, and others transcribed.

V. A quarto MS. of his Sermon Notes.

VI. A variety of detached compositions in his own hand, &c. &c.

These materials have supplied much that well consists with a full account of the life of Bengel; though, for mere biographical narrative, there was very little; nor could much of the kind be looked for; because the prominent events of his life, such as belong to more public men, are but few. But it was considered that those who respect his memory would wish to have as much as possible of his edifying remains; and that the larger class of those who were likely to welcome a new memoir of his life, would not be of the most learned description; a conjecture which was soon verified by the list of subscribers to this work. For the religious turn of thinking (in Germany) since Bengel's time, has taken such a direction among most literary men, and even among very many professed divines, that were Bengel now amongst us, he might with more propriety than ever call himself an "ecclesia monadica;" or "a speckled bird," (Jer. xii.) in the ecclesiastical world. Still the author could not well suppress every thing, which was likely to be less attractive to his less learned readers: but whatever is so, he has endeavoured to render popularly plain; and, it is chiefly on their account that he has subjoined an Appendix* of important matter. Nevertheless, some passages of this work will still fail of interesting those who are quite unlearned; the particular subject in hand not easily admitting of greater perspicuity: as in ch. i. of Part I., ch. i. of Part II., ch. ii. of Part III. &c. Whoever finds any difficulty in understanding these chapters, may omit them without having occasion to lay aside the book; as all the rest will be found both instructive and edifying.

The author has endeavoured to select from his materials such subjects as appeared the most valuable and interesting; and at the same time to bring together upon each subject whatever observations were plainest and most pertinent; so that the work contains many valuable remarks upon Education, Pastoral Theology, Pietism, Separatism, Church Government and Liturgical Services; likewise upon Author-

* This Appendix is embodied in the present work, under the author's direction.—Tr.

ship, Scripture Exegesis, the Spirit of the Times, Doctrinal and Moral Science, Prophecy, the Types of the Old Testament, &c. which will doubtless be read with pleasure by many. Bengel's thoughts upon this variety of subjects are here given just as they were found in his writings; no party or prejudice has been consulted; a true portrait of Bengel, and nothing else, was supposed to be the thing desired by the reader; and for its completion, Bengel's own writings were found sufficient.

One very important particular here demands a moment's attention. It was considered but justice to Bengel, that this work should comprise his views on the Apocalypse: for not only has his name been farthest known and most remembered on their account, but, by being misconceived or misrepresented, they have been the innocent occasion of very unfavourable opinions in the minds of some respecting him. Thus it has been confidently asserted in some popular publications, that he predicted the end of the world to happen in the year 1836: an assertion which will be found at variance with every thing he has written. In the present volume it will be seen with what correctness of judgment he contemplated the character of his own times, and with what surprising accuracy he foreshowed that of the times which have since gone by. This surely was a performance which did not entitle him to be ranked with those fanatical prophesiers who at seasons of great excitement and change have suddenly appeared like the fungi of a night's growth, and been nearly as soon forgotten. For though not one thing more than has come to pass of what he anticipated, should be accomplished; though upon all which yet remains of unfulfilled prophecy he should be found to have erred; still he would deserve to be numbered with those whom God from time to time has gifted with more than common insight into Scripture and human nature, were it only for those discoveries and anticipations which events have already confirmed. If we read with unbiassed attention his sentiments and inferences from the Apocalypse, as found in the following pages, (Part III. ch. vii.) we cannot well avoid the conclusion that he was gifted in no ordinary degree, to have spoken as he has done of future and distant times.

Nor let it be overlooked that Bengel, as he has expressly told us in these pages, "did not profess to deliver his opinion upon every subject of the kind with equal certainty;" and that he all along exhibits his views "not as articles of faith, but as things which would both admit of and require correction." As the appropriate season for trying their correctness seems nearly to have arrived, so his own anticipation is already fulfilling, that "he should for a time be slighted and forgotten, but by and by be again resorted to."

This publication will assist in evincing what further correctness may belong to his views upon prophecy: independently of which, if made use of, not for vain and curious inquiries, but as a repertory of motives to repentance or conversion, to amendment of life, and to patient continuance in well doing, it will be seasonable and useful. Practical, vigorous, and benevolent Christianity is the thing which is everywhere more and more wanted; and for the promotion of this, the compiler of the following Memoir commends it to the special blessing of Him, for whose honour and glory it was undertaken, and by whose gracious power and continual help it has been carried on and completed.

J. C. F. BURK.

THAILFINGEN,
30th March, 1831.

CONTENTS.

PART I.

BENGEL'S EDUCATION.

PART II.

HIS OFFICIAL ENGAGEMENTS.

PART III.

HIS LITERARY WORKS.

PART IV.

HIS PRIVATE LIFE.

THE

LIFE AND WRITINGS OF BENGEL.

PART I.

BENGEL'S EDUCATION.

CHAPTER I.

HIS LITERARY EDUCATION.

JOHN ALBERT BENGEL was born at Winnenden, a small town of Würtemberg, about five leagues from Stuttgart, on the 24th of June, 1687. He received the first rudiments of learning from his father Albert Bengel, M.A. assistant parochial minister of that town. He never forgot his father's "easy and pleasant manner of instructing" him, but used to speak of it with truly filial gratitude; so different was it from the method which then generally prevailed, and so much better adapted to improve the dispositions and abilities of children. But the kind and familiar tuition of such a father it was not long his privilege to enjoy; for this excellent parent* was suddenly taken from

* Of Bengel's parents some account is given in a course of Sermons on the Liturgical Epistles and Gospels, &c. by John Christopher Bilhuber, M.A. chief parochial minister of Winnenden, printed at Stuttgart in 1744; it is as follows:—

"The Rev. Mr. Bauder was succeeded by the Rev. John Albert Bengel, M.A. from 1681 to 1693, who was a man of piety and good learning, and diligent and punctual in all the duties of his office. He is still affectionately remembered by many an aged member of this church, some of whom have told me that in their early days they received benefit by his ministry which they could never forget. If ever the premature death of any faithful teacher was to be lamented here, it was him by an epidemic fever in the year 1693. Thus he "lost one chief human support of his temporal welfare, but not the providential care of his heavenly Father"; for David Wendel Spindler, a friend of the deceased, immediately undertook to superintend his education. This gentleman's qualifications for such an undertaking could only be equalled by his love to the bereaved child. But in consequence of the French invasion under Louis XIV., whose troops had already made considerable desolations in Suabia, his widowed mother's dwelling-house, which she had recently purchased, was soon afterwards reduced to ashes; and thus her late husband's library, which had been left to our little scholar, was totally lost. This, however, only served to make him thankfully acknowledge in after-life the kindness of Providence, which thus removed from him the temptation of reading too great a variety of books. Mr. Spindler, who previously to the French invasion had been master of a seminary at Winnenthal, was now obliged to remove from town to town, till in 1699 this excellent preceptor obtained a permanent station as tutor in the High School of Stuttgart. Little Bengel had all along accompanied him as a boarding pupil, and to him no removal could have been more favourable than this to Stuttgart; for, having made such progress in early knowledge that Spindler's elementary tuition was now insufficient for him, he was thus brought at once among the best instructors the country afforded, especially for those branches of education which were become almost absolutely necessary to him. His proficiency placed him directly in the senior class of what was called the middle school, conducted by Mr. Sebastian Kneer, an excellent Greek scholar, by whose valuable help he completed his elementary preparation within

that of this excellent man: for in the forty-third year of his age, and the twelfth of his well-discharged ministry at this one place, he was called away by a malignant fever then prevailing, on the 21st of April, 1693, as a good and faithful servant, to enter into the joy of his Lord. His attention to the sick by night as well as day, particularly in the adjoining hamlet of Hartmannsweiler, was indefatigable. He fearlessly entered the most infected cottages, caught the fever, and after a short confinement to his bed, was called home to God. This was indeed a trying season, for only four months afterwards our town was miserably destroyed and burnt to ashes by the French. Thus in the death of this valuable minister were again fulfilled the words of Isaiah, lvii. 1, 2. 'The righteous are taken away from the evil to come,'" &c.

His widow died at Denkendorf only a few years since, having fallen asleep in Christ, full of joy and peace in believing. She was daughter of the Rev. J. L. Schmidlin, rector of the cathedral of Stuttgart; and was a great grand-daughter of the famous Würtemberg reformer, John Brentius. Her name is still sacredly remembered and beloved by persons of this town, &c.

the short space of six months; so that at the age of thirteen he was promoted into the upper school, where, under the professors Meurer, Schuckard, Hochstetter, Erhard, Canstetter, Essich, and others, he advanced most satisfactorily in the dead languages, and gained very competent acquaintance with history, mathematics, French and Italian.

His mother, who remained ten years a widow, was married in 1703 to John Albert Glöckler, Esq. steward of the theological seminary of Maulbronn. This pious and excellent man was a real second father to him; a circumstance to which the church and learning appear indebted for the further advancement of our very hopeful young pupil, who long afterwards related that it was "by this second father's kindness and encouragement that he was enabled to proceed to the university"; so that in that same year he became a member of the theological College of Tübingen.

We do not know why his studies there in philosophy and in the higher branches of philology, were restricted to a single year, when two years was the usual time; but he "was enabled fully to make up for this at a more distant period." At Tübingen he attended the lectures of Andrew Adam Hochstetter, afterwards doctor of theology, Matthew Hiller, the professor of Hebrew, John Conrad Klemm, Rösler and Creiling. For more private study he chose Aristotle and Benedict Spinoza, and gave attention to Poiret, Leibnitz, and Bayle's "Dictionnaire Historique and Critique." The ethical treatises of Aristotle and Spinoza were valued by him as helps in moral philosophy, which he was studying under Hochstetter's public lectures. At the same time he acquired such competent knowledge of Spinoza's Metaphysics that professor Jäger set him to prepare and arrange materials for a treatise "De Spinocismo," which the professor afterwards wrought up and published. And Bengel expresses himself "thankful to be able to say, that his attention at that season to metaphysics and mathematics gave his mind a clearness for analysing and expounding the language of Scripture." He ended his philosophical pupillage with the degree of Master of Arts, at taking which he defended (as *respondent*) Professor Hochstetter's final *disputation*—"De Pretio Redemptionis," ("On the Price of Human Redemption"), when the latter was admitted to the faculty of Doctor of Divinity. Bengel, at this taking of his degree, showed such proficiency in academical studies that he was placed first of the men of his year, though most of them were older than himself.

He now entered on the study of divinity with the serious diligence of a christian student, especially as "he had long been disposed to inquire devoutly after spiritual things, and had always felt most delight in the holy Scriptures." Here he had the help of Dr. John Wolfgang Jäger, afterwards chancellor of the university; Michael Förtsch, soon after professor in the university of Jena; Christopher Reuchlin; John Christopher Pfaff; A. A. Hochstetter; John Christian Klemm; and Gottfried Hoffmann. Several of these, especially Jäger and Hochstetter, took much interest in him. Professor Jäger, for whom, as already mentioned, he had prepared materials for a treatise on Spinoza's Metaphysics, and who was now intending to compose a Church History, employed Bengel in making researches for the purpose. This being done under the professor's own superintendence, "habituated" Bengel "to that clearness of arrangement and expression which is so observable in Jäger's own works." With Hochstetter he was even more intimate: that learned man had the valuable faculty of "discerning in young persons any rising disposition to improvement, and knew how to direct it to their best advantage. He valued their youthful efforts, however weak and uninformed, which he always seconded and promoted by the kindest encouragement and advice. He would often give such a turn to any business in hand as to make young persons feel that by going on to complete it they were performing an acceptable piece of service to himself." Bengel found him a faithful and experienced guide in all his literary pursuits; and was led by him into many a pleasing and profitable exercise of the kind, to which his regular course of study would not have conducted him. Among these Bengel reckoned his doing him the honour of making him his respondent in the disputation above-mentioned, which consisted of subjects purposely selected for the occasion; likewise that he set him afterwards to superintend the correction of a new edition of the German Bible, whose summary, contents, and preface, were drawn up by Hochstetter himself. He approved and encouraged Bengel's undertaking to make the punctuation of that version, (especially from the book of Job to that of Malachi inclusive,) more conformed to the accentuated Hebrew, as far as could be done without altering Luther's own renderings. This was an employment which, while it made him more familiar with the original text of Scripture, may also be regarded as no unimportant preparative for his critical labours in the New Testament. It likewise gave occasion to his writing an essay on the Hebrew accents, which went to show, that though a general uniformity may be traced in the accentuation of all the prophetic books, yet each several book has further a distinct accentuation of its own, and that consequently the Hebrew accents, though they may not be of equal antiquity with the text itself, must be intimately connected with its genuine interpretation.

For a long time after he had quitted the university he had still the privilege of much personal intercourse with Hochstetter. Besides becoming his curate at the city church in Tübingen immediately upon his ordination, he served a curacy at Stuttgart, from 1711 to 1713, during which time his friend Hochstetter resided there as senior chaplain to the court; so that for nearly ten years Bengel had the benefit of that excellent man's familiar society, which may well be regarded as a valuable help to the formation of his future character.

Though he most attentively pursued at the university the course of private reading pointed out to him for benefiting by the public lectures upon the exegesis of the Old and New Testament, doctrinal and controversial divinity, church history, and homiletical studies, still he contrived to give also much attention to other theological works, particularly Spener's Latin treatise "On Impediments in the Study of Divinity," by the help of which he endeavoured to become familiar with the arrangement of theological topics; and deeply interested himself about the right handling of Scripture by reading Franke's "Prolegomena (or preliminary notices) to the Greek Testament;" as also his "Manuductio," or "Guide to the Study of the Sacred Writings." He perused the Old and New Testament repeatedly in the original languages, and in several versions; making use of Flacius, Glassius, Sebastian Schmid, and Hedinger, for textual elucidation; and of John Meyer's edition of the Seder Olam for its historical illustrations of the Old Testament. For catechetical purposes he studied Spener's German Exposition of the Catechism; and for the science of christian ethics, Arndt and Schomer; and though he studied the two last authors very diligently, he often wished he had read them many times more instead of treatises by others upon the same science. On creeds and confessions he made use of J. F. König's "Theologia Positiva Acroamatica," as he was attending J. Ch. Pfaff's public lectures on that work; but he afterwards studied the several creeds and confessions by themselves, and read the works of Chemniz and Spener in that department. "Such a variety of occupations gave him but little time for listening to "divers and strange doctrines," which we would often prefer to have been entirely ignorant of when we have to undergo the trouble of dismissing them from the mind. Yet he found it useful to depend less on his own isolated reading than on his free and familiar intercourse with experienced men of science, and on carefully recollecting and reconsidering their public lectures."

Having, with these studies, occasionally, during his last two years at the university, exercised his talent in preaching, and having in the twentieth year of his age completed his academical course of theology, he underwent examination for holy orders before the consistory of Stuttgart in December, 1706; held an academical disputation "De Theologiâ Mystica," ("On Mystic Theology,") at the commencement of the year 1707, (Dr. J. W. Jäger presiding as moderator;) and conducted a public disputation of students terminating their academical course of philosophy. He then quitted Tübingen to enter on a parochial charge, as provisional curate of Metzingen-under-Urach, and which he found to be a school of experience altogether new; for he was sent here, not as an assistant to an elder minister, as was usually the case with such young beginners, but into a sphere of labour entirely his own, and this from the great confidence placed in him. Hence he had to preach and catechize much oftener than an ordinary curate; and the entire care of the souls of his parish, together with the whole business of its church administration, rested with himself. What a field of ministerial knowledge and experience was here opened to him is expressed in his own Memoir, where he says, "My first fortnight's residence as curate of Metzingen convinced me at once what a variety of qualifications a young clergyman ought to have, but alas, seldom possesses, for such an office as this. How totally different is it from the notions one had formed of it at the university!"

Before he had passed a year in his country parish, he was called to take the office of junior divinity tutor at Tübingen. This situation, though quite of another kind, was far better suited to his improvement in knowledge and science, and to the general formation of that special character which he was afterwards to sustain. While it still afforded him plenty of opportunities for exercise in preaching, it required him to assist pupils in philology, philosophy, and divinity, which, with his having to preside at the regular doctrinal examinations, was likely to answer the very best purpose in completing his own acquaintance with each of those branches of learning. It also afforded him that intercourse with professors and old fellow-students which was not a little conducive to his own development. "Therefore," he observes in his own Memoir, "when one has spent some time among people out of doors, (in a country parish,) and acquired a *gustum plebeium et popularem*, become acquainted with the religious views, tastes, and prejudices of the common people, it is useful to return for awhile to college again in order to undergo a second theological education. Thus upon afterwards coming out, one is likely to labour with more matured experience and better success."

Of his progress in sacred learning at this period we have evidence in a Latin treatise which he composed "On the Holiness of God," (Syntagma de Sanctitate Dei;) which is highly spoken of in the "Corona Tübigensis," anni 1718, but was never in its original form committed to the press. The principal substance of it was embodied in his later works, as in his Commentary on the Apocalypse, 3d edit. page 310. It was a philosophical as well as theological treatise, and one of its objects was to show, from parallel passages of Scripture, that all the attributes of God are implied in the Hebrew expression קָדוֹשׁ (holy); and in ἅγιος or ὅσιος, by which it is rendered in the Septuagint; in a word, that the Divine holiness comprehends all his supreme excellency. He alleged several reasons for it in accordance with Scripture, and adduced quotations from the most eminent divines of every period, to show that it was no new opinion. But he modestly yet decidedly opposed the cabbalistic idea of Professor Neumann, of Breslaw, that every letter of the word קָדוֹשׁ contains some deep mystery, and he communicated the substance of his treatise to the professor himself, in a Latin letter. This occasioned between them an interesting correspondence, from which Bengel seems to have derived his thought of applying himself in earnest to the study of the rabbinical writings, which the professor encouraged him to do. But Bengel having been promoted soon after to the head tutorship of a theological seminary newly set on foot at Denkendorf, his leisure for the purpose was diminished, especially as he had to undertake a tour, at the expense of government, through a considerable part of Germany, to qualify him the better for his important situation.

This tour he commenced on the 7th of March, 1713, and completed it in September. He visited Nüremberg, Altorf, Erlangen, Kloster-Heilbronn, Coburg, Saalfeld, Rudolstadt, Weimar, Jena, Naumburg, Schul-Pforte, Weissenfels, Merseburg, Critz, Hanau, Heidelberg, Leipsic, Halle, and Giessen. He had intended proceeding farther into the north of Germany, but was deterred by the prevalence of a serious epidemic in those parts. He every where on his journey kept in view the great object of it, and made it his principal business to get well acquainted with the classical schools and other institutions of learning, in order to examine and compare their various methods of instruction, and the relative advantages of those methods; he obtained much interesting information for his purpose, and this the more easily, as a spirit of rivalry had arisen among the adherents to the old system, who disapproved of each other's particular plans as much as they agreed in opposing the new method of Spener and Franke. Their contention was briskly kept up in actual experiments, rather than in useless paper war, and turned upon the question, what they ought chiefly to teach, and in what manner. Spener's followers complained most of the neglect of Greek; that the Greek Testament in particular was too little even read, and still less explained by familiar remarks of grammatical, historical, and practical interest. They wished that young persons might be led on to their requisite attainments, not so much by the bare exercise of memory, as by that of the understanding; and their plan of education embraced, beyond that of others before them, a development of all the intellectual faculties, the formation of character, and above all, the fitting it for eternity. In their views of school discipline they differed from the standing method, as wishing that pupils should be always under vigilant inspection, as much during play hours and amusements as at school. Utterly disapproving of all needless restraints, and much more of every thing like harshness of authority, they desired only that serious spirit of watchfulness over the pupils' welfare, which, as proceeding from affectionate kindness and good sense, was best suited to promote in young persons an ingenuous, sober-minded, and consistent demeanour.

As this general movement upon education was very helpful to our inquiring tourist, in collecting the complaints, plans, and opinions, of the most experienced tutors, so it brought on a similar stir respecting *theological* instruction. While controversies about pietism grew warmer in many of the German provinces, enthusiastic separatists rose into considerable notice in others, and elsewhere fears were entertained lest the followers of Christian Thomasius should trouble the church with their subtle questions and opinions about natural law. Bengel kept accurate notes upon every thing he observed of this kind for his own future use. Some of them are in the writer's possession, and they evince how calm, considerate, and impartial an observer he was, and how he endeavoured to turn all to account. Hence he visited seminaries widely different from each other in their private plans and in their public confessions of faith, and made himself well acquainted with the theory and practice of their respective managers, which he describes with so much unbiassed simplicity that one is struck with the beautiful combination of his ability and modesty.

As he found this tour profitable to his general knowledge, as well as to his official purposes, we will mention an instance or two of its importance to him in his future capacity as an author.

Through his acquaintance with Mr. Stark, a very reputable professor of Hebrew, in the Leipsic University, he was confirmed in his conviction that Helmontius and Neumann were quite wrong in thinking that any hieroglyphical importance belonged to the Hebrew alphabetical characters. Stark had very seriously apprised Bengel of the dangerous errors into which such a speculation might lead, and instanced several learned persons who had thus almost reasoned themselves out of common sense. Bengel congratulated himself long after on being able to say, "that he knew nothing of cabbala, nor of alphabetical mysteries, nor of influences in astrology, nor of angelic appearances."

While he was staying at Heidelberg, Dr. Minz, of that university, drew his attention to the canons of scripture interpretation which had been published by Gerard Von Mastricht, which Minz strongly recommended to him as a clue to the intricacies of New Testament criticism. Of what importance this became as a hint to Bengel will be seen when we come to notice his own critical remarks upon the New Testament.

He heard, while at Halle, some of Dr. Anton's lectures on the Apocalypse; and afterwards got the whole course of those lectures transcribed for him. Professor Lang also, of that university, drew Bengel's first attention there to Vitringa's "Anacrisis ad Apocalypsin," or "An Impartial Examination of the Different Opinions of Writers upon the Interpretation of the Apocalypse." With that gentleman, as well as with other followers of Spener, he had several conversations upon those important developments of the kingdom of God, which they considered as approaching. These conversations suggested to his inquiring mind a train of ideas which formed the germ of his important system of Apocalyptical exposition.

CHAPTER II.

BENGEL'S RELIGIOUS EDUCATION.

EXPERIENCE shows that those who attain to true practical piety are chiefly of two classes. The one, which is the least numerous, find their whole life pervaded by a tender conscience and intimate communion with God, the small beginnings of which may be traced to the very first forming of their minds, and which has characterised, though not always in the same degree, every period of their existence. With the other, and far most numerous class, this divine communion has had frequent and long interruptions, during which it seemed to have totally departed; but has suddenly reappeared through the mighty operation of divine grace. Thus it is only the latter who can speak of any particular time of their religious awakening; for the former have always been as it were awake, though they also have had their aberrations, stumblings, conflicts, and temptations; but they have always manifested themselves from their childhood as children of God, and have been accustomed to consider and feel themselves such from their earliest years. They have grown up all along like healthy plants, having profited by their heavenly Father's discipline, correction, and manifestations of love. The most important seasons of their growth in grace have never been attended with those vivid experiences or striking changes which others can remember, who have at some period of their life quite departed from the right way, and by long spiritual slumber have so lost sight of God's paternal character, as to enjoy nothing of it; or who, by frequent repetition of wilful sins and by confirmed habits of vice, have even trampled upon their birthright, and been found amongst his open enemies.

Bengel was from early life an eminently pious and enlightened Christian. That "the memorial of the just is blessed" may truly be applied to him. Though upwards of eighty years have elapsed since his death, his memorial is to this day greatly blessed among thousands, not only in his own, but also in other and remote countries; and every where is he esteemed as one whom few of his cotemporaries, and still fewer of succeeding times, have surpassed in scriptural acquaintance with the mystery of the gospel, and in faithfulness to light received. But to attempt to point out any period when his spiritual life began, or to fix upon any one particular season as that of his awakening to practical piety, would be nugatory; for the devout consciousness of being a child of God appears to have been possessed by him from the first dawning of his mind, and to have remained with him till the end of his course.

Before he was six years of age, when he lost his father, he enjoyed such communion with God, and such a strength of faith, as to be quite persuaded he "could have detained his parent in this life, had he believed himself directed to pray for that purpose." In these his earliest years "he had many clear, pure, tender feelings and stirrings in his heart concerning God; and the texts inscribed on the church walls of his native town, from the Epistle to the Romans, concerning death, sin, righteousness, the crucifixion, &c. produced in him as a mere child emotions of great joy and peace, and left upon him very profitable and lasting impressions."

With this work of the Spirit of God within him coincided the religious instruction he received from others. "He enjoyed from his childhood the advantages of hearing and learning the word of God;" for his parents and instructors took pains early to store his memory with suitable prayers, scripture passages, and hymns. Presents of edifying books were given him from time to time as his mind advanced; and he would often purchase such books for himself with his little pocket money. These early favourites,* after he had become better able to value them, drew from him a grateful acknowledgment of "the kindness of Providence in putting in his way such things

* Such as Arndt's "True Christianity:" Sonthon's "Golden Jewel;" Gerhard's "Sacred Meditations," (in Latin); Franke's and Schade's "Introduction to the Reading of the Holy Scriptures," &c. Beside books of this sort, the frequent preaching of the parish curate, the Rev. John George Unkauf, was greatly blessed to him.

at the very time they were wanted, and the very best of their kind."

Thus with child-like simplicity he followed his heavenly Father's guidance, and submitted to God's inward and outward discipline; and though he did not yet fully understand what a high and rare privilege he enjoyed, the power of the divine word took such possession of his heart, that he had confidence in God, like that of a little child in its parent; took great delight in prayer, longed for the better life to come, loved the Scriptures, enjoyed the church hymns, and the simplest books of devotion; had a tender conscience, dreaded doing wrong, and showed complacency in every thing that was excellent.

Nor could these beautiful blossoms of his early piety long be entirely concealed from observation. Young Bengel possessed a large share of the love of his school companions and of every older person of his acquaintance. It was seen that there was something in him above his years, although the cause was not inquired after: indeed it was well for him in respect of his future development, that "his *piety* was not made very much of, so that he went on growing in grace, like "the grass, that tarrieth not for man."* "I went on in simplicity," he said, "under the idea that no one observed me, and was glad that I could proceed thus quietly." Did he then feel within him no stirrings of our common corruption?—"I was no stranger," he says, "to sudden and injurious suggestions and sallies of thoughtless, foolish levity, natural to youth, but the danger of my being led away by outward temptations was not frequent, as, in addition to our public lectures, I had always something to attend to in private, and thus was entirely preserved from idleness." At one time he had to instruct the junior scholars; at another he was busied in some recreative study or employment that was set him; at another he had some new book put in his way to read. But he most preferred spending his leisure hours in perusing that book which he had so early learnt to love more than every other—the Bible. Disrelishing all bustle and noisy distraction, he often retired for "serious and salutary meditation; for he ever deliberately preferred soberness to trifling, and loved above every thing that which had a pious tendency, finding his delight in devout, solid, and seemly words and actions, and feeling an aversion to whatever was loose, idle, and

* Micah v. 7.—That is, as the growth of the grass eludes the observation of man, though it is continually advancing under the blessing of heaven.

ungodly." Whenever he discovered any thing wrong in himself, though it was generally what no one would have noticed in him, his inward monitor instantly reproved him, and thus preserved him from stumbling upon outward temptations.

Fortified by such interior discipline of the Spirit, and kept in devout communion with his heavenly Father by the continual exercise of prayer, though he followed up the study of the heathen classics with great diligence, and almost with enthusiasm, he was not contaminated by what is found in them so pernicious to many. His lively apprehension of their beauties may be seen in his following remark upon Cicero's Orations:—"Cicero, from his earliest days, had studied mankind. This enabled him to depict so admirably their characteristic habits and passions. There is in all his orations, and especially in his philippics, such a flow of eloquence, that when one sits down to them it seems impossible to leave off. I have been afraid of reading too much of them at once, they have so carried me away."

But that he was not entirely free from spiritual temptation, while studying classical literature and the elements of philosophy at the High School of Stuttgart, may be inferred from a remark which he makes upon this period of his life. "My will was compliant; but many a doubt assailed my understanding. To communicate such difficulties to any one, in order to have them removed, was what I was too timid to do; hence I often laboured under secret anxiety, and disquieted myself with it to no purpose, by which I contracted the appearance of habitual reserve, and lost some of that ability for ease and freedom of manner which would have preserved me from seeming, as I must have done occasionally, somewhat singular. However, it often had a different effect in the eyes of others, though perfect strangers to me; for their first sight of me gave them a hope and confidence that I could feel for their mental trials, which they would readily disclose to me. And notwithstanding those constitutional ailments of mine, indeed at the very time when I was suffering under them, the gracious goodness of God afforded me such affecting discoveries and experiences of inward peace, that I felt encouraged, particularly on my first attendance at the Lord's supper, to persevere in child-like prayer; and that holy ordinance was a means of inciting me to it, and to a hearty desire of departing to be with Christ."

This simple account of his spiritual experience is not difficult to understand. His will, he tells us, was decidedly in favour of what is good; his affections found their enjoyment and repose in the gospel of Christ, as teaching us how to attain the chief good of man, and as promoting it in the most efficacious manner; but his natural reason would put in its claim, whether right or wrong, to demonstration and certainty upon truths which had already taken possession of his heart, and would prosecute that claim the more strenuously on account of his naturally superior mental powers, especially as they advanced in cultivation by classical study, and by increased spirituality and practical piety. A remark of his own is here much to the purpose:—"It would be worth while to discuss the proposition, that *conversion easily leads to heterodoxy*. It might be shown, first, that in divine truth very much depends upon the least things; and then, that through the weakness of our natural understanding we are far from being in a condition to apprehend divine truth as yet to its full extent, and consequently are bound to have great patience one with another. A raw, unconverted man, living after the course and fashion of this world, and therefore indifferent to the truth altogether, meets with no difficulty in subscribing to any form of doctrine. He takes a thing for granted, just as he finds it, and cares not for the trouble of proof. But a really converted man feels truth to be a precious thing; is disposed to inquire after it; preserves it when found; and handles it, as he would an invaluable jewel, with great care and circumspection. Finding it impossible to go on in a careless, trifling spirit, he is obliged to 'prove all things,' whatever trouble it may give him. Now as truth upon every point is not attainable without many a hard struggle, his progress is often, in the mean time, very slow, during which he may easily be mistaken for a person of heterodox opinions. But how lamentable is it when such ingenuous inquirers are thought worthy only of harsh treatment; when their brethren bear down upon them at once with puzzling propositions and perplexing interrogatories, and can think of no other method of dealing with them but the method of coercion; whereas, we ought rather to allow them the free liberty of disclosing to us every private scruple, that by their acquiring a confidence in us they may by and by suffer us to make an attempt to remove their difficulties."

Bengel's own spiritual difficulties at this period may be

conjectured from two or three notices of the kind among his papers. Speaking of the seven psalms, which are called *penitential*, and which young persons at school were specially taught to commit to memory, he notices that they "were so called long before the time of Luther, and contain very many experiences not generally familiar even to the most advanced Christians. Such passages," he adds, "occasioned me much perplexity in my younger days; for, wishing to measure myself by the measure I found in those psalms, I endeavoured to realize the same strong experiences, and could not. Many persons, perhaps, have perplexed themselves in the same disheartening manner." On another occasion he speaks of the blasphemous and bad thoughts with which holy persons are sometimes harassed, and says, "O, how many such darts have heretofore gone through my soul! They have occasioned me such distress and dejection in my younger days, as quite to alter my manner of behaviour to others; and I hardly knew how to prevent it."

We find him regretting at a later period, that during his two first years at Tübingen he had lost much time in doubts and difficulties about the purity of the text of the Greek Testament. He commonly at that time used the edition which, with an excellent preface by Professor Franke, is, in all other respects, copied from the Oxford one, which contains a mass of various readings, without showing which of them are preferable. Being at that time occupied in studying dogmatic theology, and having to look for proofs in his Greek Testament, he was perplexed with this medley of uncertainties; especially as in the divinity lectures of those days, at more universities than one, very undue attention was given to textual criticism. Our timid young student thought he stood alone in these perplexities, for he had not confidence enough to ask for their solution; and having long busied himself in them to no purpose, he found it necesary to lay aside this edition and to study the simple text. But such a season of discouragement had its advantages, for it "stirred him up to diligent prayer; and his being tempted to doubt as to the purity of textual readings was overruled into an early habit of accurately investigating every nice peculiarity of the word of God, which led him to ponder over some of its most important passages, prevented him from leaning to his own understanding, or to mere human authority, and left him but little leisure for extravagant fancifulness;" in a word, it wrought to the very best effect upon his future critical labours.

We may regard, as another advantage of this season of mental trial, his having learnt, that "the most important of all controversies are those we experience within us; of which there is no end, till the whole mind has undergone a change, and the whole man has struggled into renovation. When this is done, a host of casuistical scruples disappear at once, and we soon get rid of the remainder."* Indeed it was in more than one respect that his spiritual life became advanced by his residence at Tübingen University, especially at its theological seminary, which he entered just at the time "when the Lord had stirred up among the elder students a more than common zeal for true piety; a zeal that was followed by the most happy and lasting effect upon many." A number of well-disposed young men, having been stimulated by the example of students at other universities, (as Halle, Leipsic, &c.) had agreed to regard themselves as a society of christian brethren under obligation to diffuse among one another, and among their connexions, a practical knowledge of the written word of God, a vitally sound and actively well-doing spirit of Christianity. They wished not to waste in fashionable levities the fairest season of their life, but to encourage one another to devote the strength of its prime to the service of Him whose servants in a particular manner they were destined to be. At those years when worldly and fleshly lusts so easily fascinate the inexperienced into the snares of death, and actually impede so many in the way to happiness, temporal and eternal, they designed to strengthen one another for quitting themselves like men of God; and as early days were best suited for the formation of friendships, they wished to form such as, being consecrated by his holy fear, should insure every real blessing of that nature to the end of life.

A young man like Bengel, whom God had so early drawn to himself, and who, to use his own words of humble and grateful acknowledgment, "had experienced grace in his childhood a hundredfold more than sufficient to have destroyed the very life of sin within him," could not but regard it as a singular favour of Providence, and a great kindness of such christian friends, to be admitted into this social circle, and no longer obliged to go on as it were by himself. Doubtless he

* Bengel's words.

was welcomed by them as a valuable addition to their company, and they were glad to have among them a mind so richly gifted. As this promising combination was perfectly in harmony with the statutes of the university and of the college, and tended most happily to promote diligence in study and regularity of conduct, it was very kindly patronized by several of the professors, continued in a flourishing state during Bengel's four years at Tübingen, and was kept up by one succession of students after another through the whole of the last century. As it had been of such important service to Bengel at the outset of his manly piety, and as so many of his early and happy recollections were associated with it, he felt the most sincere joy at hearing, in 1747, that a revival had taken place in this society; * and in 1748, when he was on a visit at Tübingen, he took a most friendly part at one of its meetings.†

Besides this advantage from like-minded fellow-students at Tübingen, his residence there was particularly beneficial to him in respect of his tutors. Several of them, being men of lively faith in Christ, laboured to promote the spiritual as well as scientific improvement of their pupils; and among them we may especially name Dr. Christopher Reuchlin, and Dr. A. A. Hochstetter. Bengel speaks of the former as "a truly noble character," and says that "his lectures, and particularly those he gave just after morning prayers—indeed, whatever things he uttered at any time—were refreshing like the morning dew, full of power and full of life. He had nothing of affectation; neither used any high sounding expressions; but all was just with him as it should be; and at returning from his lectures, one felt as if returning from a sermon full of unction and energy. His manner was as instructive as it was persuasive and stirring; and whoever came to college in right earnest about practical religion, was soon made fervent in spirit by his means. He was clearly in the scripture sense 'strong in spirit;' and was instant and very affectionate in prayer. It was always profitable to get near him."

Bengel had the advantage of much intercourse with him; for it was one of Reuchlin's excellences, that he devoted himself most gladly and willingly to the students. Personal acquaint-

* Charles Henry Rieger, afterwards rector of the cathedral church at Stuttgart, was then one of the students belonging to it.

† For his brotherly and edifying address on that occasion, see Part II. chap. i. sect. 2, at the end.

ance with such a man must have been more valuable just then than ever; as he was ripening under severe trial for his approaching abrupt removal to a better world. He fell asleep in Jesus on the 11th of June, 1707, shortly after Bengel had terminated his divinity studentship; and the elegy inserted in his Memoir by some pupils who heard the last lecture he ever gave, was composed by Bengel.

Hochstetter also, who, as we have seen, was very useful to Bengel in learning, was equally so in promoting his welfare as a Christian. He was a sincere Christian himself, and a very learned divine; serving God with zeal, conscientiousness, and unwearied endeavours to extend the influence of vital Christianity. The following extract from a funeral discourse which he delivered upon the death of Reuchlin, where he strikingly describes the character of a true Christian, may serve to give us a better idea of himself.

"The children of this world," he says, "commonly use the words *godly* and *pious* in a way of ridicule. Of whatever rank or profession any one may be, if he will no longer live irrationally, extravagantly, or profligately as they do, and especially if he venture in brotherly kindness to remonstrate with his erring neighbour, that he may not suffer sin upon him; he is bantered or abused by them as a *pietist*, by which of course they mean a heretic. Nevertheless, there are such beings in the world as persons truly *pious;* persons who are in earnest to please God, having hearts of honesty, and not hypocrisy; persons who live by the faith of the Son of God; who, though they despise no man, cannot but love good order, and observe it in their conduct. Nay more, they are merciful persons, who, knowing what it is to feel christian love, evince what they feel by a sincere regard for the temporal and eternal interests of their fellow-men, go straight forward in the narrow way which leadeth unto life, and turn neither to the right hand nor to the left, to unsound doctrine or to ungodly and careless living. They are upright in their dealings, attentive to the duties of their station, and busy not themselves with other men's matters. *These* are they who are justified by Jesus Christ; their lives attest this fact; their study is to conduct themselves as the elect of God, holy and beloved; and to be holy in all manner of conversation, because he who hath called them is holy. Their upright walk before him is after the example of our Lord Jesus Christ; that example which he hath purposely left us, that we should follow his steps. And though things often go strangely with them in the present life, and they are sometimes treated as the offscouring of all things for Christ's sake, and have to pass through this vale of tears amidst many peculiar hardships and privations; still their outward tribulation, what is it but secret joy of spirit? and all the shame put upon them, what is it but their true honour and glory? Corrupt as is the present generation, we have not been without some bright examples of persons like these. Was not our departed friend, Dr. Reuchlin, a righteous man; and yet did he not seek all his righteousness in Jesus Christ? If there be any one who can contradict either of these facts, let him come forward and do so. Verily he gave all diligence to live holily, humbly, peacefully, meekly, and patiently. He could say with the apostle, 'Being reviled, we bless; being defamed, we entreat;' and he showed himself a very Nathanael, 'an Israelite indeed, in whom is no guile.' Did he 'speak the word of God?' It was 'with all boldness.' Did he visit the afflicted? He would never leave them without consolation. He set himself in opposition to false doctrine, and equally so to all unholy and hypocritical living."

A sincere minister of God who thus describes the character of a true Christian, is describing *himself*, or at least *the standard* he aims at, and to which he heartily wishes to conduct others. We may therefore safely rank Hochstetter with those by whom Bengel's youthful spirit received salutary impressions of the glory of genuine Christianity. But the benefit he thus derived from time to time by christian society, scripture, and excellent pious books, his heavenly Instructor saw fit to increase by a long severe sickness, which confined him to his bed in the year 1705, and which became so serious, that among his friends, though not by himself, his immediate death was fearfully expected. At this season of trial he enjoyed peculiar communion with God, who comforted him with the Psalmist's secret assurance, (Psa. cxviii. 17,) "*I shall not die, but live, and declare the works of the Lord.*" After he had thus passed some time under the discipline of the Cross, he recovered gradually, and was at length enabled, amidst the affectionate blessings of his parents, who had nursed him all the while with exemplary care and tenderness, to return from Maulbronn to his studies with renovated vigour, and enriched with most valuable experience from affliction. The whole residue of his years was one continued proof that his purpose "to devote entirely to God's service and glory this renewed grant of temporal life," was none of those vain resolutions which so many in affliction have made with no better effect than to deceive themselves, and to dissemble with God.

During his second residence at Tübingen, as Hochstetter's curate,* he kept a regular diary, for the promotion of his own knowledge and practice of christian truth. Every day he wrote on a separate leaf one or more thoughts that had occurred to him in meditation, reading, &c.—a practice, the advantage of which may be seen in the few instances we here bring forward.

"1711. June 25. A Christian should not leave off praying, till his heavenly Father, as I may say, give him leave, by permitting him to obtain something."

"June 26. As Böckler wrote memoirs of characters, in imitation of Velleius, so might memoirs be drawn up of scripture characters, as of Abraham, David, Joab, &c. But it requires much knowledge of scripture and of mankind to do it properly, for sacred and common biography are not the same. In the holy volume, the faults even of the best of men are impartially set down, and there we are informed how even such faults were graciously overruled to bring about good. But memoirs written by uninspired men are apt to dwell chiefly upon the *good* qualities and actions of their worthies; notwithstanding, there are times when the whole character of one and of another looks very critical."

"June 27. The greater genius and power of memory any one possesses, the more careful should he be not to neglect the cultivation of his judgment."

"June 28. That person will acquire moderation, who is ready to ask upon every occasion, Is it not time to refrain? And that person will acquire the power of silence, who on every occasion asks himself, Is it not time to be silent? But can any one excel in these things who is always quick at imagining, Is it not time to speak? Is it not time to eat, drink, sleep, &c.?"

"June 30. One's attention in hearing sermons will become more lively and fixed, either by taking notes, or by the habit of turning each matter, as we hear it, into prayer."

"July 1. In medical science there are three things in the following order; observation, consideration, application. It is so upon many other subjects."

"Aug. 1. The prohibited degrees in marriage may be com-

* See the former chapter, page 5.

pared to those consecutive tones in the musical scale which cannot harmonize, because they are too near together."

"Oct. 12. If in the course of conversation with others you find any subject upon which you are deficient, apply yourself immediately when alone to remedy the defect."

"Oct. 22. We should so arrange and contrive, as that all matters which are to occupy the attention at one and the same time may aid and support each other."

"1712. To keep the true middle way between too much activity and too much retirement, is one of the main duties of a Christian."

"The more crooked the mind, the oftener will the straightforwardness of Christ our Saviour have to cross it."

"1713. *Passiveness towards persons and things,* which is a kind of negative quality, is only of value as it respects the *activity of God.* When this finds a place in it, it is highly to be commended; otherwise it is good for nothing."

"How may I know that I am become an heir of heaven? How may I know that God is in me of a truth? When I have the earnest of the inheritance, that is, when I am habitually led by the Spirit of God, so as to walk in love, with my heart crying to him, Abba, Father! and listening to every whisper of his Holy Spirit. These are the fruits of (spiritual) baptism."

"We find in the Scriptures one and the same grand matter throughout. This is a delightful truth."

"We sit as it were in the centre of Christianity. What will God require of us, to whom he has committed so much!"

"Christ's own special commandments were no novel ones: Moses had delivered them long before. Is not the love of God and our neighbour the very substance of them? and yet the Socinians would teach us to regard Christ as a *new* legislator; yes, and as nothing more. Hence they choose entirely to overlook his priestly office; but that they may not appear to reduce him to an ordinary man, they extol his mission as "a teacher sent from God," and spin out christian morals very refinedly, as may be seen in John Crellius's 'Ethics.'"

"To abide in the Lord Jesus is very needful."

"The more we discover from time to time of God's faithfulness and truth towards us, the more do we feel urged to bless, love, and trust him, upon all occasions."

"The habit of instructing others gives a facility of communicating our thoughts in a distinct and perspicuous manner."

We may regard what we have called Bengel's religious education as finished by his tour through Germany in the summer of 1713. Ardent and successful as he was in the pursuit of intellectual acquirements, he never made these his principal, much less his exclusive object; and was disposed to avail himself of that tour in order to collect things valuable for the heart, no less than for the understanding; and "to seek out especially those excellent men, who, though rich in wisdom and goodness, had never communicated their treasures by the press." Hence he often met with persons of deep christian experience, as well as with many celebrated writers of the day; all of whom, in various ways, but in rectitude and singleness of heart, served the Lord Christ both publicly and privately, and sought to promote his kingdom by every laudable endeavour. Of these may particularly be mentioned J. E. Stolthe of Jena, Weidling of Weissenfels, L. C. Crell, the two Langs, Tennhardt, and Augustus Hermann Franke. His acquaintance with those excellent men was much more than a common exchange of civilities. He passed whole days and weeks in their domestic circles, and enjoyed the benefit of their converse when it most unbent itself. Though in them and in other valuable friends whom he had gained upon his tour, he found considerable differences upon religious points; some being zealous Lutherans, others rigid Calvinists, some Spenerians, others Inspirati, others Separatists, and one, at Altorf, of the Greek church, whose name was Alexander Helladius of Larissa; yet their very differences, considering how they agreed in the main matter of faith, hope, and endeavour, served only to instruct and edify himself. Every thing which could be urged for this or that religious opinion, his reflecting mind heard vigorously advanced by living advocates; a thing which influenced him far more safely than mere book-learning would have done, to take that happy middle course which is as distant from fanatical enthusiasm and sectarianism, as it is from cold and heartless speculation. He also conversed with many who were in evident, and even important error; but their amiable character and conduct, with their valuable and active beneficence, served only to confirm him in that noble forbearance of the true christian believer, which, as it is any thing but indifference, so is it most exercised by those whose faith in Christ, as the Saviour of all men, is the most confirmed. He returned home with his heart established in grace, humbled at having found so many far beyond himself in christian attainments, inspired with a holy zeal to follow up their examples, and enlarged in liberal-mindedness and love. And as he could not but witness, what must strike every observant traveller in Europe, the awful corruption of the world at large, especially when he heard so many pious and eminently gifted men affectingly complain of the manifold daily hinderances thrown in the way of their activity for the kingdom of God, how could he help ejaculating, with the believing Psalmist, for his country and for mankind, "O that the salvation were come out of Zion: O that the Lord would deliver his people out of captivity!"

We close our remarks on the advantages he derived from this tour, by inserting two letters which he wrote at the time from Halle, where he found real practical Christianity concentrated. The first was addressed to a young friend, in Latin, and may serve to show the progress of his *mind;* the second is to his mother, and bespeaks the improvement of his *heart.*

"*Halle*, 17*th June*, 1713.

"My dear Cousin,

"I can assure you, that the farther I have proceeded on my travels, the more good I have gained: for which incalculable benefit I would ever be thankful to our heavenly Father, and would entreat you all who love me, to be thankful with me. I shall resume the account of my journey from where I ended in my letter to you from Nuremberg, on the 23d of March. The acquaintance I have formed with persons of eminent learning at Coburg, Saalfield, Rudolstadt, and Weimar, has afforded me many advantages. With remarkable kindness they gave me much interesting information, particularly with respect to the conducting of schools and academies. Indeed, I met with most information of this sort where I expected least. On the 5th of April I came to Jena. I had not intended making a long stay there, but, by the providence of God, I was introduced to a man of approved piety, and of no common learning, who received me under his roof, and treated me as one of his family: his name is Stolthe. He has great talent for awakening and stirring up others, by which he has been useful to many of the young, and his usefulness in this way is daily increasing. Many suspect or envy him, and consequently hate him; but others are most affectionately attached to him, are glad to have his guidance in their studies, and are in closest communion with him by mutual prayer. Every Lord's day he holds a prayer-meeting in his house, and another for exposition daily after dinner. To students preparing to communicate at the Lord's table, he gives instruction for several weeks beforehand, by particular exposition of subjects from the catechism.

"I derived so much benefit from the company of Buddeus and other learned men, that I stayed more than six weeks at Jena: after which I went by Naumburg and Schul-Pforte to Weissenfels, where I passed ten days, most of the time with Christian Weidling, who was very kind and affectionate, though I had honestly told him how the friends at Halle had gained my heart more than all others on my journey. He is a pious, active, and very successful man in education. He commences all its business with prayer, and loses no opportunity of giving valuable hints and encouragements in the best sense, to his pupils. He considers it very important to recapitulate with them whatever they have learnt; rightly judging it of prime consequence for them to be well grounded in all elementary principles.

"At Langendorf I viewed with great delight an Orphan Institution, which had been established by a pious carrier, named Bucher. I came to this place (Halle) on the 29th of May, and the first boarding-house I entered exactly answered my wishes; as it is but a little way from where the professors live, and is preferred by the more pious students. And now having got here, I have so much to tell you, that I know not where to begin; for I am *at Halle*, and could easily write a whole volume about it. First, I can assure you that every thing corresponds to the expectations I had formed of this seat of wisdom and piety, and delightful indeed do I find it to experience and see for myself, all that I had learnt from printed accounts. The new king of Prussia lately visited the Orphan-house, and conferred a special privilege upon it, which already is generally known. The Royal Pædagogium is in a very flourishing condition, and quite answers the description given of it three years ago in a printed account of its formation; besides that all can now be conducted with greater convenience than ever, as the tutors and pupils are brought under the same roof, having a new large abode assigned them at a little distance from the Orphan-house. In both of these establishments I find very much that is useful to myself; but the advantage I value most, is the kindness and attention shown me by Mr. Freyer. The Seventh Report of "*The fruits of God's continued care over the Halle Institutions,*" is now in the press. Breithaupt, with the consent of the university, has holden a public (Latin) disputation with Thomasius on the subject of polygamy, from which the latter came off much chagrined, and he declares that he is misunderstood. Dr. Anton gives expositions of the Apocalypse, and lectures on the Ecclesiastical History of the Seventeenth Century; in both of which he introduces, with much unction, a variety of general remarks, that discover deep wisdom. Dr. Franke, who is much in favour with the king, has begun a course of expository lectures on the Psalms. He takes one, two, or three, of the shorter psalms each time, and goes into an accurate investigation of their meaning and object; adducing, without any prolixity, quotations from commentators, ancient and modern. To the theological students he also gives edifying lectures upon his work, entitled, "Idea Studiosi Theologiæ;" likewise, casuistical lectures upon select passages of Spener's "Theological Views and Discussions;" for instance, Discussion I. pp. 15 and 162. At private devotional meetings, and in preaching, he is often very forcible and energetic, but never forgets love. He beautifully combines earnestness with simplicity. Michaelis reads lectures on the Acts of the Apostles; and Lang does the same upon the Epistle to the Hebrews: the latter, immediately after public prayers, delivers a practical lecture upon the Sermon on the Mount. I find him a very strict and grave man, both in his life and manners, which accounts for his peculiarly tart style of writing. He also reads a lecture on the Art of Preaching, which is attended with very good effect. Here he explains texts, and shows how to sketch out a given subject. Freilinghausen lectures also upon preaching, but quite in another way. He sets the students to preach before him in a church, and then delivers his opinion upon their performances. What delights me above all is, the harmony of these men among themselves, which they study to keep up by social prayer. Good people in general at this place seem to have much more confidence in one another than I have ever seen elsewhere; and this serves better than any other means to keep alive their exemplary spiritual zeal and watchfulness, and to prevent all drowsiness and lukewarmness. I regard it as no small favour of Providence, that I witness here so many noble living instances of what the power of the Lord can effect in us, and can make of us. I had heretofore thought myself a sort of isolated Christian, left almost entirely to my own resources; but here I learn something about the communion of saints. I have this day been again to hear Dr. Franke preach, and could not but particularly notice that this eminent man, who in his usual manner of preaching is extremely sedate and seemingly cold, as soon as he comes to touch upon the grace and glory of our Lord Jesus Christ, is at once quite animated, and filled with a holy ecstasy.

"I deem it a special advantage of my journey, to have seen, in so many various instruments of the Divine Spirit, such a diversity of his gifts of grace, and such manifold operations of the power of God sanctifying and fitting men for extraordinary activity and usefulness: so that by the whole, collectively, I am better able to imagine a perfect man of God, whom no single living character can adequately represent.

"Dr. Anton, in his lectures on the Ecclesiastical History of the Seventeenth Century, takes notice not so much of those great movements in the world which interest its votaries, as of the far greater work of God, which is quietly proceeding, and silently maturing through such external events; which is what too frequently escapes the attention of common historians. With this view he notices the triumph of the truth, as brought again to light by Arndt and his followers; the inefficacy of the opposition which set in against the principles of the Jansenists; the conversion of Dr. James Reihing, who came over to Protestantism, and was elected Professor of Divinity in the University of Tübingen, &c. Professor Lang has just commenced a course of literary lectures, in which he gives memoirs of learned men, and critiques upon their writings; but I must conclude, as it is impossible for me to relate all in this letter. I will tell you more by and by, God willing, when we meet."

We append to the above letter a few passages from his travelling diary, referred to at p. 9.

"Dr. John William Bayer, Professor of Divinity at Altorf, holds private meetings of his students; at which he gives them select passages of scripture to explain, and their expositions are finally enlarged and corrected by himself. As he disapproves of too strict a mode of education, he insists rather on such superintendence and admonition as shall not remit even during those youthful recreations which his own free and liberal disposition cheerfully allows."

"Stolthe, of Jena, says, that piety is at a low ebb in Holland, because they have nothing of the Cross there. Election to grace, he said, is general; but election to glory, particular; and that the ninth chapter of the Epistle to the Romans is to be understood of the election to grace, not of the election to glory. That the merit of Christ is not the *original moving cause* of preventing grace. That tears should not be suppressed in the pulpit, as they will often speak to the hearts of some of the audience; and that ten persons at once had recently been first affected, and spiritually awakened, by such simple means. Stolthe frequently recruits himself with bodily labour. He is very prudent, and never hastily puts confidence in any one."

"Weidner, of Schul-Pforte, allows his pupils eight days for each written composition. Of every such exercise the pupil writes a copy to give to him, and reads it before the whole school, when it is corrected in the hearing of all. He has found this practice very useful."

"Isaiah F. Weisseborn, of Jena, said in his sermon,—

"*Jesus* comes not without *salvation;*

"*Christ,* not without *anointing;*

"*The Son of God,* not without *his glory.*"

"Weidling, rector of the high school of Weissenfels, teaches in a very simple, clear, and accurate manner. He maintains that history ought to be studied at an early age, while the memory is active. He corrects all written exercises *vivâ voce,* and is very kind in his method of doing it. He avoids much talk and compliment when conversing with his pupils, but they all appear sensible of his kind-heartedness."

"Aulic-counsellor Schwope, of Merseburg, said, that some do harm by giving pupils too great a variety of things to attend to at once. That phrases for their exercises ought to be suggested to them: that Hildebrand did so, and not only gave their meaning, but explained and illustrated each word of them beforehand, speaking largely upon the different meanings and applications of Latin and German terms; and afterwards dictating an exercise by way of illustration. He added, that some of the most valuable men of the day had been educated at his school."

"Greitzman, of Critz, gives his pupils choice passages in Greek and Hebrew to learn by heart. Co-rector Herzog commends Poiret as an eminent philosopher. He directs his pupils to compose imitations rather than original essays, and to write narratives instead of letters or declamations."

"Junker, of Altenburg, is a most kind man. He admires the regulations and methods at Halle. In teaching the classics, he says, we should carefully explain the peculiarities both of Latin and of German words, though it may take up much of the time; and that rapid reading is only useful to more advanced pupils. He construes first, and the pupils repeat after him. He delivers all his instructions in the vernacular tongue. He reads the Greek Testament through with his pupils in the course of a year, taking every occasion for practical observations and exhortations as he goes on. Pupils refusing to submit to order after two or three admonitions, are dismissed from the seminary, that he may have no occasion for any severer discipline."

"Godfr. Vockerodt, of Gotha, is grave and strict, but affable. He is an advocate for the study of Aristotle; and says, that heathen ethics ought to be studied historically, and in the original authors, so that pupils may be ready, upon every ethical point, to tell what Epicurus, Plato, Cicero, &c. taught."

"Kessler, of Gotha, manages to make such pupils as write bad Latin, acquire in a few weeks a remarkable facility and correctness, by reading Castellio's version of the Bible. He disapproves of expurgated classics, and of substituting the Greek and Latin fathers for heathen authors, as he considers them inadequate to the ends of classical study."

"Pritius, of Frankfort, observed, that all successful education of young persons depends quite as much on attending to the proper direction of their *will*, as on cultivation of the understanding. He speaks highly of the writings of Poiret, as leading the mind so directly to God; and recommends Spener's 'Advices.'"

"Tennhardt received me very kindly. He is moderate and abstemious; mortifies the flesh, and is much concerned for the health of his soul. He cordially hates every false way. Respecting the word *within us*, he thus expresses himself:—That it is that which works out good in the human soul, by inciting and admonishing it to what is good. That even the heathen have this inward word. He thinks that very frequent preaching, especially at stated hours, is unprofitable and vain; and that notice of it by church-bells should be given only at such times as a minister feels *inwardly disposed* to preach. He strictly insists on the *moral* obligation of the Sabbath, because enjoined in the decalogue, &c."

"Breithaupt, of Halle, is inclined to regard it as one of the signs of 'the last time,' that the present generation cheats itself with the notion of its own excellence, dreams of being on the point of enjoying the very best condition, and regards the ancients as no better than old women in comparison with itself. These, he says, were just the thoughts that men had of themselves immediately before the deluge; but as 'God is not mocked,' so he is not to be imposed on by such thoughts as these."

We now give his second letter, addressed to his mother.

"*Halle*, 25*th Aug.* 1713.

"MY MOST DEARLY BELOVED AND HONOURED MOTHER,

"My filial affection and bounden duty have long been urging me to spare a portion of time for particularly addressing your pious spirit; and, as I cannot at present pour out my heart to you in person, I do it as well as I am able by a letter. I enjoy the consoling assurance, that our faithful God and Father in heaven continues to keep up in you that desire after himself and his everlasting mercy, which has long found its place in your heart; and that he will make it still stronger and more ardent than ever. O yes, this ONE THING is that which 'our soul longeth after' in the present transitory state. The few days that may yet remain to us in this life, cannot be more happily spent than in seeking, with constant care and diligence, to become partakers of the heavenly inheritance. Great as this inheritance is, its attainment is secured, if we only heartily *desire*, *accept*, and lay hold of it. In ourselves we have neither strength nor worthiness for that purpose; nor can any prosper spiritually who have not known and felt the reality of their own wretchedness, misery, poverty, blindness, and unfitness for all good. But in Christ Jesus are freely bestowed for our everlasting possession, the forgiveness of sins, the gift of righteousness, the peace of God, spiritual rest, consolation, joy, strength, life, fulness of content and satisfaction; and we have only to prostrate ourselves before the throne, with such utterances of the heart as these:—'Heavenly Father, I am thy creature! Thou hast made me that I might have the fruition, not of these transitory things of time, but of thine own everlasting blessedness! At present I live in this world, banished, with the rest of mankind, from thy house, on account of sin! In these ways of error have I suffered myself to wander farther and farther from thee, and have spent in vanity, indecision, and doubt, the time which I ought to have employed with all diligence in returning to thee as my Resting-place. I have gone astray like a sheep that is lost. Seek me, bring me back, and take me up! Teach me thyself the right way, and meet me in it; open mine eyes; withdraw not thy hand from me; leave me not, neither forsake me, O God of my salvation! Pardon all my sin, and especially the inbred corruption of my nature. Forgive my every transgression, through the precious blood of thy dear Son! Send thy Holy Ghost, and shed abroad thy love in my heart, that so I may possess the blessed scriptural assurance that I have verily found favour with thee. Keep also and preserve me, that amidst the sufferings of this present life I may possess my soul in peace, quietness, and tenderness, in constant spiritual watchfulness and sobriety; in contentment, meekness, joyfulness, love, and hope. Teach me perpetually to seek the one thing needful; to cleave to thee with purpose of heart; to find thy word my very joy; to hold perpetual communion with thee in secret prayer, and by inward prayer without ceasing; to lay up in myself a good foundation against the time to come. O God! be thou ever *my* God; that neither death nor life may be able to separate me from thy love, &c.'—All this variety of goodness our heavenly Father most plentifully and faithfully sets before us in the gospel, and has actually made it over to us by his holy baptism; moreover, the blood and continual intercession of our beloved High Priest and Saviour will ever be available for us and in us. Let us then apply every affection of the heart truly, and at once to these very things. And because the heart is naturally so weak, faint, and cold, so unprepared and so blind, it is highly advisable to complain of this its condition to our Redeemer himself; to read his word diligently and at all seasons, even though there may be ever so many temporal duties to be minded, and to hold it in meditation under all circumstances; inquiring particularly into our spiritual state morning and evening, betaking ourselves to the closet, and supplicating him who seeth in secret for the comfort and light of his Holy Spirit. The time past of our life should also be reviewed; and we should as it were anticipate and pre-occupy what of it may yet remain, so as not to waste our treasure, the quiet and peace of our souls, by any sudden changes and emotions of the mind, by natural timidity, by vain anxieties respecting temporal things, by indiscreet mixing in worldly society, &c. 1 Pet. iii. 2—6.

"And now I commit all this to that *sure* and *certain* blessing, the gracious favour of my faithful God and yours. On him let us venture all; to him let us commit every thing, my most tenderly beloved and honoured mother! Let my dear parent only set about it in the manner I have here described; let her constantly attend to prayer, serious meditation on the word of God, and continual elevation of the heart to him; let her be careful to keep whatever good thing God in such exercises has committed to her, and give herself sufficient time for these purposes; let her try this for only three days together, then act as he shall direct her,—and I am confident she will wonder at herself, and be enabled to praise the Lord. If she set out in this way with ever so much self-distrust and simplicity, let not that discourage her; it is so much the better. I have met with many instances upon my journey, which show that simplicity is any thing but a hinderance to the operation of Divine grace. Only let us ever take heed how the heart is disposed towards him, and we shall not stumble that we should fall. For we shall then have to pour out either humiliating complaints against ourselves, or longing desires after God, or acknowledgments of our joy in him: one good thought will produce another; and for this the book of Psalms, and a much-valued devotional manual of the celebrated Arndt, entitled his 'Paradise Garden,' are among the best outward helps. How happy are we when we have God for our shield and our exceeding great reward! May he be found such to my beloved and revered mother!

"I close my letter with assuring you, that my journey hitherto has been accompanied by many spiritual and temporal blessings to me; as also, that I am quite well in health: for all which let thanks be continually given to the Most High! May he ever increasingly manifest his goodness towards us, and write in the heart of my dear and honoured mother what I have here written. Amen."

PART II.

HIS OFFICIAL ENGAGEMENTS.

CHAPTER I.

AS TUTOR OF A THEOLOGICAL SEMINARY.

SECTION I.

IN THE SEMINARY ITSELF.

BENGEL returned in September to his native province, with a variety of useful information, fully resolved to devote his talents to the service of God. Meanwhile, the buildings for the seminary of Denkendorf were so nearly completed, that before the end of November he was able to commence residence there. Accustomed not to take any step without an eye to the Divine will, to submit to it with child-like resignation upon all occasions, and to supplicate help from above, he entered on his new employment with special prayer and renewed self-dedication, and could say, "What passed between God and my soul the first night of my residence at Denkendorf, gave me good ground of encouragement for the whole period of my abode there." The following memoranda of rules for his own conduct, which have been found among his papers, may certainly be regarded as the fruit of his pious reflections of that very night; though they appear to have received some additions from his pen on subsequent occasions.

"Prayer and thanksgiving. Self-reflection. Laboriousness.

"Zealous exertion to advance the pupils of the Institution in their various departments of knowledge.

"Wise economy, especially in purchasing books.

"Temperance. Liberality to the poor.

"Looking to the Lord while engaged in the work.

"Careful observation of the least whispers of my thoughts and inclinations, as well those which arise of themselves, as those which are produced by outward impressions.

"Using all diligence to set an edifying example every where, and in every thing.

"Combating against fear and alarm of every kind.

"Perusal of the Scriptures: composition of spiritual songs.*

"Care of bodily health, especially of my eyes.†

"Devotion in prayer.

"Watchfulness against the devices of the Adversary.

"Suitable employment of vacation days.

"Writing letters at hours of relaxation.

"Early rising; retiring in good time to rest.

"Guarding against those digressions from main reading, which may be occasioned by having to refer to a variety of books.

"Much thinking; little writing.

"Letting small matters pass.

"Writing down good thoughts immediately, in an album always at hand for the purpose.

"Constantly aim at introducing profitable conversation.

"To note passages that have struck me in reading; to read them over again, and extract them at convenient opportunities.

"Careful attention to decorum.

"Frequent recurrence to these and other rules of prudence and holy living.

"Increased earnestness in listening to sermons, so as to lay particularly to heart whatever is especially delivered for that purpose.

"Withstanding all sudden strange thoughts and fancies.

"Never deferring to a more convenient season what may as well be done at the moment.

"He who has to impart wise and prudent instructions to others, must endeavour to have that clearness of ideas which will enable him to say much in few words; implying many things as pre-supposed, and leaving many others to be inferred."

---

* A few specimens of these are given in Part III. chap. xviii.

† One of his eyes, without any diseased appearance, had been dim from his childhood, so that he could not read with it. Bajers' "Regimen Sanitatis Literatorum," was his general adviser upon health.

How conducive must the faithful observance of such rules have been to "faithfulness in that which is little," as well as in greater matters; to spiritual, as well as temporal comfort and prosperity! Only thus was it possible for him successfully to attend to so many comprehensive employments in private, without suffering them to interrupt his pressing official engagements; not to mention his correspondence, which obliged him to write about twelve hundred letters annually.

The solemn dedication of the new Institution, and its commencement of labour, took place early in the following December. On the seventh of that month, the prelate, John Frederic Hochstetter, delivered his inauguration speech as its president; on the eighth, in the forenoon, Andrew Christopher Zeller, as senior tutor, did the same; and Bengel, in the afternoon, as junior tutor. His subject, which was one of peculiar interest, was luminously invested with his own manner of thinking. It was *De certissimâ ad veram eruditionem perveniendi ratione per studium pietatis,** (The diligent pursuit of piety is the surest method of attaining sound learning.) He began by remarking, how much it was to the honour of government that it had established this seminary at the present crisis, while the country was so menaced by hostile armies; † as it might be inferred, that Würtemberg regarded as *real* bulwarks her institutions of learning and piety, and considered it necessary to increase their number in the same proportion as her *other* bulwarks fell away. He then addressed the young persons who were to be received into this new nursery of theological learning, and showed what a privilege they ought to consider it to be placed at the most eligible season of life in a situation which afforded facilities for devoting all their time and strength to the noblest branches of learning. Hence it became them, as persons of integrity and prudence, to make the most diligent use of such providential advantages; for doing which, it was first and foremost indispensably necessary to be well aware what is that true centre of all valuable knowledge and exertion, around which alone every study and pursuit can beneficially revolve, and maintain such unity and consistency as are necessary to make them a real and permanent blessing. That this central and main

* The greater part of this speech is found printed in "Pregizeri Suevia et Wirtembergia Sacra," pp. 353–56.

† The French had lately taken Landau and Freiburg; so that Würtemberg was then in great peril.

matter had been ever one and the same for all undertakings in general, and for that of the sacred ministry in particular; in a word, that piety must be their focus, both primary and secondary. This was what had ever fashioned and governed the course of all the most truly learned and estimable characters; and if we admit Aristotle's position, that *natural abilities*, *instruction*, and *application*, are the three principal requisites for sound learning, then just so is fervent, practical piety, under the Divine blessing, the very life and soul of these requisites.

First, as to *natural abilities*. None but the practically pious man can develop these with that strength and that regularity which are needed for raising them to the highest improvement. For, the activity and efficacy of that grace of God which is bestowed upon the pious man, tends much more directly than the best natural tact, to help him with respect to all zeal and regular progress in science. And who can avoid seeing that there is no preservative like this against the many seductive allurements to which students, especially, are liable, and which have, in too many instances, blighted every hope and prospect of their attaining sound learning? Again, what is there like true piety to overcome our natural indolence, and to preserve the mind from disturbing passions; or that can impart to it that liveliness, force, and clearness, by which even a person of ordinary abilities, in search of the most recondite truths, will often outstrip the best gifted and most favourably circumstanced, who remain strangers to communion with God? What these can hardly learn, with all their diligence, and with the best assistances, will often present itself, as by a kind of intuition, to understandings no longer darkened with the exhalation of native corruptions and hereditary prejudices.

Secondly, with respect to *instruction*. It was a favourite maxim, even of heathen philosophers, that true wisdom begins in the knowledge of *ourselves*. Who, then, is so likely to possess this knowledge as the person that is always obliged to converse with himself in order to commune with his God? Self-knowledge is a constant attribute of true piety. Besides, it is only the pious person who will have free access at every season to the prime repository of all genuine knowledge. That repository is the sacred volume; and I say that it is freely opened to the pious alone, for none but they will faithfully follow its instructions, and consequently possess the clew to those unsearchable treasures of wisdom and knowledge which it contains. And this clew they possess for the benefit of others as well as for themselves; for whoever maintains real communion with God will be the better qualified upon every occasion to speak wisely and suitably to his fellow-men.

Thirdly, with respect to *application*. Surely it is only he who fears God that can find real content and satisfaction in his pursuits. Others may run after such satisfaction, but all their toil to overtake it in the fields of science will be in vain; and its phantom rather allures them on towards the most perilous abysses. Whereas, science itself, to those who love God, will be among the "all things that work together for their good."

He concluded with expressing it as his fervent and devout wish, that every pupil of the Institution would seriously address himself to God, imploring of Him that renewal of the heart and mind which is indispensable to real piety, and thus insure a prosperous and rapid advancement in all necessary and useful knowledge.

Bengel and his colleagues were now to enter upon the business of the Theological Seminary. The pupils were admissible from fourteen to sixteen years of age: their knowledge of Latin, Greek, and Hebrew, previously acquired at elementary schools, was here to be completed; and they were to be carried forward into the higher departments of classical and sacred literature. They were also to receive instruction in religion, in the elements of philosophy, and other necessary matters of general knowledge. In compliance with these requirements, Bengel, under the sanction of his colleagues, drew up a plan *raisonné* of study, for the use of the pupils rather than of the teachers, and entitled it, "The Denkendorf 'Dic cur hic?'" or, "Limites et Methodus Studiorum Alumni Denkendorfini;" *i.e.* "A Rationale of Study for the Theological Seminary at Denkendorf, containing the reasons for each branch of study, the limits prescribed to them, and the method to be pursued." This plan was not a mere dry catalogue of various scientific objects, but it furnished appropriate introductions to the attainment of each, and specified the advantages to be expected by the method it recommended. Another design of it was to preserve the pupils from remissness and its attendant discouragements; or else to restrain them from that youthful presumption which at first setting out, especially in scientific pursuits, is apt to prompt the notion of having attained every thing at once. Hence he detailed with brevity, but sufficient particularity, the proper routine of the several studies, together with—

1. What in each distinct branch was *indispensable,* what *useful,* and what merely *agreeable.* Thus the student of humblest abilities would be enabled to perceive, amidst the great mass of scientific matter before him, what was most requisite for himself.

2. How to profit from public lectures by diligent preparation in private, as well as by recollections of them; and what method of preparation, attention, and recollection, each department of study required.

3. Special directions how to apply the leisure time of every week-day to the best advantage. For the Lord's day, besides attendance at public worship, diligent reading of the Scriptures and of suitable pious books was recommended. Those week-days in which but few hours were thus vacant, were to be employed in preparation for lecture, and in reconsidering and reviewing what had been learnt; but those in which there was more leisure from public lectures, were to be given to more extensive private study. It was specially enjoined, that a full hour of every week-day should be spent in personal recreation, and this out of doors when the weather permitted; but that the rest of their recreation should consist of lighter reading, as in poetry, geography, history, &c.

4. Of languages, it was observed that, for present requirements, Latin demanded most attention; and then Greek and Hebrew; but the Oriental dialects, as proving of real use to scarcely more than one in a hundred, were to be studied only by pupils of best abilities, especially as acquaintance with modern languages was found to be more generally useful.

5. In order fully to answer the ends of classical literature, it was recommended to read diligently such Greek and Latin authors as flourished nearly at the same period; and the reading of Latin works, not reputed classical, was to be deferred till the student had acquired a pure Latin style of his own. Plautus, Terence, Catullus, Tibullus, and Propertius, were also to be reserved for a time of further advancement.

6. The relative benefits of each particular study; as, for instance, what advantage the knowledge of languages, logic, the science of the human mind, history, geography, &c. affords to the interpretation of writers, sacred and profane.

7. From special regard to the requirements of the Denkendorf Theological Institution, the preference among philosophical

sciences was to be given to *logic;* which, however, was to be kept as clear as possible of all trifling subtilties of the schoolmen.

8. Preparatory to the study of divinity, the Scriptures were to be carefully studied in the original languages as well as in the vernacular translation; and scripture passages proving every principal doctrine were to be recited and rendered familiar to the memory.

Finally, attention was recommended to a few general rules:—

1. Live piously, uprightly, wisely.
2. Beware of slackening in piety and diligent study.
3. Let your ONE OBJECT and endeavour in EVERY thing be, the glory of God, a good conscience, and sincerity about becoming instrumental to the good of the public.
4. Be careful to keep an accurate diary and memorandum-book.
5. Make appropriate extracts, and refer to them frequently.
6. Examine yourself from time to time, and especially at the close of each week, what progress you have made in every thing.
7. Avoid bad companions as you would avoid death.
8. But cultivate, as much as possible, the society of those who are pious, studious, and learned; seeking with all care to profit by whatever they say and do; and never value yourself upon your learning or piety.

Bengel's own earnest endeavours to promote the design of the Institution are further perceptible, from a passage written by him in the year 1740 (March 7th), which also shows that he set out with this general principle, that "the main business with a pupil is not merely to furnish him with a certain *quantum* of the various branches of knowledge, but to put him in the way of attaining a good state of thinking and feeling;"—rather to *form* than to *in*form him.

"1. With every new set of pupils I go cursorily through Cornelius Nepos, in order to accustom them to my method; though most of them may have read this author elsewhere.

"2. I then read with them Cicero's Epistles, those which are prescribed in the official publication, entitled 'the (Würtemberg) Ecclesiastical Directory.' In the course of the lecture each epistle is particularly explained and illustrated, and every pupil has afterwards to make a written translation of it.

"3. In lecturing upon Cicero's Epistles, I sometimes give

exercitia extemporanea (philological and other elucidations suggested in our course of reading), from choicest passages of the classics, such especially as appear to have the most immediate bearing upon the passage in hand.

"4. I take occasions for introducing classical antiquities and other needful illustrations, and now and then direct their attention to some book which will give them further information upon particular subjects.

"5. In the weekly *exercises,* I lay a stress upon elegance in writing, and upon writing our own language correctly. These exercises I rectify in the presence of the pupils, but more with the pen than with words. When full periods are to be formed from dictation, I call upon each pupil for his *vivâ voce* remarks, which I then correct and complete.

"In *Greek,* I employ set times for their recollecting and clearly comprehending the paradigmas and grammatical rules. We go through the Greek Testament in two years, during the first months of which I require the text to be translated quite literally; but afterwards, when I find we can get on quicker and with more confidence, I let them read off sentence by sentence into Latin. The more important passages are learnt by heart. To increase our (*copia verborum*) stock of words, I conduct them through Leusden. After the whole course of these Greek Testament lectures is completed, I lecture with them upon Chrysostom's Treatise on the Priesthood; recommending to the more advanced pupils, Nonnus's 'Paraphrase of St. John's Gospel;' and 'Macarius.'

"In *logic,* I contrive that they shall bring into application all the rules they have learnt at the town schools before they come to us. I do not go far beyond the *Manual,* but explain to them rather more at large in what respects the older and later systems agree or differ; and occasionally suggest a few thoughts which may be useful for deeper investigation by and by. I take opportunities afterwards, when lecturing upon a Latin author, or even upon the Testament, to present to them some practical exercises in logic.

"In *history,* which is lectured upon during the two last months of our two years' course, we follow the introduction furnished by Essich's Compendium; one chief object being that the pupils may both gain a summary view of the principal epochs, and notice particularly the bearings and connexions between ecclesiastical and general history."

As the tutors of the Theological Seminary were to be not mere lecturers, but *educators* of their pupils (it having been arranged as one special design of the Institution, that young persons should not be left to themselves during their hours of relaxation, as they were at theHigh Schools in general), Bengel kept in view this part of his duty with conscientious fidelity. It was with him a particular matter of conscience "to habituate the youth under his care to a reverence for holy things, and to guard them against the sins incident to their age, which are as common as they are dangerous, particularly disingenuousness and impurity." He also laboured "to imbue them as early as possible with elements and principles which he hoped would in time be found most valuable to them in the sacred ministry." And, he had taken the likeliest method of effecting this design; for the maxims on which he acted savoured nothing of the pedagogue, but were of the most liberal kind. "I am not (he said) the most rigid censor of every little failing or youthful silliness that may come under my notice. I give my pupils to understand, in a general way, that every thing of the kind has in it the nature of sin, but I do not express censure upon every occasion; for such things are almost unavoidable till young persons become seriously concerned about the inward discipline of themselves. Forbearance of this sort was well suggested to me by the manner in which the late (school) rector, Essich, acted with his pupils. When he found, upon coming into the school, that all his youths were out of order, he would exclaim, 'You naughty boys!' (as if he would say, 'Must you be always at your diversions?') All was quiet in a moment, and every one at his business. On such occasions I too have said, 'The majesty of young students is not the most important in the world; let it not forget to do homage to the majesty of God.' It is another thing when their youthful sallies have proved mischievous or dangerous; then, of course, things require to be more seriously noticed."

"Delicate as it is for tutors to resort to any of the severer remedies, on account of the danger of impairing their own influence, still among such a variety of youths as must be found in so large a seminary, a *degree* of sternness may sometimes be even necessary. Care only should be taken that all may be evidently intended for their good, and that any displeasure, however expressed, go not beyond the walls of the Institution. For this reason I am not forward to write to the parents about the faults of my young charge, &c. Where there is too much strictness, young persons are in general only the more disorderly when left for a while to themselves; indeed, our most careful management of them ought never to be unaccompanied by discrimination between what the Scriptures call 'nature' and 'grace.' If such discrimination be regarded by some persons as mere refinement, rather than as practical wisdom, we cannot help it: we can only say that experience proves its necessity. Not that we mean that children should be treated in all respects as grown persons; but we mean that Scripture makes no distinction between old and young, when it says, 'first the natural (man), and afterwards that which is spiritual.'

"It soon appears how the young people are likely to turn out; indeed, the parents themselves have often unwittingly discovered it to me when they first brought them to the seminary. Those of a cheerful, frank, and open disposition, give us no serious trouble; but good is not to be expected from such as discover disingenuousness, duplicity, and dissolute inclinations.

"Parents, early instructors, and tutors of seminaries, ought to be very careful never to be overcome by irritation, and especially never to extort subjection by any harsh means. These things only serve to harden the temper, and to render it unmanageable; whereas our simple aim should be merely to assist and set young persons right. They must necessarily at times displease me in something or other; but I never think of being at open war with them, lest I should have to put up my weapons with remorse and repentance; all I aim at is, to avoid being 'partaker of other men's sins.' It may often be right to punish a slighter fault, and to overlook a more serious one unexpectedly to the offender, whereby we may make him ashamed of himself, and gain his heart. Conscience must direct us in all such cases, and it may sometimes direct us to leave such young persons to *their* conscience. Every one must give account of himself to God. Ephrem Syrus, comparing the tutor with his pupil to a ship with its cock-boat, said, 'Let the cock-boat lie upon the shallows, if it will not come off; but the ship must go on.'

"The worst thing in our Theological Institution is, that we are obliged to retain the pupils, if they are ever so untoward; whereas, in other institutions, as in the Pædagogium at Halle, the *concilium abeundi* (dismissal) is given to those who will not conform to the rules; so that there is no need of mulct, nor of punishing by confinement. But with us, if there happen to be a single black sheep in a class, it greatly endangers the rest, and punishments are oftener requisite than is good for more ingenuous youths to witness, as it is apt to excite even in them a spirit of slavish fear. The bad ones will be offending every week, and cannot well be exempted from formal punishment, because the Consistory wonders that an unfavourable testimonial should be given to any who have not been often mulcted. It would be far better to dismiss them at once, that as they will not conform to order in one line of life, they may do better in another. There are some tutors who think they have performed a kind office in preventing a pupil from being expelled; but where is the kindness of it? They have taken pains to keep a sickly sheep in the flock with mischief often enough to the rest. Why not away with such a one? Why should he cumber the soil?"

The good effects of an education conducted upon such principles, and of Bengel's personal instructions in particular, were unanimously and gratefully acknowledged by the best of his pupils in after life. Two instances may serve for many more that might be adduced to show this. A memoir of Dr. Huber, councillor of State, which is printed in the Würtemberg Transactions, contains that celebrated man's testimony to his former tutor as follows:—

" Bengel made me acquainted with the Homilies of Chrysostom, but chiefly have I to thank this learned person for his historical lectures on Cicero's Epistles *ad Familiares*, and for his constant and persevering admonitions to virtue."

Likewise a letter addressed to Bengel by the Rev. Matt. Frederic Beckh, M. A., an excellent minister of the Penitentiary, and of the Orphan-house at Lewisburg, contains the following acknowledgments.

" Truly, I can never be thankful enough to God for the great good I owe to you, to your amiable and valuable instruction, and to your many other expedients for my benefit. The good I thus gratefully acknowledge was not merely of a scientific kind; it was practical and moral. That I did not take proper care to retain such valuables after I left Denkendorf for Maulbronn, where I lived without God in the world, I now deeply regret, and confess my shame for it to the glory of God. How often, yes, how often still sounds in my ear your word of dismissal, which you always used to leave with us as your advice after prayer on Saturday evenings,—your *Colligite animas!* * (Compose your minds!) At that time I did not enter into it, but now I do: yes, I know now what it means! But though I cannot yet say, *Colligo semper animam,* my prayer is, *Collige Domine, collige animam meam!* (Gather up, O Lord, my whole soul into peaceful recollectedness and wisdom!)"

Bengel was far from contenting himself with the services he had rendered to pupils during their stay in the seminary. As he ever showed a deep interest in them even before they entered it, so he equally cared for them long after they had left it. He spared no pains in communicating to parents who wished to know how their sons might gain the best preparation for coming into the Theological Institution, every necessary and particular instruction; and he made a point of furnishing the pupils who had left him with well digested advices how to pursue their studies to the best advantage, especially if they went to the university. He appears to have been strongly influenced to this by his grateful remembrance of the encouraging kindness he had experienced in early life from so many who had benefited him in the same way; so that, much as he was pressed with various other important engagements, he also allowed his former pupils freely to correspond with him, and to ask his opinion upon every subject of difficulty. Several availed themselves of this permission, and to a considerable extent; among whom were Jeremiah Frederic Reuss, afterwards chancellor of his University; Christopher Frederic Oetinger, afterwards prelate of Murrhardt; and Mr. Smalcalder, afterwards professor of civil law; who so endeavoured to profit by this advantage, that documents before me show letters of theirs to have been answered by Bengel every eight days. Oetinger, speaking of this in his memoir, says, "Reuss having been a favourite pupil of the great Bengel, was afterwards, while at the university, his particular correspondent upon academical subjects; and Bengel always added something relating either to his own apocalyptical discoveries, or to his own christian experience. These communications I was allowed to see from the very first, in 1724, when he wrote, *Inveni numerum Bestiæ, Domino dante.* (God has enabled me to discover the number of the Beast.) Reuss soon

* An instance of such evening admonitions, Bengel has recorded, Nov. 10, 1737. "Before our evening devotion yesterday, such a freedom of spirit was bestowed on me, that I found more access to the hearts of the students than ever. May He who granted it bestow a further blessing on it, that fruit may come forth, even fruit that may remain!"

after left the university for the family of General von Grävenitz; I then took his place, as Mr. Bengel's correspondent, and went a number of times to see him, every half year at the least, often every quarter, and sometimes more frequently, so that he once hinted to me that I came too often. I was favoured to witness the whole construction of his apocalyptical system from the very beginning; and it truly delighted me to notice all along the method and means which God made use of to advance, purge, strengthen, and establish the growth of knowledge and wisdom in that chosen vessel."

The benefit of corresponding * with so faithful and experienced a friend and instructor could not have been small; particularly as he never assumed the air of a superior, but was communicative as a father with his sons, and almost as a brother with brothers, though they were so much his inferiors in age and attainments. As love and high esteem had linked them to him at Denkendorf, so after they had left the seminary, and were now very differently circumstanced, still there was no one else to whom they could so freely and confidentially open their minds, and from whom they could be so sure of obtaining satisfactory solution of any of their difficulties. When we consider how apt are young students, through too much confidence in their own slender acquirements, to regard all new teachers with a sort of distrust, we may well suppose that even Bengel's scholars, especially with the educated spirit of inquiry they brought with them, would sometimes feel dissatisfied with the university instruction of those times, and therefore would highly value the friend who, by showing them better how to regard any subject in hand, could help them to see in what respects their dissatisfaction was misplaced, or else teach them how best to supply any defects in the public lectures by their own private diligence.

It must also have been an advantage to many of his pupils to have received from his sound and matured experience, some check to that youthful ardour which is so ready to embrace new discoveries in philosophy or divinity, merely for their charm of novelty.

To these benefits for the mind he not unfrequently added others for inferior necessities, making his epistles to poorer students ponderous at times, with considerable sums of money: so glad was this pious and enlightened man to do any good in

* Particulars of it occur in the next Section.

his power; especially as his Lord and Master, in working while it was day, had laboured to diffuse temporal as well as spiritual blessings.

Thus the fairest and most active season of his life, from his twenty-sixth to his fifty-fourth year, was spent in discharging most successfully, under the Divine blessing, the laborious office of a tutor. After this period, however, he began to feel his strength no longer equal to the work as heretofore; and it induced him to wish for a sphere of usefulness less pressingly laborious. He found it in being called to the dignified station of Prelate of Herbrechtingen, which had become vacant by the death of George Frederic Zügel. Thus, on the 24th of April, 1741, he closed his duties as tutor at Denkendorf, in the same manner as he had commenced them twenty-eight years before, namely, with a Latin speech on "The beneficial influence of Piety upon the studies of the rising generation." This he prefaced by affectionately taking leave of the governors of the institution, and especially of the prelate, his ancient and revered friend, Philip Henry Weissensee. Then turning to the young persons of the Institution, he declared how strongly induced he felt, on such an occasion, to address them upon the self-same subject which he had chosen at his entrance upon office twenty-eight years ago. He had since that time instructed twelve successive classes of pupils, amounting to about three hundred persons; but his experience during that long period had taught him nothing different from what his firm conviction had induced him to speak upon at his inauguration. For those of his pupils who had regarded the fear of the Lord as the beginning of wisdom, and had submitted to the sanctifying discipline of the Holy Spirit, had either become wise and valued men, and were now filling some of the most important stations in the church and in places of learning, or had finished their course by happy and exemplary departure in the faith; whereas those who had been averse to discipline and good order, through love of pleasure, licentiousness, evil companions, and pernicious writings, had, in despite of the mercy of every providential obstacle, forced their way to an imaginary liberty of short-lived enjoyment, and had brought upon their friends, their parents, and themselves, indescribable troubles and miseries; while all the good of which they might have been the happy possessors, now eluded their attainment; nay, many of them had come to a premature death in the service of sin, and, it was quite to be feared, had trifled away and utterly defeated the salvation of their souls.

He begged them to consider that the institution to which they were admitted was for intellectual, and also for spiritual purposes, and that the good will and ready mind with which pupils generally entered the seminary, must necessarily after a while, in a rich pasture like this, become either better or worse; so that though the change in its taking place is gradual and imperceptible, the stages of advancement in good or evil soon become observable, and increasingly rapid, because dispositions of the heart do not admit of being put on and off like garments at our convenience. It is only he who expands his whole heart to piety, that can acquire a relish for the written word of God—the depository of all genuine wisdom. The learned world are ever offering us some "new thing;" but what is deemed most valuable to-day, is found of no value to-morrow; and the more vivid our imagination of pleasure in human discoveries, the sooner is it extinguished. The inspired Scriptures alone present subjects that will never wax old. In what innumerable instances do we see them slighted or undervalued; and yet in what innumerable instances are they continually bearing away the palm of triumph! He, therefore, who prefers following his own deceitful heart, rather than the word of God, or imagines himself able to unite any immoral habit with solid science, that person is really at war with himself; for most true is the saying of Tertullian, that "Fear is the reward of every sin." Both the fear and the sin may possibly be overruled for the transgressor's recovery; but how many are found miserably entangled by both, and borne along to the gulf of hopeless perdition! For reasons like these, he trusted all his young friends would remember his valedictory exhortation, and regard true piety as their all-important business. In this way alone would they promote their own welfare, and that of the state and church to which they belonged; thus only could they give joy to himself, or to any who sincerely loved them, and thus they would do it effectually.

SECTION II.

IN CORRESPONDENCE.

1. *To a Prelate at Maulbronn.**—"When I despatched my last letter to you, young S. was here; and by his whole behaviour, his rude manners and dissipated habits, confirmed all the complaints you had made respecting him. Indeed, I fear that the conduct of most of the other youths in your establishment is no better than that of himself and his companion, and that you will have many a trouble with them during the tedious year and a half they have still to spend with you. I consider myself therefore in duty bound to write to you particularly upon this matter, for it seems to be bringing your happiness and your good name into great danger. May you, my dear friend, regard the honesty and frankness with which I write, only as a token of sincere love and faithful friendship! Your own pupils, and those of your colleagues, have a very bad character at this place; they are spoken of as idle, ungodly fellows; headstrong, foppish, dissolute, fond of drinking, quarrelling, riot, and many other disgraceful things; and the cause of all this is largely attributed to the too indulgent lenity of the prelate, and to their being permitted by the prelate's lady to have inordinate allowances of wine. How far this is true, of course I cannot undertake to say. It is enough that the report has come to the ears of our ecclesiastical superiors at Stuttgart, and is already so much circulated, that I should deserve to be regarded as unfaithful to you, if I did not tell you of it. As your vacation is just at hand, the beginning of next term will be the best opportunity for turning over a new leaf. I know your own kindness and lenity, especially towards young persons; but you know also that God is a jealous God, who is even displeased with that sort of kindness which allows fault after fault to pass unpunished, till real mischief ensues; you know, too, that young persons must be led, not only with the tenderness, but also with

* The seat of another Theological Seminary in Würtemberg; the principal tutor or head of which was a prelate of the Swiss Protestant Church.

the seriousness, of love; and that they must be early taught to bear in mind the account which they must one day give.

"Among young people at present, the cunning craftiness of seducers, and the disposition to be seduced, are increasing much faster than a tutor who has been accustomed to earlier days is apt to imagine: and those who are the first to take advantage of too much lenity, are likewise the first to throw the blame of their own misconduct upon those who had suffered them to go unpunished. It would be presumptuous in me to point out to you what is necessary to be done; you know, without any prompting of mine, how to meet these exigencies, under the guidance of divine and human prescription, as also by comparing your past with your present experience; in doing which, you will secure your own comfort amidst the pressure of declining years; that comfort, I mean, which flows from confidence in God, out of a good conscience, and from the preservation of our own respectability. I am persuaded that what I have thus ventured to write, my dear friend, is not displeasing to the God with whom we have to do; and I feel quite encouraged to believe, that neither will it be unwelcome to yourself, but quite the contrary, when, with all your sincere and fatherly love to your disorderly charge, you have tried upon them the effect of your kind and fatherly severity."

2. *To a parent who was preparing his son for the Seminary.*— "—— I think you should be rather sparing with him in Cicero's Epistles, that he may not be too soon tired of them when he comes amongst us, for we lecture in them very minutely. With a little of your own superintendence, he might go cursorily through the last six books. He might study also the Letters of Pliny, and read Valerius Maximus and A. Gellius.* These authors I think more suitable to him than others, as they contain no subject which occupies a sequence of many books. Some tutors, during lessons with their pupils, dwell much upon Latinity; but I think this unnecessary. It is better to refer them to Tursellinus, ('De usu Particularum L. sermonis,') as improved by Schwartz. While they are studying the Latin

* Valerius Maximus, a Latin historian, born at Rome, who flourished under Tiberius, to whom he dedicated his work, entitled, "Libri novem Factorum Dictorumque Memorabilium:" See Torrenius's edition, Leyden, 2 vols. 4to. 1726.

Aulus Gellius, a Roman lawyer, born A. D. 130. He studied at Athens, where he began his "Noctes Atticæ," containing observations on various subjects. This work has been translated by Beloe.

particles in that book, they become insensibly familiar with phrases and elegances; other requisites may soon be gained as occasion shall dictate.

"You must be particular in habituating your son to a good style, but rather as it respects construction and turn of sentences, than nicety in selection of words and phrases. As to the rest, which I call *minutiæ*, you need no particular information from me. You can take, at pleasure, some article of a periodical publication, or a paragraph from a sermon, or even from a Latin classic; this last he may translate into German, and laying it by for a few days, then translate back into Latin. More attention I think should be bestowed upon promptness in (Latin) writing and speaking, than upon neat composition; for the latter, with all our painstaking, is but seldom properly regarded by young pupils, and is far from attainable in every respect. You must also give him some knowledge of Hebrew, and still more of Greek. At the same time, let his attention be directed to history, geography, mathematics, and other pursuits connected with *things*, and of permanent use. I find Castellio's Latin version of the Scriptures, especially the last edition with the index, very useful (for acquiring a good general knowledge of the Latin language.) But to be thoroughly familiar with Latin, the practice of conversing in it is of great service; though I do not advise carrying this too far."

3. *To the father of one of his pupils.*—"Your dear son still goes on well, and it gives me great pleasure to assist young persons like himself. Any such tokens of your kindness as I received from you at the end of the autumn vacation, are unnecessary, after such a close family connexion has been formed between us; yet I accept it through fear of making you uneasy, and I do so with my most sincere thanks. But let me assure you that I shall think it a still greater kindness if from this time you will leave me opportunity of showing, both officially and as a friend, how much more I feel under obligation to yourself, than you can be to me. Whence our young student acquired such a liking for the violin, I know not; for my own part I prefer some musical instrument more suitable for solitary recreation, and less likely to draw young people into company; but, as he prefers the violin, I shall see that he continue to make a prudent use of it, and mean to remind him, if necessary, of "*ne quid nimis*;" &c.

4. *To the mother of one of his pupils.*—"If your dear son's real good has been promoted by what is no more than bounden duty on my part, the honour and praise for this, as for every thing else, be to God alone! May it please him to guide with his own eye, the youth of our days, and those of our seminary in particular; may he preserve them, and your dear son among them, from the many evils of the world, and grant them to increase in wisdom and grace! With respect to what he thought fit to write in commendation of me to yourself and family, I can only say, it is my earnest wish to be as useful to him as to others; that I am far from being satisfied with myself; that I am but an unprofitable servant, and best aware what still is wanting in me; but I regard his thus writing to you, as a proof of his grateful disposition, and it gives me good hope that he will always welcome and practise every thing valuable which is taught him. And may I not hope, dear and honoured Madam, that this consideration will serve to set your own mind at rest as to any needless anxiety about him? for some such anxiety shows itself in your kind letter. I also beg you to be assured that I undertake the education of honourable and pious persons' sons, quite as freely and cheerfully as I do that of others, and even more so; therefore any particular remuneration on account of higher rank, &c., is out of the question. I value more than any acknowledgments of a temporal kind, such spontaneous wishes as yours for the Divine blessing upon me. May our heavenly Father grant also to yourself and to your worthy relatives whatever his never-changing faithfulness, and your own heart's desire, in submission to his will, can bring upon you; may he assure to you what he reserves among his treasures, against that day when he shall make manifest every good word and work," &c.

5. *From his letters to his former pupil, Jeremiah Frederic Reuss.*

"*January* 13, 1721.

"The great God make me all that people think me to be, and something more; may he make me what he would have me to be."

"*February* 24, 1721.

"Either refrain, dear Reuss, from writing to me, or do not apply to me such superlative expressions. I should quietly, like a fond father, place it all to the account of your love, were I not afraid that my allowing it will bring upon me a heavy responsibility. For the same reason I wish it were not said here at daily prayers, 'our most revered tutors.' I believe that if

Herod had been displeased with the acclamation, ' It is the voice of a god, and not of a man,' he would not have been struck dead in such a horrible manner. God's honour is an awfully tender thing, and may be injured before we are aware.

" I see you are keeping the right object in view. Go on after it with all zeal, only not in your own strength. ' Our sufficiency is of God :' whose voice if any one has heard, and has begun to feel his drawing influence, he becomes less his own master than ever, though really his own master, of course he never was. But the world's vain things cannot now yield him even that imaginary satisfaction with which men amuse themselves. The study of divinity itself, to say nothing of other learning, will no longer be pursued by him for mere entertainment or intellectual gratification, but he is sweetly constrained to turn his pursuit of these things to a nobler purpose, namely, to the honour of his God, and to the everlasting welfare of the soul.

" On the *various readings* of the Greek Testament I could say more to you than this letter would hold. Take and eat in simplicity, my dear friend, the bread as you have it before you ; and be not disturbed if you find in it a grit now and then from the mill-stone. Christ and his church have ever appeared to the world's eye as clothed in weakness and mean attire; the same befalls his written word; but neither to Christ nor to his word, much as the world may be offended in either, can any real blemish be attached. I find all such *apparent* weakness and meanness perfectly reconcilable with the glory of Christ, and with the excellency of his Word.

" If the sacred volume, considering the fallibility of its many successive transcribers, had been preserved from every seeming defect whatsoever, this preservation itself would have been so great a miracle, that faith in the written word of God could be no longer faith. I have only to wonder that there is not a much larger number of those readings* than there is; and that there are none which in the least affect the foundation of our faith. You may therefore safely and securely have nothing to do with doubts, which at one time so distressingly perplexed myself."

" *Nov.* 5, 1721.

" My own thoughts respecting the soul's union with the body may be seen in my Notes upon Gregory, Sect. 141. But

* An editor of the six comedies of Terence has noticed in them twenty thousand various readings; and the author of this Memoir has noticed about five thousand in Cicero's Epistles.

you will find me more reserved upon that subject than young philosophers like yourself could wish. For at first entrance upon philosophy, we of course desire to know every thing; and it is only after long and laborious inquiries that we come to acquiesce in what, by its very nature, cannot be further inquired into. It seems to me impossible clearly to comprehend in this life the manner of the soul's union with the body; at least, I must think so, till the contrary is evinced upon better grounds than philosophy has hitherto furnished. Take, for instance, Leibnitz's theory of 'Pre-established Harmony,' and where in it shall we find any satisfaction upon such subjects? Besides, his theory itself is nothing new: you may meet with it in a treatise upon Matrimony, published in the last century, by Melchior, a clergyman of the Reformed communion.

" You will benefit by the university lectures you have still to attend, if you are careful to recollect all that is valuable in them; and if with respect to what is not so, you are equally careful to consider what ought to have been said, and in what manner it ought to have been treated; for we should learn to profit by defects and errors, as well as by excellences. But let your greatest care be to keep leanness from your soul while engaged in such occupations of the intellect; and this you may do by setting apart daily a quarter of an hour for retired prayer and self-recollection. Moulin's tract on 'The Peace of the Soul' may be of some use to you in that way."

"*Jan.* 1, 1722.

" During the season of this sacred festival, which forcibly calls to our remembrance the kindness and love of God, I have been every day so shut up with a severe cold, that I have seemed excommunicated from church privileges. But I hope to be enabled to preach at Epiphany, what I should have been glad to have preached in the Christmas holidays. You say I may make amends by imparting to you the good I have been unable to communicate from the pulpit; but you are asking bread of a hungry man. For though I have known what it is to have spiritual supplies heretofore, my liberty of spirit seems at present as much obstructed as my voice. Still you have with you the omnipresent Lord, who once visited us from the bosom of the Father, clothed in the nature, and bearing the name, of Man—a name, which before had been out of repute in heaven; but which he has now made honourable among angels, and has rendered graciously acceptable with God. Here, then, is our Light; contemplate it with stedfast eye; sweep away, if possible, out of its beams, every thing unholy and unclean; read, and pray, and praise; yea, persevere in such exercises. 'Give thyself wholly to them;' and apply all to your personal, spiritual improvement. I have read some of Franke's sermons with my family, and we have found them very edifying. He is a preacher that has always something peculiarly festal for festival days; for the subject of the season, whatever it be, seems to absorb him. Therefore I recommend to you his festival sermons most especially.

"To-day I have seemed to feed upon the hymn, 'Were thousand-thousand voices mine;' singing it inwardly at least with a feeling as if I had nothing to check the breathings of my soul. May you find the same good by it, and may God grant you whatever, agreeably to his holy will, can further your real welfare."

"*Jan.* 30, 1722.

"—— In my opinion you have at present nothing to do with imaginations of things which, though possible, are never realized. But it does appear strange to me, that philosophers, who profess and call themselves Christians, should be so shy of speaking of the 'Logos,' in whom every thing is, which is."

"*March* 11, 1722.

"You ask my sentiments on Rom. i. 21. God deserves our gratitude for all his benefits; deserves to be adored for his own glorious nature; deserves to be honoured, exalted, and glorified for his wonderful works. Grateful adoring piety then is to be the great end of all our seeking and searching after him; and without making it such, our seeking is vain and fruitless. The very attempt to think upon God, when it is not simply for his own sake, is virtually no better than to deify, either ourselves or our thoughts. The longer any go on thus averted from the true end of their inquiries, the farther must they be entangled in erroneous ideas of God, and of every thing that most concerns themselves; and the more agile their natural powers of mind, the greater will their perplexities become. While they are philosophizing upon the nature, attributes, providence, or works of the Deity, though ever so busy in inquiries professedly of a theological character, they get nothing for their pains except the frothy productions of intellectual pride. I counsel you therefore, my dear friend, to use philosophy merely for attaining the knowledge of things natural; but for any suitable acquaintance with God, let his own word be your guide; and whether employed in this or in philosophy, consider always how to advance the life of personal, spiritual, practical piety; how to find fresh matter for adoring, admiring, revering, honouring, and glorifying the name of the God and Father of our Lord Jesus Christ. Whatever is foreign to this, let it be either totally neglected as unworthy of your notice; or at best, let it be any thing but food for your soul, and used only as the coarse materials of masonry."

"*May* 21, 1722.

"Take care not to meddle with any branch of learning in a hurried and superficial manner. If you have not time for all, rather neglect something entirely, or else defer it. Keep at present to philosophy; giving only such time to divinity as a pious Christian's necessities daily require; that you may not be tempted, when the season arrives for the latter study, to neglect it for the sake of the former."

"*June* 12, 1722.

"I could wish you, my dear friend, to consider why you are so eager to search into the speculations of the *Theodicè;* * for the more we can talk upon such things, the less we know about them. Is it to promote piety? Knowledge of this sort will not at all promote our recovery from sin; and when we are recovered enough, we shall know enough; wisdom will then be spontaneously manifest to us. This is all I have now to say upon speculative philosophy; for though I meant to have said a great deal more, the desire has left me, because I know that God cannot be pleased with our too curiously inquiring into the secret things which belong to Him. He would have us humbly adore his holy purposes, without presuming to search into the reasons of them. Such heights and depths of knowledge may be precluded to us even in eternity itself; at least, it is presumptuous to attempt them at present. As God saw each of the things which he had made to be individually good, and the whole of them collectively to be *very* good; so whatever he has done must be best; and what he

* A celebrated work of Leibnitz, thus entitled.

has not done, should never be called good for a moment. Any comparison of what he has done with what he has not done, is extravagant. . . . . . . My time is too short to go with you into an examination of Leibnitz's views; but what I have said will suggest enough for your consideration. Let me then advise, that in studying philosophy, you make it your care to have every admitted principle upon the sure foundation, rather than to amass devices and ornaments for the lofty top of the edifice."

"*June* 29, 1723.

"Death has in a single month taken away two of your fellow-students; and you rightly observe, that of those who were before you at this seminary, and of those who have been here since you left us, several are already removed from the earth, yes, and calculation has long convinced me, that of every single class of pupils, a third part is lost to us, either by death, or by disappointed hopes respecting them, before the remainder have entered upon those public duties which require so many years' preparation. I am apt to regret labour spent in vain upon such a number of young persons; and if one knew who would be the victims, it would be our business to instruct them, not in the art of living and dying, but simply in the art of dying; for what could they have to do with Cicero or Ovid!"

"*Sept.* 18, 1723.

"The principle of setting out from *an adequate fundamental point* in metaphysics, appears to me quite *in*adequate, and to involve the same contradiction in that science, as the principle of *social compact* in moral philosophy. It infers only negative conclusions; consequently nothing can be built upon it. It serves merely for refutation."

"*Nov.* 24, 1723.

"I see, my dear friend, you are beginning the study of divinity with conscientiousness and self-distrust; let these put you upon diligent prayer. Be contented at first with the public lectures, and with your own private diligence in the Hebrew and Greek Scriptures. Be master of every particular in the Compendium upon which the first course of lectures proceeds; then study at large each article separately; in which you may be directed by Hoffmann's 'Synopsis,' and Buddei 'Instit. Theol.

Dogm.;' no third author for the purpose do I advise you to take in hand, till you are thoroughly acquainted with both of these. Beware of relying on the representations of human authors more than on those of Scripture. It is only in the Bible that the all-pure Spirit of God breathes; I am afraid of human theology, lest it 'savour the things which be of men.' Franke's 'Idea Studiosi Theologiæ' will give you many useful instructions. Read this excellent work through and through; twice or three times in continuance." . . . . . .

"*Dec.* 23, 1723.

"Ten days ago I lost my little boy, of three months old. It is a comfort to me under this trying bereavement to have pupils and friends like yourself. To mitigate grief, I turned my particular attention to those parts of Scripture which serve best to establish us in faith, love, and hope, while I gave myself day and night to my *general* biblical occupations; especially as I had reason to hope that my engagements of this sort would at some time or other prove a blessing to others."

"*May* 13, 1724.

"Respecting the Lord's Supper, I have already, on various occasions, written three treatises upon it.* If you desire further theological information, take up Franke's book, entitled, 'Christ the Substance of the Holy Scriptures.' This treatise excellently proves the deity of Christ. I beseech you, my dear friend, to abide by that one dictum, 'It is written;' and leave, 'It appears to us,' to the philosophers. All the real advantages which *divines* can derive from *philosophical* training may be comprised in a very small compass; its chief use to *them* is for teaching good arrangement and methodical inference. But theological verities themselves, in their harmony and beauty, are to be looked for in the Scriptures alone; it is there we find their best mutual illustration; and we must ever consider the sacred volume as its own safest and best interpreter. For this reason I have given the humble name of *Gnomon* to my 'Annotations on the New Testament;' for they simply *indicate* what lies within the compass of the sacred text."

* These are contained in Ph. D. Burk's "Pastoral Theology." (1.) Theses de Administratione Eucharistiæ, p. 427. (2.) Suggestions respecting the Admission of unworthy Communicants, p. 455. (3.) De præsentiâ Christi in Sacrâ Cœnâ, p. 578.

"2 *June*, 1724.

"Your query as to Scripture being *divinely endited* to the sacred penmen is ambiguous. If you ask whether *the very words* which they wrote were thus dictated to them, I can only remind you, that the apostles themselves have drawn the most important inferences from scripture terms and expressions of the utmost brevity and minuteness; as in Heb. ii. 8, xii. 17, vii. 3, 14; Gal. iii. 16; and that St. Peter, (2d Epist. iii. 16,) ranks also the Epistles of St. Paul among the holy Scriptures. But if your inquiry be respecting the *general* inspiration and authority of *all* Scripture, I may refer you to the proofs of it which have been collected by various excellent writers, as Hunnius in his 'Tract. de majest. et certitudine SS.,' and by Langius, in his 'Diss. περι θεοπνευστιας,' &c. &c.; but for my own part, I am satisfied with this simple position, that *the whole sacred volume is in most beautiful harmony with itself; (omnia se quadrant.)* As we cannot contemplate a globe without observing how round and complete it is; so to an attentive observer are the Scriptures of the Old and New Testament.

"On the deity of our blessed Lord, I recommend to you what Spener has written. I cannot conclude without reminding myself and you, that all doubts are more easily resolved by prayer and retired communion with our own hearts, than by any argumentative process."

In August, 1725, Reuss had written to Bengel respecting the proceedings of Frederic Rock, at Tübingen. This man professed himself inspired. Reuss, after relating his conversation with him, requested Bengel's opinion of the case. The following was his reply :—

"*Aug.* 29, 1725.

"I am still a continual sufferer, and chiefly in my head; so you must excuse brevity. I have never seen any of the *Inspirati;* but I know that persons much better informed than myself, are very cautious of giving their opinion about them; therefore it seems imprudent for me to speak positively, till I feel myself called to do it.* Indeed, I have never met with a more delicate subject than this. What you, my dear friend, said to Rock himself, namely, that he ought to

* See Bengel's opinion of Rock expressed afterwards Part IV. ch. 4.

examine whether he is called to exhort rather than to prophesy, may well engage his serious reflection. With an eye to this subject, I recommend you to read Tennhard's 'Warning to Separatists.' 1718. p. 120."

"*March* 15, 1726.

"I am learning to go through evil report and good report."

"*June* 15, 1726.

"As my object is to obtain a pure and genuine text of the whole Greek Testament, I am at present busied in various readings given by Mill and Küster, and have already begun to separate and select from the mass I have collected for the purpose. 'A time to gather, and a time to cast away.' I could wish the two times were not quite so near together."

"*Sep.* 14, 1726.

"All you desire me to do, my dear friend, is very good and excellent; but where shall I get eyesight and time?

"Last week, when I had commenced working at the Harmony of the Gospels, I found myself unawares in the midst of the Apocalypse. O that you had been with me yesterday evening! I begin to think I can ascertain the commencement of the time of the Beast. Thoughts are now crowding into my mind upon this subject, and I have been obliged to interrupt them in order to write to you. These, with some other avocations, oblige me to conclude. Farewell!"

Reuss having written to consult him about accepting a call to Petersburg, was answered as follows:—

"*Sep.* 25.

"Did you make it a matter of prayer, as soon as it was proposed to you? Did you ask counsel of your college tutors, at least such of them as you consider most in communion with God? The subject is a tender one, and I am diffident of giving my opinion, though I think it would be wrong to give none. I would therefore say, go, if you have the consent of parents, if it be compatible with health, if the time of the year be fit for it. Five years is the shortest period before you can receive any appointment at home, and as it would be right meanwhile to embrace an opportunity for foreign travel, why not the present one? It is possible that among a rude and simple people, not yet corrupted by our modern refinements, you may have better openings for advancing the glory of God, than in our own highly favoured country, which has too long been very unthankful to him. But take care, my dear friend, that it be his glory you have at heart; that you have no vain object in view; and should you arrive there, choose such engagements as are least likely to draw you aside from the knowledge of the truth. Likewise, let it be clearly understood, that you are to have the option of returning home at pleasure, into the bosom and service of your mother church."

"*Sep.* 1726.

"You ask what you should do, supposing this call be repeated a *third* time. I know not how to advise beyond what I have said to you in conversation and by letter. Consider my suggestions over again. If your dear parents give their consent, and the most pious of your friends decide for it, then comply; but determine to steer clear of all rocks, my brother, and to sacrifice nothing of the duty you owe to your mother church and country."

"*Jan.* 11, 1727.

"As I have been for some time suffering considerably from spiritual chastening and bodily pain, so as to be the less disposed either to self-complacency, or to any great anxiety of pleasing others, I was only the more gratified with your letter, my dear friend, in which you notice my key to the prophetic periods. Still, be it ever so truly ascertained, as I think it is, I do not expect it will meet with general approval.

"The subject of the Divine covenants requires a closer investigation than I can give it to-night. The very notion of a law implies maintenance of justice against transgressors, and this was certainly the design of the covenant under the former dispensation; but as it was still a *covenant*, so it likewise held out to the transgressor a hope in returning to God, though it did it only indirectly and obscurely. The grace of Christ fulfils and satisfies the Law; and the New Dispensation is given, not in covenant, but in *testament*, for our restoration by Christ to the Father. When our complete restoration shall be effected, so close will be the union of God with men, that the word *testament* itself will be inadequate; so high will be the privileges that are to crown and consummate the New Testament dispensation.

This you may see, among other Scriptures to the same effect, in Rom. iii. and Heb. viii."

"*July* 27, 1727.

"Yesterday, on returning home safe and well, I found that our dwelling had been mercifully preserved from imminent danger by fire. I was at Boll at the time, and so ill as to be laid upon Hezekiah's couch, where I could obtain neither help nor comfort from any human being. But God heard my petition, and I have thus learnt how insignificant I am, and how little loss the world would have sustained had I been removed out of it. I did not feel any wish to live even for completing my works, though I had no express anticipation of death, most dangerously ill as I was. I gave myself up entirely to the Divine disposal, and thus it was ordered that I should recover."

"*St. Thomas's Day*, 1728.

"I have spent most of the present month in examining the authenticity of 1 John v. 7, and I believe I have now quite ascertained it. Still the real place of that verse appears to me to be after the eighth. Read it with this arrangement, and see how well the verses run together."

---

6. *Extract of a letter from Bengel to S., who, from a mistaken notion of piety, was disposed to undervalue scientific cultivation, and to give up study.*—"—— As we must be renewed into the Divine image in wisdom and righteousness, so God teaches us by the written, as well as by the inward Word; and because his written Word was originally given in Hebrew and Greek, it is necessary to learn these languages. He could sustain our animal life without agriculture; yet he has appointed that man should till the ground. He could increase in us mental and spiritual light without our seeking it; yet we are obliged to seek it, and to set our faculties to work for that purpose. One appointment is never intended to supersede another, but all for mutual concurrence and mutual help. Nothing is more pernicious than indolence; it is soon succeeded by general relaxation and slumber. Activity, though it certainly may become extreme, and all extremes are to be avoided, is decidedly better than indolence, for promoting a sound state of spiritual health. Franke's 'Idea Studiosi Theologiæ' well teaches how to avoid extremes. A young minister by and by finds a variety of perplexities in his work, and then feels how good it would have

been had he laid up a little stock of knowledge, though he did not seem to want it at the time when he had opportunity for acquiring it; and afterwards it is too late."

7. *His plan of Theological Study.*—The following are some extracts from a plan he drew up at the repeated request of friends, who wished to know "in what manner a course of four or five years' study of divinity might be arranged to the best advantage."*

In section 4, he says, "As a doctrinal Manual forms the basis of the first course of lectures which the student has to attend, he should make himself quite familiar with it in all its chapters and subdivisions."

In section 6, "By no means should he attempt at forcing his unassisted reason to grasp one subject of the system after another. Let him make each given subject familiar to him *historically;* and then whatever he finds come home to his heart, without any straining of his understanding, let him adopt as a fixed principle, with careful fidelity and thankful obedience."

Section 7, "Afterwards let him sedulously peruse other compendia and confessions of faith; keeping his eye particularly on the connexion and consecutiveness of each article, especially with a view to supply any defects in his former manual."

Section 9, "A well-arranged and apposite selection of scripture proofs is far more valuable than all demonstrations by the light of nature. He who is to be a witness of Christ, has to do, not so much with *knowing*, as with '*believing*.'"

Section 11, "Let him 'give' more 'attendance' to *hearing* than to books; especially when he can hear what he cannot learn by reading. Let him get his mind well ordered, by devoutly digesting and meditating upon all he learns, and he will be able to think clearly upon whatever is to be added to it. He may be helped in this, by making what he has learnt the subject of conversation with friends; whether they are more or less experienced, it does not signify. He will thus improve in arrangement, expression, and communication; and therefore students who have ability and leisure for tuition will do well to engage in it."

Section 12, "Searching the Scriptures is as much the principal thing for any theological course, as it is for the course of

* Printed in Ph. D. Burk's "Collections for Pastoral Theology," pp. 927—936.

one's whole life. Here, however, their substantial matter, in its essential bearings, should be our chief concern, apart from all philosophical disquisition with respect to the manner or degree of their inspiration. Particularly we should accustom ourselves to regard and use them, not as an accidental assemblage of various sacred writings, but as a relatively connected whole, of which Christ is the essence, the special subject and object. Any doubtful or difficult passages should never confound or discourage us; but all those evident truths and instructions which pervade them, and which are as easy of attainment as they are essential in importance, should be perpetually commending themselves to the devout student's conscience."

Section 15, "For polemical divinity he should become well acquainted with the notions which Jews, Mohammedans, Freethinkers, &c. teach, concerning the way to heaven, in contradiction to the pure gospel. The subtilest excursions of controversy seem to turn upon the Arminian question, and here particularly Zeltnerus may be of use."

Section 19, "It is not wise for the student to purchase many books, were it only for the real loss of time he is likely to incur by them. I prefer recommending him to write down such of his own thoughts as he finds of most importance, and to secure by memoranda the most valuable parts of his reading. In books of his own, a pencil-mark in the margin will serve; and from those he borrows, he can copiously extract the substance, often in the very words of the author, with references to page and edition."

Section 21, "Finally, the less he feels the stimulus of youthful vanity, the more he will aim at what is likely to be of solid use; and he will ever afterwards be experiencing the benefit of having done so.

"I would finally advise every student to complete these summary instructions from time to time out of his own increasing knowledge and experience; and never to overlook the necessity of continually seeking the Divine blessing. It is God who giveth the increase."

8. *Extracts from his letters to different students.*—1. "It is only the student who habitually delights in the Scriptures previously to his entering upon philosophy for the clearer arrangement of his ideas, that can study philosophy to good effect; for to stand on the vantage ground of Divine revelation, is the only

security for safely considering and judging of every floating system which may meet the eye. To traverse the mazy round of such systems, one by one, and to examine them by our own unassisted reason, is like seeking our way to the metropolis, by first visiting all its environs, labouring to dry up every puddle, and to remove every stumbling-block out of the circuitous route. Surely, by going directly in the plain public road, we accomplish our journey much sooner. In the study of theology there are a thousand things, especially of a controversial kind, which we can well do without, and the necessity of knowing them is but imaginary. Most of these I would conceal, if possible, from young students altogether; and if this could not be done, I would entreat them to be the more wary and serious about discovering the simple and naked truth; the sweetness of which, once tasted and enjoyed, 'enlightens our eyes'* to surmount all remaining difficulties. We then find it more easy to perceive both sides of an argument, and we, as it were, feel our way to what is true in it. Faith depends on whatever of truth it has already embraced; (follows the guidance of a star it already knows to be that of Bethlehem;) and goes on as courageously as a blind man who leans upon a brother's arm; whereas, the acutest intellect, without faith, is liable to incessant doubt and perplexity."

2. "Our philosophical men make a great parade of I know not what sublimated metaphysical theories of the universe; but solid natural philosophy is most sadly neglected. The ancients did much the same; they disguised their real ignorance or uncertainty in the details of physical science, with a parade of general notions and *universal ideas.*"

3. "Mathematical science is a good collateral help in *certain respects;* but there are truths of the utmost importance which lie totally out of its province, and which it even tends to unfit us for apprehending and embracing. A mere mathematician, as aiming at definite ideas about every thing, is likely to remain a perfect stranger to many truths which are vital to his welfare; for as truths are of different kinds, they require different means for their apprehension. Thus, as we cannot try acoustic truths by our eyes, nor optical truths by our ears, so neither can religious truth be tried by our artificial definitions of logic, or by any human science. Who can define the human soul? But are we therefore to infer, that we have no souls? Here,

* 1 Sam. xiv. 29.

then, I may remark, that the various susceptibilities or faculties with which the human mind is gifted for entertaining various kinds of truth, have among themselves a kind of natural balance, a mutual equilibrium for mutual strength; so that whichever of them is over-burdened to the neglect of the rest, the equipoise is proportionately destroyed. Thus a too constant exercise in mere mathematics has *the effect* of impairing the faculty of *belief*."

4. "The student, by meeting with such a variety of raw notions and strained hypotheses in the works of the learned, is apt to become mistrustful of all; and thus mere learning has given rise to scepticism. But he who makes the right use of learning finds it a worthy handmaid to revelation, and an assistant to him in obeying the truth. Small, however, is the number of those who seem duly aware what an abundant variety of matter may be deduced from human learning for feeding the flame of truly spiritual piety, and for awakening a lively interest in the ways of Providence, and in the cause of God."

9. To a tutor who regretted being "obliged to employ most of his time in the care of very young pupils," he wrote:—"Console yourself for the present with Poiret's maxim, that 'the humblest engagements in this way are really the noblest; and that the highest are the vainest.' If I ought to add a word of my own, let it be to remind you, that pupils, whether younger or older, are to be managed only with prayer, patience, and love; without which, no instruction of ours, however good, will stand."

10. To one who consulted him upon subscription to the Symbolical Books, he replied:—"The Symbolical Books are a confession of faith to which our Protestant church has bound herself. The intention of subscription is, not to bind her ministers to every particular contained therein, for example, to every particular interpretation of scripture passages, &c., but simply to testify our renunciation of heresies therein opposed. Thus, respecting the whole controversy (against Flacius,) concerning original sin, the article is, 'Original sin, though it be the most deeply rooted corruption, is no substance.' He who believes this declaration, can quietly subscribe it. There is no pressing of nice particularities on the part of our superintendents; but when a person, coming to subscribe, begins to start one diffi-

culty after another, they naturally fear that they have to do with a snake in the grass. Many have desired such *general* formularies for subscription as they think would exempt from all difficulties—but this is impossible; for a formulary that suits one person will not suit another. Let subscription be made with perfect honesty, but in the spirit of christian liberty, *(bonâ fide cum libertate animi;)* and then let a man be guided by his conscience in the discharge of his ministry. If the governors of the church have any real matter against him, they will be sure to see to that; but to try every one upon all points, is a thing which they neither wish nor are able to do, especially in a great country like this. Luther would have none to be under such restrictions. He said, 'He that can really improve or amend what I have drawn up, let him do it.'"

11. *To a young civilian.*

"*March* 8, 1717.

"You ask me, my dear friend, respecting *universal positive right*:—I am willing to give you my opinion very briefly. Universal positive right is a contradiction of terms. But you may answer, are there not some things in the divine law which, though positive and ordained, are obligatory upon the whole human race, and yet their obligation cannot be inferred from the nature of the things themselves? I answer, whatever things you regard as such, they show themselves to be, not positive, but natural, by their continuing in force; whereas, had they been merely positive, they would by this time have had no force at all. There are *natural* duties and rights which are enjoined and sanctioned by divine revelation; because the light of nature since the Fall is insufficient to discover them. Those only are known by the mere light of nature which are necessary for the very existence and continuation of society; but the rest must be learnt from God's revealed word. If you mean by *positive*, those duties and rights which, though founded in the very nature of man, are *not self-evident by natural light;* I can only say, this is an improper application of the term. You may try the truth of these remarks in any instance at your leisure; and if our modern writers give you any difficulty upon the subject, let me know of it. My conclusion is, that duties and rights may be natural in one respect, and positive in another; in the former, they are founded in the nature of things; in the latter, we can become acquainted with them only from Scripture."

"*March* 15, 1747.

"—— You perceive, my dear friend, that I have not time to go much farther into the inquiry respecting those natural laws which I have agreed in my own very qualified sense of the term, to call *positive;* but I will just endeavour to answer one of your objections.

"You say, if there are *natural* laws which can only be termed *positive* in respect of written revelation, by which alone we become acquainted with them, how then are mere heathens to know them at all; and, consequently, where is *their* obligation to fulfil them? Can we suppose any such obligation to result from the originally uncorrupted condition of man, which empowered and obliged him to know them? In other words, is man in his present fallen state, bound not only to fulfil, but to know, laws and things which he would have known and practised, had he continued innocent? Certainly he is. An indubitable instance of this very obligation is attested in the seventh chapter of the Epistle to the Romans, where lust or covetousness is mentioned as a case in point; and where the obligation to resist this sin is shown to be a natural one, but the *knowledge* of the obligation is declared to be a matter revealed by the written law of God; whence the obligation is in one sense *positive.* The light of natural reason is greatly weakened by man's original apostacy. This is evident from the fact, that the very things which to one nation appear most abominable, are by another regarded as perfectly allowable and inoffensive. But that natural knowledge of right and wrong should have been in so many instances lost, surprises us less than to find so much of it in other instances preserved. And preserved it is, that mankind may at least stop short at a limit within which it is possible to turn back into communion with God. What, therefore, may yet be most 'clearly seen' and known by natural light, is just what is absolutely necessary for the very continuance of the human race, and social intercourse. All that we discern beyond this, we discern not so much by any natural light in the mind, as rather by a blind feeling in the soul, by what we may, perhaps, denominate intellectual sensation, or, more properly, moral taste, (as obligations, for example, relating to modesty,) and is, therefore, of less power to convince and persuade, and more subject to change and inconstancy, than what is known by reason and inference. Here, by the way, we may perceive into what absurdities men may wander, who set out with the principle, that what are called natural laws, originate merely in the social feeling. For were this true, nothing could be obligatory, till all *felt* to that effect. As for truths not quite obvious at first sight, if you would render them familiar by reducing them to some general principle, I will give you one which I borrow from no subtile philosopher, but from the plain and unlettered mystic Macarius—*compliance with universal order.* For such an universal order really subsists, which, descending from the Supreme Being, to the beings he has created, links them with himself subordinately, and to one another, in the relation either of equality, or of unequal rank and dignity; and every obligation or duty is the natural consequence of this universal order, how little soever our blinded hearts may be disposed to comply with it as the primeval law of our existence."

12. *To a divinity student at Tübingen, who had informed him of a remarkable religious revival which had taken place among a number of his fellow-students.*

"*Feb.* 20, 1747.

"Your letter of the 1st inst. delights me for two reasons; because I regard it as a token of your unabated love, and because it contains such very pleasing tidings to the glory of God; for you may suppose how it cheers me to learn that N. N. and others of our Denkendorf students are among those you describe as awakened to a serious concern for real Christianity. May the faithful and good Shepherd take these precious souls into his continual keeping! May he preserve and strengthen them, and cause many of his best blessings to be spread abroad by their means! As any one seeing me thus writing, might easily conclude, that surely I could not close my letter here; so how truly does our God, who commences nothing with *us* in vain, perfect it unto the end! Yes, the first outpouring of his gracious goodness is an earnest and pledge that he will complete his work of grace in all who surrender to him the willing heart, and the obedient ear. And in what I have thus said, the whole instruction you kindly desired of me, as to how this religious revival should be conducted, has summarily glided from my pen. But as I am bound to give you my ideas more at large, I advise that each of these young men be very careful to remember and reflect upon his first deep impressions, so as not to suffer that ray of divine grace to become dim which has entered his inmost soul, but to make use of it for assisting his judgment in all future experience; and then he will be at no loss to discern between what is conducive, and what is obstructive, to his spiritual welfare. Holy secret familiarity with the eternal love of God in Christ Jesus, and continual endeavours after more perfect knowledge of it, should constitute the spring of all their proceedings. By perpetually searching the Scriptures, not for mere increase of knowledge, but for blessed personal conformity to the Divine will, true nurture will be supplied to the inward man; and until solidity and stability be thus attained, it is good to let other studies, however valuable, stand still for awhile, yes, till the word of Christ has, by the exercise of faith, entered into the very constitution of the soul. That influence of divine power which is communicated by means of the simplest and plainest truths, and which gains possession of the heart as its passive recipient, without putting it to any aggressive toil, by and by sheds itself abroad in manifold excellences of personal character. I would have no one attempt to force himself into any particular sensible experience, but simply hold on in real faithfulness to what he receives. Whoever thus adopts at once a straightforward spiritual course, or rather I should say, allows divine grace to lead him on, may now safely profess himself in full communion with his christian brethren. But the simplicity and open-heartedness essential to such communion will not oblige him to tread just in the footsteps of another, much less to look out for any particular body of Christians, that he may model himself after *them*. Let him beware, however, of needlessly censuring and judging those who differ from him. The best and safest way is, to keep the eye stedfastly fixed on the great banner of the Lord of hosts, and to proceed as it shall conduct us.

"With respect to behaviour towards fellow-students and others, I would advise our friends not even to seem to court observation, either by any unnecessary preciseness, forbidding manners, reproofs expressed or implied at improper seasons, or by any other indiscreet way of showing faithfulness and bearing testimony; at the same time, neither fear nor favour should make them unfaithful to the souls of their former familiar acquaintance; no, not even upon subjects which are considered as indifferent. Show such persons, without telling them so, that it would give you joy to see every one likeminded with yourselves, nay, surpassing you in whatever you deem necessary or desirable. But the most important thing is to maintain faith in each word and promise of God. Now faith is learnt by faith; that is, it is maintained, increased, and strengthened by exercise; just as walking, speaking, writing, &c. are learnt by walking, speaking, and writing. The difference is only in this, that walking, speaking, &c. are purely physical exercises; whereas the essence of faith consists in yielding ourselves up to the influence of the Holy Spirit, in and by the word, without any physical emotions or perturbations of our own. I hardly know what more to add at present, except how much pleasure it will give me to know that the good thus begun among you is prospering exceedingly. May divine grace prevail mightily in these and other precious souls; particularly in yourself," &c.

It has been already stated,* that Bengel, when at Tübingen, in 1748, addressed a meeting of pious students of that university in a fatherly and edifying manner. The following are passages of that address:—

"During my long residence as tutor in the Theological Seminary of Denkendorf, whenever I had occasion to notice a worthy student, I was always disposed to think better of him than of myself; for such a young man, I thought, could not have let slip so many opportunities, much less have lavished away so much grace as I had done. Provide then, my dear young friends, against being obliged one day to say the same to yourselves. I have often thought, if I could begin life again, I would do better. But then I recollected with joy, that by the grace of God I am what I am, and that could I live my life over again, I should be the same poor sinner as before; consequently, the chief point after all, with myself and with every Christian, must be, 'Lord, have mercy upon me!' Yes, the Lord is faithful; therefore it shall be well with me! Much may be said of self-knowledge; but it is only as the knowledge of God and Christ is connected with it, that it is complete and right, or can be called true self-knowledge. This indeed ever accompanies the knowledge of God and of Christ; without which, whatever is called self-knowledge, be it ever so studied and elaborate, brings no honour to God. For how can God be honoured by the man who confines his attention to himself?

"O it is a noble season of opportunities for a young man while he is at college; he has so much leisure here to give himself to the word of God, and to prayer! He who makes a

* See Part I. ch. ii. p. 18.

good use of advantages like these, is laying up a good foundation against the time to come; a provision which will be serviceable to him through life. Though college discipline may hold him under some restrictions, he enjoys independence itself compared with those who are actually harnessed in the ministry. Whoever, therefore, applies these advantages faithfully, will acquire a reality of *inward* experience, which the avocations of the public ministry are never so likely to insure. For when come abroad into the world, he finds what a world indeed it is, and withal how important and difficult an undertaking is that of a minister of God, a messenger of God's sending to treat with such a world as this. So that if during his years of studentship he has really done his best to prepare himself for his future work, he will be able, without self-reproach, when engaged in it, to commit all his difficulties to the blessed God himself, and to say, 'My God! such and such do I experience the world to be, nor can I make it otherwise; but I commend it to thee. Surely, if I love the souls committed to me, thou lovest them still more.'"

"What an invaluable thing is simple-hearted, fraternal union among all who have but one and the same great common object! And its value is felt more than ever when local circumstances oblige us to live apart at some distance from each other;—when we seem to stand as it were alone."

"The main concern is to be *continually* in an appropriate frame of mind before God. As for any good we may have done, this is safely deposited among his treasures; while the ill we have done may all be repaired by one drop of the precious blood of Christ. Therefore, the less I feed my mind upon what I have done, the better; for it only hinders me from reaching on to the things which are before. We live every day upon God's fatherly goodness and mercy. This is my answer to those who complain that they enjoy only now and then a glimpse of divine grace. Though we are not always in the act of feeding our bodies; though we taste and relish food only while we are taking it; yet the body enjoys the strength of it for a considerable time. So is it with these glimpses of divine grace. That they should continue without intermission, is not necessary to the soul's health; and the grant of them at intervals administers strength for other intervals during which they are suspended. How can we arise and minister to God, if we would be always as it were sitting at table, and feeding upon extraordinary experiences? We are not sent into the world to enjoy dainties every day; if we simply desire composure and peace of spirit, I have not a word to say against it, for this is both right and requisite. Yet, even under the pressure of affliction itself, a person is often a brighter example of piety, feels conscious of more sincerity, and lives in more simple dependence upon God, than when every thing succeeds to his wishes. At all darker seasons we should exercise ourselves in casting a longing look after *the bright banner* which 'in days past' we have descried leading us in the march of the Lord's hosts. Though at present it may not be just in sight, still we know the country; so that we may act like the benighted traveller, who, though he now misses a light which he had seen at a distance, knows the direction he should take. Our natural disposition with regard to spiritual exercises is a compound of indolence, coldness, and faint-heartedness; therefore we need continually to be stirred up, chafed, and animated, by the word of God, and by prayer. As water, though naturally cold, admits of a high degree of heat; but if removed from the fire, will gradually become cold again; so our religious affections, to whatever fervour, liveliness, and vigour they may have been raised, will, if not kept awake and recruited by resh matter, insensibly abate into lukewarmness, and even coldness. Though there still be latent spiritual life, its glow is only kept up by active stirring. Hence St. James says, that 'through works is faith made perfect,' that is, through the perpetual activity and stir of practical devotion. Thus the Christian, whose lot Divine Providence may have cast upon the very worst of times, will possess more spiritual life and vigour than those who live in almost perpetually peaceful retirement. Secluded separatists are seen generally to have more light than life. Why was it that some of the ancient fathers in their solitudes complained of so many assaults from evil spirits? These disagreeables were virtually a benefit to them from God, and might not have been requisite, or at least might have been got rid of, had those good pietists remained in social intercourse with others; whereas, even in their entire seclusion it was needful they should have something for exercise. Let us, therefore, follow as tenderly as possible the leadings of God, even to the least whisper of his holy will; but not think of benefiting ourselves by going beyond our measure, (any more than by falling short of it.) As knowledge and experience render us so familiar with our bodily stature, that with light shining upon one side of us, we expect to see our shadow increased or diminished, as we move towards the light, or recede from it; so familiarity with our religious affections will enable us to discern whether our love is greater or less; will readily tell us just how much we are advancing or retrograding with relation to Him who is the Light of the world. And, surely, our christian love must ever be estimated chiefly by the relation it bears to Christ himself; as also his great love to us must always be the standard of the love we are to bear towards HIM. But the human heart is surprisingly mutable and fickle; and there is not a minute of the day or night in which some mutation backwards or forwards is not passing within it. What then should be our perpetual aim, but to realize the Divine presence constantly with us, especially as our experience of it in every way will be proportionate to the thoughts we have about it? He who, with the confiding disposition of an affectionate child, sets God always before him, goes on easily; not so easily he who regards him only as a stern lawgiver and judge. A traveller over the Alps does not find it needful to be incessantly contemplating the precipices or perils he sees around him: he keeps his eye upon the track at his feet, and proceeds in safety."

"Certainly it can be no small thing in the sight of the Divine Majesty itself, to have the charge of a handful of good persons who are destined to become the salt of a whole country, and to serve for a seed and revival in the kingdom of God upon earth. Persons are disposed enough to value the favour of their fellow-mortals; the present season is peculiarly suited for finding favour with God, as the labourers for his kingdom are so few, and the number of those who are quite devoted to him is so small. No sellers in a market can be so ready to obtain buyers as God is to receive us into his service. He is ever presenting himself to *us*, though we are not always ready for *him*. The more, therefore, is that person likely to be commended, who is ever in earnest to serve him. It is worth while to notice in this respect, how much often depends on a single happy moment of the day or night, when God is found to be specially near to us.

"Satan makes our worldly matters his pretext; for while these make inroads upon our *love*, he, by them, designs an assault upon our *faith*. But by overcoming the Wicked One, we overcome the World. Let a person who has once escaped from the snares of Satan, keep the heart, with all diligence, in the *love of God;* and he will retain the victory, and prosecute it with advantage. For who is the soldier that keeps his ground, and "abideth for ever?" It is "he who doeth the will of God;" he as truly abideth for ever, as doth the everlasting God himself. 1 John ii. 17.

"Many err in imagining there is only one way to be right in a thing; whereas, there may be many ways leading directly to the same object, all in equal conformity with the Divine will. Decided personal religion depends upon a good state of the heart, more than upon any intellectual penetration, or coincidence with others. Our thoughts bear sometimes too lightly, and sometimes too gravely upon our spiritual and practical difficulties. Only let self be sacrificed to God; let us give ourselves up, without any reservation, to his blessed and holy will; and we find ourselves blest with a new will, which may well be called, ἐξουσία τοῦ ἰδίου θελήματος, 'power over *our own* will;' (1 Cor. vii. 37;) thus we act uprightly of free choice, and no longer need to be anxious at every step lest we should do something offensive to God. For we thus live *ingenuè,* like free-born children, with a liberty nowise dangerous, the liberty of faith and love. The soul in this state may say to itself,

'Eat now thy bread with cheerfulness,
Thy doings please Him well.'

Only let not the sweetness of this be considered so essential to our life, as to make us unwilling to forego it, should God see fit to withhold it."

"The life of man in the present world is appointed to warfare and conflict. God would have conducted him to everlasting happiness by the best and easiest way, but as he became unwilling to walk in it, (and his unwillingness is now natural to us all,) the Divine appointments are like those for the Israelites in the wilderness, who, whereas they might have accomplished their journeys in eight days by the direct way, had to spend forty years about it. Let us therefore acquiesce in such appointments, however much we may long to get to heaven; for we do not yield ourselves up to the will of God, till we are quite willing to remain here as long as it shall please him, though it may be for a hundred years."

"There are many things in which we may be either totally

unsuccessful, or constantly experiencing our defects and shortcomings; but such things should not dispirit us, for God's goodness and long-suffering exceed all human thought. On the other hand, we should never say in our hearts, 'If I can but be saved, I shall be contented with the lowest place in heaven;' for thoughts of this sort flatter indolence, and he who indulges them, may soon care nothing about heaven itself. As ambition stirs men in worldly matters to advance what is called their *fortune*, and to push it as far as they can; so a far nobler ambition well becomes every christian believer. The inequality between the highest and lowest rank in this world is as nothing compared with the least degree of inequality in the glorious world above. Who is it that pauses sufficiently to consider this; and who is it that acts accordingly?"

CHAPTER II.

AS A PREACHER AND PASTOR.

Section I.

HIS MANNER OF PREACHING.

Bengel enjoyed all along from his seventeeth year,* to the close of his life, opportunities of preaching the gospel; and this under a variety of circumstances. Even while he was a student at the university, the regulations of his college required him to preach in his turn before the society; and in the vacations he occasionally volunteered the same services at Maulbronn, where his mother resided after her second marriage. He next undertook regular pastoral charges as a curate; had occasionally to preach when he afterwards became assistant college tutor at Tübingen; and still oftener during his two years at Stuttgart, where part of his duty was to assist the town clergy in preaching and catechising. Likewise at Denkendorf, though without any parochial charge, preaching was all along attached to his office as seminary tutor, except for the last two years. Finally, as provost of Herbrechtingen he had to preach there constantly, whenever he was not called to Stuttgart, to attend either the Synod, or the sessions of the Provincial Estates. But when he was elected councillor of Consistory, and provost of Alpirsbach, which required his constant residence at Stuttgart, he became exempt from such official preaching; but he always continued his private expositions and prayer-meetings there, as he had been used to do at Herbrechtingen. We are now, therefore, to view Bengel as a preacher and curate of souls, that we may not only be informed of what he actually did

* In 1704, (Oct. 28,) he preached his first sermon as a divinity student in the university of Tübingen.

in that character, but may perceive how he endeavoured to do more; for with the exception of some funeral addresses, none of his sermons have ever appeared in print; yet the compiler of this work has before him a considerable number of Bengel's unpublished writings, rich in homiletical and pastoral theology.

His sermon texts were ready to his hand in the portions of Scripture appointed for our church services. In earlier life he wrote every word of his sermons, with "very diligent preparation;" indeed he always considered this exercise as indispensable to the formation of a good preacher. But in later life, "he occasionally left a portion of his sermons unwritten, (though even *that* he took care to meditate well;) as he now wished to habituate himself by degrees to connect his thoughts off-hand, so as to be prepared to preach *extempore* when occasion might require it." Though at this he soon found himself remarkably ready, (and we know that he generally followed his maxim to "think much and write little,")* yet we find him even at an advanced age regularly composing at least a sketch of every sermon; thus, the very last he preached at Herbrechtingen, is drawn up with great particularity and exactness. He said, with special reference to preaching, that "we ought to consider it a general axiom, that grace begins where natural means can go no farther; but that as far as these means are available, we are not warranted to expect extraordinary help." That the very apostles were subject to this rule, and it was only for *extra*ordinary emergencies that the consoling and encouraging admonition was given, "Be not careful what ye shall speak:" which by no means proved that they did not meditate their addresses on "common occasions." He also remarked, that "when a preacher of the gospel forbears doing the very things for which he has excellent (natural) ability, just because he wishes to preach Christ more clearly and simply, such a man will find an abundant blessing in his work." That "it does not become us to teach every thing we know, much less every thing just as it occurs to us, but only that which is best adapted to the benefit of our hearers." That "in whatever any one wishes to be wise, let him first of all regard himself as a fool in it, and then he will be wise."

In meditating for his sermon, his custom was first to consider the text with exegetical minuteness, and then carefully to select, by the help of a concordance, such parallel passages as served to form a rich assemblage of scriptural thought and expression.

* See Part II., ch. i.

He has observed, that " in meditating for a sermon it is necessary to dismiss from the mind all thoughts of our worthiness or unworthiness, and to fix it only upon God's honour and will; so as to subside by devout prayer into calm and composed reflection, and be quite divested of self; leaving the rest to God's good pleasure."

In choosing his subject "he used to look into the appointed portion of Scripture, as if he had never preached from it before, and as if he should never preach from it again. Whatever then appeared to be the choicest part of it, and seemed more particularly impressed upon his mind by divine influences, this he took for his subject, with an eye to the honour of God, the love of Christ, and the salvation of men. Fundamental truths relating to faith, love, and hope, abounded in his preaching; nor was he ashamed of that abundance, but took it for granted that nothing can be more acceptable to truly pious souls; and that they have a just claim upon us for accommodation of their wants." He made the familiar necessities of his own soul a measure for selecting what he should prepare for others, and reserved his more learned researches for communication by the press. In his " Sketch of the Church of the United Brethren" (p. 83,) he says, " From my heart do I prize as worthy of all acceptation the sufferings of our Lord Jesus Christ, and therefore have always been glad to hear such a subject preached upon. For the same reason it has ever been my delight to preach passion sermons; and these, I may say it without boasting, have been favoured with peculiar acceptance in my congregations. I can satisfactorily show, from sketches of such sermons still by me, that the main subject of each, as well as the manner in which I arranged, treated, and applied it, comprised the very marrow of the gospel, and did not consist merely of circumstantials. Still I am acquainted with many a servant of Christ whom I far prefer to myself in this respect."

Bengel's manner of preaching, however, was anything but sameness. " At one time he would give a running exposition and application of the selected passage; at another he would elicit and dwell upon some important doctrine; at another, proceed more directly to particular practical application." He took great pains to acquire skill in concluding his sermon; for he considered that "a preacher who can come to a close when and how he pleases, is able to preach the whole sermon with much greater ease and freedom."

His manner of address from the pulpit, says a contemporary,

was "natural, simple, and almost catechetical: hence the most illiterate, and even children, could easily understand him." He says himself, in the preface to his "Sixty Practical Addresses on the Apocalypse," "Some say I write obscurely, but preach plainly. Here then are my discourses just as I delivered them;" (they were taken down in short-hand); "here is something plain."—Rhetorical flourishes in sermons, and especially any aim at popularity, he regarded as sinful; he also had no ambition to overpower his audience with sudden and violent emotions. His instruction was addressed with great humility to pious hearts; but he sometimes spoke to the consciences of the impenitent in a most impressive and awful manner, in a tone and style of holy severity. Though he never laboured at forced animation, yet when it came naturally, he made use of it. In method he took the apostles for his pattern, with respect to their previously touching upon what was for the better, and then adducing what they had to blame; hence he disapproved of the way of Gottfried Arnold, and his followers, who commenced their discourses by setting forth what they had to find fault with, and then showed how it was to be remedied." He also remarked, that "we do not find mention of our great adversary so repeatedly occurring in the Scriptures, as is now the case in common sermons, which, upon every occasion, bring us at once into a sort of contact with the author of evil; whereas the inspired teachers, in the New Testament, always set what is good in the foreground, and then earnestly insist upon our knowing and opposing every evil of the human heart; for whichsoever of these evils is overcome, in that respect Satan has no advantage against us."

The question, when the law, and when the gospel, ought most to prevail in our preaching, he answered by saying, "We must never take others for our rule in this matter. Let every one do as God shall direct him, while making the best use of his understanding and knowledge." He considered his own preaching as more didactic than awakening; and though he knew "that awakening preachers, by their fervently urging things home upon their hearers, are found to do more striking good to some," he never adopted their *manner*, because in himself it would have been forced and unnatural. He observed, that "it was best to set forth the truth in its own luminous simplicity, without having recourse to quaint, low, or technical expressions, or odd sayings." In his sermons he would sometimes read scripture passages at full length, because he thought that "we ought not to give the generality of people credit for any thing like so much scripture knowledge as we are apt to do: besides, that simple passages of Scripture prove, after all, the best and most refreshing food to those hearers who are really thirsting for salvation." With respect to his delivery, he had ever, from his early days, determined "so to moderate himself in expression, that the tongue might not go before the thoughts, or utter any thing unadvisedly; and he aimed so to guard against all levity and youthful foppery, in language and manner, as to maintain that proper gravity (σεμνότης) which holy Scripture enjoins." With equal care did he avoid the bad practice of "uttering every sentence in a raised unnatural tone of voice," so that even "in the more forcible passages of his sermons," he would elevate his voice and action in only a very slight degree. "He was particularly sparing of emotion when he preached on the passion of our Lord," because he would always have sermons of this kind comport with the gravity of the subject, and to be delivered with appropriate sobriety. For a reason of the same description, he would "never in the pulpit raise his arm at full length, but only from the elbow."—After he had preached, he used "carefully to note down any thing he had forgotten to say, that he might profitably introduce it on a future occasion;" and he always endeavoured to follow Professor Anton's* advice, to "make a beginning for the next sermon immediately after preaching the last; while your spirit is still warm and stirred within you." When any sermon he had preached seemed to have had no effect, he consoled himself in its being "of some use for humbling *himself*, and perhaps for convincing others that the grand matter of benefit to souls does not reside in the preacher."

But that a preacher with such faithfulness, and depth of sound knowledge, and of such largeness of heart, as embraced the whole plan of salvation, must have been peculiarly qualified for exhorting and instructing his fellow-christians, is evident; especially as it was no insignificant part of his character, that his call to preach the gospel was habitually regarded by him with the most decided and delightful preference, as a business which more than any other God had laid upon his heart. In the true spirit of Spener, he considered that every candidate for the christian ministry "ought to be able to exhibit the credentials of his spiritual birth, because an unconverted minister, being not a man of prayer, must be as inefficient as a bird with one wing." In this respect he had no cause to be ashamed, for he knew in whom

* Of Halle.

he had believed, and "spake" and testified, *because* he believed. He also felt much encouragement about his *public* ministrations, because he was convinced, by manifold experience, "that far more good can be done *vivâ voce*, (by personal addresses,) than by writing of books." "A good minister of a parish," he said, "has excellent advantage for getting at men's consciences; and will be regarded and made use of as a pastor, indeed, by those whose hearts are affected by the Spirit of God, and opened to receive the truth in the love of it. Only such a minister must not flatter himself that he shall ever be able to make all crooked and rough things straight and even to his mind, so as to set every member of his congregation upon the right footing. For still the greater part of them will seem to have been as it were "born in vain," (Ezra x. 3.) "Many are called, but few chosen;" but then, what one is enabled to accomplish with that few, is the more precious:"

The following are a few sketches, &c. of his sermons.

1. Sermon on John x. 27—30.

"My sheep hear my voice; &c. —— I and my Father are one."*

The Scriptures contain a variety of pleasing similitudes, which illustrate the character and blessedness of true believers. Thus in the fifteenth chapter of St. John's Gospel, our Saviour speaks of himself as the true Vine, and of his people as the branches; by which he teaches that they are related to himself in the closest manner, and are expected to bring forth the fruits of righteousness. Accordingly, and in that same chapter, he calls those persons his friends who do whatsoever he commands them; and in Matthew xii. 49, he calls them his brethren and sisters. In the fifth of the Epistle to the Ephesians, St. Paul compares the church to the body, and Christ to the head of it; and as but one soul animates and governs the human body, so they who will be members of Christ, must be all governed by his Spirit, and have the same mind in *them*, which is also in *him*. Likewise in Matthew xiii. our Saviour compares the visible church to fishes of all sorts inclosed in a net; the good part of which represent the righteous, and the rejected part, the ungodly. But there is one similitude still more affectingly striking; it is this, where Christ speaks of himself as the Good Shepherd, and of true believers as

* This was Bengel's first sermon. He preached it in the Theological College at Tübingen, Oct. 28, 1704, in the eighteenth year of his age.

his sheep. When he saith, "My sheep hear my voice;" he teaches both what their disposition is towards *him*, (they hear his voice and obediently follow it,) and what good care he takes of *them;* (he knows them; gives them eternal life; and will not suffer them to perish.) Let us better understand this, by considering—

The character and condition of true Christians; or,

I. Their nature and disposition.

II. Their glory and blessedness.

God grant it may not be without edification to us! Amen.

The words of the text are a part of our Lord's vindication of his Godhead, in reply to the contradictions of unbelievers. To show the sin of their unbelief, he appeals to the wonderful miracles he had wrought, and then exhibits the disposition or character requisite for being his true disciples, as possessing in itself that belief and love of God which his enemies were strangers to. He further shows what is the nature and disposition of all his true disciples, when he declares to his enemies why they did not believe on him, namely, because they were not of his sheep; for that it was one mark of being his sheep, to "*hear* his voice." This does not mean *mere hearing*, that is, listening to the preaching of Christ *without laying to heart* what we hear; for the unbelieving Jews had done this; but it means that his real followers do not wilfully resist the truth set before them, but assent to, and approve of it from the heart, and reduce it all to practice. To the same effect he further saith to them, "He that is of God heareth my voice; ye, therefore, hear it not, because ye are not of God."

Christ's sheep also *follow* him. The Jews knew that their (animal) sheep generally followed the shepherd; so do all spiritual sheep follow Christ in life, sufferings, and death. Whether they hear or read his exhortations to faith, and hope, and love, to the fear of God, or to any other virtue, these exhortations they follow. Do they learn how he suffered for them, and herein left them an example? They follow his steps, as St. Peter teaches us to do, in his first Epistle, chap. ii., and according to that fundamental rule which Christ himself has given—"If any man will come after me, let him deny himself, and take up his cross daily, and follow me." Let us consider—

II. THE BLESSEDNESS AND GLORY OF REAL CHRISTIANS: Christ here says, "*I know them.*" This means not only that he knoweth all their works, that he tries and proves their hearts and inmost thoughts, as we find he was able to "tell" the woman of

Samaria "all that ever she did;" and as he proved that he knows the evil thoughts of the hearts of his enemies; but it also means that he has such a *kind* and *gracious knowledge of them*, that, in the character of their Good Shepherd *he suffers them to "lack nothing;* feeds them in the green pastures of his word, restores and refreshes their souls;" and takes that affectionate care of them which we find he does; attends to and cherishes them in such a peculiar and special manner, that they shall never perish, nor shall the infernal destroyer himself be able successfully to assault them: so that they may joyfully exclaim with the Apostle St. Paul, "O death, where is thy sting? O grave, where is thy victory?" for Christ their Lord hath "given to them eternal life." What no eye hath seen, nor ear heard, and what hath never entered into the heart of man to conceive, hath God prepared for them that love him."—It is true that the children of God in this world have much to endure in temporal respects from the ungodly, and in spiritual respects from their adversary the devil; many crosses, trials, troubles, and afflictions, abide them. Through much tribulation must they enter into the kingdom of God. But the sufferings of this present time are not worthy to be compared with the glory which shall be revealed in them. "Our light affliction," says the apostle, "which is but for a moment, worketh out for us a far more exceeding and eternal weight of glory."

Are Christians such a blessed and happy people, that Christ "knows them" in that way of grace which we have been describing? ...... Who then would not wish to find himself a real Christian, one of the sheep of that Good Shepherd Jesus Christ? Who would not wish to abide under his faithful and pastoral care for ever? I doubt not we all, at once, perceive that this must be happiness indeed. Who then is there amongst us that can now comfort himself with the thought of possessing it? We answer, all may do so, who walk worthily of the name of Him, whose sheep they desire to be; who follow him in faith, love, hope, and other virtues. Let only the same mind be in us which was also in him, and suffer not the heat of trial and temptation to surprise you, because Christ himself hath tasted death, and that for *us*. Let us beware that we never depart from our Good Shepherd into ways which are not good; by following our own will instead of his. As Christ himself is represented in Isaiah liii. 7, "as a sheep that before her shearers is dumb;" so let our strength be also in quietness and confidence; and let us "run with patience the race that is set before us." O how many depart from this pattern and example of Christ! How many rather resemble the fox in cunning, the swine in low and grovelling indulgence of drinking and eating, the goat in lasciviousness, the dog in envy, &c. than they resemble the patient lambs and sheep of Christ's flock, by obediently following their Good Shepherd! How many live merely to fulfil the desires of the flesh and of the mind; how many follow the multitude to do evil, instead of following Christ! Alas! "they have their reward!" But, beloved, let us not run with them into the same foolish and perilous indulgences, how much soever they may be offended at us, and incensed against us; for to them we are not to look, either for thanks or for reward. Christ is our Lord and Shepherd; him let us follow, and we shall lack nothing. Has he not declared to us, that he knows his sheep? Happy, then, are they whom he thus knows. He knows their affliction and their poverty; he knows what they need, and he careth for them. He will acknowledge them as his own, and as the blessed children of his Father, in the last day; but he will say to the goats on his left hand, "Verily, I know you not:—depart from me, ye cursed," &c. The righteous will then be for ever with him their Lord, and him whose voice they have heretofore heard "in faith, not in sight," and have followed it, him shall they thenceforth see as he is, face to face. For this comfort of hope, be praise, honour, and thanksgiving, to the great and faithful chief Shepherd! May he lead us by his Spirit and Word, that we may walk worthily of him unto all pleasing! Amen!

---

2. Sermon on the Gospel for the nineteenth Sunday after Trinity. Matt. ix. 1—8.*

It is most comfortable and delightful to read in Moses those words of the supreme LOVER OF OUR LIFE, "I am the Lord that healeth thee." (Exod. xv. 26.) Though he created man in a capacity to need no physician, for then were his soul and body in their most beautiful perfection, and in the finest harmony with each other, yet, alas! by the fall, Adam degraded himself and all his posterity into a very different condition; for every human soul now naturally bears the disgraceful image of sin, instead of the pure and undefiled likeness of God; and Isaiah (i. 5, 6,) truly describes our awful condition, when he says, "The whole head is sick, and the whole heart faint. From the sole of the foot even to the head, there is no soundness in it, but wounds, and

* Preached at Maulbronn, 10th of Oct. 1706, shortly after his severe illness; in his twentieth year.

bruises, and putrefying sores; which have not been bound up, neither have been closed, nor mollified with ointment." The body, likewise, is become subject to the mournful change of returning to the dust whence it was taken, and of being previously afflicted with many a sickness and woe, the forerunners of death. But thanks be to God, who as the true Physician, has vouchsafed us ample remedies against this double misery. For the recovery of the soul he has provided the precious blood of atonement, through those sufferings of his dear Son, which were predicted by Isaiah, who said, " Surely he hath borne our griefs, and carried our sorrows; yet we did esteem him stricken, smitten of God, and afflicted. But he was wounded for our transgressions; he was bruised for our iniquities; the chastisement of our peace was upon him, and with his stripes we are healed." And our bodies themselves are, by our blessed Redeemer, already so benefited as to be either totally exempt from much hardship and suffering; or else such sufferings are, in the case of pious persons, changed from punishment into fatherly correction. We have satisfactory evidence, in the gospel before us, that our Saviour is the true physician, and the master of healing. For here is a poor man brought to him for recovery from sickness, and, behold, he heals him in a manner worthy of himself, and altogether divine. He recovered him both in body and soul; and he wrought this recovery in the presence of his enemies, notwithstanding all their rancorous opposition. Let us, therefore, set this miracle before us on the present occasion; and consider the cure of this paralytic—

First, As begun in the soul;

Secondly, As vindicated from the unjust conceptions of the scribes; and

Thirdly, As gloriously completed by the gift of bodily health: And O that my beloved hearers may singly and privately lay to heart the divine truth which is here suggested to us; and that God may write it effectually in all our hearts, by the power of his good Spirit! Amen.

I. *The cure* of this paralytic was *begun in his soul.* " Behold, they brought unto him a man sick of the palsy, lying on a bed." The circumstances show that the chief object of these persons was to get their long-afflicted patient healed by Christ, who had now become greatly renowned for his words and works. But he begins the work of healing in a way very different from what *they* expected; for, first of all, he heals the *soul* of the sufferer, and defers the cure of his body for awhile, saying, " Son, be of good cheer, thy sins be forgiven thee!" Sin being the insidious cause of *all* sicknesses and of every human woe, what wonder was it that Christ should first remove this hidden *root* of the malady? The man, as thus assured of the forgiveness of his sins, could now be of good comfort indeed! The wall of spiritual separation between himself and God, who is the fountain of all comfort, was now removed! We also, if "justified by faith, have peace with God, through our Lord Jesus Christ." (Rom. v. 1.) Yes, in this way we all may become assured that we are the holy children of God. Observe, here, that Jesus addresses the sick man himself by the name of "Son!" Moreover, the cure is wrought through the *faith* of those who brought him to Jesus; for it is expressly said, "When Jesus saw *their faith.*" Not as though Christ needed to *see* this work of theirs in order to *know* that they had faith; for he saw as easily into *their* hearts as into the hearts of the evil-thinking scribes. But this faith of theirs was so well pleasing to him, that he was willing, at once, to give the poor sufferer the benefit of it. It is true, that in our spiritual concerns, and especially in the matter of justification before God, none can have the special benefit of the faith of others; for "the just shall live by HIS faith."* But in temporal matters this may easily be done. A sick person may be divinely recovered and preserved through the faith which is exercised by his relatives and friends: he may be given to their believing prayers.

Our Saviour's conduct here further shows that *spiritual* welfare should always be our *first* concern; for as the soul is so deplorably infected by sin, our chief business must be to obtain deliverance from this worst of evils, even the true deliverance which is only by Christ, our great Physician. But as they that are whole feel not their need of him, we must take care to know and become sensible of the great wretchedness to which sin has reduced us; not only our original and native corruption, but our many actual sins, committed both knowingly and in ignorance. We must acknowledge and believe that we have thus deservedly subjected ourselves to sickness and bodily pain, and rendered ourselves liable to Divine displeasure, condemnation, and future punishment. Believing this, our hearts must be moved with godly sorrow and godly fear; and be affected with holy dread of all sin. Yes, we ought to feel true contrition of spirit, and inward aversion to all iniquity; we ought to be heartily sorry, not so much at being liable to punishment, as at having offended

* Rom i. 17.

against the fatherly goodness and faithfulness of our Creator, Preserver, Redeemer, and Comforter. When the heart is, indeed, thus affected; when we sincerely feel and acknowledge our spiritual diseases; then is the season for applying to our good Physician. Bring, therefore, thy contrite heart and spirit, miserable and vile as thou mayst be, to Him; disclose to Him, and disclose, if circumstances require it, to a christian friend or christian minister, thy real condition; do it without reserve; complain of thy misery to the faithful Saviour; pray to Him for help; draw nigh to Him in true faith, and he will certainly accept thee; he will heal all thy diseases; he will bind up thy wounds; he will wash thy stripes; he will make thee perfectly whole and clean, through his own precious blood; he will present thee without spot before his heavenly Father. Yes, he is willing and ready to do all this; just as in the case of the paralytic, he did not want many entreaties.

This, beloved brethren, being the only safe state for our souls, should it not be our greatest care neither to rest nor to relax till we have received forgiveness of our sins through the blood of Christ, and have become assured of our admission into the number of the children of God, whose fellowship is with Christ? Let us not rest till our consciences have become thus cheered and comforted; till we are able, on solid ground, which must be that of the truth itself, to declare with joy, that Christ's word to us is, "Son," or "Daughter, be of good cheer, thy sins be forgiven thee." This, however, is to be obtained in no other way than by the divinely prescribed and irreversible order of repentance and faith, as we may even see from the text before us. The eyes of the Lord are upon faith; "without faith it is impossible to please God." (Heb. xi. 6.)

But lest any deceive themselves by mistaking some empty dream, some vain imagination, some fleshly confidence, for true and lively faith, we must be reminded, that the faith here insisted on, is a "faith which worketh by love," and clearly manifests its reality by "good works." The faith of this sick man's friends manifested itself thus; and so did the faith of the sick man himself, for he immediately obeyed the word of Jesus.

We have high and important reasons for that *supreme* care of the soul which is here recommended. Consider with me, beloved brethren, why God hath given us this present life? Is it that we may spend our few precarious years in looking carelessly about us; in toiling to obtain the enjoyments and pleasures of this world; in merely taking care of our frail bodies; or in heaping up uncertain riches, and gaining earthly possessions?

Has he not placed us here that we may serve HIM, and be duly prepared for eternity; we, who are, or ought to be, the temple and habitation of His divine glory; and that we may learn to become inseparably united to Himself; "bound up," (as the Scripture expresses it,) "in the bundle of life" by blessed communion "with the Lord our God?" How far, then, do our personal life, conduct, and conversation, accord with this great and benevolent intention? Do we faithfully consider the high, original, and divine grandeur of the human soul, which never can be satisfied with the perishable delights of *this* life? Must we not soon, perhaps to-morrow, leave this life, and quit for ever a world into which we brought nothing, and from which we can carry nothing out? This mortal body must soon "return again to its earth;" but in what condition will my immortal spirit "return to God that gave it?" Surely it is of more consequence than gaining the whole world, to know, whether our souls shall stand in sight of his throne as before a Father perfectly reconciled to us, or as before a Judge whom we have everlastingly offended. Alas! "what profit" will it *then* be, I ask it in our Saviour's own words, "to have gained the whole world, and to have lost one's own soul?"—Therefore, let us now, "while we have time," seriously reflect and consider what our present spiritual condition really is. For is it not a fact that we have spent a very large portion of our time, perhaps the best part of it, without even thinking seriously and in earnest upon such a subject at all? Is it not true, that we have been far more serious and in earnest about possessing *this* world's goods, accommodations, pleasures, and delights, than about being "counted worthy to obtain THAT WORLD, and the glory of the resurrection?" Have we not much more "loved this present world," than made it our great business to seek that its very opposite, "the love of the Father" may be in us? Yet, hear how the inspired Apostle St. John warns us against such a state of mind: "Love not the world, neither the things that are in the world. If any man love the world, the love of the Father is not in him;" &c. Our temporal occupations, we allow, are appointed us by Divine Providence itself; but have we not been so much concerned how these occupations may be turned all to our mere *temporal* account, that in the mean time we have totally forgotten to labour for the kingdom of God? Or are we with our blessed Saviour making it our very "meat and drink to do the will of our heavenly Father, and to finish his work?" Are we not indulging high thoughts of ourselves, self-righteous thoughts, which must ever be without foundation; instead of endeavouring to be well assured of the grace of God towards us; that we are holding communion with Christ, and fellowship with his sincere disciples? Do we seriously consider that there will hereafter be a resurrection to life, if we have done good; but to condemnation, if we have done evil? O that we would be constantly remembering and reflecting that "whatsoever a man soweth, the same shall he also reap," "whether it be good or whether it be evil;"—that so inestimable "a treasure in the heavens," "a crown of glory that fadeth not away," is placed within the reach of us all, that our conversation may even *now* be in heaven, as citizens of heaven! O, if we indeed enjoyed any foretaste of this glorious inheritance, how earnestly should we be caring for our souls, and regarding every opportunity, every moment, lost, in which we have forgotten to bear that inheritance in mind and heart, and neglected to frame and order every act and sufferance with an eye to its complete possession.

We consider—

II. *Our Saviour's vindication of his manner of healing*, in reply to the unjust thoughts of the scribes. They thought it strange that this Jesus, whom they took for a mere man, should arrogate to himself the power of forgiving sins. As every sin is primarily an offence against God, so they had Scripture to prove that it is God only who can remit its guilt and punishment. Hence they considered our Saviour's language as nothing short of blasphemy. Such were the private thoughts then passing in their minds; for they did not utter them. Our Lord, however, who "needed not that any should testify to him of man, for he knew what was in man," publicly remonstrated with them upon their evil thoughts in general, and upon this in particular, and then proved, by a miracle, his power on earth to forgive sins. His reply to their evil thoughts may be considered as to the following effect:—"*Ye* choose to regard me as nothing but a mere man, whereas you ought to know that I am truly God. You have no *cause* for entertaining those evil thoughts which I see in your hearts respecting me; for I will at once demonstrate that I can forgive sins, and will now put it within your own power to believe it. Is it not evident, that to heal a paralytic with a word is a *divine* work; a work that cannot be wrought, in his own name, by a mere man? Ye shall be bound then to own a truth which is self-evident; namely, that I have power to forgive sins." And now he immediately completed his work of double healing, by commanding the paralytic to rise up and walk. Let us pause here a moment and learn how necessary it is so to order and keep our very thoughts, as not to offend God our Saviour, or to injure the righteous cause of our neighbour. It is true that men in general tacitly agree to let one another's *thoughts* alone; neither can any *human* tribunal take cognizance of men's evil thoughts, except when these issue in evil words and deeds; for God only is a discerner of the thoughts and intents of the heart, and men judge but "after the sight of their eyes, and the hearing of their ears." But to Him whose ways are not as *our* ways, our most hidden thoughts are naked, open, and amenable. It is He who "trieth the hearts and reins," and of whom it is written, "O Lord, thou hast searched me and known me! Thou understandest my thought afar off." Therefore let all the earth stand in awe of Him, and fear before him; let us dread to displease him, and fear to offend him even with our thoughts; for with these we *may* offend him grievously, when we distrust his revealed truth, his almighty power, his justice, equity, or his love in general; or when we indulge any particular lust, any secret desire which agrees not with the spirit of his holy commandments. We should always remember, that "from within, out of the heart, proceed evil thoughts, murders, adulteries, fornications, thefts, an evil eye, blasphemy, pride, foolishness; that things which defile the man and make him reprobate before God, spring from within him as naturally as noxious waters flow from a poisoned fountain. Hence we should be particularly careful not to harbour uncharitable and evil thoughts of our neighbour; much less should we condemn any part of his conduct, or misinterpret any of his actions, which after all may perhaps be good. It is very easy to sin against others in this way, and we are very liable to do it. Observe how Eli wronged the devout and pious Hannah when he hastily regarded her as given to insobriety, at the very time when she was pouring out her heart to God! How did Simon the Pharisee wrong not only the woman who gratefully bestowed the precious ointment upon our Saviour, but even our Saviour himself, when he thought, "This man, were he a prophet, would have known who and what manner of woman it is that toucheth him, for she is a sinner." How did "the barbarous people" at Melita, wrong the Apostle St. Paul, of whom, because a viper had come out of the kindling fuel and fastened on his hand, they thought, "This man doubtless is a murderer, whom vengeance suffereth not to live!" And, lastly, how unjustly did these scribes also think of our Lord and Saviour Jesus Christ.

But true christian charity, or love, obliges us to take care that we put the best possible construction upon the conduct of others. A real Christian may be actuated by pure kindness and love in reproving another whom he sees endangered by evident sin, wasting precious time in idleness, using improper language, or indulging in fopperies. Now the person in fault, though he may be older, or higher in rank, or wiser in other respects than the person reproving him, ought not to receive unkindly the well-intended admonition, but to allow it a charitable meaning; not imputing it to pride, insolence, injustice, or arrogation of superiority. Again, if we see any of our fellow-men remarkably *unfortunate*, as it is called, that is, under some providential chastisement, we are not to take it for granted that *they* must be more ungodly and wicked than *others*. If we see a person make a conscience of some uncommanded observances, or of things not absolutely necessary to salvation, or to moral decorum, we are not hastily to attribute it to self-will, pride, or particularity; but ought to bear with such a person, and to treat him with kindness and tenderness. Such are some of the requisites of that truly christian charity which (1 Cor. xiii.) " beareth all things, believeth all things, hopeth all things, endureth all things." How can an uncharitable and " evil-thinking" heart be in the least degree pleasing to God? Our evil-mindedness and wickedness are as exposed to the eye of Him with whom we have to do, as are the possibly good motives and upright intentions of our fellow-Christian whom we may think ill of. Instead of judging others, we should be constantly watching the state of our *own* hearts, that we may know how *we ourselves* are disposed towards God. We ought ever to be considering whether we have sincerity enough to come before him, and say, " Search me, O God, and know my heart: prove me, and know my thoughts;" or whether, instead of this, our Saviour has not occasion to ask us, as he did the scribes, " Wherefore think ye evil in your hearts?"

We notice lastly—

III. Christ's *completion of the cure*, in the man's *bodily recovery*. Having vindicated himself with words of power against the evil thoughts of the scribes, he proceeds to perform a miraculous bodily cure; and thus to evince, in the sight of all, his divine competence to heal an incurable disease, and consequently to forgive sins. Observe how courageously he addresses himself to the work, taking no further notice of the evil thoughts of his adversaries. Surely we may hereby learn, that in our christian course, and in the faithful discharge of every duty, we ought not to be diverted from our business by the wrong judgments and evil conduct of others about us; but to be content with the approval of God and of a good conscience.

"*Then saith he to the sick of the palsy, Arise, take up thy bed, and go unto thine house.*" This served to let all men see that he uttered no *unmeaning* language, when he said, "*Thy sins be forgiven thee;*" but that it was a word of grace from his own omnipotence; a word which could find its way to the healing of souls and consciences, by *imparting* the forgiveness it announced; a word which also the winds and seas obey; which opens the eyes of the blind, gives the power of speech to the dumb, hearing to the deaf, and life itself to the dead. This command to the paralytic conveyed to him an ability to perform it; for no sooner was it said, "Arise, take up thy bed, and go unto thine house," than the man arose and did so. And we may believe that he *continued* obedient to Christ: that he loved, honoured, and glorified him before men. Here then let us learn how *we* ought to act when God has delivered *us* from afflictions, whether temporal or spiritual. Is it not most reasonable that we should thankfully acknowledge such gracious favour, by consecrating, in every way we can, to His service and praise, our souls and bodies thus mercifully restored? Surely he has hereby given us fresh occasion for "glorifying him in our body and in our spirit, which are as certainly his," as we are his redeemed people. Peter's wife's mother, after Christ had recovered her from a fever, "arose and ministered unto" him and his disciples. We, in like manner, must "yield our members as instruments of righteousness unto God," and "present ourselves as living sacrifices, acceptable to himself through Jesus Christ." By nature we are adversaries to him, and our own corrupt nature is always indisposed even to this "reasonable service;" but the regenerating and renewing grace that speaks the word "Arise," imparts a power to do so, as truly as power was imparted to the bodily frame of the paralytic. "For we are his workmanship, created in Christ Jesus unto good works, which God hath before ordained that we should walk in them." When God has saved our life from destruction, surely we ought to say, "O Lord, I am thy servant; help thou me! so will we sing my songs in thy house as long as we live." (Isa. xxxviii. 20.) But our best way of being grateful to him, is to devote our entire lives to his praise; that we may "run in the way of his commandments, because he hath enlarged our heart." We shall then likewise endeavour to make our fellow-sinners our brethren, "partakers of the benefit." If God has regenerated and enlightened us by his word, then, as his peculiar people, zealous of good works, we are to "show forth the virtues of Him who hath called us out of darkness into his marvellous light; acting out that precept of Christ, "Being converted, strengthen thy brethren." St. Paul, like a true child of God, though in captivity before king Agrippa, said, "I would to God that not only thou, but also all who hear me this day, were both almost and altogether such as I am, except these bonds." Have we also been restored to *bodily* health? Then must we make ourselves as useful as we can to our afflicted neighbours, never forgetting that our own health was renewed for that very purpose.

Consider, beloved, that this is the will of God in Christ Jesus concerning us. It is what he expects of us; and upon this he has not left us to confer with flesh and blood. Neither are we to give it a secondary attention, and soon to forget it; but we are to seek first this business of life as long as we live. Let us, therefore, be prevailed with to engage every day afresh in whatever service our blessed Lord and Master requires, and we shall experience in due time the fulfilment of that exceeding great and precious promise made by himself, "Blessed are those servants whom the Lord, when he cometh, shall find so doing; verily I say unto you, he will gird himself, and make them to sit down to meat, and will come forth and serve them."

If as Christ's true disciples, we improve *to our neighbour's welfare* the gifts and abilities bestowed upon *us*, we shall receive from Christ the same regard and recompense as if our services had been done to himself. Yes, and *beforehand*, even in this *present* life, we may expect to enjoy invaluable advantages by faithful obedience to Him. The Scriptures every where promise this to us; assuring us that as "Godliness with contentment is great gain," so it "hath the promise of the life that now is," as well as "of that which is to come." Many a Christian who sincerely loves and fears God, and "prays" to him "without ceasing," is more prospered even in temporal things, (not to mention that he is far more *contented* and *happy* about them,) than worldly minded persons who rise early, who late take rest, and eat the bread of cares and anxieties; "for surely God gives to his beloved in their sleep." The highest ambition of worldly men is to enjoy what they call *prosperity* in this fleeting life; but pious persons, though ever so "perplexed on every side," with their "soul continually in their hand," are privileged to enjoy a double blessing; they not only attain "the kingdom of God and his righteousness," which they "seek first," but "all other things are added unto them;" the blessings of this life are given them over and above, as well as "the principal thing," the "one thing needful." And though this additional bounty may be sometimes withholden, which however is an exception to the rule, still they will be "abundantly" compensated in the heavenly kingdom, and "the more" so in consideration of what was withholden from them for "a little while," and as it were "for a moment." For they who wait for the Son of God from heaven, shall be glorified in their very bodies; which shall be "fashioned like unto his glorious body, according to the mighty working whereby he is able to subdue all things even unto himself. Then shall "they shine forth as the sun in the kingdom of their Father;" "everlasting joy shall be upon their heads;" they shall be familiar with the highest and most perfect loveliness; "they shall see God" "face to face."

May He dispose our hearts to be continually "thinking on these things;" that such may be our lives in this present world, as not to make us one day repent of the manner in which we have led them!

"Think of it, while you sojourn here,
Toil in his love and holy fear,
Nor think to mourn your choice;
But trust in his most holy word,
As your best comfort, and the Lord
Shall make you soon rejoice."

Amen.

---

3. Sermon on Acts iv. 12.*

"Neither is there salvation in any other; for there is none other name under heaven given among men whereby we must be saved."

There is abundant reason for showing such respect to Scripture as to believe that not a word in it is given of God in

* Preached in his twentieth year, in Stuttgart, at his examination for holy orders, 23d December, 1706.

vain; but that every jot and tittle of the sacred volume is conducive to his glory, and all profitable for doctrine, reproof, correction, or instruction in righteousness. This remark may even be applied to the names imposed on scripture characters, whether by God immediately, by his holy angels, or by holy men. Thus the name of *Israel* was given to Jacob, because as a prince he had wrestled with God and prevailed; thus the prophet Hosea was divinely directed to call his several children by the names of Jezreel, Lo-ruhamah, and Lo-ammi, names significative of God's heavy displeasure against the ten tribes; and thus the aged priest Zacharias was enjoined by the angel Gabriel, to give to his promised son the name of John, signifying that he was to be a preacher of the grace now about to be manifested to the world. We might mention other instances of the kind, as the name of Abraham from Abram, and of Sarah from Sarai; of Peter, whose name signifies a rock, and of James and John, whom our Lord surnamed Boanerges, the sons of thunder. But as the light of the stars is excelled by the brightness of the sun, so are the names of all others excelled by the most blessed and divine name of JESUS, at which "every knee shall bow, and every tongue confess that he is Lord, to the glory of God the Father." Therefore St. Peter assures us in the text, that "there is salvation in no other; for there is none other name under heaven given among men whereby we must be saved, but the name of Jesus Christ." Thus he represents the precious name of Jesus—

I. As peculiar to Christ alone;

II. As a name bringing salvation; and,

III. As a name full of joy for every man.

O Lord Jesus Christ! whose name is as unction shed forth, most salutary and most refreshing, mercifully grant us all to experience its grace and sweet savour, that being strengthened by its mighty power, we may zealously follow thee in life and death, through honour and dishonour! Amen.

Few as are the words of the text, our weakness can comprehend but little of their full and glorious import. Let us, however, attempt to extract something of their honeyed sweetness, and for this purpose consider the name of Jesus—

I. *As a name peculiarly appropriated to himself.* St. Peter, in this noble defence before the Jewish council, declared that there is salvation in no other. It is as if he had said, "Ye men of Israel, think what ye will of this man Jesus, who has been so despised in your eyes; and think what ye will of us his followers; yet suffer me to tell you, that it is in His name that the impotent man before you has been so wonderfully made whole, and that consequently Jesus *must* be the true Saviour of the world. Surely, therefore, you have reason to acknowledge and accept this Corner-stone, which you builders have set at nought, but which nevertheless is " chosen of God and precious;" reason have you to believe in Jesus as the Messiah that was to come, and not to wait for any other. In this Jesus, the promised Seed of Abraham, the blessed Root of Jesse, in Him alone must you seek the salvation of *your* souls. Unless you seriously apply to *Him* and cleave to *Him*, you cannot be redeemed from condemnation and the power of Satan; you cannot become free from the guilt and punishment of your sins. It is of no avail that you rest in your own national " glory," your sacred " covenants," " the giving of the law, and the service of God," the temple, the sacrifices, " the promises," and other privileged advantages; out of Christ, all these will avail you nothing. These were intended purposely to direct you to Him as the great Sum and Substance of all scripture. Equally in vain do you rely on your own works, on your imaginary righteousness by the Law; for the " just," as the Scriptures teach you, " must live by his *faith*." In vain do you depend on the Divine favour shown to your forefathers, or say within yourselves, " We have Abraham to our father," that Isaac was his promised son, and Jacob was surnamed a " prince with God;" for these fathers were themselves saved by the grace of Jesus Christ, who is the same yesterday, to-day, and for ever; they found acceptance with God through the blood of the Lamb slain from the foundation of the world. There is no other name under heaven given among men whereby we must be reconciled to God, justified, made well-pleasing in his sight, and partakers of the true and eternal salvation, but only the wonderful Name of Jesus; that is to say, Jesus himself personally, with all his invaluable merit and satisfaction, his work, his knowledge, his sufferings, and his death.

Hence, then, we also may safely infer, that the name of Saviour, the name which brings with it the glorious accomplishment of our redemption, belongs truly to none other but only to Jesus Christ our Lord. The import of his name was announced by the angel to Mary his mother, and afterwards to Joseph her husband: " Thou shalt call his name Jesus, for he shall *save* his people (whether Jews or Gentiles) from their sins." He indeed must have an arm of omnipotence who can bear and carry away the sins of a whole world, the heavy burden of the divine displeasure, the awful curse of the divine law. "No" mere "man could deliver his brother, nor make agreement unto God for him." Therefore "it behoved" "the Son of God" himself to be "manifested;" for none other could destroy "the works of the devil." (1 John iii. 8.) "God" himself had to "purchase the church with HIS OWN BLOOD." (Acts xx. 28.) "Salvation" could come to us only "by the Lord our God." (Hos. i. 7.) He, "even" he, had to "blot out our transgressions," and it could be only "for his own sake."(Isa. xliii. 25.) "Of the people there was none with" him. (Isa. lxiii. 3.) Well may we then acknowledge, that

"Not all the sons of God in heaven
One sinner's ransom could have given!—
On Jesu's name alone we call,
Our hope, our confidence, our all!"

It is true the name of Jesus existed in the names of the prophet Isaiah, of the high priest Joshua, and of that earlier Joshua, the captain of the Lord's people of Israel; for the holy fathers, by giving their children such names, meant to testify their faith in the salvation that was to come, and intended thus to keep it in remembrance. Eve and Lamech appear to have done the same at the birth of their respective sons, Cain and Noah. But names of this sort were sometimes imposed by divine authority, to foreshow the threefold mediatorial office of Christ, who, as the true Jesus, should above all others, preach the pure gospel under the New Testament, as Isaiah (the evangelical prophet) did under the Old; should "build the true temple of the Lord," the christian church; "be a priest upon his throne;" and lead us into the promised "rest," which, however violent the opposition of powerful adversaries, "remaineth for the people of God."

As this name, therefore, which is above every name, can in strict propriety belong to "*none other*" but Christ; so, without him, we have no foundation to build upon, in heaven or earth. Never then must we think of putting any thing in competition with Him; for He is the only one who can *save* us; He of all the sons of men is the only one who was from everlasting in favour with God; and only "in Him" can all the nations of the earth be blessed." Concerning which promise let us observe, that it means not that all nations, considered absolutely or merely as nations, shall be blessed in Him; for we read elsewhere, that only "he who *believeth* on Him shall not be confounded." And again, "He that believeth on the Son of God hath everlasting life; but he that believeth not the Son, shall not see life, for the wrath of God abideth on him." The Jews could not hope that their prayers would be heard, unless they turned towards the temple and the mercy-seat in it, when they prayed. Certainly *we* can never hope for any *salvation* from "God," who "is a consuming fire," except through "the Only-begotten," "whom God hath set forth for a propitiatory, through faith in his blood, to declare his righteousness in the forgiveness of sins." We are every one by nature very *ignorant* of God, and "blind;" so blind to things spiritual, that "no man can know the Father, save he to whom the Son will reveal him;" although this knowledge is verily and indeed our "life eternal." (John xvii. 3.) We are by nature "enemies;"* ungodly;† and sinners;‡ for which reason we can no otherwise be "made accepted" with the righteous and holy God, but only "in the Beloved; who in Isaiah is called Jehovah's "Servant, in whom his soul delighteth." All and every thing depends on what is contained in that declaration from his own lips, "I am the Way, and the Truth, and the Life; no man cometh unto the Father, but by me." If ever, therefore, we would enjoy favour with God, we must look for it only through "the redemption which is in Christ Jesus;" and this redemption we must apprehend and appropriate by a true and living faith. In our Lutheran church, whose authorised formularies stand clear of the erroneous notion of being justified by the supposed merit of works, such admonitions as I have here produced from Scripture, may seem not so particularly called for; but, alas! these very admonitions are grossly counteracted by many, who little suspect themselves of so doing. For to make a mere oral profession of desiring to live and die upon the merits of Christ, is surely not enough; but it is needful carefully to watch, deeply to examine our hearts, and to see that no Dagon is set up by the side of this Ark of the Covenant, that we place no reliance on frigid purity of doctrine and discipline, good as all purity is in itself. Neither must we presume upon having been born of christian parents, brought up in the Protestant church, or incorporated with it by baptism. For "the Word" itself, though

* Rom. v. 10. † Ibid. iv. 5. ‡ Ibid. v. 8.

ever so faithfully "preached," will not "profit" us, unless "mixed with faith of them that hear it." Neither must we value ourselves on the piety of our forefathers, or of holy persons who have preceded us or belong to us; for "every one of us must give account of *himself* to God;" "the soul that sinneth, it shall die;" and "the just," only, "shall live by *his* faith." As we must not reckon upon any external communion with the church, so neither must we ground our hope of salvation upon any commendation or esteem of us, though expressed by the most pious persons; neither must we depend on having regularly received the sacrament; for with all such things, God may still have no pleasure in us. Much less must any one think of resting his happiness in his isolated self, upon his mere imaginary morality, upon his decorous and regular life. For if this were at all to the purpose, then were the unblest Pharisees the most blessed of men, and Christ as a Saviour died in vain. We must likewise remember, on the other hand, that none are possessed of that real faith which lays hold of the salvation in Christ Jesus, who are not careful to live unto Him that died for them and rose again; and that they to whom sin is not hateful as the gall of bitterness, have never tasted the sweetness of His all-powerful NAME. * * * * *

---

4. Sermon, on Romans vi. 12—14.*

"He who committeth sin is the servant of sin;" and the service of sin is dreadful and miserable slavery. But its misery comes to an end, when we come "to obey the Truth;" as said our blessed Lord, "Ye shall know the Truth, and the Truth shall make you free." For when we have heartily received the grace presented to us by Him, that grace ruling in us, guides, strengthens, and establishes our will and determination to engage in his service, which is perfect freedom; and we no longer remain servants of sin. Of this important matter the apostle treats particularly, in the sixth, seventh, and eighth chapters of his Epistle to the Romans, from which chapters are selected the epistolary readings of our church for the last and next Lord's day. But it will be profitable on the present occasion to consider what lies *between* these portions; let us therefore now meditate on the twelfth, thirteenth, and fourteenth verses of the sixth chapter, which teach us that—

* Preached at Stuttgart, 6th July, 1712, a month after his 25th year.

FREEDOM FROM SIN, GRANTED TO THE CHILDREN OF GOD, IS THE MOST GLORIOUS LIBERTY IN THIS WORLD.

Here is—

I. THE GROUND OF THEIR LIBERTY. They "are not under the Law, but under Grace." Grace is a delightful word, whatever meaning we give it; but *the Grace of God* has the most delightful meaning of all. It is true that the pride of natural reason can see nothing in it; but faith can find in it all comfort and encouragement. The Grace of God purifies, animates, and gladdens the heart of a true believer. Some things are better understood by contrast. Here then the expression "under Grace," is contrasted with that of "under the Law." Now to be "*under*" any thing, is to be so influenced by its authority or power, as to have the heart and conscience taken up with it, and to be governed by it in our whole conduct. Therefore all who have any concern about God, all who think the Divine favour of any value to them, are either "under the Law," or "under Grace." But there are very many who seek not after God at all; and these, in our apostle's meaning, are neither under the Law nor under Grace; but are, what he terms, "without law." (Rom. vii. 9.) Thus there are three classes of persons in the world: persons "without law," who live in carnal security; persons "under the Law," who live in anxiety and fear; and persons "under Grace," who live in peace of conscience; who have their hearts in a state of comparative and increasing satisfaction. In one or the other of these three classes is every individual included. As we cannot properly understand the condition of one class without considering the others, let us here consider them all; that the carnally secure may learn to "fear;" the fearful become encouraged to desire the true freedom of the gospel; and those who are "free indeed," be kept from turning aside either to false security or to needless fear.

First, let us consider the state of those who are "without law;" who are neither "under the Law," nor "under Grace;" for though the law condemns them, they are insensible of it. Of this sort are most persons of the present day. They are giving unbridled freedom to "the lust of the flesh, the lust of the eye, and the pride of life." Their whole man is freely devoted to these things; they suffer no such enjoyment to escape them. One excitement after another yields them pleasure for the present, and thus they do whatsoever they will. Their principal law is not the law of God, but their own will, their "fleshly mind." If divine authority interpose with its demands, they reject it immediately in their practice, as if they said unto God, "Depart from us;" or they treat it with *general* neglect, though they are perhaps disturbed by it sometimes in their conscience. They live on in the blindness of self-love and self-complacency, and because God in his providence "keeps silence," "their inward thought is, *I shall have no sorrow.*" But when they are reminded that though he is a merciful God, he is also a righteous God, and an avenger of evil, they unhesitatingly catch at some scripture text for the quieting of their consciences, and go away at death in this false dependance, without ever feeling any real alarm about punishment in the unseen world, till they are actually "come into that place of torment." As they have made themselves perfect slaves to the desires of the flesh and of the mind, their carnal nature is become so much a component part of themselves, that they do not desire freedom, even when it is offered them. If they have now and then some complacency in virtue, such complacency soon leaves them; and they settle down upon their good wishes and good intentions, to the accomplishment of which their wilful ignorance and depravity never permit them to attain. They die without wisdom!

Surely, then, it is even a great mercy if God chasten such persons with fearful misgivings and anticipations, that he may make them acquainted with his awful jealousy and holy indignation. Now such forebodings and misgivings are actually experienced by those whom we consider as belonging to the *second* class; as persons "*under*" the pressure and bondage of "*the Law.*" All men indeed are under the Law, as bound to obey it; but we are here speaking of those who are sensible only of the Law with its terrors. It brings its demands to them, by awful convictions in the conscience. It rebukes and condemns them for all that they have done, all that they do, and for all which they have left or are leaving undone; and their conscience is here awake to God's legal and just cognizance of their most secret thoughts, words, and actions. His Law shows the exceeding sinfulness of fallen man; it threatens the conscience, and pursues it with its righteous curse. "By the Law is the knowledge of sin;" therefore "the Law worketh" to such persons nothing but "wrath." Sin to them "appears sin" indeed; and such it must appear. Hence they are very disquieted and distressed. Conscience, alarmed and terrified, engages them in a variety of religious exercises. These they follow in their own strength, (imagining thereby to retrieve what is defective in their conduct, and so to pacify the Divine displeasure.) But all such "inventions" being of no value, nothing of value can result from them. And whereas these persons once accounted no part of their conduct sinful, they now feel that it has been sinful all along, and know neither how to advise nor how to "deliver their own souls." Conscience thus continuing timid and distressed, they only plunge from one trouble and difficulty into another. They *would* do good, but cannot do it with freedom and from the heart. They "consent unto the law of God, that it is good" in its requirements; but they are "ignorant how to perform that which is good." The former state frequently merges into this latter; and he who is in this latter state frequently backslides into the former. Men strictly in either, are shut up under sin, and the only difference between the two classes is, that the latter are *sensible* that they are in this condition, whereas the former sort are *not* sensible of it. Both are in a state of captivity, but those "without law" go on willingly in their bondage of sin; while those who are "under the Law" would gladly be released, only they know not how to effect it. "The Law" serves however to "lead" these persons "unto Christ," and to bring them to believe entirely and freely on Him; which indeed is its peculiar office and design.*

Those whom it is thus successful in bringing to Christ, belong to the *third* and happy *class*, who are "under Grace." By faith in Christ they are made free from charge and condemnation. By experience of grace given, their conscience attains quietness and serenity, and the mind becomes enlightened with the knowledge of God's holy will; confidence and love now take possession of the soul, accompanied by lively hope, life, and power from God, which they experience in the progress of their willing obedience. The Law finds nothing in them now to reprehend. Past sins can no longer accuse, nor remaining corruption "have dominion." The soul is become awake and vigilant. By the aid of the Spirit of God reproving in them the very smallest deviation from perfect rectitude, they keep themselves "in all things circumspect;" and are careful to derive strength through Christ. What an all-important condition is this! Is it not the duty and interest of every one amongst

* Gal. iii. 24.

us to be concerned about it, to seek after it, and to endeavour above all things to make it our own?

Whoever desires further information upon this subject, will do well to read blessed Luther's Preface to the Old Testament, where he particularly and clearly describes these three several conditions of man with respect to the Law, and where every one may learn to which of them he belongs. Let him also make use of the sixth, seventh, and eighth chapters of the Epistle to the Romans.

Now as the two preceding classes are unhappy, so is this last the happy one. But as it concerns those who belong to the two preceding classes to take all possible pains to belong to the last, so those of the last have to beware lest they turn aside or fall back again. We are, therefore, now to consider—

II. THE DUTY OF THE PIOUS; which is, to disobey indwelling sin; to obey God; and thus to maintain their freedom.

Those who are "under Grace" are here admonished by the apostle, as follows: "Let not sin, therefore, reign in your mortal body, that ye should obey the former in the lusts of the latter," &c. Sin, like a root in the ground, remains even in the true believer; it is still active; and godly persons still feel within them the stirrings of corrupt nature. These stirrings solicit the will, and would employ their bodily members as instruments of unrighteousness unto sin. Now, whenever the will yields, sin "reigns." Then the tongue, with all the members, and bodily senses, become subservient to its rule. And when this is the case, the man is fallen back, by one declension after another, into that condition which has been described as "under the Law." In the strength of the Lord, therefore, must we rule over sin; over anger, wrath, impatience, intemperance, sloth, covetousness, &c. (Matt. v. 29.) On the other hand we must be entirely devoted to God's service, and yield "our members and bodily senses as instruments of righteousness unto God." (Rom. xii. 1.)

As this is clearly our bounden duty and reasonable service, so sin is a slavery most disgracefully unreasonable, and lamentable. Therefore though we bear about with us a body of sin and death, we must ever quit ourselves like men "*alive* from the dead." (Gal. ii. 19, 20.) For this we have always sufficient ability; because Christ's death and life work in us. Did we but entirely live "*under Grace*," we should do nothing but good; for whenever pious persons fail to act in their own character, they are fallen back "under the Law." Hence as, in strictest language, none but the really pious can do good, it is only to persons professing to be such that the apostle says, "*Therefore* let not sin have dominion over you," or "rule within you." Men without real piety can avoid for a while the *outward* commission of sin, but *inwardly* they remain under its dominion. This is why they complain of the impossibility of keeping the law of God. By that very complaint they betray their real character. Does any such person then ask, What must I do? Must I go on as I am? We answer, if sin is odious as well as burdensome to us, so that we have a sincere desire to be made free from it, in this very desire God has already bestowed upon us grace, whereby we may come before him with earnest prayer so as to meet him as it were in his work; and, indeed, we ought thus to make every possible good use of our first impressions and, to do so immediately; for as long as we "tarry" in sin, we are continuing in bondage "under the Law."

Hence we may form an opinion of the state of piety amongst us. We have the Law and the Gospel ministered abundantly; but few are seriously making use either of the one or of the other. Consequently they can know nothing of the comfort of true liberty; they are neither "under the Law," nor "under Grace." It is not too much to say, that the greater number of professed Christians are either specifically trampling upon God's law, or specifically turning his manifested grace into licentiousness. Such persons, were it possible, would take heaven from him by force, that they might escape his final judgment. There is such a general "falling away" from the practical principles of real Christianity, that whenever these principles are but alluded to, men instantly raise objections about the impossibility of practising them. Why is this, but because the true principles of our holy religion are so very opposite to the present unchristian, or rather antichristian, lives of those who profess it? They would have heaven with an adulterous heart; they would serve God only so far as suits their private convenience, or humour, their vain glory, worldly honour, or lucrative advancement. Something indeed they are willing to do, in order that they may think themselves "good Christians;" but on the whole they care little or nothing about "knowing the grace of God in truth."* For they think so lightly of his law, that if Moses could come among us every hour, he would break in pieces each time his two tables of

* Coloss. i. 6.

stone at the sight of so great a multitude of abominations and disobediences. The main inlet of this irreligion of our times begins in that improper and pernicious bringing up of children, by which they become familiar with sin and vice from their earliest years. Children of both sexes are too much left to "do according to their will," in all ranks of society, from the lowest to the highest; and this goes on from childhood to manhood. Thus who can know what sins they have not learnt to commit! And does not experience show how impossible it is to reach the hearts of such persons after they are grown up, unless they are taken in hand by God himself, and that most seriously? The worst part of their condition is the ruinous self-deception with which these most pitiably misnamed Christians confirm themselves in ungodliness, vanity, and sin, by a delusive parade of notions and forms relating to religious truths, which were only given for the personal recovery of ruined man. Led on by their own preferences and imaginations, many of them are at one time, so they think, "under the Law," at another time "under Grace," and by and by, "without Law" altogether. With these fancies do they amuse themselves when they profess a wish to become *pious:* in imagination they become so, but in reality never; for their piety has no continuance, though at times they will confess their sins, and even attend the sacrament. In order to prepare for this, some of them will pass through all the three classes as it were in a dream. On Friday they will be, what in truth they have been all along, "*without law;*" on Saturday, *under the Law;* on Sunday, *under Grace;* and these advancements are accomplished with them by unmeaning prayers and hollow-hearted fervor. By and by the whole business is again forgotten; perhaps the very next day they are led neither by the Law nor by Grace, a plain proof that their Saturday *penitence* and their Sunday *faith* were nothing better than hypocrisy and formality; certainly contained nothing of grateful and cordial submission to that influence of the Holy Spirit, which touched them, perhaps, during such religious exercises. O that the eyes of them all might be opened to behold their miserable condition! For certain it is that false self-esteem is the very delusion with which men fortify themselves, as long as they do not heartily yield to the good pleasure of their gracious King. Their "strong delusion" of self-esteem will not suffer us to reach their consciences or touch their hearts, either with the most pointed sermon upon repentance, or with the fullest preaching of grace. If we attempt to bring them to a better state by pressing upon them the necessity of more closely examining themselves, they either think this needless, or they regard us with suspicion, as if we wished to deprive them of all comfort in religion. But religion in its true sense is a thing they have never yet attained, though it is high time they should use every effort to attain it. All men have not faith, and they certainly have not. Others will contrive to satisfy themselves with their punctual and constant performance of religious formalities; many of them take wonderful pains in this way, but not after that "perfect law of liberty" which would show them "a more excellent way," and how to walk in it freely and with delight. How can we refrain from wishing for *them,* that they would "receive the grace of God in truth," "with all their heart," and give, not their formalities, but "themselves, to the Lord."

As for those whose lives testify that they are "under Grace," and who are chiefly concerned to remain so, we would exhort and encourage them to all perseverance, &c.

---

5. Sermon on Acts ii. 40.*

St. Paul, in his First Epistle to Timothy, the second chapter and fourth verse, bears a noble testimony to God's universal love; the benefit of which he himself had gloriously experienced. He there speaks of "God our Saviour, who will have all men to be saved, and to come to the knowledge of the truth." Man was created for everlasting life, but we have lost our original right to it, ever "since by one man's disobedience judgment came upon all men unto condemnation." Nevertheless the Father of mercies gave and appointed to be our Mediator his only-begotten Son, who, having died for all, God would have all men to believe in him, and hereby to be restored to the blessedness of eternal salvation. Another noble proof of this is given by St. Peter in the text before us; for here he bears testimony before the church at Jerusalem concerning God's goodwill towards all mankind; and what this apostle testified to *them,* he testifies with equal certainty to *us* also. Let us therefore consider—

* Preached at Tübingen, in his 24th year, 1711.

THE GREAT SALVATION WHICH WOULD SET US ENTIRELY FREE FROM SIN AND MISERY; by inquiring,

First, *Who are the persons that need this great salvation?*

Now the words of our text are found in that memorable sermon which St. Peter preached with such wonderful success at the feast of Pentecost; and it was to Jews at Jerusalem that he then said, "Save yourselves!" The Jewish nation had been God's peculiar, accepted, and chosen people; and to them he had committed and manifested his Word. He had given them the covenant of circumcision; and had conferred on them many most distinguished privileges and advantages. Hence it might easily be imagined, that having the means of salvation in such abundance, they needed nothing more. Nevertheless, they had also heard the personal preaching of Christ himself, and had witnessed his miracles. Surely, then, it might easily be supposed that though the rest of the world were ignorant and out of the way of salvation, this could not possibly be the case with the Jews. Yet it is to Jews that St. Peter here beseechingly addresses the words in our text, "Save yourselves!" Consequently all mankind, without exception, are in so wretched a condition, that they most urgently need the salvation of God. This inference is but too evidently confirmed by every possible testimony. The judgment unto condemnation under which men lie is universal—not only on account of hereditary corruption, but also on account of our own manifold personal transgressions. By these we have become "sold under sin"—captives and slaves to it. This is our own condition, as it was that also of the Jewish people. And as Christ declared to them, "If the Son" (of God) "shall make you free ye shall be free indeed," (John viii. 36); so can *we* be made free only by living faith in the Son of God. All our religious formalities can as little avail us for this deliverance, as could Israel's religious observances avail *them* in the days of our Lord. It is true that we, like them, have the Word of God amongst us; we hear and we may read the pure truths of divine revelation; we have a true church, with its ordinances of grace; we have the benefit of a regular ministry. These things may well be regarded as eminent favours, being so many means by which we may be conducted to the knowledge of God, to faith in Christ, and to everlasting salvation; but as long as we remain unrenewed in heart, and unamended in life, it is certain that we have never yet received salvation by these, consequently that they have availed us nothing; and it must still be said to us, and *is* said unto us, "Save yourselves!" (Neither can the most certain conviction and accurate knowledge of scripture facts or doctrines be any substitute for that vital hold which a living faith takes of salvation in Christ.) When St. Peter used this manner of address to the Jews, "Save yourselves," eight weeks had not yet elapsed since they had seen and crucified the Lord of glory. How plainly does this teach us, not to satisfy ourselves with the most perfect *historical knowledge* of Christ's sufferings for us, but to consider seriously, how we may come through faith, to actual fellowship in that salvation, which Christ, by his precious death, hath obtained to us! Yet, alas! we are too apt to be contented with a mere knowledge of the *fact.* Incontrovertibly true as it is that Christ died for *all,* consequently for *us;* and that he has in this sense redeemed and purchased us with his most precious blood; still we can never be saved by a mere conviction of the truth of this fact, nor by any mere conception of it, however correct; no, nor by any presumption upon it unsanctioned by the warranty of Scripture. Many, who place the *most confident* reliance upon being saved by Christ, are often in the very worst condition with respect to any true interest in him. Why? Because their confidence is only carnal imagination or fanatical presumption; for as long as our hearts are not turned to God, but we are strangers to repentance and forsaking of sin; as long as our faith worketh not by love, but we fail in this demonstration of gratitude to our Lord Jesus Christ;—we must remain entire strangers to his salvation, however constantly we attend public worship, or adopt every ordinance of private devotion.

Having thus seen *who are the persons that need this salvation,* we consider,

II. How IT IS CONFERRED.

As the salvation itself is glorious, so is the language in which it is here announced: "Save yourselves!" or, "Allow yourselves to be made happy and blessed." They who have to do this, are of course hitherto unblest and unhappy. And as we are all so by nature, being "all under sin," and holden in its captivity, under the curse of the law and the wrath of God, and remain so, unless we become "servants of God, having our fruit unto holiness;" therefore conscience is ever liable to terror, and often full of it, yea, often, which is more perilous still, it is insensible, and seared as with a hot iron. Thus having no confidence in God, no love to Him, we cannot be said to "call upon him faithfully." If we abide in such a state as this, what are we but slaves during our natural life; and when this life is ended, what remains but tribulation and wrath for ever! The punishment of hell, to all who persist in such a state, is inevitable; (Rom. ii. 9,) for this is to persist in being "children of wrath;" "alienated from the life of God;" "children of the wicked one." Hereby death reigns in us; the world draws us along by evil example, as by a mighty stream, to perdition; while we have nothing but darkness within, around, above, before us. Great, however, as is this wretchedness, equally great, yes, far greater, is the salvation at present within our reach. Unhappy, unblest, unsaved as we may be, God is willing to save and make us happy, if we are willing to look into and appreciate, very differently from what we are doing at present, that great salvation which is described by Christ himself as the "opening of blind eyes, and the turning of men from darkness to light, even from the power of Satan unto God; that they may receive forgiveness of sins, and inheritance among them which are sanctified by faith that is in Him." (Acts xxvi. 18.) See how inconceivably great is that salvation! But great as it is, God imparts it to all who sincerely desire to partake of it; and to them is inputed the all-availing righteousness of the Son of God, for whose sake, and by communion with Him, they become his heavenly Father's chosen and beloved children, and, by the right of children, "obtain" a part in the heavenly "inheritance" of God "with all them that are sanctified." They are privileged even in *this* world to "draw nigh to him continually" in "the Spirit of adoption," and can now worship him as a "Father," because they are delivered "from an evil conscience." And as heretofore they were the "slaves of sin," so are they now "become" blessed "servants of righteousness, over whom neither sin, nor death, nor our adversary the devil," nor his agency in this world or in the next, can any longer have dominion. They may therefore go on their way rejoicing in the power and strength of their common Lord, and have no need to be "afraid with the fear" which torments those who remain willing strangers to God. And as they are "no more strangers and foreigners, but fellow-citizens with the saints, and of the household of God," so he is daily preparing them to be made "meet," as they already are in right and title, "for the inheritance of the saints in light." God is "their portion."

Such is the great salvation which Christ hath actually obtained to us, and our possession of it consists primarily in taking hold of that Almighty hand which is stretched out to help and save us, and in allowing that hand to lift us up. God our Saviour hath appointed his sacred ministry for the very purpose that it may be instrumental to this our happiness and blessedness. Besides the preaching and teaching which Christ sends us by his ministers, we have also his written word and ordinances. We have therefore both the way and means of salvation before us; we have also instruction how to use the means, and how to walk in the way. Of both must we immediately, with all possible sincerity and earnestness, avail ourselves. Do you ask how we must begin to do it? We answer with St. Peter, "Repent, and be converted, that your sins may be blotted out." It is only by true repentance, which is a change of the mind, it is only by sincere and heartfelt conversion, that "so great salvation" can be mine and yours. Repentance, true repentance, is ever preceded by brokenness of heart, by contrition of spirit. Of the Jews we here read, that "they were pricked in their heart;" that is, the word preached went to their heart; and they cried out, "Men and brethren, what shall we do?"—Peter's address was instrumental to this preparation of heart; he had represented to them the grievous sin they had committed against the Messiah, with the sacred benefit arising from his sufferings; and they were affected by it to the most serious alarm about their own salvation, so that despairing entirely of themselves and of their best performances, they were on the stretch to know how they themselves might return into favour with God. The same experience, O man, whoever thou art, must be thine also. For though thou hast not personally "killed" either with thine own hands, or with the voice of thy suffrage, "the Prince of Life," thou canst not but acknowledge that thy sins have virtually crucified him afresh. This is reason enough why thou shouldst feel alarm at the displeasure of God, and inquire, "What shall I do?" Be ready then to surrender thyself entirely to him, and leave it to his good pleasure how to deal with thee. O do not think that such a wounded state of heart consists in having a few transient thoughts and slight impressions of our depraved and ruined condition! We must be made truly sensible of our guilt and corruption, so as to bring the matter seriously before God, and to say, "thus, and thus have I sinned!" (Josh. vii. 20.) We must assume no disguise to our poverty, shame, and nakedness; all confidence in natural virtue and good deeds must be utterly renounced, and our simple inquiry must be, "What shall we do?" Or, "What must I do to be saved?" The apostle's requirement to "repent," is also God's requirement, and means such a genuine change of heart and sentiments, as will be produced by duly considering the Divine law, listening to the voice of conscience, trembling at the righteous displeasure of God, and sincerely sorrowing that we have so wretchedly requited his most gracious and faithful love. Hence we learn to acknowledge and ever humbly to feel our sin and guilt before him; we regard ourselves as the unworthiest of his creatures, as persons who deserve nothing but shame, rebuke, and punishment. Our self-confidence, our false security, falls away, and is renounced; we desire, we implore forgiveness of sins in the name of Jesus Christ; we call upon him as our Mediator. Through the knowledge of Him we become justified, (Isai. liii. 11;) by faith in Him we receive the Holy Spirit to govern, remind, rebuke, admonish instruct, and comfort us all our days. This is indeed to be helped with "saving help;" this is to be "*saved;*" called with a holy calling, not according to our works, but according to our heavenly Father's own purpose and grace, "which was given us in Christ Jesus before the world began." (2 Tim. i. 9.) Then are our sins of every name forgiven; then is Christ Jesus known by us as having come into the world to save sinners. Only so much depends on our apprehending this most important matter rightly, that we must notice more particularly,

III. The manner of appropriating this salvation. This is intimated in the text, "Save yourselves!" which does not mean, "Save yourselves" *actually*, or *absolutely;* but "be ye saved," or "allow yourselves to be saved." For man is so ruined, that he cannot really help or save himself. The work is of God; conversion is His vouchsafement, (Acts ii. 47;) neither can we *help* Him at all in it, however we may interrupt and mar his work. We might as soon expect a slumbering man to stand, or a lawful captive lawfully to deliver himself, or a dead man to wake himself to life, as expect that we can, by our own natural strength and good works, arise to spiritual liberty and life, and really save ourselves. Place therefore no confidence in any thing short of God, who alone can deliver and save. Whoever then is concerned for his redemption and salvation, let him apply at once to God by earnest prayer, and ask for the increased influence of his Holy Spirit. As our salvation begins in the light and strength of Him who prevents us all with this gracious favour, so we must now submit ourselves entirely to his guidance and governance; wait upon him perpetually in retirement, secret prayer, and devout meditation; lay open all our sin and confusion before him, and take good care never to disturb or mar His work. (For we should remember, that God is graciously healing us, whatever be his dealings with us.) Now as many an irrational brute, however naturally ferocious, will become submissive and quiet enough to have a thorn drawn from its foot, and the wound dressed and healed,* why then should not we also as readily and willingly suffer God himself to do with us whatever he will? If we are not delivered and saved, the failure can never be attributed to the faithful Creator God our Saviour, who declares himself able and willing to do whatever is needful for us; and who asks nothing of *us*, but that we cease from walking contrary to him, and surrender ourselves wholly to the care, guidance, and governance of his Holy Spirit. For He " will have all men to be saved, and to come to the knowledge of the truth;" therefore is it with perfect justice that he will say to the impenitent, " disobedient and stiff-hearted," † " Ye would not!"

I therefore call upon you now, with the same beseeching exhortation which the apostle used, " Suffer yourselves to be delivered and saved!" " Why will ye die?" ‡ Why will ye not allow yourselves to be " reconciled to God? § Behold, even now, in this your day," God is willing to SAVE you! O, avail yourselves of the present occasion for that purpose! Who knoweth how much longer his hand shall be stretched out to you for peace? O, that my entreaty may be accepted by some of you! even as St. Peter's entreaty was accepted by many. O that in like manner, this day, some souls may be added to Christ and to his church! Verily their names would immediately be legible in the book of life. Behold, my brethren, at this moment, "the kingdom of God is come upon you!"|| Follow the attractive influence of its grace. Hearken to the voice of that grace. Confer no more with flesh and blood. Look not on the multitude of the disobedient. Ye that, under the displeasure of God, may well be suffering enough at present,

* A remarkable instance of this occurred at the London Zoological Gardens, where a tiger that had been wounded in the foot by another in the adjoining den, patiently submitted to its regular dressing.

† Ezek. ii. 4; Isa. xxx. 1; Matt. xxiii. 37.

‡ Ezek. xviii. 31. § 2 Cor iv. 20. || Luk. xi. 20.

suffer, I beseech you, one thing more; suffer yourselves to be made happy and blessed. Suffer yourselves to be "turned away every one from your iniquities;" turn away from them, not merely for a while, but seek to be endued with that power from on high, which shall uphold your goings in the paths of righteousness, peace, and pleasantness, as long as you live. Not only in the apostles' days, but now also, Christ is able to save and make happy all who will come unto God by him. (Heb. vii. 25.) By thus coming you shall be eternally redeemed from all evil.

"For, as I live, Jehovah saith,
I have no pleasure in your death;
Why will ye die? Behold, my will
Is but that men should cease from ill,
Be turn'd from all iniquity,
And live for ever blest with me.

"Consider it, poor child of fear;
Thou art not left to black despair;
Strong consolation, health and grace,
God here reveals to meet thy case;
Trust in his oath; to live begin;
Only lament and loathe thy sin."

---

6. Notes of a Sermon on Matthew xi. 2, &c. preached at Herbrechtingen, on the third Sunday in Advent, 1741.

The incomparable greatness of the Lord Jesus Christ, as it shines forth,

I. From his works.

II. From the pre-eminent excellence of his forerunner, John the Baptist.

I. His works are—numerous—wonderful—public—"full of grace,"—accordant with the prophecies of the Old Testament.

From all these shine forth his greatness. He is, "He that should come;" the Son of God; the Lamb of God; the Saviour of the world; the express image of the Father.

Application. What is to be *done* by *us?* Let the kingdom of heaven suffer violence from our repentance, conversion, faith. (Ver. 12—20.) Become of the number of Wisdom's children, (Ver. 19.) Come unto Jesus. (Ver. 28.) Present thyself before him in all thy poverty and necessities. Be not offended in him. (Ver. 6.) Let all thou hearest of him go to thy heart, whether thou hast found thy spirit much or little affected hitherto. Go thy way, and let "the works" of a *Christian* be "seen" in thee, and be "heard of" as *thine.*

II. John, the forerunner of the Lord Jesus, (ver. 9,) was a "great" man, a prophet, yea, and more than a prophet; yet was it his part to yield to and make way for Christ. This he did, gladly and willingly. How great must Christ himself be! Set a high esteem on virtues and gifts of grace, but set a much higher value on Christ himself. Every thing points to him. Be not a mere looker on, or an admirer of him; give thyself up to him, quite and entirely. To exhort you so to do, is my office and my joy, even as it was John's to exhort his disciples to the same effect. (Comp. 2 Cor. iv. 5.) O that I, "*in*" THIS "*same hour*," might be able to prevail with *you!* O that I might be able to persuade you to make a blessed use of the approaching commemoration of Christ's coming into the world!

---

7. Notes of a Sermon on Luke ii. 33—40, preached at Denkendorf, on the Sunday after Christmas day, 1713.

We have this day before us a portion of the gospel which especially addresses itself to children. I would, therefore, take pains to speak very simply and intelligibly; and I earnestly request all my young friends present, to attend to what I may have to say about our blessed Saviour, Jesus Christ; because I am to speak in his name.

Doctrine. "The holy childhood of Jesus is a pattern for pious children and young persons to imitate. It is likewise an example for us all."

Our Lord Jesus Christ, as the Son of God, had no need to grow or increase in any good quality, for he was divinely perfect as well as pure and without spot; but it is concerning him as man, that we here read, (ver. 40.) "he grew and waxed strong in spirit." As man it was that he prayed, held intercourse and communion with God; was characterized by the virtues of perfect purity, simplicity, integrity, modesty, obedience, wisdom; and that the grace of God was upon him. He grew up unknown to the world, but manifest to his heavenly Father; and he abode, meanwhile, in retirement, working with his own hands, (like other poor persons.) For *our* sakes he "sanctified himself" (John xvi. 19.) from the very first, even before he was twelve years old. During all this time he was gathering and laying up treasure, out of which he afterwards brought forth such abundant good. Come, then, dear children, and learn from his example. It is not enough to grow in years, though even this is the gift of God, and no work of our own; we likewise must "wax strong in spirit" as we advance in age. How beautiful is it, when we are not always mere beginners, but can say, "For such a length of time I have lived in Christ!" But many have never even begun thus to live. Many children are wicked. They swear; tell falsehoods; steal; give themselves to excess in eating and drinking; are immodest in their language and behaviour; are fond of idleness; lead an unruly life; hate what is good; go after bad companions, deceiving and being deceived. All such are the very opposite to what Christ was. They "grow," but it is in sin and wickedness. They "wax strong," but it is only in the flesh. They are "filled," but it is with deceit. They have "grace and favour," but it is with the children of this world, and not with "God." You, however, must not live so, my dear children! Think upon the example of Christ, and upon his love to children. Think of the angels, who watch over *you*. Commune with your own hearts and be still; "learn obedience;" shun bad companions. Learn to love the word of God, and prayer. O never imagine for a moment that these things are of no such great consequence: it is a precious thing for young people to be pious; and precious are their prayers and thanksgivings! Think only what a beautiful crown of honour, still verdant and blooming for ever, belongs to Jacob, Joseph, Samuel, Solomon, Josiah, from their youthful days. *You* are, at present, in the spring season of your life; how beautiful, if you are adorned with the hopeful blossoms of righteousness! And now is the time when you will find it much easier to give yourselves up to Jesus, than if you wait till by and by. Your hearts are not yet filled with so many vanities and cares as they are likely to be, if you delay to enter into close friendship with your Saviour; besides, you have not, at present, so much opposition from the world around you. Blessed is that person who, early in life, makes his calling and election sure. (2 Pet. i. 10.) But this often proves a hard matter in riper years; nay, even in youth a person may heap up wrath against himself. (Ps. xxv. 7; Job xiii. 26.) Think of the sad examples of Ham, Ishmael, Esau, and others.

Perhaps you think you have not power to make your calling and election sure, because you are born in sin. Or, you think you have not yet resolution or understanding enough; or, perhaps, you think you have time enough yet. Vain is every excuse of this sort. The grace of Christ can overcome and remove all such difficulties, however many or great you may imagine them. How much time you may yet have, I do not know, neither do *you;* but this I know, that none of you have a moment to lose.

What I here say to children, applies equally to parents and instructors. It is for you to encourage your children in following these exhortations, by teaching and admonishing them, by setting them good examples, by avoiding every thing that may prove to them an occasion of stumbling, &c.

Finally, my beloved brethren! we must all be willing to become as children over again. (Matt. xviii. 3.) Let no one be ashamed to acknowledge that there is still need for him to grow.

---

8. Notes of a Sermon on Luke ii. 41, &c. preached at Denkendorf, on the first Sunday after Epiphany, 1738.

"The pattern of a holy family; Jesus, Mary, Joseph."

I. The pious parents—

1. go up to the feast of the Passover every year, and take, as early as possible, their child with them;—

2. are accounted worthy of a trial and temptation;—

3. suffer anxiety together about the child Jesus.

II. The holy Son—

1. feels with his parents a sacred delight in the festival;—

2. exhibits many peculiarly excellent graces, and displays a mind and conduct eminently worthy the imitation of children and young persons.

---

9. Notes of a Sermon on Matt. xx. 1, preached at Denkendorf, on Septuagesima Sunday, 1739.

Introduction. 1 Cor. ix. 24, 26. There are many who do not press at all toward the mark for the prize of the high calling of God in Christ Jesus; there are many who run, but as uncertainly; there are some who so run that they may obtain.

Subject. The frame of mind in a Christian who is sensible of his real state and condition.

I. Such a Christian is earnest and diligent for himself. II. Affectionate towards others. III. Humble towards God.

I. He is disposed to serve God. Follows the call of God *without delay;* fully satisfied that left to himself he must be wretched. (Eph. ii. 12.) Achieves his work *with patience;* bears the heat and burden of the day, till the evening arrives; *troubles not himself* with *things beside* his "purpose;" but devotes all his power and strength to the Lord. (2 Tim. ii. 4; iii. 10.)

II. (1.) *Self-righteousness* carries *envy* with it. It cannot bear that any should stand upon an equal footing with itself. The Jews were of this character. Something of the kind appears in Peter's questions: ("Lord, and what shall this man do?" or, "What shall we have therefore?")

(2.) Faith produces benevolence and love. (1 John ii. 9—11; Rom. ix. 3. 1 Cor. xii. 26.) He that hath not these is no true believer, but a stranger to God.

III. (1.) Compliance, true-heartedness, and believing confidence, go before;

(2.) Humble obedience and subjection, with no praise arrogated to self, follow after. (Luke xvii. 10.)

He who examines himself by these marks of a christian spirit, will easily ascertain whether he is proceeding in the right way.

---

10. Notes of a Sermon on Luke viii. 4, &c., preached at Denkendorf, on Sexagesima Sunday, 1714.

We have lately discoursed on the benefit of *faith*. All of us are professed believers, and are apt to think we are really in the faith. God, indeed, is willing to awaken true and lively faith within us all; nevertheless, "all have not faith." (2 Thess. iii. 2.) Let us, therefore, examine ourselves whether we be in the faith; let us prove our own selves. Such an examination is an important one, and deserves our very best attention.

Subject. "There are three hindrances of true faith:"

I. Inadvertency;

II. Inconstancy;

III. Worldly mindedness.

I. True faith cometh by the word of God, which we must embrace with the heart as well as with the understanding. See here the necessity of attention, prayer, and faithfulness. Where there is inattention, faith is hindered; but inattention is often in those who *hear;* to say nothing of those who hear not, or forsake the assembling of themselves together; or who sleep when they should be hearing, or who suffer themselves to be thinking of other things when the word is addressed to them, &c. Without attention, the soul continues empty, uninformed, rude, and heathenish. But, even where there is not this *gross* inattention and negligence, there may be a want of *proper*, that is, of devout, attention; in consequence of which, the word never reaches the heart at all, or is "caught away out of it." Let every one, therefore, think seriously, whether he has given it such attention. How could ignorance among professed Christians have become so fearful as it is, were it not for great inattention? especially when catechism is so often publicly gone through, and so much preaching of the gospel is heard from year to year! Alas, how few comprehend what is delivered! It is often as if people had been preached unto in an unknown tongue.——In all such instances there can be neither faith nor salvation. Now, as the heart is fickle enough and deceitful enough of itself, what must it be in those who give *advantage* to an enemy that is lying in wait to deceive! Here is a reason why so few have ever begun sincerely to believe in Christ. Many, I know, are ready enough to plead their want of better capacities, or their want of having been better taught. So much the more earnest should be their endeavours now to learn; and so much the more earnestly should they pray God to teach them. O let us be persuaded not to treasure up wrath against us by false excuses.

II. We must, therefore, not only hear, attend to, and receive the Word, but we must also *keep* it. Wherever this is done, the consequences will be happy ones; even joy and peace in believing. As a root must have sap and nourishment in order to strike deeper into the soil, put forth branches, and bear fruit; just so do men need constancy, perseverance, and patience. It is because they allow themselves to want these that they make no progress, and in time of temptation fall away, frequently upon the most trifling occasion.

III. We must learn entirely to deny ourselves, and always to have our affections consciously under God's control. Faith teaches nothing less; it is by these means that the peaceable fruit of righteousness is yielded perfect and ripe. But worldly cares, love of wealth, sensuality, intemperate conviviality, choke the word and render it unfruitful. These very things are at present some of our greatest hindrances in religion, among the poor as well as rich. For, alas! how many, who are poor in things temporal, are still poorer in spiritual respects, and "going about hardly bestead and hungry, behold not the dawn of the morning,"* not the least prospect of meliorating their spiritual condition!

* Ps. xlix; Is. v. 14. Isa. viii. 20—22, Lutheran version.

How truly awful for the immortal soul! None then need go far to inquire, why is there so little real Christianity? The inquiry is plainly replied to in Prov. xxiv. 30, &c., and Heb. vi. 12. Think of this, ye, whose hearts are in any degree awakened. Have pity on your own souls; for Almighty God is willing to show mercy and pity toward *you*. Many may be saying in their hearts, "As I am so poor and wretched in this world, surely I shall have my happiness in the next." Most sincerely would I rejoice with every one who is likely to have it; still let us pause and reflect on what the apostle St. James, (ii. 5.) tells us, that it is only those poor persons who are rich in faith that are chosen to become heirs of God's kingdom. Therefore, all is not done by merely coming to church, or attending outward ordinances. Multitudes went far from their homes after Christ, into the wilderness, and even heard him personally address them there; but it was all of no use to those of them who laboured only for the meat that perisheth; to those who had not faith. Do you ask, How shall I *have* faith? Be seriously *concerned* to have it. Hear the word, and keep it in a honest and good heart; bring forth fruit; persevere; pray constantly and fervently; love not this present world; "sow not among thorns;" break up the fallow ground; expose to the sun the noxious weeds; cast away the stones; receive the good seed of the word; pray for the continual dew of God's blessing; cherish and obey the grace of Christ within you; desire to have this grace more abundantly. "He that hath ears to hear, let him hear."

---

11. Notes of a Sermon on Luke xvi. 19—31, preached at Denkendorf, on the first Sunday after Trinity, 1739.

Man is a traveller, arrived at a crossway, where one direction, steep and difficult, leads upwards to the city of God; the other, easy and agreeable, leads aside and downward to destruction and perdition. Faithful is the friend who warns any of their imminent danger: take it then kindly of me if to-day I attempt to speak

Of man's true wisdom; which is, "to depart from hell beneath:" and let us consider,

I. We have THE RECORD of that wisdom;

II. How to use it aright; and,

III. The blessed advantage of so doing.

I. "They have Moses and the prophets; let them hear them;" said Abraham, in the parable before us. *We* have *more* than Moses and the prophets; we have the words of Christ; with the writings of his apostles and evangelists. All this is an inestimable benefit, which greatly distinguishes us from many other nations who have it not. Surely, then, we are "without excuse" if we walk after the imagination of our own hearts; if we follow the multitude in the broad and descending way; if we live not after the word of God.

II. The necessity of "repentance" was acknowledged by "the Rich Man" himself; but that is not sufficient; we must add to it our *obedience:* this Abraham did, before Moses and the prophets existed; but the Rich Man did not do this, neither did his five brethren do it, neither did the multitude of the Pharisees do it. The necessity and nature of the obedience required is taught abundantly in the scriptures of the Old Testament itself; yes, in Moses and the prophets. See Isaiah lxvi. 2; 2 Chron. xxxiv. 27; Jerem. xxxvi. 24.

III. (1.) Thus "*hell,*" that dreadful "place of torment," is *avoided;* and, (2.) "*everlasting consolation*" is *obtained.* Think of the WIDE difference between these two things. A "GREAT gulf fixed" distinguishes them. O do not, like the Rich Man, "receive thy good things" *here!* Matt. xvi. 26.

A Funeral Address, delivered at Denkendorf, at the interment of Provost Knoll; Feb. 4, 1727; in Bengel's 30th year.

Job xvii. 1.—"The graves are ready for me!" *

My mourning Brethren!

By the name of brethren do I take the liberty to address every one of you, foregoing all complimentary appellations of this world; for Death knows nothing about *them.* I would speak to you from the words of Job, "The graves are ready for me." This was the language of one who, with the exception of Jesus Christ himself, stands pre-eminent among those who have endured the cross of afflictions. He uttered it at a time when his troubles were at their greatest height, when he had entirely renounced this present life, was quite resigned to die, and regarded himself as a person "dead already." Now, as people

* Lutheran version, "The grave is there!" or, "The grave is ready!" or, "Here is the grave!"

usually expedite the burial of their dead, because they are no longer fit to remain above ground, so Job would seem to deal with himself; therefore he exclaims, "The graves are ready for me!"

Another grave, my distressed and beloved friends, yes, one grave more is now ready, and one more departed friend is made ready for it. Ah! my brethren, it is the grave of our late revered provost, John Everard Knoll.

A celebrated Grecian actor,* wishing to affect his audience by the representation of a character† deeply mourning over the violent death of her brother, took privately with him from the grave the bones of his son, lately deceased, and hereby, in an unfeigned and natural manner, impassioned his own feelings, and then those of the spectators. So could my private grief easily put an emphasis upon the sorrows with which I now address you; but the affliction comes with sufficient keenness of itself; and this large assembly have all cherished such affectionate regard for our departed friend, that my greater need and difficulty is to *banish* sorrow, rather than increase it. For us it is enough, more than enough, that the grave is ready, by reason of a loss like ours.

As late as the close of the past year, our worthy provost had enjoyed such favourable health, that during the last eight days of December he went through considerable exertion without fatigue; but his first public ministration in the present year was his last; and with it he closed the services of nearly half a century. The entrance of the new year was to him accompanied by the inroad of death upon a beloved and faithful female relative, who had many years resided under his roof; and within a few days more he was himself stretched on a death-bed, so unexpectedly, that he had not time to say, "The graves are ready for me!" No, not on *that* occasion; but he had said it often enough long before. During a large part of his life, whenever he thanked his friends for their good wishes upon a new year, or upon his birth-day, he used so to express himself as to make it evident that he contemplated every year as his last; and how many interesting addresses and observations upon mortality and eternity have I heard him utter, when, some time since, he was laid aside by the rupture of a blood-vessel! Indeed his own salutary thoughts of death quite animated and attempered his holy life and conversation. Could we all have overheard the language of his soul during his latest moments,

* Polus at Athens. † Electra.

and witnessed what he then brought forth from his treasure, as the best experience of his whole life, how little necessary would it be for me to utter another word over his grave!

His earlier days were plentifully graced with the fruits of diligence; his ministry was characterised by laboriousness; and his zeal was tempered with care and prudence. His social intercourse was ever on the footing of kindness, and his very seriousness was full of cheerful forbearance. His liberality ran abroad in silence and secrecy, and his hoary age was one thankful acknowledgment of the Divine hand that had led him all his life long. Among his other good qualities, it was not the least that he was so very humble before God as a sinner, and as an unprofitable servant.

Will all, which can be thus truly related of him, perish in the grave here made ready for him? Certainly not. Surely, then, we have no real cause for sorrow; but great cause for comfort, encouragement, and hope. Besides, his is not the only grave that has been made ready here. For more than six centuries this edifice has stood, erected after the pattern of the holy sepulchre at Jerusalem; and many a mortal tabernacle of exalted personages, of knights and pilgrims, has here been interred, because, in the dark middle ages it was imagined that the slumbers of the tomb were more secure and blessed within such consecrated houses of God; and ever since the Reformation, when this convent was appointed to Protestant uses, many of its presidents have found their resting places here, down to the very father of our departed friend; so that not merely a grave, but *graves*, as the text speaks, have been made ready here. To say no more of those, we are reminded to notice one which still continues empty; I mean the holy sepulchre of "the Lord" himself. Thus, the very thought of the grave, the very thought of the way of all flesh, which at present forces itself upon us, may serve to bring home to our hearts COMFORT, ENCOURAGEMENT, and HOPE.

But suffer me to add one thing more. It has been given out, that pilgrims of all denominations, who go to the holy sepulchre, so called, in Palestine, feel, as soon as they arrive there, a transport of sacred awe, and quite an altered state of mind. Be that as it may, I am confident that a lively, spiritual consideration of the facts connected with the now empty sepulchre of the Lord Jesus, may serve to make a blessed alteration in ourselves. Therefore, to fulfil the office entrusted to me this day, I would solemnly ask of every heart here present, are we in readiness, as was our departed friend, to leave the body we carry about with us in the cold, deep bed of the grave? Some may be shocked at such a question, and not very well pleased with me for putting it; nevertheless it may prove a precious balm and embalming unto others. For there are those who, by the grace of God, can joyfully resign themselves to the thought of a sudden departure. Some, indeed, have been quite forward so to do, as were the ancient martyrs. Oh what a blessed change! the more sudden, the better! The rash, however, and the presumptuous are occasionally bold enough to venture upon it, while holy persons, who tremble for their own salvation, may, "through fear of death, be all their lifetime subject to bondage." But as I wish, in the best way I can, to thank every one of you for the affection you have shown to our dear departed father, receive from me, brethren, a token of my thankfulness in this present earnest entreaty and admonition, that upon every occasion, to the very end of your lives, you would endeavour to think upon the graves among which we walk, as if you were thinking of your own, and be wisely prepared for it in ever waiting for your Lord, and in waiting *upon* him. Thus shall you experience more than a recompense for the respect you have this day come to pay to the memory of the deceased; you shall experience how God himself can remunerate.

Now, then,

"The grave is ready there!
Let the full ripen'd son to his father repair!
Glory, honour, and peace, from their rod and staff bloom,
Near Jesus' tomb,—
Which few had more watchfully heeded than they.
Let them rest from the burden and heat of the day!
Safe treasur'd the hire of their work will be found,
When God shall break up the repose of this ground,
And the voice of archangel proclaim in the air,
'No more graves there!'"

Section II.

HIS MAXIMS FOR PASTORAL CONDUCT.

1. A pastor of souls ought not only to be persuaded of the truth of what he preaches, but also to be divinely persuaded of his own call to the ministry of reconciliation. He should be able, so to speak, to show the register of his spiritual birth. He should have fully made up his mind to live only for the

furtherance of the Divine honour and glory; to live faithfully to Christ, and to serve Him; to go into the kingdom of heaven himself, and to gain as many as possible to be partakers with him of the heavenly calling. He should purify himself, even as Christ is pure, and keep himself free from the bands of those sins which most easily beset him; so as carefully to "give no offence in any thing," and thus be the better qualified upon all occasions "to take forth the precious from the vile," (Jerem. xv. 19;) having nothing to do with the one, and upholding the other.

2. A minister of souls should go about his work with christian fortitude; be much among his flock, and not suffer himself to get discouraged. For this purpose, let him lay to heart that no Third Sunday after Trinity returns,* without occasioning, most probably, a new overflow of joy in heaven at the recovery of some one sinner to God, by the "holding forth" of the good tidings of "the word of life;" and, surely, one such fruit of his labour, though gathered even less frequently, is an occasion of extraordinary consolation. Again, that whenever things seem to go heavily, all may turn to our own profit in the end; may serve, at least, to keep us from presumption; may assist us, if we improve the trial, in becoming better acquainted with ourselves; may render us more humble before God, and induce us to wrestle in prayer for more of that witness of his Spirit, which can quiet all our doubts and anxieties. Thirdly, that God, we may be certain, has to exercise no less patience with ourselves, as believers of the gospel message, and as commissioned to preach and apply it, than we have to exercise with our hearers. How long has he to wait and look to us before any thing appears in us, that is suitable to, or commensurate with, his own glorious design in commissioning us! With what wisdom does he lead us on, in order to produce out of so much defilement in our motives, and so much infirmity in our aims, even a little that is truly valuable! And should not our patience and long suffering be learnt from his? Fourthly, that a minister has not to blame himself for living in a degenerate age, that will endure so little strenuous exertion to be made; while overflowings of ungodliness, particularly in oppressing and grinding the poor, make it the less wonderful that so little is effected by the preaching of the gospel; when rulers, often enough aware of existing abuses, are backward to apply the proper remedies; and thus allow the weaker part of society to be devoured

* Alluding to the Gospel appointed for that Sunday, in the Lutheran Church. See also our own Liturgy.—Tr.

by the stronger. Fifthly, that God (Ezek. ix. 4) causes his mark to be set upon every one of those who sigh and cry for the general and particular abominations of their country; and, that he will spare them in the day of his righteous visitation, as a man spareth his own son that serveth him. (Mal. iii. 17.) Sixthly, that such a minister may be refreshed and comforted, by considering what God may be doing by any of his brethren elsewhere, provided he has the humility to rejoice at any promotion of God's cause by their means, as if it had been effected by his own instrumentality. This will be making the good of *others* his own; and will prove that popularity is no aim of his. Seventhly, that though his people may not become really awakened by his zealous proclamation of the gospel, they become a little softened and civilized by some clearer notions of spiritual things. Professor Franke declared, from long experience, that he had always found that the parishes which had good men for their ministers, became gradually more civilized and orderly. Though God may grant more of spiritual ingathering to one minister than to another, this is no proof that the less successful minister is the less valuable with Him. Some surgical instruments are used constantly; others, but occasionally; yet the latter may be as valuable as the former. If the falling of a tree require fifty strokes, and one man give three, another five and forty, and another finish the business with two strokes more, we do not debate which of these men did most to fell the tree, which of them ought to have most wages, or which, at least, knows how much he has contributed to the work. Nor have we any more reason to be jealous about our own private importance in the great work of converting our fellow-sinners.

3. When we have opportunity of doing any spiritual service to others, we must not spare or excuse ourselves, or hang back through scrupulosity; though, as a general rule, it is good to know what our ability and resources are, that we may not spend ourselves prematurely. To have but two hundred florins a year for expenditure for ten years together, is more than to have four hundred once for all. Yet the person who undertakes the sacred ministry, must not regard for a moment his worldly convenience, honour, ease, or pleasure, in comparison with the great end of his high calling. Let him remember, that it is a short course we have to run in this life, and that we need not desire to have every temporal matter just to our convenience, but may well be content to take things as we find them. If we can

improve such things, we may; and if not, we should never be anxious about it, nor even think of contrasting our condition with that of those who are more prosperous; rather should we compare it with that of others who are less so. Whatever afflictions overtake us, we should not forget that it is the world that we are in, as long as we are in this life; and we should commit ourselves, with childlike submission, to the Divine disposal. And it is worth while to notice, that, as our ministerial life consists of two portions, the past and the future, so, though our *better* days, as we are too commonly apt to call them, are past, yet our remaining ones are bringing us every day nearer to the happy consummation. It is also far better to adapt ourselves to our situation, than to wish to have it adapted to *us*. In the latter case, we only labour in vain, and make our life irksome; but in the former, we have the graceful advantage of seeming as if we had been made for our situation. Those generally get through life best, whether in a civil or religious capacity, who conscientiously fulfil the duties of their station, and meddle with nothing beyond it. They may be but little noticed in their lifetime, so quietly do they make their way along; but they are missed when they are gone.

4. A minister of souls ought to show the way of salvation plainly and clearly; to teach repentance in the most friendly, affectionate, and compassionate manner of inviting persons to forsake every false way, and turn into the only right one. Our desire to declare the whole counsel of God may tempt us to fear lest we should thus deal almost too tenderly with some; but when we recollect what sort of people the ancient prophets had to address, and yet what beautifully evangelical testimonies they delivered, we may see at once that it is best to follow their example. And, with what persevering, patient, and tender affection did the apostles beseech men! (2 Cor. v. 20.) Let such be our pattern. If people learn nothing *better* from us than what they are already familiar with, they will be content to remain as they are; which shows how necessary it is that the good tidings should be commended to every man's conscience, in the manner of an ambassador sent to disclose one delightful message after another.

5. A pastor of souls must be like a parent. Let him think of the parent bird, that takes her young ones under her wings, and suffers them to hop upon her back. We can never expect to get the confidence of our people by overbearing manners or temporal constraints; no, nor by any thing short of long-suffering,

love, and tenderness. Friendly intercourse with them often effects much more than all the reasons, demonstrations, and sermons in the world. The traveller unwraps his mantle, not when the cold wind blows strongly, but when the warming sunshine smiles. It is better here to have a single dove flying towards us of its own accord, than to see ever so many driven into the enclosure. How desirable is it to get our people to feel so easy with us, that they can ask or tell us any thing with open-heartedness and simplicity! It is desirable, indeed, to have even the unconverted thus confiding in us; and we should aim at it. Therefore,

6. A christian minister ought not to shun friendly intercourse with worldly persons, on any suitable occasion; only he should take care to "be not a partaker of other men's sins." Some good will ever be done, where what is testified, or rather ratified by him, *out* of the pulpit, agrees with what he preaches *in* it. Much that he has taught may seem not remembered by others, yet benefit will often, by and by, come out of it. Many a flake of snow, and even many a layer of it, may be absorbed by the moisture of the ground; but, at length, as it continues to fall, the whiteness of the fields shows that it is gaining the ascendant. Therefore, *sparge! sparge! quam potes:* (go on scattering the good seed wherever you can; lose no opportunity; and do your best.)

It is difficult to preach home to such a mixed multitude as our congregations at present consist of. When we preach the law, and "rebuke sharply," then are many of our hearers very apt to think only of others, or to make a little exception here and there in favour of themselves, especially about matters in which they know they are the less guilty. When we preach the gospel, they listen to it, and, perhaps, think of it; but that is all. What then is to be done? Go on, and preach, "in season, out of season," &c.; but be not disappointed if you fail to make everybody pious. You will, "by *all means,* save some."

7. Maintenance of brotherly communication and fellowship with true Christians should never be neglected or lightly thought of by the christian minister; otherwise his pastoral work will degenerate and subside into a kind of easy mechanical employment; whence it is that many seek only their ease, glide into a mere secular life, and "mind earthly things;" although it is very difficult to say what good those pastors have ever been remarkable for doing, who have grown, by their office, remarkably rich. As the hand cannot say unto the eye, I have no need

of thee; so neither can the eye say this to the hand. We may regard common pious people as the hand; which, as it is often of essential use to the eye itself, by many humble and laborious services, so, pious persons, though of very ordinary stamp in other respects, are able both temporally and spiritually to benefit him who watches for their souls; and they can also be really helpful to him in his work.

8. Many become seriously impressed, and "pricked to the heart," under sermons, who yet derive no special comfort from the word of grace, till it is communicated to them in private conversation. Therefore, *visiting* those committed to his charge should be considered by the Christian minister as any thing but a light matter; for he can often do much more good by his private visits, than by his public testimony. He should, therefore, let his people see that he is always willing and ready to attend privately upon any and every one of them; and he should allow and encourage them to be as free with him as their confidence in him can make them. Moreover, he should let them feel, at his visit to any house, that the presence of neighbours is quite agreeable.

9. And then, with respect to those who make use of him as their spiritual friend, he should be careful to do nothing of his own will, and to omit nothing which the will of God requires. As to any *hopeful* characters among his flock, let him seek *proper seasons* for intercourse with them; that is, when they are not so likely to be diverted or distracted by their worldly avocations; but, as to the *untoward*, he must endeavour to bring home the word of God to them at all seasons. By kind and familiar conversation, he may induce them first to talk about things indifferent, that they may come, at length, of their own accord, to be open about things which they were not directly questioned upon. Wherever he has plenty of daily opportunities for this, it is best to consider what moment may be most favourable. But when such opportunities occur but seldom, or where he is likely never to have another, he should not suffer the present to pass by without delivering his testimony. For, the thought of having neglected it will be very painful, should the person unexpectedly die; whereas, there will be comfort in remembering that we carried a testimony of the truth to his conscience. We should keep ourselves unanxious; otherwise we spoil much of our work. Therefore, we should undertake and determine every thing with God rather than with ourselves; that we may be able to say, "Lord, I have done that which thou commandest me." An answer

from Him will be sure to arrive at its proper time. A single word which we may happen to drop, before an unconverted person, nay, even a look, or a mere point of tacit understanding between him and us, will sometimes be decisive for such a person's conversion; for we may often, without knowing it, hit the nail upon the head. One said to a person, whose wife was taken ill, "Your house is now consecrated!" or, "You have now a sanctuary in your house!" and that casual remark fastened on the person's mind. It is a great advantage to be able, in our most familiar conversation, to throw out suitable thoughts in a natural manner.

10. Nothing must be thought too insignificant for our grand object. That object is, that we may win souls; and how few soever we may have the charge of, we must show them that we really think it worth any trouble to lead them to Christ.

11. We must never entirely slight or neglect any one. Whatever his sin, fault, or failing may be, we should try to make him acquainted with it, sensible of it, penitent, convalescent. Successful or not, we should still consider whether he has not some good qualities, which we may turn to the best account. But the "christian world," as it is called, which, in the present day, is but too much like the world itself, will have every body perfect at once, under the penalty of severe slight and neglect; what wonder then is it that so few will confess their faults one to another? what wonder that hypocrisy and dissimulation prevail every where? For he who openly discovers a single fall, is directly put too much at a distance, if not slighted and neglected altogether. O how differently does the long-suffering of a holy God deal with *us!*

12. *Sometimes* a sharp rebuke answers the purpose best. Pastor Wiegleb, of Jena, once said to a man who came to him for advice, "You are one of those who are a disgrace to the town." The man felt this, and actually amended. Another, in his youth, overheard a reproach vented against him by a mere girl. She had said, "A pretty covetous priest he'll make by and by." This so stung him that he was ever afterwards disposed to "take heed and beware of covetousness."

We should endeavour, where we can, to weaken strong and pertinacious credulity; for it strangely nurses infidelity itself. As it is very different from christian belief, so there is a kind of foolhardiness belonging to it; whereas, people of genuine faith are impressible, tractable, willing to be reasoned with, and yield to conviction.

13. (Every chain of reasoning should have links of equal strength.) It is of prime importance not to reason upon proofs or motives, weak and strong, promiscuously. (Their unequal strength is likely soon to discover holes in the tissue, and to insure a verdict that it is badly woven.) For the stronger parts are then of little other effect than to sharpen people's attention to the weaker; and while these bring the stronger under suspicion, the whole is in danger of neglect and contempt. Therefore, it is better to adopt one kind of tenacious and conclusive proof, which cannot be gainsaid.

The following extract of a sermon, preached by Bengel in the hospital church at Stuttgart, for the benefit of the orphan house in that city, on the fifteenth of July, 1712, which was one of the days appointed for public monthly humiliation and prayer, may here be suitably inserted, for its illustration of the last of the above remarks. The sermon was upon Psalm v. 5—7, and showed—"*What a motive for true repentance and amendment of heart and life is found in God's awfully revealed hatred and wrath against sin.*" In applying the subject, at the conclusion he said:—

"Let us lay aside the evil mind, put away the iniquity of our hearts, and be led by the Spirit of God. His guidance is not grievous. Let us put on the mind of God. Let us shun the vain pleasure of ungodly society; indeed, where the heart is purified, a man cannot, for very love and holy charity, behold the wicked without jealousy. No; the children, friends, and servants of God, cannot look upon the mass of corruption that is in the world, without poignant grief; and are glad to discover any means likely to remedy it. Now, to mention only one instance of this corruption; it is notorious into what immorality and excesses our youth degenerate, wherever faithful superintendence and careful education are wanting, to imbue them with the fear of God, and to habituate them to virtue and industry, "yea," to "every good path." Without this, they generally become profane, depraved, dishonest, addicted to falsehood; and form the very characters that draw down upon themselves and upon a whole people, that wrath of God which is described in our text. Christian parents, therefore, cannot do a better and more valuable service than by endeavouring, most seriously and perseveringly, to wean their offspring from evil habits, and to accustom them to good ones. For the same reason, christian rulers can institute nothing more laudable and useful, nor evince love to their country in a more noble manner, than by projecting ways and means for imparting useful education to a multitude of destitute orphans; neither can benevolent Christians, who would return, as it were, some thank-offering of their temporal substance to the Supreme Lord and Giver of all, better apply their charity, than by contributing in this way, as much as they are able, to the rescue of young persons exposed to so many and great dangers. Hence, it is to be regarded as one of the many inestimable favours vouchsafed to our own times, corrupt as they are, that in various parts of our country, many benevolent persons have been raised up to establish and support orphan institutions, though with slender means at their commencement; and that already, through such institutions, a considerable number of children, who might have contributed not a little to increase the wrath of God upon the present age, are now brought up in his holy fear, to respectable and useful employments. And may we not reasonably hope, that, eminently distinguished by the Divine blessing as these institutions are every where become, no pious persons will be so insensible of their value as not to acknowledge them worthy of all possible assistance and encouragement?

An institution of the kind has been for some time projected in this metropolis, but its advancement has resembled that of the second temple, strikingly noticed in the first chapter of the prophet Haggai. Nevertheless, we may confidently hope that it will receive support by the unanimous, ready, and willing help of the pious, who are the best persons to look to for such a work; and we may be sure that "from this time" God "will bless" it, if we persevere with sincere zeal in what, as having commenced it in his name, and as having dedicated it to himself, it is no longer at our option to abandon. They, therefore, who delight in "whatsoever things are lovely and of good report," will consider well whatever is proper to be done in the present instance. We cannot here anticipate all the opposing and distrustful thoughts by which one or another may feel cramped in his liberality and bounty, much less can we here meet such thoughts with any reply; but we will hope that there may be no necessity for doing it. Whoever is constrained, by the love of Christ, to put forth liberality upon other occasions, will be taught by the same love to take a warm interest in our infant institution. What is given to it from such a motive, though, like seed cast upon the soil, it may not immediately yield its expected increase, will certainly produce the fruit of righteousness in due time; and they who mean to share the joy of such a blessed reaping time, need not take long in considering whether they will take advantage of the present season for sowing. For whatever is given in simplicity for the Lord's sake, is only such a lending unto the "Lord of all" as he will again repay; especially when the thing is done in the hope and expectation which true faith inspires. Let every one then, whose heart is inclined to contribute *at all*, resolve immediately to contribute *something*, and he will never have occasion to repent of it. But our chief concern is, that every one who would gladly see this house builded, and the stones and timber ready prepared, yes, and lively stones, also, brought together for a spiritual house, would supplicate for it the Divine blessing, as upon this all the rest depends. Let him also pray, that those into whose hearts God has put it to commence this work, may become yet more lively, willing, and watchful to promote it. And devoutly is it to be wished, that by these means, as well as by others still more efficient, a people may be trained and prepared for the Lord, to serve him in faithfulness, and to abominate ungodliness; that instead of loving unrighteousness more than goodness, they may become imitators of God, as dear children, yea, even of our own God, of whom it is here written, (Ps. v. 4,) "Thou art not a God that hath pleasure in wickedness; neither shall evil dwell with thee," &c. With this view, then, may all of us cooperate to the best of our ability, not only *temporally* and in behalf of others; but, above all, *spiritually*, to the best of our ability, *for our own personal salvation*, and *for that of our families and connexions*. Thus will it be our blessed privilege increasingly to taste and see that the Lord is good and gracious. Surely it will be well with them that serve God acceptably, as the verses which follow our text plainly declare. (Ps. v. 7, 11, 12.) With sacrifice of this sort God is indeed well pleased, (Ps. xv. 1, *seq.* 9;) and he will fully manifest that he is so, "in that day." "Wherefore let us have grace wherewith we may serve him acceptably," &c. Heb. xii. 28, 29.

14. Some characters are so reserved, that the more we endeavour to ascertain their spiritual religion, the less open they appear to be with us. We must wait, therefore, and be quietly content to wait a good while without seeing any fruit. That patient waiting for God's time and seasons, which is so recommended by Taulerus and other writers, is now too little thought

of, by many who are apt to overdrive themselves, as well as others. Nevertheless, such waiting often brings with it, when God's favourable moment arrives, more benefit than we can get by our own officious toil of many months ; and the good effect is more lasting than any thing we can obtain by forcing or devices of art. There are some persons so constituted, that with our consideration of this, and of the great temptations of this present evil world, it appears better to let alone what is proceeding in their minds, and to leave it, as it were, in the bud, rather than try to force its growth : that having time fully to develop itself, it may open to the kingdom of light, perhaps just at their departure from this life. Not that I think it wise to talk too loudly upon such a matter ; but to those who are concerned in the care of souls it may not be without its use and consolation. At all events, let us do every thing with as much suavity and cheerfulness as possible, leaving the rest to our chief Shepherd ; and thinking with Moses, "Have I conceived and borne all this people ?"

15. Where there is life, there is life. I mean, that if our hopeful persons are too much petted and dallied with, they are apt to look for it, trust to it, become indolent, and at last require, as it were, to be carried like children. *Abraham*,* a father of the church in the fourth century, left the members of his flock to get on for themselves, after he had brought them so far as to unite cordially in the confession, "We believe in God the Father, and in his Son, Jesus Christ." Our Saviour said to his disciples, "It is expedient *for you* that I *go away*." The Spirit of the Lord caught away the evangelist from the Ethiopian eunuch, who, after he had been baptized, "went on his way rejoicing." Acts viii. 27.

As a young tree will thrive none the better for my continually pruning it, digging about it, &c. and, as a little child that runs very well upon level ground, is only the more likely to fall if I perpetually call out to caution it, so is it if we are ever urging those under our spiritual care to *actus reflexos ;* (*i. e.* to trouble themselves about sensible feelings of their state of grace, and of their growth of holiness.) There are those whose whole christian business consists in *actibus directis*, (in free and direct proceedings, to which they are instigated by their faith and love ;) and whereas they thrive the best, so they would only become disheartened and bewildered by our pressing them about such reflex matters. Nevertheless, others may be all the better for this

* One of the earliest Christian monks.—See the Author's *Merkwürdige Reden der Altväter*, p. 111.

mode of treatment; nay, they may absolutely want it; consequently, a minister should have the gift of sound discrimination.

16. What is the main requisite for one who has the care of souls? It is what is so often expressed in the Psalms by the word יָשָׁר, *yashar*—straightforwardness of principle; ("this one thing I do!") It is a disposition of soul that may be compared to a straight line, having nothing *awry*, nothing *doubling;* a disposition neither to soar nor sink; that knows only its *straightest* way directly onward to "the mark."

17. Ye, beloved brethren, who have the care of souls! Let us have our own souls filled with the love of Christ. This will make us lively and active, bold and ready, always well furnished for our work; and will best help us to ascertain in our fellow-men their real state of mind, and to see how to recover them. *We should commune among one another with more confidence and intimacy;* never forgetting, that it is *with fellow-men*, and *fellow-redeemed*, that we have to do. People, in time of pestilence, or of any other public calamity, lose sight of their smaller and private matters, their prerogatives, external preferences, and distinctions. So should we behave to one another; so should we deal with our fellow-mortals, our fellow-*im*mortals: this is the way to take them, as it were, captive; and to do with them what we will.

It is, in every respect, good to be ready at acknowledging our infirmities, but not to be always at it, like many who become mere complainers. We ought to "make mention of God's righteousness;" we ought to "glory in his grace;" and not to let complaining, or any thing else, choke up such inexhaustible springs within us.

Is any commendation bestowed on us? let us be sure to trace it all to Divine grace, and then it will only serve to deepen our humility, and yet to stir us up more wakefully to every duty.

18. I very willingly leave every one's private matters of faith to himself, though these may be weak, or even false, provided he come only to the true conclusion. A very young child, in attempting to walk, would hold itself by its own clothes; and if it thus get to the other side of the room, we may well let it enjoy this imaginary help. O, with what tenderness of sympathy ought we to treat the souls of our fellow-men! By putting them too forbiddingly upon the stretch, we only prepare them to recoil in an opposite direction.

19. We never interfere with a person as to where he may

choose to go and refresh himself with his glass of wine; and in like manner there are occasions when we must let our people alone as to their extra-gratifications of a spiritual kind. Nevertheless, a pastor of souls must be any thing but indifferent about pious members of his flock absenting themselves frequently from his own ministry; as this may look as if he had been dealing to them hay, straw, and stubble, instead of the bread of life.

20. With respect to private meetings for edification, it were to be wished that our more hardy and zealous soldiers of Jesus Christ were not too much restricted and cramped by acts of the legislature, framed under colour of civil order; but were freely permitted the privilege of improving such time as others lavish upon worldly diversions, to their own mutual edification in the word of God. I compare these meetings, in no invidious sense, to a fresh swarm of bees, settled upon some tree; now let them be skilfully hived, and not rudely dispersed. To do the latter is more than a pity; it is indiscreet.*

21. I do not understand objections against such private meetings. Why are Christians to be obliged to stand apart, and each one to keep his piety to himself? This is as if, at seeing persons travelling in company on the highway to the same place, I were to desire them not to go together, but to keep at the distance of at least a musket-shot one behind another.

22. Sickness implies life; and surely even in morbid piety there is *some* spiritual life. It is the *ungodly* who are *dead* while they live. (1 Tim. v. 6.) Why then should ministers reject or neglect those children of God in whom they perceive that something or other is not quite after due order? Should they not rather endeavour to help and recover them—to heal that which is lame or sick? Ezek. xxxiv. 4; Heb. xii. 13.

23. Many are disposed to make far too much of such meetings, and seem almost to think themselves a better sort of people, because they join in such a special religious exercise. But as such can have no exclusive claim to piety, so neither are all of them really pious. There are excellent Christians who do not attend meetings of this description, and there are hypocrites who do. (We ought, however, to think favourably of them in general, and to remember, that) though as lookers-on we are at liberty to form our opinion of them, yet we are not to be their judges. "Destroy not the work of God." As we leave every one to

* Thus Bengel wrote in 1741, two years before the Würtemberg Act was passed concerning Private Assemblies, to his friend Weissensee, the General Superintendant at Denkendorf; which perhaps contributed not a little to the mild wording of that Act.

manage his temporal concerns in his own way, so in all such matters of religion as are less essential, we can and we ought to let people alone, that principal matters may be the better attended to on both sides. With respect to those who experience some inconveniences from the world on account of attending such religious meetings, we need not be anxious to run immediately to them with comfort; for such inconveniences are good and salutary. A little rudeness or ill-humour of domestics towards my children is not to make me hasty in siding with the latter, or in taking much notice of it; indeed such things may have spared me some trouble as a father, in teaching them proprieties.

24. When seriously disposed persons band together, but are not united upon fundamental points, as is the case in the present day, there is at best much unedifying discussion, and much nonsense talked; nay, it is well if ludicrous scenes do not ensue. But "the wisdom from above is first *pure*, then *peaceable*." (James iii. 17.) Souls must become *prepared* for one another, and then their union has its value. It is a good thing, however, when Christians thus thrown together, with much remaining imperfection and error about them, have some check of circumstance which keeps them from breaking out with their personal peculiarities, so that, after all, they really help forward one another. But if a minister finds some in his flock who are always halting and undecided, let him be for bringing them to the point at once:—"Tell me whether you prefer to hold by Christ or by the world?" Do they answer, that Christ is their decided choice? then let him tell them they must alter their conduct in this or in that respect. For some, when suffered to go on haltingly and slovenly, are apt at length to think that they cannot do better. Should such serious and plain dealing with them prove of no avail, some trial or other will, by and by, show their real character; for then they will either relapse entirely, or break through their difficulties, and become decided and devoted Christians.

25. When any christian community is characterized by coldness or lukewarmness upon really spiritual subjects, the natural consequence is lack of vital warmth for sustaining that close communion and familiar intercourse, which are so desirable among its individual members, and which ought surely to be found in a community of persons really born again. And this will be particularly the case when there is not sufficient solid basis of sound knowledge and christian experience for the foundation of such

mutual confidence. Where these things are at all wanting, the time for full and primitive communion is not arrived.

Much is requisite for solid union among fellow-Christians. As they must all have a good proportion of knowledge and experience, so it is necessary there should be among them some who have "the spirit of judgment," or "the eyes of their understanding" so "enlightened," as to be able to counsel and conduct their brethren; who, without such aids, will often justle one another. But let each look carefully to his own personal conduct, that, when they come together, their brotherly freedom may not degenerate into absurd exhibition. Alas, it is but too common, even among Christians, to act without simplicity; and they who ought to show themselves the honest servants of the Lord, and members one of another, are apt to speak only to please; to neglect the duty of faithful and affectionate admonition, expostulation, or rebuke; and to be sadly backward to stir up and encourage one another. Some appear to carry about with them neither humility nor love—nothing of the mind of Christ; and can be distinguished as belonging to the same community, by nothing more than formal exterior adherence. If this be any thing better than stage personation, I should be glad to know in what respect it is so.

In true communion of christian brethren, there must, of course, be communion of prayer, besides rules and regulations upon a variety of things. But they ought not to be bound too strictly to formalities of time, place, and circumstance; for the stricter such ties are made, the sooner they break. Many keep to uniform rules, because they first began so, and do not like to appear changeable and unstable; especially as they flatter themselves that they made a good beginning. The more intimate and confidential we become, by mutual fellowship in spiritual exercises, the more carefully must we beware of aping one another. In walking together, it is not necessary nor even convenient for one to put his foot just where another has put his. They can go straight on in company, by steps of their own choosing, and still be near enough. Neither must any one of the party think of *pushing* others forward; but all and each must agree in mutual submission to the guiding spirit of their common Shepherd, who once breathed, and breathes still, upon every one of his true disciples. But many in the present day are erring more and more, from this blessed dependence on the Divine presence, into winds of doctrine or gusts of feeling which they themselves have raised. In personal religion they move indolently and lukewarmly, and need to have their pastor always about them, for their preservation from false security, and from forgetting vital and solid christian communion. Such, however, as have no truth and sincerity at heart, will not abide this faithfulness of their minister, but will soon fly off.

26. If he cannot obviate the prevalence of open "abominations," let him, at least, "sigh and cry" concerning them to God, and take every occasion to testify against them earnestly, though meekly; but let him not harass himself with anxiety about its success. As a landed proprietor will often put into court a protest against some invasion of his rights, though he knows that no immediate good can result from it, so a minister should persevere in bearing witness to the truth, though he cannot see what good it will do; for seed cast upon the waters may be found after many days, and meanwhile he has delivered his conscience. A rivulet is always available for the purposes of human life, whether actually used for them or not, or whether even noticed as useful for them.

27. As to what is plainly contrary to the revealed will of God, a faithful minister will testify against every thing of the kind, and will do it with such seriousness and explicitness as that all may clearly understand him. He will never suppress his testimony through fear of man, especially as the unconverted will bear many an unpleasant truth to be spoken to their face. Every reproof, as it must produce some pain and remorse at the time, may excite momentary irritation; nevertheless, people afterwards become ashamed of themselves, and return to reflection. But we must be very careful always to temper our rebukes with sound discretion, for which the following cautions are needful: 1. Guard against attempting palpable impossibilities, or what will evidently be of no use, as without such discretion we can never insure respect and influence; for if once we begin to take a wrong aim, our best success in time past will avail us nothing. 2. Be not sensitive to take any thing as a personal offence to yourself, for this is but one of the many ways in which man "disquieteth himself in vain." All personal affronts, real or imaginary, we must make up our minds never to regard for a moment. 3. Be careful to take the right opportunity; for to sting unseasonably will only increase the rancour of him it affects; as it will seem more like an attack, than like christian reproof. 4. If we have only just heard of something unplea-

sant, which refers to a time long past, we must not immediately go and talk to the person about it; it is better to wait and observe him till the evil reappears, as this will furnish occasion for expostulating with him upon his general conduct and disposition, without dwelling too much upon any single instance. 5. We should be unprejudiced, affectionate, tender, and compassionate; for if persons can but be made to feel that we are sincerely concerned for them as fellow-men, their hearts become softened and kindly inclined towards us. 6. Our very *manner* is a thing of importance. A kind *no* is often more agreeable than a rough *yes*. 7. We must not indiscriminately address all as open and gross sinners. This will even increase self-complacency in the hearts of many; they will think they know more good of themselves than we know of them. "Surely I lead a regular life;" "I am not so bad as some that I am acquainted with," &c.

28. As to matters of comparative indifference (ἀδιαφόρα), such as playing, dancing, and the like, we shall do well to consider, that arguments against these things have often been overstrained. Here we must not always judge of others by ourselves. We cannot give them our own eyes to see with, nor just our own views of things. There are persons who have so grown up, that their hearts are callous as leather, and sometimes as dry bone. Now natural hilarity and buoyancy of spirits are to me far more tolerable than the forbiddingness of an unfeeling, unsusceptible, unbroken, and impenitent heart. The former is an unlike counterfeit of the Divine happiness: the latter is the very opposite to this. Some have learnt to esteem many a thing sinful, which is but a bare ceremony or adjunct of common worldly civility, and which occasionally serves to check the outbreakings of sin itself. It is true, we do not take such things with us to heaven; but our having conformed to them gives us no particular painful recollections after we have turned to God, though we have now learnt to feel the *general* vanity of our past life. They are at most but the natural accompaniments of an unconverted course, which as naturally leave us at our conversion. We must not, therefore, make too large demands upon others all at once; much less insist with any bitterness of spirit, or with too legal strictness, upon putting down the gaieties of dancing and the like; still less must we give out sweeping rules upon such subjects; but must endeavour to direct every one to his own conscience, and warn him against doing whatever is unfavourable to peace of mind, or promotive of self-rebuke. The patriarch Job, who evidently "had his children in subjection with all authority," did not absolutely prohibit them

from social festivities, but he prayed for them. And we have more reasons than those of Job to pray earnestly for our people, and to do it at the very time when their vain amusements are going on. Such intercessions would not fail of bringing down benefit to some of them; whereas, to lay down the law with respect to their indulgences would only serve to irritate and provoke. But these remarks are not intended to discourage my brethren from giving their own views of such amusements at proper occasions; neither from plainly declaring, that as people are resolved to use their liberty to the utmost, and will not admit the *dangerous tendency* of their habits, they are like those who will walk as near the edge of a steep and hollow river bank as possible, and that they have abundant cause to beware, lest by approaching too near the world's madness and folly they ingulf beneath it their own interest in a better world; or by indulging in its unprofitable and vain dissipations, they sport away their part and lot in the kingdom of heaven, and receive only in this life "*their* good things:" indeed, that they may well regard as a certain sign of their unconversion, their preference for, and delight in, such things as these, and that they will learn to view them in a very different light if ever the Spirit of God effectually influence their hearts, &c.

But a minister must take care not to let the misconduct of some bad members of his congregation influence his opinion of the whole; for though nothing but the croaking of frogs is to be heard upon the pool's surface, we are not thence to infer that there are no fish beneath.

29. A minister should not only in the pulpit, but privately at opportunities, insist upon the necessity of practically renouncing the world; but he is not to consider himself bound at all times to rebuke every sinful habit or practice the moment he perceives it. Here, as in every thing else, he must follow the guidance and influence of the Spirit of Christ. And thus at one time he will be still and silent, and only sigh before God; at another, he will feel himself "pressed in spirit" to address the conscience of an offending brother—and he may then do it with powerful effect. When we are conscious of such strong inducement to admonish and rebuke, it is not right to defer it to a more convenient opportunity, as hoping to temper the unpleasant subject with some seasonable congratulation or good wishes, that we may some day have occasion to express; neither should we endeavour to compass our object by any other circuitous method. But breathing conscious integrity of motive, if we have "a word of" admonition or "exhortation," we should, without disguise, "say on."

Experience has too often taught us that any other method is far less likely to succeed.

30. A minister must have respect to the good order of the church as a body, and must, for its sake, be particular in obeying its rules; by which he is more likely to keep his flock watchful over their own conduct, and submissive to general order. He must, likewise, be very accurate and punctual in all exterior conformities; otherwise, from his variableness here, people will infer that he is as variable and wavering in his doctrine and instructions. But, with regard to preaching, I think he should not be so strictly uniform, as to want freedom for adding, after he has concluded his sermon, any few apposite remarks which may then occur to him. Communications of this sort should also be delivered like those of friendly conversation, rather than as part of a formal address. Macarius tells us, that in ancient times any of the audience were allowed to put questions to the preacher in the midst of his sermon, and that, though such questions were not always apposite to the subject in hand, they were immediately replied to. Such a simple practice might be revived with benefit amongst us.

31. Concerning ministerial intercourse with the sick and dying members of the flock, my official situation has prevented me from having very extensive experience in this way; but, from what I know of it, I may add the following observations:

Compassionate regard for the sick, and prayer for spiritual wisdom to use it aright, will be always the safest guides of the faithful minister in this part of his work. There are appropriate selections of scripture passages and devotional pieces, both in prose and verse, which may serve for directing the sinner clearly and fully to Christ, as well as for encouraging the penitent believer to look for complete redemption through his precious blood, and to apply to God's paternal love towards us *in Him.* With a manual or two of this sort, we may draw the attention of the sick person to such of their contents as are best suited to his condition and most familiar to him, and then endeavour to interest his heart in their meaning and their application to his present state, rather than interrogate him at once whether he has lived accordingly or not. We should afterwards drop some remark, that may imperceptibly induce him to make free acknowledgments concerning himself; for it is very desirable that he should become inclined, of his own accord, to compare his present with his past condition. Where no gross hypocrisy has prevailed, it is not desirable to insist upon beginning every thing over again, nor to suggest that all his former stirrings under preventing grace may have had no reality. Rather, should we take every opportunity to help up and support him, according as he more and more clearly perceives his own poverty and wretchedness. Besides, in doing this, we shall be able, from time to time, to make those special applications upon which so much depends. Persons decidedly ungodly, especially if self-accused of having led a dishonest or profligate life, are often under a kind of secret despair; and this makes it, at the very outset, our business to convince them that there is still a hope of salvation for them, if they are but in earnest to obtain it. Their despondency is sometimes expressed in exclamations, "that they are lost," that they are "quite given up to the devil," &c. Here, then, we have fit occasion for fully declaring to them the sinful and ruined state of mankind in general, and of themselves in particular; likewise, for setting before them the perfect freeness and fulness of the grace of God. We may, according to circumstances, commend to them either repentance or faith, or submission and resignation to the Divine will, with any other requisite; and we should be concerned all along to have them deeply interested about these things. Sometimes we need to be cautioned not to exceed proper bounds in our addresses to the sick; for though many, after recovery from serious illness, have acknowledged that what was said at their bedside came most acceptably, and did them good, others have found conversation troublesome and harassing. Therefore, upon all such occasions, it requires much discretion to know when to speak, and when to be silent. We should endeavour to ascertain, from the patient himself, which of these is the more convenient or agreeable; and, whenever he is able and disposed to talk himself, we should let him have his way.

If his sufferings prevent our addressing him as one needing to be brought to the knowledge of his sins, we may, by praying with him, suggest thoughts and expressions suitable to his case. Persons, when they are thus presented, as it were, to God, by intercessions uttered for them in their hearing, become more ready to join in with a voluntary confession of their faults, and with self-accusations, than when we try to draw such things from them, especially in the presence of others.

Some sick persons, particularly if advanced in years, are apt to regard young ministers as having less experience than themselves, and as unable to be of much use to them in spiritual matters, though they are grateful for their good intentions. Such prejudice it is desirable to remove, by convincing them, that as all ministers are but God's instruments, it is not on these that we should depend, but on the truth itself. Sometimes it is also useful to remind the sick, that we come to them for no selfish purpose, but simply about the welfare of their souls—that we cannot possibly have any thing to gain or lose, by setting such or such views of gospel-truth before them.

The time of their receiving the Lord's Supper is an excellent opportunity for opening to them the treasures of Jesus Christ.

All notions of *opus operatum*, all dependence on religious performances, and on this in particular, must, if need require, be declared futile and vain; our great endeavour, before and after, as well as at the time of showing forth the Lord's death, should be simply to lead the sick person to turn to God in Christ, and to stay the mind upon him alone.

A minister ought, with all sick persons, to watch favourable moments, that he may lose no opportunity of effecting some good, if not to the sufferer, at least to those about him. He should, therefore, before and after the decease of any person, endeavour to impress the relatives and friends, that the chief thing is not simply whether strong consolation is imparted to a dying person, but whether his heart is interested in the main matters of the gospel; whether he shows something more than mere general assent to it; whether he has a real relish for spiritual things, and longs for more of them; and we should seriously intimate, how many, it is to be feared, have no such longing or relish for divine things, but die in a state of spiritual insensibility; that we have no reason, however, to fear this for any who persevere in prayer, and are glad to receive scriptural exhortation and encouragement.

"*Baptism over the dead,*" (1 Cor. xv. 29,) seems to have been the baptism of those who embraced Christianity just before their death. "*Pulling out of the fire,*" (Jude 23,) means, rescuing with a degree of holy violence and importunity, when a slow and soft remonstrance was ineffectual, those who were in imminent danger, and "nigh unto perdition, whose end" (had they thus continued) "was to be burned." For our Saviour's warning, that "there are few who find the way to life," must not discourage the messengers of salvation. Let them be only the more earnest to stir up their people to diligence and faithfulness.

It is my firm belief, that few genuine conversions ever take place on a death-bed. The sick person was either under the influence of grace, though in a less perceptible manner, and it was manifested at last, or he died in his inveterate state of mind. Still, it may be observed, that many uneducated persons are upon the true foundation, though unable to express themselves to that effect, for want of regular instruction in early life; yet God often imparts to such persons, in their last moments, a liberty of spirit and utterance beyond what they ever before enjoyed, and sufficient to show that he has not let his children sail away quite *incognito.*

We should remind those who presume upon having time enough to think of their conversion when they come to die, that people in dying circumstances, though ever so sensible of their danger (which itself is not a very common thing), find it extremely difficult to acquire a consciousness of being heartily turned to God; for they are under perpetual misgivings lest their care about it is only because they are apprehensive of dying.

We meet with some persons who are always ready to weep, but who cannot exactly tell why; and their inability to explain their feelings only distresses them the more. These we may advise not to suppress their tears, but freely to pour out their hearts before God, reminding them how sufficient it is that God himself hears and understands them.

Many, of mere natural tenderness, quite set their hearts upon their children, and are so anxious for their welfare, here and hereafter, that they seem to neglect the working out of their own salvation. Such we must endeavour to divert from needless anxiety, by assuring them that when we get into eternity, "every one of us must give account of himself to God;" that "all souls are his;" and that every *natural* tie between parent and child, husband and wife, &c., is dissolved at death.

At some death-beds it may be worth while to consider, whether the *peaceful* departure of the sufferer may not be hindered by the unforgivingness of an offended neighbour or relative; and that he may fall asleep in peace when the offended person has expressed reconciliation.

32. To these advices for visiting the sick, we add others, which Bengel addressed to the sick themselves, in the hearing of friends, who wrote them down.

To a dying man he said, "My dear brother, try to find your way into the love and light of God. Make use, my brother, of that right and privilege which Jesus Christ, the beloved, hath procured for us revolted and rebellious creatures. Let the Spirit of Grace be mighty in your own weakness, (not only by sustaining you under it, but by entirely sanctifying you,) by working in your heart groanings which (cannot be uttered like those of nature, but which) reach into that eternity whither God is drawing us, and whither we are journeying; where our great Redeemer is for us entered, and where there are many already with him who have gone the same way before us. I commend you, my brother, to the faithful and covenant-keeping God. Let us join in prayer, one for the other!"

To a young lady dying of consumption, who, showing her emaciated arms, complained how long she had been wishing that God would take her home to himself, he said: "This is like one of my pupils, who lately was very eager to go home for the vacation, but could not till he had attended the last lecture. No doubt you think you have nothing more to do in this world; but you should believe, that even after we have packed up and made ready, God has still some exercises for us, to prepare us fully for eternity. He would have us wait, and bear a little longer, till it is his good pleasure to loose and let us go. Now, to abide in patience and comfort of this belief, is a sacrifice acceptable to God, and our reasonable service."

Bengel was with some christian friends at the death-bed of the Rev. Mr. Grammlich, chaplain to the Court, at whose request was sung the hymn which thus begins:—

"Rest, ye ashes of the dead,
In your quiet, lonely bed,
Till the last great day arrive,
When the Lord shall bid you live,
In beauty rise, and feel it given
Freely to breathe the air of heaven;" &c.

Bengel repeated over again to his dying friend every striking expression of the hymn, and then spoke of the glories of the city of God, which he said "must be most beautiful, as is evident from the words, 'God is not ashamed to be called *their* God, for he hath prepared for them a city.'" His friend was thus carried in his thoughts to such a view of the majestic holiness of God, as made him exceedingly to abase and loathe himself. He sobbed, turned away his face, and poured forth acknowledgments of his own wretchedness. Bengel replied, "It is true, we are only unprofitable servants, and it well becomes us to confess how guilty we are, and to implore God's free grace and pardon." This was immediately done by the dying man, with many strong emotions and tears. Bengel then proceeded: "When we faithfully acknowledge our guilt and misery, God deals bountifully with us, as the King of kings, and forgives our ten thousand talents at once." The afflicted person soon became more serene, and thus continued to the last. Bengel parted from his friend with affectionate mutual benedictions, and with mutual laying on of hands. The latter sweetly fell asleep in Jesus two days afterwards, and was buried by the side of Hedinger, who had been the means of awakening him to a sense of real Christianity. His interment there was appointed by the late excellent Mrs. Sturm; for Grammlich, she said, "had long consecrated that spot for his own resting-place, by the many prayers and tears he had there poured out at the grave of his friend Hedinger."

Respecting a person whose mind was in a state of much perturbation and debility, he said,—"I listen patiently to all that such persons have to communicate, as it may serve to suggest some salutary reply; besides, it helps to make one better acquainted with the wretchedness of human nature. But if any are so shut up by depression and melancholy that they cannot unburden their hearts to me, or even enter into conversation, then I pray with them, and get them to repeat after me. They are often much relieved in hearing their own utterance."

33. Those wretched contentions which sometimes happen between husband and wife, arise from irritable tempers, and sometimes from matrimonial unfaithfulness. In the former case, we must show what an advantage is given to Satan when Christians, forgetting their warfare against him and his cause, begin to turn it upon one another. As for matrimonial unfaithfulness, we must testify that it directly tends to extinguish all knowledge of God. Generally speaking, a pastor will do well to notice this abomination occasionally in his preaching, and pointedly to attack it, by dwelling upon it for some time; for a deep stain will not vanish at one superficial rubbing. In former days, men wrote more against special vices than they do at present. The notion now too much prevails, that if the general depravity of our nature be directly taught and learnt, particular sins will fall away of course. But surely we may sometimes eradicate the whole of a noxious shrub by pulling at one of its tough branches. Besides, there are persons with whom all else would be right if they did not but "lack one thing." Therefore be not weary, ye ministers

of souls, in rightly *dividing* and dispensing the word of truth. The atheism of the present day, which shows itself to be on the increase, not only in private profligacy, but in open and avowed repugnance to every serious thought and reflection concerning the living God, can only be properly encountered and overcome by unremittingly holding forth the word of life in all its bearings.

34. When we remind the rich of their duty, to excite in them mercy towards the poor, it were to be wished that we had opportunity at the same time of talking to the poor themselves about righteousness and fidelity; as the poor are so apt to throw all blame upon the rich, and the rich upon the poor. How much better would it be if both classes would seek God together, and the one mutually support the other by interchange of kind feeling and good actions. Whereas, now, many a rich person declines giving alms, because they are often squandered away at beggar's lodgings in "drunkenness, revellings, and such like."

35. A minister of souls should make his especial care those two classes of his flock which may be called the first and the last—I mean the children and the dying. The first, because in them he may look for the largest outpouring of blessing upon his labours; the last, because so little time remains for the fulfilment of his ministry to *them*.

36. Admission (to the Lord's supper) of such a mixed multitude as commonly attend it, has much perplexed many well-disposed ministers;* and certainly the devout sighs it occasions them are hastening on the help of the Lord (to the distracted church). If it be inquired, whether it would not be better that some ministers should even suffer themselves to be expelled from their office rather than be obliged to administer the sacred ordinance indiscriminately, whether their communicants "discern the Lord's body" or not, I would reply, that as to defend the truth didactically is one thing, but to set about doing thus in our usages is another, so the state of society will still bear in some measure the former of these, whereas the latter will be, as it *has* been, always liable to abuse. If a minister have scruples of conscience about unworthy communicants, let him speak with each of them privately; and having fully represented to them the responsibility they incur by partaking of such a holy ordinance, let him leave

* Bengel had, probably, here particularly in his eye two Würtemberg clergymen, Rueff of Dürrmenz and Seeger of Lomersheim, who, having left their scruples of conscience with the Consistory, stated that they were ready to admit all persons, and even profligates, if the Consistory chose thus to order it. But the latter declined the proposal.

it to them to act as they think proper. He can thus set his rail at the church porch rather than at the Lord's table. But at distribution of the elements let him proceed with serenity and cheerfulness; as if he would pour out at once the whole efficacy of the blood of Christ to his communicants; as if he would fain lift them once for all into the heavenly kingdom.

As coming to the Lord's supper proves in many cases a means of conversion, ministers should particularly observe to utter the words of Christ's institution with such emphasis as befits the state of each recipient. Not that I mean it is an article of doctrine that the Lord's supper is *an appointed means of conversion;* for this is not the special intention of the ordinance.

The form of declaring absolution, as used in the Church of Würtemberg, is beautifully impressive, and better than any other that I am acquainted with. That of Saxony, where the minister lays his hand upon each person separately, does not please me. If a minister have a person before him in really spiritual distress, it may be well and reasonable to lay both hands upon him, and even more; but to do this indiscriminately, is not only injurious with regard to the ungodly and profane, but even with regard to persons truly concerned about religion in all other respects, but not yet impressed about the use of that solemn rite. Indeed such an abuse of it tends to deprive it of all its force and significance. If there are none present who are capable of appreciating the blessing of God's own absolution, of what service is it for his most powerful witnesses to announce it? But where there are any in a state to receive such an announcement, there the word of God will have its good effect, even though it may be uttered by very unworthy ministers.

37. The primitive Christians had their "feasts of charity," which preceded every celebration of the Lord's supper; they also assembled together at other times for affectionate christian communion. These institutions have, in some places, been revived of late; and, though it has been done perhaps a little too boldly and prematurely, still such things in our days may be regarded as a preintimation in the ways of Providence of what will certainly become general in the latter-day glory of the christian dispensation.

And even *separatism* itself may be contemplated in the same cheering light. For there will be one day such an entire separation of the good from the bad, that not a particle of what is bad will be discoverable among the good. Those who are really drawn (unto Christ) by the Father, have a keen sensibility upon this matter; and here in the main they are right; though every one of them does not consider how much longer the mixture of good and bad has been seen and borne with by their heavenly Father than by themselves.

38. Some, when they have begun to lead a converted life, are ready to think that nothing which proceeds at all upon the old beaten track, nothing which belongs to the usual routine and order of things, can possibly be right for them. Hence they can think only upon changes and alterations in every thing. The good people at Berlenburg are of this morbid temperament, and look for a change in "the kingdoms of this world;" indeed, this is almost their idol in religion. Whoever comes to them with prophecies that the kingdoms of this world will soon be dashed in pieces, they quite hug him. *Seitz* is, therefore, every thing with them. He considers himself to be the angel sent to measure the Holy City, and whom the two witnesses are to second. Consequently, he styles himself Zerubbabel. But whoever expects himself to be made signal use of by the Almighty, must be humble.

Surely he is a foolish traveller, who, having a plain beaten track before him in the open country, prefers a slippery and dangerous one close by a ditch or river. Yet this is the way in which many of the reputedly pious lead their lives (and are thinking to get to heaven).

39. Those who think God is to be worshipped with only spiritual feelings, are certainly as mistaken as others who would satisfy themselves with external devotion. I freely admit the great importance of what is taught concerning those remarkable instances which have been appealed to as answers to inward prayer; and I equally admit the value of what is called the word within us; but great prudence is necessary for properly teaching and applying these things, as here there is a danger of tempting God, and of giving way to the deceivings of our own hearts. The passage in John vi. 45, "They shall be all taught of God," (compared with Heb. viii.) is not to be understood as meaning that there should be no need of receiving instruction by human instrumentality, for then even the apostolical epistles would not have been needed; but this promise simply points at the peculiar superiority of the New Testament dispensation as compared with that of the Old Testament. God saw it good to appoint for the Old Testament church a system of constraint and coercion; but

upon that of the New Testament he bestows a free spirit, which makes it much easier to understand divine things; and they who drink into the spirit of the new dispensation, and are guided by the written instructions of Christ and his apostles, find their way much plainer and smoother. They acquire at once a readiness and aptness for knowledge and practice, which, under the old dispensation, were to be attained only by long discipline of instruction communicated through prophets and teachers. The passage in 1 John ii. 27, refers to false doctrine, which true Christians had no need of being *taught* to discriminate (for they could discern it at once). The awakening, which is wrought by the power of the Divine word in individual persons, without the instrumentality of the regular ministry, is one thing; but whether without such instrumentality we are to expect a whole church to be planted, is another. Nevertheless, it is not in all cases indispensable that every minister should have been a student at the university. Ordained, however, they must be. For to be ever so true a believer in Christ, is insufficient of itself to confer a right to all the offices of the church of God. We are sure that what we thus speak is the declared will of our Lord himself, ana that his apostles so ordained in all the churches. Christ ordained his apostles, and these ordained others as elders or ministers. The church has power to choose her own ministers; but *ordination* to "this office and ministry" itself cannot come from *her* as a body—it must be derived through her ministers; hence Paul left Titus to ordain elders in every city. The laying-on of hands was intended rather for the imparting of spiritual gifts, than for simple ordination. Though the measure in which these gifts are now bestowed is much less comprehensive than it was in primitive times, still the imparting of them has not entirely ceased; consequently, the laying-on of hands continues allowable and proper. But the person who receives it must also be in a capacity to receive the gifts signified by it, otherwise this solemn rite is useless; and, where such capability exists, some good effect is wrought, even though the person performing the rite be a mere hireling. I have no objection to regarding this rite as sacramental in the general, (though not in the special, use of the term;) for it is an outward (and visible sign ordained by Christ himself, as a) means whereby God imparts his grace unto men (and a pledge to assure them of the same).

40. The *mystics* first appeared about the end of the fourth century, or the beginning of the fifth, in connexion more parti-

cularly with one who styled himself Dionysius Areopagita. When the philosophy of (Platonists and) Aristotelians, and the scholastic divinity which sprung out of it, began generally to overspread the church, a number of worthy persons, desiring to keep aloof from theological jargon, retired into *themselves*. Every mystic had a certain portion of light, and by this he determined to abide; but into the general economy of God, as dealing with men collectively, they collectively had no insight. Consequently they lived in *abstraction*, and took no part whatever in the public business of society. They lived in obscure times, and had enjoyment for themselves, but not for others. By and by, when the schoolmen made every thing to depend upon syllogistic speculations, the mystics themselves Platonized about every thing in an obscure and mute sentimentality. Still they could not have denied that whatever real good belonged to them was owing, under God, to their having enjoyed originally the nurture and admonition of their mother church. As for our refined mystics of the present day, where should we now have seen even one of them, if their ancestors under Charlemagne had not been brought to their Christianity by the power of the sword?

It is a question, whether Christ's name itself would continue to be remembered upon earth, had he not instituted the eucharistic commemoration of his death; though we may be unable to comprehend in what *degree* this ordinance can contribute to the "remembrance of" *Him*.

41. Our separatists consider themselves experienced Christians, and we must put up with it. There is, however, in the greater part of them, much high-mindedness, self-will, and pugnacity. Many of them remain quite men of the world; and if as a body they had some good thing among them at first, the good was intermixed with so much alloy, as gradually to have disappeared. No doubt there are among them righteous individuals known to God, but such are to be sought chiefly in the first generation of them; children and children's children commonly degenerate. God, however, makes use of separatism to accomplish his own good purposes; for instance, to serve as a standing protest against radical corruptions in our church, particularly against our "lewd ones of the baser sort." Still it is certain, that pious persons, both ministers and people, may serve God with a pure conscience in the very heart of our degenerate church; and, corrupt as its multitude is, I can find in it a larger number of such pious persons than are to be found among our separatists. The

latter ought to consider, that a conscientious minister, who can get through only half of his arduous work, is better than one who does nothing. They, however, will have every thing exactly to square with a certain pre-conceived rule and plan; and if this cannot be effected, they will fly off and leave all at a stand. A remark of Cicero is but too applicable to their conduct: "Nothing is more disagreeable than the censoriousness of idle lookers on; rather let *my* respect be reserved for those who have fallen in the engagement." (*"Nil minus fero quam severitatem otiosorum; plus vereor, qui in bello occiderunt."*)

But we may well bear with them, if we only consider that they want a correct insight into the general economy of the kingdom of God. It will soon be otherwise. In our conduct towards them, I think we should regard them as we do the non-franchised inhabitants of a city, who, as serving none of its offices, enjoy none of its corporate privileges. No compulsion or coercion ought to be used with them; we are neither to oppress, nor judge, nor abuse them; but to leave them freely to follow their own principles, as far as such principles are not contrary to the general laws of civil government. Even when they refuse to have their children baptized, we should leave this to their own responsibility; yet if we have opportunity, we should testify to them in love our own sentiments and views, with the reason why we believe and act in one way, and cannot believe and act in another. But we are not obliged to concede to them the accommodations specially appropriated to our own church-membership; for instance, the interment of their dead in our parish church-yards. Here we are necessitated to wear the appearance of some unneighbourliness. The church-yard is a fee belonging to the collective church members, as such; consequently a real separatist can have nothing to do with it. But if he regard the accommodation of burial as a mere piece of civil respect due to every body, we may lower his tone by asking him, Why he here faces about to look after the world's respect, for upon his own principles he has turned his back upon it. If he rejoin, that it is a common ecclesiastical right, then it cannot be his, for he has separated himself from the ecclesiastical commonwealth. Besides, as the whole earth is the Lord's, surely it does not essentially matter in what particular spot of this earth one is buried; only our separatists should never think of being buried side by side with so many ungodly persons, so many hypocrites, formalists, and the like.

42. But were I a minister of any parish where our separatists are found, I would endeavour to be made manifest in their consciences; I would live and teach so as to give to none any occasion of stumbling; I would warn my people not to use harsh language against them, not to judge them; I would point, not at their bad qualities, but at their good ones; I would encourage the practice of every kind of forbearance towards them as fellow-citizens and fellow-men; but familiar interchange with them upon spiritual matters I should discourage. Any kindnesses of a temporal nature I would be ever ready to show them, and would endeavour to raise up among my own people such characters as might convince them that upright and blameless persons can still be found in our church, and can conscientiously remain in it. In this way I think I should be taking the right method for inducing them to submit themselves, if not before, yet possibly after, some trials or temptations may have overtaken them.

43. It is very convenient that every country clergyman should add some valuable study to the faithful discharge of his ministerial duties, many and various as those duties are. I advise this, in order that he may not imperceptibly centre too much in himself; but that by learning how the kingdom of God, in manifold ways, is proceeding elsewhere, he may feel himself either stirred up and encouraged, or abased and ashamed, or instructed and directed, as his case may require.

44. Upon matters of business, wherein a clergyman may have to bear some official part, or to give advice with official persons, let a few prudential maxims be kept in mind: as, 1. Honesty is the best policy. How often have I noticed persons of much *finesse* and contrivance, awkwardly situated at a deliberation upon some matter of importance, through their not being then sufficiently confided in, when they really meant to give honest advice. 2. If we are engaged officially with persons in authority, suppose upon some case difficult to be decided, let us not wait till they are obliged to counsel *us*, but proffer, with all due modesty, one or more propositions of our own. Gentlemen with whom we may be thus engaged, are not always prepared upon every measure; and, therefore, will the more readily accede to a judicious proposition that may be made to them. The same observations apply to sitting in Consistory, or at the Sessions of the Provincial Estates. If our opinion, previously well digested, be given seasonably, it is easier to guard it by anticipating any

objections against it, or to defend it after they are made, than to have to start objections and maintain them, against an opinion given by another. 3. Though we may be aware that the measure we have to propose is one we shall not be able to carry, still we should take occasion to express our sentiments and reasons for it; discovering no displeasure at being obliged to yield a point upon which perhaps we may be better informed than are many of the persons about us; and quietly submitting to remain in the minority; especially if the debate is upon something non-essential. This is always one of the best means of gaining a respectful hearing and attention at the next meeting. And let us be thankful not to have too much business thus entrusted to us, when what we had in hand we could not accomplish to our mind. 4. Whatever looks superfluous or overdone, whatever to others may appear forced, with all our own approbation of it, we should learn to avoid. 5. Let us never even appear to favour a bad cause upon any account; rather let us endeavour to gain for honest men an opportunity of freely uttering what they may have to say; and never let such men feel any manner of restraint before us. Let us also particularly guard against being ourselves impatient of listening to what others have to say. By giving every one full time to speak, we shall be better able to discover who it is that may have any *unworthy* end to answer.

Section III.

PASTORAL LETTERS.

1. *On Blasphemous Thoughts.*

Having been consulted how to advise those who complain of unclean and blasphemous thoughts, supposed by them to arise from satanic influence, he replied as follows:—

" Satan may occasionally bear his part in such thoughts, but we must take heed of attributing them too hastily to *him*. There is enough in the human heart itself to suggest such filthiness, especially to persons of a lively imagination, although very few who are thus harassed will ever be communicative enough about it. With those who will open their minds to us, we should not directly attack the evil itself, but turn it to the occasion of learning their spiritual condition; so as to help them in a general way, through repentance and true conversion to God; aiming thus to dislodge, not merely a few ramifications, but the whole substance of the disease: as surgeons, to cure some particular part, endeavour to rectify the general system. Unless this be done, we may relieve the person, but not effectually. To insist, with such morbid minds, upon their bearing and improving their affliction into more humility and purification, is not a good method of treating them. They must be brought to feel the necessity of an entire change of mind; for one opposite serves to expel another, as darkness is only to be dispelled by light. Against the whole tide of blasphemous suggestions, we should wish to get raised, as soon as possible, the breath of praise to God. Let it whisper at least from human lips, if it may not yet sound with the voice of melody. Whenever any hideous idea enters the patient's mind, bid him to regard himself as merely passive under it. If he learn to do this, and indeed he may become expert at it with the quickness of thought itself, then all discord within him will by and by be attuned to this string, and will be as if he only heard the hated and abhorred blasphemies of another, and they will not be finally reckoned to him as his own. It is good for him, however, to be always communicative about such things, and to manifest that the trouble he feels is not for himself only, but for others who have so much to endure in sympathising with and consoling him. Openness of this sort is the way to get more than a common share of sympathy from those who have to drag on with us, and it induces them to make much more considerate allowance for us."

2. How may Christians, who have "left their first love," be enabled to recover it?

Bengel replied:—

"*May* 3, 1748.

"Our Lord Jesus himself shows how to recover our first love, in the fifth verse of the second chapter of the Apocalypse. Here three things are enjoined as requisite for the purpose: 1. *Remembrance* (of our former condition); 2. *Repentance;* and 3. *Doing our first works.* The first dawn of divine grace upon the soul is sufficient to light us along to the end of this life; but we are not to expect that it will always affect us with the same delight in God, as it did at our earliest experience of it. It is in His account as valuable as ever, and it is as excellent as ever for our own use. Therefore, we must not stand still and complain of not receiving a uniformly delightful increase of it; but must patiently proceed with the measure of it we possess, and leave it to the good pleasure of God to shine upon our path in his own good time."

3. *To a Person suffering by Hypochondriasis.*

"Your malady may be traced chiefly to bodily temperament, but it has increased for want of spiritual advice at the time when God first sent it upon you for your soul's health, and by your having thus cumbered and troubled yourself about many a thing foreign to the purpose. Whereas your imagination and feelings, having become more tender and susceptible through weak health, ought to have been occupied with the image of Christ; for want of this, you have pored upon your own infirmities, instead of meditating upon that tender and infinite love which our heavenly Father manifests to us in Christ Jesus. And now no good is to be done by all these convictions of bitter things against yourself, much less by any mental worry and perplexity. The only thing required is to look away from self altogether, and to think upon and trust in nothing but the love of God, in his tender mercies over all, in his promises, in his benevolent government, in his saving grace, which hath appeared unto all men, in the full atonement or reconciliation made by our blessed Saviour; who received sinners and ate with them, &c. while he walked upon this earth; to learn, I say, to trust and glory in such things, and patiently to wait for and expect their personal application to yourself; meanwhile remembering that your single soul cannot be a burden too heavy for the mighty God and gracious Saviour, who has been ever meekly bearing with so many before you. Should your endeavouring thus to go from self to Christ speed less easily and fully than it might do, still be patient, for God himself is patient with *us*, which is the very reason why our case is not desperate, and why we may even yet obtain much useful instruction and benefit from past endeavours, which we are apt to think have been fruitless.

"It is only with grace that the heart can be established, so as to have the discordant multitude of our clamorous thoughts silenced. A life of communion with God carries along with it the best antidote against all gloomy suggestions. We must regard His mere mercy as our only refuge, and constantly make use of it. A single ray of this influence of grace will cheer at once all sad and anxious recollections, however many they may be; the Lord is faithful, he is greater than our heart."

4. *On Conversion.*

"*Nov.* 18, 1742.

"And now with the good hand of God upon me, I will endeavour to answer your inquiries. They are,

"1. What is conversion, and what properly belongs to it? It is the turning and submission of a soul, hitherto sunk in self-ignorance, self-love, and idolatry to the creature, consequently hitherto alienated from God; it is the returning and submission of such a soul to Him, and to his good and holy will, for the sake of His honour and glory, and for the sake of its own health and salvation.

"2. Whether conversion and awakening be the same? Conversion is more than awakening, as the fruit is more than the blossom; for God may awaken a man, and he may forthwith sink down again into the slumber of sin and death, so that though awakened thus again and again, he is still unconverted. But when he follows up the awakening, then he is converted.

"3. Whether personal conversion is not to be understood somewhat differently now, from what it was among the primitive Christians; our circumstances under the Divine economy having become different from theirs? I answer, that "the mark," the object, the end of conversion, must ever be the same; though the point where conversion begins, or from which it sets out, must vary with different classes of men, as idolaters, Jews, nominal Christians, &c.

"4. When persons profess to be converted, how are they to be proved,—that we may distinguish real faith from a thousand other things which are either flattering and imposing, or perplexing and revolting? For instance, how shall we be able to distinguish bad spiritual symptoms from failings which are known sometimes to be owing to bodily disorder, bad training in childhood, natural temperament, education, &c.?

"Prevalent evil symptoms of a purely spiritual nature are easy to be perceived, and as it were felt with the hand; for here persons go on boldly in sin, without any fear of God before their eyes; but a state of grace is not so easily discernible in those who have naturally a tender feeling about good and evil, nor in those who have a natural equanimity in sudden emergencies and in the presence of overbearing persons, when others would not be able to maintain their composure. Neither are persons who are converted always qualified to prove others; and it is very dangerous to imagine ourselves so qualified. It is far more safe to come to no opinion about the condition of many, than to deceive ourselves or be deceived by others in a single instance. For between the two classes in whom either a state of sin or a state of grace is clearly discernible, there are very ambiguous characters, whom we must leave entirely to the decision of God; many in whom what is good and what is bad are strangely intermixed or alternated; many who are really better or really worse than we should imagine from their exterior conduct. It is true, that we can speak abstractedly as to what is compatible with real faith, and what is not; but to pronounce upon the person of an individual is a very different matter. We should always be much more severe in examining ourselves, than in judging of others, &c.

"5. May a fixed time ever be referred to as the commencement of true conversion? Yes; when a state of open sin has been exchanged for decided obedience to the grace of Christ, the very day of such a change, or even the hour, or perhaps moment, may be referred to. But when the transition has proceeded by slow degrees, and many false steps and backslidings have intervened, a person finds it very difficult with respect to himself, and still more difficult with respect to others, to point out the time when evil or good gained the ascendant. The surest reference is, to be always taking care to have scriptural comfort in God with respect to what we are at the present moment, and to commit all the past to Him who knoweth all things. Who can ever settle the question of conversion without this; or even have his mind properly settled at all?

"6. How may we most scripturally express ourselves upon our own state of grace? All that we can possibly utter upon this subject is contained in one sentence of St. Paul: 'Nevertheless, I obtained mercy:' or, 'The Lord hath called me out of darkness into his marvellous light:' or, 'Though such and such was I; yet I am washed, I am sanctified, I am justified, in the name of the Lord Jesus, and by the Spirit of our God.'

"Let any one but 'come to the light,' and his general character will always show itself: whereas, by making too nice distinctions about what are called degrees of grace, we are only encouraging hypocritical people to ape and cant. Besides, as there are many, on the one hand, who have a sort of emulative or imitative religious zeal which 'cometh of evil,' (κακοζηλία;) so, on the other hand, there are many really upright but diffident persons, who continue in hurtful suspense about their state of grace, because they cannot see in themselves just the very marks of it which others can *talk* of. But though a genuine singing bird, in its unfledged nonage, may be easily mistaken for another that will never be vocal, yet its growth gradually betrays its nature, and by and by it sings from instinct. Here then I take my stand. Every one is at liberty to speak with all the edification he can give to himself or to others respecting the condition of his soul: but we are not to overrate disclosures of this sort. Better is it to look after the *fruit*, at seasons when the tree may be expected to show its nature."

5. *To a young Clergyman who had requested his Advice and Consolation upon some distressing Points of Conscience.*

> " Only his kind paternal heart
> Can yield us balm for every smart."

" My very dear Sir,

" As I am one who can believe you and feel for you, so I certainly desire to set your mind at rest. Old things that adhered to you are passed away: let then a thoroughly renewed state of mind shine forth in all your life and conversation. Do but commit your concerns entirely to God, and who knows that he will not make your good example shine in the very places where formerly you gave occasion, as you fear, for offence and scandal? Any express acknowledgment to the parties concerned, of every little offensive circumstance, would in your case answer no good purpose, and might give pain to others: whereas, compensation for a single thing of any value that you may have appropriated, and that honest acknowledgment and deprecation upon which forgiveness ensues, may be of real and blessed service to others as well as to yourself. You go so far as even to think of making amends for fruit purloined by you in boyhood from your schoolfellows, and in youth from your fellow-students at the Theological Institution; but in my opinion every thing of this sort is absorbed in the universal law of love. For suppose any one in youthful levity had purloined the like from yourself, would you ever think of requiring or accepting compensation? And may we not fairly expect the same good feeling from those to whom you were a young defaulter, whether they are persons who fear and love God or not? Rather give alms of what you possess, two, three, or four times the value of the little matters purloined, and supposing the persons who once missed these should have vented displeasure and bad wishes against the unknown delinquent, pray to God to bless such persons with yourself. If any sincere friend of your youth continue offended with you, take some opportunity of delivering before him such an awakening testimony, as, being the very opposite of former conversations between you, may serve to revive in him religion and friendship at once: or by sending him your best wishes through some mutual acquaintance, give him occasion for such good reflections as may issue in true kindness to yourself. Where personal intercourse can be had, I should prefer it to all explanations in writing; but we must remember, there are different ways even of making use of that. So much for the present in reply to your valued letter, which I now return you immediately upon having thus quite done with it, that you may be the more certain you wrote it to a faithful friend. If you feel a wish to consult me further about this or any thing else, with a view to composing and settling your own mind, I beg you will be perfectly free with me.

"I think it necessary to distinguish between different perplexities of this nature, in order to get rid of some of them by self-denying submission to the discipline of Providence; and to be free from others, by cheerfully and actively discharging the duties of life. 'The peace of God rule in your heart!'"

6. *Being consulted by a Clergyman how to advise a Person under great Trouble of Mind, on account of some very scandalous Sins, not publicly known, he replied:—*

"I need more knowledge of this person's particular circumstances to give you a full and satisfactory reply; but whatever they are, the immediate question is, how to advise one who appears unsettled rather by a single clamour of conscience, than by any general and true repentance.

"First, then, direct the person to look to the supreme God alone, and to make up matters with him in serious and real conversion; crying to him under the sense of his 'heavy hand,' 'O Lord, forgive the iniquity of my sin!' throwing together as in a mass the whole tissue of past sin, original and actual, and supplicating unceasingly for total remission through the atoning death of Jesus Christ. The sins of a whole life, thus confessed and sincerely forsaken, need not keep such a person away from the Lord's table.

"Having thus gone to the root of the matter, your parishioner will come to know more decidedly how to act in respect of the outward man, which is henceforth to be brought into entire submission to the righteousness of God; and will see, without any self-accusation before the civil authorities, whether it be His will that such authorities should have any thing to do with the matter; or whether it shall please Him still to send only private chastenings of his own immediate infliction, as He has done hitherto. As no temporal punishment, especially from magistrates, can make atonement for sins to God, so the soul may be saved without any such civil punishment.

"If your inquirer say nothing more about self-deliverance to public justice, you will do well not to recall any such thought; but if such a thought be persisted in, circumstances must determine what advice is to be given. Whatever may be pleaded in extenuation of offences like these before a human tribunal, the person must however take care not to plead any thing of the kind before God. If your diocesan be a man acquainted with the gentleness of Christ, (see John viii. 6—11,) perhaps you might further ask his counsel in the business; but do it personally, rather than by letter."

7. *Another friend of Bengel, having been consulted by a person under great remorse of conscience, previously asked advice of Bengel, who thus replied :—*

"*March* 23, 1736.

"Most sincerely would I return you such an answer as shall accord with the holy will of God, and serve to tranquillize in the best manner, that is, thoroughly to recover, the person in question. The Mystery of the Annunciation, which is this day commemorated, shows what a glorious state is, by the incarnation of God, recoverable to fallen man, who was originally created in the Divine image. What you have communicated to me, is indeed the reverse of all this, to a most revolting degree. The person whom it concerns has truly cause for the deepest self-humiliation before God, for turning the alarm of conscience, about one sinful disposition and act, into a thorough recollection and consideration of all that the conscience has never yet been awakened to feel; in a word, for impartial self-examination, and due consideration of the whole state of the heart and life. For this purpose I should recommend diligent attention to the word of God, with laying to heart how holily and awfully he speaks of such and such besetting sins; with serious and repeated meditation upon suitable passages of Scripture, and with humble supplication and prayer. The fifty-first Psalm may serve as an appropriate model for such prayer; together with those well-known Church hymns, 'Jesus, thou strength of contrite hearts,' &c., and, 'My God, this heart I bring to thee,' &c. The person should likewise be fully persuaded, upon scriptural grounds, that no repented sin is too great to be blotted out of the book of God; and that any who truly apply to our Saviour Christ, the physician of souls, may still, as multitudes have done already, 'wash their robes, and make them white in the blood of the Lamb.' Consequently, asking, seeking, knocking, supplicating, waiting, are the only means for gaining effectual relief, not merely from the guilt of one alarming, overbearing, depressing sin, but from the whole body of sin, with all its roots, branches, and bitter productions.

"I would not have this person to communicate the subject in hand to any one else, except perhaps to an enlightened, pious, and confidential minister; and this only if it be necessary for obtaining repose of mind and peace of conscience. But I would have such person to feel it a bounden duty of love, to warn any that may appear endangered by similar temptations. Moreover, the being not put to shame before the world, should form an additional inducement for simple and humble resignation to the chastenings of God, in whatever way he may be pleased to inflict them; whether as personal, by his own immediate hand, or by any of the circumstances of his providence around us. Through this self-resignation to the Divine will, combined with entire self-renunciation, God will have the glory of his supreme holiness, wisdom, and goodness; and the desired peace of mind will be experienced. May He manifest throughout to this chastened sufferer his own mercy and truth! But O, what a turbid fountain is the human heart, even in those who are awakened to a sense of sin, and of their need of the gift of righteousness! In our common intercourse, which is sometimes edifying, and sometimes only appears so, we are all, alas, too little disposed to notice how much in us still remains to be overcome; and in this respect we think far too favourably of one another. One person also is too easy and superficial about himself; another in the same respect is too precise: whereas we ought to deal with our inward man as servants do with a long-neglected room, which they are bidden to render habitable and comfortable. They set about carefully sweeping and cleaning it; but they do not go to the heap of dust and rubbish which they have thrown out of it, in order to pick and gather up what is *less like* mere filth and rubbish. The whole having been thrown away and done with, that is enough. Now God intends his word to be a panacea. If we sincerely seek him, he is found of us; and then, whatever in us is sad, gloomy, dark, worthless, deadly, or infernal, will die away and disappear, provided we are instant in prayer and humble waiting upon him. For he is both Light and Love; and by presenting ourselves before him, we become sensible of the coldness and darkness of our nature, and then of his bringing us out of this state, by his only-begotten Son, into union with himself: and the disquieted person you speak of will experience all this, by only being in earnest about it. Should that troubled spirit perceive any thing like returning joy or serenity, let this cheering visitation of God preserve it; that is, let the person well observe and bear such a visitation in mind, in case of another plunge into the depths of trouble and trial; regarding what God has already done as a pledge of that peace which shall by and by gain the entire ascendant. Thus will all shocking or appalling imaginations disappear, without need of any personal struggle against them, and the yoke of sin will of itself gradually dissolve and melt away (because of the anointing).* But O for true humility through the remainder of the pilgrimage! and it will be well not too soon to lay aside even trembling before the face of the Lord. Surely the remembrance of guilt remitted, while it ought to be a stimulus to holy exertion, should continually admonish us not to be high-minded, but to fear; and thus to pass the time of our sojourning in this world; (forasmuch as we are redeemed not with corruptible things, &c., but with the *precious* blood of Christ, &c.)"

8. *To the Count M. of Saxony.*

This nobleman desired to have the sentiments of some Protestant divine upon the following thesis:

" To a rational and truly christian man, perfection and felicity are brought about by frequent adversities and cross incidents, sooner than by a long succession of pleasant and prosperous events."

" This was to be proved by reason and by revelation, after giving correct definitions of—

* This seems to allude to the 27th verse of the xth chapter of Isaiah, in the Hebrew.—Tr.

"1. A rational man;
"2. A truly christian man;
"3. Perfection; and
"4. Real felicity."

Bengel answered:

"He who all his life possesses the written word of God, and judges of every thing by the use of his rational faculties (being, as he is, a man and not a horse), will hereby learn, not only what can be learnt by mere reason itself, but something, or rather much, beyond; and this in a noble, vigorous, and divinely-favoured manner, without any self-complacent thought respecting his own natural powers. For (as man fell by unbelief, so) God brings us back to himself, not by absolute knowledge, but by faith. Our unassisted reasoning faculties still retain some traces of the great Master-builder's original work; but those three great articles, creation, redemption, and sanctification, which are taught in Scripture, are so connected together, that without the light of revelation we must have remained unacquainted with our origin, our end, and the means of attaining that end, whatever natural wisdom we might have imagined ourselves competent to. Consequently, it is accordingly as we learn, or do not learn, from the written word of revelation, that we learn, or never can learn—1. who is really a rational man; 2. who is a true Christian; 3. what is perfection; and, 4. what is real felicity. None but a true Christian is really a rational man; and such a man seeks perfection, not *in himself*—for this would not only be *un*reasonable, but perverse and hurtful—but he seeks it IN CHRIST; in whom also he obtains real felicity, by the way of self-denial, and by the way of tribulations and temptations, which are auxiliary to self-denial; and because he can attain such real felicity only through a course of trial and probation, he does not attain it in its perfection till he is arrived in the other world. To such a man the proposition at the head of these remarks is so clear and evident, that he wants no proof of it, but only a more accurate and convenient way of expressing it. He is satisfied with that cumulative Scripture testimony which is pointed out to him by the index to many a Bible, and in many a compendium of divinity, in a section entitled 'The Cross;' and of such cumulative Scripture testimony he knows by experience the value. By the force of such testimony apostates are reproved, and sent* empty away, on

* Ps. lxviii. 6.—TR.

account of their preference for temporal enjoyments, through indulging in which they had already become quite satiated to weariness; or else afflictions prove the means of disengaging them from their undue attachment to things temporal, and of exchanging their excessive self-love for the love of God. The same manifold testimony of his word serves also to purify the saints, while it exercises and preserves them."—Consider Psalms xxxvii. xlix. and lxxiii. Hosea ii. 6, 7; v. 15; vi. 1. Luke xvi. 25. Acts xiv. 22. Rom. viii. 17, &c. 2 Cor. i. 9; iv. 7, &c. 2 Tim. iii. 12. Heb. xii. 1—11, &c. &c.

9. *On the early death of one who had been an honoured instrument in promoting the kingdom of God.*

A friend having in a letter complained rather too strongly of the premature death of such a person, Bengel replied:

"When God thus hastens the departure of useful persons, we may well think it is meant often as a rebuke and chastening to those who have not duly appreciated the favour of his having sent such faithful labourers among them. At the same time, it is frequently in goodness and mercy to the deceased themselves; for they are taken away from present evil, and from the evil to come. And then we should consider, that all the successive generations of God's children amount to one general agency in his cause; so that as one generation passes away, another is found to have taken its place, to carry on the work of God. Thus there is a never-ceasing growth proceeding in the field of the church of God, and he is always repairing its seeming losses; whereas the persons whom he will have to be thus disposed of, are meanwhile gathered in and saved. Whenever, therefore, any of Wisdom's more valuable children are taken away, this is no real harm or loss to the church universal; for such persons having answered the purpose of God thus far, by having finished the work assigned them, others come forward and tread in their steps. Moreover, people often are not sensible what a treasure their worthy teacher was, till he is gone, and an unworthy one succeeds him. They then begin to amend of their own accord, and to edify one another; which they had neglected to do while they had God's faithful commissioner among them, and were haggling with him."

10. *Storr to Bengel.*

John Christian Storr, when chaplain to the Court of Stuttgart, wrote to Bengel (*Sept.* 5, 1748), as follows:

"As your Christian love constrained you to take a kind and paternal interest in the trials I had to encounter at the close of last winter, in consequence of a sermon I preached at the carnival—when your judicious christian advice, I can assure you, supported and encouraged me not a little—gratitude bids me submit to your inspection the manuscript of that sermon, which I send you just as it was written. I got it back only a few days ago, and will now give you a further account of the result, which indeed is more like a new trial to me than a termination of the old one. Consequently I have again to beg the help of your advice and prayers.

"On the 30th of last month, as it was the birthday of the prince's intended bride, and I had to be at court, lord privy councillor Bilfinger took this opportunity of bidding me to call on him, and said he would then return me the manuscript of my sermon. I called upon him the next day: he was very affable, and began by saying, he had so long deferred this private conversation with me because he wished to spare my feelings. He proceeded to state his reasons why he thought I ought to alter my manner of preaching before the court; and said, that I must at least desist from using in it such expressions as *carnival, pleasure-house, masquerade*, &c. His principal reasons were—1. that though he was willing to call the carnival, and every thing of the sort, a frivolity, yet it was not sinful; it was only a kind of court-assembly, convened in compliment to the duke, consisting of persons belonging to the court, and of reputable inhabitants of the city. It was an occasion, certainly, of temptation to improprieties; and improprieties sometimes took place at it, but not so many as were imagined and talked of; so that, by denouncing *the carnival* in my sermons, I, in fact, made a direct attack upon the duke, and this in public, which surely was very unjustifiable. It was likewise an attack upon others as well as upon his highness; for however guiltlessly, or from necessity, any one might attend upon the occasion, I denounced every such person before the whole church, representing them in a more unfavourable light than they deserved; and thus gave gratuitous offence, defeating my own object, which was professedly the promotion of love and good will; for it was altogether contrary to charity to preach in that manner. Whereas, if I took no notice of the carnival by name, but simply rebuked improprieties which happen at it, I had acquitted my own conscience, and none could have any cause of offence.—2. That it was an incontrovertible rule of prudence, which divines themselves were bound to observe, to prefer a greater good before a less; and such a rule obliged us not to hazard the general cause of God for the purpose of gaining a point of less importance.

"To these objections I replied, that the things in question are certainly offences, which it is one test of our confession of Christ to reprove; and that what may seem to us a very small matter, may in his sight be a very great one. That the christian standard is not moral expediency, but the Cross; and that this alone can determine what is permissible and right. That even what is called *a trifling* word, is often of importance to faithfully confessing Christ; and therefore to make a man thus an offender for a word, is an infringement upon christian liberty.

"To this my lord director rejoined, that 'moral propriety, and not the cross, ought to be the standard for things of this sort; that the cross of Christ is the standard only for a high degree of self-denial: therefore I ought not to sit in judgment upon others, and condemn them for being below the standard of my own feelings; much less ought I categorically to declare that they are *sinning against God;* but only to endeavour to affect, allure, and induce them to go on voluntarily to higher degrees of advancement. That even in *confessing Christ* (as I called it) obvious rules of prudence like these ought to be observed; and their having been disregarded by any former divine was no precedent for *me*, as it only showed that others, as well as myself, had exceeded their commission. That it was merely my own *private* liberty which would be thus restricted, and no possible injury done to *christian* liberty.' He added, that the duke had even commanded my immediate dismissal from the service of the court; but that he had interceded with his highness, that he might be allowed some previous conversation with me; for that between ourselves he apprehended very serious consequences to the Protestant liberties of the country from indolently conceding such an important step to the duke; and that I ought to consider the dilemma to which, with the best intentions, I was reducing, not only the Consistory, but even the Privy Council, if I gave them occasion to forbid from the court, and perhaps entirely to silence, a clergyman of their own communion, at the command of a catholic prince. That this might be paving the way for his highness's general interference with our church affairs; so as, for instance, to prohibit the whole body of our clergy from uttering any censure whatever against sinful sports and pastimes; not to mention many other disastrous consequences, of the same sort, to which my conduct might furnish the first occasion. What, then, was the clear line of duty in such a case? Let us be thankful (he said) that it is only two or three verbal expressions that are disapproved of, and therefore relinquish them at once. But should I persist in using them at the next carnival, I must prepare for the worst. He concluded by saying, that as I was now informed that my method did no good, I ought to try another.

"I replied, that servants are not to be concerned about the consequences of doing the express will of their supreme Lord. That to do His will had been my single motive in the business; but that my wish not to endanger the public good, is quite as sincere as my willingness to endure any hardship touching my own private interest. Painful therefore as it would be to me to bring my superiors into any dilemma upon *my* account, still that I could not promise to make considerations of this sort the rule of my conduct. Would it not then, I asked, be more advisable for them to remove me immediately by their own act to another station, than await the possibility of any such further command from his highness? That in this way my own conscience would be at rest, nor would any of the above dreaded consequences be brought about through scruples of mine, such as I could not but feel had become too great for my present official situation.

"To this he merely answered, that no one desired to burden my conscience in any respect; that they would rather I should of my own choice remove to any place I pleased, than that religious benefit to the court congregation should continue to be impeded.

"Such is about the substance of a conversation which lasted two hours.—And now, O my God, what shall I do? It is thy cause, and thy ministry, O Lord! Help thou me!—And what is your own opinion, my worthy and beloved friend? Such things as you here see alleged against me have at least this good effect, that they stimulate me to pray that I may possess more light, mercy, and sympathy in behalf of my congregation, and especially in the business of preaching, and delivering my testimony. But I cannot bring my mind to make any such promise as that proposed to me. I seem to be in the condition of a confessor, with respect to this place and the country at large. Many through my testimony have already been deterred from attending the carnival, and many have even scrupled to prepare carnival dresses for others. What an occasion of stumbling shall I then throw in their way, if I consent never to use again the above censured expressions! But if I do use them again, and proceed as I have done, I am to be accounted a mere obstinate fellow, and even the originator of bad consequences to the public welfare. It is true that it will be nearly four months before another carnival; but at the previous bringing home of the bride princess, I expect that the same obnoxious causes for animadversion will come in my way.

"Now as I have already humbly petitioned the court to change my station, I can certainly allege this on the next occasion in my own defence; but that does not fully satisfy me. I should be sorry to leave my present situation before it is the Lord's will that I should do so; and you can believe me when I say that I prefer being found faithful to the last, whatever I may have to suffer; but whenever the Lord himself shall intimate to me, 'Arise, and flee to such a place,' I wish to obey. Meanwhile I can only supplicate,

> 'Counsel me after thine own heart,
> O Jesus, Son of God.'

It will be a great relief to me to know your own sentiments upon the matter. May God put it in your heart to show me what is the good pleasure of his will!"

Bengel's Reply.

"*Sept.* 9, 1748.

"My much esteemed and very dear Friend, in the grace of Christ,

"Between what *has* happened and what *may* happen, you have at least some breathing-time for consideration. Therefore let me advise, that during this interval you cast yourself and every thought about futurity into the bosom of HIS holy and blessed will, who so often delivered David in the field of danger from the hand of Saul and Achish, and what is more, from the temptations of sin. Even by your own shewing, I see that all has gone on very well hitherto: and should another onset come before you expect it, my opinion is, that you should stand to your former declaration, that God's will concerns you above every thing else; —that, as it is farthest from your wish to make any public mischief, or give any embarrassment to your superiors, you mean to weigh and consider with the utmost care whatever you may have to say in your addresses; but that should your spirit be affected by the power of the Divine Word at witnessing any thing in fearful opposition to the latter, so that the unpleasant emotion should unavoidably influence the language of your sermon, you cannot bind yourself by any promise now required of you to acknowledge such a thing to be either indecorous or inappropriate. So much may suffice for your answer to *others*. But now if you weigh the whole matter with yourself apart, I think you will find that you may, with a safe conscience, and entirely of your own mind, desist from using the expressions that have given offence, were it for no other reason than that in *having* used them you have already testified *what* it is you have to object against, and thus far satisfied your purpose. God's honour of course forbids us to suffer our mouths to be stopped; but if the world be determined not to accept our reproof, be it so. We may, and must, give them their way at their own hazard; only let them understand *why* we do it. Meanwhile, let us address home the more special message of the Word to those who are not living in open sin, who show hopeful signs of amendment, or love the salvation of God in Christ Jesus. Besides, our expressive silence at the world's obstinacy is sometimes more forcible than our persisting to rebuke, provided our consciences tell us, (as theirs must tell *them*,) that our silence is not owing to the fear of man; and whenever we do warn them, we may deliver our testimony in such an appropriate manner, that none who are not wilfully obdurate can well avoid applying it to themselves. I have read your sermon, but it gives me nothing further to remark. The approaching bridal festivities for the new princess will, I hope, notwithstanding your own fears, be different from a carnival, as they will not bring together the very lowest of the people.

"As I stand aloof from the contest, I am likely to view the more impartially these vain amusements. Now I regard them as, in a manner, less sinful in worldly people than in real Christians. There are many vanities, which, though inconsistent of course with the mind of Christ, yet, as *directly* opposing no specific precept of his word, stir no particular uneasiness in people's consciences, and may by and by drop away of themselves. So that a christian minister is not here bound to try the partialities of others by his own taste and feelings; still he should go on testifying to the world that 'the works thereof are evil.'"

11. *To a person discouraged by spiritual difficulties.*

"*January* 17, 1751.

"I sincerely feel for you under your present discouragement, but am not at all surprised that you as yet realize so little of the peace of God; your uneasiness being but the natural effect of your seriously considering the life you have led hitherto. The causes of this distress, though you have enumerated such a variety of them, all amount to one and the same; and you only perplex yourself the more by pondering them separately. Our own hearts are deceitful enough to suggest that the door of mercy is closed against us; and they do this, just because they are so indolent and backward *to knock* (at that door) and to lay hold (of mercy). As your own heart, therefore, is your worst enemy, complain of that also to the Lord Jesus; show him *all* your trouble; ask not only his forgiveness, but boldness and access through him to the grace of God. Whenever any disquiet crosses you, from within or from without, stay not to parley with it; but take a passage of Scripture or a psalm or hymn for your meditation; for instance, Micah vii. 9; Jer. xv. 16; xvii. 5; and pray fervently over such passages. Only turn a deaf ear to every suggestion of despondency, and you will find peace. Seek the light of God's countenance, and your darkness will be made light before you: thus also will you be more pleased with others, and others will be more pleased with you. Whatever doubts may distress you, disclose them to your worthy minister, and take his advice. May Divine mercy keep and direct you!"

12. *To a Clergyman under severe mental trial.*

"*February* 20, 1729.

"The account you have confided to me of your sufferings of conscience, excites in me much interest and sympathy; and most sincerely do I wish I may be enabled to say something to your comfort.

"A person who has sinned with greediness may easily entail a burden upon his spirit, which may not be removed till after a long time of poignant suffering. When the citadel of the heart has been allowedly thrown open to Satan, that subtle and malignant foe spares no pains to keep full possession; and if he is unsuccessful in this, he will endeavour to harass, by all possible means, the delivered possessor. And here you yourself have reason to say, 'Righteous art Thou, O Lord!' Let me, however, entreat you to seek no peace for yourself, short of that which certainly comes from God, and leads to him. Though you may think it impossible to pray, yet pray. Though you may think it impossible to endure, yet endure. Though you may think it impossible to abide unto the end, yet abide unto the end. Though you feel that the grace of God is not in our power, yet for this very reason surrender yourself entirely to his power and grace; till a look from the countenance of Christ himself shall beam upon you. (Micah vii. 7.) And in the mean time be guarded at all points against every false consolation which the world may hold out to you; for hereby the soul's sufferings become only stirred up the more. Will bad thoughts arise within you involuntarily? turn them out at once, by complaining of them to Him who knows them all. Keep always in your recollection what the Scripture says about giving glory to God. Be much in scriptural meditation, prayer, and praise. Prescribe not to the Lord of all, either the time or manner of your deliverance from bondage: if you can get no hope immediately, learn to hope at a distance, or by a side glance. Do you think, if you have been such a sinner as you speak of, you are in a condition at once to *bear* the pure and joyful light of God? Bless him rather that he makes you feel obliged to take refuge in himself, like a person running away from fire and sword. For even this severe dealing with you is but kindness in the end: it is a token that he is 'not willing' that you should 'be condemned with the world.' The very thing we had foolishly undervalued when it was within our reach, we are often obliged to get circuitously afterwards; and this that we may be recovered and saved. (Luke xv.) Only never look away from the Saviour; but let your 'eyes be continually looking unto him,' though you may not have heart enough to come immediately to his feet, and, as it were, to meet his eye 'with open face:' thus doubt not but you will be received into God's gracious favour. As far as my poor prayers and intercessions can be of use to you, you have them. Farewell."

CHAPTER III.

HIS ENGAGEMENTS AS A PRELATE, A COUNCILLOR OF CONSISTORY, AND MEMBER OF THE PROVINCIAL ESTATES.

His latter years remarkably verified the common observation, that whereas worldly honour (like one's own shadow) flies from us if we pursue it, it pursues us if we run away from it. He was " never minded to make for himself days and hours of convenience and pleasure, to lay up many good things of a temporal kind, or to get into high places of honour." His " diligence was rather directed faithfully to do whatever his hand found to do, whether it were a great matter or a small, according to the ability God had given him. He was inclined to compare his condition rather with that of persons in humbler station, than with that of persons above him; and thus found contentment no difficult virtue. He committed his ways to the Lord; and, with singleness of heart, he pressed toward the mark for the prize of the high calling of God in Christ Jesus, to whose disposal he resigned every care about a rough course of life or a smooth one."

But notwithstanding this resigned state of spirit, he was gradually promoted to the highest ecclesiastical functions and dignities of his country. Upon resigning the tutorship of the Theological Institution in 1741, he was appointed to the prelacy of Herbrechtingen, and to the station of Aulic Councillor. In 1747 he was chosen a member of the *General* States Assembly; in 1748 he was advanced to a seat in the *Special* Assembly; in 1749 he was made Councillor of Consistory, and Prelate of Alpirsbach, and created Doctor of Theology in 1751. It will be interesting and instructive to trace him from one honourable station to another, and to notice his conduct in each.

He used to say, " We may learn from the example of Isaiah (vi. 8) how to conduct ourselves on receiving any important call. When the prophet heard the voice of Jehovah, saying, ' Whom shall I send, and who will go for us?' (who will be my messenger?) he was ready at once to consent, saying, ' Here am I;'

but he did not omit to add, '*Send* me!' that he might not go without the Divine will. A 'ready mind' is much more pleasing to God than that of one who must be constrained into his service; as was Moses, to become the shepherd of the children of Israel. Therefore we *may* and *ought* to offer ourselves to God for any commission wherewith he may be pleased to entrust us: only we must wait until he *send* us, and wait to know what our place or appointment is; at the same time remembering, that as we are but human instruments at best, there is a possibility of running before he sends us, or when he does not want us. As we can be nothing *more* than his instruments, the less we mingle with his work what is merely *ours*—in other words, the more immediately we depend for our sufficiency upon God himself—the more direct is our progress to its complete fulfilment. A person of good talents may certainly, by diligence, enterprise, and favourable circumstances, bring to pass what he has determined on merely of himself; but just because he did not properly regard the will of God in the matter, does he find no blessing attending it. Nay, if he be even a converted person, consequently under the general influence of good principles, and really designing to work for the kingdom of God, still, if in any specialty he act merely by a will of his own, if he vainly imagine it is himself that must support the ark of God, he mars his undertaking at once; he brings down no blessing upon his ministration, though it be in God's service. This also is too likely to be the case, when a person, ever so honest-minded and pious, is pushed forward into the sacred ministry by relatives or friends, though his own will did not take the lead. Why are people so active in their own counsel and strength?"

With such sentiments, Bengel considered it his christian duty to let all his friends know, that, however contrary to the spirit of his own times, he had made up his mind to apply for no preferment or dignity whatever; but patiently and retiringly to await what God should be pleased to make of him by the instrumentality of his superiors; a principle upon which he always acted. Thus when, a few years after his settlement at Denkendorf, he was invited to stand for the Greek professorship at Tübingen, he deferred acknowledging this mark of respect till the professorship was filled up; believing that by thus waiting he should learn the will of God upon it more certainly than if he hastily caught at it, or hastily declined it. He had more difficulty upon another decision of the kind in the year 1720. Having received a call to the divinity chair in the University of

Giessen, at the instance of the privy councillor Smalcalder, of Hesse-Darmstadt (whose acquaintance he had made some time before), and of his relative, George Michael Seeger, M. A. who was then tutor at Darmstadt, in the family of the Baron von Löwenstern, he delayed giving any answer till he heard that a Mr. Meuschen had obtained the professorship. He then wrote a letter of thanks; but this letter was returned to him, accompanied by another from Seeger, saying that the report of Meuschen's election was unfounded; so that he was obliged to come to a decision of his own, which we find in the following reply to Seeger:

"Your letter of the eighth of May reached me at the proper time; but I deferred answering it because I was at a loss how to reply upon the matter it contained: I therefore followed the method which I have for some time adopted under such circumstances. When I was written to about taking the Greek professorship at Tübingen, I purposely delayed returning my grateful acknowledgments till I learnt that the appointment was filled up. In like manner, when I heard that Mr. Meuschen was to be the new divinity professor at Giessen, I then wrote to you; and yesterday my letter came back from Stuttgart, with another from yourself, still bringing to me the same proposal. But I have also received a letter from my wife, which says; 'Our dear father is of opinion that, with all due thanks, you should *decline* it, because, every one of us being in a weak state of health, we are unequal to such a journey and change of situation; and he thinks our worthy mother was quite distressed at hearing any thing said about it.' Though I generally sleep more soundly than when my little people are at home, last night it was otherwise, for want of the quietness of mind I had enjoyed while I supposed that Meuschen was elected. But that I may give no further trouble to our honourable privy councillor, who has enough to engage him without my increasing it, I wish my definitive reply to be made in the categorical emphasis of NO; with, however, my very best thanks for kindness so highly valued by me; and with my sincere wish that the Most High may so order the counsels and measures of our excellent friend, in this and every other business, that he may have all the satisfaction in it he can well look for. But how hidden or how few must be men of God in the present day, if this gentleman feels it necessary to look out, from such a distance, for an insignificant being like myself to come and occupy a station of so high importance!

"In addition to the family objections in my wife's letter, to which I cannot but assent, I have also many a scruple of my own. I am satisfied God has sent and placed me here. I am prospered here in every way; am become familiar with my work; and am enabled freely to apply my liberal allowance of spare time to wholesome exercises, studies, and employments. But, in so responsible a station as a professorship of divinity, what a demand of laborious preparation and engagement would come upon me, especially at the outset! and the more so, as for a number of years I have given no great deal of time to theological labour of *this* kind, important as it is in its proper place. In my present obscure and humble station I do not eat my bread quite unearned; but were I in a higher one, there might be occasion to say, Why does he stand in the way of a more efficient man? Here, also, in my native Würtemberg, my dear partner and myself have parents still living; and my own dear mother, who cannot expect to live many years longer in this world, would be uncomfortable at losing my society. Indeed, all the endearing links of brothers, sisters, relatives, and of many kind and affectionate friends, so twine about us here, that I think you will agree with me, that unless we have some very imperative reason for it, we ought not to quit such a favoured neighbourhood for a situation among perfect strangers; many of whom also may be likely to view us with an invidious eye, especially in a part of the empire where many from our own country, after settling there awhile, have found themselves glad to return home again.

" P.S.—*Stuttgart*, 1*st July*. Hither have I arrived to fetch home my family, and so have brought this letter with me. As I could not trust the subject of it entirely to my own judgment, I contrived yesterday to hold a little meeting for consultation, in the garden summerhouse of the Estates Assembly Chambers. My council consisted of my wife and our respective parents, who sat by my side upon the bench, with two dear friends opposite. My letter was read and approved; but besides the objections I had stated in it, several others were now brought forward. My mother, indeed, resolves to write to Mr. privy councillor herself. My own will I submit to hers; and mine and hers to the will of God. As I am quite satisfied that it is with his will that I am stationed at Denkendorf, I pray that he may not permit me to leave that station *without* his will. I do not know what more to say about the matter, either against it or for it."

After it had been thus decided, as in the former instance, two professorships at Tübingen successively fell vacant by the demise of Hoffman and Bilfinger; and it was again on both occasions reported that Bengel was to take one of them, namely, the professorship of divinity. When Hoffmann died in 1728, Bengel wrote to his intimate friend Marthius as follows:—"Is it not almost a want of christian modesty in me to say, that it seems as if the settling who is to take this professorship was likely to have much to do with the future course of life of your humble servant? At all events, I must beg you very earnestly to beseech God that it may please him so to dispose in this emergency, as shall best conduce to my own and others' welfare. I am not ambitious to outshine my neighbours at the university, or in the world at large; there is another glory that far excelleth, which you and I are longing for, and which I have a humble confidence that we shall attain."

In the same spirit of resignation did he act again with respect to a professorship at Tübingen, which became vacant in the year 1735. And thus he still remained stationed for the present, as tutor in the theological seminary of Denkendorf.*

But in the year 1740, Drommer, the prelate of this place, died, and Bengel's services as tutor had been now of so many years' continuance, that he had substantial claim to some office more becoming his advancement at least in age. He was asked, of course, whether he would apply for the vacant prelacy, upon which subject we here give extracts from two of his letters to particular friends.

"*April* 8, 1740.

"Who will be Drommer's successor amongst us is not yet known. I endeavour to keep myself stayed and faithful within

* On one occasion of its being proposed to him to take the divinity professorship and presidency of the Theological College of Tübingen, he thus wrote to a friend upon the plan he meant to follow in case he should enter upon these important offices:—

"I should use much diligence in preparing for every public lecture, and be continually going through a complete course upon the various branches of biblical study, that students might be thoroughly informed as to the general scope of holy Scripture, and the matter and object of each particular book of the inspired volume. I would enter upon the regular business of the professorship, directly after my being appointed, just as a person would do who had been long familiar with it, and thus lose no time. I would be communicative as a brother with the most dependent students, not indeed with that familiarity which breeds contempt, but yet freely conversible with them, and would appoint times of open access to me every week, so that if any one of them wished to speak with me quite privately, he might have opportunities for doing it. But things not of so private a nature it would, I think, be better to attend to when several are together, that all might be benefited alike. Some questions might be asked me privately, which I might find it good to answer afterwards in the presence of several, without naming who put them to me. I would endeavour to establish mutual confidence amongst them, and take particular care that those on the foundation of the college should have such ample and suitable provisions, that no pretence might exist for extra feasting. To obviate any excesses of this sort would demand my first attention, otherwise I should not interfere in it."

the lines of the Divine will concerning me. I would spend the remainder of my pilgrimage as shall best comport with furtherance of the honour of my Redeemer, and with my hope of blissful entrance into his everlasting kingdom. With this desire I earnestly request you to pray for me, and you know that such a request of mine is not a formality."

"*December* 16, 1740.

"I have just been giving to our ecclesiastical dignitaries a detailed statement of my present situation in the seminary, and now feel quite comfortably prepared either to receive a new prelate over my head, or to be advanced to a new station, if God so order it; for He alone is the patron I look up to. If He manifest further long-suffering towards such an one as me, I shall praise him for it; but let him do with me what seemeth him good; I shall still bless him. The termination of my pilgrimage cannot be very far off; what will it signify whether the remainder of it lie through a valley, or over an eminence? Opportunities for making good use of my time, I have plenty already, if I am not wanting in diligence; whereas, to whom more is given, of him will more be required."

The result was, that his ancient and faithful friend, Weissensee, prelate of Blaubeuren, should be translated to the prelacy of Denkendorf. The directory, it seems, felt that if an officer so valuable as Bengel *must* have a superior there set over him once more, the latter ought to be some intimate friend of his own. This appointment, however, was intended only as a temporary measure; as Bengel no longer ought to be suffered to wear out his declining strength in the tutorship of a theological seminary. As he had spent the best part of his life in the duties of this office, with unexceptionable and exemplary fidelity, the vacant prelacy of Herbrechtingen was shortly afterwards given him, as a station of comparative *otium cum dignitate*. Therefore, on the 23d of April, 1741, he took his leave of the parochial congregation of Denkendorf, then of the whole theological seminary the next day, and spent part of the following day in private farewell visits, which he found the more affecting, as now were expressed to him more plainly and warmly than ever, the great love and esteem he had gained amongst all around. He left Denkendorf on the 26th of April, accompanied by his wife and children, with the family tutor. They reached Herbrechtingen the next afternoon, and on the Sunday following he preached his entrance sermon. The text, which was out of the Gospel for the day (John xvi. 5—15), gave him the desired opportunity of discoursing upon the excellencies of God's Word which he was called there to preach and promote. He introduced his subject by a reference to Psalm li. 12—14, in which he showed that David's petition, "Create in me a clean heart, O God, and renew a right spirit within me," must be made our own and principal petition, if ever we mean to become blessed citizens of God's heavenly kingdom. And having then remarked, from James i. 16—21, that the new birth, by which we obtain a clean heart and a right spirit renewed within us, is the fruit of "the Word of Truth;" he opened his subject by stating, that the main excellencies of the Word committed to him are, that, by this Word, the Holy Spirit,

1. Works fundamental conviction *within* us; and then,
2. Guides us into all truth.

In the *first* part, he reminded his audience how consolatory to our Lord's disciples, sorrowful as they were at his going away, must have been the promise, that he would send to them the Holy Ghost, the Comforter; to reprove (or fundamentally convince) the world, of sin, of righteousness, and of judgment. He then showed how this promise was punctually fulfilled, is still fulfilling, and ever will be so. For as the Jews were of "the world," though they had once been chosen to be the peculiar people of God, so all Christians are originally of "the world," and therefore need to be fundamentally convinced of the ruin and corruption of their nature; of their need of the Redeemer; of his actual appearance upon earth; and of their own deliverance from the power and domination of Satan. He further stated, that his commission among them was to be a worker together with God, for this very end; and that, as he wished to fulfil it with joy, he prayed that God would vouchsafe him for that purpose the aid of his Holy Spirit. That as, in no other way but this, he expected salvation for himself, so, on their behalf, he could not but pray, and earnestly desire, that they might receive the Word of God, and become fundamentally convinced of the Truth by its means.

In the *second* part, he showed that the Spirit of God guides us into all truth, that is, brings us under the effectual influence of those good tidings, the sum and substance of which is, Jesus Christ. He added, that this effect is wrought only in true believers; that is, those, in whom the fundamental conviction above-mentioned prepares the mind and the heart for willing and cheerful obedience, yes for uniform fidelity, as a matter of conscience, in things great and small. That such persons are no longer "carnal," but "spiritually minded" (Rom. viii. 5—16), and have the real life of Christ within them; they keep his commandments, and abide in him (1 John iii. 24). That he considered it a gracious favour from God, and a blessed commission, to have to tell them of these things.

Thus entered Bengel, in the name of the Lord, on a station very different from his former one; he had exchanged a life of long toil and activity, for one of comparative rest and quietness; and that constant intercourse with ardent students and with learned men, from which he had hitherto derived such benefit, was now superseded by a life of comparative solitude. He had also left the busy vicinity of the metropolis (for his Denkendorf being but three leagues from Stuttgart, he would sometimes pleasantly call it the suburbs), for a remote and country seclusion. The literary works he had undertaken were now nearly completed,* and he considered himself to be already approaching so near the end of his course, as not to be likely to venture afresh upon any similar undertaking. Here then he experienced such a sort of void, that the longer he lived, the more tedious did the bare concerns of this world seem, and the more desirable the attainment of his heavenly home. On the 20th of September, 1741, he writes: "I have been undergoing, for several days past, an experience comparatively new to me; so much more than ever do I feel myself to be like an empty vessel, as my work of nearly thirty years is fast running to its close; but it is good for me to learn the littleness of all our human efforts." Nevertheless, he gradually accommodated himself to his new condition; and on the 20th of May, 1742, he writes: "My solitude affords me advantages for meditation on the Apocalypse, and upon other subjects more aloof from the noise and distraction of human opinions; indeed, the leisure I enjoy, after so many years of incessant business, would seem strange to me, if I did not learn to improve it. I must needs have some probationary exercises to go on with, while I remain in this life."

* On the same day that he was elected prelate of Herbrechtingen, his "GNOMON" received its *imprimatur*.

This learned and pious man's work was not yet done; he had only shifted upon a resting station, where he could enjoy more quiet for literary labour, recruit his strength for new activity, and give it to those immediate employments of the ministry, which, as he sought after them with exemplary earnestness and piety, now increased upon him daily. The impressive sermons preached by him and by his excellent coadjutors soon stirred up such a feeling in their congregations, that many with wonder and delight expressed that they had never heard such preaching before. Persons thus awakened to the value of real Christianity soon wished for instruction in personal religion beyond what they could gain from public discourses; and the more eager they were to listen to these, the more they felt their need of private spiritual application. They therefore waited upon their faithful pastor, requesting him to satisfy their desire for the truth; and he readily complied with their request. He commenced regular meetings for edification, similar to those he had held at Denkendorf, and he now expounded, first the four Gospels throughout, and afterwards the Revelation of St. John. His Apocalyptical expositions were undertaken principally at the urgent desire of Oetinger, and this was the origin of Bengel's well-known "Sixty Practical Addresses" upon that prophecy, which were published from notes taken by his hearers, with his own corrections and improvements. From his expositions of the four Gospels, taken in notes by Mr. Käuflein, who was tutor in his family, we here insert a few fragments.

From his private Expositions at Herbrechtingen.

ON THE GOSPEL OF ST. MARK.

Ch. i. 16. When we have most to attend to worldly business, we are apt to think we are farthest diverted from *the right way;* whereas, upon these very occasions, we may be really nearest to it. It was in the midst of *temporal* occupations that fishermen were called to the intimate discipleship of the Lord.

Ch. i. 35. There is something very precious in the *morning* hours. If at such seasons we leave the company of our very best relatives and friends, and retire awhile for silent prayer, we shall find our spirits refreshed, as the fields with the dew of the morning.

Ch. i. 37. It is only when a Christian has collected his mind by prayer, that he can find himself enabled to make any beneficial impression upon others. Then he *will* be enabled to do it, and often with great effect. For the heavenly unction upon him will give forth a sweet influence, which needs not a multitude of words. As one who has just been engaged in a quarrel, shows it by his very appearance, so does the sweet composure of communion with God betray itself in those who have been enjoying it.

Ch. ii. 10. How many troubles may a single sin often bring upon us! How will it be if people go on in sin till all their transgressions shall rise up against them as in battle array! Let us then at once become acquainted with Jesus. There is forgiveness with *Him.*

Ch. ii. 15. Thus can even a feast be made the occasion of leading those into the kingdom of God who are now far from it. Here we see Jesus holding kind and familiar intercourse with people of the humblest rank. Hereby they came in contact with virtues that win the heart; namely, with undefiled innocence, gracious goodness, and benevolent earnestness to help others in the right way. Let us study to imitate Christ in all this.

Ch. iii. 5. What is this hardness of men's hearts? It is being so devoid of spiritual feeling, as to mistake good for evil, and evil for good. O let us therefore labour to abide in Jesus, stedfastly and immovably, that the mists of our worldly-mindedness may be scattered by the mind of Christ rising like the sun within us.

Ch. iii. 28—30. There are many sins against the Holy Ghost. The most horrible is that of blaspheming Him; for this is *crimen læsæ majestatis*, a sort of high treason against the Majesty of heaven. Such a grievous sin the Scribes committed by a single saying; but then they had been long ripening into such depravity, and never could have been guilty of it all at once. In Matt. ix. 10, 11, we may see something like the commencement of it. While some chose to utter the dreadful blasphemy, others perhaps heard it with an approving laugh, and thus made themselves partakers in the horrible sin. How dangerous then is it to consort with ungodly persons, among whom no check or restraint being felt, sins of every name are the more easily incurred.

Ch. iii. 34. Here we may learn, that they who have entered into spiritual life, through the grace of God the Father, are to be regarded as Christ's brethren and friends, because they really are such. But what a relationship is this! And here observe that Jesus does not except from this relationship the very lowest and meanest of mankind. Therefore let every one of us who would enjoy such an unspeakable honour, give himself up at once to "the will" of God "the Father."

Ch. vi. 2. The people of Nazareth stumbled at outward circumstances, and this kept them back from faith. The same thing frequently happens now. What though we enjoy some little advantage above our neighbours? If we make a mirror of it, we then look the wrong way, and thus getting wrong in our direction, we stumble and fall. And we must take equal care not to be led away by our partialities; as, for instance, by excessive admiration of any sermon, exposition, piece of poetry, or whatever may happen to strike and dazzle us. What the Scripture calls "stumbling," or being "offended," is any such shock to our faith as hinders us from properly recovering, rising, and advancing; and all because we unduly regard things exterior and circumstantial.

Ch. vi. 4. (Instead of "despising" humble appearances, or "the day of small things," especially as to the work of God's servants,) we must learn to infer and expect greater things from less; but if so, forasmuch as we have such abundant testimony of the actual death, resurrection, and ascension of Jesus, and of his session at the right hand of God, &c., what will not that sinner have to answer for, who persists to the end of life in his rejection of the divine message upon these subjects!

Ch. vi. 50. "*It is I.*" ("I am he.") This satisfied and consoled the disciples. When any true disciple at present has become so intimately acquainted with the Lord Jesus, that if he say unto that disciple's soul, "It is I," or "I am he," or "I AM,"* he can become immediately satisfied and consoled, how good is it! He said the same on another occasion, namely, to his enemies in the garden of Gethsemane; but it produced a very different effect. When the soul is already favoured with a sound constitution, any temporary disorder in it may easily be rectified by a single saying of Christ. It is with faith as with a kindled brand, which, when it is only in a sleeping glow, may be put into a flame by a single breath.

* Ἐγώ εἰμι, "I am," "It is I," "I am He;" the expression in the Greek Testament being one and the same for each rendering. This observation explains that of Bengel in the next sentence; for in the two cases which he here adduces, the two Greek words need little more than to be turned into two German words of the same meaning, each for each, and the German expression, like the Greek, admits of either signification.—TR.

Ch. vi. 56. Why did they desire only to *touch* the border of his garment? for it is not said that they wished to get *a piece* of it. The Saviour's own presence was what contented *them*. Here is no Romish faith in relics. When religion degenerates into human inventions, we may be sure that God has no more to do with it.

Ch. vii. 6. The Lord Jesus kindly took his disciples' part against the Pharisees. The disciples were unfledged pupils, under his own wing, and therefore must be protected. What a blessing is it to be really *his* friends, however exposed and helpless we may be in other respects.

Ch. vii. 7. Here we may see at once what true worship is. The heart must be near to God. Communion with Him is all our salvation. Is this what we are chiefly endeavouring to maintain? It is true He is a consuming fire; but we may draw near to him by that "new and living way" which "the kindness and love of God our Saviour" have "opened to us." (If in this way we approach him,) then we may say, O God! thou art *my* God! Then is a man's accusing and terrified conscience, which drives him from God and from himself, made tranquil and easy. God can then gain the heart; and all its humble and meekly submissive approaches to him become accepted as a service with which He is well pleased. As a man's heart is, so is he. (It is the state of *the heart* that must, after all, determine what we really are in spiritual respects.) Though we may have amassed treasures of understanding about the letter of Scripture, all this is but as so much household furniture, (in the midst of which a man may remain as insecure or as wretched as ever. We read of an apostle's hearers, that they were "pricked in their heart," and so converted. In like manner) we must be "pricked in the heart" (by a conviction of sin; deeply affected by a sense of our ingratitude to God, our guilt, pollution, helplessness, and misery;) in order to apprehend and lay hold of Jesus in his love. All will then terminate in the firm conviction, that Jesus is the Christ, the Anointed of God.

Ch. ix. 31. Jesus knew, beforehand, the whole amount of his sufferings, in all their connexions and bearings; and therefore never foretold them without likewise foretelling his resurrection: neither did he foretell this without foretelling his sufferings. Thus does true faith apprehend the latter and the former as one entire matter, and makes very much of every thing pertaining to either. Here is something for exercising the heart; something which must never be lost sight of in the darkest night of affliction, or in the clearest blaze of a terrestrial noon; for it is to guide our feet into the way of peace. As we hold a candle to the flame till it is fully lighted, so must we hold ourselves to this subject with affecting meditation. If we do not keep our souls up to it, and much more if we never come to this light, we shall remain what we have been hitherto, unchanged and unamended. But when the heart begins to speak out, "Lord, thy considerate mercy in dying for sinners was a considerateness in behalf of *me;* and thy resurrection for the justification of sinners, was for the justification of *me;* and thus hast thou effected *my* restoration to life eternal, not less than the restoration of *others;* then we are at THE POINT where the heart becomes touched and softened, and now a spring of principle opens within us which had no existence before." He is the most welcome to Christ who thus applies to him with the least delay. O that such truths as we here see connected together may take fast hold of our hearts, that we may be slaves no longer to any thing that is incompatible with the high privileges and character of true believers!

Ch. ix. 33. While his disciples were constantly *about* him, they went on pretty well; but there was good reason for his leaving them sometimes to themselves. Souls committed to our own charge may be kept from many a fault while they are conscious of our watchful oversight, though their heart still remain unamended. Observe what direction your thoughts and feelings most readily take, when you are alone; and you will then form a tolerably correct opinion of your real state.

Another province of employment was opened to Bengel by the high consideration in which his learning and piety were held by people of all ranks, both far and near. When he was only tutor in the Theological Institution, persons of various countries and conditions applied to him, either upon subjects of literary interest, or upon matters of conscience; and he was always ready to oblige every one, as far as his time, learning, and abilities would permit. But after he was raised to the prelacy, he was more sought than ever; and though he had increased leisure for correspondence, he soon found it quite occupied in answering inquiries that daily poured in upon him. But as his leisure and capacity for it were regarded by him as entrusted talents, he most conscientiously and wisely studied to improve the trust, as may be seen in the third section of our former chapter, and as we shall further show in this part of his memoir. He had also now better opportunities than ever for doing good by *personal intercourse.* During the first years of his prelacy, he had always an assistant minister, whose "sermons" became "sensibly improved," after being associated with such a man as Bengel. Several also of his former pupils contrived to get appointments near him, that they might continue to benefit by intercourse with their revered tutor. Oetinger, who came to reside at Schnaitheim in 1743, says he settled there on that very account; as did also Burk, who in 1742 took charge of the parish of Bolheim; his friend Käufelin did the same, for in 1746 he got appointed to the assistant ministry of Herbrechtingen. Two other of his pupils, Bardili and Ehrenreich, had settled in the neighbourhood before his arrival. And his intercourse with the excellent Cosman Frederic Köstlin, Master of Arts, and dean of Heidenheim, which commenced in 1747, was a real blessing to both parties, as well as to others.

Persons farther off, and a considerable number from foreign dominions, especially from the church of the United Brethren, as Weinel, Büttner, Lieberkühn, Layriz, and Timäus, found their way to distant Herbrechtingen, for the sake of intercourse with him. He was also commonly referred to when the neighbourhood was visited by great persons, (some of princely rank,) to whom respect was to be paid by a convocation of the chief inhabitants. Bengel was never disposed to court any favour by flattering the great; but he availed himself of these occasions to deliver, if possible, some testimony to the *power* and *saving strength* of the gospel.

Another demand on his present attention was the education of his two sons, Victor and Ernest, whom with a few boarding pupils he instructed partly himself, and partly by an able family tutor. His correspondence also was increased by a part of his family now residing in distant places, as his daughters were married.

All these occupations, however, were comparatively no more than a sort of recreation for a few years; for he was soon to enter upon far more comprehensive engagements.

Before we particularize the new circumstances awaiting him, we shall notice an incident which, while it betrays how carelessly certain things were attended to in those days, shows also Bengel's conscientious aversion to unmeaning formalities. It was not till after he had been about three years actual prelate of Herbrechtingen, that his bond of office in that station was sent to him for signature. It was drawn up in the ancient form, specifying all the particulars of his obligations as prelate, and setting forth three principal matters,—obedience to the sovereign, ministerial requirements, and superintendence of the management and application of the estate property assigned to the support of the Theological Institution attached to the prelate's jurisdiction. Bengel was surprised at finding the third of these particulars included in his obligations; especially as no opportunity had yet been given him for obtaining information as to how the property was managed and applied. But though he was one of the last obtrusively to interfere in matters of this sort, he saw at once that our forefathers had good reason for inserting such a charge in the bond, as the superintendence and control of a resident prelate was likely, in many ways, to be a useful check upon the stewardship of the establishment. Therefore, not to appear inclined to raise needless scruples, he subscribed the bond, but added to it the following supplementary explanation; that "he was conscientiously disposed to perform all dutiful obedience to his sovereign, and meant to remain a loyal subject to the end of his life; likewise he was most happy to take the charge of every church duty belonging to his station; but as for superintending the temporal concerns of the prelacy, he could not promise to be of any use in this respect to its Theological Institution, as being too remote from his residence; for that many an explanation upon various matters would require his being there on the spot at the time of their occurrence, and could not otherwise be obtained. He thought, therefore, that he ought to remain non-interferent upon such matters; at the same time he would be careful to act as a fellow-worker to the general good, by attending diligently to the duties of his ministry, which he could the better do if exempted from every temporal avocation of the kind."

He sent the bond with this explanation, accompanied by a letter which stated yet more particularly his reasons for it, to the consistorial director Schäffer. The directory had nothing to object against his declining to interfere in temporalities, and thus far his mind was set at rest with regard to the past. But with respect to the future he did not seem to be quite satisfied; for in the year 1745 we find him writing to Lang, the prelate of Blaubeuren, requesting him to move in the Synod a general deliberation upon the subject. In this letter he says, "Upon receiving the formalities of my office, and signing the bond, I felt it my duty, for the sake of my oath of consecration, to add an explanatory note to my signature. The extensive power of our ancient prelates over their respective districts is now vested in the Ecclesiastical Commissioners; these at least have all the exercise of it in the present day. This state of things we, who, from our fathers before us, depend upon the auspices of his most Serene Highness, have no intention to alter; neither would it be of any benefit to the church to attempt it. But it would be very much for the interest of the sovereign that prelates should be fully acquainted with the disposal of these ecclesiastical revenues. It would be valuable in its place, just as members of a joint trust are valuable to one another. I have no fault to find with the present steward; but considering the circumstances of our times, I could probably show from experience more clearly than many, the importance of such a regulation. Prelates who reside so far from their Theological Seminaries as I do, cannot, of course, form an opinion about these temporalities so accurately as those who reside on the spot. Let then all the prelates who have this advantage throw together what they know about the circumstances, and communicate it to the rest of us, for reference in any case of our own.

"I am quite of opinion that we had better even resemble the ancient Egyptian monks in their solitudes, than be reinvested with that power of Germanic prelacy, which owes its origin to the imperial wand of Otho the Great. Let those, however, who find places and opportunities to recover for the *general* good the primitive and better state (of ecclesiastical superintendence), not be negligent about it; for I have already discovered, by facts which have come within my own observation, that the vigilant superintendence of a worthy deputation from among the common overseers of the flock, has been not without its advantages to the general welfare; and why may we not hope that more such advantages are attainable by it?"

These are the sentiments of one who knew how to combine zeal and fidelity with prudence and moderation; and was as free from any precise officiousness, as he was from indolent indifference. As he had treasured up no ordinary share of learning and piety, it would have been a public loss had he not been drawn forward to assist officially in the most important business of his country. The Provincial Estates were sensible of this, and chose him, in 1747, a member of their General Assembly, and in 1748 a member of their Special Board. Upon this subject he thus expresses himself in a letter of the 29th of June, 1747: "My call to the States Assembly was unsought, but when it came, I did not refuse it. May all who love me, lend me the support of their fraternal and affectionate prayers! I have just passed the sixtieth year of my pilgrimage; and, having of late completed one work after another which God's providence had committed to me, I had thought to put my furniture into a narrower compass, (and to set my house in order.) But now I am brought unexpectedly into a wider circle of more arduous engagements than ever, having to learn what it is to watch over and assist in the welfare of a whole country, and of the church comprised in it; and this not merely in a general way, but in a great variety of particular business. Still, He who is ever faithful and true, will carry me through this large range of difficult duties also."

In the same manner did he express himself, when in 1749 he was elected Councillor of Consistory, and Prelate of Alpirsbach; which obliged him to leave Herbrechtingen, and reside at Stuttgart. "I enter upon my new and unsought office, trusting in the Divine mercy. That my call to it has occasioned mutual encouragement and congratulation among worthy and pious people, gives me comfort and joy in one respect, but shames and awes me in another, as knowing what I am in myself, and what a world it is we have to do with; a world in which it is not easy to answer even the moderate expectations which men may form of us. However, I shall thus become less and less in my own eyes, and more desirous of attaining the everlasting rest."

We add one more short extract, which is from a letter which he wrote to Chancellor Ch. M. Pfaff, D. D., in acknowledgment of the honour of a diploma tendered to him by the University of Tübingen.

"The information I have lately received respecting the intention to confer on me the degree of Doctor in Divinity, could not but surprise me, considering of how little account I am obliged to esteem myself. However, while I recognise God's gracious favours with gratitude, and my own nothingness with humility, I also regard the dignity of such an honorary degree, not only as highly valuable for the quarter from whence it comes, but particularly so as a means of furthering the usefulness of those who, after a long course of persevering study and labour, desire to benefit others upon a large scale. With regard to myself, as I have already reached so near the end of my pilgrimage, and besides, cannot think of standing upon an equality either with one who fills such an office as that of Visitor of the University, or with another who is first Chaplain to the Court,* I feel that it is simply from the humble respect and obedience I owe to my most gracious prince, and in submission to the heads of the university, who have adjudged such an honour to me, that I accept without hesitation this unmerited token of their regard."

He ended his official engagements at Herbrechtingen, on the 19th of October, 1749, with preaching before a very numerous audience upon the Gospel for the twentieth Sunday after Trinity, from the twenty-second chapter of St. Matthew.† He commenced with introductory observations on 2 Cor. i. 24,—" *We are helpers of your joy;*" and said, " The aim and tendency of the whole gospel of Christ is to produce joy. Unconverted reason has very different notions of it; but what I have affirmed of it is the real truth; and there is no joy without it. Only *where* God's communion is, *there* is joy. Thus the Psalmist declares, (Ps. xvi. 11,) ' In Thy presence is the fulness of joy; and at Thy right hand are pleasures for evermore.' The Christian's condition has joy in it already, as well as joy in prospect; moreover, it is real and substantial joy. He who is invited to become a true Christian, is invited to this joy at once. What has been my own aim all along amongst yourselves, but only this, to draw you into fellowship of the gospel of peace and salvation; and what is this, in other words, but to be a helper of your joy? For he helps his neighbour to true joy, who helps him to Christ. This I also wish to do on the present occasion.—' *Wherefore,*' (I appeal to you in the words of the apostle to the Hebrews, iii. 1,) ' *holy brethren,*—PARTAKERS OF THE HEAVENLY CALLING! *consider the Apostle and High Priest of your profession,* CHRIST JESUS.'—' HOLY *brethren*' are those who surrender themselves entirely to the will of God, to believe, do, and follow, even in tribulations and adversities, just as the Lord would have them. This ' HEAVENLY CALLING ' is a call issuing *from* heaven, and inviting us *to* heaven. *From* heaven does it come, because Christ is ' the Lord from heaven,' who, as his Father's great Apostle, calls us *to* heaven. For to this very end did he come into the world, that he might ' *bring us to God.*'—I there-

* Two clergymen holding these situations had been nominated to the degree of D.D. at the same time with Bengel.

† For recovering this sketch of his sermon, we have, together with the notes he used in the pulpit, some passages taken down at the time by several of his hearers; one of whom records in a memorandum, his having " failed to write many important things which Bengel uttered, and many of his connecting expressions;" and that he was " unable to describe the power of the Spirit which prevailed in the delivery of the discourse."

fore purpose giving a summary repetition of that heavenly calling, which I have hitherto been bringing to you, and to remind you,

" 1. Whereunto we are called;

" 2. Through whom the call is made; and,

" 3. What is the issue of it.

" O God! Help, that I may now speak what I can maintain and continue in. Let no unprofitable word proceed out of my mouth:

" And as I am now to speak in this place for the last time,

" So grant power and impression to what I utter, as my last words! Amen.

" *First*, let me remind you,

" WHEREUNTO we are '*called*.' *This* is in Scripture represented as a *marriage;* consequently as something pleasant and joyful; and indeed as a joy designed for very many. We are called to *one communion and fellowship in* GRACE; to a GLORY wherewith God, the King of kings, purposes to honour and rejoice his only-begotten Son. It is a *heavenly* and *royal* grace whereunto we are called. It has all along been 'hid in God,' but the more hidden it is, the more precious and glorious is it. We may well find comfort in the consideration that the guests invited are *so many*, and that the King, who sends forth the invitation, is *able to supply the wants of all.* Likewise, *all is now ready.* Under the Old Testament men were taught to *expect* this marriage; but under the New Testament, all is made ready. It is also a *real marriage* GRACE; for God calls to us by the prophet Hosea, saying, (ii. 19, 20:) 'I will betroth thee to me for ever: yea, I will betroth thee to me in righteousness, in grace, and in mercy: yea, in faithfulness will I betroth thee unto me.'—God is gathering to himself a CHURCH, which, through the fellowship of Jesus Christ, is to be called, THE KING'S DAUGHTER, and THE BRIDE, THE LAMB'S WIFE.

But, alas, how do we hang back, and fall short of these exceeding great and precious blessings, of which to enjoy but a single glimpse, is happiness and salvation begun upon earth! Many know nothing whatever of this joy; they know only the foolish joy of this present evil world. They may have their joyous days, and may rejoice in looking forward to them for months beforehand, and may talk of them still longer afterwards: nevertheless, they deceive their own souls; for theirs is not *real* joy; and awful is it to be obliged to think that many have nothing better hereafter to all eternity! Even the *sorrow* of godly persons has more real *joy* in it, than is contained in all the joy of *this* world; for godly sorrow harmonizes with the will of God. What then will their joy amount to, 'when the times of refreshing shall come from the presence of the Lord;' when 'all tears shall be wiped away from their eyes!' Who is there that ought not to have, once for all, the most sincere and ardent desire to attain the beatific vision and realization of all that which we embrace at present by belief alone; by a belief, however, which is warranted by the testimonies and oath of God!

"Having seen *whereunto* we are called, let me remind you,

"2. THROUGH WHOM (we are all called); we are to expect no *other* messenger from heaven. Christ having come, once for all, began to preach and proclaim peace, by his gospel. This proclamation is to be carried on for ever by the christian ministry. Christ's ministers brought it first to Israel. The Jews were *then* in a *special* sense, 'the guests.' Afterwards, during, and subsequently to our Lord's sufferings, the invitation was made more pressing and forcible; *then* it was said, 'All is now ready! Come unto the marriage!' But as 'Israel would none of it,' the invitation was to be sent 'to others.' The Gentiles were not only to be '*guests*,' but to constitute, in a very large measure, the mystical BRIDE. Thus has the message now reached *us;* and even through him who at present addresses you, is that invitation sent to yourselves. This is the two hundred and eightieth time of my preaching to you, besides the sermons which my assistants have preached; and if there be any of you who have not been individually invited by those sermons, I desire now to invite all such, and I do it. I have warned, allured, and called: I do it once more; accept the call as if I spoke to each of you apart, for the last time, in the most earnest manner, saying, accept, I beseech thee, even thou, the call I bring thee; it is God's invitation to everlasting joy, through Jesus Christ thy Saviour!

"3. What is the ISSUE of this heavenly call and invitation? —There are guests who continue to put off accepting it, perhaps for the sake of a field, a house, a farm, or an article of merchandise; and there are others who can even mock, revile, or kill, the messengers of grace. Inexcusable as this is, experience has ever shown it to be the fact. The nearer this grace is brought to any inveterately wicked heart, the more embittered is that heart against it. Neither is the result more favourable in the case of numbers who receive the invitation and come. For "both good and bad" are found among the guests. They never *were* all *really* alike, nor ever *will* be. Therefore after they are gathered together, the awful separation follows. The man who had not on the "wedding garment," who had neither Christ's righteousness *upon* him, nor a heart renewed by Christ *within* him, is an image of all those who receive the grace of God in vain. Many will have it that their common civil life has nothing to do with their religion. Imagining they have done their duty to God, by attending church, and so forth, they conclude that God makes no further inquiry into their religion or conduct; and this delusion they palliate with every kind of ingenious excuse. Yet what but consequences the most awful can be expected from such folly as this! The particular character of the guests who *are* found worthy, is not here mentioned; it is enough that they are regarded as "called and chosen and faithful" guests, and that it is the Lord who thus regards them, &c. "The Lord knoweth them that are his," &c. &c. Let us then conclude by affectionately commending each other in prayer to God.

"As Thou, my God! hast been by me and with me during all my former life, as also during the years I have sojourned in this place, so, of thy mercy, be thou with me for the time to come, till thou take me home to thyself, into thy heavenly kingdom. And O, be thou with all those whom I am now about to leave; be thou with the inmates of the seminary, and with the members of the parochial churches; with all of every rank and age and sex! Bless likewise all who have been accustomed to hear thy message in this place, and those of us who may have heard it this day for the first time. Bless especially those who have met so often at the house and in the closet of thy servant for exercises of prayer, praise, and meditation in thy word. Of a truth, Lord! I have never said that only such are to be considered as accepted guests, or that even they are all rightly and piously minded. Thou, who alone searchest the hearts, thou only art able to discover them all, and to assign to each "his own place" and final destination. For this cause, O Lord, do I commit and commend them to thee; that it may please thee to purify and sustain them, to confirm and establish them. Unto thee I commend the whole church. What thy servant hath taught privately in conversation and confidential intercourse, the same hath he taught in public; and he humbly beseecheth thee to grant that whatever hath been thus spoken by him for thine honour and glory, and for thy name's sake, may bring forth manifold "fruit that shall remain;" and that whatever of human infirmity or impurity hath been intermingled, may be cast into those depths whereunto thou castest the sins of every sinner that repenteth. Again do I commend myself and all who are here assembled, O Lord God of faithfulness and truth, into thy hands, and unto the word of thy grace! To thy holy name be praise, thanksgiving, and adoration, now, and for evermore! Amen."

At the conclusion was sung,

"Be honour, glory, and exalted praise," &c.

from the Old Würtemberg Collection.

Henceforth it became Bengel's particular official business to assist in the direction of public affairs of the highest moment to the church of his country. As there are found among his papers some observations of his own respecting the rights, property, and power of the church, we here introduce them.

"If (says he) we would form a proper notion of the church, we must not form it, as is commonly done, by setting before us the primitive church as a model. The apostles, in speaking of 'the church,' intend not so much the church as it then existed, glorious and beautiful as it was; they meant rather the church in the abstract, or what it was designed of God to become hereafter. Eph. iv. 11—13. Christianity has never yet attained that perfect form which it is to have by virtue of the Old Testament promises.

"The light of the apostolic age was soon in the wane. With the exception of a few of the most ancient christian writings, which appeared immediately after the times of the apostles, we are constrained to say of all the rest, that the true doctrine of Christ and concerning Christ, with that of love, moderation, and sobriety, is not discoverable among them, so manifestly are they tinctured with what is harsh, rigid, and austere; the real depth of the Divine oracles and mysteries, the sweet, soft, and gracious manner of the apostles are no longer there; and as time advanced, the departure became still greater and more striking.

There *must* then be something better to come; indeed it is something truly great which God has graciously kept in store for the latter days. Lightly as many may be disposed to think of the present times, the truth is beginning to take deeper root than ever. Many verities, for which the apostles and primitive Christians laid down their necks, have for some time been fully admitted by the world, and more and more of them are continually shining forth in so clear a light, that men no longer find any thing to object against them, and hereby the worldly interest is driven further and further off its ground, though its advocates, like men in a besieged garrison, are always on the alert to devise new pretexts for it, and to fence all their outworks to the best of their ability. Indeed, as far back as the time of *Arndt*, a new and important era began to dawn. Arndt prepared the way for *Spener*, who contrived to carry home the truth to the hearts of multitudes by his institution of private meetings for edification. This method of diffusing the power of the gospel we may regard as a 'gift from above' peculiar to our times; and the exercise of it is by no means to be discouraged, as it is quite in conformity with God's great providential appointments. For the Lord, pursuant to his purpose of drawing all men unto himself, first selected a small people, a single branch of the family of Abraham, and to them he gave special laws and a great variety of peculiar forms, to fix their attention and allure them to God. So, the christian minister, who would convert even a village in the present day, proceeds first to seek out a few of that village, and bring them into communion with one another; not, indeed, to the exclusion of the rest, but rather to induce the rest to observe and inquire concerning what is going on, that his invitation may by and by be able to reach and gather *them* also.

"Arndt, as well as Spener and his followers, had to endure some enmity at first, from those who called themselves the orthodox, who arrayed against them all the fiery zeal with which they had waged war upon papists and other sects; but, since the rise of Wolf's philosophy, and because of the popularity with which it has gained ground, they are obliged, in order to withstand it, publicly to advocate sound principles; yes, those very principles which they could not find it in their hearts to endure in the person of Spener, and in the school of Halle.

"Still I do not think that the *moral* reformation, now begun, will proceed as did the *doctrinal* reformation of the last age; but rather that God will remove the 'unrighteous and the seed of the ungodly' out of the way, by his own overwhelming judgments; while a remnant will be saved, from which a people shall be born that shall praise the Lord.

"The amount of good, which for some time has been increasing so gloriously, is beginning to be at a stand. The pietistic character, which took its form at Halle, is rather too contracted for the times we live in. Zinzendorf will not be able to accomplish his plan of conducting every streamlet of the living water into one reservoir, out of which he designs to irrigate the whole world. Indeed of what use would it be to abandon the professing church and leave it, like a carriage in a slough, where its leaders have blindly driven it? Much less can it be of any use to treat that church with unmingled reproach and bitter invective; for this surely is as contrary to the spirit of the gospel, the spirit of love, as is separatism itself, which would suffer it to retrograde into the regions of dark and barbarous heathenism. Therefore we should allow every thing in it to stand, that *can* stand; whatever is of any use, let it *have* its use; and whatever we can improve to real benefit, let us improve it. Only may Christ not be forgotten as our single dependence, boast, and glory, Christ in every matter, and upon every account; and then they, who really meet in *him,* are *one.* If ever it was the safest thing to be good friends with all who love the Lord Jesus Christ in sincerity, and to keep clear of every thing like party spirit, a spirit always detrimental to the "One Thing needful," that time is now. It is no longer a question whether disorder and corruption be great and enormous, (the existence of which is pretty generally admitted and felt,) but how to treat the disorder in the wisest manner, how to counteract its baleful effects. We are not for asserting that our church is a pattern of purity, far from it; for it is at present quite a medley, a confused, discordant, undisciplined mass; and all upright minds, especially among our parochial clergy, witness its declension and disorder with real sorrow. Nevertheless our church is a church of Christ: for we are to consider, not merely what is wanting in it, or what is by human fault perverted from its right use, but what God still possesses, maintains, and upholds in it. Our case is the same in this respect with that of the Old Testament church. The Israelites, with all their corruption, were still the people of God, and were called such, because God had his own ordinances among them. We must not then be too eager to adopt every objection that may be brought against our mother church, worldly as her children so generally are; neither must we forget the privileges we retain in those common public prayers and songs of praise, which she gives us so many opportunities of enjoying. Corrupt as her condition is at present, it is to her, under God, that we owe the preservation of the Scriptures, and our familiarity with their contents; without her, the whole history of Christ would long ago have been regarded as fabulous. Therefore we ought to make the best of our present circumstances by endeavouring to improve the good we still retain; and at the same time to pray without ceasing, that the Lord may come quickly and make all things new. Such have been ever the sentiments which I have thought it right to uphold. The church is specially under the conduct of the Holy Spirit; and what we have most to pray for in its behalf is, that He may descend from heaven into the hearts of its rulers, and through them into the whole community. Now just because the church is sunk away from the Spirit into world and flesh, therefore is our Israel at present given into the hands of hard taskmasters; and the Romanists are not altogether mistaken in asserting, that temporal rulers among Protestants possess undue dominion in *spiritual* things. To name only one instance; there is with us a very great extenuation of church property; and to this evil our own good Brentius* himself contributed. Hence Dr. Jäger, when he had occasion, (in his lectures,) to speak of any lost privilege of the church, used to say, 'here is another thing which God has given up to the rulers of this world.' True; and they may use it as they please; but a time will come, when God will call them to account for it, and the recompense awaiting them will be a fearful one.

"The lawyers of Böhmer's school have written much to prove the right of temporal interference in spiritual affairs: (de jure principis circa sacra.) This is precisely the foul blot of their writings. More is thus devolved upon temporal rulers than they are able to bear; consequently it is shifted off from themselves to their legal counsellors. The (ecclesiastical) consistory is executive as subordinate to the prince, and the prince submits to the authority of his law advisers. The divines themselves sit in consistory, not as pastors or representatives of the church, but as councillors acting in the name and on the behalf of the supreme magistrate. The lawyers, especially those of Thomasius's school, generally oppose *them* when they bring forward any serious motion for the reforming of abuses. The lay community are readily allowed to act more at liberty (in church matters;) because it is expected that out of gratitude for it they will the more easily submit to other invasions of their privileges.

"It is true that in the time of the apostles, the monarchical form of church government was the best; because through such

* John Brentius, the Würtemberg Reformer, and Bengel's great-great grandfather by his mother's side.

men of God the Holy Spirit descended into the rest of the christian community. But as there are, and must be in our days, failings of so many kinds in the rulers of the church, the democratical form is now far preferable; especially when the question is, how the individual minister of any congregation is to be spiritually and effectually aided? For in this respect particularly, as well as in others, the admission of secular interference has made sad havoc in the church of Christ.

"I would have every statesman, who is so ready to retrench the spiritual authority of the christian ministry, examine well his own conscience. The directors of our Consistories are here incurring a serious responsibility before God, which they must one day give an account of. For the New Testament church is *corpus vivum*, a corporation that never dies, I mean, that it has an unbroken succession, which can no more be restricted to certain countries, places, or persons, than to periods of time. Thus there always resides within herself the power of self-renovation and self-government; and while in reality she abides under the government of the Holy Spirit, she is, as it respects any claims over her from this earth, independent and sovereign in her own right. Consequently, no other spiritual pre-eminences ought to be heard of among her members, except that the more any one has of the graces and gifts of the Spirit, the more valuable, available, and eminent is he; and that interference of civil authorities, to which the church, as she now is, has succumbed, ought to be always on the discreet side, in permitting most liberty to those who show most faithfulness and most of the Spirit of Christ; and in committing to their wisdom and experience more than they commit to others; as also in being equally zealous to retrench the power and influence of hirelings. Far from tying up the hands of pious ministers, they should address them thus:—'You have now a church committed to your charge; deal with it as you expect to answer for yourself concerning it before God.' To the churches of such ministers they ought likewise to say,—'If your pastor refuse any of you admission to the Lord's Supper, remember you cannot demand of him what is against his conscience; but you are at liberty to apply to any clergyman elsewhere, that may be willing to admit you.'

"The mixing up of secular policy with the concerns of the church, is but labour thrown away; for when all is done, that was so seriously purposed to be done, it is found to be not what was wanted. Our numerous ecclesiastical constitutions, many of which were originally well intended, are now, though I would speak of them all with respect, become no better, in general, than a kind of *percolatio culicum* (straining at gnats, and swallowing of camels.)—The camels men cannot but see, and yet are either unable, or unwilling to remove them out of the way; though were this done, every other thing desirable would soon ensue. To such a truth we should openly bear testimony; especially when we see so much hurt done to souls by the mere doctrines and commandments of men.

"Our Consistories and Synods are not insensible of existing evils, though they would rather not adopt coercive measures; but in their consciences they think those ministers right, who desire a more strict church discipline. Whether the former ought not to have the heart to put their own hand to the work, is another question. Now, if these gentlemen wish to show that they are convened, not only according to the laws of the country, but also in the Holy Ghost, they ought to speak out at once to the civil authorities, and to say,—'Your own assumption of the power of the keys, and your converting it to a mere temporal and jurisdictional right or prerogative of your own, is the very occasion of those abominations which prevail throughout the land, in the desecration of the Lord's Supper, cursing and profane swearing, lewdness, &c.; and the plunder you have thus assumed, we awfully regard as resting with your responsibility, till you choose to restore to the ministers of Christ himself, the prerogative with which he has invested them, and them only.' Were this done in the power of the Holy Ghost, it would certainly work to some good effect. But were the question, who shall be admitted to the Lord's table, decided, as it ought, *at the vestibule*, so to speak, rather than *within* the church, then would it be found necessary to begin deciding it, first with respect to the ministers themselves. The reason, however, why God permits so much corruption to take its course, is surely because his own authority and influence have ceased to be acknowledged amongst us, as if there were no more for him to do. Nevertheless, he will soon come and melt down all such things into another mould, by the refiner's fire. Meanwhile, let us, as being satisfied that those who are in authority are often blamed undeservedly for doing what there is reason enough to do, abide, in respect of church discipline, by the following rule:—Take general care to remove every sinful *practice* from each individual member; and if this cannot always be effected, let our endeavour be, that the evil shall do as little mischief as possible; and if the evil will work notwithstanding, let us however set a guard upon its extension.

"We have no regular administration of true discipline in the church, because we have no *materia ecclesiæ;* I mean, that real Christians, as its genuine members, constitute no *regularly organized body for that purpose.* Therefore, external formalities must not be too strictly urged by our parochial clergy; for the true remedy lies deeper than all such things; and this they must take care to know and remember."

As it was one business of the consistorial council to improve, from time to time, the Liturgical Psalm and Hymn Book, and to compose forms of prayer for any remarkable public occasions, ecclesiastical or civil, Bengel's views upon these subjects will be seen in the following extracts; which we shall close with a public prayer, composed by him upon an occasion of murrain and pestilence.

"Good forms of prayer are valuable; but when the heart has been put in tune by their means, it is better that they should give place to extemporaneous petition. Still, even prescribed forms may be prayed with the heart, so as to come out of the heart: and, on the other hand, persons who are for praying always 'from the heart,' as they call it, that is, without any prescribed form, may, and do, come insensibly to use what amounts to form; only with this difference, that *their* formularies take their shape from the devotional habituations of these persons themselves; whereas they are not more beneficially impressive than the written forms of others. Books of prayers adapted to slender attainments, have generally most popularity; but, in such books, vanity and devotion often seem to go hand in hand; at one time the strain of their devotional expression is excessively weak; at another, quite seraphic. This tends to make any more grave and concise delivery of devotional sentiments less easily relished.

"It would be delightful to have one Psalm and Hymn Book universally adopted; but in this the humbler classes ought to be chiefly consulted. We should inquire among such people respecting hymns which have been found remarkably useful; for which the suffrages, so to speak, should be collected from house to house. We might thus obtain a beautiful and excellent assortment. Every man to his own taste; but for mine, many of the Herrnhut hymns are too jingling; the older compositions (as those of Luther, and others after him,) suit me much better; they allow me to think and recollect, before the next rhyme comes in, whereas, when so many rhymes chime one upon another to please the ear, all is too sweet; though I admit that when the versification is too cramped and concise, we are equally inconvenienced *that* way, but with a multitude of rhyming *words,* there is danger of having many unrhyming *things.*

"I have long thought that if the *uncouth* expressions in some old hymns, as in that which begins, 'Uphold us Lord!' were not read in the text, but allowed to stand as the *keri* in the margin, two sorts of Christians, of very opposite tastes, might thus be easily accommodated.

"As for the diminutive '*Jesulein,*'* I object not to the use of it in the old Christmas hymns, where the word has certainly a peculiar pleasantness, a kind of charm that touches the heart; but in other and modern hymns, where it is used chiefly for the sake of the rhyme, surely it is unseemly and improper. During a considerable part of my life, I have been in the habit of closely examining the sacred expressions of Scripture, and have very frequently had occasion to notice them to my pupils in the Theological seminary, where the common hymns and prayers were made use of. I have thus contracted a sensitive relish for those expressions, very distinctly from all others. If I had courage to engage in such a work, I could speak with a better grace of my having long ago collected materials sufficient for a treatise upon this subject, showing how far the phraseology of Scripture ought to be our model in the choice of expressions for prayers and hymns; and evincing by examples, what exquisite delicacy characterises the language of the apostles and prophets, which, by the way, can only be attributed to their divine inspiration.†

"It would be a good arrangement in a church hymn book, to class the hymns according to the respective times in which their authors lived. This would serve to distinguish their peculiar gifts of grace, as also the growth or decay of such gifts in the church of Christ.

"Church music, when not plain and simple, may delight the ear and imagination, but obstructs the true melody of the heart. The prevalent notion that it is a means of awakening devout feeling, is the very same that has introduced a multitude of

* The diminutive termination is used in the German, as in other languages, to express tender endearment.

† A more particular discussion of this subject, by Bengel, is found in his *Weltalter* ("Age of the World"), pp. 280—304.

ceremonies without end; and is to be dreaded like the commencement of a dropsy."

A public Prayer upon an occasion of Murrain and Pestilence.

"Almighty God, heavenly Father! all things are in thy hands; and thou doest according to thy will in the army of heaven, and among the inhabitants of the earth. All, whatsoever liveth, hath life and favour from Thee; but when thou takest away their breath from man or beast they die, and return to their dust. Health and sickness, plenty and scarcity, life and death, are at thy disposal. By whatever thou givest to the children of men, thou wouldst draw to thyself those who have departed from thee, and wouldst amend the lives of those who fear thy name. Thou hast hitherto abundantly manifested thy grace towards us, that we may obtain everlasting salvation through thy Son, our Lord Jesus Christ, and therewith enjoy thy blessings even in this world. But, forasmuch, as instead of yielding to thee that obedience which is so justly due, we have departed farther and farther from thee; thou hast made us to feel thy chastening rebuke, or to see it in those around us, or to hear it at a distance. Wars and rumours of wars have approached our borders; the ripening fruits of the ground have been destroyed by tempests; our cattle, in multitudes, perish by disease; and even our fellow-men, both old and young, some in large numbers together, others singly and almost unnoticed, are swept away by infectious sickness; and though not hid from thee, it is hidden from us, what further awaits us. Thou, O Almighty God, canst in a moment consume thy rebellious people with a word; or send such spiritual and temporal distress, that we should choose death rather than life. It is by thy mercy, O God of all grace, it is by thy long-suffering and forbearance, that we live, and have space afforded us for considering the things which belong to our peace, and for laying hold of the gracious hope set before us in Christ Jesus. O grant to us a submissive, meek, wise, and understanding heart, that we may feel thy hand, know thy counsel, and not imagine that these calamities have come upon us by chance; much less submit to our sufferings under the false notion of fate and necessity. Preserve us from intemperance, obduracy, pride, and rebellion of spirit; from wantonness and envy, from murmuring and unrighteousness; and work in us true repentance and conversion towards thee, with lively faith, holy importunity of prayer, childlike obedience to thy blessed will and commandments; and cordial, active love towards one another; that thou mayest remove thy plagues far from us, and see it no longer needful to inflict them. Assist those who counsel and promote the public good; and grant them grace to adopt, upon every occasion, those measures which shall conduce to the temporal and spiritual well-being of all. Show thy mercy upon those who are suffering affliction, O Thou, who art the hope of all the ends of the earth, and of them that are afar off upon the sea. Renew thine image upon our souls by thy Holy Spirit, that thy good pleasure to do us good in all things, may proceed without obstacle. Let the supplications of those who love thy salvation in Christ Jesus, prevail above the curses and imprecations uttered by the ungodly upon man and beast. God be merciful unto us, and bless us; cause thy face to shine upon us, and we shall be saved. Amen!"

We have no details of his active engagements, either in the State Assembly or in the Consistory, beyond two extracts of letters; the one addressed to Jerem. Fredr. Reuss, then at Rendsburg, the other to prelate Weissensee, of Denkendorf. These, however, are sufficient to show with what *sort* of business he was then occupied; and a passage from his own memoir of himself discovers the spirit in which he attended to it.

"With my increasing years and engagements, I feel increasing need of help from the Divine mercy; therefore I earnestly desire the intercessions of those who love the salvation of God, and particularly do I crave yours, my dear respected relative. God do with me according to his own good pleasure, and supply my lack of service by more able and active labourers. Many and various matters come before us in the Consistory; and, though under a catholic prince, we in some respects have even a larger share of liberty. In the Consistory we fill up vacancies in the christian ministry, appoint masters to the various schools, see to the supplying of curacies, hold examinations of divinity students, and Whitsuntide examinations, and promote pupils from one class to another in the Theological institutions. These seminaries, the University College at Tübingen, as well as establishments ecclesiastical and charitable, demand constant inspection; and we have to keep up friendly communication and correspondence with foreign churches, universities, &c. We have also to deliver reports from time to time to the civil department of government, upon miscellaneous causes and matrimonial cases. The Consistory, and the four general superintendents, constitute the synod; and these superintendents act as its commissioners during every recess. There is also business to be transacted with the university at the visitation seasons; and, besides what comes before us at our consistorial sessions, we have daily occasions for communicating, personally and by writing, with parochial ministers, candidates of theology,* and others."

To Weissensee.

" *March* 31, 1750.

" Were I the mighty man which you, and probably you alone, take me to be, I should be for making far greater demands upon myself than I now can do. My deep sense, however, of my own weakness, brings this comfort with it, that I can enjoy my present situation with an indulgent conscience, as I did not come into it by any ambition of my own. When it requires me to give my sentiments, I speak as conscience dictates, and having done this, I have only to look on, and see what God is pleased to effect. Such is my privilege, and I make use of it. But you, my happy, aged friend, who are got so near to the desired haven, are enjoying the comfort of your agreeable retirement, though still obliged to acknowledge that the waves of this polluted and polluting world will sometimes beat over your cloister walls upon your youthful charge, preserved and separated as they are by such an excellent enclosure. I too, at Herbrechtingen, had thought to have escaped from the world for ever; whereas now you see me transplanted even to Stuttgart, where I find myself more deeply rooted than ever in a morass of secular obligations; for, in my declining years, I have to commence a sort of noviciate in temporal things, after I have already spent so large a part of my life in those which were chiefly spiritual."

In the sketch of his own memoirs, which we have already several times referred to, he says:—

" Habitual self-renunciation made every change of employment easy to me, which would otherwise have been quite difficult and irksome; but my settled object all along was to assert and promote the honour and glory of God. Towards my sovereign I ever desired to carry the mind and disposition of an obliged and grateful subject, a faithful adviser, and conscientious, diligent member of the State Assembly of my beloved country. Towards superiors I conducted myself as an inferior; and towards

* A candidate of theology is what we should term in England *an unbeneficed clergyman.*

equals I endeavoured to act as proportionately to our equality as I knew how; while I considered inferiors as those for whose sake persons above them ought to lay themselves out. I have regarded myself, in these three relative conditions, as ever in duty bound to promote good, and to diminish evil, according to the best of my ability; and, provided such ends were attained, I never cared who was the instrument."

But notwithstanding his many occupations at Stuttgart, he still exercised there a kind of pastoral ministry to what may be called a little private church. For, as he had to reside there at stated times, for attendance at the Synod and Diet, before he removed thither as an inhabitant, he held private meetings for edification in his Stuttgart abode, and found in that city, persons, among both the sick and well, who thirsted for the truth of the gospel. To these, therefore, while yet prelate of Herbrechtingen, he began gladly and willingly to impart instruction, exhortation, and comfort, from his own abundant christian knowledge and experience. A letter which he wrote to colonel Franke, at that period, may here be suitably introduced; in which he says—" I am drawn out, for the first time, from my long retired habits, into a much engaged and stirring kind of life. Just lately I have had to reside in Stuttgart for several weeks, and next week I must be there again, besides what I have afterwards to do, if I live and am well. All such avocations, while they open to us more and more of the vanity of the world, ought proportionately to confirm us in closely following the Lord Jesus Christ, who once passed through this same world in a manner so worthy of himself, and so well pleasing to his heavenly Father. During my visits at Stuttgart, I have met with not a few who diligently seek Him that seeth in secret, and who abide patiently upon *Him*, notwithstanding all secular interruptions and discouragements; and I was particularly delighted, not only with what I had heard of His Serene Highness the Prince of Mecklenburg, but indeed with what I have found him to be; for at Stetten I enjoyed the long desired pleasure of conversing with him. This prince honours THE LORD, and THE LORD will honour *him;* and will lead him to true *exaltation* by the way of true *humility*.

APPENDIX.

Some Letters written by Bengel as an Ecclesiastical Representative.

Having in the year 1747 been consulted respecting a young man who had gone over to the Roman Catholic communion, he replied:—

"*Stuttgart, June* 25, 1747.

"I shall be glad if my advice or endeavours can be of any service in the matter, upon which you have kindly written to me. The young man you speak of is, of course, not to be the subject of any compulsory measures, but we must seek to bring home the truth to his heart; all other expedients will be of no use. It might, therefore, benefit him to receive, from some one who has influence with him, a letter, written after earnest prayer for divine direction, to the following effect:—'Your case, my dear friend, is not singular. Others have been misled in the same way as yourself. The arguments and motives which have determined you to this resolution, are not your own, but have been suggested to you by others. Whether it was in conversation, correspondence, or study, that you have been thus influenced, is of no importance; but it is certain, that you have not a true idea either of Popery or Protestantism, but will in eternity, if not (as I heartily hope you may) before, be convinced, at what a wrong conclusion you have arrived. What was there in all the aspersions that have been thrown out against Luther, whom you will see, notwithstanding, in the great day, at the right hand of the Judge of all, to the utter confusion of his cruel revilers; what was there in all such aspersions, to hinder yourself from making the best use of the saving grace of God in Christ Jesus, apart from every human invention? or what was there in them to prevent yourself from living amongst us according to the gospel? Take heed what you are doing; for you have to give an account to God: and in warning you, I have done my duty. Remember that 'there is a way which seemeth right unto (many) a man, but the end thereof are the ways of death.' My wish for you is, that you may find the way of life; and this is to be found, not in following any particular party, but in the word of truth.'—Such is the manner in which I should endeavour to reason with him. May God give counsel and understanding; and vouchsafe his mercy to this mistaken person."

From the Count Erdman Henry von Henkel, to Bengel.

"*Pölzig, January* 12, 1750.

"Reverend and dear Sir,

"I would assure you in few words how often and how much I have been really edified by the recollection of my first happy acquaintance with you at Stuttgart, which took place as long ago as the year 1727, in the palace of Her Serene Highness the Duchess of Würtemberg. It is a recollection which has been kept alive by every thing I have often read and heard of you from time to time. I have now taken the liberty of applying to you for information, which I should be glad to get as early as possible, respecting the Rev. Mr. Storr,* one of the assistant ministers of St. Leonard's, in Stuttgart. I am satisfied as to his christian piety, but I want to know whether he is competent, in learning and talents, for the professorship of divinity now vacant at Halle, by the decease of Dr. Clauswitzen. The party adverse to real Christianity in that once highly favoured nursery of so much unspeakable good, has been of late plotting decidedly against her best interests, so that there is reason to fear lest the professorship should be preoccupied by one who, instead of caring for the cause of God or the extension of his kingdom, will use every exertion to hinder and subvert it. Of all the residents there is not one whom we can think of proposing to this office. Those who are most pious, and preach the gospel in power and purity, (and God be thanked, there still are some at Halle who do so,) have either not sufficient learning and experience, or not every requisite talent, neither are they sufficiently popular. As for the more learned of that place, they are so conceited of their turgid philosophy and rationalistic teaching, that they can regard little else as of any value. In plain opposition to the method of St. Paul, and of the other faithful servants of God, they are preaching themselves and not Christ, certainly not in the power of the gospel. Indeed they are almost unwilling to mention his name; they publicly profess the wisdom of this world, and of the princes of this world, which is foolishness with God, instead of the 'wisdom of God in a mystery.' Some hold principles, if not atheistical, certainly of naturalism and deism. Such principles they are not ashamed to avow in their public lectures, and with the younger part of their audience they gain much popularity in that way. Serious as is the want of worthy and pious subjects

* Father of Dr. Gottlob Christian Storr, afterwards senior chaplain to the Court of Würtemberg.

of His Majesty in such a place and in so important a station, the enemies of the truth are endeavouring further to avail themselves of it, for aiming, in any direction they can, a fatal thrust at this our favoured university; by introducing into it, and recommending to the king's notice, either some person tainted with the Wittenberg heresy, or some fine talking rationalist; indeed they are even procuring them from other universities. Of these unwelcome strangers is one Dr. Chladenius from Erlangen, a bitter adversary to the truth, who lately almost obtained the best prospect of holding this vacant professorship, through the active influence of his patron the university curator; but as the latter died suddenly a few weeks since, and as the new curator is a more enlightened man, the way at present appears still open for another competitor; and as secret advice has come from Berlin that a candidate of the Würtemberg school should be proposed, this, Rev. Sir, is the occasion of my applying to you respecting Mr. Storr. Knowing that you have at heart the cause of God our Father, and of His Son Jesus Christ, I am confident that as you are ready to lend it any help you can, you will consequently assist us towards securing the worthy object we have here in view.

" With sincere wishes that the Lord, even our own God, may crown with his unspeakable blessing, all your endeavours in your new situation, even as he has prospered all your former labours,

" I remain, &c."

BENGEL'S REPLY.

To the Right Hon. Erdmann Henry von Henkel, Count of the Empire.

" Most honoured Sir,

" Your obliging letter reached me yesterday, but up to the present moment I have been unable to command leisure for giving it such a reply as it immediately requires. Your Excellency's remembrance of me for more than twenty years, the kindness with which you assure me of it, and your pious wishes for me in my new situation, cannot but affect me in the most gratifying manner. For my own humble part I can add, that my high esteem of and sincere attachment to your Excellency have ever continued undiminished.

" Such a professorship, and at Halle, is indeed of no small importance, and may God make the succession to it an instance of his peculiar favour!—I am very happy to give you my sentiments respecting Mr. Storr. Though I am not aware that he even looked forward to a divinity professorship, or that others ever thought of it for him, I certainly consider him admissible to such an office. He is a man of spiritual wisdom and understanding; intrepidly zealous for the honour of God; and so meek and gentle that he may well gain every one's heart. He has a penetrating and judicious mind, betraying no strained labour of thought or display in reasoning; and with a clear and easy delivery he has also a dignified, temperate, and pleasant manner. At first hearing him, perhaps, we should think him better fitted for the pulpit than for a professor's chair; but what he may want in reading and controversial divinity, he could easily acquire at such a place as Halle, so as to come up to the standard of its very best divines; for he is a well-grounded theologian, and in such a situation he would have the assistance of colleagues, so as to be able meanwhile to make himself familiar with all essential matters, as occasion shall require. He has never printed any thing, except his well-known funeral sermon, and a preface to Arndt's "True Christianity;" but he is preparing for the press a collection of sermons for the poorer classes. He was assistant minister at St. Leonard's, only for a short time; but has since, for six years, been chaplain to the Court. Last year he received a call to Frankfort on the Maine, which he declined by the advice of superiors, who have a particular hope and object for him here at Stuttgart. Freely as I have thus spoken of his real qualifications, in dutiful compliance with your Excellency's inquiries, my official responsibility obliges me, with equal frankness, to say how necessary it appears that we should keep him, if possible, here with *us;* upon which I am persuaded your Excellency will agree with me, if I only state to you the circumstances of this place. Here he has easy access and considerable influence amongst high and low, strangers and natives; and the extraordinary number of persons who crowd to hear him, may be considered as one sign that he is made manifest in men's consciences. His removal too from us would be a heavy demand upon his own family feelings, as he is going to be married to the only daughter of a Würtemberg councillor, residing at Esslingen, though I know he is no slave to such considerations. I am not aware of any other circumstance adverse to your proposing him.

"It might do no harm to send his name to Berlin, if it be so managed, that any proposal coming from that quarter to himself may be rather as to whether he would like such a situation, than as a formal call to it. And should his Stuttgart people not consent to part with him, his having been invited away will only quicken their attachment to him, and thus help to increase his influence and usefulness among them more than ever; but if they *can* give him up, I too shall be willing to surrender him to our beloved university of Halle.

"May God from the fulness of his grace in Christ continue to bless your Excellency; and whereas there are in these days so few who are seeking his kingdom in the truth, may you be only the more abundantly invested with righteousness, peace, and joy in the Holy Ghost, &c."

In the year 1750, the Consistory of Würtemberg deliberated upon preparing a new Compendium of divinity, more adapted to the present state of knowledge and to the academical lectures, than that of Dr. John Wolfgang Jäger, published in 1702, which had been hitherto made use of. One member, whose choice was approved by a considerable number of others present, observed, that Professor Israel Gottlieb Canz had attempted to supply this want, by publishing his "Compendium Theologiæ purioris," &c. But several of the Tübingen professors objected to this work, as having been put forth for general adoption without due consultation of the Consistory. This induced the chancellor Pfaff to write to Bengel as follows:—

" (*Tübingen,*) *September* 10, 1752.

"Dr. Canz's Compendium has lately appeared amongst us without having been submitted to the censorship of our university; and I cannot conclude that it has been submitted to, much less approved of by, the Consistory, because I find in it passages quite at variance with the doctrines of our Church. Such passages, had he communicated his manuscript to me, I should certainly have requested him to omit; but I also find in it omissions of many things which surely ought not to be omitted.——Dr. Canz cannot but know that I am his very good friend; but his propensity to obtrude *philosophic* reasonings upon christian theology, has always displeased me. I write this with no improper feeling, but sincerely wish that some divine, who has more tact and knowledge for it, would compose a suitable compendium. Even if our opponents should not some day endeavour to bear us down with affronting *quotations* from such books as his, our giving the least countenance to them will amount to a departure from the Augsburg Confession, and consequently to a forfeiture of our privileges of the peace of Westphalia."

Bengel answered.

" *Stuttgart, September* 19, 1752.

" Honoured Sir,

" In order to return you a proper reply respecting Canz's Compendium, I had an interview with the president of the Consistory, and with privy-councillor Von Zech; from which I have to state, that the book has not undergone the censorship of the Consistory, nor do they or the other authorities here, intend to give it their sanction. Their wish simply was, to have a compendium more suitable to enlarged and scriptural research; and the Consistory will feel obliged by your privately communicating this their wish to the rev. author. Their president intends to be at Tübingen in a few days, so that you will then have a good opportunity of proposing to him whatever may appear desirable upon the subject."

A friend having written to Bengel concerning some attempts made to effect a union between the Reformed and Lutheran churches, he replied:—

" *January* 9, 1722.

" With regard to the arguments, alleged on either side, respecting this politico-ecclesiastical union, (for I can think it nothing better,) I do not trouble myself about them. The publications which I have seen respecting it, appear rarely to proceed from minds of a heavenly mould. Were St. Paul himself now to descend from paradise, upon a mission to Protestant Christendom, he would find far other work to accomplish than that of civil coalescence between Lutherans and Calvinists. Yet this is the best that such a union would amount to, were it ever so compact; for how can the unity of the Spirit be wrought out among so many, while so few of them *have* the Spirit? The division itself I regard as a severe fatherly rebuke upon us, which may therefore not be without its beneficial effects. For whereas we Lutherans reject the notion of absolute, unconditional decrees, we as it were constrain its advocates to hold out representations more moderate, and more conducive to their own practical and experimental piety; but, on the other hand, if ever the doctrine of decrees in general shall fall into disregard amongst ourselves, the majority of us will decline into what is no better than mere rationalism, having by and by lost all belief in God's universal grace.*

* For other letters, which have some relation to things touched upon in this chapter, see "His Observations upon the Church of the United Brethren," chap. xv. Part III. of this volume.

Part III.

HIS LITERARY WORKS.

CHAPTER I.

INTRODUCTION.—HIS OWN ACCOUNT OF THE PRINCIPLES HE OBSERVED AS A WRITER.

Bengel wrote much, and to the purpose; for besides his *new editions* (which, in most respects, were very improved ones) of various ancient authors, we have about thirty *original* publications of his own. These are also of considerable bulk, notwithstanding his remarkable habit of condensing, which was not so peculiar to the writers of his day. His works contain a great variety of extensive and elaborate research, in several important departments of knowledge; namely, classical and biblical philology, exegesis, criticism, chronology, and divinity doctrinal and practical. Yet he was never a professed author; that is, he "never was induced, by confidence in his talents and acquirements, to choose any literary ground for trial of strength or display of sentiments;" but every occasion of what he prepared for the press was imperative. These occasions arose out of his official requirements; the subjects he wrote upon "presented themselves legitimately all along in his way of duty as a tutor; and if he further considered and studied them at his leisure, it was in the hope of getting more knowledge of the truth, and of being more invariably directed by it." For after having given attention to any subject, he did not feel obliged to content himself just with what was absolutely called for in his work of tuition; but continued his inquiries from a sincere desire for the advancement of sound knowledge, especially of scriptural divinity.

He used to say, that "we ought to be very careful about composing new books," for that "every book should add something to the reader's information, or at least to the improvement of his heart; but how many do neither!" That "every book ought to contain something original; and whoever has nothing of the kind to impart, ought not to write. Yet how many publications are there in which we find not a single new observation!—I have often prayed, and do pray to this day, that God would keep me from useless labour; and I see that all along he has so carried me through my various and difficult employments, that were I to begin them over again, I could not despatch them in less time than I have done. As it is wrong not to undertake the employments for which God has best fitted us, it is equally so to seek by them our own gratification, instead of the public good. It has long been my rule to write nothing which, at my dying hour, I might have to repent of: but to adhere to such a rule one must cut off, as it were, the right hand, and pluck out the right eye! For many of our thoughts charm us, when they are first conceived; O yes, and if we preserve them, they will please others also; and yet it may be our duty to discard them."

By adherence to such principles he aimed at securing himself against two faults very common to writers; that of venturing upon a work manifestly without a call, because without proper ability, or with no better motive than vanity; and that of deficient respect for the public, in sending out a work unentitled to their notice, because containing what they knew before.

The conscientiousness with which he never forgot his resolution of meeting the exigencies of his pupils at every stage of their progress, preserved him from a fault too truly alleged against many writers; that they abuse the learner's industry with superficial matters, such as they could sweep together just before delivering each lecture, and which have very little to do with the deep and difficult inquiries they had professed to set out with.

When he had completed any work, he was never in haste to put it to the press, but reserved several for ten or twenty years together; for he said, "should it turn out to be his duty entirely to withhold what had required so much time and labour, still it would be no loss to the public: and as to himself, though his works might eventually be useful to others, their chief advantage was often the regular and sober employment of his own mind in composing them. That learned men when they have once set their faculties in motion, are very liable to waste the strength of them upon empty and fanciful speculations; therefore all intellectual labour ought to be according to the strictest order and method, and not to spend itself like a mill running on when the meal is out." Hence, before he published any work, he considered it on all sides, " especially how it was likely to meet those who were entire strangers to the subject;" and it was always his rule " to submit every such work in manuscript to the critical inspection of superiors and persons in ecclesiastical authority; inviting them to make alterations wherever they could shew him better." With this view he also held extensive correspondence upon a variety of subjects with private individuals; and said, " I am glad to be able to avail myself of the counsel and assistance of kind friends, besides what is afforded me by some in their public capacity, who have to revise my books officially. Experience has taught me that such helps tend to make my way open and easy. I meet with obliging and reasonable censors; and if in one place and another, of my writings, something requires alteration, what harm is it? There is plenty of occasion for the omitted matters to be brought forward in a better way at some other time; and if there were not, I have the comfort of remembering that nothing was begun or completed in my own will; so that I may the more surely expect the divine blessing upon what I have given to the public. It is often one reason why men of learning commit such great blunders in their writings, that before publication they do not communicate upon them with others. Is it not more agreeable to come to a good understanding upon any subject, by putting this confidence in one another, than by and by to have people debating point after point in reviews or at one's elbow?"

He felt abundant reason for his being so indefatigably diligent as a writer; and remarked, that " though it is unnecessary to be always making books, even upon good subjects, yet as so many are published only for vain and sinful entertainment, whose rapid sale evinces how ungodly are the generality of us, though we bear the name of Christians; while, for instance, there is many a play which can hardly be printed fast enough, as if people were not as responsible to God for time spent in reading as for time spent in other employments: therefore it is the duty of those who seek His honour and glory, if they have the means of providing sound nurture for precious and immortal souls, to be always on the watch to introduce something of a valuable and wholesome kind, that such pernicious trash may not take up all the room in God's world; but that some relish for his saving word may be preserved, at least among a few. And as ' the wise and prudent' are generally so refined or overcautious, as not easily to incline to, or at least not to venture upon any such undertaking, therefore God, who sees it necessary that something good should be given to the world, gives it by the ministration of comparative 'babes.' As for myself, I can say that I have endeavoured from time to time to keep in the back ground; for it would have been far more agreeable to my natural feelings to have passed along through this life without noise or notice. But it has happened otherwise."

"When a man begins to have his name cried up in the world, he becomes subject to a new set of feelings which are unknown to others. His sensations may be compared to those of a criminal in the pillory, especially if, as an author, he is mightily basted by opponents. The most painful of such feelings arises from being not only disparaged by men of the world, but even suspected by those who are really spiritual; so as to be dreaded among them as dangerously unsound. This is indeed heart-grieving; and it is well to be conscious, upon such occasions, that countenance from fallible men was not the thing we had reckoned upon; and to be able to say, 'All is under God's direction;' I will therefore 'be of good cheer,' and 'in patience possess my soul.'"

CHAPTER II.

HIS NEW EDITIONS OF SOME CLASSICAL WORKS, AND GREEK FATHERS.

1. The earliest of his larger publications was a new edition of Cicero's Epistles. These were connected with his official tuition. They had been appointed by the Cynosura Ecclesiastica,* to be used by the lower Theological Seminary, for its instruction in Latin. His undertaking this new edition, originated in his own preparatory studies for lectures upon that work; during which he gradually amassed a quantity of expository and critical annotations. These happening to meet the prelate's eye at his visitation of the Seminary, pleased him so much, that he encouraged Bengel to continue them, so as to get up a new edition for the use of the pupils. Thus as he could not well decline such an undertaking, he set about it. His principle was, "I must work while it is day; I do what my hand findeth to do, without much caring what it is, provided my eye and heart are aiming at what is best in the end. And then, though the *what*, the *how*, the *why*, the *wherefore*, or the *whereunto*, may be all along unknown to me, God knoweth how to turn all to his own holy purposes. 'Only be faithful,' is my motto; even if it concern but a jot or tittle. Indeed some of the most important exegetical discoveries, or their still more important results, are made by conscientiously attending to apparent minutiæ. One day's feeble work of ours may be as much with God as that of a thousand years; so greatly to our account can he make all things turn, provided we honour him by aiming always at his glory."

Such views served to make him patient and faithful. Hence he cheerfully bestowed the minutest requisite carefulness, upon disquisitions the most trifling in appearance; and though this often exacted of him the severest labour of mind and body, he never spared himself; but would say, "I feel the effects of my critical laboriousness, especially of the intense application I have found necessary for adjusting my chronological calculations. Yet

* "The Directory (or Book) of Ecclesiastical Order."

where is the harm if one of us wear out himself a little, provided it is not done wantonly or wilfully? Though ever so great a personage has fallen in battle, people generally remark that he did not fall *in vain.*'

In the year 1719 appeared the fruit of his six years' studious occupations, entitled,

"M. Tullii Ciceronis Epistolæ ad diversos, vulgò *Familiares;* recognitæ, et iis instructæ rebus quæ ad Interpretationem, Imitationemque pertinent: operâ Johannis Alberti Bengelii: Stuttgardiæ sumtu Jo. Benedicti Mezleri."

This work was in no respect a mere reprint of preceding editions, though he carefully availed himself of whatever he could find in them to enrich his text and annotations. But he every where wrought his materials over afresh, with the diligence of an independent mind. In his Appendix to the work (pp. 735—762), he gives an account of the pains he had taken for obtaining a correct text; and here appears at once the future great critic upon the New Testament. Many peculiar excellencies of this edition were owing to his having always kept his eye upon the wants of his pupils. He added to it a couple of neat maps, one of Italy and Gaul with part of Britain, the other of Greece and Asia Minor; with several carefully prepared indexes, the first giving a very accurate account of the occasion and time of Cicero's writing each letter; the second was an index of proper names, with references to where they occur; the third was lexicographical, exhibiting the *copia verborum* of the work; and the fourth was an arrangement of the epistles according to their subjects, showing how to use them as valuable specimens of very various epistolary composition. Appended was a dissertation upon the advantages of studying this classical work, and how to make the best use of the present edition; first, for a thorough understanding of the text, and then for imitation of the writer. It, therefore, particularly explained the use to be made of the summaries of contents prefixed to each epistle, and of the notes subjoined at the end of the latter; as also how to use the different indexes; and showed the method to be observed by tutor and pupils before lecture, as well as during and after it, for gaining all the advantages which this book can furnish to beginners in Latin, in history, and in rhetoric. So that there are few editions of any classic author, which, without at all favouring indolence, supply such real helps for well comprehending every bearing of the text. He closes the work with observations quite characteristic of himself. Having done his best to render it useful, valuable, and pleasing to his pupils, he thinks it right to add a few words of warning with this inscription, "*ne quid nimis*" ("take heed of excess.") Here, therefore, he exhibits the possible dangers of philological study to personal Christianity; and, among other things, remarks, that "there is no bodily or mental labour which may not be made injurious to our secret and perpetual communion with God. Even scriptural researches may, without needful discretion, very easily occasion in learned men an indifference to true godliness, instead of nourishing any desire for it, or delight in it. As mere 'knowledge' of every kind 'puffeth up,' so human ideas are apt to captivate human beings, and thus to check in the heart all easy and favourable germination, growth and influence of divine truth. This is seen in those who are devoted to science and literature. Hence Mercury (the interpreter,) is as much opposed to Christ, as is Plutus or Mammon; for such a fascinating ascendant does mere learning hold sometimes over men, that hereby they lose all relish for the salutary truths of the gospel. That this should be the case with excessive lovers of classical literature, is not to be wondered at; for the spirit of heathen wisdom ever was, and ever must be, a spirit of presumption, vanity, worldliness, selfishness, and sensuality; and yet there is in it something uncommonly catching and infectious to those intellectual persons, who are not established in spiritual religion. This flattering and dangerous influence of classical philology is strikingly described by Erasmus in his 'Ciceronian Dialogues,' and by E. Leuchner, in the fifth chapter of his 'Gymnasiosophy.' On the whole, then, it is absolutely necessary that the student should prepare himself for every pursuit, of this sort especially, with serious heartfelt desire, and admiring reverence of, that wisdom which is from above; and should be particular about 'keeping his heart' in such a state, 'with all diligence,' from day to day. He, who is thus minded, will be competent, as to whatever comes in his way, to attend to it with faithfulness, sobriety, and good effect; for the pernicious parts of his reading will then not injure him; and the good will be of more than ordinary benefit to him; he will also derive many an advantage from classical writers, which the writers themselves never contemplated. By such easy and agreeable study he will also contract those habits of attention, observation, accuracy, and perseverance, which will be of excellent use to him when he engages in studies of a less interesting and alluring form. He will have acquired likewise a readiness in Latin expression, so as to have no need to envy the most elegant Latin scholars; and, above all, he will become daily more desirous and susceptible of divine things, as by following these advices, he never loses his relish for the majestic and all-commanding simplicity of revealed truth."

After thus editing Cicero's Letters, he completed a translation of them into German. This also he had intended, with Weissensee's assistance, to have published;* but was prevented by having now undertaken works of a more extensive kind, and more intimately connected with the cause of Christ. He had also, during the earlier part of his residence at the seminary, collected materials for a new edition of Ovid's *Tristia* (chiefly after the Verpoortinian edition,) and upon the same plan as that of his Cicero's Epistles; likewise materials for a similar edition of Persius; but neither of these were ever published.

2. The next work he edited was Gregory's Panegyric upon Origen.† This too was occasioned by the necessities of his pupils; for they had to read some father of the church, as an accompaniment to the study of the Greek Testament; and he selected the above work, with the consent of the directors of the Institution: "first, because Gregory has there shown, by his own example, that a youth of an inquiring spirit can find no true and solid satisfaction in all the heathen philosophical systems, many as may be their advantages and claims of interest to those who study them for other purposes; but is compelled, by a sense of his own needs and necessities, to seek refuge in the substantial truths of Christianity.—Secondly, because the 'Panegyric' contains verities of the highest importance, which, as most fully

* "After completing," he said, "my researches among the classics and the fathers, my next undertaking was the New Testament. Daily relish for the sweet language of divine inspiration had now superseded with me that of all other dainties, though I was not insensible of their charms."—It was in the very midst of his classical occupations, in the year 1717, that he wrote to a friend,—"I have more need to be stirred up by you, than you by me; for I often find my (spiritual) strength at a very low ebb among these dead heathen (classics.) But my toil becomes lighter every day, and the Divine wisdom has hitherto so preserved me, while busied in these little things, that in the main I get no harm. Neither among my young flock have I frittered away my *jus postliminii* (*i. e.* I have not become estranged from beloved theology by my duties as a classical tutor;) indeed, I hope soon to have the privilege of pasturing less interruptedly among gratifications more solid and substantial."

† Bengel's title of this work runs thus:—"Gregorii Thaumaturgi Panegyricus ad Originem, Græcè et Latinè; et omnibus qui sapientiam, ut illi, Christianam, vel cum linguâ Græcâ, vel etiam citra eam docent, discunt, et colunt, eo accommodatus instituto, cujus ratio in prooemio explanatur; operâ Jo. Alberti Bengelii: Stuttgardiæ, sumtu Jo. Bened. Mezleri, 1722."

responding to the soul's inquiries, far surpass all others in moral efficacy.—And, thirdly, because it is here demonstrated what great care is needful for any thing like sound scriptural exposition, and that those only can become good expositors, who have the eyes of their understanding enlightened by the Spirit of God."

Thus did the present work afford Bengel a valuable opportunity of impressing upon his scholars, the decided superiority which that holy faith they were destined to preach, holds over every human system; because the latter, being but inventions of blinded natural reason, are as destitute of the most needful kind of truth, and still more, of all completeness in the same, as they are of all satisfactory credentials: whereas, the very opposite is true of the system of Holy Writ; as, the more deeply its fundamental verities are inquired into, the more richly and abundantly do they reward our diligence.

He followed the example of former editors in furnishing the Greek text with a Latin translation; and gave an appendix of appropriate notes from G. Vossius, Is. Casaubon, D. Hœschelius, and L. Rhodomannus, with many original notes of his own.*

3. From the following extract of a letter to Weissensee we learn, that, as early as the year 1715, Bengel had thoughts of publishing, for the use of his pupils in the Theological seminary, a new edition of Chrysostom's Treatise in six books " Upon the Priesthood."

" *Denkendorf, Aug.* 15, 1715.

" I find it will be useful, when I have gone through the Greek Testament with my students, to connect with it some other author, as a lecture book; and, with my present class, Chrysostom's seven select Homilies, printed at Tübingen in 1709, with a preface by J. M. Jäger, appear to me very suitable for the purpose. I think, however, that that ancient and eminent father's noble and concise work, 'De Sacerdotio,' would do still better, as being rich in elegancy of words and phrases, much commended by writers ancient and modern, and decidedly the best production of his pen. I prefer it as especially excellent upon the pastoral office; and it may make upon my young people an early

*Buddeus expresses his opinion of this work, in his " Isagoge," p. 109, as follows:— " Quæ editio ut summo studio adornata, ita, et ob notas variorum selectas, ac complures novas, imprimis est commendanda."—(*i. e.* " This edition merits the highest commendation, as well for the beauty, and most critical accuracy of the text and version, as for its judicious selection of notes from various commentators, combined with many new ones of its own."

and deep impression of the sanctity and vast importance of that ministry for which they are designed. I even think of preparing a Greek and Latin edition of it, with annotations and indexes, and have collected a variety of materials towards it, for it is more than a century since it was printed in Germany. Meanwhile I must wait for the appearance of Montfaucon's promised edition of the whole of Chrysostom's works."

This last observation shows why his own publication was so long delayed. Though the first volume of Montfaucon's edition came out in 1718, and contained the treatise "On the Priesthood," yet Bengel's inquiries for it at Strasburg, and among various booksellers in Germany, were unavailing. He was therefore obliged at last (this was in 1724) to apply to Bernard de Montfaucon himself, who had the kindness immediately to send him the treatise in a set of proof sheets; (as a whole first volume could not well be separated from the rest, and to purchase all the volumes would have been too expensive for Bengel.) The delay, however, gave him opportunity of carefully collating the preceding editions, and for availing himself of some valuable manuscripts which had not been noticed in them.* The form of this edition resembles that of his "Gregory:" containing the revised Greek text, and the Latin version at one view, on opposite pages. The notes are at the end, and consist of a compressed selection of the best remarks of preceding commentators; many new notes of his own; and some of the best thoughts of the best writers on pastoral theology. In all which appendages he endeavoured to confine himself to what was most absolutely requisite; as it was one of his rules for editing an ancient author, that we are not to act as architects, who plan, perfect, and accomplish their own original ideas; but like some tasteful and diligent gardener, who sets off the native and appropriate beauties of a spot of ground in their simplest and most attractive form. To this work he also annexed an interesting tract, entitled, "Prodromus, N. T., &c.," which we shall have to notice in the following chapter.

* His work is entitled, "Joannis Chrysostomi de Sacerdotiô libri sex, Græcè et Latinè, utrinque recogniti et notis indicibusque aucti, eo maximè consilio, ut cœnobiorum Wirtembergicorum alumni, et cæteri, qui N. T. Græco imbuti sunt, ad scriptores ecclesiasticos suavi gustu invitentur, facilique methodo præparentur. Accedit Prodromus Novi Testamenti Græci rectè cautèque adornandi: operâ Jo. Alberti Bengelii: Stuttgardiæ, apud J. B. Mezlerum et C. Erhardum, 1725."—In the year 1825 there appeared (as if for a memorial of the value of this edition, after a hundred years,) a beautiful stereotype impression of its Greek text, published by Charles Tauchnitz, [of Leipsic.]

Moreover, he wrote " Annotations upon Macarius," whose Greek text, with its Latin version, he improved in various important passages, and elucidated upon many points of philology and divinity. These annotations Dr. Pritius had intended to insert in an improved edition of his favourite Macarius, which his death prevented him from completing, so that it never was published. Lastly, Bengel wrote, " Annotations to Ephrem Syrus," which were left in the same condition.

CHAPTER III.

HIS CRITICISM OF THE GREEK TESTAMENT.

Section I.

*SOME ACCOUNT OF GREEK TESTAMENT CRITICISM TO BENGEL'S TIME.**

In order to do him justice as a critic in this department, it is but right to take a brief review of what had been done before him. The earliest printed Greek Testament was that of the celebrated Aldus of Venice, who, in 1504, sent from the press the first six principal sections of St. John's Gospel. It was not till 1516, the year before that from which we usually date the commencement of the Reformation, that any thing like the entire Greek Testament was printed. But in that year the first edition of the kind was published by Erasmus, partly from MSS. which he had met with at Bâsle, and partly from collations of the Latin version. Its rapid sale multiplied it to four quickly succeeding editions; in each of which he still availed himself of fresh MSS., though he seldom furnishes any particular references to them.

In 1525 the Alcala Bible, (Biblia Complutensia,) which had been completed under the superintendence of Cardinal Ximenes, received the Pope's *imprimatur*. This edition contains the advantages of the Vatican MSS., with those of a codex Rhodiensis, and doubtless of such MSS. as were then discoverable in Spain.

Robert Stephens (Stephanus,) made it his object to combine the excellencies of these two principal editions, and of others less noted, (as of Asulanus's Venice edition of 1518), with his own collations from MSS. in the Royal Library of Paris. Thus

* In this and the ensuing sections we follow, principally, his own historical account of New Testament Criticism in his "Apparatus Criticus," and Dr. J. Leonard Hug's "Introduction to the Scriptures of the New Testament," vol. i. p. 54, &c.

he published his first edition in 1546; a second in 1549; and a third in 1551; to which his son added another in 1569.

Theodore Beza, the celebrated scholar of Calvin, prepared, about the middle of the sixteenth century, a fourth *principal* edition of the New Testament. He availed himself of all preceding editions; likewise of MS. materials in the Stephens' family; and moreover, by the favour of Queen Elizabeth, he obtained the benefit of a fine collection of MSS. treasured in England. Thus was his work valuable as containing the advantages of all MSS. hitherto discovered in Italy, Spain, France, Switzerland, and Britain. His first edition was published at Geneva in 1555, from the press of Henry Stephens, and was repeated in 1576. A third appeared in 1582, a fourth in 1589, and a fifth in 1598. Numerous impressions of Beza's text, occasionally altered by that of Robert Stephens's own third edition of 1551, came out after the year 1624, from the offices of those eminent Dutch publishers the Elzevirs and the Wetsteins; and were most favourably received on account of their typographical beauty and convenience, as also of the Latin versions annexed, chiefly that of Arias Montanus. By such means did these gentlemen contrive to give no ordinary measure of credence to an opinion which had been very confidently put forth by themselves, that theirs was the generally received text. All this, however, was insufficient to discourage several learned Englishmen from commencing a deeper research in New Testament criticism, which in the course of time shewed Beza's editions to be less and less satisfactory. Our new laborious critics were, first Brian Walton, then Dr. John Fell, and afterwards John Mill. Walton, who was the leading editor of the London Polyglott, published in 1657 the fifth volume of this great work, which contains the Greek text of the New Testament after Stephens's third edition, with the various readings of the famous Alexandrian manuscript. Fell sent forth a new edition of the Greek Testament in 1675, in which he not only availed himself of all preceding criticisms, but gave the results of collations of very many additional MSS. then newly discovered in England, Ireland, France and Italy; together with the various readings of the Coptic and Gothic versions. Still more extensive and meritorious was the thirty years' labour of his scholar John Mill, who collated over again nearly all the MSS. then known in England, and got collated for him on the continent a very considerable number of others, some of which had never yet been consulted. He was also the first to discover settled principles for this department of criticism, and to make use of them with advantage. His Greek Testament was printed at Oxford in 1707, (the last year of Bengel's studentship at the University,) and another edition of it at Amsterdam, in 1710. This latter was superintended by Ludolph Küster, a German, born in 1670, at Blumberg, in the earldom of Lippe; was enriched with additional collations from Paris manuscripts; and was reprinted at Leipsic in 1723.

The firm of Wetstein and Smith at Amsterdam, wishing not to be outdone by their English rivals, had printed, in 1711, a new and carefully corrected copy of the Elzevir edition,; which was meant to have some recommendation of novelty from the various readings it contained of a Vienna MS. together with the forty-three critical canons of Gerard von Mastricht. But these new canons of Greek Testament criticism, which Bengel, in 1713, had become acquainted with at Heidelberg, were far from satisfactory to his inquiring mind: indeed the manifest weakness of many of them would naturally but serve to call forth his abilities to aim at finding something better for his own satisfaction. He was further induced to attempt this by considering that his great grandfather by his mother's side, Dr. Matthew Haffenreffer, was one of the few Germans who had ever prepared any substantial editions of the Greek Testament. He had sent from the press of Theodore Werlin of Tübingen, in 1618, a handsome edition in quarto, with the Latin version of Erasmus annexed, and with the benefit of some Greek MSS. to which, however, he gives no distinct references.

Section II.

BENGEL'S EARLIER CRITICAL ENGAGEMENTS.

It has been already mentioned that Bengel, during the years of his studentship, became intensely interested about the various readings of the New Testament. As it is not surprising that, with the inadequate means he possessed for clearing up such difficulties, before the publication of Mill, he should have found here a labour to which no young student was equal, so he was obliged to allay his doubts with the Christian believer's axiom, that the providence of God must certainly have guarded His Fountain of revealed wisdom from all such corruptions of human error, or human wickedness, as would withhold from us any of the essential truths of our common faith. The time, however, arrived, when he had no longer to believe, but was enabled to see, that this was the case. Having officially to go through the whole Greek Testament every two years with his pupils, he was led to inspect a great variety of its editions, especially as those which many of the pupils brought with them from home did not exactly agree together. Thus originated in his very lectures the first stirring of inquiries which brought him to critical collations and amassings, and these his indefatigable private diligence soon multiplied very considerably; for even in the year 1721, he could observe, as we have already seen in one of his letters to Reuss, that the various readings were much fewer than might have been expected, and that not one of them was of any such moment as to shake in the least degree the fundamental articles of evangelical faith.

Hitherto his critical and exegetical remarks had made up but one miscellany, though it now far exceeded what he wanted for his pupils. This treasure, especially the exegetical parts of it, having been noticed with very great satisfaction by his friends, they strongly urged and encouraged him to go on and complete it for publication and more general use.* Thus he continued with unwearied industry to augment, arrange, and correct his exegesis, and to gather about him, more and more availably, the criticisms of predecessors in the same pursuit. But these he found less and less to be depended on; as he soon saw that to obtain a pure original text demanded, though not a discovery of any manuscripts of the apostolic, yet a collation of the oldest and most valuable ones which the world contains. And he reasonably expected that many such of great value might still be found in several European libraries which critics had less explored, as in Germany, Switzerland, Hungary, Russia, &c. He, therefore, first made private applications wherever he could have access, or thought it likely to procure assistance. Nor were these exertions unavailing; for his materials now so accumulated, that as early as April, 1725, he was prepared to promise a critical edition of the Greek Testament; which he did in the tract entitled "*Prodromus Novi Testamenti Græci rectè cautèque adornandi,*"

* Among these persons were Christopher Zeller, prelate of Lorch; Christ. Matth. Pfaff, chancellor of the University of Tübingen; and his foreign correspondents, Whitby, Le Clerc, Bajer, and Reineccius, who all sent him repeated exhortations to proceed.

annexed* to his Chrysostom on the Priesthood. Herein he states that he had resolved to publish under the title of GNOMON, an exegetical commentary upon the New Testament; and besides this, to prepare upon it a critical work in which special use would be made of the labours and suggestions of Walton, Fell, and Mill; (whose bulky publications, not having been reduced to any popular form, were then but little known in Germany;) also of the most recent works of Gerard von Mastricht of Holland; of the German critics, L. Küster and J. C. Wolf; and of Bengel's own collations of manuscripts, newly discovered. He announced his design here to reprint carefully in the Greek text, whatever, as belonging to it, had been most approved of and confirmed by preceding editors; and to insert in its margin such of the most interesting lections as had been hitherto confined to manuscripts. Moreover, as Stephens's references, with his divisions of the chapters into verses, betrayed too much haste, and were very unsatisfactory, especially in the Epistles of St. Paul, he intended to use his best endeavours for supplying something better of the kind. Likewise instead of Gerard von Mastricht's forty-three canons, he purposed to give a single canon of his own, which should be perfectly simple, consisting of four words only, and admitting of general application. He added, that he had not lightly undertaken a work of such difficulty and liableness to misconception and detraction; but that, having been first impelled that way by official emergencies, he was persuaded at length by friends to prepare for publication what, after ten years' painful suspense, had served to set his own mind at rest. Finally, though he had materials, he trusted, already sufficient for real usefulness to the public, yet feeling it his duty to give the work as much ripeness and perfection as he could command, especially as having undertaken it for the honour and glory of Christ our Saviour, he was induced to request that those who had the means and facilities, would promote his access to additional materials, exegetical or critical, by at least informing him where such rare materials might be found. If any should scruple to risk these literary treasures from their depositories, he begged leave to remind them, that though it is not usual to expose such valuables to hazard, especially out of public libraries, they are equally liable to be damaged or destroyed by fire or water though locked up at home;

* This tract is also found in the Appendix to his "Apparatus Criticus," 2d edition, p. 625, &c.

whereas, they may be preserved uninjured, while travelling abroad under the eye of God, for whose honour and glory they should be sent forth, &c.

Copies of the "Prodromus" became circulated with his Chrysostom, through many a city and country; nevertheless he got several hundred others printed apart, and distributed wherever they were likely to answer his purpose. Various friends were active in circulating them, but especially Weissensee, who here most kindly availed himself of his extensive connexions abroad. But at many a door the knock was given in vain, especially at the Theological seminaries of Upper Suabia; the answer was, either, "we have nothing at all of the kind;" or, "we have no access to the libraries." Even from Halle no other encouragement was returned, except a hint which led to the discovery of a valuable collection of ancient MSS.* But such disappointments only enhanced the helps which arrived from other quarters, and which were as follows:—

P. J. Crophius obtained him the use of seven Strasburg MSS., more or less perfect. The seventh supplied important emendations for the text of the Apocalypse.

Zachary Conrad von Uffenbach, a member of the Senate of Frankfort, furnished him with four Greek MSS. of different books of the New Testament, and two MSS. of the ancient Latin version.

J. C. Iselin and J. L. Frey, of Bâsle, engaged in collating for him three Greek MSS. of their university library.

Matthias Marthius, the Lutheran pastor at Presburg, procured him, of the ecclesiastical council there, the loan of a beautiful vellum MS. of the four Gospels, which had once belonged to Prince Alexius II. Comnenus, (Emperor of the East, A. D. 1180.)

George Bernard Bülfinger, M. A., who was at that time in the service of the Russian government (afterwards a President of Consistory in Germany,) having obtained permission of the Archbishop of Novogorod, and from the Synod of Moscow, employed, under his own superintendence, Fr. Ch. Gross, to collate a Muscovy MS. of the Greek Testament, containing many a lection quite peculiar.

Christian Weiss, of Leipsic, sent an accurate collation of seven Latin MSS., which all belonged to the library of that city.

The ducal library at Stuttgart, and the imperial city library at

* See below, in his correspondence upon literary subjects.

Reutlingen, furnished Latin MSS. for collation; and Maturinus Veyssiere de la Croze sent a careful selection of the most important passages of the New Testament from Armenian and Coptic MSS., which supplied deficiencies in Mill's collations of those passages. Other materials of inferior importance we here omit to mention.

SECTION III.

*WETSTEIN, BENGEL'S RIVAL.**

While Bengel was making this valuable collection of critical materials, and was already engaged in collating and arranging, "a vigorous and active young man, who possessed more than a common share of various knowledge and attainments, began," says Leonard Hug, "to entertain thoughts of getting the start of the Würtemberg theological tutor. His name was John James Wetstein, of Bâsle." He was born there on the fifth of March, 1693; became a divinity student in the university of his native city; applied himself early to the study of criticism and antiquities; and at the age of twenty, with John Lewis Frey for his moderator, held a public academical disputation *on the various Readings of the Greek Testament,* in which he maintained the practicability of ascertaining the pure reading of the original text, perfect and complete. He afterwards made for the purpose an extensive tour in foreign countries, chiefly in France and England, during which he examined and collated many MSS. of the Greek Testament, and a considerable number of versions. Being in London in the year 1716, he there became personally acquainted with the learned Richard Bentley (a friend of Mill, who died in 1707), and informed him of the critical apparatus he had collected. He was urgently advised by Bentley to undertake an edition of the Greek Testament; but, excusing himself as being so young a man, and for want of time on his tour, he offered to Bentley, if he would undertake it himself, the use of his whole apparatus. This inclined Bentley to set about it, and Wetstein, on his return to Bâsle, sent him other materials besides, from the libraries of that city. Bentley now issued pro-

* Upon this subject, and for comparison with our account of Wetstein, we refer the reader to a book entitled, "*Joh. Jac. Wetstenii Prolegomena in N. T.*," ed. Joh. Salom. Semler, Halæ, 1764, p. 476, &c.; and the *Acta*, or "Discussions and Proceedings respecting the Errors of J. J. W." &c., Bâsle, 1730-4.

posals for his intended publication, which were accompanied by a specimen of it. This was in the year 1721. But notwithstanding that engagement to the public, and his being thus amply provided with collations of MSS. from France, Holland, and Italy, no such edition ever appeared; for Bentley had fallen out with his coadjutor, Conyers Middleton, and could not keep upon the best terms with Wetstein himself; but the chief obstacle was his disgust at having been refused by government a permission to import from France the paper he preferred for printing the work. Bentley's undertaking being thus abandoned, and Wetstein having the critical collections again at his own disposal, the latter was earnestly solicited by his relatives of the same name, who were booksellers at Amsterdam, to prepare those criticisms for insertion in a reprint, which they were about to make, of Gerard von Mastricht's edition. At their instance, and with encouragement from the above-mentioned John Lewis Frey, he began with renewed activity to increase and arrange his materials. This he did especially from the year 1726 (the third year since the publication of Bengel's *Prodromus*,) when his brother, Peter Wetstein, who had just returned from Amsterdam to Bâsle, entreated him, in the name of their Dutch relatives, to oblige them by immediately preparing and forwarding some specimens of his work, together with his Prolegomena, that they mght without delay advise with other learned friends upon the subject. The Prolegomena, with these specimens, were published in 1730 *anonymously;* but this precaution did not secure their author from three years' persecution on account of them, particularly at Bâsle, his native place. Of that persecution we shall relate a few particulars, and how it originated; because it will show the suspicion with which critical works upon the New Testament were regarded in those days, and how desirable therefore it was for the advancement of sound knowledge, that a person of Bengel's approved piety should just then have been engaged in this sort of criticism, as also what reason there was for all Bengel's modest caution about it. The originator of Wetstein's persecutions was the same Professor J. L. Frey who had been the first to encourage his entering upon enlarged critical pursuits; who had procured him opportunities of giving public lectures on the Greek Testament; and had maintained particular intimacy with him up to the year 1728. Wetstein, in his own account of the controversy, has not explained why the professor became so suddenly altered towards him. In assuming that Frey allured him to the field of criticism, and to a more free manner of exegesis, for the very purpose of circumventing him, he surely speaks too strongly, and only renders himself suspected of personal animosity. It is more probable that Frey's disgust arose from Wetstein's not attributing to him any of the honour of his publication, although, as Wetstein's senior, and as a professor of several years' standing, he had from time to time very extensively assisted him with critical communications. Wetstein had also previously made himself a good many enemies, by attacking, in his usual style of severe sarcasm, several of the most respectable clergymen of Bâsle, some of whom were Frey's near relatives. He had accused them of confounding, in their sermons, prayers, and hymns, the distinct personalities of the Godhead, by applying the term *Father* to the Son and Holy Ghost; and by concluding their prayers addressed to the Father with the following final clause: "Hear us, for the sake of thy sacred wounds," &c. Frey at first had sided with Wetstein in this censure; but the latter having, it seems, afterwards pushed the matter too far, Frey at once declared to him his opinion, that such censoriousness could proceed only from one who was tinctured with Arianism. After this, and probably many similar rejoinders on both sides, the rupture became entire. When they met one day in the Bâsle university library, Frey began objecting against Wetstein's announced edition of the Greek Testament, that it was likely to be too expensive, &c. and then alleged, that Wetstein's criticisms proceeded upon wrong principles relative to the discrimination of ancient manuscripts, &c., and consequently could never be relied on. Wetstein denying this, endeavoured to convince Frey that every critic, with his eyes open, can pronounce at once upon the antiquity and value of any such manuscripts, if he only noticed that in the more modern ones the Greek circumflex was expressed by a curve, but in the most ancient ones by a figure, exactly like a Roman v inverted. Frey denied that there was any such certainty of discrimination as this, however plausible it might seem, (and maintained that the circumflex in question is all along an *angular* figure;) whereupon Wetstein appealed to J. Grynæus, then present, and requested his decision. He immediately gave judgment by saying to Frey, "Certainly, doctor, if this circumflex 'is all along an angular figure,' the angular in many MSS. looks very much like a *curve*." Frey thus went home doubly offended; and eight days afterwards, happening to meet Wetstein again in the library, who had Montfaucon's edition of Origen's Hexapla before him, he asked him, if he had "any thing new there?" Wetstein replied, "I have discovered a most ridiculous error of J. C. Iselin's, which has got into Breitinger, of Zürich's "*Proposals*" for a new critical edition of the Septuagint. He promises collations of Bâsle MSS. which have no existence at Bâsle." Wetstein, who had naturally a strong propensity to ridicule, might have said this with more than usual of his satirical bitterness, because the announced work was likely to stand very much in his own light, as he had long been making elaborate preparations for a similar one; and it is easy enough to suppose that he was secretly displeased with Iselin and Frey, from knowing that they had furnished Bengel with collations of Bâsle MSS.

But, as he thought he had seen Frey express a smile of pleasure at hearing of Iselin's alleged blunder, he was the more surprised to learn that, immediately afterwards, Frey had privately accused him to Iselin of having made the latter appear ridiculous before a whole company of students; nor was he less surprised, when he found that the former had even got an injunction passed by the Senate to forbid his continuing to examine manuscripts in the university library. Neither was this all; for Iselin and Frey now went so far as to lay a memorial before the Senate, signed by every parochial clergyman in the city, and by other divines of the university, petitioning that J. J. Wetstein, assistant minister of St. Leonard's, be *prohibited* from publishing his criticisms of the Greek Testament, forasmuch as it was a useless, uncalled for, and even dangerous work. It was urged in support of the petition, how he had advanced the most trifling and puerile particularities, of a grammatical stamp indeed, but perfectly foreign to all good criticism; that such an edition was totally uncalled for, inasmuch as the Codex Alexandrinus, which was his chief critical oracle, had been printed often enough; and that it might well be considered as *dangerous*, because Wetstein had presumed to embody in the text, at pleasure, any, however unsupported, lection he met with. Thus there was reason to fear he was claiming a right of censorship over Scripture itself, in support of his own hypothetical and groundless fancies; especially as they had even learnt that he was prosecuting his criticisms under a Socinian bias. Lastly, that several passages of Scripture, which are express upon the divinity of Christ, had been assailed by him with critical suspicion.

Such complaints, however, though reiterated to the Senate, and not without endeavours to draw the very people of the town into the controversy, having proved ineffectual, his opponents managed to get possession of memoranda which the students had taken down at his Greek Testament lectures; and from what these notes contained upon doctrinal points, they contrived to frame such accusations as led to his being summoned to submit the whole mass of his written criticisms to the Senate's inspection, and to answer personally to a long list of objectionable tenets which he was accused of maintaining. Compliantly and adroitly as he replied to every question, it was at length decided, that he taught opinions adverse to the doctrinal system of his church, that he inclined to Socinianism, and even favoured the views of Rationalists. For instance, that though he admitted the inspiration of the Scriptures, he held their infallibility as relating only to principal matters. It was further proved against him, that in his public lectures and discourses he had spoken too freely about scripture obscurities, and of the common people's inability to understand them; that he had ridiculed in certain companies the belief of satanical existence; had explained away demoniacal possession as nothing more than a physical malady; and had acknowledged that in catechizing he had designedly passed over those passages of Scripture wherein the devil is mentioned. That in a sermon upon the tenth Commandment he had expounded concupiscence as a thing not sinful; that in his church prayer he habitually omitted the expression "making satisfaction," under the pretext of its being a *difficult* expression; and that the most suspicious part of his conduct, was his having forbidden his students to deliver up the notes they had taken of his lectures; and his having made alterations in such parts of them as he thought would give offence. These proceedings against him issued in his being suspended from the ministry, and he went away to his relatives in Holland, where the Remonstrants appointed him to the rectorship of a high school, as successor to the aged John le Clerc, upon condition that he should previously return to Bâsle and retrieve his license. He complied; and having prevailed with the Senate to rescind his suspension, on the 8th of October, 1732, he was again declared capable of ecclesiastical functions. Nevertheless, his controversy with Iselin and Frey did not end here; for remote from them as was now his place of residence, they so kept up animosities, that Wetstein declared it was owing to their opposition that the publication of his Greek Testament had been delayed for at least twenty years.

SECTION IV.

CONTINUATION OF BENGEL'S CRITICAL RESEARCHES.

Bengel having, in the year 1729, submitted his work on the Greek Testament, together with his "Apparatus Criticus," to the censorship at Stuttgart, and to the Theological Faculty of Tübingen, received licenses for their publication, which were conveyed in terms very honourable and encouraging to himself. Shortly after this, he found Wetstein's Prolegomena come out together, with the specimen of that critic's intended edition of the Greek Testament. A work of such importance for its copious collations, of course he could not neglect to examine; especially as he was aware that so travelled a scholar as Wetstein must have greatly the advantage of him in extent of materials. He therefore once more paused about his own publication, till he had carefully sifted the whole of this newly presented mass of research. In the subsequent announcement of his work,* he says, "The new edition promised in the 'Prodromus' is, by the Divine help, so far completed, that it may be considered as almost ready to be presented to the public. But as my arrangement required further consideration, and has in consequence been altered, the whole will be found distributed into four distinct works. First, I shall send out a larger edition of the Greek Testament in quarto, which will be succeeded by a smaller one in octavo; the larger will be accompanied by another work entitled 'Apparatus Criticus,' giving a particular account of every reading I have adopted; and then, in a separate volume, I shall publish as soon as possible my exegetical annotations, which though completed in amount, do not appear sufficiently matured for the press."

With regard to the readings adopted by himself in the text, he reassures any anxious inquirers, that, with some exceptions in the Apocalypse, which was a book peculiarly circumstanced, he had not admitted a single expression that had not been embodied with it in printed editions; and he had the more confidently made this a rule with himself, because research had convinced him that any reading not adopted by former printed editions,

* This announcement was entitled, "Notitia Novi Testamenti Græci, rectè cautèque adornati, quod perbrevi publicandum justis conditionibus recipiunt Jo. Georgius et Christianus Godofredus Cotta, bibliopolæ."

even though it might have probability on its side, was always of minor importance. Finally, in composing his "Apparatus," he had carefully considered and weighed each of the forty-three canons of Gerard von Mastricht; and that the promised canon of four words would be found in that "Apparatus." This announcement was accompanied with specimens of the form of the text in quarto, as also of the "Apparatus Criticus." Accordingly both made their appearance, followed by the smaller Greek Testament, in the year 1734.*

The arrangement of each edition is exhibited in its title-page, and both of them were found to agree in every particular with the announcement and specimens; neither were they much inferior as to type, correct printing, and good paper, even to those of Amsterdam.

As the minor Greek Testament was without the "Apparatus Criticus," its preface gave a brief account of Bengel's researches, and of the principles upon which he thought it right to conduct them. In the concluding paragraph of this preface he inserted an adage, which, though brief and in quaint Latin, excellently shows how to search the Scriptures with the greatest benefit:—

> "Te totum applica ad Textum;
> Rem totam applica ad te."
> "Keep thyself closely to the text,
> And apply the whole substance of it to thy own edification."

The "Apparatus Criticus" consists of three parts: the first explains what New Testament criticism is; its difficulties, with the best means of overcoming them; and gives a concise but sufficient history of this branch of knowledge down to his own time. The second part shows, by way of introduction to each portion of the New Testament, the resources of criticism for such several portions, with references to editions, manuscripts, and fathers. Here it was his object to determine more evidently the relative value of the different MSS. by their antiquity, origin, and greater or less degree of correctness, as also what collations, more or less accurate, they had undergone. Next are detailed all the principal

* The quarto edition has the following title, "'Η ΚΑΙΝΗ ΔΙΑΘΗΚΗ, Novum Testamentum Græcè, ita adornatum, ut *textus* probatarum editionum medullam, *margo* variarum lectionum in suas classes distributarum, locorumque parellelorum delectum; *apparatus* subjunctus criseos sacræ, Millianæ præsertim, compendium, limam, supplementum et fructum exhibeat: inserviente Jo. Alberto Bengelio: Tubingæ, 1734." The octavo was entitled, "'Η καινὴ Διαθήκη, N. T. Græcum, ita adornatum, ut in textu medulla editionum probatarum retineatur, atque in margine ad discernendas lectiones genuinas, ancipites, sequiores, ansa detur: Stuttgardiæ, 1734."

various readings themselves, in the order of chapter and verse, with evidences for and against them. Then, as to passages of more immediate importance, he examines, with impartial and scrupulous care, each evidence, external and internal, in favour of this or that particular reading. Thus the following Scripture passages are especially attended to: Matt. vi. 13; John i. 1; viii. 1—11; 1 Tim. iii. 16; 1 John v. 7. Lastly was given an introduction to the Revelation of St. John, a book subjected to many more various readings (though it exists in fewer MSS.) than any other book of the New Testament; but oftener found in the MSS. which Bengel's exertions had brought to light, than in others. Here, therefore, he had the more to do in consequence of the very great imperfectness of all the hitherto *printed* editions of the Apocalypse. The third part of the Apparatus defended criticism in general, and the present criticisms in particular; especially as every care had been taken to keep the latter within the golden medium. Yet he would not dissemble how much still remained to be done for perfecting the general criticism of the New Testament; he therefore, in conclusion, earnestly called upon those who had time, ability, and opportunities, to contribute their help in this laborious but most useful study.

SECTION V.

OPINIONS PRONOUNCED UPON BENGEL'S CRITICISMS.

The reception of his work among the studious fully answered his expectations; nevertheless, while many of the better disposed were thankful for the advantages it afforded, insomuch that the minor edition of the New Testament was soon out of print, there were others of a very different mind. "Certain ministers of God's word" scrupled not to insert in one of the periodicals entitled "Early Gathered Fruits," (No. 4, of the year 1738,) a stricture containing the following remarks.

"If every book-maker is to take into his head to treat the New Testament in this manner, we shall soon get a Greek text totally different from the received one. The audacity is really too great for us not to notice it; especially as such vast importance, it seems, is attached to this edition. Scarcely a chapter of it has not something either omitted, or inserted, or altered, or transposed. The audacity is unprecedented."

The writer of this stricture was probably John George Hager, M.A.; he, at least, it was who afterwards used very much the same language in a disputation which he held at Leipsic.

Quite another sort of objections was raised in an article of the *Bibliothèque Raisonnée*, published by the Wetsteins of Amsterdam; (see vol. for 1734, p. 203;) which article was known to have been written by J.J. Wetstein himself. Here it was stated as a principal *defect* of Bengel's work, that he had *not* adopted lections *enough;* not even all which he considered the true ones; that he had gone only upon a half measure; and that half measures, particularly in criticism, had been always of little or no use. That it was one and the same thing here, whether we gently intimate or whether we speak out; whether we note our preference for one lection standing in the *text*, or for another standing in the *margin;* all still depended upon the general question, Are we or are we not freely to use our critical resources? The right of using these had never been disputed by the Protestant churches or by Rome herself; for as it rests on the surest foundation, so all editors of the Greek Testament had ever acted upon it. Cautious and prudent, however, as they had been in so doing, this had not secured them from censure and persecution: for even Erasmus had been rewarded with the reputation of being an Arian; and Robert Stephens was obliged to fly to Geneva to escape a burning at the stake, &c. Therefore Bengel's excessive prudence and caution would be any thing but serviceable to him; especially as he too, in editing the Apocalypse, had found it necessary to abandon these his favourite virtues; so that it would have been better had he relinquished such caution altogether, and adopted into the text, whether from print or manuscript, whatever readings he considered to be the best. That the four worded canon proposed by Bengel "*Proclivi scriptioni præstat ardua,*" ("the more difficult reading is preferable to the easier one,") was quite ambiguous and unsupportable, as any reading countenanced by a majority of MSS. is surely the one to be preferred; hence Bengel's work, as presenting a collation of only twelve, could be of no very great value. Wetstein lastly threw out a sarcastic slight upon Bengel's promised exegetical annotations, (the Gnomon;) but he concluded with acknowledging, that *Bengel's edition of the New Testament was the best that had ever yet been printed.*

That Bengel should publish some reply to opinions thus more or less unreasonably passed upon his work, seemed necessary from the circumstances of the case, especially as that age was characteristically fond of learned controversy. He had also another reason for so doing; for "critical labours being (as he had observed) so toilsome and dry, doubly entitled the labourer to a temperate and equitable judgment upon his productions; consequently it was but right that he should defend himself against unreasonable detraction." This he undertook to do in several pieces as follows.

In reply to Wetstein's strictures he wrote, "A Defence of the Greek Testament, edited at Tübingen in 1734." This defence he inserted in the preface to his "Harmony of the four Gospels," published in 1736. Count Zinzendorf having read the "Defence," had recommended it to his friends in Holland; for he met with it in his tour through that country, and was very much pleased with it. From Holland, therefore, Bengel received a request, which there is reason to suppose came originally from Bâsle, that he would by all means republish it in Latin, for easier access to foreign countries. Bengel then revised and translated it, and sent it to Amsterdam for admission into the "Miscellanea Critica," a journal published there; its admission, however, having been, for some special reason, refused, two of his friends, Professor D'Orville and Jerome von Alphen, undertook the printing of it.* Bengel in this defence dismisses several minor objections, and proceeds as follows:—1. "That Wetstein was incorrect in asserting, that the edition in question had been prepared with the help of no more than *twelve* MSS.; it contained his own collations of *seven* Strasburg MSS., *one* Byzantine MS., *one* at Warsaw, *one* at Moscow, *two* at Uffenbach; with collations made by others of *three* at Bâsle, and collations of *seven more*, besides the collations of L. Valla and of J. Faber Stapulensis. He had also collected upon the ancient Latin version of the Old and New Testament (the Vulgate,) sufficient to render it a very easy task to make a complete recension of that version. Above all, by impartially collating *every lection of printed* editions, he had reduced the whole controversy to a much narrower compass, upon very many passages.

2. "Why the canon 'Proclivi Scriptioni præstat ardua,' should be deemed ambiguous, he was the less able to understand, as the terms of which it consists had long been used, and by the oldest critics; especially too as he had given his own meaning in thus

* "Io. Alberti Bengelii Defensio N. T. Græci Tubingæ, anno 1734, editi. Lugduni Batavorum apud Conradum Wishoff, 1737." It was also reprinted in the Appendix to the 2d edition of the "Apparatus Criticus."

combining them; and had shown the comprehensiveness of its application.

3. " As to his never embodying in the text (except in that of the Apocalypse,) any MS. reading, though appearing the more correct one, he admitted it was a rule he had obeyed for *prudential* reasons, rather than from *absolute necessity*. He considered it, however, not so cautiously *narrow* as was represented; for as the many printed editions of the text serve to correct one another, all imperative need of reference to unprinted MSS. is hereby, except in a few instances, entirely done away. His caution, though censured, was also most justifiable, as tending to satisfy very many considerate persons who had expressed, not entirely without cause in relation to such matters, their dissatisfaction with critics in general. Had he not used that caution, greater evil might have ensued than even was apprehended in the strictures of this journal, namely, an increased perplexity in the minds of many about the certainty of the text; a perplexity keeping pace with men's natural eagerness for novelty, and which at present was the more to be dreaded, as Wetstein's own example gave indeed some occasion to fear, that the public might, by and by, have the text of the New Testament modelled, first after one system of theoretical divinity, and then after another; unless some stand, like that objected to, were made to prevent it.

4. " That the exception he had indulged in his revision of *the Apocalypse*, was defensible on two accounts; first, that its contingent of various readings was much greater than that of any other part of the New Testament; and secondly, that fewer MSS. of this than of its other parts had ever been collated, or even been discovered; so that his restricting himself to *printed* editions here, would have been rather out of place.

5. " To the ridicule attempted against his yet unpublished 'Gnomon,' he had only to say, that the more his materials had increased, the more had he found it necessary to divide his notes, critical and exegetical, into three distinct works, namely, *Text*, *Apparatus*, and *Gnomon;* and that the last was now in the press.

6. " As to Wetstein's notion, that the correctness of readings should be determined by a majority of MSS., it was absurd in itself, and contradicted its abettor's own *Prolegomena* of 1730; as also his preface to the second edition of Gerard's New Testament, published by the Wetsteins in 1735. That to ascertain the authority of any MS., it was necessary to have consideration of its *origin;* a thing which often gives preponderance to one,

beyond a hundred others. Were this mode of estimating them allowed and acted upon, there would be so little occasion for fearing any *numerical* reckoning, that rather he would wish it to be made; and that meanwhile he would venture to pledge himself that even a majority of manuscripts would in general confirm no recension so fully as his own.

7. " Though he had no wish to inquire into Wetstein's motives for getting up such a hasty reprint of Gerard's Greek Testament in behalf of the firm of his relatives, he could not forbear making a few observations on the character of this new edition. Hasty, indeed, he was obliged to call it, because it retained all the typographical errors of the first, and even added one more, in stating that a hundred MSS. had been collated for that first edition, whereas only a single MS. had been collated for it; and because Wetstein had given this second edition a preface, which betrayed very diligent availment of Bengel's " Apparatus Criticus," and more approval of it than had been expressed in the *Bibliothèque raisonnée*," &c.

To the other strictures which appeared in the " Early gathered Fruits," and in " Hager's Disputation," he replied, partly in German and partly in Latin (in 1739), through a journal entitled " New Literary Notices from Tübingen." " As the former of these strictures had attempted to show, by specimens of Bengel's criticisms on the text of the Apocalypse, how much he had departed from the received one; and as the reviewer had hence concluded that the other books of the New Testament had been treated much in the same manner, which was surely, he said, to be lamented, as such an endeavour to throw uncertainty over the text was putting weapons into the hands of infidels; Bengel, therefore, showed that Erasmus, who undervalued the Apocalypse, so hurried it to the press, that he had suffered many evident errors to remain, and had even substituted for the original Greek text of the concluding part of this book, a translation of his own into Greek from the Latin Vulgate. That " though the genuine Greek was afterwards brought to light, and printed in the Spanish (Complutensian) Polyglott, this spurious Greek of Erasmus was still propagated by other editions; so that it was high time the Apocalypse should undergo a most accurate revision, aided by the variety of excellent materials which had been gathered, not only from versions and from the Fathers, but also from newly-discovered manuscripts. Unreasonable, then, was it that the Apocalypse, the only book in which he (Bengel) had deviated from the printed readings, should be produced as a specimen of his having presumptuously altered the text of the New Testament. He therefore now solemnly called upon these 'ministers of God's word,' to examine the whole of his work most strictly; and then, in a future number of their journal, either to point out in what passages he had deviated from any printed *edition*, or else to acknowledge their having borne false witness against him."

"As to the objection that he was putting weapons into the hands of infidels, he could only reply, that the sum and substance of the New Testament having remained complete and uninjured in all its existing copies, whether manuscript or printed, and whether more accurate or less, the infidel could have no advantage, unless furnished with it by those very critics who underrate a proper revision of the text; for, by indiscreetly restricting such sober liberty, they leave the sacred text exposed to every rash and presumptuous judgment. Besides, infidels cannot possibly be ignorant how many various readings have been put forth; which, instead of finding increased by his own revision, they would find fewer for objecting against than ever. That other strictures, to which he had been compelled to reply, upon this same work of his, had accused him of uncritical *caution* and *diffidence;* whereas the present called upon him to show, that he had not proceeded with uncritical *temerity*. It turned out then, on the whole, that he had kept the middle way, and consequently the right one. That all truth, even in reaching its own ministers, had to undergo, first, temptation within the bosom of him who sends it forth, and then, gainsaying and contradiction from without; yet, sooner or later, according to the persons it has to deal with, it proves at last victorious," &c.

In the other and *Latin* portion of this reply to the "Early gathered Fruits," he chiefly controverts Hager's notion, that in Acts ix. 5, the *paraphrastic*, and not the *close* reading, is the correct one. He shows that the close reading is favoured by the greatest *number*, *variety*, and *antiquity* of MSS.; that is, he omits no proof which could be demanded for its support. So that, whereas Hager alleged this as an instance of his improper treatment of the Greek Testament, it was evident, he said, that Hager had nothing here to object to at all, as it was now clear that he (Bengel) had acted, not according to his own arbitrary pleasure, but according to the most approved principles of criticism.

Before there was time to put in general circulation this German and Latin reply to Hager's Strictures, the alarm which this opponent had excited, served to nip in the bud one of the fair fruits of Bengel's industry. For after Muthmann and Steinbart had agreed to publish, at Züllichau, a German original Bible, with the Greek Testament, according to Bengel's revision, annexed, and had announced their intention in Proposals of Oct. 1, 1738, they were so vehemently attacked from various quarters, respecting this appendage, that they changed their purpose, and, instead of the text of Bengel, chose that of Reineccius. By the appearance, however, of Bengel's defence, the alarm was so far allayed, that they applied to him to compose for their work a tabular index, displaying, in parallel columns, the more important variations between the text of Luther, the Greek text of Reineccius, and that of Bengel.* This table was very serviceable in justifying the correctness of Bengel's revisions; so that none could help seeing that they supported Luther's version much more closely than did the lections, which hitherto had been most commonly adopted.

Other controversial business awaited him through the proceedings of Count Zinzendorf, who probably never anticipated, much less intended, any such thing. But the count had made a translation of the New Testament, and had issued printed specimens of it, in which he acknowledged that he had availed himself of Bengel's revised Greek text as his principal standard for the work. This acknowledgment provoked a great outcry against the count's new version, especially through a publication entitled "*Theophili à veritate*, or, Biblical Scandal, given by Zinzendorf." Moreover, the editors of the "Early gathered Fruits" thought this a good opportunity for entering their own protest once more against Bengel; as they had been prudently silent about him ever since his solemn challenge to them in the "Reply to certain Ministers of God's Word," above mentioned. Accordingly, in their fifth number of the year 1741, one of their remarks to that effect was—"Zinzendorf acknowledges his own new version to have been framed according to Bengel's Greek edition obsequiously throughout, notwithstanding he knew, or might have known, how much censurable matter has been discovered by sound divines in that edition." To this fresh piece of detraction Bengel replied in an augmented reprint of his Answer to

* This table is also inserted in the second edition of the "Apparatus Criticus," p. 678, &c.

Hager,* from which for brevity's sake we extract but one remark, viz. that "the need of a thoroughly revised text of the Greek Testament is now greater than ever, because not only are the earlier vernacular translations undergoing revisal, and new editions of them, each to a large amount, are successively issuing from various quarters, but missionaries are also beginning to translate the Scriptures into the common dialects of India and other countries."

In the hope of contributing some assistance to such an important undertaking in behalf of the heathen, he about this time transmitted, by pastor Kleinknecht, a copy of his Greek Testament, with various annotations in his own handwriting, to the Danish missionaries at Tranquebar, who were then preparing a version of the Scriptures in the Tamul dialect.

Lastly, the Roman-catholic party attacked him violently, on account of his criticism in general, and that of the Apocalypse in particular. One of them, the Rev. Thomas Adelbert Berghauer, in a publication of A. D. 1746, entitled, "*Bibliomachia*, or, an Expedition and Review of many lamentably adulterated Bibles," asserted that "Bengel had moulded the Greek of the Apocalypse into a quite novel form, and with his slashing and murderous pruning knife had most wretchedly hacked, decomposed, and nullified the original text." Bengel's reply† was given in an appendix to the 58th—60th of his "Practical Addresses on the Apocalypse;" and showed, by a demonstrative chain of argument *ad hominem*, that "as for the vulgar objection of his being a Bible-murderer, a corrupter of the Scriptures, and so forth, because he set a high value upon sound criticism, it was just as applicable to the editors of the Complutensian Bible, Cardinal Ximenes and his coadjutors, with their patron Leo the Tenth, as to himself. That the charge of his having maltreated the Apocalypse, was evidently repeated after Hager; and showed that his work had never been carefully looked into, otherwise his clerical opponent must have seen, that the text here agrees much more closely with the Vulgate and Complutenian text, than with that commonly received among Protestants."

He then makes some general remarks upon this scurrilous pamphlet, and observes that the author had very appropriately entitled it "*Bibliomachia;*" for its special and infelicitous

* Printed at Ulm, 1745.

† It is also found in the second edition of the "Apparatus Criticus," p. 748, &c.

business was *war with the Bible!* It was a congeries of open blasphemy against the word of God in *all* Bibles, catholic or protestant. But "the writer of it," he added, "must give account to Him who is ready to judge the quick and dead, as St. Peter himself declares; and let this serve as an answer to the dedication of the 'Review,' now lying before me. But, my protestant readers! what do *we* say to this *Biblical Review?* Does it not fulfil St. John's word in the Revelation, concerning the beast and Babylon? Is not this enemy of the Bible drunken with the wine of the great city? How blood-thirstily does this zealot write in his spiritual intoxication, when he says, that '*the catholic church has a strong arm, and a spiritual and temporal sword, to bring to obedience all heretics, as well as her own rebellious children, if they rise against her with their wrong-headed and obstinate fancies, having their flaming pride lighted up by the Bible!*' What would have been our fate all along to this day, had none of the Roman Catholics, especially of those who were high in power, possessed a nobler cast of mind than this; and, above all, had not the faithful God always restrained the wrath of such zealots; who, deaf to the clamours of conscience and humanity, and foolishly imagining themselves always in the right, and us in the wrong, think cruelty sweet, and even please themselves with the idea that (by persecuting us) they are doing God service. Surely many prophecies to this effect, and especially in the Apocalypse, must now be on the point of fulfilment: and well may we arm ourselves with the patience and faith of the saints.

"O that this may be the last occasion of my standing in the gap to vindicate the precious original text of the New Testament! The children of peace cannot love contention; it is troublesome and painful to them to be obliged to contend even for the truth itself. (Gal. vi. 17.) May the Lord Jesus diffuse among us his peace, his grace, and his glory, ever more and more! Ruling even in the midst of his enemies, till he shall have subdued all things; yea, unto Himself!"

Much as he wished to have no further occasion for defending his critical works, his wish could not yet be gratified. For Provost Kohlreif publicly challenged him to a most uncritical measure; namely, to hush the enemies of criticism by admitting that even the various lections were given by inspiration, in order to meet the necessities of various readers. This he felt obliged to answer; and he took the seasonable opportunity of showing its absurdity, in his "Vindication of the Holy Scriptures," published at Leipsic in 1755. Part I. sect. 20.*

Wetstein also had started afresh against him, by inserting new objections in the second edition of his Prolegomena, in 1749, and by adding the same to his Greek Testament, which came out in 1751.† But this piece of acrimony, replenished as it was with tedious minutiæ and personalities, Bengel, happily for himself, never saw. Indeed, the cause of sound knowledge would hardly have gained any advantage by a continuation of the controversy. For Wetstein had now introduced into it so much of an extraneous nature, that he seemed almost to have lost sight of the main object which Bengel desired to keep in view; namely, of deciding whether a reception nearer to the Vulgate be not the more correct one;—whereas, Wetstein, who had once taken the affirmative side of this question, in agreement with Bentley, had opposed it of late in the most determined manner. On that one point both parties were now so entirely at issue, that no adjustment was to be expected. While then we leave unnoticed Wetstein's additional rejoinder, it is still necessary to justify Bengel's character from one illiberal imputation, that of acting with disingenuous dexterity or double dealing. Bengel, in the preface to his "Harmony of the Gospels," having inserted a letter of Frey respecting Wetstein, which letter was "not in German, *like the rest of the preface*, but in Latin," Wetstein maintained that this was done with the view both of pleasing the Bâsle *literati*, and of not offending the *illiterate* German pietists. Now the most cursory glance at that preface discovers the wickedness of such an imagination; for there we find numerous Latin quotations, which are *also* left untranslated, because it was presumed that the book would have its *learned* readers. What double dealing, then, could there be in his leaving untranslated this letter of Frey's?—But it is time to cease noticing the ungracious attacks which Bengel's critical work upon the New Testament drew upon him from various quarters. Rather let us pass on to the honourable acknowledgments awarded him by others for his labours and services. As an instance of the rest, we will attend to one whose eminent erudition entitles him to much respect. Dr. Joh. Leon. Hug, professor of divinity in the university of Freiburg, in his "Intro-

* See also the second edition of the "Apparatus Criticus." p. 760.

† See also the more recent edition of Wetstein's Prolegomena, published by Joh. Sal. Semler, in 1764, with Annotations by Semler; pp. 399—430.

duction to the Writings of the New Testament," (2d edit. vol. I. p. 313, &c.) speaks of him as follows:—

"Bengel is the first German who has laboured creditably in this department of learning. While for many years he was engaged as a tutor and lecturer, he was quietly pondering the text of Mill, and early availed himself of Latin and Greek MSS. for consultation. But his valuable industry did not stop here. He proceeded to make numerous collations, and hereby developed more and more his original talent for criticism. For this he was neither indebted to his friends about him, nor to the expensive and valuable helps procured for him, but to the resources with which his own mind was endowed. By long and indefatigable attention, he became quite familiar with the various phenomena of the sacred text, and so well acquainted with the peculiarities and usages of heterogeneous critical documents, that from his own observation he drew out new principles for the profitable application of critical learning. He was the first who classified MSS. according to the incidental agreements which he discovered in their general features and in their particular lections. He discerned in them respectively a common similarity and uniformity, sufficient for evincing two distinct classes; one of which he termed the *African*, and the other, sometimes, the *Asiatic*. His observations having thus conducted him to a simplicity of research, and his classification of so many various witnesses having converted them into compact and conspiring parties, he elicited from them certain general principles, whereby he set in motion that present march of criticism which will now proceed, even supposing his own editorial works could ever be forgotten. Wetstein is, in my opinion, deservedly to blame for having neither valued, nor so much as comprehended, Bengel's admirably luminous principles of criticism."

In harmony with these sentiments, has been the general reception of Bengel's critical writings to the present time: and though Biblical criticism became after his death materially advanced every ten years, first by Wetstein, and subsequently by Griesbach and Matthiæ, Bengel's octavo Greek Testament has gone through five editions.

There was published at Oxford, in 1742, (*è TheatroSheldoniano, edente Johanne Gambold,*) *Novum Testamentum Græcum, textu per omnia Milliano cum divisione pericoparum et interpuncturâ, J. A. Bengelii;* and in 1745, when the authorized Danish version was revised by command of his majesty the king of Denmark, the text of Bengel was preferred as the standard for that purpose.

A second edition of the "Apparatus Criticus" was published in 1763, by Philip David Burk, "curis beati auctoris posterioribus aucta et emendata;" (enlarged and corrected by the latest labours of its pious deceased author). It contains Bengel's supplementary criticism on the New Testament, with which are embodied his collations of a written copy of another MS. of the Apocalypse. This MS. having been destroyed by a fire at Copenhagen, the copy of it was communicated to Bengel, by J. L. von Mosheim. A particular review of this second edition of the "Apparatus" is found in Dr. John Aug. Ernesti's* "*New Theological Library*," vol. IV. part ii. p. 109, &c. We shall better learn its value by noticing a few of the principal matters referred to in that review, with Ernest Bengel's counter statements† and observations upon it. The reviewer speaks as follows:—"The *Apparatus Criticus* of the late prelate Bengel, is one of those books which do honour to our church and country; and though in its general drift and particular remarks it is not without defects and errors, and is far short of a perfect work, nothing of the kind yet published by any member of our own church will bear comparison with it. Its first appearance drew forth great opposition amongst us; for Scripture criticism had been previously very little attended to. The science had hitherto been regarded as dangerous, and even mischievous; but public opinion about it has gradually become quite altered; and Bengel is now not only celebrated in foreign parts, but his merit has been more and more perceived and acknowledged by ourselves; especially since our countrymen have begun in larger numbers to study and engage in works of criticism. This is evident from the first edition being now out of print, and from those continued and frequent inquiries after it, which give good reason to expect a quick circulation for this new one.

"By comparing the number of pages in the two editions, the augmentation of the second does not appear considerable; for the first consists of six hundred and twelve, and this second, which is of the same type, contains no more than six hundred and twenty. Much, however, upon critical subjects may be furnished

* Professor of Divinity at Leipsic; the well known author of valuable editions of Greek and Latin classics. He died in 1781.

† *Vide* E. Bengel's "Elucidation," &c.

within the space of eight quarto pages of letter-press.* It is to be regretted, that the excellent author either never saw Wetstein's Greek Testament, Bianchini's Evangeliarium, and Sabatierius's Italian version of the Old Testament, or else did not choose to make use of them.†

"Of several pieces in the Appendix, the following here deserve to be noticed :—

"1. 'An Essay on the duty of preserving the purity of the Greek text of the New Testament;' (*Tractatio de sinceritate N. T. Græci tuendâ ;*) which contains a reply to some remarks upon Bengel's work inserted by Dr. Michaelis, in his *Tractatio de variis lectionibus N. T. cautè colligendis et dijudicandis;* ('Essay on the duty of caution in collecting, and deciding upon, the various readings in the Greek text of the New Testament.') Bengel sent it in manuscript to Dr. Michaelis himself, who printed it at Halle with his own observations, in 1750. Bengel said of it to his friends, that 'he could answer Michaelis's remarks, but would not; lest so amicable a contest should lose its agreeableness by prolongation into a controversy.' If the tract of Dr. Michaelis should ever be reprinted, this piece of Bengel's might be usefully annexed to it.

"2. *Clavicula N. T. Græce ex iteratâ recensione nuper edita;* ('A small Key to the Greek Testament, a new edition, repeatedly revised;') which was written chiefly in reply to some strictures of the late Dr. Baumgarten, and is occasionally rather harsh.‡ Baumgarten, though he had not made criticism his particular study, did not want acumen and a pretty good acquaintance with his subject; neither is it unjustly that he upbraids Bengel with having introduced readings of minor importance, and omitted others of greater; nor could Bengel give him any other answer but that it did not belong to his plan to exhibit every particular

* Ernesti altered this remark in part x, p. 490, to the following:—" It was by an oversight (?) that in the review of Bengel's Apparatus, twelve *leaves* were mentioned instead of twelve sheets; by which it appears that the new edition is a larger work than the old one." This alteration, however, is still more erroneous than his original remark; for he was correct in saying that the second edition contains 620 pages; but this is with the omission of the whole of the Greek text of the New Testament, which was inserted in the first edition; consequently there was a *much greater* enlargement than the reviewer had noticed.

† The former of these alternatives is the more probable; and may be accounted for by considering that Bengel, in the latter part of his life, with his new official engagements, his infirm state of health, and his strong anticipation of the nearness of his end, could no longer follow up literary labours with the attention of his earlier years.

‡ The alleged asperity will not easily be perceived, if the manner in which Baumgarten attacked Bengel be impartially considered.

lection;* an answer which shows how necessary it is for such of his readers as wish to be thorough critics, not to limit themselves to his *Apparatus*, but to seek out more extended and comprehensive repertories of criticism.† Bengel, however, has respectably answered the objections which Baumgarten made to his criticisms upon some passages in the Acts of the Apostles, in the Epistle to the Romans, and in the Epistle of St. James; and here his work contains a number of important additions.

"3. *Tabula lectionum variantium N. T.*; ('A Table of the various readings of the Greek Testament;') which is the most useful part of this Appendix. It is well known that the excellent author, when he published his '*Gnomon*,' had changed his opinion of some readings; which was not to be wondered at. Here then we have his final judgment upon the whole.

"But notwithstanding all the defects which may be pointed out in this 'Apparatus,' it is a highly valuable compendium of criticism on the New Testament, for those who have not leisure or inclination to explore further in such a field of literature. We have always recommended it to students, and we do so still."

* It is true that only this *general* answer was given by Bengel in his *Clavicula*; but a particular refutation of such objections will be found at proper places in the revised text of his *Apparatus Criticus*.

† Bengel was fully sensible of this, and acknowledged it even in the first edition of his *Apparatus;* at the same time he remarked, that a work presenting the whole apparatus of criticism in every minute particular, was not his object; though he wished such a work might exist.

CHAPTER IV.

HIS GENERAL PRINCIPLES OF EXPOSITION.

Exegesis was, more immediately than criticism, a part of his official business; and having to go through the New Testament with his pupils every two years, he conscientiously prepared expository remarks for each lecture. This led him necessarily into criticisms; which he laboured to reduce to a regular system for the press, before he published any thing exegetical; and though the latter was what his friends urged him first to send out, he waived it for the present, because he saw that the study of criticism was too little valued; though, as one of the departments of theological knowledge, it then needed cultivation more than the rest. He also considered, that as so many valuable comments had already appeared, no new expositor ought to come forward without well digested materials; whereas, for his own part, he should not be able to feel himself thus competently furnished, till after the persevering labour of a number of years. With these views he had been accumulating observations for above twenty years together, so that he could the more readily give forth, in due time, the fruit of very extensive researches. These may be considered as of two kinds, namely, general and special. His "Gnomon" upon the whole of the New Testament, and his German translation of the Greek Testament with its annotations, comprise his *general* researches; and those which we term *special* are found in his chronological and apocalyptical writings, and in his several defences of them. That his chronological and apocalyptical writings frequently run into one another, was because the fore-appointment of *times* as well as of *events* entered indispensably into Bengel's views. His first expository publications were some concise tracts on the Apocalypse, inserted in various theological journals; afterwards, in 1736, he published his "Harmony of the Gospels;" and in 1740, "An Exposition of the Revelation of St. John;" as specimens of more enlarged expositions promised to the public. His

"Ordo Temporum" was published in 1741; his "Gnomon," in 1742; his "Cyclus," in 1745; his "Age of the World," in 1746; his "Sixty Practical Addresses on the Apocalypse," in 1747; his "Testimony of Truth," in 1748; the "German New Testament," in 1752; and the "Vindication of the Holy Scriptures," in 1755. As we cannot thus notice his expository works in the order of their publication, without repetitions and interruptions, therefore, to bring the subjects as nearly as we can to that order, we shall notice first, his *chronological* and *apocalyptical* writings; and then such as relate to the New Testament generally. As introductory to both, we shall exhibit a few lineaments of his character as an expositor, by referring to remarks scattered in his writings, and particularly to his essay "On the right Way of handling Divine Subjects," which he prefixed to a volume of sermons by J. Chr. Storr, published in 1750, on the Liturgical Portions of the Apostolical Epistles.* In this essay, he draws a striking contrast between his own views of scriptural exegesis, and those of the Neologians;† and observes, "that the most important, best, and greatest thing that can befall us in this transitory world is, not the most eminent and permanent possession of science, talent, riches and power; much less the most plenary gratification of sense and appetite; but such grace and strength as will enable us to live faithfully, and meekly submissive to the holy and blessed will of God in Christ Jesus, so as to find ourselves in the way of attainment unto life everlasting. On the part of God, it is HIS WORD which is the means of substantiating this; and on our part it is FAITH; by the combination of which simple means we are brought into communion with God, and of course to endless happiness. Whatever, therefore, He tells and teaches us in his word, we are to suffer ourselves to be told and taught. Though there can be no doubt that our first parents were originally endued with the knowledge of God, of human nature, and of all creatures, and with ability to use this knowledge for their happiness, even *then* God gave them *his word* for the exercise of their *faith*. The patriarchs too, and the people of Israel, were led on by the *word of God*. It was for the assistance and support of *faith*, that He caused his word to be committed to writing by Moses, by prophets and apostles. During the sundry

* The essay was reprinted in the second edition of his German version of the New Testament; (p. 1000, &c.)

† Compare his Letter (given above), addressed to a Young Civilian.

times in which these testimonies were committed to writing, God gave such witness of himself, by stupendous public miracles, and by glorious public manifestations of his power and presence, that no Israelite could entertain any doubt of the truth of such written testimonies. This confirmed assurance of Israel's faith was continued on to the faith of Christians; and thus He, who had named himself the God of Abraham, Isaac, and Jacob, was now called the Father of our Lord Jesus Christ; whose manifestation in the flesh, and whose written testimonies of that manifestation, are confirmed and established by their accordance with all the Scriptures of the Old Testament; by his own exalted declaration; by incontrovertible witnesses who saw, heard, and wrote accounts of all; as well as by a multitude and variety of stupendous public miracles. The Scriptures, moreover, carry in themselves independent and convincing evidence of the truth, validity, and sufficiency of all the narratives, doctrines, promises, and threatenings they contain. Truth is its own witness, and exacts our assent. I recognise the hand-writing of a friend, without needing to be told who has written to me. We want not the stars, much less a torch, to show us the sun; it is only the blind that cannot see it.

"By the written WORD then, must every thing stand or fall. If the word of a fallible mortal is sometimes so much to be accounted of, what inestimable value must be attached by the Almighty himself to His own word, to all and every part of it; though the ruin of heaven and earth should be required to bring it to pass! It also possesses a supernatural efficacy. Sometimes it is beforehand with us; its power is felt, as it were, unawares, especially by persons who have never been familiar with it; it takes men captive, and kindles faith within them, before they have even thought what faith is, or considered whether they will believe, or why they should believe. This is a very different thing from conviction by moral, historical, or mathematical inference. Still we are bound to use the word of God as *a means;* worthily of itself, and suitably to the purposes for which it is given—namely, for our conviction and persuasion to believe and obey it. And in order to do so, we must inwardly reverence and attend to it; carefully investigate and prove all things; humble ourselves always more and more before God; receive the truth *as* truth, grace *as* grace, justification and salvation *as in the highest degree desirable and welcome;* yield obedience to the Divine will in every thing, to the best of our knowledge;

earnestly and diligently call on the Father of our Lord Jesus Christ, for the aid of his Holy Spirit; seek to make his way known upon earth, and acceptable to others; not rest in fair and promising beginnings, but perpetually endeavour to grow in the grace and knowledge of God our Saviour. They who are thus disposed, will certainly have the heart established with grace. (John vii. 17; viii. 31, 32; Rom. xii. 2.) They, and they only, attain the true wisdom, fellowship with Christ Jesus, and communion with his saints; are sealed by his Holy Spirit of promise unto the day of redemption; and gain an earnest and foretaste of that fulness of joy which they shall possess at his right hand for evermore.

"It is of unspeakable advantage for all ranks and conditions to enjoy together public exercise of the word of God in their assemblies, and hereby to grow familiar with it. The simple text of Scripture ought, therefore, to be more diligently read in our churches. But there is likewise great advantage in scriptural exposition, and in experimental and practical applications of Scripture by preached sermons and printed works: whereas mere productions of the imagination, however ingenious—mere elaborate and elegant compositions—bold and daring inferences—swollen, forced, and fiery words, which after all have no vital warmth—such impertinences are any thing but to the purpose. When edification is made to consist in feeling that we admire fine invention, excellent reasoning, or beauty of language—which, alas! is all the edification which seems to belong to or to be sought after in many *pulpit discourses*, as they are called,—the whole amounts to nothing better than what St. Paul styles 'making the cross of Christ of none effect.' It is a destruction that wasteth at noon-day, in these reputedly enlightened times.

"The Scriptures supply us with many precious things, over and above the fundamental truths of salvation. The books of the whole sacred canon, such as we now have them, were not handed down to us by chance or accident; neither are we to regard them only as a manual of sayings and examples, or as isolated relics of antiquity, from which no perfect whole, no comprehensive and finished plan, can be educed; but as a matchless, regular account of God's dealings with man through every age of the world, from the commencement to the end of time, even to the consummation of all things. They indicate together one beautiful, harmonious, and gloriously connected system. For though each scriptural book is in itself something entire, and though each of the inspired penmen has his own manner and style of writing, one and the self-same Spirit breathes through all; one grand idea pervades all. Surely, then, it becomes us to accept with reverence, gratitude, vehement desire, and teachableness, ALL AND EVERY THING which God here lays before us; and not of vain conceit to reject or strike out any portion or particle as useless. For, in the word of God, one thing ever serves to illustrate and confirm another: what God effects in individual saints, and what he effects for his people at large, are mutually and marvellously interwoven; and a single glance at that vast economy which stretches itself out over all, is of infinitely more personal consequence to us than to know the most interesting cabinet secrets of all earthly potentates.

"Many a forced interpretation of Scripture is incurred by making haste to clear up every difficulty that lies on one side of a subject, and stumbling upon greater difficulties on the other. These should be distributed, as nearly as possible, to either side alike; which would leave us certainly a narrower space between them, but would serve the more to keep us in the middle and straightforward, that is, in the safest and shortest, direction.

"Experience, especially in these times, shows how dangerous it is to contract the attention to any point of Scripture apart from the whole. Thus we may err by a factitious glorying in grace, or dwelling upon one matter of faith to the disparagement of the rest (in the way that some really christian brethren have treated the subject of our Saviour's passion); or we may attribute too much to fallen nature's light, by adopting only such Scripture statements as we can explain and vindicate by human reason. The latter of these errors distinguished a sect in Italy before the Reformation, which was then very small, but which has now fearfully extended itself over France, England, and Germany. Numbers have hereby come to deny the very existence of God; while those who would make the best of it consider religion as nothing more than decency and propriety of conduct; and will not even hear of an atoning Christ, or of our righteousness in him, or of the work of the Holy Spirit (on the heart), or of any thing taught exclusively by revelation and above natural reason. Those who have settled down into the desperate resolution of not referring to the word of God as their standard of inquiry, it is better always to let alone; not a pen should be put to paper on *their* account. Persons of this stamp will hardly ever be set right by argumentative deductions, however legitimately inferred. The great work of true illumination and conversion, when it takes place in such persons at all, begins rather by a ray from the word of God at once, or upon occasion of some sudden affliction of a temporal or spiritual nature. But we ought to guard others against them, for the preservation of those who are more worthy the name of God's human creatures. This, however, is best done by applying his written word in its own simplicity. There are others, who, with all their respect for revelation, are still for carrying the exercise of our limited reason beyond its legitimate bounds; which necessarily leads to a multitude of errors. To such persons the following plain thoughts may be of service:—

"1. Reason is a noble and invaluable faculty of the soul; it is an instrument for perception of things spiritual and physical within us and around us. 2. Nevertheless, all the properties of this faculty are become most affectingly deranged and corrupted, so as now to be subject to very great ignorance; yes, to many doubts and errors. 3. But, notwithstanding this perversion and corruption of the reasoning faculty, we human beings still retain a high preeminence in the visible creation; we are not sunk to the grade of horse or mule, but remain *men*, and retain the capacity of perceiving and understanding things presented to us. 4. The things which reason perceives, are many and various; some of them are also of a mysterious nature, but have nevertheless been known to the wiser sort among the heathen. 5. Some truths reason perceives of itself; such, for instance, as a heathen, finding them in the Scriptures, may easily assent to, without regarding the Scriptures as Divinely inspired; others it perceives by scriptural revelation *alone*, and accepts them upon the *authority* of that revelation, by the exercise of a property which is very familiar to it upon common natural subjects, and which is called *belief*. 6. Therefore, in perceiving truths *out* of its own natural reach, but brought to it by Divine revelation, reason is to be regarded as merely *instrumental:* whereas, in perceiving truths which are *within* its own natural reach, it is to be considered as *principal;* for in these it makes and employs its own inferences; but in the others it is to us nothing more than a transmitting medium. 7. There are some truths which, though reason can of itself perceive to a certain extent, it is helped much more clearly to perceive by the Holy Scriptures; here, then, also it is rather instrumental than principal. The truths I advert to are those which relate to the existence of God, his attributes, operations, and benefits; the existence of separate spirits, both good and evil; the existence and attributes of the human soul, and its union with the body. How far reason would conduct us of itself upon these subjects, can now no more be determined than we can determine how far the light of a lamp would reach if we had perpetual sunshine; indeed, the scanty light which the heathen have had upon many things, came originally by tradition from the Scriptures or divine revelation. 8. Human reason is most at home in things *physical* and *material.* From these it can deduce many a profitable inference and invention for the life that now is. 9. But as godliness is profitable for all things, having promise of the life that now is, and of that which is to come, so this most profitable thing in the world, consists in knowing God, the Creator and Disposer of all things. 10. Good and evil are also in some measure discerned even by the natural mind and conscience. 11. But there are matters of infinite moment upon which natural reason furnishes no data whatever to proceed upon. In mathematics, natural philosophy, and logic, we may very safely acknowledge every prerogative claimed by what is called 'the new* philosophy' (of Wolf); but upon divine subjects it is quite another thing; here we have need of the most reverential caution, lest our natural reason arrogantly assume principles of its own invention to proceed from, or measures and rules of its own to work by; for in matters of pure revelation it is, and can be, nothing more than secondary and passive; it is a mere transmitting medium (like this refracting atmosphere, for our communion with the great luminary, over which it has no control). 12. When Scripture directly testifies any thing in plain words, Reason has nothing to do with arbitrating upon its *possibility;* for her own comprehension is so very limited, that though she may be able sometimes, or even frequently, to say a thing is *possible,* it is but seldom she can pronounce a thing to be *im*possible, even in a *physical* respect,—to say nothing of things supernatural. 13. Therefore we do not rightly handle divine subjects, when, borrowing from Scripture what can be learnt *from Scripture only,* we proceed to show its possibility by our own

* Bengel has observed elsewhere, that speculative philosophic systems have always very quickly become obsolete; whereas, practical truths have been preserved by their constant recurrence and use in common life. Yet, subjects remote from ordinary understandings are capable of frequent reappearance in a new dress; and thus it is that what are called new systems, are often nothing more than new modifications of what has appeared and disappeared again and again.

mere reasonings; for this looks like attempting by natural knowledge to supersede faith in the Divine testimony; and when we have done all that can be done in this way, the sneering infidel can quite as readily produce his *rational* arguments, contradictory to and equally valid with our own; yes, and falsehood, poised against truth in such unlawful scales, may very easily be made to preponderate. If a missionary, who has brought to a heathen country truths necessarily thus borrowed from Scripture, were to attempt to render them influential upon pagans by arguments of mere reasoning, experience would soon teach him that any thing but success was to be looked for by such a method of proceeding. 14. To bring an unbelieving person to true and practical faith, is a work of Divine power. Consequently, the first thing to be done with such a person is, to set before him the great *matters* of faith, and *the duty* of his own implicit assent and consent. Here we ought to use no circumlocution, no endeavour to come at him by methods indirect; especially if he be at all disposed to acknowledge the Divine authority of holy writ.

"The moral influence experienced from any particular truth which we have embraced by mere natural reason, is weak as compared with the influence which that same truth produces when afterwards embraced by faith; for 'when faith cometh,' a power always accompanies it which is quite supernatural.

"Reason will even affect the most recondite subjects, as if it could do something with them; it would discover, devise, and settle every thing: but faith embraces what is plain and easy, and by her own moral simplicity she remains unperplexed at what is intellectually abstruse. Never let me think of exhausting any sacred subject. I must resolve to work on for God, calmly awaiting whatever he may be pleased to disclose. It is thus I have come by what little knowledge I possess; and have learnt by experience, that through endearing to ourselves this calm and passive submission of spirit, so as to seek it and pursue it, we attain in good time to far clearer light than ever we could have enjoyed by our own too forward and prying exertions. 15. He who in the true spirit of faith keeps himself up to the word of God, will find, as he goes on, that he is learning how to treat divine subjects appropriately and naturally. I mean, that even his natural endowments become softly and sweetly blended with the grace bestowed on him. Indeed faith, while it always communicates a teachableness and tractableness to its possessor, sheds from him upon others also the benign influence of those qualities; so that even the advancement of learning is much indebted to influence of this sort; and it was *in Christendom*, and by means of *Christians*, that the sciences first began their present triumphant course. 16. When reason's native powers are too highly extolled, other human capabilities are of course lauded in the same proportion; one consequence of which is, that men learn to *trust in themselves:* and this is one among the sad signs of the present times. 17. But what is most to be lamented is, that people are insensibly sinking into deeper and deeper ignorance of the influence of divine grace, and are even learning to regard all scriptural doctrine respecting it with a suspicious eye; and this to such a degree, that could Pelagius himself appear among them, he would surely mourn over our modern Pelagianism."

The above remarks strikingly show how opposite to every thing like the rationalism and naturalism of the present day, were Bengel's sentiments upon the inspiration of the Scriptures, and their legitimate exposition. His remarks, which we shall next adduce, will inform us how far he considered it right to use the liberty of Scripture exposition, with regard to the Lutheran system of divinity as then in use, as also in reference to church confessions, and allegorical or mystical systems of interpretation.

"The truth of God must be our dearest object, whether the popular system accord with it or not. Far be it from us to wrest or force Scripture into compliance with any favourite hypothesis. It never can be right to invent dogmas, and then go to Scripture in order to prove them.

"It is better to run all lengths with Scripture truth in a natural and open manner, than to shift and twist and accommodate. Straightforward conduct may draw against us bitterness and rancour for a time, but sweetness will come out of it. Every single truth is a light of itself; and every error, however minute, is darkness as far as it goes. Though there is much Divine forbearance with human errors, every error is something contrary to the Divine glory and honour; to these, truth, and truth only, is that which conforms. Here then is an argument for prizing the most simple truths as invaluable jewels.

"He who professes nothing more than what is agreed to by his party, may proceed unopposed, though he defend it with novel arguments, stronger or weaker, of his own, or with arguments borrowed or deduced from any novel system of others.

But he who conscientiously, and simply "for the Truth's sake," endeavours to make farther advances in the knowledge and confession of the Truth, must not expect to be exempt from trials and temptations. For if his attention respect *the things taught*, rather than *the persons who teach*, so that he cannot suffer himself to be influenced by any respect of persons, it will be impossible for him to avoid giving offence in one way or another. This, at least, has been my own experience.

"Every Divine communication carries (like the diamond) its own light with it, thus showing from whence it comes. No touchstone is required to discriminate it. It comes, indeed, with additional and more *immediate* demonstration of the Spirit to the faith of him who receives it cordially; but its *general* demonstration is given as a precious deposit to the church at large, and abides as such in the written Word.

"We ought immediately to apply ourselves to learn whatever, by diligent research in the fear of God, and by calling upon Him, we may become enabled to learn; we ought to do this at once, rather than delay under the notion of waiting for extraordinary illumination or influence; lest by and by we should come to fancy that we want neither book nor human teacher. Under the New-Testament Dispensation, God bestows his Spirit upon men, that they may first prove all things for themselves, and then freely proceed to the business before them. He does not bestow and then take away, but he bestows for our accumulation; and so he continues to bestow and to add. On man in general he has conferred intellect and reason; these he does not take away or supersede in the person whom he converts and enlightens, but will have him make use of them. He has moreover given the Bible. This also we are to make use of; and in so far as this may suffice, he bestows no additional revelation.

"What is commonly styled Lutheran orthodoxy in the present day, deviates in many particulars from the Old Lutheran divinity. Hunnius, Grawerus, and Calovius contributed much to this deviation; and their rigid and nominally orthodox followers in more recent times, at Wittenburg and Hamburgh, once wished to draw up a new confession, that might serve to get rid of the Pietists. (This was acting in character.) Moreover, the nominally orthodox cannot call us in question upon points left undecided in a church confession, however offensive they may find them. And yet, the Augsburg Confession is a great work, considering the dark times in which it was drawn up. The other confessions also are of such a tenor, that they ought to be studied, if only on this account, independently of their historical importance. But never let them be converted into barriers to stop the increasing stream of divine truth, which surely ought to swell and spread more and more as time advances. Unreasonable would it be to wish the sun not to mount up from the east, because we had light enough to read by at four o'clock in a summer morning.*

"It is one unquestionable principle of exposition, to introduce nothing *into* the Scriptures, but every thing *from* them, and to overlook nothing which is really contained *in* them. Indeed, the longer we live, the more occasion have we to beware of our own hearts, our busy minds, and our imaginations; and to keep close to the simple word of God. We must be particularly cautious of nursing *every* thought or idea that is started within us, however conformed to Scripture it may appear; and we must never lose sight of the connexion and analogy of revealed truth as a whole. Especially requisite is care of this sort in studying the Apocalypse, wherein most expositors have erred by confining their attention to distinct portions, and interpreting these by their own imagination; instead of taking the whole book together, and attempting the interpretation of one part by its connexion with the rest. Again; some methods of exposition are too controversial—others too mystical or allegorical. But the true commentator on divine revelation will fasten his primary attention upon the *letter*, (literal meaning,) but never forget that the *spirit* must equally accompany him.

"There are ascetic persons of strong feeling, who indulge in mystical meditations; others of an opposite character, are all for book learning, and absorb themselves in erudition. These two classes heartily revolt at each other. I am something between both, and please neither of them; being regarded by the former as a mere scholar, and by the latter as a mystic and enthusiast. It is all very well, as it shows that I am not aiming to 'have glory of men;' for we read of some who 'have their reward.'

"We must never devise a more spiritual meaning for scripture passages than the Holy Spirit intended; but, considering God to be virtually addressing us, in his word, we should concern ourselves first to understand Him, and then how to communicate it to others. He is great, and past finding out; no wonder then that he does not teach us every thing in this life, which is but a

* Compare (above, Part II. ch. i. 10.) Bengel's letter on Subscription to the Symbolical Books, Confessions, &c.

pilgrimage; though he discloses enough for our direction and progress. More than this would not be useful just now; it is reserved for home.

"If we wish to be wise above what is written, or to know more upon scripture subjects than what the Scriptures, as a whole, give out to us, we depart from the word of the Cross, from the simplicity of faith, and from what qualifies us for assisting to 'make wise the simple.'

"Many habituate themselves to such a sort of inward feeling, and peculiar mode of expression, upon secret and mysterious subjects, that their understanding loses its susceptibility of inference and proof, however conclusively drawn from the sure word of prophecy, or from facts of history. But nothing is too external for minds in a spiritually sound condition; they can bring themselves to converse with *any* of the revealed works and footsteps of God. To regard *any* thing of the kind as nugatory, would, in their account, be to find fault with 'the Holy One of Israel.' As in every point and waving line of creation and providence, so in every jot and tittle of the written word, yes, in every bearing of both, however seemingly unimportant, they can learn to find some force and significance of its own.

"The properties of Scripture may be summarily enumerated as follows:—1. All of it is clear and intelligible enough to persons who sincerely desire to conform the heart and life accordingly. 2. The word of God is found to be of special effect upon the human heart, for conviction, conversion, instruction, and comfort, in all ages and nations; and hereby evinces—3. its Divine authority; whence it follows—4. that it is the standard for determining every controversy in matters of faith. 5. It is *perfect*, as containing whatever is necessary to be known and believed in order to salvation. 6. It is also *profitable*, as containing nothing irrelevant or useless. 7. The providence of God has watched over it, so that it retains its purity unsullied, and can be enjoyed now, as it ever could be from the beginning.

"The means and ordinances of grace have a twofold respect to the compound nature of man. This twofold respect is something which, God having joined together, we must neither sunder nor lose sight of; but we must not mistake the transparent substance of the precious but earthen vessel, for the substance of its *more* precious and heavenly contents; nor the glittering and well-conformed scabbard, for the sharp two-edged Sword of the Lord.

"The *historical* matters of Scripture, both in narrative and prophecy, constitute, as it were, the *bones* of its system; whereas, the *spiritual* matters are as its muscles, blood-vessels, and nerves. As the *bones* are necessary to the human system, so Scripture *must* have its *historical* matters. Yet it is precisely because these are not found in the apocryphal book of 'Ecclesiasticus,' and in that called the book of 'Wisdom,' that these books have been mistaken for canonical, by those who can enjoy nothing but what to them appears exclusively of a spiritual character.

"If our observation be confined to our own spiritual experiences, and we take no notice of the manifold, wonderful, and massy exhibitions which God gives of himself in the grand total of the world and of the church, it is easy to raise questions upon every thing. So, if we have nothing to do with any book, inquiry, or exercise, except such as run upon subjects specifically religious, we contract a wrong, because delicate and morbid, habit of mind. Externals, like the integuments of vegetables growing or gathered, have their use. Lay by some sorts of seed *in the husk*, and they dry all the better for it, and are much fitter for sowing.

"The sum, then, of the above remarks is—1. That the Holy Scriptures are the sole repertory of that complete system of truth which man, as a being appointed to obtain everlasting salvation, needs to be acquainted with. 2. That every, even the minutest, scripture detail has its importance in the structure of revealed truth; and natural reason has often the power of seeing and tracing that importance, but never the power of choosing or rejecting any such matter at pleasure. 3. That the expositor who nullifies the *historical* groundwork of Scripture for the sake of finding only *spiritual* truths everywhere, certainly brings death upon all correct interpretation. 4. That the Scriptures best illustrate and corroborate themselves; consequently, those expositions are the safest which keep closest to the text. 5. That the *whole* power and glory of the inspired writings can be known only to the honest, devout, and believing inquirer. 6. That much in Scripture is found to stretch far beyond the confines of reason's natural light, and far beyond even our symbolical books. Still, whatever of the kind is evidently declared in Scripture, ought to be received as a part of the system of divine truth, notwithstanding all reputed philosophy, and all reputedly orthodox theology. On the other hand, every theological notion, which is not evidently deducible from Holy Scripture, ought to be regarded with religious suspicion and caution."

It is hardly necessary to say, that such sentiments as these rest upon a thorough conviction of the real inspiration of the Scriptures. Bengel, however, considered their divine inspiration as distinguishable into two kinds. He says—" The kind of inspiration vouchsafed to the *apostles,* appears somewhat different from that imparted to the *prophets* of the Old Testament. The age of the prophets may be regarded as years of minority—that of the apostles, as the period of riper years. To the former was dictated every word they were to speak or write: the latter had greater scope in this respect; still, their writings are as much the word of God,as are those of the prophets. Even in our own meditations, we can feel how easily the appropriate words for expressing them will come of their own accord. Thus, the very thoughts with which God inspired the apostles, furnished them at once with competence and propriety of expression; else, how could they, as 'unlearned and ignorant men,' have had the command, which we see they had, of language so full, beautiful, and every way appropriate. A minister of government may have two secretaries: one a mere writing clerk, to whom every word is dictated; the other well acquainted with his lord's mind, and thus enabled to express it accurately in words of his own; so that what he has thus expressed is as much the will and pleasure of his principal, as if it had been written by verbal dictation."

Having seen upon what principles of exposition Bengel proceeded, let us just notice him as making use of them in his study. Here we find him surrounded with the choicest works of those who preceded him in the same department of knowledge. For though he was not rich, and in pecuniary respects his authorship did very little for him,* he laid out much of his money upon books;† but he had always the prudence to expend it principally upon such as were the most valuable for sound learning, and at the same time the most scarce. Those which he wanted only for once reading, and such as he could conveniently borrow, he did not purchase, but made from them accurate extracts, which he neatly arranged in common-places. As it was not, however, his " care to get together a mere assemblage of other men's opinions,

* He once said—" It is well that I am not thus working for my bread, or I should long ago have been obliged to take to some other business."

† He said—" I certainly could have spent a less quantity of money in this way; but we do not *live* by money; neither does the respectability or credit of a family absolutely depend upon money."

so he was still farther from desiring to depend solely on his own reflections."

His favourite expositors upon the New Testament were Luther and Hedinger;* but dearer and more important to him than either was Scripture itself. "The word of God," he said, "is always valuable and savoury in its own pure and simple form; but when saturated with human explanations, it is apt to cloy."

He used prayer for becoming collected and fitted to his work; and the success which attended and crowned it, often drew from him grateful praises and thanksgivings. Thus, when his *Gnomon* was sent him completed from the Tübingen university press, on the 28th of March, 1742, his spirits were quite raised to thank God and take courage; and he sang that evening the well known hymn—

"O Thou, who our best works hast wrought,
And thus far help'd me to success,
Attune my soul to grateful thought,
Thy great and holy name to bless;
That I to thee anew may live,
And to thy grace the glory give.

"I thank thee, Lord;—my gifts are thine;
More than I sought hast thou bestow'd;
Then let me henceforth claim as mine
Nothing unpromis'd by my God;
Henceforth, O make me more and more
Humble in mind, in spirit poor."

When he began the revisal of his "Exposition of the Apocalypse," he said, "O what cause have I to ask continual help of God in this important business!"

He wrought not like a hired servant working only for others, but his heart and mind liberally enjoyed the fruit of his labours. Thus we find him saying: "I have been quite delighting myself for some time in the Epistle to the Colossians. How dazzlingly does the incommunicable glory of the Lord shine forth in this epistle; and yet what striking condescension does he here display towards ourselves!"—"I experience particular enjoyment of the second Epistle to the Corinthians. St. Paul, when he wrote it, was continually exposed to *perils of death;* and yet the epistle breathes nothing but *life.*"—"I have often been in such a frame of mind, that those chapters of the Book of Proverbs, in which I had formerly looked for no connexion at all,

* He also acknowledged, that "conversational remarks which he had often silently listened to, had helped him to many a useful reflection for his annotations."

have appeared to me as though their sentences followed one another in an order truly beautiful."—On 1 Tim. vi. 12, he said, "O God, thou hast called *me* to eternal life; thou too hast laid hold on *me;* withdraw not thy hand from me, until *I* have laid hold on that eternal life."—On 2 Cor. vii. 1, "O God! impress more deeply on my own heart thine exceeding great and precious *promises*, that I may *perfect holiness in thy fear!*"

CHAPTER V.

HIS CHRONOLOGICAL WRITINGS.

PROCEEDING now to a more particular account of his works of exposition, we begin with his chronological writings, and first with his "Ordo Temporum."* The object of this work, as its title imports, was *to exhibit the whole line of chronology which pervades the historical and prophetic books of the Old and New Testament, from its commencement to its termination; and thus to cumulate proof that the Scriptures form one beautifully connected and credible whole.* In the preface he shows, by a series of examples illustrative of each other, that "as the many numerical specifications found in Scripture have a peculiar claim to our attention, because they belong to Divine Revelation, so they have a mutual connexion, which conducts us on to one great and important final point—the day of Christ's appearing. That to this object the historical as well as prophetic books severally contribute; and that by attending to their intimations with simplicity and a desire to learn, we shall find an agreeable path through the obscure labyrinth of their chronology. This path he had attempted to trace; and, in so doing, had suggested a method of explicitly handling whatever appeared most essential and useful."

But he considers it necessary to give a few preliminary advices.—1. It was not to be thought, that he presumed to foretell or determine the period of the last day, though many of his investigations seemed to touch very nearly upon it. 2. He requested that, upon matters of this sort, his work might not be prejudiced by the notion, that futurity is intended of God to be hidden from us entirely; or that it is useless and dangerous to attempt determining any thing about it, &c.; for that such a

* Its whole title is, "Jo. Alberti Bengelii Ordo Temporum, a principio per periodos œconomiæ divinæ historicas atque propheticas ad finem usque ita deductus, ut tota series et quarumvis partium analogia sempiternæ virtutis ac sapientiæ cultoribus ex Scripturâ V. et N. T. tanquam uno reverà documento proponatur. Stuttg. apud Christoph. Erhard, Bibliop., A. D. 1741." (The second edition, considerably enlarged, was printed at Stuttgart by Joh. Benedict Metzler; curante Eberhardo Friederico Hellwagio.)

notion savoured too much of judging Holy Scripture itself by our own fancies and presumptions. 3. He wished that his book might be carefully read through, before any opinion were given of it. 4. He requested the reader attentively to discriminate between what he stated as *possible*, and what as actual and *certain;* also, 5. between what he expressly attempts to prove, and what he but cursorily hints at. 6. He desired that judgment might be formed from *his own words*, and not from sentiments reported to be his. 7. He hoped that persons unskilled in calculations would spare themselves the trouble of attempting to find out by any other method, what cannot be ascertained except by calculation. 8. And that the reader would not spend too much time in endeavouring to digest the tough corticating threads of the chronology, but would take care to enjoy the delicious kernel enveloped in them.

The work then commences with an accurate table of the whole chronological line from Adam to the time of the apostles, very useful for the elucidation of essential matters in the body of the treatise. He next proceeds to treat of the notifications of time which are scattered throughout the books of Scripture, and shows how they may all be viewed in intimate connexion as unbroken links of one common chronology. As it will be sufficient here to notice the results of his inquiries, we refer the reader for further information to the book itself. The pre-adamite hypothesis he considers as a mere dream, refuted by Gen. i. 26; ii. 7; v. 1; yet he thinks it probable that the commencement of time corresponds with our autumn; that man's state of innocence was of very short duration; and that the Israelitish day of atonement (the tenth of the seventh month,) is the anniversary of the fall of man.

	Years.
By Genesis v. he reckons from the creation to the deluge - - - - - -	1656
— Gen. xi. From the deluge to the birth of Abraham - - - - -	290
— Gen. xxi. 5. From the birth of Abraham to the birth of Isaac - - - -	100
— Gen. xxv. 26. From the birth of Isaac to that of Jacob - - - - -	60
— Gen. xli. 46; xlv. 6; xlvii. 28. From the birth of Jacob to that of Joseph - - -	90
	2196

		Years.
	Brought forward - -	2196
By Gen. l. 26.	From Joseph's birth to his death -	110
From thence to the departure out of Egypt	-	140
		2446

He obtains the last computation in this series, by comparing Gen. xv. 13, with Judith v. 8, (Lutheran version,) and Acts vii. 8, where it is stated that the seed of Abraham, commencing with Isaac, were to be "*strangers*" four hundred years. Isaac then, having been born within this period, was sixty years old at the birth of Jacob, who was ninety years old at the birth of Joseph, who lived a hundred and ten years; so that there remain a hundred and forty years to complete the four hundred.

Now, by referring to the seventeenth verse of the third chapter of the Epistle to the Galatians, where it is stated that the Sinaitic law was given four hundred and thirty years after the promise made to Abraham, we find from the call of Abraham, in his seventieth year, to the giving of the law, four hundred and thirty years exactly.

The only difficulty is that suggested by the fortieth verse of the twelfth chapter of Exodus; where the four hundred and thirty years seem to be reckoned (not from the birth of Isaac, but) from Israel's beginning to sojourn *in Egypt*. But that this is only a chronological *diastole*,* is evident from various considerations, particularly that of scripture genealogies.

Thus, from Adam to the Exodus we have 2446 years. By 1 Kings vi. 1; 2 Chron. iii. 2, there were 480 years from the Exodus to the fourth of the reign of Solomon; or 487 to the completion of the temple. These 487 years are distributed as follows:

		Years.
Deut. i. 3, 4.	The sojourning in the wilderness -	40
Joshua xiv. 7, 10.	The conquest of Canaan - -	5
Judges iii. 11; iii. 30; v. 31; viii. 28; ix. 22; x. 2, 3, 8; xii. 9, 11, 14; xiii. 1. 1 Sam. iv. 18; vii. 2.	Period of the judges, and of Samuel and Saul - - -	391
		436

* A chronological *diastole*, is a figure of speech (common in Eastern languages) which *dilates* into a longer period of time the substance of what *actually* transpired within a shorter one. Examples of the kind occur in the sacred writings. Thus Matt. xii. 40,—"The Son of Man shall be in the heart of the earth *three days and nights*."

		Years.
	Brought forward -	- 516
1 Kings ii. 11. 2 Sam. v. 4. 1 Chron. xxix. 27.	Reign of David -	- 40
1 Kings vi. 1, 38. 2 Chron. iii. 2.	Solomon reigned to the commencement of the temple, four years; and from thence to its completion, seven years	11
		487
	added to the above	2446
Thus the temple was finished in the year of the world		2933

Two considerable difficulties having here arisen, 1. from the appearance of 79 years more in the book of Judges, (iii. 8, 14; iv. 3; vi. 1; xii. 7; xv. 20; xvi. 31;) and 2. because his calculation seemed to omit the reign of Saul, which, by Acts xiii. 21, was of forty years' continuance; Bengel shows by an induction of particulars, that those 79 years may very well be included in the above-mentioned period of the judges; since whoever had been divinely called to act as judge, upon only a single occasion, bore, we may say, the style and title of a judge for the rest of his life; or, in the language of the Bible, was said to have judged Israel so many years; though he never afterwards *acted* as chief, either in a civil or a military capacity.

Thus was it shown that the actual duration of Saul's reign was but three years and a half; that consequently *four* instead of *forty* years is perhaps the true reading in the twenty-first verse of the thirteenth chapter of the Acts of the Apostles; and that king Saul's three years and a half may be included in the 391 years of the judges. Yet, supposing that St. Paul *did* ascribe forty years to the reign of Saul, then he might mean, not his personal reign, but the whole time of Samuel the prophet, to the beginning of the reign of David.

But he further brought the statement of Acts xiii. 20 into harmony with the above chronological distribution, by means of a reading, which, having the authority of several valuable MSS., refers the 450 years therein mentioned to the preceding verse; the sense thus being, not that the judges governed during 450 years, but that the period from the birth of Isaac, or, in other words, from the time of Abraham's "seed being a stranger in a land that was not theirs," (Gen. xv. 13,) to the time of the partition of Canaan, was 450 years. Then, by 1 Kings xi. 42, and 2 Chron. ix. 30, he finds the conclusion of king Solomon's forty years to be Anno Mundi 2963.

The years of the kings of Judah, to the eleventh of Zedekiah, are, according to the Books of Kings and Chronicles, 393 years.

But the reigns of the kings of Israel were to be reduced to chronological harmony with those of Judah. For this purpose he divides into two unequal parts, the whole period from the revolt of the ten tribes to the taking of Samaria by Shalmanezer. The *former* portion of this period reaches to the death of Joram king of Israel, to which date the collective reigns of the kings of Israel give ninety-eight years, and those of the kings of Judah ninety-five. Assuming the latter number as the more exact, he adjusts this difference of three years by supposing, as fairly deducible from the text, that the years included in the reigns of those kings were not always *entire* ones. In the *latter* portion of the above period the collective reigns of the kings of Judah give 165 years, and those of the kings of Israel 143; so that here we have a difference of about twenty-two years, which he adjusts by a closer examination of the text; whence it appears that, for some unknown reason, twelve years of Jeroboam's reign are not reckoned; and that the government of the ten tribes, prior to the reign of Hoshea, in which it was utterly overthrown, suffered an interregnum of nine years, through an Assyrian invasion.

The kingdom of Judah survived that of Israel a hundred and thirty-three years. Thus, by adding the above 2963 to 393 (that is, to 95 + 165 + 133), we have for the year of the world, 3356, when Nebuchadnezzar burnt Jerusalem, in the nineteenth year of his own reign (Jer. lii. 29; 2 Kings xxv. 8). And here scripture chronology connects itself with that of profane history, just where the latter has its dates so clearly ascertained, that we can the more easily forego what the Old Testament no longer furnishes.* For we can now refer to the canon of Berosus and

* "The history contained in the Old Testament is throughout distinct, methodical, and consistent; while profane history is utterly deficient in the first ages, and full of fictions in the succeeding ages, and becomes clear and precise in the principal facts, *only* about the period when the Old-Testament history ends, &c. It is further worthy of remark, that this same nation (the Jewish), who may not have lost so much as one year from the creation of the world to the Babylonish captivity, as soon as they were deprived of the assistance of the prophets, became the most inaccurate in their methods of keeping time; there being nothing more erroneous than the accounts of Josephus and the modern Jews, from the time of Cyrus to that of Alexander the Great, notwithstanding that all the requisite aids might easily have been borrowed from the neigh-

Ptolemy, which, with what may be collected from Josephus, supplies the information required. According to those writers, Nebuchadnezzar (Nabocolassar) began his reign 604 years before the vulgar Christian era, or in the 4110th year of the Julian period; whence it may be inferred, that the eighteenth year of Nebuchadnezzar's reign, or A. M. 3356, is the 587th before the Christian era, or the 4127th of the Julian period.

He then distributes the interval of 587 years A. C. as follows:—

	Years.
Nebuchadnezzar's reign continued, after the burning of Jerusalem - - - - - -	25
Evilmerodach (Ilvarodamus) reigned - - -	2
Neriglissor (Nericassolassarus) - - - -	4
Nabonidus (Nabonadius) - - - -	17
To the edict of Cyrus - - - - - -	3
To the rebuilding of the Temple - - -	15
To the arrival of Ezra in Judea (Ezra vii. 1), in the 7th year of Artaxerxes Longimanus - - -	63
To the arrival of Nehemiah in Judea (Neh. ii. 1) -	13
To Alexander the Great - - - - -	113
To the persecution under Antiochus Epiphanes -	164
To the reign of Herod - - - - - -	128
To the real year of the Birth of Christ - - -	37
To the commencement of the vulgar era - -	3
	587
To these add - - -	3356
And we have	3943

years, from Adam to the commencement of the vulgar Christian era.

Having thus seen in what manner Bengel arranged the chronology of the Old Testament, we must take some notice how he harmonized it with the periods mentioned in prophecy. Let the following passages be attended to for the purpose.

I. By comparing Jer. xxv. 11 with Jer. xxix. 10, 2 Chron. xxxvi. 21, 22, and Dan. ix. 2, he shows that the text warrants us to consider the prediction of the seventy years' captivity as denoting, not so much the Jews' captive residence in Babylon,

bouring nations, who now kept regular annals. Whence it appears, that the exactness of the sacred history was owing to Divine assistance."—*Rev. Hartwell Horne's Introduction to the Scriptures*, vol. i. p. 190, fifth edition.

as the whole period of their servitude under the Babylonian yoke; which commenced *one year before* Nebuchadnezzar came to full possession of the throne, while he governed as crown prince in the reign of his father; (comp. Dan. i. 1—5; xi. 1; Jer. xxv. 1;) and lasted during

43	years of his own reign,
2	under Evilmerodach,
4	under Neriglissor,
17	under Belshazzar, or Nabonidus, and
3	more to the Edict of Cyrus,
—	
70	years.

Consequently it began in the third year of Jehoiakim, after he had revolted from Nebuchadnezzar, but was now reduced to entire subjection under him, 2 Kings xxiv. 1—3.

II. The period of seventy years' captivity, mentioned in Zech. i. 12, is not quite coincident with that spoken of by Jeremiah; but must be computed from the siege of Jerusalem, A. M. 3354, to the second year of Darius Hystaspis, A. M. 3424. Again, the period of 70 years in Zech. vii. 5, is distinct from both, and is to be computed from the destruction of Jerusalem, A. M. 3356, to the fourth year of Darius, A. M. 3426.

III. The 390 and 40 years in Ezek. iv. 5—9, end together. The former commenced A. M. 2966, in the fourth year of Rehoboam, 2 Chron. xi. 17, and ended A. M. 3356, when Jerusalem was burnt under Nebuchadnezzar; the latter began A. M. 3316, the thirteenth year of the reign of Josiah, and ended also in A. M. 3356, the eleventh year of the reign of Zedekiah.

IV. The prediction in Daniel ix. 24—27 (of the seventy weeks distributed into periods of 7, 62, and 1,) Bengel thus paraphrases: "Know this, that from the going forth of the commandment, shall the Jerusalem, which is to last until Messiah the Prince, be building during *seven* weeks; then shall the streets and walls be restored, and preserved in repair, though in troublous times, for *sixty and two* weeks; and after the expiration of the sixty-second week, shall Messiah be cut off and be no more. And (to rebuke the nation for this rejection of the Messiah,) the people of the Prince shall (afterwards) come and destroy the city and the sanctuary; but he shall confirm the covenant with many for *one* week; and *in the half of the week* he shall cause the sacrifice and the oblation to cease."

Bengel, in the *first* edition of his "*Harmony of the Gospels,*" page 71, had understood these seventy weeks to mean seventy septenaries of years, or four hundred and ninety common years; and had reckoned their commencement from the seventh of Artaxerxes to A. D. 36; so that the last septenary would begin in A. D. 27, with John's appearing in the wilderness, and Christ's entrance upon his public ministry. But in his "*Ordo Temporum*," and in the *second* edition of his "*Harmony*," page 99, he gives another solution, as considering that he had found in the Apocalypse the true key to these numbers; namely, that the seventy weeks are equal to 555$\frac{5}{9}$ common years. As analogous to this, he adduces Ezek. xl. 5, where a measure somewhat larger than the ordinary one is used for prophetic notation. Agreeably to this computation, he finds the point of time to be reckoned from, in the words of Daniel, which speak of "*the going forth of the commandment*," and which he refers to Zech. i. 7, as also to Ezra iv. 24; and thus considers the seventy weeks as commencing with *the second year of Darius.* Now this Darius, as appears from the most approved chronologies, is Darius *Hystaspis;* and it is further evident, from Ptolemy and Eusebius, that the *second* year of this Darius is the 519th year before the vulgar Christian era. Accordingly, the first seven weeks (+ 54 years) reach to the 455th year before this era; that is, to the first year of Artaxerxes Longimanus, consequently they include the reigns of those Persian kings who encouraged the rebuilding of Jerusalem, and reach just to that period when Haggai (ii. 9,) and Zechariah (ix. 9,) testified, that in *this* temple and in *this* city the Messiah should appear.

During the succeeding sixty-two weeks (or 492$\frac{4}{63}$ years), the streets and walls were entirely set in order, and continually improving. This period reaches to about the end of A. D. 28, the year of that feast of tabernacles mentioned in John vii. 2. (Comp. "Harmony of the Gospels," 2d edit. p. 349.) If by "the people of the Prince, be meant the people of Israel, we know that from the time of Christ they began to cooperate in the final destruction of their city and temple. (Matt. xxvii. 25; Acts v. 28; Luke xix. 40—44.) The Roman armies, however, may be meant by this expression.

In the last prophetic week, we find the latter part of Christ's ministry, his oblation of himself, (Matt. xxvi. 28,) the commencement of the New Testament ministry, (Luke xxiv. 27,) and that full adoption of the Gentiles into the christian church, which is related in the tenth chapter of the Acts of the

Apostles, and which took place A. D. 37. By the way, it is clear from this statement, that *during the whole period of Christ's public ministry there could have been only three passovers.* This is one of Bengel's most important chronological points maintained in his "*Harmony of the Gospels.*" Several other facts likewise come to light by this investigation of the period of Daniel's seventy weeks; and among those facts is the important one, that our Lord's nativity took place three full years before the vulgar Christian era. As to the *time of* the year in which it occurred, Bengel considered the ancient tradition correct—that it was the twenty-fifth of December; and for ascertaining the year itself he observes, that "there are three principal points in the gospels, by which it is connected with profane history. These are: 1. That by Matt. ii. 1, both the nativity and the flight into Egypt were in the reign of Herod the Great. 2. That by Luke iii. 1, John the Baptist began to teach and baptize in the fifteenth year of the reign of Tiberius. 3. That by Luke iii. 23, Christ was about thirty years of age when he was baptized by John, and commenced his public ministry. Now Herod the Great died in the 43d Julian year, a little before Easter. The death of Augustus was sixteen years afterwards; and Tiberius immediately succeeded him. Hence it appears inferrible, that Jesus, who was born some time before the death of Herod the Great, must, at the time of commencing his public ministry, have been about *thirty-two* years of age; John having begun to baptize somewhat earlier. Now as here occurs a difficulty which chronologers have tried by one forced method and another to remove, Bengel thought it most easily solved by understanding the sixteen years of Augustus and the fifteen of Tiberius, &c., as periods *not wholly complete.* Thus he obtains 3972 years from the creation of the world to the death of Christ. The Acts of the Apostles he finds to comprise the succeeding period of twenty-five years, reaching to A. D. 55 = A. M. 3997; so that the conversion of St. Paul took place A. D. 37, and his abode at Rome between A. D. 53 and 55. The time of writing the New Testament Scriptures is stated as follows:—The Gospel of Matthew in A. D. 39; Mark, A. D. 41; Luke, A. D. 46; John, A. D. 63. The two Epistles to the Thessalonians, A. D. 48; the Epistle to the Galatians, A. D. 49; the Epistles to the Corinthians, the first Epistle to Timothy, the Epistle to Titus, and the Epistle to the Romans, A. D. 52; the Epistles to the Philippians, Ephesians, Colossians, Philemon, A. D. 57; to the Hebrews, A. D. 58; the Acts of the Apostles, A. D. 59; the second Epistle to Timothy, A. D. 66; the first Epistle of Peter, A. D. 58; the second, A. D. 59; the Epistle of James, A. D. 60; and the Epistle of Jude shortly after. The Apocalypse, A. D. 96; and St. John's three Epistles, not long before his decease, which took place in A. D. 98.

Bengel proceeded to fix the periods which, during the writing of the New Testament, were future, by first refuting the notion of being forbidden by Scripture to attempt to fix them. Some, he said, would urge this opinion from those sayings of our Lord in Mark xiii. 32, Matt. xxiv. 36, Acts i. 6, 7; and from his having admonished his disciples to watch, as persons who were never to know the time when the last day should come. In the two first of these passages, the stress, he said, lay in the *present* tense; "no man *knoweth* the day nor the hour." In those days, NO man, not even the Son himself, *did* know; but he afterwards knew it, for he revealed it in the Apocalypse. The true meaning, therefore, is, that, with respect to the time of Jerusalem's destruction, Jesus could say, that some persons of that generation should live to see it; but, with respect to the day of his appearing in judgment, he could not for the present communicate any thing more particularly. And as for the passage in Acts i. 6, 7, the stress lay in the single word "*you;*" therefore it was quite inferrible at the time, that further disclosures would be made to those who should come after. The passage itself further shows, that we are not precluded from *all* knowledge of the future, but only from knowing those times and seasons which the Father hath reserved in his own power. That it was quite unscriptural to insist that no periods or events have been predicted for men's clear ascertainment beforehand; for the world in Noah's time was forewarned of the very year when the flood came. To Abraham a promise was made that, within the space of a year exactly, he should have a son; and the four hundred years during which his seed should sojourn in a land that was not theirs, were revealed to himself and his descendants long beforehand. The seven years of plenty with the seven of famine in Egypt, and the seventy years of servitude under the yoke of Babylon, were all previously made known, &c. &c. Surely, then, the twenty prophetic periods of time in the Apocalypse had not been specified for nothing. It might be observed, that the dispensations of God's providence in general, have ever directed men's minds to futurity, and kept them in expectation of temporal events to come. God gives a promise for believers to depend upon; and they are to persevere through all difficulties until its fulfilment. By this method God continues to evince his governing providence, truth, goodness, and faithfulness unto men; and his children under this discipline evince their long-suffering, patience, love, faith, hope, earnest expectation, moderation, and sober-mindedness. Such was the Divine conduct with Abraham; and such afterwards with the whole nation of Israel. From Egypt they were taught to look and long for the possession of Canaan; and with every prediction, under their kings, concerning the Babylonish captivity, was almost constantly connected the promise that it should continue only seventy years. The seventy weeks of Daniel were predicted to commence immediately upon the liberation from Babylon, and to terminate in the public appearance of the Messiah. A similar process is observable under the New Testament dispensation, from its very commencement. The earliest Christians were stirred to watchfulness by a forewarning of the destruction of Jerusalem, though not of the nearness of the general judgment; for it is rather from the *certainty*, than the *nearness* of our Lord's coming, that we are exhorted to watch. The Apocalypse, which was written not long after the destruction of Jerusalem, gave assurance, that at least a thousand years should elapse before the judgment day; but still men were exhorted to watch. Prophecy proceeds in a gradual manner;—the patriarchs looked forward to *the glorious issue of* Christ's expected coming, for *this* issue has ever been Divine revelation's grand object; but the events of ages intermediate were to the patriarchs a blended mass of confused imagery. The prophets who came after them, saw such future events more clearly; still more so did the apostles, especially the last of them, St. John. Now the same remark applies to the gradually developed interpretation of his book, the Apocalypse. The more general disclosures of this book were ascertained from the beginning; and its more special ones have become plainer and plainer all along, proportionately to the respective exigences of succeeding generations, and to the light bestowed upon them. It will, therefore, be nothing strange if, in our own age, clearer views upon these subjects should be found than in those of our forefathers; for believers have all along received such additional information, as, being suited to their own times, was sufficient to secure them against any danger of being turned aside from the common faith.

Having thus vindicated the study of prophetical chronology, he educes some general principles for following it up; and first states it as his opinion (from Heb. ix. 26; 1 Cor. x. 11; 1 Pet. i. 20, iv. 7; Habak. iii. 2,) that the time of the New Testament dispensation will not be so long as was that of the Old; an opinion which Luther likewise expressed in a note upon 1 Pet. iv. 7.

"The Bible," says Bengel, "divides the duration of this world's economy, either into *two* parts, '*the beginning*' and '*the end*' (1 Sam. iii. 12; 1 Chron. xxix. 29); or into *three*, '*the beginning*,' '*the midst*,' and '*the end*.' In the former case, the whole time of the New Testament dispensation falls within the second half, and is called, 'the last time,' and 'the end of the world' (1 Pet. i. 20; Heb. ix. 26; 1 Cor. x. 11); but in the latter case, Christ's first coming is in '*the midst*' of this economy, fulfilling the prophetic petition of Habakkuk, ch. iii. 2. Now by attending to the connexion of these two expressions, the *beginning* and the *end*, we find incontrovertibly, that the time of the *New* Testament dispensation must be shorter than the period of 3940 years, the duration of the *Old* Testament; consequently the world would endure at farthest not beyond 7880 years." And as in Bengel's time, A. D. 1740, there had elapsed already 5690 years, and still the twentieth chapter of the Revelation, with several previous matters of the prophecy, remained unfulfilled; and as, according to this inspired book, two thousand years are yet in prospect, the events which are to precede what is foretold in that chapter must be very near at hand. For, add two thousand years to the current year, 1740, and you have A. D. 3740; from which it is evident there *can* be only two hundred years before the prophecy of that chapter begins to be fulfilled. Now if, following an analogy very common in Scripture, we suppose the duration of the world itself to be involved in the number *seven*, that is, to continue 7777 years, the unfulfilled events which are to precede the two thousand years must be comprised within the short space of ninety-seven years, and will have transpired by the beginning of the year 1837. With this agreed that interpretation of the Apocalypse, which he could not but think the correct one, as he considered the number of the Beast to be the true key to its chronological interpretation, and this number to denote six hundred and sixty-six *years*, synchronical with the forty and two months. Accordingly, the year 1836 would terminate the *nonchronus* (Rev. x. 6—11,) of 1036 years, which began in A. D. 800; with the "*short time*" (ὀλίγος καιρὸς,) of the third woe, (Rev. xii. 12,) which amounted to 888$\frac{8}{9}$ years, having commenced in A. D. 947; and the 3$\frac{1}{2}$ times (Rev. xii. 14,) of 777$\frac{7}{9}$ years, which commenced A. D. 1058; whence it would appear that by the close of these periods, all things precursive of the millennium will have come to pass.

Such are the principal matters of his chronology of sacred history and prophecy, as arranged in his "*Ordo Temporum.*" We have only to add, that in this work he exhibits the relation between the Sabbatical years and the years of Jubilee, and compares them with astronomical observations; of all which he has further spoken in his "Cyclus." We shall next proceed to give an account of other of his writings, which treat still more particularly of the chief portions of scripture chronology; and then take some notice of his controversial writings on the chronology of apocalyptic prophecy.*

We conclude the present chapter with a brief view of his "*Harmony of the Gospels.*"

In its preface he states, that this harmony turns upon the im-

* Of the former sort are—

1. His "True Harmony of the Gospels; exhibiting in their natural order the Memoirs, Works, and Discourses of Jesus Christ our Lord, for establishment of Truth, and for exercise and edification in Godliness." Tübingen, published by Christ. Henry Berger, 2d. edit., 1747.

2. "An Exposition of the Revelation of St. John, or rather of Jesus Christ; translated from the original Greek, illustrated by prophetic numbers, and presented to all who regard the work and word of the Lord, and desire worthily to prepare themselves for the great events which are near, even at the door." By John Albert Bengel, 1740; Stuttgart, published by John Christ. Erhard; 2d. edit., 1746; 3d., 1758.

In connexion with the last-mentioned work, we may notice some portions communicated to various journals before the whole work was printed; also the Latin Exposition of the Apocalypse, as given in the "Gnomon," and likewise, particularly for the sake of their appendices.

3. The "Sixty Practical Addresses on the Apocalypse, suited to edification; with appendices or gleanings, so interwoven, that the whole may be regarded, either as a second part to the 'Exposition of the Apocalypse,' or as another 'Confirmed Testimony to the Truth.'" Stuttgart, published by J. C. Erhard, 1747; 2d. edit., 1788.

4. "Cyclus, sive de Anno Magno solis, lunæ, stellarum consideratio, ad incrementum doctrinæ propheticæ atque astronomiæ accommodata." Ulmæ ap. Dan. Bartholomæi et filium, 1745.

Of the latter sort, namely, his *controversial* writings, are—

1. "The Age of the World, or an Investigation of the Scriptural lines of Chronology, and the Seventy Weeks of Daniel; illustrative of important texts and salutary doctrines, to the praise of the Great God, and of his sure Word of Prophecy." By John Alb. Bengel. Esslingen, pub. by Fred. Christ. Schall, 1746.

2. John Albert Bengel's "Confirmed Testimony to the Truth; comprising a variety of necessary matters respecting it; intended especially as an Answer to Messrs. Kohlreif and Drümel." Stuttgart, pub. by John Nicholas Stoll, 1748.

3. Dr. John Albert Bengel's "*Vindication of the Scriptures,* against the Appendix to Kohlreif's 'Wine-press of Wrath,' and Koch's 'Clearance and Purifying for Confirmation of Truth.'" Leipsic, printed by John Christ. Langenheim, 1755.

portant fact demonstrated in the work itself, that between the baptism and crucifixion of our Lord, there could have been no more than three feasts of the passover. With respect to the arrangement of the work, he further states, that he had prefixed a *summary* of the four gospels, noticing each *apparent* discrepancy between that of St. Mark and St. Luke; after which he had given the text itself in Luther's version (with appropriate running titles and sectional divisions,) so printed, that what was related on each subject by the several evangelists, might be seen at once in parallel columns. At the close of every portion he had subjoined annotations, serving either to justify the correctness of the harmony, or to convey some other useful instruction. To such as might find too little for edification, he offered the following advice:—"Whatever you read here, whether concerning God, the Saviour, the Spirit of God, the holy angels, or the followers of Christ, read it for the purposes of admiration, thankfulness, repentance, faith, growth in knowledge, and of doing the will of God. Whatever defect or evil you perceive in any characters here presented to you, take it as a warning. Does the narrative conduct your attention to a variety of circumstances which took place in connexion with our Lord and his apostles? consider yourself interested in such circumstances, and, as it were, placed in the midst of them; for instance, when it is said in Mark x. 49, 'He calleth thee,' think, Jesus calleth *you;* or so treasure up, by meditation, the particulars of each transaction, that some general useful instruction may be the result. Does any good and cheering consideration arise in your heart—any sweet and tender emotion? turn yourself with it to your Saviour, just as if you were one of those who personally conversed with him when he was upon earth. Thus will you acquire a readiness in communing with him by ejaculation and prayer, better than from the use of any devotional manual; though I have no wish to depreciate such prescribed and valuable helps. God grant us more and more light and strength out of the fulness of the Beloved, in whom he hath graciously made us accepted!"

In the preface of the second edition, he says, "this revised work is the same in its main points with the first edition: for I abide by what I have said of the three passovers, and of our Lord's having adapted his discourses to the portions of Scripture publicly read among the Jews on their Sabbaths and festivals. But in other respects I have made considerable alterations, which will not be regarded by reflecting persons as beside the purpose. For no one can communicate to-day, what he is unable to learn till to-morrow. Opinions given of one's book, with more matured consideration used by its author, serve often to enlarge or rectify one idea and another. And as every author ought to be free from any favourite prejudices, so he ought to endeavour, with each new edition, to benefit his readers as much more as he is able. Since my first publication of this kind, others have wrought considerably in the same department, and have had regard to my deductions. What therefore has further occurred to myself, after weighing what they and others have said, I have conscientiously inserted here, to improve or defend my observations. But it is far from my wish that any, even the most ignorant, should rely solely upon what I have written; indeed I wish that none of us may rest upon mere human authority; but that we may wisely learn to 'prove all things.'"

It is worthy of notice that Bengel, by the present work, performed an essential service to theological science, in abandoning the notion, that each evangelist intended to relate every event according to the exactest order of time; and yet in keeping far aloof from the arbitrary liberties to which some writers have resorted, through a forwardness to account for apparent discrepancies.

A work printed at Leipsic anonymously in the year 1765, entitled "A History of the Life and Ministry of our Lord and Saviour Jesus Christ, compiled after Bengel's 'Harmony,'" and moulded into one running text, with a preface by Crusius, served to extend the usefulness of the present work; as did also Dr. Gottlob Christian Storr's adding Bengel's *Table of the harmony* to an edition of the Lutheran Bible which he published at Tübingen in the year 1793.

CHAPTER VI.

HIS EXPOSITION OF THE APOCALYPSE.

No book of Scripture has had so many expositors, at least so many incorrect ones, as the Revelation of St. John. But ought this consideration to deter from further attempts to disclose its mysteries, and from the hope of ever arriving at its true interpretation? Or are Christians at least bound to let the book alone, till its interpretation shall manifestly appear of itself, in the historical events of the christian church? Bengel certainly did not think so, nor could he see it his duty to think so. As his researches had fully satisfied him that this book is a genuine writing of the beloved disciple, so he believed that the particular providence of God, which had watched over all the canonical books in general, had especially watched over this last of them, and had a wise and good design in adding it to their number. But if it was not in vain that the book had been extant for so many centuries, surely it was intended to be studied; moreover, if we are justifiable in deferring the understanding of prophecy, to the time of its complete fulfilment, then were the Jews justifiable in rejecting the true Messiah. Bengel therefore believed the possibility of arriving at a correct interpretation of this book of prophecy, even before its complete fulfilment; and this he believed so certainly, as to venture to say, that an expositor who concerns himself only with its predicted *events*, and not also with their *dates*, is a useless interpreter of any thing predicted in it. For it was not without design that twenty specific periods of time are inserted in this inspired book. (Its Divine Author has connected them with their respective predicted events, and) "What the Lord has" thus "joined together, let not man put asunder." Bengel thus regarded the explication of the dates or periods not only as practicable, but essentially requisite, quite as much so as that of the subject matter. But he thought it probable, that the development of such periods would become clearer and more satisfactory as time advances; and that at present it was enough "to be able to show, that each past generation had received as much insight into the Apocalypse as was requisite for its own particular use." Convinced of this, he regarded it as the duty of every fresh expositor to follow up the discoveries possessed by the age he lives in, by carefully concentrating every scattered ray of light already thrown upon it, and waiting in patience and humility, if God peradventure shall grant any further light upon it, even to such an insignificant person as himself. This had been his own way of proceeding. As early as before the year 1724, he had expounded the Apocalypse with the rest of the Greek Testament to his pupils at least six times, and before the end of that year had nearly completed a body of annotations on the New Testament, which he designed to publish under the title of "Gnomon;" though up to that time those of them he had affixed to the Apocalypse were all of a borrowed kind. But just then (to use the words of a contemporary writer respecting him,) "did the Lord grant such light to spring up unto him, that the portal to the Divine structure of the Apocalypse became open to his view." He used to speak of this valued vouchsafement as connected with the following remarkable circumstances. When about to prepare a sermon which he was to preach on the first Sunday in Advent, 1724, his thoughts were led to the twenty-first chapter of the Revelation; and recollecting Potter's view of it, who understands in a mere general sense of architectural enlargement not only the measuring numbers mentioned in the 16th and 17th verses, but even the numbers mentioned in the thirteenth chapter, the question all at once arose in his mind, "What if Potter be right in the former case, but not in the latter? What if indeed for the kingdom of God in its full and glorious accomplishment, no chronological bounds, according to our notions of time, can be affixed; though such *be* affixed to the previous great tribulation which directly conducts and breaks open the way to this glorious consummation? If such be the fact, then will not only the forty and two months of the Beast's blasphemy, (ch. xiii. 5, 6,) but likewise the number of his name, *six hundred three-score and six*, contain a precise and definite *period* of TIME; and these two expressions denote one and the same identical period." The idea came so forcibly to his mind, and so occupied it, that he could not continue his meditations upon the text he had chosen for his sermon; which however proved no loss either to himself or to his congregation, so beneficial was now the influence of those great and glorious things which were anticipated as couched in the above mystical periods.

From that moment he set about tracing, at his private leisure, the golden line of scripture chronology, prospective as well as retrospective; and thus more and more clearly perceived the glorious harmony of the Apocalypse with the history of the world and of the Church. Here also he found the use of a discovery he had made in Greek Testament criticism; that in Rev. vi. 11, the true reading is simply χρόνον, a *time*, or *period;* and not χρόνον μικρὸν, "a little season." *

His pleasure was only equalled by the humility with which he entertained the whole disclosure as an unmerited vouchsafement of God. This we shall afterwards see from some extracts of his letters, and at present from the following to J. F. Reuss:—

"*Dec.* 22, 1724.

"It is impossible for me to withhold from you a disclosure, which, however, I must request you to keep entirely to yourself. By the help of the Lord I have found the number of the Beast. It is six hundred and sixty-six *years*, from A. D. 1143, to A. D. 1809. This key to the Apocalypse is of importance, and even consoles me with respect to the repeated losses of my infant children; for those who are born in this generation are entering into troublous times. You, also, my dear friend, may well make ready to meet such times; for wisdom will be greatly needed. But 'Blessed be He that cometh! (in the name of the Lord.' Ps. cxviii. 26; Luke xiii. 35.)"

"*Jan.* 20, 1725.

"Some are urging me to publish on the number of the Beast; others dissuade it.† For the sake of the Roman Catholics I am not in a hurry about it. To every thing there is a season; a time to wait, and a time to hasten. It was with great pleasure I lately noticed Luther's remark upon Rev. xiii. 18; for I find that he too interpreted the number of the Beast as denoting 666 years for the period of the papal temporal domination; only according to him, that period commenced under Hildebrand in A. D. 1013."

* Μικρὸν, Lectio *certissime* delenda. Griesb.

† Having at length seen it his duty to publish it, he afterwards wrote, "It does not surprise me that many are so prejudiced against my apocalyptical discoveries. It is something quite strange to us to be obliged to adopt new truths. We directly feel as if upon slippery ground. Writing upon events which are yet to come is quite a different undertaking from that of history. The latter can bring credit; the former *must* bring obloquy and contempt; for it is proscribed by the world, by the learned, and even by the godly. But truth is of more importance than one's credit or any thing else. We must not be deterred from uttering truth, by any concern as to what people will say of us."

"*May* 11, 1725.

"I am still working at the Apocalypse, and daily see more and more the coherence and harmony of its particulars, so as to suspect more strongly than ever, that if holier persons remain incurious about the signs of the times, it will fall to the lot of some very unworthy individual to discern those signs, and make them known to the world."

This last declaration may be illustrated by the following, which bespeaks his sincere humility. "While I am computing the periods of sacred chronology, I feel astonished beyond measure that God should thus impart light concerning them to such a poor feeble creature as myself; indeed, if I at all stagger about my own computations, it is only when I wonder how it at length comes to pass that *I* should be the person to unfold such high and holy matters to the world."

Having arranged to his satisfaction the chief parts of his apocalyptical system, he applied most of his leisure and strength to the completion of his critical works; though his correspondence with intimate friends, and especially with Marthius, shows that he was still endeavouring after increased knowledge upon apocalyptical subjects.*

He first published upon these subjects in the year 1727, in the sixth volume of Schelhorn's *Amœnitates literariæ*, Art. 3, under the title of "*Discipuli de temporibus Monitum de præjudicio hermeneutico* (*dies prophet:=365 dies vulgares*) *accuratiorem Apocalypseos explicationem etiam nunc impediente;*" or "A word from an humble disciple upon the prophetic periods; concerning the prejudice, that a prophetic *day* signifies a natural year; showing how that prejudice hinders any clearer elucidation of the Apocalypse." This communication was conveyed in language rather obscure, perhaps intentionally so. But shortly afterwards he expressed himself more plainly, in a brief German treatise, entitled "Principles for an accurate and unforced exposition of 'The Revelation of Jesus Christ.'"† This work soon drew so much attention, that he was very strongly urged from various quarters to give his views of the Apocalypse more at length; which he set about doing in a treatise consisting of two preliminary essays, which he inserted in the tenth number of a periodical conducted by J. J. Moser, of Frankfort, 1734, and entitled, "Things new and old concerning the Kingdom of God."

* See below, ch. xvii. 6, the extracts from his correspondence.

† It is reprinted in Beverley's "Corrected Index of the Times," 1729.

The first essay was "On an accurate and unforced System of Interpretation for the Apocalypse:" and the second, "On the present Continuance of the Third Woe; and the necessity of giving heed to it; evinced chiefly from the twelfth and subsequent chapters of the Apocalypse." He announced in the preface, that he was preparing for publication a new version and exposition of the Revelation of St. John, from his revised Greek text; but as a considerable time would elapse before he should be able to venture such a work upon public notice, he was willing, in compliance with the wishes of some christian friends, thus to communicate a kind of specimen of it; and should any, who love Christ's appearing, find that these essays cast a single ray of light upon what remains obscure in the prophetic word of God, he hoped they would help him by prayer to derive out of the fulness of the Lamb that was slain, whatever should still appear wanting in the treatise. Meanwhile he trusted that no friends of this mind would give him credit for such impertinent and unprofitable things as had been attributed to him; *much less would entertain a high notion of his performance;* he having all along maintained and inquired intó nothing but what Scripture had already delivered to his hand; for it was by the simple search of Scripture that he had been led into these subjects quite unexpectedly, nay, almost involuntarily. Finally, he hoped that with fervent prayer and close consideration of the prophetic book itself, they would with all needful discretion try whatever was here laid before them, and convert it to their real benefit."

The treatise first speaks of the high importance of the Apocalypse, as a book which has been mighty through God among christian believers, especially in seasons of general distress and perplexity; and which will be so again, probably at no very great distance of time. It then takes a brief survey of the whole prophecy; noticing the three first chapters as its introduction, and the other nineteen, as its main substance; the former relating "*that which*" the apostle "*saw,*" and "*that which is;*" and the latter, "*that which shall be hereafter.*"

The fourth and fifth chapters engage our attention upon the Great Author of the prophecy, and upon its general scope; the succeeding ones give the histories of future times; the sixth containing the four first and three last seals. But before the seventh seal, is *the preparation,* (ch. vii.); the seven angels with seven trumpets, (ch. viii.); the four first, and the three last with the three woes, are announced here, but commence in chapter the ninth. The seventh trumpet is the most important, and displays the dragon with the two beasts; as also the kingdom of Christ in heaven and earth. Here precede, first, *the preparation*, in chapter the tenth; secondly, *the summary contents*, (ch. xi. 15, &c.;) and lastly, *the account itself*. In this we have, first, the *adversaries;* consisting of the *dragon*, (ch. xii.) *the two beasts*, (ch. xiii.) and *the great harlot*, (ch. xvii.); secondly, *their overthrow;* (which indeed begins in chapters xv. xvi.)—then, (but in an inverted order,) *the harlot*, (ch. xviii.) *the beast* and *the false prophet*, (ch. xix. 11,) and *the dragon*, (ch. xx.)—are taken out of the way; thirdly, after gradual advances, under the trumpet of the seventh angel, (ch. xi. 15; xii. 5—8; xiv. 1, 13, 14; xv. 2; xix. 1; xx. 4,) we have *the final completion of Christ's kingdom*, (ch. xx. 11; xxii. 5;) and then *the conclusion*, exactly corresponding to the *introduction*. The fulfilment of such parts of this prophecy as have no specification of dates or times, was to begin *quickly*, (ἐν τάχει.) It did so, namely, in the Apostle St. John's own time; it has been going on through each succeeding century ever since, and will do so unto the consummation, and end of the world. Therefore in the dates or periods here presented, we have nearly the total sum of the world's remaining duration. These periods are so important a concern in the prophecy, that its right interpretation is impossible without them. Now we find they are in the seven denominations of *hour*, *day*, *month*, *year*, *season* (καιρὸς,) *time* (χρόνος,) and *age* (αἰών.) To interpret these, we must distinguish when common days and years, and when such as are prophetic or mystical, are intended: we must also find the key to their computation. Some have thought they denote only common time throughout; (as that a day here spoken of, is always a common day;) others are for prophetic or mystical computation exclusively, and assert, that every prophetic day is a common year. To either of these acceptations there are insurmountable difficulties; the sum of which is, that a *prophetic day* is found to be *much shorter* than a common *year*, and *much longer* than a common *day*. So that probably the truth lies in a *mean reckoning;* which makes a prophetic day to be about half of a common year. We are conducted thus far, by considering merely the explanations given by former expositors. Let us now advance a step further, by means of the text itself. This, in ch. xiii. 18, invites us as follows: "Let him who hath understanding, *count* the number of the Beast; for it is the number of a man; and his number is six hundred three score and six." Here is something to be *calculated;** but *we require for our calculation two numbers at the least.* Accordingly this thirteenth chapter furnishes us with one other number, and only one; it is that of the forty and two months. We must therefore assume this for our *second* number. But before we begin to reckon, it may be proper to inquire, what noun, understood in a grammatical sense, can belong to the *numeral* expression 666. The answer is, that it must, *according to the context,* be a noun denoting computation of *time.* Moreover the *neutral* form of this *numeral* as found in the best *Greek* MSS., and its *masculine* form, as found in the *Latin* Vulgate, direct us to the word "*years,*" as the understood noun for it to agree with.

Thus the numeral expression 666, denotes 666 *years;* and these, as the text implies,† are *common* years; while the forty and two months denote likewise 666 years; and with these two expressions, we may frame the following proportion; $42 : 662 :: 1 : x$; according to which, one prophetic month is $= 15\frac{6}{7}$ common years. Thus we have the key to all the other computations. Now if it be asked which of the periods we consider *mystical,* and which *common;* we reply, that those which elapse previous to the number of the Beast, (for example, *those which precede the third woe,*) we consider *mystical,* (the number of the Beast forming as it were a connecting link, half visible and half secret;) but *those which belong to the finishing of the mystery of God* we understand *literally.* And this decision is analogous to the manner in which *other things preceding the third woe* are expressed, for they are expressed *figuratively;* whereas, things which follow it are expressed in common language.

Bengel, soon after he had published this sketch of his plan, was induced to insert in the "Spiritual Reporter," (comp. xv. xxiii. p. 1235—37,) an apocalyptical article in answer to Seiz, who had determined the fulfilment of all these prophecies to as early as the year 1736. Next to this, Bengel published his "Exposition of the Apocalypse." In his preface to the first edition, he states, how he had obtained the key to his computations: and that the longer he made use of it, the more clearly was this sacred book opened to him; and that in consequence of the pressing requests of friends, and the false reports circulated by ignorant or ill-designing persons respecting his method of interpretation, as also lest his conscience should be hurt by with-

* Ψηφισάτω, "let him calculate."—Rev. xiii. 18.

† Ἀριθμὸς γὰρ ἀνθρώπου ἐστί.—Rev. xiii. 18.

holding from the public what had come to his notice unsought for, he had at length resolved to publish this full "Exposition," after having heard, examined, and profited by a great variety of opinions, elicited upon his Plan by the Essay he had published in 1734, "On an accurate and unforced system of interpretation for the Apocalypse." He added, with as much modesty as integrity, that he did not wish his "Exposition" to be regarded as any *infallible revelation,* which he should be supposed to have been favoured with, but simply as the *natural fruit and result of his honest inquiries and researches in the word of God;* in which view he humbly offered it to the examination of the public.

The work itself consists of a new version of the Apocalypse, with a running exposition, preceded by an introduction, which contains a general view of the whole prophecy; and followed by a conclusion divided (in the third edition) into seven sections; 1. A table of the chronology. 2. An humble attempt to determine more accurately the times of the Beast. 3. Characteristics of genuine interpretation. 4. An account of men's expectations from age to age in reference to prophecy. 5. Prophetic exposition with respect to its influence on men's actions. 6. Examination of some other prophecies. And 7. Salutary advices.

The "Exposition" was intended as a distinct work from that comprised in his next publication, the "Gnomon;" as this, which was in Latin, was more particularly for matters interesting to persons acquainted with the learned languages; whereas the "Exposition" set forth what might become intelligible and profitable to all; so that both may be used either together or separately.

In the introduction above mentioned, is found a more copious analysis than he had before given, of the contents of the Apocalypse (see above, p. 287,) with explanatory remarks. But previously to discussing the periods, he directs the reader's attention to the following notices, deducible from the simple showing of the text;—that the *first* woe came to its end before the rise of the Saracen empire; that the *second* woe denotes the Saracen dominion; that the *third,* though long ago commenced, was not yet expired; and that these are fundamental matters essentially connected with a system of correct interpretation.

He then proceeds to a more particular investigation of the chronological periods; resuming the inquiry he had commenced in an Essay already noticed; and speaks as follows:—"Since by comparing together the two most common, but opposite systems, we have been led to conclude that in all probability a prophetic day is about half of a natural year, let us now further consider that that conclusion makes the forty and two months of the Beast to be about half of 1260 = about 630 years; which tends to confirm the supposition already expressed, namely, that the number 666 denominates *years*.

"Let us make use of the result thus far attained, for the purpose of discovering all the *other* apocalyptical periods. This is to be done principally by comparing with the number 666, the 1000 years mentioned in the twentieth chapter. At once we perceive that this latter number bears to the former the relation of 3 to 2; and by a little additional thought we obtain the following interesting proportion: 3 : 2 : : $999\frac{999}{999}$ years : $666\frac{666}{999}$ years; consequently a unit of $666\frac{666}{999}$ must be $1\frac{1}{999}$ year. And this may be one reason why the word *years* is not added to the numeral expression, '*six hundred three score and six*,' in the sacred text. *Unity*, in each of these denominations, with the appropriate fraction annexed, (thus, $111\frac{1}{9}$,) very little exceeds the ancient Roman century, which consisted of 110 years. Mention is made of a 'half-time' in the text itself, and there is reason for supposing a *half-time* to be *exactly the unity we here speak of, with its appropriate fraction;* so that we may exhibit the apocalyptical periods according to the following scale:—

A Half-time - - - - - - - - - -	=	$111\frac{1}{9}$ years,	ch. xx. 4.
A Time (καιρὸς) - - - - - - - - -	=	$222\frac{2}{9}$	
A Time and a half - - - - - - -	=	333	
Two Times - - - - - - - - - - - -	=	$444\frac{4}{9}$	
A Half-period (half χρόνος) - - - -	=	$555\frac{5}{9}$	
The Number of the Beast - - -	=	$666\frac{6}{9}$	ch. xiii. 18.
A Time, Times, and Half a Time	=	$777\frac{7}{9}$	ch. xii. 14.
A Short Time (ὀλίγος καιρὸς) - - -	=	$888\frac{8}{9}$	ch. xii. 12.
A Thousand Years - - - - - - - -	=	$999\frac{9}{9}$	ch. xx. 2.
The 'time no longer,' οὐκέτι χρόνος, or no whole period between	=	$999\frac{9}{9}$ and $1111\frac{1}{9}$	ch. x. 6.
A Period (χρόνος) - - - - - - - - - - - -	=	$1111\frac{1}{9}$	ch. vi. 11.
An Æon, or double period (αἰὼν) - - -	=	$2222\frac{2}{9}$	ch. xiv. 6.

"Thus *an accurate consideration of the text* discovers a regularly ascending series of periods as here stated. The difficulty, that a 'short time' (ch. xii. 12,) should denote the long space of $888\frac{8}{9}$ years, is done away by considering that our computation is by half-times, (viz. $111\frac{1}{9}$.)—Now the ancients used to reckon no less than *seven* to the completion of a time, (καιρὸς;) hence four *times* (or $222\frac{2}{9}\times 4$) might easily be denominated 'a short time,' ὀλίγος καιρός." The application of this key of *times* to the apocalyptical dates and to those of history will be seen in the following table, to which a few particulars are added, which obviously could not be found in Bengel's "Exposition," that we may take a better general view of his chronological system.

CHRONOLOGICAL TABLE.

Anno Mundi.	Events.	*Ante Christum.*
1	The Creation of the World - - -	$3940\frac{39}{40}$
2593	Beginning of "The Midst," (or middle period,) of the world's duration, Habak. iii. 2 - -	1347
3889	Beginning of the latter portion of the world's duration, 1 Peter i. 20 - - - - -	51
$3940\frac{39}{40}$	Birth of Christ.	
3943	Beginning of the Vulgar or Dionysian Era -	A. D.
4038	Opening of the Apocalypse in the reign of Nerva	96
4040–4059	The *First Seal*, ch. vi. 2. Victorious reign of Trajan - - - - - -	98—117
4040	The *Second Seal*, ch. vi. 4. War with Decebalus in Dacia, &c. - - - - - -	98
4040—4054	The *Third Seal*, ch. vi. 6. Scarcity under Trajan	98—112
4040	The *Fourth Seal*, ch. vi. 8. Calamitous events of every kind, from the time of Trajan; especially inundations, earthquakes, pestilence, conflagrations - - - - - - -	98
4040—5151	Ch. vi. 11. Period (χρόνος) of $1111\frac{1}{9}$ years, from the persecution of Christianity under Trajan, to the persecution of the Waldenses by the papacy	98—1209
4056—4077	Ch. viii. 7. *Trumpet* of the *First* Angel. Rebellion of the Jews; and sanguinary wars with that people - - - - - -	114—135
4192	Ch. viii. 8. *Trumpet* of the *Second* Angel. Irruption of barbarous nations into the pagan Roman empire - - - . - -	250
4257	Ch. viii. 10. *Trumpet* of the *Third* Angel. The Arian Heresy - - - -	315
4337—4452	Ch. viii. 12. *Trumpet* of the *Fourth* Angel. Gradual decline of the Roman empire, which comprised all the then known world - -	395—510
4442	Ch. viii. 13. Flight of the *Eagle** which announces the *Three Woes.* Diligent inquiries into the Apocalypse. - - -	500

* *Angel* in our English version; but *Eagle* is considered the genuine reading; ἀετοῦ πετομένου. Lectio indubie genuina. Griesb.

Anno Mundi.	EVENTS.	*Anno Domini.*
4452—4531	Ch. ix. 1—12. The *First Woe*. Severe oppression of the Jews in Persia, which lasts five prophetic months=79 common years - - -	510—589
4531—4576	A *pause* between the *first* and *second* woes; which lasted 45 years. Activity of Mahomet -	589—634
4576—4789	Ch. ix. 15. The *Second Woe;* which lasts one prophetic year, month, day, and hour;=213 common years. Havoc commenced by the Saracens - - - - - -	634—847
4789—4889	*Pause* between the *second* and *third* woes; which lasts a hundred years - - - -	847—947
4742—5778	Ch. x. 6. Commencement of the *non-chronus*, (or a "TIME *no longer*,") which lasts 1036 years -	800—1836
4742—5742	The Germanic Roman Imperial Dominion, established by Charlemagne; which lasts about a thousand years, and "letteth" (stands in the way of) the rise of Antichrist. 2 Thess. ii. 6, 7.	800—1800
4882—5559	Ch. xii. 6. Twelve hundred and sixty prophetic days;=677 common years; from the completion of preparatory institutions in Bohemia, for the diffusion of vital Christianity in that country, to its almost entire extinction there after its rise and diffusion in other countries by the Reformation - - - - - - -	940—1617
4889—5778	The *Third Woe;* ch. xii. 12, lasts (ὀλίγον καιρὸν) "*a short time*," 888$\frac{8}{9}$ years - - -	947—1836
5000—5778	Ch. xii. 14. The "time, times, and half a time," (or 3$\frac{1}{2}$ times,) in which the *Woman* nourishes and supports herself in the northern countries of Europe; a period of 777$\frac{7}{9}$ years - - -	2d Sept. 1058—1836
4882—5000	The *most* helpless time of the *Woman*, now fled into the wilderness; wherein she was dependent on the nourishment and support of others, and chiefly of princes - - - -	940—1058
5000—5559	*More favourable* time, when she becomes nourished, and nourishes herself. Revival of learning; invention of printing; Reformation - -	1058—1617
5589—5778	The *most favourable* time; wherein she *nourishes herself* with continually growing strength (though under oppressions), so that she can nourish others also. Pietism; Bible societies; missions, &c.	1617—1836
	The Beast out of the Sea; the papacy, as completed by Hildebrand, lasts forty and two prophetic months, ch. xiii. 5, 18, or 666$\frac{6}{9}$ years. The beginning of these cannot be fixed till their close; the two most probable periods which may be assigned, are either	
5015—5682;	from the beginning of the reign of Hildebrand to the death of Clement XII., under whom the	

Anno Mundi.	Events.	*Anno Domini.*
	weakness of the papacy against the emperor manifested itself - - - - -	1073—1740
	or from	
5085—5752;	from Celestine II., the first who was elected without any voice of the people, until again a change shall take place in the relative position of the pope towards the city of Rome. (Decree of Napoleon of the 17th of May, 1809, by which the papal jurisdiction was abolished) - -	1143—1809
5682	The *non-existence of the "Beast out of the Sea,"* begins with the termination of the period 666; probably *the "Beast out of the Earth," the "false prophet,"* ch. xiii. 11, begins just then, or even earlier - - - - - -	1740
5556—7777⅐	Ch. xiv. 6. The angel with the Everlasting Gospel; the measured everlastingness (αἰών) continues 2222⅔ years; Arndt or his followers - -	1614—3836
5577—5769	Ch. xiv. 8. The angel who announces the Fall of Babylon; Spener, or his followers - -	1635—1727
5682—5778	*The Harvest* and *the Vintage.* The sweeping away of many good and bad men from the earth, ch. xiv. 15—18 - - - - -	between* 1740—1836
5772—5778	Ch. xi. 3. *The prophesying of the Two Witnesses;* which lasts 1260 common days - -	between 1830—1836
5772—5778.	Ch. xi. 2. *The last Treading-down of Jerusalem;* which continues forty and two common months	between 1830—1836
5772	The *rise of the Beast* out of the bottomless pit -	about 1830
5773—5774	The Beast *takes his throne upon the seven mountains;* where he must "continue a short space," ch. xvii. 10 - - - - -	1831—1832
5774	*The Power of the Ten Kings (one hour,)* ch. xvii. 12, lasts one prophetic hour; that is, eight natural days - - - - - - -	1832, from the 14th to the 22d Oct.
5773—5778	*The seven Plagues,* ch. xvi. Divide into *four* and *three,* and run out quickly, in the days of Antichrist - - - - - -	about 1831—1836
5775	The ten kings *lay Babylon* (Rome) *waste;* in an agreement with the Beast; ch. xvii. 16, ch. xviii.	1833
5774—5778	The last raging of Antichrist; which continues about three common years and a half - -	1832—1836

* The reader, upon coming to this part of the table, is requested to take notice, that Bengel, in speaking to the years between 1740 and 1836, has expressed very various conjectures [*B.*] (so as not to have professed to speak *positively*, either of the year 1836 or of those very near it. Some slight flaw in the system, which may still conceal from us the awful year intended, should be so far from encouraging any to think lightly of the general matter, that we should be only the more circumspect and piously inquiring; as there is enough in the system to warrant our expectation that the time is very near at hand.)—[*T.*]

Anno Mundi.	Events.	*Anno Domini.*
5778	*Conflict of the Beast out of the Bottomless Pit with the people of God; and his overthrow at the appearing of the Lord;* ch. xix. 11—21 - -	18 June, 1836
5778—6778	*Thousand years binding of Satan;* ch. xx. 1—3 -	1836—2836
6778—6890	*Loosing of Satan* for "*a little time*" (μικρὸν χρόνον), a period of 111⅑ years; ch. xx. 3 - -	2836—2947
6778—7777⅑	Thousand years' reign of the saints in heaven; ch. xx. 4 - - - - - -	2836—3836
7777⅑	End of the world, and Judgment - -	3836

Explanations of the above chronological table may be collected almost entirely in Bengel's own words, from his "Exposition of the Apocalypse." Its principal matters are as follow:—

"The book of the Revelation divides itself into *three* parts: first, the *introduction;* secondly, the *body of the prophecy;* and thirdly, the *conclusion.* The contents of the three first chapters, as preparative of all the events that follow, form the introduction; and first, we have the personal preparation of the inspired writer himself. This holy man, though he had been faithfully exercising his apostleship more than thirty years, yet before he could receive such high disclosures, must submit to purification. Next, we have the preparation of the *angels,* (or overseers,) of the seven churches, as also that of those churches themselves. Both parties are to be brought into better condition by repentance; therefore it is testified to them that the Lord knew the work of each individually, whether good or evil had the ascendant, or whether both were equally balanced. What was good in them, was, by the way, confirmed and strengthened. This preparation of the seven churches is *an example* to the Lord's servants in every age and on every occasion; therefore it is here introduced with perfect right and propriety; but we cannot, without violence to the text, understand it as likewise prophetic of seven periods in the christian church. Seven glorious promises are respectively annexed to it for the encouragement of each angel of the seven churches.

"After these preparations, the Lord again addresses himself to John, saying, that he would 'show him things which must be hereafter' (ch. iv. 1.) Here commences the body of the prophecy; which opens with a manifestation of all power in heaven and in earth, as given to the Lord Jesus Christ. This is set in full view, first, *generally* (ch. iv.) then, *by the seven seals;* the *four first* of which relate to *visible* events, that commenced soon after the revelation was given.

"The riders on the horses represent, not so much any particular *persons*, as rather *events*, that should take place in the four regions of the Roman empire, rapidly succeed each other, and occupy but a short period. The *first* of them points at the victories of Trajan, subduing Arabia Petræa, Armenia, Assyria, and Mesopotamia; and attracting embassies even from India, to respect the Roman conqueror. The *second* intimates the sanguinary war carried on in Dacia, against Decebalus; the *third*, the Egyptian scarcity; and the *fourth*, the earthquakes, inundations, pestilence, and conflagrations, by which, from the time of Trajan, multitudes of the human race, within the Roman empire, were swept away. What was fulfilled, under these *four* seals, all within the few first years after St. John wrote, served to establish the credibility of the whole prophecy, by giving a fourfold proof that all was under the dominion of Christ, and that he was fully able to dispose the future after his own counsel, agreeably to what he had here foretold. The *three last* seals relate to the *invisible* world, which is equally under the government of Christ. *First*, and under the *fifth* seal, appear the martyrs, who had lost their lives by the persecutions that raged under the Roman emperors. Their cries for vengeance import, that Rome had not, under the four first seals, suffered any *peculiar* trouble. They are directed to wait till the other martyrs shall have been added to their number. In the middle ages, the church had rest from persecution; but towards their close, the popes, who now occupied the place of the Cæsars, began those persecutions of faithful Christians, which they have ever since abetted, and will continue to do till their city has filled up the measure of her iniquity. Under the *sixth* seal, appear the departed souls of the wicked, awaiting in terror the day of judgment. Preparatory to the grand sequel, the 144,000 of Israel next appear; and after this, an innumerable company of all nations and kindreds and people and tongues, who should be delivered out of 'the great tribulation' and temptations that would commence soon after the date of the Apocalypse. Hereby is intimation given, that even in the most distracted and troublous times, the Lord will preserve a people to himself in all quarters of the earth! The *sealing of the elect*, in chapter the seventh, may be regarded as *preparatory to the all-important seventh seal* (under which the representatives of the invisible world, and especially angels, are again set forth); so likewise the holy '*silence in heaven*,' recorded in chapter the eighth, which, as it seemed to John, lasted about half an hour, may be considered as *more specially preparatory* to that important period. The angels now make ready for the full execution of the great commissions given them, which they then execute singly and successively. The trumpet of the *first angel*, (ch. viii. 7,) relates to the *Asiatic* '*earth*,' and denotes the dreadfully raging *rebellions of the Jews*, which commenced in the reign of Trajan, but were chiefly carried on in the reigns of his successors; and in particular, the rebellions conducted by the false Christ, Bar-cochab. The *second* (ch. viii. 8,) relates to *Europe;* which from Patmos would appear encompassed by '*the sea;*' and announces *the irruptions of the Goths*, and other barbarous nations, into the Roman empire. The *third* (ch. viii. 10,) relates to the *Arian heresy*, the founder of which 'fell from' the 'heaven' of the church, when he diffused his blasphemous doctrine amongst a great multitude of adherents, particularly in Africa (the land of torrents and inundations,) and hereby occasioned many sanguinary conflicts. The *fourth* (ch. viii. 12,) comprises *the then known world, and signifies the disruption of the old Roman empire*, which, A. D. 395, was divided between Arcadius and Honorius, and which Alaric, Attila, Genseric, and Odoacer ravaged, one after another. By the *woe crying eagle* are the seven trumpets divided, as by a break, into *four* and *three*, like the former partition of the seals. The eagle's *triple woe* is coincident with a period about A. D. 500; when Andreas Cæsariensis in Asia, Primasius in Africa, Apringius in Spain, and Cassiodorus in Italy, wrote much upon the Apocalypse. With this *triple woe* is next contrasted the everlasting gospel, as signifying, that the triple woe, in announcing temporal plagues, intimated also great mischief to souls. The *fifth* trumpet (ch. ix. 3,) relates to *the blind zeal of the Parsees for their own eclipsed and darkened philosophy*, which instigated them to raise a very severe persecution against the Jews, that continued seventy-nine years. This was also *the first woe*, and was stirred up by *the destroyer* out of *the bottomless pit*, who afterwards rises up as the Antichrist. The twelfth verse intimates a state of respite, or comparative quietness between the first and the second woe. This respite lasted forty-five years after the twentieth of Mahomet. During that period, the whole Saracenic woe, and the Popish, in part, were already in a state of preparation. The *sixth* trumpet announces *the Saracenic slaughter*, as now commenced, under the caliphs Abubeker, Omar, Osman, and Ali. It began upon a small scale, but grew more and more terrible, till it was broken up, A. D. 847, before the city of Rome. By this plague were the nations of Christendom chastised, especially for the image worship (ver. 20,) which had leavened nearly the whole mass, and which such severe chastisement did not prevail with them to abandon, for they continue it even down to the days of the two witnesses. In ch. x. an angel stands up, who solemnly swears, that although the three foes of Christianity, *Satan*,—who is now thrust down to the earth, the *Beast*, that rises up out of the *sea*, and the *other Beast*, that arises out of the *earth*,—will now bring on the *third woe*, yet no further period of 1111$\frac{1}{9}$ years should elapse, before the finishing of the mystery of God, the consummation so often foretold by his servants, the prophets of the Old Testament, and which was to take place under the trumpet of the seventh angel, now just at hand, (ch. x. 7.) But before the consummation, a series of many kings (ch. x. 11,) was to arise, the most important of whom is the Germanic Roman emperor; consequently this 'non-chronus,' *no period*, or 'time no longer,' commences A. D. 800, with the establishment of his imperial power, under Charlemagne. This power (together with the other kingdoms formed about the same period, as that of France, A. D. 752, that of the Roman ecclesiastical state, A. D. 755, that of England, A. D. 819, &c.) comes to its dissolution before the end of the *non-chronus* (in 1836,) preparatory to which, the imperial, and these regal powers, will have undergone great transformations. Here, by the way, we see refuted those interpreters who restrict the fulfilment of nearly all the Apocalypse to a few of the years of Antichrist. That the eleventh chapter pertains to a later period than the order of the book would seem to intimate, is evident from the seventh verse. We therefore waive for the present the *particular* matter of this chapter. By its fourteenth verse it connects itself with the twelfth verse of the ninth, and with the eleventh verse of the tenth; agreeably to the positive assurance which had been given, that Jerusalem would become converted (to God and to his Christ.) After the Saracen arms had encountered violent opposition, especially from the Germanic empire, during the hundred years' *respite*, which was to succeed to the *second* woe, then the *third* woe breaks out rapidly. At the trumpet of the *seventh angel* is heard (ch. xi. 17,) the hymn of praise sung by those in heaven, in reference to the scope and end of the *tribulation*, which at this period is coming upon the earth. Then a new scene of a very important kind is disclosed. First, there appears (ch. xii. 1,) *the woman clothed with the sun*, that is, the church of God and of his Christ, as originally and principally from Israel, but now from the Gentiles also, formed, planted, edified, spread abroad, and maintained toward the east and west, and such as it shall much more appear hereafter, especially when 'the natural branches' shall have been grafted in again upon their own olive tree. Here, therefore, she is represented in the glorious attire in which she shall come forth out of the wilderness, when a christian government of the world ('the sun,') the Mohammedan power ('the moon,') and Israel ('the twelve stars,') shall constitute her adorning. Her 'being with child,' denotes, that in the age of Charlemagne commenced a kind of foreshowing that all nations will become her inheritance; and her 'crying,' intimates the waiting and painful longing of the saints, that the kingdom of God might be speedily accomplished. But against this accomplishment, which now seems quite near, *a great red dragon with seven heads, ten horns, and seven diadems,* sets himself in violent opposition. Hereby is represented the devil in all his wrath and power. His drawing after him the third part of the stars, intimates the apostasy of multitudes of teachers from the true faith. This apostasy took place in the years 847—947, when the Manichean heresy, and profligacy with it, wrought dire mischief to the church. The man-child is a figure of Christ's kingly dominion; hence its birth is here implied to be an event invisible; and its being caught up to God, signifies that Christ's kingly dominion in the period of the *seventh trumpet* is a thing at present hidden from the world. The *flight into the wilderness* refers to the transition of Christianity from Asia to Europe, especially to its *northern* parts, which till that period had been a spiritual wilderness, in comparison of countries that were included in the Roman empire, and which had long since received the gospel; for Christianity, at the very period of its suppression in the East, began its progress in Germany, Hungary, Bohemia, Poland, Russia, Sweden, and Denmark, by the labours of Ansgarius, Cyril, Methodius, and Herbertus, in the ninth century. This was the 'preparing of a place appointed for' the woman; and the preparation became completed in Bohemia, the more special place of her refuge, in the year 940, when Duke Boleslaus, at the urgent desire of Otho the Great, obliged his princes to receive christian instruction. Christianity in these countries required at first the immediate fostering care of their princes; it was '*nourished*' by them, and continued to be so, during twelve hundred and sixty prophetic days, from

A. D. 940 to A. D. 1617, but was gradually passing in the mean time into another condition. The *most helpless period* of the woman was from A. D. 940 to A. D. 1058; then began the time, times, and half a time, (or 3½ times,) during which, from A. D. 1058 to A. D. 1617, the woman was at first partly to 'nourish' *herself*, and partly to be 'nourished' (*by others;*) but was afterwards herself to be *the* NOURISHER, from A. D. 1617 to A. D. 1836. Within the *second* of these three periods, from A. D. 1058 to A. D. 1617, we find the revival of learning, the invention of the art of printing, the Hussites, and the Reformation; and in the *third* (from A. D. 1617 to A. D. 1836,) we have pietism, protestant Bible societies and missions, and a beneficial energy extending itself to foreign and far distant countries.

"The 'water as a flood,' (ch. xii. 15,) which the great 'serpent cast out of his mouth after the woman,' represents the Turkish power that in the Asiatic 'earth' received its check and limitation by the crusades and subsequent events; and that was to be further checked and limited in the last half period between 1725 and 1836, chiefly from Russia and Persia; and at length to be entirely evaporated by the Divine judgments. The *persecution*, in ver. 13, relates to the oppressive vexations which those who had embraced Christianity in the north (of Europe) should suffer from their pagan countrymen. The Great Serpent himself,—namely, Satan, who, though despoiled of his original glory, had kept till then his place in 'heaven' as the accuser of the saints,—was now, after his conflict with Michael, cast down to the earth, where he is to practise for 'a short time,' 888$\frac{8}{9}$ years. That to the woman were given for her flight two wings of an eagle, denotes, that her flight was to take place in a period during which the Eastern Roman empire was standing. What is said in the seventeenth verse, refers to Christians concealed in various parts, especially in the East, who, though much oppressed for a time by infidel rulers, are by and by to grow into considerable importance.

"The *Beast*, which appears in ch. xiii., has a twofold rise; first out of *the sea;* then out of the *bottomless pit.* In the former he makes things evil and troublous; but his time for doing it is short. He is a secular power with spiritual pretensions, and arises *not very long after the termination of the second woe;* but his second and last form, which is out of the bottomless pit, will survive the desolation of the great city of seven hills. He is evidently the Papal Hierarchy, which commenced principally with

Gregory VII., and has all along asserted dominion over every country of the earth; demanding a reverence intimately prejudicial to Christ's sovereignty, and at times peculiarly blasphemous, with respect to it; whereby, as well as by its own persecuting and sanguinary spirit, it has most materially assisted him who is a liar and murderer from the beginning, and who has ever been Christ's most determined adversary. The wound inflicted on the head of this Beast, and afterwards healed to the wonderment of the whole earth, signifies the deadly conflict which the papacy sustained against the Germanic Roman emperor; whereupon the astonished world was, at the mere good pleasure of this papal power, led on to crusades, councils, pilgrimages and jubilees. A variety of afterlude of the same description may also here be intimated as forthcoming at subsequent periods. His '*war with the saints*,' may be seen in the history of the Albigenses and Waldenses of the *thirteenth* century; of the followers of Wicliff and Huss in the *fifteenth;* and of the protestants in the sixteenth and succeeding centuries; likewise in the persecution of individual believers of the Romish communion itself, by the bloody and fiery awards of the Inquisition. The ascription of '*great power*' to this Beast, in ch. xiii. 7, may more particularly refer to its remarkable extension by the discovery of America, and by subsequent missions to India and China. The Beast out of the sea continues forty and two prophetic months, or $666\frac{6}{9}$ years; but *the commencement of these cannot well be ascertained till they are found to have elapsed.* Their termination may be either at the rise of the *Second Beast;* or under the *fifth vial;* or at the *seating of the Woman upon the Beast;* or at his *rising out of the bottomless pit;* or at *his final overthrow.* I have tried various computations: one from A. D. 1073, the beginning of the reign of Gregory VII.; another from A. D. 1077, when the emperor Henry IV. was humbled by this same pope; another from A.D. 1080, when this Gregory VII. nominated Rudolph to the imperial throne. Accordingly I find the termination of the $666\frac{6}{9}$ years, the end of the Beast (out of the sea), between A. D. 1740 and 1750, during which period the papacy will have suffered very considerable hardships and diminutions. Another computation which I have tried, was from A. D. 1143, when Celestine II. was elected to the popedom; as he was the first thus elected, without the concurring voice of the people. Likewise from A. D. 1159, when Alexander III. mounted the papal throne, and became renowned for his contest with the emperor Frederic I. &c. but I have come to no certainty upon the subject. Perhaps the right method is to reckon *several* risings of this Beast; one from the elevation of Gregory VII., to the weakening of the papal power in respect of the emperor; another from Celestine II., to the weakening of the same power in respect of the people of Rome. The Beast, considered as to his seven heads, is the papal power transmitted through a long succession of popes; but when "*the last head,*" and especially the Beast himself, as "*the eighth,*" shall rage, he is become a personal individual. The "*horns*" are ten kings existing in this same *last* period.

"The *other* '*Beast,*' (ch. xiii. 11,) arising '*out of the earth,*' (which earth is probably Asia,) is also here called '*the false prophet.*' He is the armour-bearer of the former Beast; and rises about, or after the termination of the 666 years. He is the power which most of all supports and defends, for its own selfish interest, the dogma of papal supremacy. At first this power might be that of a party, an *order*, or the like, but in the last period, it is concentrated in a personal individual. It speaks as a dragon, or great serpent; that is, poisonously, fierily, overbearingly, cruelly. Its chief work consists of seductive signs and wonders. It has the semblance of a lamb: sets forth itself as being perfectly christianlike; right catholic; meek and virtuous. Time will show whether this is not *Jesuitism*, (with which the characteristics here given strikingly coincide,) or at least *Freemasonry;* that of Persia in particular; especially as in the last times, Popery and the Socinian heresy (a denial of the proper deity of Christ), will run into one another, and the latter will at length bring things to their crisis.

"The mysterious secrecy affected by Freemasonry, shows that there is no good in it. It appears to cherish neither *faith* nor *hope;* and as for *love,* it has only an empty show of it. The fraternity it boasts of, has, like that of the Jesuits, the approval of the high ones of this world; a circumstance which may well be suspected as one certain mark of false doctrine and a false church. Indeed it seems desirous to demonstrate, once for all, that perfectly virtuous integrity can subsist without Christ.

"The tyranny over conscience which the Romish communion has hitherto exercised, is but the prelude to a far worse religious tyranny that shall one day arise, when '*the mark*' (of the Beast) shall be forcibly imposed, and which may be either a distinctive sign in the person or dress; or a constrained subscription to certain articles; or both. For if this mark, which is to be indispensable to all buyers and sellers, mean nothing more than that a Christian, when he has heartily turned to God, can no longer get on so well with the world, as he could in his unconverted state, this is a mark which has existed ever since the time of Christ and his apostles. That reverence should one day be exacted to a *speaking image*, will not seem strange if we consider how zealously, even in these *rational* and *illuminated* times, image worship continues to be supported by the Romish church.—According to verse 13, the false prophet '*doeth great miracles;*'* and their being wrought '*in the sight of men,*' may mean, that they are miracles wrought only in appearance, with design to astonish and seduce the beholders. God having, once for all, established the true doctrine, we are certainly to put no confidence in any miraculous pretensions incoherent with it, (Deut. xiii. 1; Matt. xxiv. 24.) Lawful and prudent suspicion of alleged miracles, and discrimination with respect to them, are things totally absent from the Romish communion; so that the signs and wonders of the false prophet find no difficulty of reception within it. It is also important to notice, that many Jesuits, (and even Gregory VII. long before them), have been much addicted to magic. In contrast with these worshippers of Antichrist, we have now reappearing, in ch. xiv. 1, the 144,000 Israelites before noticed, (ch. vii. 4); but here they are no longer exhibited as inhabitants of this world; they are translated to the other, and beheld in a state of glorious security.

"By the *three* angels who next stand up, must be meant, at least the announcement of three great and important messages to the church and to the world; the angels may likewise represent the personal human instruments of those messages, who probably receive special help to their work by the invisible ministry of angels. The *first* I think to be ARNDT; and the expression '*everlasting,*' here applied to the '*gospel,*' may bear a reference to the measured everlastingness, (*αἰὼν*) which I regard as equivalent to two *periods*, or 2222$\frac{2}{9}$ years.† Ascription of such importance, to Arndt, appears justifiable on account of the extensive diffusion of his writings, and this in so many languages; or rather, on account of their remarkable usefulness

* Σημεῖα μεγάλα.

† See the series of apocalyptical periods already given in this chapter.

in the church of Christ. The *second* angel I think to be SPENER; who became the great instrument of reviving the study of New Testament prophecy.

"The *third* angel is not far distant; his commission will consist of warnings (and threatenings of the severest punishments) against honouring the Beast with any spiritual or external reverence. In the character of his mind and purpose, he seems to be nearly allied to Arndt and Spener. The messages of the three angels will be fulfilled inversely of the series of their delivery; for the mark of the Beast is, *historically,* first in the series; then, the fall of Babylon; and lastly, all nations whom Jehovah hath made, shall come and worship HIM, and give glory to his name.

"With the warning of this third angel, we have a beautiful contrast in the thirteenth verse; where a consolatory voice proclaims, '*Blessed are the dead which die in the Lord,*'—just at the period when the Beast is raging, in the height of his power, against the Most High, and so many are being put to sundry kinds of death.

"In ver. 14—20 are figured by THE HARVEST and THE VINTAGE, two visitations going abroad before the outpouring of the vials. By the *harvest*, the righteous are gathered into 'the garner' of heaven;—by the *vintage*, the ungodly and profane 'scoffers' are hurried into the wine-press of wrath. The loud *cry* of the angel may represent that of multitudes too closely pressed and thronged; as intimating the reservation of vast numbers for some particular purpose. When at length the judgments shall have commenced, they will proceed the more violently for their past delay; in the mean time good and evil will ripen on together. How long it will be to this period is not determined. It is enough to know that it is near at hand. The frightful deluge of blood extending over so many miles, (ver. 20,) will take place in the country round about Jerusalem. There follows in ch. xv. that sign by which the wrath of God will be accomplished. Hitherto he had borne with his enemies in much long suffering; but now his wrath is come upon them to the uttermost. It goes forth swiftly, and where it smites, it smites effectually. Meanwhile, at the very season when things on earth are coming to such an awful issue, we hear in heaven a breaking forth into joy and praise, at the very prospect of these judgments of God; because they will serve to awaken *universal* attention, so as to stir up the heathen to conversion. With verse 5, a new stage of vision commences, to which the first verse was preliminary. The seven golden vials (ver. 7,) constitute, *not the third woe itself,* but the preparation for it, (ch. xvi.) The third summons which goes forth, is to the angels to pour forth the vials of the wrath of God, and seems to imply, that the vials will be discharged in very rapid succession; for we find no more periods appointed to run out. The *sores* under the *fifth* vial are of the same nature with those under the *first;* and as the *first* is *subsequent* to the mark of the Beast, so the *seventh* immediately introduces the judgment upon Babylon. The judgments of the trumpets affect *temporal* kingdoms; the judgments of the vials, which are arranged exactly in the same order, affect the *Beast* now invested with the power of those kingdoms. The judgments of the four first vials come to pass more rapidly in succession than those of the three last, a considerable time being requisite for the standing of the '*darkened throne of the Beast,*' and for '*the kings of the whole world;*' from the going forth of the '*three unclean spirits,*' to the arrival of '*the great day of God Almighty;*'—as also for '*Babylon;*' from her '*coming into remembrance before God,*' to her '*drinking of the cup of wrath.*'"

"The *first* vial (ver. 2,) chiefly concerns *Asia*, and brings with it burning pains; the *second* is poured upon *Europe;* the *third*, upon *Africa*, especially *Egypt;* the *fourth*, as being 'poured upon the sun,' affects the whole world. It may also intimate extraordinary heat in the atmosphere, and fiery phenomena in the heavens. The *three last* vials are mutually connected; at least they all relate to the *religious* community. For the *fifth* affects the '*Seat of the Beast,*' and his devotees, the apostate Christians. His seat at this period may be vacant. The darkening of his throne is unintermitted; yet during it we find he retains his kingdom for the present. But subsequently, when the woman is seated upon the Beast, we are told fully and decidedly, that the Beast 'is not.' The *sixth* vial applies to nations dwelling in the country of the Euphrates; consequently to the *Turks*, if their empire be not already suppressed. There will likewise be a great revolution in the countries of Persia and India, and in the whole region from thence as far as Palestine. The Mohammedan 'kings of the East' do not *bring* the plagues, but blindly rush *into* them. By this time, the three adversaries, the Dragon, the Beast, and the False Prophet, become quite leagued together, and each will send forth a spirit of his own. These three unclean spirits will be active in obscuring every idea concerning God as our Creator, Redeemer, and Sanctifier: and hereby will 'gather the kings of the whole world' into the service of their three respective masters, (ver. 13.) But all will terminate in a result the very opposite of what they had designed. The warning of the fifteenth verse, and which as it were unexpectedly breaks in upon the narrative, bespeaks its own importance to all persons concerned in the events which are speedily to follow.

"The great plague, with which the period of the seventh trumpet terminates, is coincident with that of the seventh vial, and is characterised by a tremendous earthquake, which will reduce the earth into a state adapted to the good things which are to ensue. With all this, however, Rome still remains; but Jerusalem is divided into three parts. And here may be the place for what was anticipated concerning Jerusalem by chapter the eleventh. Our Saviour expressly foretold, that the Jews should be led away captive into all nations, and that Jerusalem shall be trodden down of the Gentiles, until the times of the Gentiles be fulfilled, (Luke xxi. 24.) This treading down has already lasted 1700 years; consequently that of forty and two months here mentioned, must be another, namely, the *last* treading down, which is just at hand. Accordingly, the time will come for Jerusalem to be increased to seventy thousand inhabitants, and for its temple to be restored; which time precedes, by a little, the overthrow of the Beast of the bottomless pit, (who will have made war against the witnesses;) and *may* occur within the years 1830—1836. The 'forty and two months' are common months; as the 1260 days of the witnesses are common days, coincident with those months. The witnesses are styled 'the two olive trees, and the two (sevenfold) branch-lights standing before the God of the earth,' because they are filled with the oil of joy of the Holy Ghost. The return of rain after the days of their prophecy, that is, at their death, denotes, that apostate Christians, Jews, Turks, Infidels, and Pagans, will rejoice and exult as if their leader had gained a glorious victory, upon the cessation of that testimony of Christ which was borne by the witnesses. But their joy will, 'after three days and a half,' be changed into terror, at the resurrection of these witnesses, and at their ascension into heaven; when the tenth part of the city will also fall by an earthquake. This terror, however, has a salutary issue; for the remnant are converted. And now, the treading down of the holy city has ceased. Satan, indeed, once more (see Zech. iii. 2,) before he is taken, seeks to assault it with his temptations, and to seduce the nations to whom the outer court is given; but he will be taken captive.

"Chapter xvii. John is now rapt in spirit into another region, namely, that of Rome, here called a wilderness, as being remote from "the glorious land,' and estranged from true Christianity. Rome is exhibited to him under the figure of an harlot, sitting upon the Beast (whom we here find gorgeously arrayed,) and riding upon him; but she is at length annihilated by this Beast, and by his ten horns. These *horns* properly pertain to the Beast's *ultimate* period; but the seven *heads* are seven successors who resemble them in their system of rule. *They* exist *as kings*, one after another, upon the seven hills of Rome. At the time of Antichrist's coming, five of them are fallen; the sixth stands, but in great weakness. The seventh, when he comes, proves also the eighth, on account of the *additional character* he acquires by rising out of the bottomless pit as 'the man of sin,' the very Antichrist. As the *seventh*, he is only as one member of a body corporate; but as the *eighth*, he possesses superadded dignity. He will then be an individual person, a 'man;' by whom new abominations, worthy of the bottomless pit, will aggrandize the blasphemous and antichristian power of the papacy, after this power has been for some time remarkably diminished. Whether this man will be a *Jew*, as old tradition has it, or a prince out of any of the chief regal families, time must show. In his last most infernal raging he will continue about three years and a half. The ten *horns* (ver. 12,) are *ten new secular rulers*, (possibly five Eastern, and five Western,) who at this time obtain dominion together; but immediately, perhaps at a general congress, after 'one hour,' (which may be a prophetic hour, consisting of eight natural days,) they deliver up and sacrifice their power to the Beast, who thus becomes so potent, that he will even wage a violent war against Christ, (the Lamb, ch. xix.) But before this, will the great Prostitute, the city of Rome, be judged by those kings; herself with her princes, her rich and *eminent* patricians, having become hated by them. After the fall of the Germanic-Roman empire, that is, shortly after A. D. 1800, those kings will do more to check the secular power of the papacy, than ever had been done to this effect in former times.

"In chapter xviii. we have that most impressive announcement of the fall of Babylon. Frequent and violent controversies, about the nature of its fulfilment, show that the fulfilment itself is still future. Shortly before it takes place, all such real Christians as are concealed in this Babylon, are bidden by a voice from heaven to 'come out of her, that they may not be partakers of her sins, and that they receive not of her plagues.' Every feature of her in this chapter combines in showing clearly, that *Rome* is intended; that city, which preeminently, both under the pagan emperors, and under her popes, has to the very last embrued herself in more bloodshed than any other city ever did. From Rome have issued all the well known sanguinary decrees for the destruction of heretics; she was the authoress and instigator of the bloody persecutions carried on against the Waldenses, the Hussites, and the French Huguenots. We need name only the horrid Bartholomew massacre, the thirty years' war, &c. &c. &c. The single agency of the Inquisition has consigned to matryrdom several millions of the human race, *for her sake alone.*

"Chapter xix. The awful destruction of Rome is succeeded by another joyful Hallelujah in heaven; and the inspired John beholds the Son of God in his triumphant perfection of power and dominion; for now is he manifested to destroy utterly his enemies upon the earth. With respect to the nine kings in particular, whereas they take not warning at the fall of Babylon, but all along surrender themselves only more and more to the seductions of the Beast and of the False Prophet, a conflict of the latter with the Son of God, terminates in the ejection of both those adversaries into the lake of fire; but the refractory nations, who, notwithstanding all this, still refuse his easy yoke, and will not have him spiritually to reign over them, become ruled with a rod of iron. Probably the empire of Russia, which meanwhile will have attained extensive power, may principally constitute that rod of iron.

"The subject of the twentieth chapter follows up that of the preceding, closely in the order of time. The devil arrives at the third stage of his punishment. In the first, he lost his principality; under the seventh trumpet he remained awhile '*in heaven,*' and was soon thrust down to the earth; but here, we behold him cast bound into the bottomless pit, there to abide a thousand years; after which he will be loosed for a little season, and then cast into the lake of fire. Here, by the way, it is evident that the thousand years are yet future; otherwise we do violence to the whole prophecy, and have no space for the running out of the measured everlastingness or æon of $2222\frac{2}{9}$ years, which commenced A. D. 1614;* not to mention that history

* See the table of events above given in this chapter.

has hitherto furnished us with no period of a thousand years that will bear the application of what is herewith foretold. Satan, during this predicted millenium, will be disempowered from seducing the nations, that all the good which he had obstructed may proceed without interruption. Every other enemy will *then* likewise be 'out of the way;' Babylon will have been desolated, the Beast with the False Prophet being in the lake of fire; the kings who adhered to them will be overthrown and destroyed, and much other disorder will be 'brought to nought' by the seven vials, &c. Nor is the Woman thenceforth secluded in the wilderness, but the whole earth lying open before her, the gospel will demonstrate itself in its full power; so that Jews and Gentiles will every where become worshippers and true followers of the Lord. The kingdom will become that of God and of his Anointed one, (ch. xi. 15); and thus 'the mystery,' of which he had given the glad announcement to his servants the prophets, 'is finished,' (ch. x. 7.) In all this is implied not a little; viz. an overflowing fulness of the Spirit; most abundant demonstrations of Divine grace; a serene, holy, combined, harmonious obedience and service of His universal church; fruitful, healthy, peaceful times; vast increase of the holy people; cheerful longevity; exemption from the much suffering which men heretofore drew upon one another and upon themselves, by wilful sin and folly, &c.

"But still the saints will have to walk by faith and not by sight: the conflict with sin in the flesh will still remain; nor will death have been yet swallowed up in victory. Many a sore temptation, though not from Satan, will continue to be common to men; and watchfulness will not cease to be always needful. The law in Matt. v. 8, all along abides in force; likewise the everlasting gospel, (Rev. xiv. 6); and the showing forth of the Lord's death till he come, (1 Cor. xi. 26.) Rulers and magistrates will still hold commission, but will treat as brethren those over whom they are set. The ordinance of marriage will abide; agriculture, with every *useful* art and business, will be retained; only whatever of the kind is subservient to vanity, pride, and luxury, will be utterly done away.

"Upon the termination of this happy thousand years, 'Satan will be loosed' again for a 'little time,' (μικρὸν χρόνον.) This 'little time' may, according to the analogy of the other periods, be $111\frac{1}{9}$ years; so that the 'short time,' (καιρὸς ὀλίγος) namely, $888\frac{8}{9}$ years, and this little time taken together, amount to just a thousand years. When, therefore, this additional period is fulfilled, and Satan's attack, which will be forwarded through the instrumentality of Gog and Magog, is defeated, the great adversary is then arrived at the *fourth* stage of his punishment, for he is cast into the *lake of fire.* But immediately upon that loosing of Satan, commences the gradual resurrection of the martyrs; who, in union with Christ, shall reign *in heaven* a distinct thousand years, extending to the *general resurrection. This*, with the final judgment that speedily ensues, is described in ver. 11, &c. as taking place at a period subsequent to that distinct millennial reign in heaven which will have been enjoyed by the risen saints. The awful period is not definitely pointed out, but will very quickly follow this second millenium.

" Chapter xxi. discloses the everlasting glory and blessedness of the renovated universe; and now the '*New Jerusalem*' shines forth. In attending to the description of it, which is here given by St. John, we have need to keep our thoughts in the deepest reverence, that we may neither expound it too corporeally, nor spiritualize away the significant force of the words. That the New Jerusalem will have a *place* as well as a *name*, is evident, because our souls will inhabit risen *bodies;* which must needs be relative to space. But whether the *dimensions* of the city, which are computed like material ones, be intended as really such, and not rather as figuratively expressing the accomplished number of the elect, I will not attempt to determine. The latter appears probable, from the New Jerusalem being styled 'the Bride, the Lamb's Wife;' and because, to justify so strong a personification, it cannot be a place *merely.*

" The sixth verse of ch. xxii. ushers in,

" III. *The conclusion of the whole prophecy.* This concluding portion is fraught with reflection, and is well worthy of it. It contains various paragraphic pauses, beautifully corresponding with those of the *introduction.* For there as well as here, the things which are to come to pass, and the things we are to observe and do, are testified in the same order; first the grand matter of God, generally; and then of the Lord Jesus Christ, particularly.

" The divine attestation to the words of this prophecy is affixed by the Lord Jesus himself, in ver. 7—by the angel in ver. 9, 10—and by the apostle (ΣΥΜμαρτυροῦμαι) in ver. 18, 19. Moreover, here is a distinction between the predictions of the Apocalypse, and those of Daniel, (xii. 4, 9, compared with viii. 26,) concerning '*The Time of the End.*' The words in Daniel were *closed up* and *sealed,* as referring to very remote futurity; whereas, here it is said, (ver. 10,) 'Seal NOT the sayings of the prophecy of this book; for the time is at hand.' The predictions of the Apocalypse serve to explain and illustrate those of Daniel.

"Verse 11 teaches, that forasmuch as the strongest motives to repentance and conversion are to be found in this revelation, therefore, whosoever will not yield to such motives, has now to see to it, whither the way he has chosen is leading him. Here then is a reason why, as an expositor of this prophecy, I must keep back nothing, but must clearly and freely lay open all. I may make no impression where I had hoped to do it, but I shall find that I have done it where I did not expect it. For what those who 'are full' regard as insipid, may be savoury and vital to others in a time of need. And what may be thought over-curiousness at present, will hereafter serve to the praise of the Divine glory.

"The awful Commination which here prohibits the smallest addition to, or diminution from, the words of the book of this prophecy, was peculiarly necessary; because, in the prophetic writings, so much depends on a single, apparently trivial, word; and because, in writings of this kind, any perversion of the true meaning is not so easily discovered, as in books of historical or other information."

CHAPTER VII.

APOCALYPTICAL INFERENCES AND ANTICIPATIONS.

BENGEL'S inferences from prophecy were not the dry notions of a mere biblical scholar; but the living convictions of a christian believer. Thus did his apocalyptical system so enshrine all his principles of life and conversation, that only through that medium could he contemplate either political events and designs, the condition and affairs of the church of Christ, or those of science in general. Hence it is quite requisite to the true delineation of his character, to exemplify in some degree these his habits of reflection; especially as we are furnished with a considerable number of his apocalyptical anticipations, which are not only well deserving of notice, but are even of intense interest, for their gifted farsightedness upon scriptural vantage-ground.

He observes, that* "apart from all the details of chronological computation, we cannot but think ourselves approaching very near to the termination of a great period; neither can we get rid of the idea, that troublous times will soon supersede the repose we have so long enjoyed. At the approaching termination of any great and remarkable period, many striking events have been found to take place simultaneously, and many others in quick succession; and this after a course of intermediate ages in which nothing unusual has occurred.

"The condition of the church at present,—retrospectively of the dark ages universal popery, and prospectively of the glorious millenium,—is of a middle character. Evangelical truth has since the Reformation been merely conducted down to us by a chain of generations, none of which have been very remarkably affected by it; the vast majority in each having, as it were, settled on the lees. But we have now for some time begun to witness a variety of new and extraordinary emergences; as *visions, inspirations, sects,* &c. A time of general agitation, concussion, and collision, has

* We here follow chiefly the Appendices or "Gleanings," belonging to the 25th—40th of his ".Sixty Practical Addresses on the Apocalypse:" but we insert in proper places other passages also, which have come to hand from his letters, diaries, &c.

commenced, but the consummation is not yet. Signs however exist, which plainly enough intimate that something still more extraordinary will soon transpire. Of the fathers of the ancient church, Bernard, who lived in 1110, is accounted the latest; and from 1140 to 1160 was the thickest of the darkness. Then came Waldo, Wiclif, Huss, Luther, Arndt, Spener, and perhaps a seventh. This was the *cock-crowing,—the period of dawn.* By and by the crucible will yield its gold.

"Should nothing perfectly novel and upon a grand scale emerge within the next three or four years, (from 1740,) there will be another interval of comparative calm, which will last for a considerable time. As long as nothing extraordinary befalls Rome or Jerusalem, things in general will proceed pretty smoothly; but while they continue much as they are, the news in the journals will be alternating and fluctuating every quarter of a year. *One novel scene of things and then another, will be perpetually engaging public notice,* till the children of men become ripe at length for a visitation from Him who is higher than the high ones. When events have arrived just at the finishing of the mystery of God, we shall hear the striking of that clock which has so long been silent. I mean that partly *before,* and partly *at* this period, many events of a terrible, yes, and also of a joyful kind, will rapidly succeed one another.

"What is good appears to be also ripening for the harvest. Whereas our more recent sects have now, as I may say, disclosed all, even the noblest mysteries, and this so freely and indiscriminately, that babblers themselves are found able to begin imitating and counterfeiting them, there remains nothing more of the kind to disclose. Things cannot well be pushed to a higher pass than they are.

"As aged people are fond of repeating the history of their former years, so the world, as waxing old, appears to dote upon her own personalities. Witness the present craving appetite for books of narrative, and for tales of olden times.

"That the world itself begins to be ripe, may be seen also in the following circumstances. The manner of doing evil, and of abetting it, has more and more the show and importance of an art or science. The sins against the seventh commandment are rapidly gaining ground. How very many in our days are evil reported of as to that matter! What must be the end of these things? And yet they will grow worse and worse, when with men's inherent lusts the grand seduction of Antichrist begins very generally to cooperate. We shall soon see fornication more lightly thought of in Christendom than it was and is among the heathen. Adultery is already regarded as a piece of gallantry; indeed, excesses and crimes still more against nature, are not unheard of. Whatever iniquity among the higher ranks is practised upon a larger scale, or in a more *refined* manner, every lewd fellow of the baser sort aspires in his *humbler* way to imitate; and, thus among high and low, the bands of moral restraint are relaxing more and more; for superior persons, by yielding license to others beneath them, can walk after their own lusts with less outcry and molestation. I consider it as another sign of the radical corruption of our church, that when faithful ministers openly reprove and boldly rebuke such abominations, they are instantly vilified as assaulting private character; and are even threatened with prosecutions not dissimilar to those which were carried on against the primitive Christians before heathen magistrates.

"Our church, to speak generally, is become, in *the collective body of its members*, so corrupt a mass, such a pernicious leaven, as is sufficient to infect the whole world. With the exception of the few who cherish within them a spark of divine life, the rest of us have all the faults of a heathen wild olive-tree. The aspect of the present season in the church indicates the approach *of winter;* for ours is a poor frigid slumbering age, which needs an Awakener; and surely an Awakener is coming.

"Our newswriters and journalists, who have always been scribblers for pay, have contributed much to the present corruption of the public taste. Their pages will serve to show the complexion of the age we live in; that there is a spirit in it which every day more and more decidedly favours scepticism, and sets itself in opposition to Divine Revelation. The Bible (with all the parade about it) is a lamentably neglected and despised book; yes, and many who show it some regard, have learnt to handle its contents so improperly, that they cause many more to stumble, to err, and to go astray. The abilities of reason and mere nature are so exorbitantly magnified by the most, that the bulk of Christendom will soon be unable to understand the very meaning of faith, grace, or any thing supernatural. The memory of those great and holy men of old, whom the Omnipotent made use of for such mighty acts of his benevolence and supernatural interposition in his people's behalf, is now so irreverently treated, that lo! one statistical sciolist summons a 'Joseph' to his council board; another questions a 'Moses;' and a third cross-examines a 'David,' (all, chiefly for what is termed their *political* conduct;) and what God himself accomplished by the mere instrumentality of such sacred men, is perversely construed by others into state management, and is thus referred to by some of the present age, in justification of their own public artifices or intrigues. The mere fancies and imaginations of minds so corrupt and so 'reprobate concerning the faith,' are printed off with unscrupulous levity, and circulated by the trade, for the sake of mammon, for the alleged *diversion*, but real depravation of the human intellect. And even public teachers and private tutors, as well as governors and rulers, are captivated by the mischief, and it runs down abundantly to the very lowest ranks. Hereby wholesome discipline and instruction lose all their efficacy, notwithstanding the boasted progress of wit, intellect, and ability in our days. Many even attack the Lord himself, the Saviour of the world; and one trembles to utter the impieties which are vented by audacious and numerous individuals. Systematic ungodliness has thus attained such a growth, that writers against the fundamentals of our common faith will very soon be publicly rewarded by pensions. Some, indeed, are already privately supported and encouraged in this way.

"The humour of the times has quite dismissed one article of faith, namely, respecting the person and work of the Holy Spirit. That which relates to Christ, (his deity and atonement,) is likewise on the decline; and even that of the creation of the world hangs only by a fibre. Men covertly sneer at religion, as nothing more than (an old engine of state policy, or) a curb for the lower classes; and very many persons of the sacred office, having no better opinion of it, regret that they cannot, with the rest, live quite in the mode. We see every where a subsidence into merely civil morality and natural decorum; and any thing beyond is held to be a fair object for (some kind of) ridicule; yes, (even among the ordinary ranks, as well as in more polished society,) the great visitation of God himself in Christ Jesus is treated with remarkable levity. Men seem to make it a point of secular interest so to manage in all they do and say, as that nothing peculiarly and really savouring of religion, nothing concerning God and Christ, may be traceable in their conduct. People in our days are excessively sparing and cautious of giving their open and explicit testimony to any power they may have felt and experienced from the Word of God.

"The spirit of *freethinking* and of gross infidelity has already found its way down to the lower orders. We may frequently hear even uneducated persons jesting upon such sacred subjects as the resurrection of the body, &c.

"Carnal security, self-assurance, and the imputation of cant and hypocrisy to real piety, are now visible among all ranks and conditions; are associated with coarse profligacy on the one hand, and with refined infidelity on the other. One might well imagine that Satan himself could neither refine with more subtilty, nor deal out coarseness with more effrontery; yet all this is but as child's play in comparison of what will ensue by and by. Men are now but novices to those who will appear in the last age of general profligacy, when fleshly security and scoffing at religion shall have gained completely the upper hand; when it will not be so much as dreamed that the end is so near; when the dream will be, that all things shall continue as they were from the beginning of the creation. But even that season will have a few who shall continue in the faith, and in patient waiting for Christ; though their numbers will be small indeed, compared with the multitudes then wholly given to infidelity.

"Were it not for our laws and civil authorities, real Christians of the present day would have experienced, before now, very little better treatment from their nominal brethren, than what the primitive church received from its pagan countrymen. But when the '*restrained* wrath' shall once have broken its barrier, there will be cause enough to wonder at the consequences. The continuance of many a valiant and useful servant of God amongst us, is no sufficient argument of the good state of things in general; for let it be remembered, that the greatest number of holy prophets that ever appeared in Judah at one time, appeared at a period of the greatest national corruption and nearest impending ruin.

"The splendour of courts in the present day, only reminds one of worm-eaten furniture gaily varnished over. In former times, like a vigorous and healthy person, it had a fresh and natural brightness of its own. Compare, for example, the days of Everard III. of Würtemberg with our own age, (1740.)

"Things are proceeding in the world like the weather of this month of February. It is fair and foul alternately; and the alternations will go on till healthy and pleasant spring settles in. And as winter does not *produce* the vernal season, but is gradually dislodged by it, so is it with the experience of the church as a body, and with our own individual experience.

"The approach of better times for Christianity may be compared to the gradual peep of verdure through the dissolving snow, with here and there a green patch more or less conspicuous. The large wintry covering spread over all the nations, and which *we* are waiting to see dissolved, consists of Mohammedism, Popery, and Infidelity. These are alike, as amounting to one and the same usurpation over immortal souls; only in one direction its force is purely temporal; in another, it is unchristianly secular; and in the third, it is at open war with all divine revelation.

"The Great Tribulation, which the primitive church looked for from the future Antichrist, is not arrived, but is very near; for the predictions of the Apocalypse, from the tenth to the fourteenth chapter, have been fulfilling for many centuries; and the principal point stands clearer and clearer in view, that within another hundred years, the great expected change of things may take place. Even though within the next five years the Beast's chronological number should still remain unexpired, such a failure in our apocalyptical calculations is no more than the crack of a pane in the window of a large edifice. Still let the remainder stand, especially the great termination which I anticipate for 1836. Let the periods intervening issue as they may—they are only the woof of my system, not the warp: the latter is good, though the former, I am well aware, has its defects. On every point I do *not* insist with equal assurance; but I lay the total, such as it is, before the public; and let posterity consider it for themselves—correcting some parts, and confirming others, as experience of fulfilment shall direct. I have long made up my mind as to my explanations of the Apocalypse,—that they will seem to have come to nothing, soon after I am dead, and that my very name, as one of its expositors, will fall into disrepute,—nevertheless, a time will arrive when the truth of my allegations will be recognised with the seal of public approval.

"Should the year 1836 pass away without any such remarkable change in public affairs as I have anticipated, some fundamental mistake in the arrangement of my system must be sought after. Should even my exposition of the prophetic periods in general be ultimately found erroneous, still my practical application of the matters of those periods will stand good and be serviceable; and not less valuable in its place will be found, I trust, my exhibition of the *structure* of the Apocalypse; indeed I cannot help thinking that the two inquiries, namely, into the structure of the subject-matters, and into the determination of the periods, serve materially to illustrate each other. And my province is not so much to declare future events, as to display the relative bearings of the apocalyptical system. Perhaps I could tell the world more plainly than I am disposed to do, in what manner a variety of future events will turn out; yes, how they will shape themselves in the course of the next century; as also how they will succeed one another. But men have warnings adequate to all necessary purposes; quite as adequate as if the events were rightly computed to an exact period or year.

" I have watched the condition of our times, and am convinced, that the art of political government is forming more and more methodically into a system from which all holy fear concerning the judgment of God is meant to be carefully excluded. And here indeed we outdo the ancients. *Their* governments had their religions, however false. Among ourselves also prevail sins, which the prophet complains of respecting Sodom; namely, pride, luxury, indolence, and contempt of inferiors. Those of lower ranks, who can by any means keep pace with the higher, are permitted to come up with them; and this permission is imagined to atone for every thing else. Surely we cannot feel at home in such a world as we now find it; at best it is but as an inn upon the road; and the summons, 'Arise, and depart, for this is not your rest, because it is polluted,' surely cannot be unwelcome, when it comes. For folly is practised exceedingly in our own days; because it is taken for granted that we can know nothing about futurity; and because, to superficial beholders of God's providence, all is at present uncertainty and suspense; but when *the great breaking up* shall begin, what things are there of an awful and important kind that may not be expected to follow one another in quick succession!

" I am not particularly inclined to inquire about future temporal things, as such; I inquire rather about the good or evil with which the church will have to do, whether temporally or spiritually; and I look beyond it all to the great result. What may befall even Germany itself, is in comparison only as a little rivulet to a mighty stream. Germany, however, will have its part to act at the great issue now in prospect.

" As to the question, whether flight to some distant country, from the terrors of Antichrist, will be advisable, and if so, when, how, and whither is it to be effected; my opinion is, that flight is a thing not to be thought of, neither at present, nor perhaps at any future period. The Christians, at the destruction of Jerusalem, were otherwise circumstanced; the Lord's 'people,' (Rev. xviii. 4,) that will in that day be found in Babylon (Rome,) will also be in a different case from his people elsewhere. But local refuges which promised the greatest security, may have the least; and where things seemed to menace tribulation and anguish, there may be peace. The true preparatives for all security are shown in Rev. xiii. 10, 18; xiv. 12.

"I continue to think, that were the present war (1741) between Frederic II. (King of Prussia,) and Maria Theresa (Queen of Hungary,) now to conclude in ever so firm a treaty of peace, still something worse will ensue. What if a treaty should be formed between France, Hungary, and the emperor (Francis I.,) jointly to attack Prussia?—It strikes me also that Prussia may very possibly become a channel of Antichristianism.

"The western empire continues *about* a thousand years from A. D. 800; consequently, about sixty years more from the present time, (1740;) beyond which, we have no confidence concerning it. Let it only be considered whether the *French* crown will not one day become the *imperial* one. The very letters, which spell in Greek the number of the beast, seem to look that way; for they will form the two words Γάλλος Καίσαρ, 'a Gallic Emperor.' And though no such emperor should be the immediate successor of the present emperor of Germany, (Charles VI. 1741), still I believe that France certainly will obtain the Cæsarship (of the western empire.) I also believe that the (western) emperor, though not just the present reigning one, will have yet greater power, before that he, (as the ὁ κατέχων, 2 Thess. ii. 7, 'he who now letteth,' or prevents the rising up of Antichrist,) 'shall be taken out of the way.'

"Likewise, the German bishoprics and abbacies will be converted to secular uses; but of what sort does not yet appear. Certainly, however, before the fulfilment of Rev. xvii. 12, great changes must come to pass with respect to kings and states. The maps of Europe, &c. will then have a very different appearance from that of our present ones, and the older delineations of territory, &c. will be rendered useless. Indeed, many large countries, especially those which were under the stride of Gregory VII., will in process of years, by means known only to God, become desolate and comparatively void. How otherwise can they all at once receive *ten* new masters? Those which were portions of the old Roman empire, as Italy, Spain, Portugal, France,

Britain, Greece, &c. will suffer important revolutions, till at length the ten toes of Daniel's great image, which are also the ten horns of the Beast, will make their appearance. It looks as if the five western ones would issue from the house of Bourbon.

"Whithersoever the Roman empire anciently extended, there has the modern Roman or papistical power been chiefly dominant. Consequently Sweden, Denmark, and Norway, pertain not to the ten horns of the Beast. In Germany, the state of things is, in this respect, of a mixed character; for here the Romans have been at one time masters, and the Germans at another. That corner of Germany which is compassed by the Danube, was not so much visited by the light of the gospel in the earlier periods; hence it was its privilege to enjoy it at the period of the Reformation. Spain, Italy, France, &c. were replenished with abundance of evangelical truth, in the earliest times, but were not faithful to it; and even when the gospel visited them by the reformers, they remained insensible of its value; therefore will those 'bands' which they have preferred to wear, 'be made strong,' (Isai. xxviii. 22,) and become the more rigidly adhesive.

"Probably the Latin language will not be much longer employed so extensively and generally as it still is. Cultivation of learning will soon take another turn, and assume *quite a modern* character. The volumes hitherto written upon jurisprudence, and even the writings of Spener and Franke, will, in the great approaching change and transformation, sink into disrepute. Arnold's works are more likely to subsist; though, I fear, his too large deviations (from the established christian system,) by which he fails to urge with sufficient prominence the distinguishing doctrines of the precious gospel, will somewhat detract from his usefulness, or even work positive harm.

"The complexion of the times may be discerned by what sort of books obtain the quickest sale. The popular works of the present day are all kinds of tales, true or false, of the strangest things; intended solely for transitory amusement and excitement. To convey by them any thing of a spiritual kind, it must be worked in with such art and ingenuity as will promise entertainment and delight in the perusal; beyond which, as nothing is sought, so no real improvement of the heart is found. As for our present writers in general, they are exceedingly cautious in touching upon any spiritual subject, especially that of the Holy Spirit's work upon the heart; indeed, writers who are regarded by our philosophers and divines as over pious and enthusiastical, are as deficient as the rest in this respect. With many paragraphs and whole treatises which are lauded as quite spiritual, the φρόνημα σαρκὸς, the vain, self-loving, carnal mind of our corrupt nature, shows itself so fearfully mixed up, that people are likely soon to lose all discrimination of what is spiritual and what is otherwise.

" An opposite extreme has likewise begun to show itself. What some are forward to teach about ' the *inward* Word,' (or, ' the word *within*,') is likely to occasion much fearful evil, as soon as *philosophy* shall officiously take such a subject in hand. Persons who are always dwelling upon that subject, are impatient to get possession of the kernel without its fostering shell; every such appurtenance is with them an impertinence; in other words, they would have Christ, without the Bible. But notwithstanding this favourite refinement, they are insensibly approximating to an opposite extreme, and they will arrive at it. For as it often happens that extremes meet, so are fanaticism and gross deism found at last to coincide; and mischiefs symptomatic of the one and of the other may already be seen occasionally in one and the same beclouded mind.

" The manner also in which *the Apocalypse* is handled by its numerous expositors, may well justify some fearful apprehensions; especially on account of the great discordancy of such expositors with one another, which so perplexes and wearies most readers, that they become indifferent to the whole; for they conclude that no correct and useful exposition of the kind is practicable, or else that, among so many, it is impossible to decide which is the right one. Not a few, with some appearance of moderation and prudence, interpret prophecy in so generalizing a manner, that they teach little beyond what was known already; as, that the church of Christ has many enemies, but will never be destroyed; and so forth. Others would persuade us, that any thing but popery is foretold in the Apocalypse; and that this book of prophecy relates entirely to the future Antichrist, or else is exclusively upon the destruction of Jerusalem by Titus. Hence, in these times of great temptation, when we are needing every means of spiritual health, one important specific which God has given to promote it, is deprived of all its peculiar virtue; and the Divine testimony against popery is overlooked or nullified, at the very period when such a testimony is more requisite than ever. Is it then any wonder, that persons having no spiritual discernment, should become so confused even in their search after truth, as to fall easily and unsuspectingly into the hands of popery itself? But the controversies hitherto maintained about ecclesiastical matters are comparatively but a mock fight. We see in them as yet no bloodshed; but they will be more serious by and by; and men must hold themselves in readiness for trials far severer than the present.

"As there are streams which take their rise in countries mutually remote, but which, meeting farther down, form a mighty river; so, in the present day, multitudes of circumstantial occurrences which seem to have no mutual affinity, but rather to be as incompatible as they are heterogeneous, will be found to have met and coincided in the great and terrible season of tribulation that is not far off. Some one subject occupying the heart, inflates men so, that they become over confident; or perhaps it has the opposite effect, of making them too diffident and timid. By and by some additional thing helps to darken the understanding or bias the judgment; hence, what knowledge they had in hand to guard them against seducers or seductive objects, loses much, if not the whole of its influence; after this, it becomes a matter of indifference; and by and by is perhaps suspected as a delusion of former weakness. Thus 'all that is in the world,' works together for the more easy ingress of the '*false* prophet,' and for the triumphant success of his stratagems. Alas! what must the aggregate of such cooperations overflow unto at length!

"The papal power at this present time (1740) is sustaining the effects of a severe shock, and beginning to experience a momentous change. Still the abject adoration paid to its personal representative will continue, though his own individual authority is likewise evidently on the wane. Papists themselves are far from being satisfied with respect to their church. They see plainly enough that they are in a difficulty; but they are not so ready to acknowledge it. Some of them have said to me, 'You are too severe upon us in your Exposition of the Apocalypse.' But I have expressed nothing stronger than what is in the text. The confidence *(fermete)*=which God here gives me, startles many of them, so as rather to damp the boldness of their opposition.

"It has been correctly remarked upon the papal system, that it has not yet completed its antichristian character, by denying the Father and the Son. But though Socinianism and Popery at present appear mutually aloof, they will in process of time form a mighty confluence, that will burst all bounds, and bring every thing to a crisis. We may expect it in the following way: the residue of heavenly influence on the professing church, as a body, will have utterly evaporated; its holy things having been already more and more prostituted to the spirit of this world. And the Holy Spirit being thus withdrawn from the camp at large, the world will deem its own victory and triumph secured. Now, therefore, a spirit of liberal latitudinarianism will prevail every where; a notion that every one may be right in his own way of thinking; consequently all is well with the Jew, the Turk, and the Pagan. Ideas of this sort will wonderfully prepare men for embracing 'the false prophet,' whose *patron* (1 John ii. 22,) is neither far behind him in his approach, nor far off from the next generation.

"Mohammedism and spurious Christianity will gradually liquefy into each other, and out of this stagnant corruption will emerge the false prophet. Had any such change in the religion of the Caliphs, as could have made a figure in history, attended the transfer of their sceptre to the Ottoman Porte, I should not be disinclined to consider the rise of '*the Beast out of the earth*' as already *past*, only his miracles and signs are as yet *future*.

"Mahomet may be regarded in a twofold character, both as a philosophically eclectic theologist, (who has culled and adopted just such truths and tenets as pleased himself,) and likewise as the founder of a vast, but very novel and peculiarly sectarian denomination of political religionists. In this latter respect he will gradually become, with his overt religionism, quite obsolete; but in the former, the Beast out of the earth may not improbably replace him. An inclination to certain tenets of the Alcoran, seemingly pointing at such a transfer, is already discernible over the wide field of Christendom in various quarters.

"One sign of a near approaching general change is, that men have begun to relinquish their natural and hereditary forecast for remoter posterity. They who devote any considerable amount of their substance to benevolent purposes, are doing it not so much by founding durable establishments in real property, as by money expended in hope of a quick and sure return. This is seen in missionary institutions, emigrations, diffusion of the Scriptures and edifying books, multiplication of schools for the higher and lower orders, &c. In all such events, it is not difficult to discern the hand of God, (as operating for a very peculiar purpose.)

" The order observable in the great prophetic announcements clearly intimates, that at present (1740) the age of missions to the heathen and to the Jews is not fully arrived. As for the Jews, they are to expect no amendment of their condition, till they become provoked to jealousy by the conversion of the Gentiles. The Romish stumbling-block must also first be removed out of their way, and the Mohammedan abomination must likewise dissolve from before them. But though it is too early for the *general* conversion of Jews and Gentiles, it appears a sin of omission on the part of protestant churches, that they have not begun long ago to send missions to both. I, at least, cannot help thinking, that endeavours of this kind would have been far more noble, than the hitherto excessive painstaking of protestants to settle every subtle question in polemical divinity, or rather, to gain themselves only credit and celebrity in controversy. No modern church but that of Rome had formerly any missions, and hers were such as the heathen nations did not particularly welcome. Missionary work has at length been undertaken by protestants, later indeed, but with greater purity. There are now several pieces of fallow ground broken up in the East and West Indies, which already promise to make good our present failures in Europe. And the time is not far off, in which shall be seen greater and purer things than these. When once the Lord Jesus shall stretch out his hand, a larger portion of inheritance shall be given him. At present much toil and time are expended, before even a few among the heathen can be brought to true Christianity; but *then*, a nation shall be born in a day. Verily, all nations whom thou hast made, shall soon come and worship thee, O Lord, and shall glorify thy name.—Ps. lxxxvi. 9; Rev. xv. 4. Long enough has Rome been an impediment to this.

" The Apocalypse displays a continually westward progression of the great public movements; and history shows, that the establishment of modern universities has all along taken the same direction. After the sacking of Constantinople, learning emigrated from thence to Prague; and after this place had become celebrated for its university, a whole hive from it migrated to Leipsic; from whence learning progressed to Halle, and then to Göttingen, still more westward, and so extended beyond the limits of Germany.

"I am quite aware that much remains to be inquired into respecting scripture chronology; but something may be further done to the purpose by those who come after me. Persons, quicksighted and enlightened in the Scriptures, will no doubt be raised up far more in number than our present scanty few; and will have an ear open to the intimations of those sacred oracles, which, from the time when Moses penned their first paragraph, down to the last *Amen* of the Apostle John, gradually swelled into one summary display, as well as glorious instrument, of God's grand economy of the world. Yes, and a period is approaching, when the pure millenarian doctrine will be duly regarded as an article of the true faith; and then teachers will be so well acquainted with the whole detail of the Apocalypse, as to make it the subject of common juvenile instruction; how little soever may be taught from it at present, and however singular we may seem for taking it in hand.

"Our general system of the Apocalypse will appear to stand upon lawful or unlawful ground, according to the different views of each observer. If our exposition of this book of prophecy be not generally based upon truth, then how much besides, which has commanded great regard and attention hitherto, must at once fall away *with* it; and then where is any thing like the truth to be found! But if it rest upon fundamental truth itself, then what have the Romanists, the Separatists, the Petersenians, and others, to say to it? For which among them all can possibly think as I do? New wine must be put into *new* bottles."

CHAPTER VIII.

HIS SIXTY PRACTICAL ADDRESSES ON THE APOCALYPSE.

After he had published his "Exposition of the Revelation of St. John," persons requested him to address them upon this prophetic book at his Sunday evening prayer meetings, at Herbrechtingen. He did so; and much having been taken down by various hearers, was put together, and widely circulated. But as the whole consisted only of imperfect notes, and was very incorrect, he retouched and filled up what they had written; after which, others copied and further circulated the work; so that it proved very acceptable and blessed to many. Hence numerous requests were made to him for its publication by the press, especially from persons who had read extracts of it in the collections of abbot Steinmetz, of Kloster-Bergen. Thus Bengel printed, in the year 1747, his "Sixty Practical Addresses on the Apocalypse;" in the hope that their more general dissemination would not be fruitless. To render them still more complete, he inserted appendices or gleanings, in which he took occasion to answer objections that had been made against his apocalyptical exposition, as well as to express his sentiments on what had appeared to require additional research.

As edification was the leading intent of these addresses, they deserve the consideration of those who are disinclined to enter into the particulars of historical and prophetical chronology; as also of persons who imagine contemplation of the Apocalypse to be rather a hinderance than a help to practical piety. That we may show what appropriate matter Bengel found in it "for the use of edifying," we shall here quote a few extracts from the work itself, in the hope of inducing some to read the whole of it.

"The Apocalypse, as we learn from the first verse of it, was written for our learning and admonition, as '*the servants of God*,' and of Jesus Christ our Lord. It was written for such persons of every rank and condition, but not for strangers, enemies, or spies. Those who are idly curious to know what may sooner or later come to pass, at home or abroad, are not the persons to receive an answer. None but Christ's faithful servants can learn truly to profit by this book of Revelation. Their hopes, their prayers, their earnest expectations, their humility, their love, their joys, are all so finely interwoven with their heartfelt considerations of what shall be hereafter, that hereby they receive fresh incentives to active benevolence and mercy, and thus attain their full growth in manly piety.

"Christ's saying—'*Blessed is he that readeth the words of the prophecy*,' is virtually contradicted by many objectors. This need not surprise us in the children of this world; but when persons, who in other respects are *spiritually* minded, persuade themselves, and endeavour to persuade others, that by a diligent search of the entire book, no advantage is gained to spiritual religion, they are making a spurious and unblest attempt at spiritual refinement; an attempt which our Lord here at once, by the word 'blessed,' rebukes as with a thunderbolt. Surely, they who familiarly know his voice, will not thus 'turn away from him who' here 'speaketh' to them 'from heaven.' Rather ought we to accept this heavenly gift and vouchsafement, with as much of godly simplicity on the one hand, as of caution on the other; and the caution should be, not to value ourselves on partaking of a benefit which so many undervalue and lose. There is no room here for carnal glorying; but only for humility, holy fear, and deepest reverence.

"('Unto Him that loved us, and) WASHED US FROM OUR SINS (in his own blood,' &c.) As all filthiness is unseemly and uncomfortable, so he who can relish *sin*, which is the filthiest of all things, is surely like some insane person, who can revel in mire. Whatever temporary gratification the fleshly mind may experience in anger, wrath, bitterness, discord, strife, extravagance, intemperance, or impurity, these and such like sins not only are something foul and indecent, but prove troublesome afterwards to the flesh itself. And certainly the soul never enjoys any true comfort, ease, and complacency, till it is effectually purified from such things; for till then it cannot endure to look upon itself. Let those who continue strangers to such comfort, never leave off seeking till they have found it.

"Christ's saying, 'AS MANY AS I LOVE, I REBUKE AND CHASTEN,' (iii. 19,) has nothing too hard in it; nothing too severe. Would there be either love or mercy, think you, in letting persons sleep on while their house is on fire; or in excusing ourselves from disturbing or alarming them, because they are enjoying their sound repose? Sinners will be always unwilling to have their false security, peace, and felicity, interrupted; and for this very reason should we entreat the Lord not to spare us, but rather to rebuke and chasten us whenever he sees us inclined to relax from his instruction and discipline. In our seasons of spiritual prosperity it is good to bespeak of the Lord Jesus the performance of such an office of love upon us, if ever we should become disposed to lapse from under his healing care.

"Many little imagine how possible it is for our blessed Saviour to have complacency and delight in us; and how much it becomes us heartily to desire it, and to endeavour after it. Persons in general think of nothing beyond mere duty and obligation; thus making their service for Christ no better than that of cold vassalage, done, because it *must* be done. But they who seriously lay to heart that it cannot but be, so to speak, a delight unto Christ himself, for his saints to act agreeably to his own good will and pleasure, would perform many a duty in a much nobler spirit; and persons who are daily familiar with such thoughts, will go on with their daily duties in much more confidence towards him with whom we all have to do; yes, they will live in much more communion with the Lord Jesus; and this communion with him will be as that of a man with his friend. Let us but heartily consent to enter into such an intimacy, and we shall immediately find Christ's own voice encouraging us. Up, then, and meet him directly, and without delay; coincide with him in every thing.

"Chap. iv. 1—6. In considering such symbolical representations, we must carefully remember, that no visible form can be attributed to God's essential nature. This is only a representation suited to the scope of the prophecy. God has at sundry times showed himself in divers manners; but he is ever invariably the same; unchangeable in all his attributes. O how must the glory of the Almighty appear in heaven, where he discovers himself to his creatures in his own sanctuary! What delight, joy, and gladness, what adoration, reverence, and songs of praise! We in *this* life should be looking as it were after nothing else, but the attainment of that beatific vision. In whatever situation, here upon earth, those twenty-four elders might once have lived, it is certain that they are now inexpressibly exalted, and replete with bliss. I may venture to say, that they made no great figure before the world; and even in their own eyes they might not have seemed destined tc so elevated a preferment, or consecrated to become hereafter such chosen vessels of honour in the Divine glory. Let us all, up to our own measure, order, and time, yield ourselves to God, as instruments of his truth; yes, as vessels of honour unto himself, upon every occasion; and this with singleness and simplicity of heart, conscious of no reserves, or exceptions: yes, let him do with us just as seemeth him good. (How great soever may be our advancements in piety and knowledge of the truth,) there is always something greater beyond us; something, too, which surpasseth all understanding; yes, though 'the elders' occupy glorious stations in heaven, there are many stations more glorious still to be attained.

"O, it is base and wretched to be charmed and captivated with this world;—to lose ourselves in it by departing in heart from the Lord, and obeying unrighteousness, lusts, and temptations to various improprieties. This is making ourselves more and more unmeet for the inheritance of the saints in light, for the enjoyment of the pure glory of God. Those heavenly citizens before us have ended every conflict, and are now enjoying everlasting rest, glory, and honour. It is only here below that we have any conflict; that we have to overcome what is dark, sinful, perplexing, and annoying. It will be far otherwise in that blessed world above, &c.

"Chaps. xii. and xiii. &c. He who has intercourse with papists ought to be prudent. For instance, it is far from good to get into disputations with them. Let us leave this to others; for there will be always enough persons ready for it. Private protestants do best here in saying nothing to them; their disputings with them in the market or at the *table d'hôte*, &c. will never do any good. Let it be seen, without parade or help of words, that we carry about within us the power of godliness; that we are savingly acquainted with Christ, and the love of God; and that we have a lively hope of the heavenly inheritance in the communion of his saints. But should they, in familiarity with us, ever say, 'We and you are Christians alike; hold with *us*, and let not our *small* differences of sentiment perplex and trouble you;' then we must be very circumspect; particularly as popery professes to be much more softened and moderate now, than in former days. We may be certain that no *noisy* zeal against it will be of any avail. A true Christian will maintain unimpaired charity towards all, be they ever so mistaken; but it will be continually necessary that he should be prudent, wise, watchful, firm, and undaunted; whether at present we are within the period of the first beast, or already are come into that of the next, namely, of the false prophet, which is immediately to follow. O what a season of general seduction will this be! And there is no way of anticipating it by flight to other countries; for in endeavouring this, we may rush into the very midst of the temptations and troubles.

"Rather let us learn, as long as we may, the word of truth; and whatever suitable instruction from the gospel is suggested to us, let it serve to soften and melt our very hearts, that the spirit of it may dwell in us richly in all its wisdom and power; and that we may abide in communion with God, and with those who have fellowship with the Father, the Son, and the Holy Ghost. For as it is the Dragon that opposes the special glory of the Father, so does the Beast oppose that of the Lord Jesus Christ; and the False Prophet that of the Holy Ghost. Against those three adversaries must we have recourse to the 'Three that bear record in heaven.' Thus will God get him honour by his weak and helpless children.

"Chap. xiii. 10. This sentence is a warning to opposers of the Beast, that they be not tempted to employ against him any secular force or violence; indeed, nothing of the kind can add strength to their cause. Faith and patience alone must be the armour of the saints. He who uses any carnal weapon against the Beast or his abettors, not only effects no good, but will be the first to go into captivity. So it has been found in several cases already, especially a little after the death of Luther. So likewise it happened to the Reformed in France, only forty years ago. They fought bravely against the troops of Louis, but they suffered for it in equal proportion themselves. Let such things be a caution to those who in the approaching tribulation or persecution may be disposed to take up arms in self-defence, or to make any personal resistance whatsoever. He who has not yet entered into such trials, can easily give good advice to others; but when we are actually in the midst of them, we shall require much wisdom, faith, and patience, to prevent us from doing either too much or too little. God help and direct those who shall have to submit to the oppression, as well as those who shall have to advise them! Certainly it is better to endure patiently the most vexatious life, than to lead ever so many into captivity. It is better patiently to be faithful unto death, than to put our hand to the sword. Patience and faith, prayers and tears, were the only weapons of the saints in the first ages of Christianity.

But though they accounted themselves as sheep for the slaughter, to suppress them was impossible; moreover, Christianity at length gained the ascendency. In like manner, God can still deliver his believing, patient, and holy people out of all trouble; only let them not attempt to take such work out of his own hands. He who regards himself as the property of Christ both in soul and body, and proves by doings and sufferings that he really is such, that person is already holy and blessed in his deed. None but such a person will manifest true patience and faith in severer conflicts; but such a person *will* manifest them, that Christ may be glorified in him. (Neither need he be anxious about the future, for) sufficient strength will be supplied to him according to his day. We have no personal stock of such strength, like that of fruit and wine stored up for the winter; but in God's treasury all is safely reserved for us against the day of need. Let us be only faithful to the requirements of each present hour, and leave the rest to God. Whatever is for our good will arrive in due order; the Lord will hasten it in its time.

"Chap. xxii. 6—11. 'HE THAT IS UNJUST, LET HIM BE UNJUST STILL.' This, of course, does not mean that any Divine connivance at the continuation or increase of wickedness will ever take place; it only means that whoever, notwithstanding the great notices and signs he has received concerning things to come, and of their approaching period, still forbears to do good, shall be left to himself, (to eat the fruit of his own way, &c.) O it is awful indeed thus to be given up to a reprobate mind, for to do whatever we will. Those whose heart is waxed gross, may call such a license, liberty; but to be 'free from righteousness,' surely is any thing but liberty; it is the most abject vassalage to Satan. Far rather let us beg of God to put and keep us under the severest discipline all our life long, than be inclined to follow our own devices. It may seem to ourselves an incomprehensible mystery, that God should thus leave to man the awful choice of life or death; but, whichever of these we may prefer, God will be glorified, though in very opposite ways. Let us imagine two persons sojourning through this life together. The one spends it in unrighteousness; and by force or fraud obtains large temporal possessions; though he had previously enough for himself and family. He is unfaithful as a steward of God's property; he is devoted to filthy lusts. But even in this life he cannot help experiencing much disgust and loathing; because he finds such poor pasture for the flesh, and because, as far as enjoyment is his object, he attains during his whole life but very little. The other diligently follows every good work; lives in righteousness and true holiness; and puts a holy violence upon himself under every temptation, that he may keep a pure conscience and persevere without weariness unto the end, in the practice of all goodness. To this man is ministered an entrance into the everlasting kingdom of our Lord and Saviour Jesus Christ; to the other is given an irresistible command to depart into everlasting fire. Yet how stood once the balance between these two characters? Perhaps that balance at one period of their earthly life amounted not even to thirty silverlings of profit or loss, or even to a single day's pleasure or self-denial. The decision of a single moment has sometimes been the only thing required to strike the balance, to determine the preponderance, the final, the everlasting choice; just like the momentary decision one has to make at coming to the point of two parting roads. *Now,* then, is the accepted time; behold, now is the day of salvation. To-day is Christ testifying in our ears, 'Surely I come quickly.' (Rev. xxii. 20.) Of every one who has preferred unrighteousness and uncleanness will be exacted an account of all he has ever heard or been taught to the contrary. But let the person who is aroused by the nearness of the time, and who is waiting for a salvation that is at hand, go on with a good courage. Let him practise righteousness yet more and more; let him live more and more entirely in holiness; let him be righteous '*still:*' and holy, '*still.*' His labour is not in vain in the Lord."

"It is one important advantage of attentively and habitually contemplating God's general economy and government of the world in all ages, that hereby we lose sight of our own petty self-interests and private grievances, so as to be less liable to selfish anxieties; for we are occupied with things of superior interest; we are taken up with observing how God's great universal work advances, and how his purposes are hastening to their accomplishment. Godly and devout occupation of the mind in this way is also one help against the natural dread we have of death. In like manner I have found it to be one benefit of studying sacred chronology, that while I have been careering in thought over the billows of departed ages, and have been borne along on the current of time from century to century, the doings not only of private individuals, but even of the greatest monarchs, have appeared to me as 'a very little thing;' as the mere passing of a wave in the great ocean scene.

"The more extraordinary appear any supposed faculties of the *inspirati* and others of the present day, the more needful is it for every child of God to live in self-recollection, self-possession, and deep humility; to be continually fulfilling the law of Christ; to be adhering closely to his word; to be trusting in that word to the very letter.

"God has often given a promise for his believing people to feed upon, and yet interposed many circumstances apparently quite adverse to its fulfilment; the fulfilment has nevertheless been brought to pass; it has arrived suddenly, and when least expected. The case is similar just now, with regard to the coming of Christ; and our business is to go on, living upon the promise of his coming. Upon our so doing depends the exercise of every christian virtue."

CHAPTER IX.

A BRIEF REVIEW OF ALL PRECEDING APOCALYPTICAL INTERPRETATION, WITH REFERENCE TO THAT OF BENGEL.

WE have already mentioned, that Bengel, in the conclusion to his "Exposition of the Apocalypse,"* gave "some account" of its earlier interpretations; in which he showed the views and expectations which had been formed and entertained from age to age by persons in general, and by pious persons in particular, with especial reference to "The Revelation or Manifestation of our Lord Jesus Christ." Of this "account" we shall here furnish an abridgment; and then shall add, not indeed an account of all the interpretations which have appeared since Bengel's time, or even which have more or less adopted his as their model; for this would be too extensive; but only a concise statement of the *principal* continuations and *additional developments of that system* which he was the first to set forth. He observes, that "All the prophecies, even of the Old Testament, had Christ for their chief object; and contained some points of reference to events more remote than that of his *first coming*. Accordingly many scriptures were fulfilled by his appearing in our flesh, as our Lord himself repeatedly intimated, Luke xxiv. 47; but after he had advanced his disciples so far as to know and own him to be the promised Messiah, he led them on from this fundamental knowledge, to the prospect of things which he would hereafter bring to pass for the salvation of the world. Thus he foretold not only his sufferings, crucifixion, death, resurrection and ascension, but likewise his yet future coming again. In the last days of his ministry, just before his passion, he referred them to the scriptures of 'Daniel the prophet;' and, announcing the destruction of Jerusalem and of its temple, he expressly predicted, that this would happen before the passing away of that generation; but that the end of the world would not be yet. He also intimated to John, that that disciple should tarry till He, the Christ, should come. Now because the Christians of Thessalonica, and others, expected

* Part IV.

that the Lord's second coming would take place before the destruction of Jerusalem, St. Paul, in his second epistle to them, predicted a previous great apostasy, and the disclosure of the 'man of sin,' as events which would precede that second coming; as events also which themselves would not come to pass, till 'he who *letteth*,' i. e. obstructeth the standing up of Antichrist, should 'be taken out of the way.' Thus was 'the end' announced to be much more remote than many at that time had supposed. As for the destruction of Jerusalem, it did take place before the passing away of that generation to which Christ foretold it. John also survived all the other apostles, and, till near the close of the first century, waited for the fulfilment of that special promise which Christ had given to him. And how was it at length fulfilled? He received from Christ a peculiar revelation and manifestation of him as the king, Messiah, and of the glory of the kingdom; all which he has particularly described in the Apocalypse. But even by this revelation, 'the end' itself was shown to be distant *at least* a thousand years beyond St. John's time; likewise by the same revelation it appeared that there were now *three* future objects to be looked for; namely, 1. Antichrist. 2. The blessed millennium; and lastly, the end of the world. The first of these, viz. the coming of Antichrist, had been supposed to mean only the collective persecutions which the church endured under the Roman emperors, from Nero to Gallienus; and the persecuted Christians consoled themselves under their severe sufferings, in the hope that the second of these objects, the blessed millennium, would speedily arrive. But the longer this hope continued to be deferred, the more did the doctrine concerning it become mixed with Jewish fables; and this at length brought it into suspicion and contempt. When Christianity, in the age of Constantine,* was made the religion of the empire, a notion began to be entertained that the millennium must have already commenced; men dated its commencement from Christ's nativity or crucifixion; and dismissing the opinion that Antichrist had come, they regarded this event as still future, and expected the appearance of Antichrist to take place at the termination of their own imaginary millennium. Mistaken as this notion was, it became by and by subsidiary to the important discovery, that the secular papal power which arose in the eleventh century, was very intimately related to

* A. D. 323.

Antichrist. Some indeed publicly asserted at the very beginning of this century, that the time was near, when 'the man of sin,' the personal Antichrist, would manifest himself. This was taught in the churches of France, and first at Paris; and was believed by very many throughout Christendom. The number 666 was found to express in numeral letters the name of Benedict IX.; A. D. 1032—45. All this, however, was at most but a prelude to things yet future. But when Gregory VII. advanced the claims of papal domination to the utmost, the generality of honest, upright, and simple-hearted writers, (says Aventinus,) asserted, that the reign of Antichrist had now commenced; still many correctly expected something worse than the worldly papacy. But after the periods reckoned upon had elapsed, without any thing decisive appearing, the 1260 days were thought by some to intimate so many natural years that were to precede the days of Antichrist, and a subsequent commencement of flourishing times to the true church; an interpretation which, however, was condemned at the Council of Arles, A. D. 1260. Others abode by the opinion, that the tribulation under Antichrist *had* commenced, and they looked for its termination to take place after the 3½ times of the Woman; that is, after 350 years, by their reckoning. With this opinion the Waldenses, as also the followers of Wicliff and of Huss, consoled themselves; expecting their own deliverance to take place by the year 1383, and afterwards by A. D. 1420. Though even the latter period was too early, it coincided with the dawn of the Reformation. Of a different opinion was Pope Innocentius III. He said THAT THE NUMBER 666 DENOTED 666 NATURAL YEARS: but he interpreted them of the period of Mohammedism; against which, as hereby conceiving it to be near its end, he stirred up a crusade, A. D. 1213. Thus through interpretations devised in favour of the papacy, the doctrine of the millennium became gradually involved in very great obscurity, which, however, was in some degree irradiated by the partial light of the Reformation. For Luther, having also perceived that the number 666 certainly denoted so many years, interpreted it as referring not to the Mohammedan or Turkish, but to the papal power. He believed also with many, that the duration of the world, from its commencement, would be only 6000 years; and hence considered its end so near, that he could see no space for any *future* millennium. Therefore he regarded the millennium as having begun with the New Testament dispensation, and as having terminated with the reign of Gregory VII.; from which period he dated the commencement of the 666 years. Thus we see he was aware of the following nine important particulars; important, because they all contribute to a right interpretation of the Apocalypse: 1. That the *first* Woe is *great;* the *second, greater;* the *third,* the *greatest.* 2. That the *second* Woe commenced in the seventh century, with the Saracens. 3. That the *third* Woe is the papal power. 4. That this commenced with Gregory VII.; and that it, 5. lasts 666 years. 6. That the *third* Woe, and the *seven vials,* are contained under the *seventh trumpet.* 7. That the expiration of the *third* Woe is synchronical with the seven vials. 8. That the thousand years are natural years. 9. That the thousand years cannot be synchronical with the period of the Beast. If we add to these, 10. Another particular declared in the writings of Franciscus Lambert, a friend of Luther's, that the thousand years must be *subsequent* to the period of the Beast, then we have the whole ground for a right interpretation. But this particular was not much regarded at the time; for most believed that hereby the end of the world was made to be too distant; moreover, the frantic Chiliasm of the Anabaptists served to give millennarianism the appearance of a heresy in the eyes of the whole protestant church, and to introduce the most strange and contradictory interpretations of the Apocalypse.

" Spener was the first who renewed the look-out for better times to the church of Christ militant here upon earth. He maintained the hope of these better times, and defended it with great seriousness, firmness, and assurance, to the day of his death; but he refrained from all particular determination of the prophetic periods. A path, however, was thus again opened for the coming forth of the truth upon the subject; and it *did* come forth, and continued to gain strength, and to press forward. From that time, expositors separated into distinct classes. Some, looking solely for the predicted *events,* left the periods altogether unconsidered; or, fastening upon detached passages of the Apocalypse, applied them arbitrarily to events with which they fancied them to accord: while both parties, leaving unexplained the more important portions of the prophecy, more easily incurred very material errors. Others, though they endeavoured to ascertain the prophetic periods, failed, by taking it for granted that these are to be all computed by vulgar reckoning; and thus, in a very forced manner, inlaid the whole distance between St. John's time and that of Antichrist, with their typical interpretations of the epistles to the seven churches, but considered all the events subsequent to the opening of the first seal to be yet future, and, generally speaking, contracted them within too narrow a space; but others, contrariwise, imagined them all to have been long ago fulfilled in the judgments inflicted on the Jews and pagans: again, others found insurmountable difficulties, by assuming that a prophetic day in the Apocalypse must mean a natural year. Campegius Vitringa came nearest to the truth, for he was the first to proceed midway, between supposing either that a prophetic day is a natural year, or that it is simply a natural day. By his help also, we return to the original arrangement; 1. Antichrist; 2. the Millennium; 3. the end of the world. But I have endeavoured to proceed midway more accurately than Vitringa; and to comprise and concentrate the substance of what the true church of Christ in all past ages, and in despite of so many and various interpretations, has upon good grounds agreed in, respecting the exposition of this prophecy; so that I trust I am the less likely to have missed the truth."

Such is Bengel's account of interpreters who preceded him. We shall now attempt to show what has been done since his time; proceeding upon the same assumption which he regarded as the only true one, namely, that the Apocalypse, a portion of the inspired Scriptures, written by the apostle St. John, is a prophetic history of the kingdom of God, composed according to the connexion of future events, and according to the order of their respective periods. It is hardly necessary to mention that some modern writers have rejected the Apocalypse as spurious; that others have regarded it as only an interesting *poetical* composition; or that others have pronounced it to be unintelligible and useless, until it shall have its fulfilment in the events. It may therefore be desirable first to notice what some intelligent writers, who agree with Bengel about its principal matters, have found to blame or amend in particular parts of his system, as well as what they have thought fit to do towards extending the knowledge of that system. Among them we have to recognise foreign labourers with those of our own country. The first of the former was Dr. John Robertson, an English physician, who published by subscription a volume of extracts, translated from Bengel's work upon the Apocalypse.* The subscribers to

* "Bengelius's Introduction to his Exposition of the Apocalypse, with his preface

that publication amounted to six hundred persons, of considerable distinction in England; and it was set on foot chiefly at the instance of the Rev. John Wesley, the founder of the Methodist connexion. This translation improves somewhat upon the original, in having many longer paragraphs divided, and passages more simplified; as also in containing all the most valuable of Bengel's notes to the purpose, obtained from the "Gnomon." In Denmark, John Hammer composed a treatise, entitled, "Synopsis Explicationis Bengelianæ Apocalypticæ;" and translated the "Sixty Addresses" into Danish, to which he requested J. F. Reuss to write a preface; who, however, advised him to get printed and prefixed for that purpose, Bengel's little piece entitled, "Discipuli de temporibus."* These same "Sixty Addresses" were likewise translated into Wendish, by John Lahode; but we have no information as to whether those translations were ever printed.

In Germany, the "Exposition of the Apocalypse," says Bengel, became rapidly circulated; and while many authors undertook to examine and illustrate it in a variety of ways, many others were busy in writing against it. His cotemporaries, Müller of Dresden, and rector Jäger of Kyrn, near Treves, drew up tables after his apocalyptical system; but the latter thought it right to differ from Bengel in some respects, as in maintaining that Antichrist has been typified for several centuries, by his precursors the popes; that the two witnesses will in like manner have many special precursors; and that consequently their 1260 days are to be understood as a prophetic period, (commencing from about A. D. 1156, and ending about A. D. 1833,) as likewise their forty and two months; which he thought apply to a treading down, not of Jerusalem, but of the nominally christian church. Moreover, C. Charles Lewis von Pfeil, and John George Bührlin, pastor of Arlesried, published Bengel's system, the former in verse, the latter in question and answer.† As this catechetical work was cheap, and drawn up very plainly and simply, it became extensively circulated, and passed through several editions. Bührlin kept to Bengel's views in every respect; only he expressed the same opinion which many others

to that work; and the greatest part of the conclusion of it, &c. Translated by John Robertson, M. D. London: 1757. Ryall, Fleet-street."

* See above, chap. vi.

† Bührlin's work appeared with the title of "The Substance of the Revelation of St. John, or rather of Jesus Christ, drawn from the writings of the late John Albert Bengel, D. D., and arranged in question and answer." Schaffhausen, 1772. 8vo.

had previously entertained, namely, that Bengel himself might be the *third* angel. (Rev. xiv. 9.)* He also expected the number 666 to terminate in A. D. 1784; and that the period of the non-existence of the Beast would last till A. D. 1832. In a new edition of this little book printed at Reutlingen, by Kurz, in 1827, we learn that Ernest Bengel (our prelate's son) found fault with it, because, that after asserting what was no other than Bengel's own opinion, namely, that the first millennium will commence in 1836, and terminate in 2836, and that the second will commence in 2836, and terminate in 3836, it denied that Bengel held this opinion; and added, that though Menken of Bremen, and many others, had affirmed that Bengel had advanced it, yet Bengel had gone no farther than to speak of a primary millennium and a secondary millennium, running on collaterally. Now it is true that a notion of this sort was held by several of Bengel's scholars; but whether Bengel taught it himself, will best be decided by the following extracts from a letter which he wrote on the ninth of January, 1746. "In the first millennium, the time is not purely good throughout, and in the second, it is not purely evil throughout. The judgment upon Gog and Magog will be attended with good, (Ezek. xxxviii. 23,) and the last period of carnal security will, it is to be hoped, not take up many or even entire centuries. I ground my belief of a second millennium, not merely on the absence of the grammatical article, in Rev. xx. 4, but also on the following observations. We find that a millennium will have elapsed previously to that seduction of Gog and Magog, which will issue in their final overthrow; and yet that there will be a millennium extending to the general resurrection. I find the termination of the first millennium to be the commencement of the second. This I infer by comparing the third and seventh verses; for between these, there is formed by the fourth, fifth, and sixth, a beautiful *simultaneum*.† The doctrine of 'the midst of the years,' and that of the two millennia, confirm each other. In saying this, we are not to be considered as citing a thing to prove itself, or as reasoning in a circle; for we may demonstrate the truth of a whole matter by taking the parts, and considering

* What Bengel thought of this opinion will be seen below, in the account of his character; Part IV. chap. iii.

† He explains the word simultaneum, that it is an elegance whereby, of two things pointedly referring to the same period of time, the one is divided, and as it were split into two parts, while the other takes us by surprise by appearing parenthetically between such parts.

them in the way of mutual illustration and corroboration, just as we proceed to make out a piece of writing composed in cipher." These passages decidedly show that Bengel had no notion of two contemporaneous or collateral millennia; neither could he have held it, for it would have been at variance with his whole system.

Another very popular work upon the Apocalypse was that of his son, entitled, "An Expository Paraphrase of the Revelation of Jesus Christ, according to the late Dr. John Albert Bengel's 'Exposition of the Apocalypse,' and to his 'Sixty Practical Addresses,' by Ernest Bengel, M. A., pastor of Zavelstein: Leipsic, printed by Ulrich Christian Saalbach, 1772;" a new edition of which was published at Reutlingen, in 1825. This paraphrase closely abides by the whole of Bengel's interpretations. Likewise the following works coincided with Bengel in principal matters, but varied from him in minor ones. 1. A Treatise "On the True Use of the Apocalypse, by Fehr; with a preface by Crusius." 2. "An Introduction to a more clear Understanding of the Apocalypse, (or Revelation of Jesus Christ,) in its chronological and historical predictions; showing that Bengel's system of interpretation is the true one. In two volumes. By George Frederic Fein, privy councillor of Baden. Karlsruhe, 1784." A second edition was published in 1808, by Macklott. This edition introduces historical and mathematical reasoning, to confirm Bengel's system of interpretation; and indeed what may be said in favour of it, is nowhere so fully brought together, and so clearly arranged, as in this work. Fein likewise adheres to Bengel throughout, with the exception of a few unimportant alterations of dates; thus he states the *second* Woe as having commenced A. D. 630, instead of A. D. 634; and the Nonchronus, A. D. 750, instead of A. D. 800. Only, as to the messages of the three angels, he considers the *first* as denoting the Reformation by Luther; the *second,* as denoting Bengel's (widely diffused) elucidations of the Apocalypse; and the *third,* as yet future. At the same time he leaves out the measured everlastingness or æon of $2222\frac{2}{9}$ years, because he could not see any showing for it in the text; and for the like reason he shrank from any attempt to ascertain more precisely the end of the world. Of a similar kind were several works of the Würtemberg prelate, Magnus Frederic Roos.* They were grounded upon

* These are as follow:—

1. An Exposition of those prophecies of Daniel which extend into the period of the

Bengel's interpretation, and were designed to accumulate its historical and scriptural proofs, or to set them in a new light. They also contained examinations of other prophetic parts of Scripture, and elucidated the agreement and coincidence of these with the Apocalypse.* Some of his other works † showed in a plain and easy manner how to make use of the Apocalypse, for improvement of heart and life; and appealed to public events of the most recent date, as attesting the chronological and general correctness of Bengel's system. The following are Roos's own views: 1. That the non-existence of the Beast, (that is, of the papal power in its Hildebrandic consummation,) commenced A. D. 1740; since which time, he says, this power has become so weakened and exhausted, that it no longer carries the great Harlot, (the whole Romish church,) but is carried or supported by her. 2. The work marked No. 5, in our preceding note, gives an account of a political Propaganda, a philosophical order or community established since the year 1786; the twofold object of which is, *the agitation of the whole human race*, to be attempted as soon as the preparations for it shall be matured; and the collection, meanwhile, of as much money and as many adherents as possible, in order to vindicate the people on every occasion against their governments, and to do every thing for bringing about a general toleration of *all religions*.

Against these and similar interpreters of the Apocalypse there appeared in 1788 an anonymous and very acute opponent, possessed of sincere reverence and high esteem for this book of Scripture, the genuineness of which had been well proved by Dr. Gottlob Christian Storr, in his "New Apology" for it, published five years before. This opponent was John George Pfeiffer, M. A., who published his pious work without even a notice where it was printed. It was entitled, "A new Attempt at the safest Understanding and Use of the Apocalypse in general, and of its Prophetic Periods in particular." As the best objections

New-Testament Dispensation; and a comparison of them with the Revelation of St. John, according to Bengel's Interpretation. Leipsic, 1770. Second edition, 1795.

2. Reflections on the Present Times, by the aid of the Apocalypse, 1786.
3. Plain and edifying Discourses on the Revelation of St. John, 1788.
4. A familiar Exposition of the Revelation of St. John, adapted to edification, 1789.
5. Instructions for Christians how to conduct themselves at the present crisis, 1790.
6. The important events of the present period elucidated by the prophetic word of God; with intimations of what will soon take place according to it. Minden, 1793.

* See particularly Roos's "Exposition of the Prophecies of Daniel," &c.

† As the "Familiar and edifying Discourses," and the "Instructions for Christians," &c.

which have yet been alleged against Bengel's system are here collected together by Pfeiffer, we shall state them as a sufficient specimen of all others.

" Bengel's system," says Pfeiffer, " rests chiefly on the following suppositions: 1. That by the number of the Beast are signified 666 natural *years*, the duration of the Beast's existence. 2. That the forty and two months of the Beast are a *mystical* (or prophetic) period, likewise amounting to 666 natural years exactly. 3. That this interpretation of the number of the Beast, especially as viewed relatively to the happy millennium, is the key to all the other periods occurring in the body of the Apocalypse. 4. That all the apocalyptical periods admit of being arranged in a series of regularly increasing proportions, which series has a dominant respect to the number *seven*. 5. That the mean length of a year is 365 days, 5 hours, 49 minutes, and 12 seconds.

" Now all these suppositions are unfounded, and contradictory to the text, to history, and to experience. For, 1. What Bengel premises at setting out—namely, that the number 666 must originally have been expressed in words, rather than in ciphers, and that those words must have been in the neutral form—is uncertain; as numerical quantities were frequently expressed in ancient times by ciphers. 2. He believes, without any authority from the text, that by this number is signified the *duration* of the *Beast;* whereas it is merely said, that in the *name* of the Beast, a name appointed to distinguish him (according to a mode of designation not uncommon in ancient times), the number 666 might be counted, by them that are wise; that hereby they might be aware of him. 3. If, as might easily have been supposed, by this Beast were signified the papal power in its condition as it was first consummated by Pope Hildebrand, still its number here specified could not mean 666 natural years; for, as Hildebrand lived about A. D. 1073, the Beast's number must have run out, and his non-existence have commenced in 1739-40: whereas, in fact, the papal power, though diminished, continues to this day. Neither has the *False Prophet* yet appeared; the two last heads of the *Beast* are still wanting; the *harvest* and *vintage* have not arrived; nor do we see any thing new or extraordinary at Jerusalem, &c.; all which events, however, are to *precede* the Beast's non-existence. That Bengel had felt this difficulty; and, to remove it, had constructed various hypotheses, as that the number 666 might be made to commence in times somewhat later; yet he allowed, at last, that its commencement could not be exactly determined till its end should have transpired. But surely it was inconsistent now to make the point of this period's commencement so uncertain, when in fact he had previously assumed it as so certain, that in comparison with it every other date was to be regarded as of only secondary importance. 4. The text shows nothing of the forty and two months being equivalent to 666 years, the assumed period of the Beast's *continuance;* on the contrary, it is to be suspected, that those forty and two months denote the period of his *greatest predominance.* But supposing they *are* to be understood as a long mystical period, still, if it be uncertain, as we have shown it is, what the number 666 denotes, it is impossible to compute by these two quantities, however we may suppose the forty and two months to be equivalent to the 666: neither can we set out with such an equation as $666y = 42x$, both of these being *unknown quantities.* Certainly, if the 666 really denominate *years*, there is no difficulty in computing the years of the Beast; for then we have only to reckon from them the length of a prophetic month, as Bengel has done, (making it $15\frac{6}{7}$ years.) 5. We search the Apocalypse in vain for data to justify any *other* such periods as those defined by Bengel. The textual words which he considers as expressing several of them, it is far more probable, were not intended to denote any *definite* period at all; (for instance the word χρόνος, which he calls a *period;)* and it was quite an assumption of his own to set down the thousand years, as one proportion relative to the number 666. Indeed could any such relation be made out between the two numbers, it would stand not as Bengel states it, namely, $666\frac{2}{3} : 1000 :: 2 : 3$, but as follows, $666 : 1000 :: 2 : 3\frac{1}{333}$; yet the former of these statements was all that Bengel had to allege for his regular scale of periods, however much that scale might have been admired. 6. The text nowhere *shows* any regular proportions of the kind as existing between the several apocalyptical periods; neither is the scale which Bengel has made choice of the only or the more probable one that might have been devised; nor does it comprise *all* the periods found in the Apocalypse. As for the number *seven* being *dominant* in them, this was an assumption partly from the numbers found in the text, 42, $3\frac{1}{2}$, 1250 days (=42 months); and partly, 7. From the *premised* length of the tropical year, which is assumed in contradiction to the latest astronomical discoveries; but were it otherwise it makes nothing for the truth of his system. Should it be argued, that the accordance of that system with the structure of the Apocalypse, as well as with history, is strong evidence of its correctness, still it must be granted, 1. That it is the plan of the Apocalypse to foreshow a continued series of events relating to the kingdom of Christ all along, down to the period of its consummation; and that those events, with the exception of some great intermediate blank periods expressly noted in the text, were to begin happening immediately and in quick succession. Between them, however, are inserted by Bengel so many and such important periods, that things which were certainly to take place in *quick succession*, are made by him to appear of secondary moment, in comparison of what he thus inserts. 2. Some periods which his system gives out, accord very well with history, but the rest are very far from doing so; indeed it may be shown, that there is no occasion for any such assumption of mystical years, months, or days, as Bengel has made, could *we* be content to remain ignorant beforehand of the duration of the chronus, the non-chronus, and the 3½ times of the woman; for durations they doubtless are, though known at present only to God. Moreover, the 3½ times will admit of computation, after a portion of them shall have expired."

The former of these two objections, namely, that Bengel's computation of the so called *prophetic* periods, does not throughout accord with history, Pfeiffer maintained as follows: "1. Bengel computes the chronus of the *fifth* seal to be $1111\frac{1}{9}$ years, from A. D. 98 to A. D. 1209; whereas, according to the text, it is to last unto the judgment upon Rome; for the martyrs are not here desiring to know when they shall have the company of their other brethren who shall be killed, but when the Lord shall appear for the avenging of their own blood and for their relief. Thus the *continuance* of this chronus must be to a period at present unknown; but its *commencement* may be more fitly dated from the age of Constantine, in the middle of the fourth century, when Christians might easily have thought, that as their religion had now gained the ascendant in the Roman empire, all tribulation was henceforth to cease, and that the millennial kingdom was about to commence.* 2. The '*short time*,' in Bengel's reckon-

* To the objection, *that the first martyrs being informed of having to wait for their companions during a period of* $1111\frac{1}{9}$ *years, is not confirmed by subsequent history; for that neither history nor the text warrants the supposition of two periods, the one complete, and the other incomplete;—whereas Bengel's dating his chronus (of the fifth seal) from* A. D. 98, *implies as much; for, from the expiration of this chronus in* A. D. 1209, *to the year* 1836, *a very considerable* INCOMPLETE *period will have*

ing, amounts to 888$\frac{8}{9}$ years: but this number is much too great, compared with the duration of the other periods; and too little, as compared with history. For it is not to be expected that all which Bengel reckons upon happening before A. D. 1836, will actually do so. Moreover, his hundred years' respite between the *second* and *third* woe is not agreeable to the text, which says, it '*cometh quickly.*' 3. His seventy-nine years of the *first* woe are not fairly deducible from history, but are thrust into it. Neither, in strictness, will the text bear application to a comparatively unimportant persecution carried on against the Jews; for events in the history of the church, which are much more important than this, must, if we adhere to Bengel's exposition, be regarded as omitted in the Apocalypse. 4. The 213 years of the Turks are fixed gratuitously; a much longer or shorter period might have been chosen with equal propriety. 5. The non-chronus of 1036 years is far too long, compared with the other periods. 6. The 1260 days of the nourishment of the Woman, or Bengel's 677 natural years, are a period the commencement of which he has fixed quite arbitrarily. 7. The 3$\frac{1}{2}$ times, or Bengel's 777$\frac{7}{9}$ years, are too short a period in respect of his '*short time*' of 888$\frac{8}{9}$ years, and coincide with no period of sufficient note in church history, but seem to have been chosen to fit in with A. D. 1836. 8. It appears from the text, (namely, from the dissimilar designations of the periods,) that of the two millennia which it announces, the one does not come *entirely after* the other, but that the greater part of their duration will be contemporaneous; so that even with his hypothesis of the New-Testament dispensation continuing a less time than that of the Old, it is possible for the millennial reign not to begin till considerably after the year 1836."*

"Much, however," continues Pfeiffer, "as may be thus objected against Bengel's exposition of the apocalyptical periods, it possesses merit of the highest importance to the elucidation of the Apocalypse. The peculiar and progressive harmony of the whole

elapsed;—to this objection Bengel replied,—that the avenging of the blood of the martyrs, and the time of its taking place, have two degrees of announcement. The *first* is, that after the lapse of a chronus of 1111$\frac{1}{9}$ years, another band of martyrs should be added to the former. In the *second* degree of announcement, the addition of the new band is a sure and joyful sign of the promised vengeance; and the particular *time* of this vengeance is afterwards fixed by those periods which commence with the tenth and twelfth chapters of the Apocalypse.

* What Bengel would have said in reply to all this, may partly be conjectured from his literary correspondence in ch. xvii., where he answers many similar objections. We shall therefore reserve our own opinion for the conclusion of that chapter.

prophecy, its connected and orderly structure, has, generally speaking, never been set forth so admirably as it has been done by Bengel. He has triumphantly refuted those who imagine that the whole of the prophecy was fulfilled in the first christian age; those who would extort seven periods of prophetic history out of the epistles to the seven churches; and those who presume they have found the key to the mystical periods, by taking each day for a year. He has refuted also the older popular systems, which make these days to be uniformly but common natural days. He has clearly evinced that the Apocalypse both foreshowed what came to pass in the first centuries, and most especially foreshows what shall come to pass in the latter years before the full accomplishment of the kingdom of God. He has rightly maintained, that the announcement to the souls under the altar in the fifth seal, is one, not of a little time of waiting, but of a chronus, a period for long protraction of the Divine vengeance. That the angelic announcement sworn by Him that liveth for ever and ever, that there should be time no longer, (ch. x.) follows as a contrast to that previous long protraction; and that by virtue of this sworn announcement, the tribulation must shortly and finally discontinue. That the blissful state thereupon ensuing will not be deferred to any thing like a too distant period. That this shorter period begins *before* the 'short time' assigned to the Devil, but expires *with* it; and that the Devil's '*short time*' commences earlier than the 3½ times of the Woman, but ends *with* them. That these 3½ times must be mystical; and that they commence *before* the rise of the Beast out of the sea. That they coincide with the forty and two months, and extend through the duration of the Beast, and on to the taking of the Dragon. That the 1260 days of the Woman are a period quite distinct from the 3½ times; and that the forty and two months of the Beast are quite distinct from, and prior to, the brief continuance of his *seventh head.* Likewise it must be conceded to Bengel, that by the Beast out of the sea, is to be understood a secular power making spiritual pretensions, and existing in such intimate connexion with the city of Rome, that all the abominations which have been practised in her, and by her means, from the time of the persecutions of the primitive church by the Roman emperors, down to our own days, will be visited in the Divine visitation upon that power. Only it cannot be granted that the papacy, in its condition as consummated by Hildebrand, is the peculiar kingdom of the Beast; rather it is the kingdom of the Babylonian Harlot, and which prepares the way for the Beast's kingdom. That we, at present, up to the year 1788, and indeed for a considerable while yet to come, are still within the period of the '*waiting;*' for it will be a long time before all the martyrs who are yet to be slain, shall have been put to death. But how long it will be to the time of the *Seventh Seal,* when the fulfilment of the kingdom of God shall commence in all its vigour, never more to be intermitted, is not to be ascertained beforehand. Only thus far we may conjecture, that though the seven heads of the Beast out of the sea should be seven secularly-spiritual rulers in succession, the whole periods of their collective reigns, with all that is to happen from its commencement to that of the millennial kingdom, may take up no more than 40 or 50 years: chiefly because it is probable there will be persons who will outlive all the events prophesied of from ch. vii. to ch. xiv. of the Apocalypse."

Thus far are the observations of Pfeiffer. He made them in the very year of the French Revolution; an event, which awakened fresh attention to Bengel's system among persons who observed the signs of the times. Of these we may notice Dr. Jung-Stilling, who, several years before, had anticipated that the prevalence of naturalism, or atheistical and deistical infidelity, would shake and subvert the thrones of princes.* He regarded himself as called upon to give a further development to Bengel's apocalyptical system, and to show that *naturalism* (as a renunciation of belief in divine revelation,) and *jacobinism* (as a resistance to all legal order and authority,) are dread harbingers of the approaching Antichrist.† He accorded with the *chronological* part of Bengel's system throughout; for he considered that the above-noticed work of his friend Fein had so evinced and established it, as to leave nothing for the most rigid calculators to object; he either knew not of Pfeiffer's anonymous publication, or, more probably, he concluded that recent events had so decidedly verified the system of Bengel, that Pfeiffer's assertion, that much of it rested upon conjectures rather than upon scrip-

* See his instructive tale, entitled, "The History of Sir Morningdew."

† He advanced these views chiefly in the following works:—

The Nostalgia, 1794, continued.
The Gray Mentor of Christendom, 1795, continued.
The Christian's Pocket Book, 1807, continued as an annual.
The Christian Philanthropist, 1807.

But especially in his work entitled, "The Victories and ultimate Triumph of Christianity, being a familiar Exposition of the Revelation of St. John." Nuremberg, 1799; and in the supplement to it, printed in 1805.

ture proofs, was no longer worthy of notice. Stilling likewise regarded divine revelation as above all the rules and formalities of human learning; and it was quite consistent with his whole manner of thinking, to deem it highly probable that Bengel had received from Divine Providence a more than ordinary insight into the mysteries of the Apocalypse; an insight not attainable by any mere research or reflection. Indeed, he acknowledged in the supplement to his " Triumphs of Christianity," that he regarded Bengel as the *second* angel in chapter xiv. 8, of the Apocalypse. This, however, did not prevent his considering Bengel's exposition as yet incomplete, nay, as occasionally erroneous, through the over-concern of its author to reduce all into systematic arrangement. He also considered various passages of it capable of further development, improvement, or correction. Such improvements he now attempted, by endeavouring to show, that the Beast out of the earth had already appeared in *Jesuitism;* that the Hildebrandic hierarchy had been gradually tottering to ruin ever since the appearance of the French Freethinkers, particularly those of Voltaire's principles; whereby the number 666 was coming to sundry successive periods of its close, all corresponding respectively to sundry successive and important epochs of its commencement; and, in particular, that things were continually approximating to a domination (anticipated by Bengel) of Roman *patricians* over the pope. That the harvest and vintage had commenced in the French Revolution; but as this revolution was only a prelude to still greater ones, so the harvest and vintage would extend beyond France to whole countries around; and, in an awful manner, gather in many, " both bad and good," from time to time, even until the Lord's appearing. That the seven vials are to be accomplished figuratively, and not, as Bengel supposed, literally; that they signify events which were to be brought to pass more or less by the spirit of political revolution; events, by which God would fulfil his judgments on the antichristian world, and thus promote the coming of his glorious kingdom. The *first* vial, he said, was the *revolutionary* spirit diffused over *European* Christendom, in the year 1789. It was specially directed against those who by false illumination were making ready for the Beast of the bottomless pit, that is, who bear the spiritual mark of Antichrist; for that this approaching antichristian Beast is that secular hierarchy, which will soon bear on its open front no bigotted superstition as heretofore, but decided infidelity. The *second* vial (according to Stilling) denotes great oppression of maritime countries by revolutionary intrigues and stratagems. The *third*, the sanguinary character of the revolutionists. The *fourth*, a manifest falling away of the power of religion from Roman Catholics and Protestants; so that they will lose sight of every motive and encouragement to good. The *fifth* applies to the papal power, which will terribly suffer by the revolutions. The *sixth* seems to relate to revolutionary commotions in Turkey; and, with the *seventh*, the rage of rebellion will reach its crisis; all the bonds of civil society will become loosed, and nowhere will any real property or security be found. The great metropolis of rebellion will then be split into three parties, and the other cities fall to pieces; but Rome will yet all along be spared, as being reserved for its own signal judgment. At length the nations will destroy themselves and one another by civil commotions and foreign wars; but will not even think of conversion to God.

Thus far could Stilling's system partly accord with that of Bengel; but there were other points in which he departed farther from it: as 1. He agreed with Pfeiffer, that the period of "*waiting*" (ch. vi. 11.) did not commence in A. D. 98, and end in A. D. 1209, but began after sincere Christians had for several centuries been longing and praying for the kingdom of God. But he quite agreed with Bengel, that this period consists of 1111 years; and he placed its commencement between A. D. 689 and 725, when Christendom was growing more and more rapidly corrupt by the adoption of pagan customs, and was menaced with absorption by the Saracens. 2. He embraced an opinion, which both Bengel and Pfeiffer had rejected; namely, that the messages to the seven churches in Asia, typify seven periods in church history; but he so argued for this opinion, that the reasons which Bengel and Pfeiffer have urged against it, are equally forcible against Stilling's defence of it. 3. He considered the two millennia to be not partly contemporaneous (as did Pfeiffer,) but entirely so; and this chiefly, because it enabled him to recur to the old opinion, that the world will continue only seven thousand years, and that the last thousand will be sabbatical. The latter idea was such a favourite one with him, that when he became acquainted with the "Æra Jubilæa" (jubilee era,) of John George Franke, and found in that book that Christ, according to this writer's computation, was born in the year of the world 4184, (and not, as Bengel said, in 3940,) he maintained in all his subsequent writings, that the millennium must commence in the year 1816.

Here it was that he most departed from Bengel; as also contradicted his own former opinion, which was, that after the end of the millennial reign, there will be a period of about 164 years, for the war with Gog and Magog; not to mention, that the more his own longing desire for the kingdom of God led him to speak of its arrival as close at hand, the more he thus exposed his system to objections. Doubtless, he would have done better, had he contrived to add nothing more to Bengel's system than what we first mentioned; and had he deduced from thence alone all those forcible, encouraging, and edifying admonitions which he addressed to men's hearts and consciences, at a season of such peculiar exposure to the infection of infidel and revolutionary mania; or if, adopting Pfeiffer's view of the subject, he had considered the revolutionary times to have been foretold in ch. vi. 12—17, which he might easily have done, in strict accordance with his own method of interpretation. (See his "Triumphs of Christianity," p. 209.)

A middle way between Bengel and Stilling was lately tried by the Rev. Fred. Sander, pastor of Wichlingshausen, near Elberfeld, in his work entitled, "An Attempt at Exposition of the Revelation of St. John;" (Stuttg. pub. by J. F. Steinkopf, 1829.) This writer accords with Stilling that the messages to the seven churches foreshow seven periods of church history, but he rejects the notion of a second millennium; and leaving the general system of apocalyptic periods as Bengel had settled it, he briefly states his opinion that the number 666, the duration of the papal power, commenced in the reign of Pope Alexander III., and in that year of his reign when his title became generally acknowledged, namely, A. D. 1177; and that it lasts to A. D. 1843; consequently, that the millennial kingdom may be expected to commence in A. D. 1847, and not before. He further shows, by what appears to be clear argument, that, considering the present condition of the world, with reference to things ecclesiastical and spiritual, the great change predicted in Scripture must certainly be very near.

One part of Bengel's system was explained in a peculiar manner, by Pastor Friederick, of Wingerhausen.* It was his opinion, that many prophecies of the Old Testament, which are

* This was in an anonymous work, which does not even state where it was printed, but which passed through several editions. It is entitled, "A Look into the Times of Antichrist, which was obtained through Scripture Prophecy, in the year 1800, by, and for the benefit of, the faith and hope of the people of God."

supposed to have been *spiritually* fulfilled by our Saviour's first coming, refer to a second coming of Christ, just before the beginning of the millennium; and will *then* be *literally* fulfilled. His treatise, therefore, relates chiefly to the restoration of the Jews, the establishment of their worship at Jerusalem, and the great blessing which will then be found in the midst of them. Here he decidedly differs from Bengel, who considered that the land of Canaan will, just before the millennium, be no place of refuge, but a very theatre of the severest tribulation; and who did not expect the conversion of the Jews, till after a great earthquake shall have befallen Jerusalem. Friederick further differed from Bengel in practical application; for he says (p. 9), " Whoever would escape from the darkness (of Europe, &c.), let him follow the two candlesticks, and the light they bear; for where can the church at such a period stand more securely, or more full of light and spirit, than in the land of Canaan, under the government and priesthood of the two witnesses? When, therefore, antichristian ordinances and constitutions shall be set up in European countries, when Babylon itself begins to *republicanize*, and even to *enforce* its new constitutions, let men withdraw from such antichristian countries, and not be dazzled by promises of liberty, or the like, so as to stay any longer among them; but let them withdraw, *as soon as ever the Lord opens the door, into the land of Israel.* But while the lesser Asia, Syria, and Canaan, remain under the Turkish yoke, we have no authority from scripture prophecy to go thither, neither will it be practicable or advisable."

All this is quite contradictory to Bengel, who considered that in Germany the antichristian troubles will be but as a rivulet to the aggregate of their mighty stream; that men will not be able to find earthly refuge anywhere; and that, in seeking it, they may run directly into the midst of the tribulation; that the kings of the East, in particular, by marching toward the Holy Land, will enter blindfold into the midst of the plagues, &c. Neither does Bengel's system at all countenance Friederick's notions concerning Palestine; but it admits that the Jews have reason to expect speedy re-establishment there.

Finally, in confirmation of Bengel's surmise, that " the correct period may, after all, be ascertained upon false principles," (or upon principles which would appear false according to his system,) it may be observed, that the writings of Ph. F. Leutwein,

M. A.;* those of Augustus Friedmann Rühle von Lilienstern, (in his "Discovery of the very near Appearance of the Personal Antichrist,"—Frankf. 1820,) and several similar writings of others, *all quite differing from Bengel in their mode of computation*, accord with him in expecting that between A. D. 1830 and 1840, Antichrist will practise his misrule.

* "The Nearness of the General Temptation," Tübingen, 1821. "The Beast that was, and is not." Lewisb., 1825.

CHAPTER X.

HIS " CYCLUS."

In this little volume Bengel attempted to show that there was a real coherence in his progressive scale of apocalyptical periods. As 1 *period* (chronus) in this scale, amounts to $1111\frac{1}{9}$ years, and as he had adopted the conclusion of astronomers in his time, that the mean tropical year consisted of 365 days, 5 hours, 49 minutes, and 12 seconds, he inferred that after 252 apocalyptical *periods*, that is, 252 times $1111\frac{1}{9}$ years, or 280,000 years, a cycle of the solar system would be completed; in other words, all the planets would then have returned to the same relative positions to one another and to the fixed stars, from which they set out at the creation. And he conceived, that hereby the calculations of astronomy were verified in a manner which had never before been noticed.* But as more recent astronomers have found the mean tropical year to be 365 days, 5 hours, 48 minutes, and 44 seconds,† Bengel's cycle can no longer be maintained. He himself, however, was far from insisting upon it as proof, and earnestly invited others to give him their opinion of it; though none ventured to do so. The work is now only of use to show his unwearied diligence upon any subject which he deemed serviceable to the cause of truth: it is also an instance of his great acuteness. Could it have been confirmed by the latest astronomical calculations, it would have very strongly supported his system of apocalyptical chronology; though the two things are not so *necessarily* connected, as to stand or fall together.

* See also the work of John Gotthold Böhmer, chief assistant minister of St. Peter's, Budissin. It is entitled, " Dr John Albert Bengel's Cyclus; or particular Reflections on the great Year of the Universe." Leipsic; by Ulr. Christ. Saalbach, 1773. Also Privy Councillor " Fein's Introduction" (already mentioned,) chronological part, pp. 135—152, &c. Likewise Stilling's Appendix to " The Triumphs of Christianity," pp. 51—58.

† Bonnycastle, (in his " Astronomy," 7th edit. 1816), states the tropical year at 365 days, 5 hours, 48 minutes, 45½ seconds. Sir John Herschel, in his recent and celebrated work on Astronomy, states it to be 365 days, 5 hours, 49·7 seconds. Here then is still a variation worthy of notice; and deviating less widely from Bengel's datum.—Tr.

CHAPTER XI.

HIS CONTROVERSIAL WRITINGS UPON APOCALYPTICAL CHRONOLOGY.

I. His "*Age of the World*," was not (he says,) to be considered as a translation of his "*Ordo Temporum*." Though some things are repeated from it rather copiously, and others briefly, yet much is entirely new. Neither was his "*Age of the World*" intended to be a complete refutation of every objection raised by learned persons against his "*Ordo Temporum*." But it takes occasion, from their objections, to set controverted points in a clearer light. It is in seven chapters. The *first* discusses the importance of that historical and prophetical line of chronology which pervades the Old and New Testament. Among a variety of matters which we have already adverted to, the work has the following additional thoughts:—

"The particular dates mentioned in Scripture, if we look at them merely apart, may seem at first like something we could dispense with; but if we trace them by the clew which Scripture itself furnishes, we find a connected series of proportionate periods conducting us towards their ultimate object, the day of Christ. It is only when we keep close to this method of tracing them, that we perceive why many an important event has no date affixed to it, while others of less importance are accurately dated. All this was evidently from design; and that design was to continue the line of chronology. In like manner, the pervading appearance of this line is one noble proof of the internal, intimate, and indivisible connexion of the Old and New Testament,—a proof which may especially be adduced in refutation of Jewish infidelity."

The *second* chapter treats of the *periods* of the world, from the creation to the kings of Persia; and contains a train of argument to prove, that Dean Kohlreiff's computation gives 567 years too many.

The *third* relates to the *middle periods;* and notices the objections which James Koch* had made to Bengel's system, especially to the second part of his Old Testament chronology, which discusses the seventy weeks of Daniel.

The *fourth* treats of "the last periods of the world;" distinguishes true millenarianism from false; and considers the authority and importance belonging to terms and forms of expression in Scripture. Kohlreiff's loud complaint of abatement in the zeal of orthodox Lutherans against millenarianism is here first animadverted on; together with what the Dean had considered as valid objections to the millenarianism of Bengel, who is glad to find an abatement of the zeal above mentioned; and states, that pure millenarian doctrine, which is of no worldly and earthly character, but spiritual and heavenly, is perfectly agreeable to Holy Scripture. He then remarks, that all lovers of the revelation of Jesus Christ, and of its true exposition, must surely rejoice with himself, that so prompt and diligent an opponent had not been able to bring forward a single objection of any weight. That this spoke in favour of his own chronology. That, from christian regard and respect, he wished the undue warmth with which this writer in his advanced years had defended his own sentiments, might subside into meekness of wisdom; that, by the same word and truth of the Lord, which he appeared so much to value, he might be sanctified entirely; and that the impressive testimony which he had borne on various occasions by his writings, &c., against the offences of this present world, might thus have its more effectual triumph. To this chapter were added, remarks upon the terms and manner of expression used in Scripture; showing that, as by the way they strikingly harmonize with the character of inspiration belonging to the whole sacred volume, so they ought to be made our own standard of expression in prayers, praises, sermons, and common life. He had introduced these remarks, because the word *chiliasm* was used in the Lutheran church as but another name for *heresy*. Whereas the doctrine of a future thousand years of peculiar blessing to the church of Christ is, by Rev. xx., a scriptural doctrine. It is only men's *false* descriptions of this blessed millennium that are *unscriptural* and heretical.

The *fifth* chapter is entitled, "The observable extent of the Scripture Line of Chronology." It notices two reviews (in main points very favourable ones) of the "Ordo Temporum;" and adds a few corrective observations.

* See his "Elements of a Safe and Correct Chronology."

The *sixth* chapter replies to several groundless objections of a reviewer (in the "Authentic Details," part 33,) against Bengel's chronological system in general, and against that of the Apocalypse in particular.

The *seventh* concludes the work, by commending the preceding investigations to the attentive consideration of sincere Christians.

II. Of his "*Confirmed Testimony to the Truth*," the *first* part was a rejoinder to Dean Kohlreiff's reply.* The most important objection which Kohlreiff had made against Bengel was, where he says, in sect. 7, that Bengel's views of the millennium must necessarily tend to a dreadful dissettlement of all true religion; for, that in his express mention of the spiritual privileges which are to be retained in his millennial kingdom, he never says one word of the continued use of the Scriptures, the symbolical books, the sacrament of baptism, the confessional, the ministerial office, or the Lutheran religion, hereby proving himself guilty of very ominous omissions. Bengel replied: "This is a heavy charge indeed, and may well serve to set every body against me. In expressing anticipations, however, of the millennial kingdom, I have mentioned things which could not possibly be thought of apart from the continued use of the Scriptures and the sacred ministry; neither is that the only occasion whereon I have intimated that I could not attempt to mention and settle every thing. But with those three inseparables, the Bible, baptism, and the ministry, Kohlreiff has arbitrarily rivetted three other matters which, especially in their modern form, are comparatively recent, and of less importance; and the continuation of which, to the end of the world, he cannot evince from Holy Scripture. Is it then a dangerous unsettling of religion, if I do not maintain their continuance into the millennium? Was there no religion till the symbolical books, the confessional, and Luther had appeared?"

We need not go on with the remaining particulars of this controversy; for Kohlreiff, with all his occasional vehemence, adopted here, for the most part, very weak and obtuse objections; not to mention that we have already noticed a much more important opponent; and shall meet with several others in Bengel's literary correspondence.

* Kohlreiff had replied to the strictures in Bengel's "*Age of the World*," by "A collateral Treatise on the World's long duration; inferring and maintaining the same from the true Chronology of Scripture, against that of Mr. Bengel, which involves a double Millennium."

The *second part* of the work reviewed objections raised against his general exegesis, and particularly upon prophecy.—1. His exposition of the seventy weeks of Daniel had been questioned by Baumgarten in his "Illustrations of General History;" by Dr. Clauswitz, who thought that every calculation of the seventy weeks ought to proceed upon *nine postulates*, one of which was, that "by years and weeks are meant no other divisions of time than were commonly expressed by those terms among the Jews." The other postulates, Bengel said, made nothing against him; on the contrary, he could show, that his exegesis granted more than they required. Having then to do only with the one here adduced, he showed, that it could not in reason apply to the prophetic periods, especially to Ezekiel xl. 5; consequently it could not require him to renounce his interpretation.

2. James Koch, in his work entitled, "*Attention to the sum of particulars, proved to be as necessary in learned Controversies as in judicial Trials*," had brought several objections against Bengel's "Age of the World;" and had proposed another interpretation of the seventy weeks of Daniel, making them simple (weeks or) septenaries of years, and intercalating between them, at different places, a distribution of 119 years of jargon. Bengel remarked, that such a mode of proceeding was in the highest degree arbitrary; that either the series of the seventy weeks must remain unbroken, or any one has a right to intercalate what he pleases.

3. He examines, by the way, some objections against particular passages of his New Testament criticism.

4. He adverts to the controversy into which he had been drawn by Drümel, who had maintained against Schöttgen that the day of our Lord's crucifixion was Wednesday. Bengel was requested, through Schäffer, for his opinion, and his answer, which, with Schäffer's remarks, was printed at Leipsic in 1746, was entitled, "Proofs that the Day of our Lord's Crucifixion was Friday." Drümel published a reply, entitled, "A continuation of the Proof that the Day of our Lord's Crucifixion was Wednesday;" and challenged Bengel roundly to refute him. The challenge appeared in the second volume of the "*Acta Histor. Eccles.*" Bengel, therefore, inserted in the present work what further he had to say upon the subject, as follows:—"By comparing the four Gospels together, we get quite a journal, as it were, from our Lord's death to his resurrection, inclusive; and this journal evidently gives no more than *three* days. Now, upon considering what days of the week these were, we perceive

that our Saviour's death can be assigned to no earlier day of the week than Friday; for the expression, "the day of the preparation," (παρασκευή,) always signifies, when thus grammatically *absolute*, the preparation for the weekly Sabbath. Besides, it is certain that Christ rose on the first day of the week (Sunday;) and the fourteenth day of the month Nisan, which is the first day of the Passover, (Matt. xxvi. 17—20,) fell that year on the Thursday. As for the objection, that, by this reckoning, Christ abode not three whole days and nights in the sepulchre; it may be replied, either that the expression, "three days and three nights" is not to be understood strictly, which we may see intimated where it is said, "on the third day he shall rise again," (Mark ix. 31; Luke xviii. 33;) or that the expression, he shall be "three days and three nights in the heart of the earth," (Matt. xii. 40,) is to be understood so extensively, as to include Christ's previous depth of *humiliation.*

The *third* and last part of this work contained confirmations of some principal points in "The Revelation of Jesus Christ;" and was drawn up in question and answer. But we may here properly pass over it; having already dwelt so largely on his apocalyptical exegesis.

III. Of his "Vindication of the Scriptures," the *first* part contained another rejoinder to Kohlreiff; and the second, another to James Koch. For Kohlreiff had published, in the year 1750, another violent controversial piece.* Here, with all the wrath and bigotry of a stiff orthodoxical champion, who feeling his defeat, still hopes to embarrass his opponent, he had raked together a number of unfair inferences from Bengel's expressions, and thus represented him as a vain-glorious vapourer, a most unsound expositor, a critic who designedly deteriorated and wrested the word of God, a despiser of Luther, an idolatrous devotee of Spener; in short, a most dangerous sectary and millenarian. Bengel in his preface observes, that "wise and discriminating persons, who have read Kohlreiff's gross perversions of truth and justice, will think this labour of mine unnecessary; and I almost agree with them that it is so. Controversial writings in general effect but little good; on the other hand, we have no time to lose; and the

* "The Winepress of Wrath in the Last Times; or a plain Interpretation of the 34th, 35th, and 63d chapters of Isaiah; with a new Appendix, drawn up for the honour of Scripture; wherein the Herbrechtingen millennarianism is exposed in its naked knavery, and in its hostility to the Lutheran Evangelical Church. By G. Kohlreiff, Licentiate of Ratzeburg."

labour spent upon them might be better employed. Still it is but reasonable that I should be considerate of others who may need to have Kohlreiff's errors refuted, and may look to me for some answer to his objections against those truths which I have defended. Such are the persons I may be useful to; and I shall adopt the shortest method of attempting it; namely, by omitting to notice all personalities, and paying attention simply to the matter in hand." In the reply itself, Bengel acknowledges it to be quite true that he was bound in conscience deeply to venerate the memory of one who had long since happily departed in the faith of Christ, and whose name was embalmed in the affections of thousands, namely, the beatified Spener; and he chose to speak thus emphatically of him, because many others were so very scrupulous of doing it. At the same time, he was far enough from having the slightest inclination to undervalue Luther; and though he had ventured to make a new German translation of the Greek Testament, even in this he had acted agreeably to the mind of Luther himself; for Luther had expressed a wish that every city might have its own translator. As for the taunt of millenarianism, it might apply as easily to Kohlreiff as to himself: for that *he* also had found in the Revelation of St. John, a prediction concerning a thousand happy years, which he considered as already fulfilled. Conscientiously could he (Bengel) subscribe to the Augsburg Confession, as declaring those to be in error who say that a *temporal* kingdom will be possessed by the saints and the godly, and that *by them* the ungodly will be rooted out of the earth. If, moreover, by millenarians are meant those who teach that the partakers of the first resurrection shall spend their millennial reign upon earth in all sorts of corporeal gratifications, then he, for his part, was as far from being a millenarian as any one of his defamers. Indeed, his own scriptural statements respecting a far purer millennium had already been the means of opening the eyes of many short-sighted persons, who had availed themselves of unscriptural millenarianism, for the indulgence of every dreaming fancy. Hereby had a kind of good been done, which antimillenarians would find it difficult to point out in any opposition of theirs.

The *second* part, containing a reply to James Koch,* went chiefly to show, that this writer, in endeavouring to support his

* See Koch's philosophical "Essay on clearness and accuracy in historical arrangement and chronology; showing their extreme importance to sound reasoning and morals."

proposed exposition of Dan. ix., had committed anachronisms. For example, he had post-dated the Jewish sabbatical year, by *one* year; the date of the crucifixion by *two* years; and, for the rest, had persisted in his dismemberment of the period of the "seventy weeks." It would be superfluous to detail the particulars of the controversy; only it is worth observing, that at p. 195, Bengel expresses himself as abiding by the opinion which he had all along given respecting the commencement and termination of the *period of the Beast*, (the number 666.)

CHAPTER XII.

HIS EXEGESIS OF THE NEW TESTAMENT.

It has been already stated, that Bengel wrote two expository works upon the New Testament.* The first of them was intended to assist students of all nations in acquiring more accurate knowledge of the christian Scriptures; and the second, which contained his German version of the New Testament, was intended to impart to general readers the benefit of his criticisms and exegesis. Both were the fruit of many years' diligent research. For as early as the year 1706, he had begun collecting "*Annotationes, Additiones, et Animadversiones*," upon Hedinger's Greek Testament. Having, since the year 1713, gone every two years through the Greek Testament with his pupils in the Theological Seminary, he at length, in 1722, determined upon preparing and publishing a brief exegetical commentary upon it. He brought the work to the end of the Apocalypse, within two years after this; but kept it by him eighteen years more, before he gave it to the public. He did the same by his German translation. It was not till December, 1741, a few weeks after he had finished his preface to the Gnomon, that he could bring himself to undertake this translation at all; and it cost him so much more consideration before he could send it to the press, that he wrote the preface to it only a few days before his death. It may be asked why he thus delayed, especially when friends were all along so anxiously expecting the works, and his opponents, as Wetstein and others, were amusing themselves upon his dilatoriness. We answer, that, with respect to the Gnomon, Bengel wished previously to send out his *Apparatus Criticus;* for he considered sound criticism to be most wanted, because very few persons in Germany had as yet given requisite attention to this laborious sort of learning. And with respect to his

* 1st. Gnomon Novi Testamenti, in quo, ex nativâ verborum vi, simplicitas, profunditas, concinnitas, salubritas, sensuum cœlestium indicatur. 4to. Tub., 1742.

2d. The New Testament, for Growth in the Grace and Knowledge of our Lord Jesus Christ; translated from the revised original Greek, with practical observations. 8vo.; Stuttgart, 1753.

German version of the New Testament, he too well knew what strong prejudices prevailed among the German protestant divines of his day, against the publication of any new vernacular translation of the Scriptures; consequently, that such a thing could not be done without causing much commotion and alarm. Hence he long doubted whether it was worth while for him to occasion such a stir among his brethren; especially as the Lutheran version possessed general correctness, and the desired alterations affected no material points of doctrine. This induced him to keep back his own translation, in the hope that others who should be better qualified than himself might make the attempt, (1742.) But being disappointed in this, he at length thought it his duty to publish it; which he expressed by remarking, that he had become more than ever convinced that many a rendering in Luther's version is incorrect. That Luther not having had the advantage of a sufficiently revised text, had overlooked in some passages the true arrangement of the words, &c. That improvements in this respect ought to be undertaken; which it was to be regretted that the Canstein Bible Institution had not done; and that, as occasion for such improvements existed, others might as well be added to them, (1743.)

The title-page of his GNOMON expresses at full its nature and design, namely, to set forth the majestic *simplicity* of the word of God; to point at its unsearchable *depths;* its impressive *conciseness;* its wonderful *adaptation to all practical uses.* All this he attempted by elucidating, from other parts of Scripture, the exact meaning of words and passages; and by keeping his eye constantly upon every finer shade of sacred expression. He thus essentially distinguished himself from most preceding expositors; and though herein he adopted a method of exposition which was very laborious, he thus brought the reader's attention still nearer to its important object. This valuable peculiarity in his exegesis, he very appropriately touches upon in a letter to Dr. Chr. M. Pfaff, in 1724. "With the revised original text I mean to furnish exegetical remarks, in which I have no inclination to appear as a teacher of mere dogmatical divinity, much less to start any thing controversial, or to inculcate just the prescribed duties of Christianity with strictness and accuracy. Neither do I wish to show myself versed in scripture antiquities, analysis, or grammatical nicety; still my exposition will be found to unite in some measure all these departments. For I intend to show the meaning of each passage, either immediately from the words themselves, or from the context, or from the analogy and harmony of each several book, or even of the whole volume of the New Testament, as circumstances shall require. It will be also seen that in needful cases I have referred to the Septuagint, the Greek Fathers, and profane authors. The modest title of '*Gnomon*,'* will, I think, best suit the work; for my annotations are so far from being intended to preclude the reader from increased research, that I wish rather to put him upon investigation of the text itself, by merely showing him the way how to set about it. My design is also to refute and to discard from the reader's attention those expositors who put upon *isolated* passages of Scripture, their own affected, forced, (or mystical) constructions, in order to grasp at impressiveness.† Instead of any such thing, I mean to insist upon the full and comprehensive force and importance of Scripture in its whole connexion. I shall first, to the best of my ability, give my own thoughts upon each passage, and then avail myself of the critical and expository remarks of others."

In his preface to the work itself, he speaks much to the same purpose; points out the close connexion between his exegesis and his criticisms; and gives his long-promised examination of Gerard von Mastricht's critical principles. He then assigns his reasons for adopting a mode of exposition which aims at noticing every particular of the divine word. That it is no more than a part of that reverence which we owe to a divine revelation; not to mention that the New Testament has peculiarities of expression, which, while perfectly familiar to its writers, are much more allied to biblical Hebrew, than to classical Greek; all which of course requires to be accurately studied in its own manner. Besides, there is a general uniformity belonging to all the sacred books, over and above the special peculiarities of each. It is also intimated by the sacred writers themselves, that an important expressiveness belongs sometimes to the smallest words and particles. He next states how he has treated each portion of the New Testament. That he has arranged his harmony of the *Gospels* by the leading fact, that only three passovers occurred during Christ's public ministry. That the Acts of the Apostles and the Epistles

* Index, or Pointer.

† This shows that Schröckh was mistaken, when in his "Biography of Eminent Literary Men," (2d edit. 1790,) he considered Bengel's mode of exposition to be the same as that of Cocceius.

illustrate each other. That he has prefixed to each portion a summary account of its contents, which would be very serviceable to the diligent reader. That he has considered the objections recently made by Dr. Joachim Lang, against his German annotations upon the Apocalypse, and has answered them with the respect he felt due to this venerable person; with whose friendship he had been honoured ever since the year 1713.—He then adverts to some passages, respecting which he desires his own work may be compared with those of preceding expositors; as Matt. xxiv.; Acts xiii.; Rom. xii.; Heb. xii.; 1 Pet. iii.; Rev. x., &c.; and after stating that he considered it desirable to intersperse a few practical remarks among his annotations, he concludes by expressing a wish, that the work may be useful in checking that peculiar misapplication of sacred passages, which was now fearfully prevalent (among cold nominal Christians, as well as heated religionists;) and in serving to awaken many from a neglect, not to say contempt, of Scripture consultation.

In a letter to a friend, he expresses a hope that the "Gnomon" may, by the Divine blessing, be a means of reviving a more general taste for the study of Holy Scripture. "Its notes," he adds, "are brief, and have many references inserted, which will give frequent occasion to the diligent reader to pause; but whoever will make himself familiar with the preface, the index, and the synoptical tables, and will then study a portion of the annotations, as occasion shall require, will soon be able to comprehend me."

He had great pleasure in seeing these wishes and hopes fulfilled. "I have much comfort and encouragement," he said, "in finding that persons who had begun to seek the truth by other helps, have expressed a kind of holy delight in making use of the Gnomon. This gives me the more satisfaction, because they could never have felt that delight, unless they had occasionally worked through a large quantity of literary matter comprised in my work."*

* A living writer speaks of the work as follows:—

"Bengel's Gnomon is a rare performance of the kind, concise, original, vigorous, eloquent, and sprightly; it is an erudite exposition, delivered in a spirit of fervent christian love. It evinces the deepest reverence for the sacred text, and a most profound acquaintance with its contents. With remarkable simplicity and humility it follows the drift of the inspired meaning, and induces the soul to open itself, even to the softest of those breathings of the Holy Ghost, which pervade the written word. Its full but artless description in the title-page, bespeaks the true tenor and spirit of the work. A plenitude of sound knowledge, hallowed and animated by deep piety, here sheds itself over the very words of Scripture, and serves to elicit from every part

This commentary was soon held in such estimation by many in Holland, Denmark, and England, as well as Germany, that its second edition was called for in the year 1759, and a third in the year 1773. The second was published under the revision of his son-in-law, the Rev. Philip David Burk, M. A. Dean of Kirchheim; and the third was superintended by Ernest Bengel, M. A. the author's son. The three editions were also distinct works. That of Dean Burk contains numerous exegetical and critical additions, from notes by Bengel, left in his own handwriting, and never before printed. The third edition also contains the *exegetical* portion of these; but those which were *critical*, were transferred by Ernest Bengel to a second edition of the "Apparatus," which was now likewise called for; and he added to the Gnomon instead of these, an examination of the more recent objections which had been levelled at his father's exegesis; and particularly, of those published in the "*New Theological Library*," by Ernesti.*

A considerable variety of popular works, founded on the Gnomon, served to extend, both at home and abroad, especially among the laity, the usefulness of Bengel's exegesis. One of the earliest of these was published in London, A. D. 1755, by the Rev. John Wesley, M. A. (the founder of the Methodist connexion.) It was entitled, "Expository Notes upon the New Testament." Mr. Wesley remarks in the preface, that he "had intended to write merely a few notes of his own, from a simple consultation of the Scriptures; but that after he had become acquainted with Bengel, that great luminary of the christian world, lately gone to his rest, he altered his plan, because he was convinced that he should much better serve the interests of our holy religion by translating from the Gnomon, than by writing many volumes of his own notes. He had therefore given in English a great number of Bengel's excellent annotations at full length, and had abridged, and compressed the substance of many more. Subjects of pure criticism he had omitted entirely, but

of it the inherent glow of its interior divine illumination."—*Evangelical Church Chronicle*, edited by Dr. Hengstenberg, of Berlin, vol. ii. p. 228.

Haman likewise thus expresses himself:—"I am at present studying with much benefit Bengel's Gnomon upon the New Testament. It is an exegesis altogether *sui generis*. No expositors, or very few, have caught the *full* import, impressiveness, and spirit of Holy Scripture. In this respect, Bengel's commentary is one of the best of its kind."—*Haman's Works*, vol. iii. p. 15.

* A reprint of Ernest Bengel's (third) edition of the Gnomon, has been published at Tübingen, this year (1836,) in two handsome volumes, 8vo., under the superintendence of Dr. John Christ. Fred. Steudel.—Tr.

had inserted the chief matters which could be excerpted from it. He had likewise received without scruple into the text, those readings which Bengel had noticed as most approved by the testimony of MSS. and versions, and had added that author's synoptical tables, which exhibit at one view the subject and contents of each portion of the New Testament. Of similar works in Germany, there were two in particular, which being got up in the same manner as Mr. Wesley's, considerably furthered the usefulness of the Gnomon. These were—1. "The New Testament, in Luther's version, accurately retouched after the original Greek, with expository notes." The revision of Luther's version, as also the notes, were obtained principally from Bengel's expository works on the New Testament. This work (in 4to.) was edited by Daniel Christian Gottlieb Michaelis, pastor of Lichtentanne, with a preface by Dr. Crusius, and it was printed at Leipsic, by U. Ch. Saalbach, in 1764. 2. "A Paraphrase of the New Testament, by Ernest Bengel, M. A., in 2 vols. 8vo. Tübingen, 1784." These two works were substantially alike; but the former follows the Gnomon in taking the text verse by verse; *inserting* sometimes expository remarks, and sometimes *appending* them separately. The latter embodies *every explanation* into a running paraphrase of the text; by which method, however, the reader is apt to be wearied. Both these works comprise the remarks of the Gnomon, with others from Bengel's different writings.*

Rosenmüller likewise, in his Scholia upon the New Testament, adopted many observations from the Gnomon.

II. As to his German *Translation of the Greek Testament*, he states with simplicity, in the preface, why he was at length induced to undertake and publish such a work. "That he had no intention it should prejudice that of Luther, neither was there any necessity that it should. That the Church has need of multiplied versions of the sacred writings. That their multiplication is sanctioned by the practice of the earliest times.

* A *third* work on the general plan of the Gnomon, but more free and original than the two above mentioned, as well as more exclusively for edification, was printed in 1828, at Tübingen, by L. F. Fues, entitled, "Reflections and Meditations on the New Testament, for Growth in the Grace and Knowledge of our Lord Jesus Christ;" by Charles Henry Rieger, Councillor of Consistory, and Minister of the Collegiate Church of Stuttgart.—Author.

This work had remained many years in manuscript; in which state it was read at prayer meetings, by persons who revered the memory of its deceased author. From what the writer has seen of it, having read a considerable part of its harmony, and the Epistles to Timothy, it appears a singularly excellent work.—Tr.

That Luther himself wished a great many more translations besides his own might become current in the Protestant Church. He then notices the principal requisites for any good translation; that as it ought to be made from a correct original text, so it ought to give the sense as complete in every way as possible, and to be as much in the vernacular idiom as the majestic simplicity of the sacred original will admit of; while the greatest care ought to be taken to lose none of its majestic simplicity in our common familiar phraseology. That in such respects a *new* translation, at least for private use, might be considered as wanting; for as Luther had such an imperfectly revised text to translate from, his version of many passages was not sufficiently close to the meaning; besides that many of his expressions had become obsolete. That he (Bengel) had now endeavoured to remedy these defects, and to produce a translation more exactly conformed to the original. To complete which resemblance, he had supplied annotations, which were further intended to edify pious persons in the grace and knowledge of our Lord Jesus Christ. But he had been sparing of remarks exclusively practical, because the Scriptures themselves supply every want of that kind. As the common distribution of the text into chapters and verses had so long and so generally been adopted, and was of use for reference, he could not well omit it; but as it was manifestly faulty in many places, he had endeavoured to rectify it by proper breaks and paragraphs which would easily catch the eye. He had also prefixed to each portion of the New Testament a summary table of its contents. Should any one feel disappointed at not meeting with more edifying matter in this *preface*, he would observe, that a servant waiting upon guests at a great supper, who duly trims the lamps furnished by the master of the house, that they may burn the brighter, performs a more acceptable service to the guests, than if he kindled any single taper of his own to add to the light. That such was the service he here aimed at: for he had written this preface merely to show the use that may be made of his version and notes. But for those who preferred reading a regular introduction to the New Testament, or to real Christianity, which is the substance of it, he could write nothing better than what Arndt, Spener, Schade, Franke, and others, had written already. That these excellent men, following closely the plain directions of Scripture itself, had shown that it must be perused with prayer, with attention, with sincere longing for salvation, and with genuine obedience of spirit and conduct; and that it was his own earnest desire and prayer, that those readers who were really seeking edification, might be disposed to study the pure text of the New Testament, with such a preparation of heart as the above writers had recommended.

Very manifold and extensive was the Divine blessing which accompanied this work. As in the year 1769, its second edition was called for; so in 1765, there had been published by an anonymous author, with a preface by Dr. Crusius, " The History of our Lord Jesus Christ, compiled from the Four Gospels, according to Bengel's Harmony and Version, and enriched with his Annotations." Likewise in the year 1766, there was published at Stuttgart, " A Scriptural Manual of Devotion," by the Rev. W. F. Schaber, M. A., a parochial clergyman. This work consisted of the short ejaculatory petitions, &c. which were interspersed among Bengel's annotations. An edition of *Luther's* version of the New Testament, with Bengel's annotations, was also published at Tübingen, by Mr. Hartmann, in the year 1767, &c. And even to the present time, Bengel's own version continues to be used in many private devotional circles throughout the kingdom of Würtemberg.

CHAPTER XIII.

HIS THOUGHTS ON DOCTRINAL AND PRACTICAL SUBJECTS, SET DOWN APART IN THE COURSE OF HIS EXPOSITORY RESEARCHES.

WE learn from his "Principles of Exegesis," noticed in our fourth chapter, that conscientiously as he adhered to the confession of the Lutheran church, he thought nothing ought to forbid our continually endeavouring to gain a still purer and more perfect knowledge of revealed truth; that he could not be responsible for the correctness of all and every interpretation put forth in our symbolical books; and that he reserved to himself the rightful liberty of uttering any further truth which he might find disclosed to him in the holy Scriptures. It was by researches conducted under this sense of duty, that he found reason to embrace the doctrine of a *scriptural* millennium, together with other sentiments theoretical and practical, the chief of which may be seen in the following detached extracts.

"The Apostles' Creed consists of two parts. The *first* treats of the Trinity: the *second* of the Church, and of the divine blessing attached to it.

"The words Godhead and Divinity, have not precisely the same meaning. Godhead, signifies the divine essence; Divinity, the glory and dignity belonging to it, and, strictly speaking, to it alone.

"The word 'holy,' properly means *separated, or set apart;* and, when applied to God, it denotes his own incommunicable excellence; that brightness of the glory of his essential attributes, which in a manner throws all creature-essence into the shade; and in which he always abides infinitely apart and distinct, not only from whatever is impure, but also from whatever is created. The divine *holiness* is therefore synonymous with the divine *majesty*. When the words holiness and glory, which singly are often used in one and the same signification, are coupled together, then the word *holiness* expresses God's hidden and unsearchable excellence; and the word *glory* denotes the revelation and display of God's holiness to his rational creatures.

"There is no reason why we should not suppose an allusion to the Trinity, in that divinely prescribed formulary, 'The Lord bless thee and keep thee,' &c. though there is little here except what we may call the *predicates*, to intimate the distinction between the three Divine Persons and their offices. The more therefore do I value every *plainer* intimation of this distinction, which is found in Scripture.

"'His glory is in Israel, and his strength in the clouds,' (Ps. lxviii. 34.) What a gloriously rapid transition of thought is here! Let it be observed by, and become familiar to, those, who, on account of the immensity of the creation, feel it difficult to believe, that our own comparatively minute globe can be so dear an object of God's providential care.

"The word *Person,* corresponds to the Hebrew פָּנִים (*Paním,*) and to the Greek *πρόσωπον*. Even the Jews called the Messiah מַלְאַךְ פָּנִים (Malách Paním, the Angel of the Presence.) In speaking of the *Trinity*, we are obliged to use some such expression, to convey our meaning. Defective as it is in some respects, yet, as we have none more suitable, we have no reason to think that God is displeased with our using it. We know in what condescending language he addresses himself to our capacities; and may therefore believe that he will bear with our weakness, though it fall far short of the true representation of himself. We shall soon know, in the heavenly world, even as also we are known; and then the very Scriptures themselves will appear to have been worded to our comprehension after the manner of a little child's first book.

"The expression, '*The Son of Man*,' always denotes the *visible* condition of Christ; whether in his humiliation, or exaltation. Thus St. Stephen exclaimed, 'Behold, I see the Son of Man,' &c., and the Day of Judgment is called the Day of the Son of Man. We also read of 'speaking a word against the Son of Man.'

"The notion which our present Herrnhut brethren entertain, that Jehovah, in the Old Testament, means God the Son, the Messiah, is surely contradicted by Heb. i. 1, where God's speaking to us in these last days, *by his Son,* is contrasted with his having spoken in time past unto the fathers by the prophets.*

* But does not the preceding paragraph from the writings of Bengel help to explain this notion of the Brethren? For there he had said, that the expression, "The Son of Man," denotes the *visible* condition of the Messiah. But was he visible *as the Messiah*, till he became incarnate? Now that by Jehovah of the Old Testament, might often be meant the Messiah, appears confirmed by 1 Cor. x. 9.—Tr.

"There is a faith which apprehends *the eternal power of the Godhead:* and a faith which apprehends *the grace of God in Christ.* The latter is the faith which saves and makes us happy; the former does not. Yet even the former is something very different from that prevalent vague notion which deifies mere nature. It is also very different from that abstracted and jejune idea of omnipotence, in which deistical infidels settle down with all the positiveness of certainty.

"It appears to me that the reason why our brethren, who are denominated the 'Reformed,' stumble so violently at what the Lutherans teach, respecting the omnipresence of Christ's human nature, is, because the former give it such a gross meaning. The Lutheran church quite believes with them, that Christ's human nature has as certainly a distinct locality 'in the heavenly places' at present, as it had formerly upon this earth. Brentius is one of those who have spoken the most lucidly upon the subject. See the reply which he wrote soon after Luther's death, to the magistrate of Wesel.

"Luke xi. 13, 'If *ye then, being evil,*' &c., is one of the best proofs of the doctrine of original sin.

"The greatest number of the Scripture types, prefigure Messiah's priesthood and kingdom. Such types were not for human use alone. God himself did, as it were, 'rest in' the gracious purpose, that his Son should come and *restore* (or *make good*) all things. Hence, in the very midst of awful predictions of destruction, we abruptly meet with some promise concerning the Messiah. Adam is the most distinguished shadow of Christ; but rather in the manner of contrast than counterpart. Aaron and David may next be mentioned, as Christ's most strikingly typical prefigurations.

"The manner of *prophetic* foreshowing in the Old Testament, resembles a landscape picture with its foreground occupied by fields, trees, cattle, busy persons, &c., all distinctly delineated on a large scale; but in its background, you descry long ridges of distant hills, and beyond them chains of mountains all diminutive; so that many objects appear grouped very narrowly together, which in the reality of nature are at a wide distance from one another. By the prophets, in like manner, are things which immediately or soon should come to pass, described clearly and definitely: but those which were seen far distant in futurity, are only adumbrated briefly, and in perspective masses. A foreshortened view may serve to express my meaning.

"Even the types were a kind of prophecies. These, as well as the prophecies, had Christ for their chief object (either the grace and the truth which were to come by Him; or else his judgments on the ungodly). The tenet that the prophetic visions and predictions have each more than a single fulfilment, needs explanation. A prophecy may admit of several *accommodations;* but its *specific fulfilment* can take place but once. The prophecies and the types mutually compose a perfect system of *promise;* a system in which the predictions, from the beginning of Genesis to the close of Malachi, swell along in number and particularity; and in which the body of the types apart may be regarded as a chamber of imagery.—I also compare the types collectively, to an adumbration on the canvas, which the artist by and by fills up with appropriate projections of light, shade, and colouring.

"Even the implied or declared INSUFFICIENCY *of* ritual *sacrifice,* was to believers, under the Old Testament, a figured intimation of better things to come; and a little light of this kind threw more brightness into the obscurity of their times, than we, who are of the day, can well imagine. They had also the oral instructions of their prophets, to assist their understanding of such things. The divine promises grew more definite and full, as time advanced; like the transverse circular streaks in the heart of a tree; where we see that the farther downwards any segment of it is inspected, the more definite and broad in the grain of the wood are such streaks as they approach *the root:* so the divine promises had *a reality* in them from their commencement; but as they descend through ages nearer to their consummation and fulfilment, we find them gradually increasing in perspicuity, definiteness and particularity.

"The whole comprehensive structure of prophecy and type, as mutually illustrating each other, has, to my view, many a cloud hiding it here and there. I only see parts of it. Therefore, in attempting to delineate it, I must do as those who would draw a map of some imperfectly discovered region. They plan down upon their scale a few places whose latitude and longitude they have ascertained, and leave blank spaces for other parts which perhaps are of more importance. Inquirers hereafter may be able to fill up the vacant spaces.

"Much has been said about the word *satisfaction* not occurring in Scripture, (relative to Christ's atonement.) But in the fortieth Psalm, Messiah testifies what surely can mean nothing less: 'In sacrifice and offering for sin, thou hast had no pleasure; then said I, Lo, I come to do thy will, O God.'

"The circumcision of the holy child Jesus, has its essential significance, not in the shedding of his blood on this occasion, but in the parting with a portion of his flesh. As both the performance and the undergoing of this ceremony were not confined to the priesthood, but allowed to and enjoined upon all classes, so our Saviour's undergoing it, constituted one part of his 'fulfilment of all righteousness,' (as 'made under the law;') but was no special part of his great sacrificial blood-shedding atonement.

"The efficacy of the death of Christ is not fully enough enlarged upon by doctrinal expositors in general. Many of them run off immediately to a trope or figure; that is, they understand by the blood of Christ, either all his merits collectively, or else the single act of his pouring out his soul unto death. Even in the most impressive treatises upon this subject, more is urged respecting the holy and *beatific fruits* of his precious blood, than about those distinct operations which bring such fruits into being. Whereas, we derive from the death of Christ, not only deliverance from the guilt of sin, but also a communication of *new vital powers;* which evince their efficacy by good works. The former is called *justification* by his blood; the latter is obtained by those who 'eat the flesh of Christ and drink his blood,' (John vi.) Hereby all his true disciples become most intimately one with him; partakers with himself of everlasting life. The life-blood which was shed at his death, as a satisfaction for sin, was spiritually carried by him into the Holy of holies, at his ascension; that it might warrant and impart cleansing and perfection to every true believer's conscience; and that such might be enabled to enjoy the application of those inestimable benefits; especially in the holy eucharist. Here then we may observe, how sadly these sacred truths are abused by the Romish inventions of transubstantiation and communion in one kind.

"As purification from sin is sometimes attributed, in Scripture, to the blood of Christ, we are to understand it, according to the context, either as operating by moral influence upon us, or else as achieving, in the natural order of God, our spiritual cleansing. Occasionally both are implied. Our faith likewise actuates us by a moral influence; but in the order of God, it is the primary means whereby we apprehend Christ as our divine Justifier and Saviour.*

* On the above representation of the efficacy of Christ's blood, Bengel observes, "If any thing in the Gnomon will provoke objections, it is what I have expressed in this way upon Heb. xii."

"Three distinct offices are commonly attributed to Christ; namely, of prophet, priest, and king. Trogillus Arnkiell was correct in subordinating the first to the two last. But I go still further; for I consider Messiah's priesthood itself as subordinate to his regal office. Christ 'abideth a king for ever;' but a priest as well as prophet, only to the end of time. His priesthood is for the recovery of fallen man to God; but a period will arrive, when this will have been entirely accomplished; yet his regal administration will still abide in full vigour. These are not mere academical thoughts: I find them in Scripture. It is fearful to observe how men in our universities 'spoil' themselves 'through philosophy and vain deceit,' upon the most sacred subjects; how they make shipwreck of their faith, either by their own inventions in theology, or by the definitions and systems of others; and how such things lead them away from the Scripture standard of thought. Surely in this respect I far prefer my own humble retirement to any academical eminence.

"It has been asked, ought the Lord's Supper to be administered to children? I think a middle course in this case, as in many others, the best. Custom is here against us; otherwise there would be no need to wait till our youth have attained to just a certain age; but we might administer to them as soon as they have a competent acquaintance with their Saviour, in faith, and love, and hope.

"It is true that the moment of our departure from this world decides our condition for ever: but many, I believe, abide in uncertainty till the day of judgment, as to what that condition will be. Thus the souls of hypocrites may be entertaining false hopes and imaginations, up to the very hour of Christ's appearing. This is an awful thought; and therefore it is well to make, in good time, our entrance into the everlasting kingdom sure; for as the decidedly flagitious, who in this life are full of infidelity and iniquity, probably depart to hell at once, so we cannot doubt that the *decided* servants of God become, at the moment of their death, entirely happy; for they are no sooner absent from the body, than they are present with their Lord. But between these two decided classes there is an indefinite variety of gradations. And though there is no *third* fixed condition after death, any more than there is a third term between yea and nay, the places of abode, in the separate state, are not only *three*, but thousand-fold.

"It is a fundamental error to think that mere death will of

course meliorate our condition. The body turns to corruption; but the soul which in this world chooses to discern and devise every thing in its own strength, will hereafter be tormented with what may be called a thirst, or aching void within it; for the longer it abides, as it will abide, in its own vain imaginations, the more will it be continually harassed by them. O what distracting torments must be experienced by many in another world, simply in consequence of the vain and perverse fancies which they allow themselves to persist in at present; for in the after state they will not be able to get rid of them! For as a river, after having reached the ocean, carries to a considerable distance out at sea its own current and complexion; so will many persons, after having reached the ocean of eternity, retain (alas, how long!) the false and vain imaginations to which they had suffered themselves to be addicted in this life.—Charity hopeth all things; but how can charity itself oblige us to hope that all who die are happy, merely because they are dead? Is it not charitable to express a fear that some of them may have gone to perdition?

"There are those who seem the less concerned about the happiness of a future state, because they hear that the most abject of their fellow-men are as admissible to it as themselves.

"That popish teachers venture to answer for the salvation of any who take to their religion, is strangely inconsistent with a tenet of their own church, that no one till after death can be assured of his salvation.

"After death an immeasurable advancement in our condition immediately commences, and continues till we arrive at that fixed state wherein we shall be found at the last day. But after death, all probation is at an end; we stand in our lot. And though a soul then advances in greater and swifter gradations than it can do in this life, still it is in its own class; along with this is it carried forward, and is no contributor to its own progress. And though there may be changes of condition in them that are lost, those who have died in unbelief will be in a state of everlasting disadvantage, compared with those who are saved.

"Considering all that we experience, and that is revealed to us, respecting the divine mercy, we may fairly believe, that there is an economy for the poor ignorant heathen, apart from that with which *we* are concerned. St. Paul would not undertake to give any final decision about *them.* 'What have I to do with them that are without?' (1 Cor. v. 12.)

"*The restoration of all things* is not a fit subject for (public) disputation. That the word αἰώνιος, (*eternal*, or *everlasting*,) has two significations, is undeniable; and thus the scriptural expressions, κόλασις αἰώνιος and ζωὴ αἰώνιος, (*everlasting punishment* and *life eternal*, Matt. xxv.) seem to bear unequal meaning. Yet it may be doubtful, whether those who, at leaving this world, go away into 'everlasting punishment' with a belief in 'the restoration,' are not sensible of more misery than those who die without any knowledge of it. Generally speaking, it would be strange to tell a malefactor that he will get a pardon under the gallows.

"On the *absolute* eternity of future punishments, it is worded n the *Latin* edition of the Augsburg Confession, 'qui statuunt,' 'who determine;' but in the *German* it is, 'who teach.' The latter pleases me better; as, in holding this doctrine, we ought to take particular care to 'have it to ourselves,' and not to force it upon others; for it is considered an undecided point.

"An opinion prevailed in the ancient church, that the condemned will obtain pardon of God through the aggregate intercessions of the elect. But this appears quite unscriptural; for we read, 'these shall go away into *everlasting* punishment.'

"'*Until thou hast paid the very last mite.*' Now I would have this word 'until,' to mean until; and this 'paying,' to denote *paying indeed.*

"There will be no remission till such a payment is made; the whole of it will be exacted and enforced. But surely the expression *until*, cannot mean the same thing as an *absolute* eternity. Many would reckon upon a great jubilee after the lapse of 49,000 years; but such a period is much too short; for, out of the limits of our terrestial world, a larger measure must be taken of every thing. Still there are sacred truths which forbid us to insist on the eternity of hell torments with that emphasis of *absoluteness* which we find in the well-known hymn, 'Eternity, thou thund'ring word,' &c.

"The *resurrection* is necessary for bringing things to such an issue, as that God may be all in all.

"The distinction between the *vapid dregs* of wine, and the *powerful spirit* produced from them, is as nothing, compared with the distinction between man in his *mortal*, and man in his *glorified* condition.

"'*In Adam all die;*'—but this is so far from an obstruction to our becoming '*in Christ all made alive,*' at the general resurrection, that as certainly as our death in Adam precedes it, so certainly is it conducive to it.

"It may well be questioned, whether, in the great day of reckoning, the debts remitted to the righteous will not be found to make a heavier sum than that which will be laid to the account of the unrighteous. Certain it is, that the sins of the former have many more refinements than those of the latter.

"There is many a sweet truth relative to our communion with departed saints. Such truths, however, must not be used as principal sustenance, but rather as spice and seasoning; for faith *must* continue *faith,* as long as we are in *this* life. And with respect to nominal Christians and infidels, who indulge a natural aversion to every thing spiritual, one may well regard it as a mental darkness, proceeding from the righteous rebuke of Him who is all-wise and all-faithful, that notwithstanding the numerous testimonies which from time to time have been put forth by the unseen world, concerning its own reality, &c., which testimonies have for ages all along increased in number and clearness, such persons, in general, have never come to any specific, public, formal and full hearing of witnesses; but instead of so doing, whenever they have had presented to them any authentic case, (of apparition, trance, vision, &c.) have evidently preferred hushing the matter up, or extenuating it as much as possible, through fear of having one seeming reason less for abiding in their practical unbelief. Accordingly, we must not be forward to relate any experience of our own concerning the invisible world; but let every one, who in *this* way also has received assurance of its reality, enjoy his assurance *upon that footing,* to himself. For (there is quite enough about it in Scripture to which we may appeal openly, and) we are always safest in keeping to the word of God, as on this we may ever depend. Yes, and it will discover to us, especially in the New Testament,—now that 'our forerunner,' the great 'Breaker,' (—he who alone dissolves the bands of death, and rends the veil,) having 'descended into Hell,' is 'ascended' (and 'gone before us) into Heaven,'—his word, I say, will discover to us such glorious things—relative to the departed righteous, respecting their communion with God, ay, their communion with their brethren too, here on earth—as may well content us for the present.

" If those who dread the very possibility of seeing apparitions of departed spirits, really knew how precious the life that now is appears in the estimation of such as have departed from it in an unblest condition, and are experiencing its reverse, surely they would put away their timidity; for such departed spirits may well be supposed to have a greater horror of coming among the living, than the living can ever have of being visited by *them.* Therefore it is best, with regard to all thoughts of this kind, to mind our own business, to live without anxiety, to have no prying curiosity or wish to learn any thing of ghosts, nor any susceptibility concerning them, but to act as if we had nothing to do with them.

" It is probable that no apparitions of souls can happen beyond a limited period from their departure, nor perhaps beyond the time when the last tie between soul and body is broken. Souls that have been quite immersed in sensualities loosen much less easily into absolute liberty from the bands of matter;—like a garrison company surrendering a strong fortress, who have first to pass out of the citadel at various gates, and then to surmount one entrenchment after another, before they have utterly evacuated their long-retained enclosure.

" Our *spiritual* senses do not in strictness operate, as it were, organically, or through the medium of each corresponding bodily sense; and yet there is a kind of analogy between the former and the latter. For spiritual senses there *are;* and this not by a mere figure of speech. Likewise they are respectively distinct. The influence of divine *light,* the influence of God's *kindness, amiableness,* or *sweetness* of character, that influence of his which either *draws* or *instigates* us, all these are *felt* severally operative upon us from time to time; and we are sensible of them, as *distinct* and *definite* operations; yes, and are consciously susceptible of them in a variety of ways. The *savour of life unto life,* spoken of in 2 Cor. ii., is of this description.

" It is the general custom in Christendom to bury the dead with their feet to the east. This originated in the simple notion of rising with the face to the east at the resurrection; a notion which was borrowed from the Jews praying with the face turned towards Jerusalem. Hence the principal door-way to our old churches is at the west end, that persons might enter with their faces to the east. This way of depositing the dead serves at least innocently to remind one of the future resurrection. Nor is it absurd to suppose, that the Lord who ascended from the

Mount of Olives on the east, may reappear in that direction." (Zech. xiv. 4.)

The case of a woman who was considered a demoniac having been related to Bengel, he thus replied:—"We should not be too hasty in believing it a case of that sort, but should endeavour to get at the real state of her mind, by addressing her like any common patient, that she may betray what state she is in. We should take a proper season for it, when she is as composed as possible; and should be very careful about addressing her; having inquired of her parents whether she is more gentle in the presence of few or many. She may be asked, whether she is wishing to be set at liberty, and to serve God with purity of heart. We should talk to her about purity, about walking in the light, &c.; but not say too much at a time. We may also try the use of music, and the melodious singing of devout and amiable children. Prayer should be offered up for instruction, duly to value the blessing of deliverance from such bondage; and the promise in Matt. xvii. 20 should be relied on, that there may be more perseverance in supplication for it. Whether this be a really physical possession, it is difficult to decide; I cannot suspect the case to be a mere cheat, because the unhappy person acts against her worldly self-interest, which would rather prompt her not to give up the dissolute trade she has followed. She may probably have often felt the rebukes of conscience during her many years of open sin; she may have heard of persons having been delivered unto Satan on account of their excesses; and thus sudden compunction may have come upon her, and have led her to think herself really possessed; so that her morbid imagination may now make her think herself constrained, like one possessed, to use evil language, and make laughing grimaces; or she may even think herself controlled by some evil being instigating her to these strange utterances and grimaces, and preventing her tongue from uttering the words of prayer which her friends endeavour to make her repeat. Though there may be no actual possession (and we are not at once to attribute it to common disease, especially if other circumstances belonging to possession are found to attend it), still it is evident that Satan is not inactive in it, but obtrudes into it much of his own operation; so that, be its origin what it may, there is special need of divine help, to know how to deal with such a person. But without further symptoms, and those of an external kind, it is, on the whole, by no means advisable to treat her as a person possessed."

" In Rev. xviii. 2 we observe *human* unclean spirits distinguished from those of *devils.*

" Surely, there must likewise be a real distinction in the spiritual constitutions of men themselves, namely, of those who die happy, and of those who die unhappy. The former seek, and have within them, the grace of God in Christ Jesus; the latter neither seek it nor have it. Not that the seeking of the former is ascribable to themselves: even this was the effect of divine grace.

" More importance attaches to the death of Christ, than to the obedience paid by all the saints, from the beginning of the world to the end of it.

" It is harsh to talk of a ransom for souls paid to the devil (though several of the Fathers had such a notion). It is no barter of this sort, it is 'mighty power' alone that redeems them, the power of Him who 'hath *abolished* death;' καταργήσας. 2 Tim. i. 10.

" I would ask those who scruple at justification by faith alone (which faith is the very life of my spirit that I derive from the word of grace), what then *is* the proximate means whereby we are made partakers of Christ? Surely, the very nature of the case admits of no *other* means but *faith.*

" That both justification and faith are only means to an *end,* and that sanctification *is* that *end* (with wisdom and redemption belonging to it), is agreeable to the sense of St. Paul, in Rom. iii. 31; viii. 1. These, namely the *means* and *end* together, we *have* IN CHRIST JESUS, 1 Cor. i. 30; it is He who helps us to both. Hence Breithaupt considered the great aim of all theology to be, our final recovery into the very image of God.

" Justification and sanctification are regarded by many, not as a simple thread spun out from the same principle, but as a twist of two threads, each of which is *(sui generis)* of its own kind.

" Two opposite errors are very common: that of persons who give the name of *grace* to every thing, even to endowments purely *natural;* and that of others, who studiously avoid acknowledging a single instance of divine grace or displeasure.

" In the parable of the ten virgins, the fire of the lamps represents the gracious light, warmth, and purification which we passively receive of the Spirit of God; but the oil is what must be obtained by diligent prayer, and in faithful obedience, in the way of *nourishing* and *increasing* this light, warmth, and purification. The same is expressed without a parable in the second epistle of Peter, ch. i. Here, in the third and fourth verses, we see what corresponds to the fire of the lamps; and in the fifth and sixth verses, we see what the recipient of that preventing grace is expected to add to it.

"The Thomasians have done much harm in making intellectual error of so little consequence, and in laying all stress upon the will. And yet their own will was not good. When once our natural opposition to the divine will shall be laid aside, then surely a large portion of our religious services will consist in intellectual exercises and intellectual advancement. For do we not most substantially honour an excellent artist, by being able and willing to enter into a thorough examination of his performance? How otherwise would it be in our power to render him due praise and commendation? Hence the supreme felicity of a future state is called the beatific *vision*.

"How much more precious is the single moment of our first awakening to discern God as a Father, than the greatest number of years spent in ignorance of it! Yet the beginning of such an awakening is generally rough and severe, so as hardly to seem like an indication that the Lord is drawing us to himself. Be it so; nevertheless, what a blessing is it to have the old rotten foundation of *self* thoroughly discovered and broken up; and all our doings and experiences beginning, in consequence of it, to run on consistently and smoothly, so much more consistently and smoothly than ever heretofore, and resembling a peaceful pellucid stream! The great matter is, so to rest upon Christ, with correct and scriptural views, as to have honest, faithful, and obedient hearts. Thus we become able to build up others also, which if we constantly aim at, and use our own right position of mind, as one necessary means for the purpose, we shall never want work of the kind. The business constantly in our hands will be, either the amendment and improvement of ourselves, or the amendment and improvement of others.

"A thorough change of *sentiment* in morals and religion is really a rare thing; for we are more easily convinced that we have *acted* wrong, than that we have *thought* wrong.

"True Christians are really happy persons, though they owe not their happiness to those things which worldlings feed and live upon. They have many solid pleasures even in this life, but it is the hope of a better life to come that gives such pleasures themselves their principal relish.

"As from every point in the circumference of a circle we can imagine straight lines converging to the centre, not one of which, of course, is exactly coincident with another of two on either side, however near all the three may be together; so is each individual drawn towards God, into communion with him, by a way more or less peculiar to that individual.

"In what respect is a child of God assured of his finally persevering, through faith, unto salvation? 1. All is of God, from beginning to end; and with him the means and the end are but one connected chain. 2. On man's part, assurance of forgiveness, and assurance of perseverance in grace, are not the same thing; for, 3. that which 'dureth but for a while,' is not perseverance. 4. The truest believers must undergo probationary trials, conducive to their preservation; 'tribulation worketh experience,' &c. 5. The nearer we approach the mark, the firmer will our assurance become, and the greater will be our triumph in it. 6. Even an apostle says, 'I am persuaded that he is *able*,' &c. 7. Thus we escape from the dubious position of the Romanists (who say, that a man cannot be assured of his present state of grace;) and from the opinion of the Calvinists (that it is impossible for real believers to fall away.) 8. It is best not to ponder too much over such future contingency, but to run with patience the race which is set before us, to do it with simplicity and godly sincerity, and leave the rest to God. Faithful *to himself* is he that calleth me, who hath upholden me thus far, and thus long, and 'who also will do it.' 9. He is faithful likewise *to me*, he is faithfulness itself, and therefore will certainly perform what he undertakes and promises; 'because thou hast kept the word of my patience, I also will keep *thee*.' 10. True believers are *happy* the moment they die; but there is a great difference between the *degree* of their happiness *then*, and that which shall be manifested *hereafter* at the last day. We shall appear with him in glory; but, hitherto, the glory of the Son of God *himself* has not so manifestly appeared, as it shall appear hereafter.

"We may be quite assured that it is impossible, while we live out of the order of God, and in an impenitent state, to have any correct knowledge of our election to life eternal. We must first be converted to the living God. On the other hand, all who are now living in the exercise of repentance and faith, cannot be assured absolutely and equally of their election; because many of them have not yet gone through the trials of the cross, in order to be found approved.

"Many never discover *the general amount* of their sins till they are upon a death-bed. They may have received *remission* in full; but they *must* come sooner or later to know what the amount remitted is. To this effect we read, Rev. ii. 4, 'I have somewhat against thee.'

"Sin, as *plaintiff*, is defeated by the advocacy of Christ; but this hinders not its continuing to act against us as *defendant*. We sometimes meet with high-notioned persons, who think they have so got the better of it, that they may regard it as a slain enemy. We must suffer them to have their humour; only let us not overlook what experience teaches. We should be very humble and sober, lest we dogmatize either way; for it is possible to contrive a set of neatly arranged theological truisms on opposite sides, and which may strike the mind at first hearing; but such things edify not.

"The adage, that 'Satan flees before a holy man,' is true only in so far as a holy man continues watchful; for if he grow secure and careless, Satan will find him empty, swept, and garnished.

"While we are in this tabernacle, we have always something in ourselves to subdue and get rid of. But work of this sort does the Christian no harm; nay, our very *conflicts* with sin are preferable to the cheerful carnal security of those who dream that they have overcome all; especially as such conflicts need not shake our confidence in the grace of God.

"What is it that best bespeaks us in earnest, as men of real faith? When we secretly, spontaneously, and unprompted by others, are seeking the Lord, and bringing our sincere desires before him; especially when we do this with all natural readiness of mind, that is, without purposing in a cold formal manner about it. This is a way of acting, which no hypocrite can enter upon; though he may do every thing else as well as ourselves. They who thus far are seeking the truth, who are thus sincere and straightforward, will yield themselves up more and more to the guidance and government of the Spirit of God; and the inward cry of their souls to do so, becomes the key-note of all harmony and consistency in outward matters. Without this, no one can upon *every* occasion be a guileless character; but one is liable to slip at some time or other into dissimulation or hypocrisy. It is the sincerely praying man, and no one else, who will (entirely depart from evil, and) make thorough work of doing good amongst his fellow-men.

"Are there not many persons who, though willing enough to

perform a variety of services to God in public, neither open their hearts to him in the closet, nor come to a decided accordance with him there? The all-important matter, that on which every other matter depends, is the harmony of our will with the will of God. This will insure a holy quietness of spirit upon every thing else. Consequently advancement in the spiritual life is to be looked for, not so much in what are called sensible experiences, as far rather in a regular orderly activity, which is, in other words, letting our light shine by faithfulness in our calling; by a careful and circumspect walk and conversation; by liberality and charity upon every occasion, &c. *Good* works are such as a believer practises *in the order of God.* It is not absolutely necessary that they should always be immediately connected with sacred things, properly so called; it is enough if our cordial aim be always to coincide with the will of God, and to promote his honour and glory.

"Our endeavours to honour God are never more pure and sincere than when we learn to forget *self.* But what a comprehensive little word is this! Even those who have forsaken all to follow Christ, who wish for no offices of distinction, who hold no appointment, nor receive any pay for what they do, and yet are really doing much for the kingdom of God, even they may be under the influence of strong selfish motives; yes, they may be absorbed in them. It is true they have made, and are making, great exertions; still some self-complacency, some small return of human approbation, some kind of food for self-love, they cannot easily forego.

"The more any one blindly suffers his character to be formed merely by his own way of thinking, so that he gropes on, in this way, exclusively and obstinately, the more unlike he becomes to the real image of God in man, which is characterized by a noble placid openness to the light of truth. Surely it becomes us to present ourselves continually before Him who is truth itself; to come to Him as empty vessels, that require to be continually replenished, and put to use by the indwelling power of Christ; otherwise how can we be adapted to any thing essentially good? We should therefore be yielding our every thought to his influence, as constantly as if we were molten mirrors, cast on purpose to reflect his image, or as wax purposely softened in order to bear its impress. A soul possessed of true faith in Him, is docile, tender, impressible, compliant; it learns to care so supremely and entirely for *him,* as to be ever secretly longing to depart and to be with him. Indeed, its home-sick desire is sometimes very strong and painful, so fain would it be at its Father's house in a better world.

" It is great delusion to reckon to our own desert the gifts which God has vouchsafed us, and then to dream of a title to more. Our having been thus favoured, ought the rather to humble us, considering that all is a trust, and that much more has been committed to us already, than we could have had any right to expect.

" It may well be thought no light matter that most of us have never done any thing like the amount of good we ought to have done; but that the main business for which Providence has fitted and appointed us, has been regarded rather as a by-work, while things of far less moment have been preferred before it. How important is it, to beware of attending too much to one thing, and too little to another!

" Besides using constant prayer for general purposes, we should be ready, upon *every emergency*, to commit ourselves entirely into God's hands; otherwise we shall insensibly follow the bias of our own inclinations.

" I cannot say I like to hear any conductor of social prayer say, ' Let us sigh' (to God.) Devotional, like natural sighing, is something too spontaneous to be thought of beforehand.

" To pray, is to be engaged in a kind of *audience*, as well as *converse*, with God, 1 John v. 15. It is more than an utterance of our requests; it includes a waiting for his answers. Let us be inwardly retired, self-observant, and waiting upon him; and, though we hear no voice, we shall experience a plain, certain, and consoling reply. God makes this reply, not vocally, but by those acts of his providence and influences of his grace, whereby he relieves our necessities. When we listen to the petitions of the needy, we do it, not for the sake of hearing them talk, but for the sake of rendering them some help.

" It cannot be *proved* that the Lord's-day comes so exactly in the place of the Jewish sabbath, that it must be in all respects observed according to the Old Testament ritual. Neither is it quite certain that the primitive Christians kept the Jewish sabbath as well as the Lord's-day. But the obligation of sanctifying one day in seven, has never ceased in the church.

" The military profession is one of difficulty to a converted man, and one which he will not be forward to prefer. But whoever is thrown into it against his will, may consider,—1. That John the Baptist did not direct the soldiers to quit it. 2. That there are instances of pious soldiers recorded in the Scriptures. 3. That the commandment, '*thou shalt not kill*,' is not so absolute as to forbid '*the powers that be*' to 'bear the sword,'(Rom. xiii. 4;) also, that God himself directed the Israelites to go to war, and concerning the wars they were to conduct. 4. That it cannot rest with private persons to determine whether a war be just or unjust, especially as the guilt is generally equal on both sides; whereas, the soldier acts merely in obedience to superior authorities, and upon their responsibility. If he can quiet his conscience on such grounds, he may; but if he cannot, let him refer the matter to God, and quit the profession, as soon as a lawful opportunity occurs.

"The married state is generally that in which we can best surmount hardships, and attain the happy end of life with many refreshments by the way. He, therefore, who has no particular calling or occasion forbidding his entrance into this condition, ought to marry. God often teaches us more by our domestic experiences, family illnesses, deaths of children, and the like, than we can learn by any independent speculations, however spiritual these may seem. It is in the married state that I have had my most serious afflictions, but with them my strongest consolations. Therefore I consider it as more than a mere permission, that a pastor should be 'the husband of one wife;' to me it seems all but a matter of necessity. A pious family, comprising and combining the sweets and benefits of every human condition, created and ordained of God, may be compared to a cheerful hive of bees; but a monastery or nunnery full of unmarried persons, is more apt to remind one of a gloomy nest of wasps. And yet so serious a concern is marriage, that if we consider all its bearings upon time and eternity, we cannot wonder that some anxious persons are never able to resolve upon it; or that, having a special delight in spiritual things, they should be the more disinclined to become instruments of perpetuating our sinful race; nevertheless, marriage is an ordinance of the good and benevolent Creator. The relation between Christ and his church in eternity itself is prefigured by that of marriage, which would hardly be appropriate, had this 'estate' been other than 'most holy.' Indeed, could it be anywise unholy, how could it ever become 'honourable among' the children of God, and be attested as such in holy writ? The pure Nazarites themselves, under the Old Testament, were not to be unmarried. Thus, I think, that arbitrarily to reject this ordinance of God, unless one's unmarried condition can, through constant prayer, be made really subservient to advancement in holiness, is a thing for which it will be found difficult to answer.

" Many precepts of the Sermon on the Mount are expressed in general terms, and require time, place, and circumstances, to show their proper application. And this, whatever it be, can never vary from any special instructions delivered in other parts of Scripture.

" As *every* propensity to love and serve the creature more than the Creator is a kind of idolatry, why does the Scripture especially give covetousness that name? 1. Worship, properly so called, consists more in *affiance* than *affection.* It is affiance in uncertain riches, rather than in the living God, that characterizes the lover of money. 2. He who commits other sins, commits them chiefly in single acts, from time to time; but covetousness preoccupies and engages the *whole man;* it dictates his every *communication.*

" *Friendship* is not one of the special topics of practical divinity, but brotherly love *is;* which both *includes* friendship, and gives it additional charms."

CHAPTER XIV.

EXEGETICAL REMARKS ON PASSAGES OF THE OLD TESTAMENT.

As his inquiry into sacred chronology demanded his particular examination of the whole Scriptures, we find him setting down in the course of that inquiry, some interesting and often edifying remarks, upon passages in the Old Testament. The following are among the number.

" The notion that chaos originally comprised the heavens as well as the earth, was borrowed from the Metamorphoses of Ovid, and in process of time found its way into systems of theology. Ovid appears to have learnt it from some obscure tradition. But *Scripture* does not blend the *heavens* with chaos; we read only, that '*the earth* was without form and void,' (Gen. i. 2.)

" Scripture places the origin of evil just where our own sad experience finds it; namely, in the appetency to 'know good and evil;' to know what pleasure is to be found by one thing and another, and how it relishes. The secret of our monstrous lust of knowledge is *unbelief*, or distrust of God; as if he had omitted to give us *every* good, because he *grudged* us something; as if he had some design to withhold or forbid what might yield us further enjoyment.

" I do not think that the coats which the Lord God made for Adam and Eve, were skins of *sacrificial* victims; they were merely garments to cover the body.*

" It makes indirectly for the truth of scripture narrative, that traces of sacred history which occur in pagan writers relating to the deluge, to Joshua, and to other persons or incidents, are

* כְּתְנוֹת עוֹר "vestis cutis," (sc. Adami and Hevæ) Chald. "Vestes honoris," *i. e.* "nuditatis." But this interpretation appears untenable, on the ground that there is convincing reason to believe that sacrifice was originally ordained of God, and that the clothing here alluded to, was that of the skins of the victims offered, and was typical of the hiding of human shame, and the comforting of human helplessness by the benefit of the sacrifice of Christ. (See professor Nicoll's discourse on Gen. iv. 7, where it is satisfactorily evinced *from the words themselves*, לַפֶּתַח חַטָּאת רֹבֵץ that sacrifice was originally of divine institution.) Moreover, the ו conversive of the future, with which Gen. iii. 21. commences, expresses, *by its nature, a consequent* upon what had been (as there

far *less pure* than the accounts of the inspired historians. Otherwise it might have been suggested that these pagan writers *borrowed* from Scripture; whereas, now, the case speaks for itself; namely, that the facts reached them by independent and very ancient traditions, which in process of time had become more and more corrupt and fabulous.

"It is nothing absurd to suppose, that antediluvian records might have been preserved by a variety of means till long after the deluge; as in excavations of rocks, &c.

"Abraham is commended in Rom. xiv. for his stedfastness of belief in the Divine promises. It may be asked, how this accords with the wish he recoils into, concerning Ishmael, in Gen. xvii. 18. This, however, did not proceed from any doubt entertained by Abraham, relative to God's promises concerning Ishmael, (Gen. xvi. 10,) but simply from a tender paternal solicitude to see Ishmael, like himself, honoured personally with some signal token of the Divine favour. This is clear from God's answer to him, (Gen. xvii. 20.)

"We find certain remarkable events in the sacred writings, as the call of Abraham, the deliverance from Egypt, &c., *often repeated* and referred to; apparently because, while all things are alike present to God, (in all ages,) we are too slow of heart to notice from what very small beginnings he has wrought and accomplished his noblest works.

"It was a very consistent piece of sacred dignity in Jacob, that, when presented before Pharaoh, he gave him his patriarchal blessing. In like manner, as it would have been unbecoming in Moses to have *thanked* the 'cunning workmen' in the name of God; therefore he *blesses* them.

"To be 'gathered to one's people,' is a sweet expression, especially as we may find it used when the custom of depositing the dead in the sepulchres of neighbours or ancestors is not at all referred to.—(See Gen. xlix. 33.)

"Joseph is one of the most beautiful examples in Scripture. In most other saints of sacred history, we meet with manifest faults; but in Joseph we see nothing but what is pure and blameless. Samuel is a similar example. The bad conduct of

is every reason to believe) implied in the preceding sentence, which was, that Eve, as the mother of all living, would be the mother of Him who should bruise the Serpent's head, yea, of Him who should be the restorer of *spiritual life*. So that ver. 21. may be translated, "*Therefore* to Adam and to his wife did the Lord God make coats of skins, and clothed them." Comp. Witsius's Economy of the Covenants, Book IV. ch. i. sect. 31.—*T.*

his sons is not attributed to any misconduct of his. The people's saying to him, 'Thy sons walk not in thy ways,' was, no doubt, distressing to him enough, and yet could not be taken otherwise than as an implied commendation of himself, (1 Sam. viii. 3—6.)

"We cannot but wonder that of all Jacob's sons, not one, during that long interval of years, disabused him respecting Joseph; and yet this was the 'Holy Family!' What a poor idea then must we entertain of mankind in general! How deplorably great must *their* corruption be!

"'Ephraim and Manasseh.' What an importance is attached even to little things in the kingdom of God! Here, for instance, in the circumstance, that the patriarch prefers Ephraim (the younger) before Manasseh, (the elder.) In Jacob's blessing we may also perceive what a weight belongs to any blessing uttered by the true servants of God; for they are persons who know Him, and who live in the 'power and strength' of communion with Him.

"The Israelites did not fraudently obtain the jewels, &c. which they received of the Egyptians, but honestly demanded them; and the Egyptians virtually honoured the people of Israel at their departure, by liberally presenting them with these accommoda-tions for their journey.

"Repeated instances in the conduct of Moses clearly show that God, so far from being offended, is rather well pleased, when in a proper and becoming manner we expostulate with him, or 'put him in remembrance' of his promises, &c.

"Levit. xvi. The day of atonement in the Old Testament, was not a festival.* Three annual festivals only were appointed, and they were to be solemnized with gladness. But this day was to be set apart for calling sin to remembrance, and we may suppose it to have been the very anniversary of the fall of man; for I find no particular national sin of Israel expressly named upon it. It was, therefore, a day of solemn remembrance for sin in general; the sin of mankind.

"The two he-goats on the day of atonement, prefigured Christ. The slain one was a type of Christ's sacrifice for all our sins; pointing out that he was to die for them: the other, being let go into the wilderness, prefigured Christ as the living surety of our forgiveness. As a single goat was insufficient for both purposes, two were made use of.

* See Matthew Henry's Note upon Lev. xxiii. 2.—*T.*

"God's general treatment of his people in the wilderness, was that of a father. He led them step by step. He could have announced to them the manna *before* they 'fell a murmuring,' but that their *heart* was to be made manifest. Their first offences were rebuked very gently, with words alone; but after the delivery of the Law in Sinai, where they had sworn fealty and allegiance, their transgressions no longer were, nor could be, so mildly dealt with.

"The language of Deuteronomy, which is addressed to the new generation, in their earlier days, treats much of the kindness and *love of God*, whose righteous 'severity' had been already manifested towards their fathers.

"The *particular* reason of *several* of the prohibited degrees with respect to marriage, is unknown; it is enough that God knows it. I cannot agree with some, who in these days refer the prohibitions to mere propriety in nature. Heretofore there has been too much strictness observed upon such matters; but now a perilous liberality of indulgence is beginning to prevail among us.

"The worship of God in spirit and truth was practicable, even through the multifarious ritual of the Old Testament, but true worshippers could hardly have helped perceiving, that there was 'some better thing' to come.

"Israel possessed the land of Canaan, under Jehovah, as his feudatories; hence they were annually to present to him of their cattle and of the fruits of their ground, by way of homage and quit rent.

"Job xix. 25, &c., will bear the following translation. 'But I know that my vindicator liveth, and that he will at last set me up above the dust. But those who so vehemently persecute me,* must be cut down for this, and I above my flesh shall see God. Yea, I shall see him for myself, and my own eyes shall behold him, but no more as a stranger to me. My reins are consumed in my bosom.' I adopt this rendering, as taking every Hebrew expression in its ordinary meaning, without forcing it; as harmonizing naturally with the context; as maintaining the same impassioned feeling which pervades the rest of the speech; as being of a piece with the other speeches of Job; and agreeable to the scope of the whole book. The sense here given has also been established by what has already taken place since Job's time; it is not dissonant with revealed truth in general, nor

* וְאַחַר עוֹרִי by which Bengel seems to understand, "but (those who seek) after my life," (literally after my skin or body.)—*T.*

with any particular part of the doctrine which is according to godliness; but Scripture elsewhere in plain language, and in many places, speaks to the same effect.

" Jephtha had vowed, that whatever first met him (on his triumphal return from battle,) should be devoted to the Lord. As his daughter was the first to meet him, she was therefore to be consigned to perpetual virginity, which, as precluding her from offspring, would render her civilly *dead*.

" The high priest's garments seem never to have been replaced by new ones, but to have lasted till the destruction of the temple. The people of the east in general take extraordinary care of their raiment, preserving it, neat and clean.

" The deed of Phinehas (Num. xxv. 6,) ' was counted to him for righteousness,' though certainly not *ex intuitu operis*, on account of the act itself; but there was in it a kind of pure faith; he would see and hear of nothing else, so great was his zeal to vindicate the honour of his God.

" Balaam was a sort of *propheta civilis*, (a worldly prophet or diviner,) and not ' sent' to the children of Israel. This is very commonly overlooked.

" Samuel offered sacrifice, though he was no priest, but only a Levite. Moses did the same; for they both of them ranked *above* the priests, because God had given them commissions extraordinary.

" Nadab and Abihu (Lev. x. 2,) offered strange fire before the Lord; probably while they were under the influence of wine. Therefore (in verse 9,) the use of wine was instantly prohibited to officiating priests.

" With the age of Samuel commenced a new period in Israel's history. *Before* him the nation had had no prophet except Moses; but, *after* him, there was a numerous succession of prophets.

" Michal (2 Sam. vi.) imagined that David ought, on such an extraordinary occasion, to have appeared in state and regal distinction, instead of being clothed in the humble garment of a common Levite.

" In what difficulty and embarrassment do we see David in 1 Sam. xxvii.! One would have thought that his faults and errors were much greater than those of Saul; but he abode stedfast in the Lord. Saul's great guilt was not his persecution of David, but his unbelief towards God.

" As a swan, plying equally with both feet, gains upon the

water, however turbulent, so David's spirit, with all his faults, struggled along through every difficulty. Whatever cross occurrences he had to pass through, and they were many and various, his spirit set in one general direction; he took one mainly straightforward course, and thus he held on to the end of it.

"What a noble spectacle do we meet with in 1 Chron. xii. 18! It is military service conducted in the spirit of faith. David could well understand such a speech (of Amasai.) Most of Israel's northern tribes came over to David on this occasion.

"How industrious and active, even in advanced age, was David, that favoured servant of God! (1 Chron. xxix.) He did all in his power towards building the future temple.

"Goodness is not hereditary: tried and found approved must it be by the cross. Solomon had a David for his father: this was no small advantage to him; nevertheless, in the issue it did not benefit him.

"It has been questioned, whether Solomon was saved at last. I think he was; for it was an express part of the promise, that should David's son commit iniquity, still God 'would not suffer his mercy to depart from him, nor his faithfulness to fail.' 'O the depth!'

"1 Sam. xvii. 26. Upon sectarian principles, Old-Testament believers ought not to have acted as they did. Thus they ought to have said, what is all this multitude of unconverted people to me? Goliah is serving them right. They are an ungodly mass. Their very king is a worthless character. Shall God work a miracle to save such a people as this?

"How many difficult and even culpable shiftings were made by Jacob and by David, before either of them reached the mark! This consoles me about many a disaster, yea, and fault, of God's true servants at present.

"It is possible that Hiel (the Bethelite), who rebuilt Jericho (1 Kings xvi. 34), had never heard Joshua's curse (Josh. vi. 26). The Book of Joshua was not read in the public assemblies.

"To know, from the Books of Kings, that every king mentioned as the son of a predecessor, was the lawful heir of his body begotten, we must observe, that the name of such king's own mother is never omitted, but expressly mentioned after that of his natural father.

"One instance in which the word Jehovah *must* have been articulated by the common people, was in their confession against Baal, (1 Kings xviii. 39.)

"The nations of Mizraim and Cush, descendants of Ham, who provoked his father's prophetic curse, are expressly mentioned in Psalm lxviii. 31, as trophies of Christ's redemption. If nations such as these, were to have a part and lot in the Saviour, surely he is the Redeemer of ALL mankind.

"The xliv—lxvi chapters of Isaiah, proceed connectedly and sublimely upon creation, redemption, and sanctification. The person who devoutly reads them to that effect, will meet with admirably fine thoughts to animate, encourage, and strengthen him.

"The Hebrew word תּוֹדָה, 'todah,' (*praise*, literally, *confession*, or acknowledgment.) is beautifully emphatic. In praising a fellow-creature, we may easily surpass the truth; but in praising God, we have only to go on acknowledging and *confessing* what he really is to us. Here it is *impossible* to exceed the truth; and here is *genuine* praise.

"In the fifteenth chapter of Ezekiel, God puts forth a parable of the vine-tree; and speaks of its wood as 'insufficient for any work, or even for a pin to hang any vessel thereon; how much more when the fire hath devoured it,' &c. In the fifteenth chapter of St. John, Christians are likewise compared to vine-branches. And a true Christian is indeed a great blessing to the world, even in temporal respects, as vine-branches are very profitable while they bear fruit. But if he abide not in Christ, but decline into a worldly spirit, he is no longer even the valuable *temporal* man he was; as the vine-branches, severed from the green and bearing vine, are not fit wood even to form a peg, and are good for nothing except fuel.

"We cannot prove from the gospels, that by the coming of 'Elijah the prophet,' as foretold in the fourth chapter of Malachi, John the Baptist is *exclusively* meant. As the Pharisees erroneously held, that the real Elijah's coming would usher in that of the Messiah, there is a delicate peculiarity in our Saviour's expression, '*If ye will receive it*,' (Matt. xi. 14.) John came in the spirit and power of Elias; but it cannot be evinced that he was Elijah himself.

"Some may be inclined to doubt, whether the Book of Esther was written by an inspired person; because, in ch. ix., we have so many words that appear tautology. Nevertheless, the impassioned joy and gladness of the writer may account for this; for gladness is commonly lavish of words.

"Apocryphal writings first became appended to the canonical

books of the Old Testament by a blunder of its Greek translators at Alexandria. Then, by and by, the note specifying their apocryphal character, being carelessly omitted in transcribing, they would in the course of time come to be reckoned with the canon! See what great mistakes may ultimately grow out of a single oversight.

"The second Book of Maccabees is a very weak document. The Jews in those days had received and embraced many notions from the heathen nations around; yes, even that of offering sacrifices for the dead *(lustrationes mortuorum.)* Hence the passage in ch. xii. appears to me a poor sanction of prayer for the dead. I think we have no scriptural warrant for it. It is *possible* that, during a few days after the death of any beloved friend or relative, we may be allowed to pray for them; and Luther has even recommended it; but beyond this we can have nothing of the kind to do. Neither can I think that departed spirits intercede for *us.* They are resigned to the will of God concerning themselves and others. That remarkable passage on prayer in 1 Tim. ii. 1, contains no mention of such a thing; and silence of this sort has its weight.*

"It is good to have to pass through humiliations and a lowly condition; and that our course in this life should be like that of a homeward-bound ship, direct for the haven, and leaving behind it (though in a different sense from what is meant by those Epicureans in the fifth chapter of Ecclesiasticus,) no track of its pathway in the waves.

"No preacher of righteousness can ever so entirely expose and confound profligates and worldlings, as they will one day expose and confound themselves; yes, in the manner here described, Ecclus. v."

* From this passage in Bengel's writings, compared with a paragraph in our preceding chapter, we may safely conclude, that there is no truth at all in the report that a former maid-servant of his confessed upon her death-bed, that she had seen him often go alone in his canonicals into the empty church at Herbrechtingen, and had observed him through the keyhole, on one such occasion, preaching very earnestly to departed spirits; and that Bengel, finding he had been observed, desired her to keep it a secret.

APPENDIX.

A few detached Remarks on Passages of the New Testament.

"2 Tim. iii. 4. How is it that our youth are so very different from those of former times? What no young persons would once have dared to think of, ours freely rush into without prompting. Alas! how προπετεῖς, precipitate, and headstrong do we find them! This is another sign that the harvest and vintage are very near.

"2 Pet. iii. 12. 'The day of God!' What is it, but the day of eternity. Majestic expression! Yes, eternity is here intimated as one clear unbroken day.

"1 John iv. 2, 3, 15. See how the apostle all along insists upon this single truth, 'Whosoever *confesseth* Christ, is of God.' But we should rightly understand what is meant by 'confessing,' and how dependant this is upon faith. It means, and especially also in the Epistle to the Hebrews, a decided and entire abandonment to that which we have made up our minds to; yes, that therein rests our total complacency and delight. If we knew the real character of those who in the present day so superficially confess Christ, did they only discover to us the interior of their hearts, alas! should we not find them (without this devotedness to Christ, yes,) empty of every thing of the kind? Times are altered since the days of St. John. For then to confess Christ with the mouth was a great thing, (it implied a renunciation of the world;) whereas now, to be known not to accede to Christianity, would prove no small inconvenience even in the world itself.

"The sacred tears of those who never weep about matters of this life, nobly attest the truth and power of the christian religion, (Acts xx. 19, 31; Matt. xxvi. 75.)

"Persons who are only imperfectly acquainted with christian truth, are, notwithstanding, vividly sensible sometimes of its beauty, (Mark xii. 28, 32—34.)

"Mark vi. 20. The secret remorse and anxieties of the wicked, together with their real respect for persons truly pious, are so many attestations to the truth and reality of religion.

"The apostles are commonly thought to have been rather

elderly at the time they were called to be Christ's disciples. But this appears a mistake; for Peter, the oldest of them, had a mother-in-law, (who could wait upon them) (the rest were probably at that time unmarried;) and Peter may be supposed to have been born after our Saviour, who addresses all his disciples as their superior in age (τεκνία.) They appear to have been plain, uncultivated persons, not indeed of an uncivilized stamp, but of a homely, blunt, and rather rough character. We may suppose so from Peter's beginning to attack the multitude with his sword, and from his imprecations shortly after. Probably at the beginning of his course he was a character not very unlike one of our honest Hamburg watermen. Hence it is *no* wonder that these disciples got so often into faults, which their Master as constantly rebuked. But it *is* a wonder that our blessed Lord should have improved them as he did in so short a time, though he still rebukes their backwardness in this respect.

" Luke xii. 37. ' Verily I say unto you, that he will gird himself, and make them sit down to meat, and will come forth and serve them.' This promise I regard as the greatest of any in the Bible; and I take the words in a kind of literal meaning, that is, as a bridegroom on his wedding-day scruples not to wait upon his guests, and to converse in affectionate familiarity with them all, so will Jesus act in the world to come, when the marriage of the Lamb is come.

" 1 Thess. iv. 13. As Scripture was given principally for believers, it speaks of *their* resurrection *expressly*, and of the resurrection of the unjust only *by the way*.

" Acts xvi. 21. The world has been always ready enough to embrace the doctrines of *philosophers*. But the doctrines of the gospel contain what is revolting and mortifying to the pride of our corrupt nature; this very peculiarity, however, is one internal evidence of their divine origin.

" One peculiarity which always attends evangelical truth is, that all who cordially embrace it, in whatever age or nation, bring forth the same fruits of the Spirit, and have the same conflicts, trials, and experiences.

" There was a wide difference between the condition of the Corinthian church and that of the Colossians. The former had been favoured with many gracious gifts (χαρίσματα) and superior knowledge, by which they became ' puffed up' (τετυφωμένοι). For this rising of the flesh, the apostle pricks them again and again, to reduce many of them to more humility and natural christian simplicity. The Colossians, on the contrary, appear to have been very rude in knowledge; he, therefore, much insists upon *knowledge* itself (ἐπίγνωσιν) through the whole of his epistle to *them*. With the Corinthians there were mountains and hills to be brought low; but with the Colossians, there were vallies to be filled."

CHAPTER XV.

HIS REMARKS UPON THE CHURCH OF THE UNITED BRETHREN.

In the last year but one of his life, he published these remarks, entitled a "Sketch of the Church of the United Brethren," having had for several years a variety of official communications with that church. This was the only one of his publications that was designed, not for framing any thing new in doctrinal or practical knowledge, but to express his opinion upon what was already framed to hand, but which at that time appeared to need the amendments it suggested. As it was occasioned by passing circumstances, it has been variously misunderstood; though, in truth, it was one of the most important and beneficial works of his life. We will, therefore, here particularly notice how it originated, and what was the effect of it.

It is well known, that Count Nicolas Lewis von Zinzendorf, about the year 1722, granted a settlement upon his estate at Berthelsdorf to a few pious refugees from Moravia and Bohemia, members of the church of the Brethren in those countries, a church which for ages had weathered the storms of persecution, by which, however, it had now become almost annihilated. The new little settlement, to which the brethren gave the name of Herrnhut,* may be regarded as the parent scion from which have sprung all those other communities of the Brethren, that have spread abroad, and proved so great a blessing to various parts of the world. To its first handful of colonists were soon added other refugees, alike driven by violent oppression from their native homes in Moravia and Bohemia; and their number was still augmented by persons from various countries, who had become dissatisfied more or less with the views and discipline of their respective churches, and whom one common desire of christian liberty had thus brought together. But as no civil, much less any religious, community can enjoy in a state of anarchy the blessings of order and prosperity, they of course found it necessary to deliberate at once upon having common fixed

* The watch of the Lord.

principles, rules, and regulations for discipline. A considerable majority of the settlers having belonged to the church of Moravia, where they had been accustomed to a discipline more personally scrutinizing than that of any other protestant community, desired permission to continue the same in their new settlement; and as the other settlers were dissatisfied with their own respective churches, not from any indifference to religion, but from being disposed to a more inward, serious, and lively exercise of it, there was no hindrance to their becoming *thus far* delighted with the views of their Moravian brethren. But it was not so easy to bring about unanimity in *doctrine*. For though the members of the new community, with very few exceptions, were all protestants, yet with respect to the protestant denominations to which they belonged, they consisted of Moravians, Lutherans, and Reformed; and these distinctions were subdivided by the private and peculiar sentiments of many among them. Hence the easiest means of their coalescence, allowing for the impossibility of a multitude seeing exactly alike in every thing, was to have a leader, of sufficient character and influence to mould them, by little and little, after a plan of his own, which should not be decidedly opposed to either of the Confessions subscribed at the peace of Westphalia; as otherwise it could expect no toleration even from our protestant churches. Such a leader did Providence give them in the benevolent nobleman who had so kindly afforded them a place of shelter. Count Zinzendorf, from his early youth, had ardently desired to become active for the advancement of the kingdom of God; and was endued with such abilities and dispositions, as would not admit of his spending his life in occupations merely secular, much less of his confining it to the common benevolence of a fatherly nobleman among his tenants and dependants. His really noble spirit required a larger sphere of signal and active service for the kingdom of God. The occasion was now presented to him, the Herrnhut community having invited and chosen him to preside over them. This was in the year 1727; and he resolved cheerfully to devote to their welfare the rest of his life. He had already been the chief manager of their temporal concerns; but his religious exertions among them had been only those of a private man; and he had appointed the Berthelsdorf pastor, Rothe, to officiate as their minister. In 1733 he invited also the assistance of Mr. Steinhofer, a Würtemberg clergyman, whose acquaintance he had made on a tour through that country. This was the first occasion of the Count's intercourse with the church of Würtemberg. But as Steinhofer wished that his own engagement at Herrnhut might not hinder his returning at any time to officiate in his native land, the Count thought it expedient to get the Würtemberg church to recognize that at Herrnhut as a sister community; which he hoped would also be serviceable to it on many other accounts; therefore he went to Tübingen, and presented through Mr. Steinhofer to the Theological Faculty the following inquiry:—"Whether the brethren of the Moravian church at Herrnhut, as agreeing with the Confessions of the protestant church, might be allowed to consider themselves as in ecclesiastical union with the evangelical church of Würtemberg, though they should retain their own well known form of discipline, as it had been established among them for three centuries?" Now, as it was unknown in Würtemberg that many members of the Herrnhut community varied at that time from the *doctrinal* system of the protestant church, (for the subsequent assimilation of their religious opinions had hardly yet begun to work,) the Theological Faculty felt it the less necessary to hesitate in giving their assent, especially as the Count had gained the hearts of all by his amiable and conciliatory conduct. Bilfinger then drew up the reply in such favourable terms, that the Count reckoned at once upon finding the church of Würtemberg an affectionate and thorough-going patroness of his little community. Upon this occasion it was, that Bengel became personally acquainted with him on the third of April, 1733. Mr. Oetinger, who had been a pupil of Bengel, had related to the Count at Herrnhut much respecting his former tutor, as well as about Bengel's apocalyptical system, and had prevailed with the Count to go with him to Denkendorf upon a visit to Bengel. Here Bengel laid before the Count in a connected manner his views upon prophecy, and particularly upon the Apocalypse.* The Count, at first, so admired all, that he even called Bengel the prophet of the age; but found himself † afterwards so hard pressed by some of Bengel's particular representations and remarks, that he discontinued the conversation; though, had he gone with Bengel farther into the subject, he might have found some important respects in which both parties were agreed. For they were very closely assimilated in many things. Both loved God from their

* See Spangenberg's Life of Zinzendorf; p. 791.

† See Oetinger's work, entitled, "Conversations between John Conrad Dippel and Count Zinzendorf in the Invisible World;" p. 5.

earliest days. Both revered the memory of Spener and Franke, and considered the present race of Franke's scholars at Halle incompetent to meet the spiritual demands of the times. Both agreed in believing that every thing relating to the great doctrine of atonement by the blood of the cross, was already deplorably neglected by modern Lutheran divines,* and that this neglect would increase more and more. Both regarded the whole protestant church as sadly corrupted, and as verging more and more to decay; they also together lamented the very great declension of church discipline. But in deciding upon the best method of furthering true religion, suitably to present peculiar necessities, they widely differed. Zinzendorf considered the Lutheran church to be already past recovery; and thought it his duty to call upon her few pious and believing members to form themselves into a new community, and withdraw from her at once, even though it should exhaust her of all her remnant life and savour of christian doctrine. With respect to the new church then to be formed, he would have it most closely bound up with the interests of Christ, by undeviating simplicity of adherence to the doctrine of atonement, and to constant preaching of the word of the cross, as the supreme matter, the very life and soul of all evangelical instruction; in order that such a church might be impervious to the infidel spirit of the times, and prove a salt of the earth to the heathen as well as christian world. Bengel was of opinion, that such a proposed germination, development, and, by and by, universal spread of one renovated, lively, and wakeful little community, intended to supersede every other, was an idea far from agreeing with the method of God's dealings with mankind, and, therefore, it was in vain to expect its realization. He anticipated that God, in his own good time, having made due riddance of the unholy and infidel dregs of Christendom, would constitute his renovated church out of the small surviving remnant. He further maintained, that not even any such distinct and separate community as Zinzendorf wished to form, could be admitted to share the glories of the millennial kingdom, without undergoing, with the rest of Christendom, much further improvement, during a severe sifting time and purification. He likewise intimated, that as it was insufficient for strengthening a church

* Bengel once observed (it was in 1744) that "the present race at Halle had become rather too degenerate to cope with the spirit of the times. That the dignity and seriousness of Spener were no longer there; nor any equivalent in their room. That the good men of that school ought to bestir themselves a little, if in such times as these they wished to answer the intentions of their founder."

against the grand apostasy, singly to hold forth that chief essential doctrine, the atonement by the blood of the cross; so, to invest this with a sort of isolated favouritism, to the comparative neglect of other divine truths and instructions, appeared rather like a piece of narrow worldly policy, or seemed at least to come short of that respect which is due to the *whole* tenor of scripture. Not to mention, that by favouritism of this sort, we rob ourselves of many other most valuable helps to godliness; as also, that, by inordinately descanting upon the blood of Christ, we may cause many needlessly to stumble at that important doctrine itself. Besides, that we may hereby come to overlook the particular means for encountering the approaching temptation of the whole church militant; which particular means can only be ascertained by carefully observing *all* the ways of God in the development of his kingdom. With such sentiments, Bengel could not feel that he should be justified in giving up the Lutheran church as yet; but thought it would be much more right to send forth an appeal to all its members, entreating them to give their most serious attention to the scriptural developments of the kingdom of God, as their safest preservative against the future great apostasy, and as their best preparation for the important changes so near at hand.

The difference of sentiment between Zinzendorf and Bengel was certainly here very considerable, and was sufficient, at its first discovery, to put these sincere and worthy men upon separate tracks. But as it was one of Bengel's resolutions, never to commit to the press his thoughts upon any subject till he had some special call for it, he did not publish his "Remarks" upon the Brethren's church till eighteen years afterwards. Meanwhile he followed, as did also the Count, that course which they considered that Providence had appointed them. Zinzendorf, having found that his services to his community were not likely to answer his wishes, without a regular commission to act among them as an ordained minister, went privately to Stralsund, in 1734, and submitted to a divinity examination from the consistorial authorities,* for testimonials of orthodoxy, with a view to ordination. The result was so favourable, that he even thought of establishing a theological seminary in the spirit of his own communion. Having learnt, on his recent tour through Würtemberg, that some of the ancient abbeys of this country were unprovided with

* These were Dr. Gregory Langemach and Dr. Charles Joachim Sibeth.

prelates, he was induced to petition the reigning duke Charles Alexander, for the prelacy of one of those establishments, with permission to found in it a theological seminary. But his petition was, though in a very gracious manner, refused, in consequence of the (catholic) duke's apprehension, that to comply with it would appear like unfaithfulness to his mother church. However, as Spangenberg, whom the Count had deputed upon this business, still found the chief clergy of Würtemberg, and particularly the chancellor, Pfaff, of Tübingen, so kindly disposed to favour his plans, the Count thought it worth while, on the second of November, to write to the Würtemberg consistory, stating, that, having "addicted himself," after the apostolical pattern, (1 Cor. xvi. 15,) "to the ministry of the saints," he had resolved, in the name of God, to receive ordination to the sacred office; and hoped that the reverend members of the consistory would grant him that divinely authorised help, as well as afford him, upon all future occasions, their spiritual counsel and assistance. As their reply (of Dec. 10) turned out greatly to his satisfaction, he soon after went to Würtemberg, and petitioned the Theological Faculty of Tübingen, that he might be immediately ordained. This was complied with; and, on the following day, the Faculty having sent out their *programma*, the Count was permitted to preach in the collegiate church, and in that of the hospital at Tübingen. He was now one, as it were, of the clergy of the church of Würtemberg, and sometimes called himself a Würtemberg divine. In the year 1739 he went, for the third time, into that country; preached with great acceptance in several of the towns he passed through, as Pfallingen, Hirschau, Hall, and Heilbronn; and delivered testimonies of his faith at other places. He became still more closely connected with Würtemberg, by Steinhofer's having taken a share in the ministerial charge of Ebersdorf, near to Berthelsdorf;* and likewise by Oetinger's spending a considerable time at Hernnhut. Oetinger endeavoured to persuade the Count and the Hernnhut community to more comprehensive scriptural inquiry, particularly through Bengel's views of the Apocalypse; but the majority did not think it necessary to seek stirring motives from *future times*, as they considered that to love Christ with a (στοργή) pathetic feeling, was better than any incitement from mysterious subjects too

* Steinhofer was in the way of being appointed copastor at Berthelsdorf; but some unexpected obstacles prevented it.

deep or too high for them to attain unto.* Bengel, who continued equally fixed in his own persuasions, modestly refrained, as long as he could, from publicly expressing himself at issue with this community; especially as so many of the reputed orthodox were then seeking to glory over them in controversial pamphlets, deeming themselves, with reasons more or less conclusive, bound to deliver their testimony against them. Therefore Bengel long preferred declining to interfere, as "he had no wish (he said) to earn commendation at the brethren's expense." But he expressed to intimate friends, in conversation and by letters, his sentiments respecting the Count and his plans, to the following effect:—

"Undoubtedly there are many truly pious and excellent persons among the people of Herrnhut. They possess the pure word of God; they have much exercise in it by oral and written communications; they have a daily practice; they allow no scandals or abuses, and enjoy full liberty of conscience; many of them have also shown great grace in enduring the cross. When men have really earnest desires after God, they are always in the way to firm footing; and in such respects I should be glad indeed to see every one diligently imitating them. We need only peruse any hymn of the Herrnhuters, upon the subject of faith, to see at once, that *Timotheus Philadelphus* † does them injustice. I should be glad to invite Timotheus himself to compose any such hymn, or a better one. There is a precious thing among them,—it is their love to one another, and to all men. As individuals, they are excellent; they only want, as I have often observed, to be conducted right, as a community. I have long noticed, that the sickly wish of seceders has always been, to adjust every single hair; and what is Count Zinzendorf now aiming at, but to mould together a neat braiding of the same? Yet, in my opinion, the time is not come for such work as this. Before we can erect an edifice, we must get together and prepare the materials. Too much haste may be the worst speed. Extremes are always dangerous, and the middle way is the safest. I love that good nobleman from my heart, and think often about him. If he had but some private good adviser, the occasions that so cramp his proceedings might be prevented. Two things in him are very commendable. He has received christian

* Thus Oetinger expresses himself, in a letter to Bengel.

† Dr. John Kaiser, a separatist and follower of Jacob Boehmen.

refugees from Moravia, has hived them into a happy community, and upholds among them such excellent discipline, as may well shame others out of their disorders and perplexities. And then, he has sent missionaries to foreign parts, where the name of Jesus Christ was unknown; so that what has been effected in the Isle of St. Thomas, and in Greenland, &c., is in my view a real subject for praise. Only, it offends me that the baptized in those places so frequently omit in their letters the name of the Father, as our Creator and God. Neither can his introduction of such novel phraseology in religion be right. It looks as if he thought the doctrinal system of our church insufficient, or not good enough. The human heart is so variously corrupt, that it requires special instruction, not merely in one or two, but in all points of christian truth, that men may become delivered effectually out of their miserable condition, and be led on in the right direction. To the essential and primary doctrine of the atonement by Christ's precious blood, my own heart most fully assents and accords; indeed every true Christian, from Luther's time to the present, has been distinguished by deep attachment to it. In evidence of this, consult only the work, entitled, 'An improved collection of things edifying to the church of God.' But when any one aims, like Count Zinzendorf, at what is either novel or exclusive, it is clear, that he is led aside by imaginations of his own, as if he thought no part of a clock so useful as the dial-hand; or no food, the whole year round, so wholesome as the richest marrow. The apostles surely knew the worth of Christ's satisfaction and merits as well as we can do; and yet, in all their addresses and epistles, we see how beautifully they apply doctrine to every variety of practical inference."

It was not till the year 1742, that Bengel had occasion to write a particular statement of his scruples respecting the brethren's church. Mr. J. J. Moser, a councillor of state, happened to be residing then at Ebersdorf, while the congregation which attended the royal chapel of that town were taking measures for adopting the constitution of the United Brethren. Moser, who was a strict adherent to the school of Halle, had long anticipated such a compromise; and he apprehended from it, what would be fraught with oppression and danger; namely, the exclusion which one member and another of that congregation would then become liable to for conscience sake. Therefore he wrote to Bengel, stating what he had learnt by experience to fear would be the event of any coalition of this sort, and requesting his best advice in case it should be effected; or rather, how to prevent it from taking place. We meet with Bengel's reply in the appendix to his "Remarks" on the Brethren's church, p. 520, &c.; and the tenor of it was, that the Count's kind reception of the persecuted Moravian brethren, deserved indeed to be regarded as a work of christian love; only the plan he had laid down and begun to act upon, appeared rather too comprehensive, and he was endeavouring to model the whole community after his own system of christian teaching, which system was not comprehensive *enough*. For if the Brethren are to have a notion that their standard is the one to which all sincere Christians ought to repair and to adhere, this surely would be carrying matters out too far. The word of God did not first go out from *them*, neither had it come to them only. The kingdom of heaven was not so limited to *them*, that every one who has received a right sense of things by means of others, must be deemed behind in his spiritual progress, until he is incorporated with themselves. Their enterprise reminded him of the forcing of plants in a hot-house, where a few certainly may be brought to a sort of perfection before their season; but it is the open garden that yields the abundance and the sweetest of them, only a little later. That, respecting church communion with the Herrnhuters, we are not obliged to be satisfied at once with every one who bears this name; "let him first be *proved*." By such proving, he adds, "I doubt not we shall see very many of them well deserving of our *brotherly* love, kindness, and confidence. But I cannot refrain from commending to them the catholic spirit with which a sound Christian, as holding the supreme head, adheres to all Christ's faithful members, without partiality, whether they belong to Herrnhut or any other denomination."

A second occasion for writing his express opinion upon these subjects, was, that his former pupil, J. F. Reuss, who held a government appointment in Denmark, had consulted him how to act with regard to an application which the Brethren had made for permission to establish one or more of their settlements in that country. His reply consisted of a few brief remarks,* substantially the same as he had sent to Moser. But having since received information of special peculiarities in the Count's doctrinal system, he added, that he could not approve of the Count's

* See his Sketch of (or Remarks on) the Brethren's Church, p. 456.

seeming to insist too little on the doctrine of Christ's resurrection, on the word of prophecy, on the observance of the moral law, and on the high value of biblical knowledge. Neither could he approve of his using ambiguous expressions respecting the doctrine of the Trinity. Bengel further subjoined a few particulars upon the conduct to be observed towards the members of that church; as that no compulsion of conscience, nor any thing resembling persecution should be adopted; that, as ministers of the gospel, we ought diligently to inculcate whatever, as preferred in the Brethren's church, is scriptural: but to be equally careful to teach other scriptural matters, which the Brethren do *not* dwell upon with sufficient distinctness and perspicuity. That we should also be particular in showing *wherein* the *true* communion of saints consists; that every Christian ought to live agreeably to it; also in what manner and by what means this is to be done. That preachers coming from the Brethren's communion into a foreign country, ought not to be permitted to preach, until they have first been proved, and have given sufficient assurance that they will keep within the limits of ecclesiastical order. That a clear understanding should be had with our native people inclined to that communion, as to what particular advantages they anticipate from connecting themselves with the Brethren's church, and how far they must be connected with it, in order to partake of those advantages. Likewise that they ought to be informed what *dis*advantages are to be apprehended. That we should labour with love, prayer, meekness, wisdom, word and deed, to get established between the Herrnhut Christians and right-minded persons, concerned for their own and others' edification, such a sort of fellowship as will secure the very advantages which the latter may have fondly anticipated from a more strict ecclesiastical union with the former.

These remarks were extensively circulated without his knowledge, and at length came under the notice of Zinzendorf himself, who wrote strictures upon them, which he sent to Bengel by Jonas Paul Weiss, and even printed them with Weiss's letter, in the third volume of the Büdingen Collections, sect. 17, p. 734. This communication gave rise to a more frequent and particular correspondence between Bengel and the Count; in which it was Bengel's principal aim to persuade the Brethren's church to accept friendly warnings against every appearance of deviation and error; to regard such warnings as proceeding from no censoriousness of his, but from real christian love; and to make a faithful use of them as coming providentially in season for their benefit. And he expressed his earnest hope, that the Count would never be carried away by his extraordinary talents, into plans too comprehensive or diffusive; as it was only in proportion to his abiding in humility, that his little community was likely to prove a blessing to the protestant church and heathen world; whereby, indeed, it might serve as an oasis to many, though it might not be able to diffuse just its own verdure through the whole of Christendom.

But Bengel never published any thing in reply to Zinzendorf's strictures, till he printed his "Sketch of (or Remarks on) the Brethren's Church," which was seven years afterwards. For he adhered to his resolution, of taking time for consideration in the love of God.

Two of the Count's more intimate friends, Lieberkühn and Layritz, waited on Bengel, at Herbrechtingen, in the spring of 1745, when he freely gave them his sentiments at large upon the subject in question, and observed, that it was by no means a duty to follow implicitly the will and ordinances of the Count; that his people ought still to retain their christian liberty, else their church was likely to settle down into a monarchical instead of aristocratican (presbyterian) constitution. He conceived a very favourable impression of these two strangers, particularly of Lieberkühn; and even said to him, "If the Count's fellow-labourers are all like yourself,—if they will act upon their own best judgment, and not in servility of respect to others, things will certainly go on better." Soon after this, he remarked to a friend, that he had "learnt to be more cautious than ever in giving his opinion of the Herrnhuters; not that he regretted what he had already done or said respecting them, but because so much that is really beautiful and excellent was proceeding among them; and because God, in bringing about any good to sinful man, is not bound to produce it free of every imperfection. When we consider those who in the esteem of ages have seemed to be pillars, and observe in how many points they have shown themselves to be but men, we may well indulge admiration at the variety of that manifold wisdom, goodness, and long-suffering, with which God has made use of such persons for the accomplishment of his own great and benevolent designs. Recollecting what I have recently expressed in conversation with two Herrnhut fellow-labourers, (who of course will carry it to their brethren,) I think it needless to proceed at present in writing about them, and shall not do it, unless some strong reason compel me."

In his reply to a second letter from his friend Reuss, he recapitulates his former observations respecting the Brethren, and then answers Reuss's inquiry, "Whether home-born persons, who had embraced the Moravian persuasion, ought to be allowed to establish themselves into branch communities." Bengel's answer runs thus:—"The whole Moravian community of foreigners and natives, is a lump leavened throughout; and seems disposed to become something better still, by extending its influence to places hitherto uncultivated. Such new settlements I contemplate with mingled fear and pleasure; with fear, lest the original parent mass should dry up and be neglected, when its ramifications at a distance come to thrive more. Still I cannot but indulge the pleasing hope, that new and flourishing offsets may serve to provoke many of the old stock to still holier jealousy. It has been often a dormant idea of mine, that if I had to guide the helm of a christian establishment, I would first be careful to find out in what districts of my superintendence a zealous minister here and there already resided: and these I would allow to obtain coadjutors likeminded with themselves, wherever they could find them. Over such I would have to be appointed for their dean, the man of their number whom they judged to be the worthiest; then I would appoint as the chancellor of their deanery, that layman in whom they could place the most confidence; and they should have full power to choose their own assistants, schoolmasters, superintendents of street districts, and of families; likewise to adopt such regulations as they could agree upon to be the best, for the furtherance of evangelical instruction, and the maintenance of church discipline, &c. The great difficulty after all would still consist in practical particulars out of doors; how to meet aggressively the manifold ignorance and indifference of the raw multitude. This, however, does not form a part of your present inquiry, which relates only to persons who are seeking what is good; so that I can the more easily say to you something positive in answer to it. Such undertakings then (of the Moravian brethren) ought certainly not to be discouraged; only they call for much prudence (on your part.) A small commencement, and nothing more, might at first be permitted them by way of trial; and their leading persons should be prevailed with to subscribe some plain, definite, and reasonable points of agreement, for the prevention of any erroneous and strange doctrines. But you might allow them freely to adopt whatever regulations their brethren at Herrnhut have already acted upon with good effect. All correspondence with that settlement could not well be interdicted; but you might reserve to yourself the right of watching its intention and result," &c.

In the year 1746, Mr. Becherer, the parochial minister of Dornhan, in Würtemberg, who had written a pamphlet of strictures upon Zinzendorf, requested Bengel's opinion and advice previous to its publication. The pamphlet related chiefly to the Count's views of the doctrine of the Trinity. For the twelfth supplement to the Brethren's collection of hymns having now appeared in print, as also another of their publications, entitled, "The present Form of the Kingdom of the Cross," had excited considerable notice, because these works represented the doctrine of the Trinity in a manner that could not but offend all orthodox Lutherans.

Bengel then advised Becherer to keep to that one subject; and having given him hints upon the best method of arranging it, he supplied him with some communications for it, and reminded him not to forget prayer, love, meekness, humility, and self-renunciation.

Early in the next year, the Count made another attempt to effect a union of his own community with the church of Würtemberg. Though in the various settlements which he had established, he had gathered around him chiefly protestants, that is, persons of the Moravian, Lutheran, and Reformed churches, still he dreaded falling under the suspicion of forming a religious medley, or of introducing any kind of innovation. Therefore having arranged those of the two churches last mentioned into two distinct classes, which he designated Bands, or Forms, he wished each of these to be subject to the general superintendence of some German consistory, and thought he could not do better than commend the Lutheran portion to the church of Würtemberg, especially as this church had (in 1733) shown itself so kindly disposed towards him. He therefore sent an address (on the 27th of March, 1747,) to the Würtemberg consistory, as also to its president, G. B. Bilfinger, the substance of which was to this effect:—"That whereas, at his ordination, he had solemnly promised to maintain all intimate connexion with the church of Würtemberg, and whereas from Weissmann's Church History, recently published, it might be seen that the real condition of the Brethren's church was very imperfectly known in that country; therefore, to acquit his own conscience of any faulty concealment of the truth upon this subject, he felt it a duty to propose, that the consistory, at their next synod, should depute commissioners, say Bilfinger, Fischer, Bengel, Cotta, and Cantz, to hold an ecclesiastical visitation of the *Lutheran* portion of his community, in like manner as the King of Prussia's principal chaplain in ordinary, Cocchius, would be deputed to visit the *Reformed* part." This address occasioned much deliberation among the Würtemberg clergy, who for the present could only resolve that Weissman and Bengel be requested to communicate their sentiments upon it to each consistorial member privately. After this, the Theological Faculty transmitted to the privy council a document drawn up by Weissman, which stated that they thought such a visitation unnecessary, as there was already sufficient evidence before the public, that the Brethren's teachers had in many important respects departed from the doctrine of the Lutheran church. That even their aversion to subscribe the Confession of Augsburg, showed, that such a visitation was not likely to be attended with any favourable result. That it was to be considered how disparagingly the Count, in his discourses and hymns, had expressed himself concerning the Lutheran church and its ministers in general; having stigmatized this church as a very *Laodicea*, whereas he had represented his own community as a *Philadelphia*, and, of course, infallible; therefore it was impossible to give him credit for wishing to hold pure communion with the church of Würtemberg; and that he desired this connexion merely to answer his own purposes. Consequently it would be imprudence and folly to grant him the right hand of fellowship, which would only increase the umbrage already taken by the other Lutheran churches at the reply of the church of Würtemberg, given from Tübingen, in 1733, (in favour of Count Zinzendorf, &c.) And that if such a deputation as he requested were even sent with full commission to Herrnhut, they would probably be as far as ever from gaining any satisfactory knowledge of the (Brethren's) community, &c. Accordingly, the consistory transmitted the following decision to the Count, on the 19th of March, 1747. "The visitation you desire, appears to us unsuitable, and insufficient either to convince the evangelical Lutheran church of the accordance of your institution with her principles, or to effect those changes for its conformity with her, which such a visitation might find necessary. We recede not from our answer given you on the 13th of April, 1733; but we must remind you, that it was given on a presumption of your accordance with the whole system of the Lutheran church; whereas, many things, which have subsequently appeared in your doctrine and discipline, are at open variance with it. We therefore take this opportunity of deferring to you, whether you are willing to produce, for the satisfaction of the evangelical Church, a full and authentic account of the doctrine and discipline of the Brethren's community, which shall be so explanatory of both, as to sift, one by one, the objections before the public, and entirely to do away the offence which has been so generally taken at your innovations in christian instruction, or, at least, at your peculiar and questionable mode of imparting it." Unfavourable as was this reply, professor Timæus, the Count's emissary, continued some time longer in Würtemberg, endeavouring to promote his cause, chiefly in private conferences; after which, in the beginning of June, he went to Herbrechtingen, where he had personal interviews with Bengel; who gives an account of them in a letter to consistorial councillor Fischer, dated January, 1747. "I was willing to hear every thing professor Timæus had to say; but at intervals I explained to him, at his request, the main points of doctrine which I had set forth in my expository writings. During the Friday afternoon we conversed together for some hours, and went into all principal matters. I held him, as you had desired me, to the doctrinal articles; I pointed out to him the incorrectness of Zinzendorf's New Testament translation specimen, (second edition.) I next conversed with him about God, in respect of his manifestation of himself in the works of creation, and in the New Testament; of the Λόγος (Word,) and the reasons of this appellation; of the Holy Spirit; and, in particular, of the impropriety of applying unscriptural expressions to the third person of the blessed Trinity. Upon many points he was obliged to leave the Count undefended; many others he reserved for further consideration; but upon not a few he remained immovable. I expressed to him my opinion, that the matter in debate contained such a strange mixture of good and bad, that, unless genuine remedies were speedily applied, it was likely to issue in some great evil. We conducted our conversation, as we had agreed to do, with openness and mutual forbearance. Our most essential desideratum was *de normâ veritatis*, or the rule we are to adopt for distinguishing what is true from what is specious. As to this, he agreed with me that nothing ought to be received or admitted contrary to the instruction of Holy Writ; but he thought that believers, especially as a community of saints, have the power from their own spiritual stock of light and strength (from which, he said, even the prophets of the Old Testament deduced the testimonies they delivered,) to become acquainted with truths which are not expressly mentioned in scripture; one of which he considered to be, that a kind of maternal character belongs to the office of the Holy Spirit. Here we see the general principle of all their peculiar tenets; and if they cannot be persuaded to abandon it, any other endeavours to set them right will be only superficial and useless. At the conclusion of the above conversation, I thought it requisite to drop a word of caution and advice, especially upon the necessity of converting the Count's *monarchical* regime into an *aristrocratical* one. He thought that the church of Würtemberg had foregone a great blessing, by refusing to send commissioners to the Brethren's synod; and I tried to persuade him that this was but an imagination of his own."

By a letter which Timæus wrote to Dr. Reuss, Bengel's son-in-law, who was very much attached to the Brethren, it is further seen in how amicable a spirit this conversation was conducted. "I was last week at the house of your dear and venerable father-in-law, and stayed with him two days and a half. The Saviour was with us, for we had met together in His name: and I believe that our conference will be blessed to my benefit and his own, as well as to the common good."

The year 1748 brings us again to notice Mr. Steinhofer, at Ebensdorf. The growing approximation of the church in that town to the Brethren's constitution, seemed likely to bring about a union between the two communities; which Steinhofer had neither inclination nor ability to prevent; but he wished to make every possible provision against its becoming injurious to any party, and indeed that it might be as beneficial as possible to all. To effect this, however, was no easy matter; for he was hampered, he said, between the door and the hinge; between the party at Halle, and that at Herrnhut; a situation which perplexed him not a little; as the Halle party, with state-councillor Moser at their head, decidedly opposed his proceedings. Moser, after the union took place, left Ebersdorf in disgust; and others soon followed his example. Moreover, the Herrnhut party themselves took umbrage at Steinhofer shortly after; so that, in 1748, he was obliged to return to Würtemberg, and seek another appointment. Meanwhile, Moser, and the rest at Halle, used all their influence to prevent his obtaining it, and wrote to Würtemberg, how it was rumoured among the Ebersdorf Herrnhuters that "Steinhofer had left them, only that he might raise communities in Würtemberg for Zinzendorf, and consign them over to *him*, as he had done themselves." Happily for Steinhofer, neither Bilfinger, Fischer, Bengel, nor the other authorities in the Würtemberg church, paid much attention to these insinuations. They cited, indeed, Steinhofer before them, but finding nothing against him, merely required him to subscribe a declaration, (dated Jan. 31, 1749,) that he had no design of introducing the Herrnhut system into the church of his own country. They also enjoined him to hold no private meetings; but allowed him to visit *families*, as a minister of edification; and gave him without hesitation the parochial charge of Dettingen-under-Urach; leaving it at his own option to publish any explanation as to why he had left the Herrnhuters. The Halle party, however, boisterously insisted on his doing this; but some of the Würtemberg dignitaries abovementioned, privately advised him to let it drop.* Bengel undertook to appease the party at Halle, as appears from the following extracts of his letters to Urlsperger, the senior of the Augsburg consistory:—"June 16, 1749.—I beg you to mention to abbot Steinmetz, that I have endeavoured, in the best manner I could, to effect a right understanding respecting Steinhofer, and that I shall continue to do so. I am confident that he has withdrawn *in earnest* (from the Herrnhuters.") "Aug. 4, 1749.—Steinhofer continues at his post, as if he had never left us. He has withdrawn from the Count in earnest, and has gained much experience."

Moser, however, wrote to Steinhofer a very harsh letter, in which he told him, that it was his bounden duty to make a

* Steinhofer speaks of this, in a letter (22 June) to Weissensee, as follows:—"When I proposed the question, in the proper place, whether I ought to publish an account of my reasons for withdrawing from the Hernnhuters, I found myself directed to make no stir about it, but composedly to leave all to the quiet working of that church order and superintendence of my station, to which, by God's providence, I had returned. One of them, whom I consulted, said, that he would not have me at present express any dissatisfaction against the Count; neither would he have the Count exposed to the world by my publishing in print what had been already inquired into by himself and his colleagues, enough for every official purpose.—Another said, 'What our consistory have agreed to think of you upon the subject, is a stronger testimony in your favour than a hundred publications of your own. Besides, it is a matter which concerns only ourselves and the Würtemberg church, and upon which we do not allow others to prescribe *for* us. Therefore if any are not satisfied with the careful consideration *we* have given it, and with the decision we have agreed upon, let them apply to *us* for their further satisfaction.' All this confirmed my resolution to decline printing any thing upon the subject."

public retractation; but the latter persisted in his silence, being encouraged by his consistorial superiors to follow his own peaceful inclinations, and to prove the orthodoxy of his faith, by publishing works of edification rather than controversy. In such works he has beautifully combined the erudition of a true Würtemberg divine with that spirituality and love, for which the Brethren's church had always been remarkable.

We have already observed, that Bengel, in the year 1745, had determined to print nothing relative to the Brethren's church, unless some particular occasion should require it. Such an occasion, however, had now appeared; for, in 1747, he had been informed, that a report prevailed among the United Brethren, that he had absolutely pledged himself to publish no remarks respecting them. As such a report seemed rather to expose himself to suspicion and obloquy, he thought it a duty he owed to the protestant Church to testify, that among Lutherans there still existed many, who had been preserved from adopting the sentiments of natural-religionists; yes, and who knew and confessed the grace of God in truth, although they had not yet joined the church of the United Brethren. Moreover, he considered himself especially called upon to justify the true interpretation and legitimate use of the Apocalypse, against the sentiments of this community. Bilfinger likewise had desired him to draw up a statement of the principal points at issue between the Brethren and the Lutheran church, that the former might have occasion to explain themselves. Steinhofer also had requested him (in 1750,) "not to relinquish the treatise (upon the Brethren's principles and proceedings) which he had undertaken several years before; especially as the doctrinal system at Hernnhut had now assumed a form very different from that of their predecessors, and contained many assertions of a more liberal but lax description, which no one hitherto had ventured to examine, and which might be the more beneficially inquired into by Bengel, because his manner of writing was not of a controversial tone, but scriptural, edifying, and practical." Thus was he induced to renew his attention to a work he had long ago begun, so as to remould and commit it to the press, with the additional information he had in the meantime received; all of which he applied to the purpose with his usual and characteristic discretion. The work* consisted of two parts: the first, in three

* It was entitled, "A Sketch of (or Remarks on) the Community, denominated 'The Church of the United Brethren;' in which their doctrine and general constitution

chapters, treats,—1. Of the doctrinal system of the Brethren, according to its gradual development, since the year 1741; here it is shown in what respects Count Zinzendorf, in his discourses and hymns, had departed from Scripture, and from the Lutheran church. 2. Of the Büdingen New Testament, especially its second edition; and how far the Count had sought to accommodate his translation of the New Testament to private views, by departing from the exact meaning of the text. 3. Of the Brethren's way of interpreting the Apocalypse; showing, that their appeal to many passages of it in support of their own sentiments, was in consequence of their not rightly understanding this sacred book.—In the second part, after noticing the Count's particular object, and the danger to be apprehended by the evangelical church from the present position of the Herrnhut community, he adds a wish that the Count might prove really serious in his late modified statements and expressions. He next notices the *bands*, (*i. e.* the arrangement of the Brethren's church into companies, under the denominations of Moravian, Lutheran, and Reformed,) and shows, that by this arrangement the medley of religious professions was remedied only in appearance. For if each individual member were left to the particular and private persuasion which he had brought with him to Herrnhut, it would be needful to form besides, he knew not how many subdivisions; whereas the real object of the Count was, after all, to assimilate the whole heterogeneous mass to a mould of his own; so that the appointment of these three bands was a mere specious contrivance. Bengel concluded with expressing what he thought was likely to be the result; but recommended that no further animadversions should be made upon points which Spangenberg, in his last public explanation, had omitted or retracted; that forbearance of this kind might help to bring them round into the right direction; and that it would be well if, in framing their doctrinal system, the Brethren's church would generally prefer Spangenberg to their other advisers. The appendix contains Bengel's *earlier* reflections and remarks upon this church. Nor can we omit to notice, that Bengel, in his preface to the work, addresses particularly all devout members of their congregations; and adds a few words to "the children of this world." He tells the *latter*, that in all these concerns there

is examined; the good parts of each distinguished from their opposites; and Spangenberg's Declaration carefully considered. By John Albert Bengel: In two parts. Stuttgard; published by John Benedict Metzler, 1751."

was nothing for *them* either to ridicule or to be offended with; but that *their* business was seriously to consider, that trials and temptations of a heavier and far severer kind might await *them.* He begged they would maturely reflect on that declaration in Scripture, 'If the righteous scarcely be saved, where shall the ungodly and the sinner appear?' That they needed *a renewed mind* to enable *them* to judge of matters like these; and he hoped they would consider and apply what they read in this work of his to their *own* amendment.—To the *former* he says, "Hear me, that God may hear you. It is not an enemy, but a sincere friend, that holds out to us the truth for its own sake. I would hope to be made manifest in your consciences, though by ever so slow degrees. Be not afraid to read and examine this 'Sketch' of remarks upon your church, lest you should have to answer to God for inattention to truth which it contains. Peace and mercy be with you! How shall I rejoice to be found hereafter to have been one of the helpers of your joy!"

As to the *effect* of this publication, some, even of the Brethren's church themselves, widely differed in sentiment upon its contents. Frohberger, in his "Letters upon Herrnhut," p. 67, says—"The noblest and best deserving opponent of Count Zinzendorf was the honest and pious abbot Bengel. He drew up a treatise on the Brethren's church, with much more meekness, love, and conciliation than belong to other controversial works on the subject; and there was reason to think it was useful to the church of the Brethren." On the other hand, pastor Böttinger, in the year 1759, says of it—"Bengel's 'Sketch' of remarks is a very dangerous work; it goes to undermine the doctrine of Christ's atonement. Scripture, according to *his* showing, speaks of *other* means against sin, besides the sufferings and blood of Jesus."* Another, and still different opinion of the work, was expressed by Fresenius, a *senior* at Frankfort, and an adherent to the school of Halle. He says—"The 'Sketch' of remarks is quite to the purpose, and contains many well-pointed observations; but I can hardly help thinking, that in some places it handles the Count rather too tenderly."

Neither the Count, nor Spangenberg, nor any member of the Brethren's church, undertook roundly to answer it. Here,

* This refers to p. 91 of the "Sketch," where it is said, "There are other efficient means for extinguishing evil and unclean imaginations, besides representing *to the senses* our Saviour's scourging and crucifixion; inasmuch as every beam of scripture truth carries its own influence for enlightening us in the knowledge of God and of ourselves; for humbling, cheering, and invigorating us," &c.

however, it is but justice to observe, that from the year 1740 to 1750 was certainly a most critical period to that church; and that serious endeavours were made by its members gradually to return from their various aberrations. Spangenberg, in his life of the Count,* speaks of several siftings by the great adversary, against which, principally after the year 1748, the Count saw himself obliged to make his stand. He also relates, that the Count this same year resolved upon avoiding whatever was peculiar, eccentric, or at all likely to give unnecessary offence,—indeed, upon making as little display of every thing as possible:† and that he declared to the public, (in the 8th number of the "Dresden Literary Notices," p.127,) that "he could from this time no longer authorise his own writings hitherto published, till they had been reprinted with his amendments, remarks, and explanations."‡ He assigned as his reason for this, that "it had been his own case, like many other writers, to publish thoughts which he was quite taken with at first, but which he was afterwards ashamed of and retracted; and that it was not in his power to correct the whole so entirely at their first revisal as he would have done." He condemned and destroyed all the copies which he could collect of the twelfth supplement to the hymns, and gave this public testimony upon the doctrine of the Trinity,—"That from the moment he saw how his expressions relative to the Father, the Son, and the Holy Ghost, were taken, he was shocked at it, and abandoned every expression of the sort. He desired that wherever such were found in his writings, they might be erased, and that no one in future would repeat them. That he abhorred unscriptural speculations upon the mystery of the Godhead, and was thankful to the Saviour of all men, that he had escaped the fire uninjured." And now the Brethren's church, in a formal and solemn manner, declared to the Saxon Lutheran Commissioners deputed to its synod in 1748, to the British Government in 1749, and to that of Russia in 1762, its adherence to the Augsburg Confession; and it published at length by Spangenberg, in 1778, what the Würtemberg divines had so often wished to see,—a particular and

* Pp. 1682, 1755, 1769, 1914, 1941.

† P. 1739.

‡ To the same effect Spangenberg says in a letter to prelate Roos, A. D. 1781, that "Bengel's work could now prove nothing further against the Brethren, as it every where related to the writings of the Count, all of which, so far as they were left unrevised by himself, he had renounced, some years before his death; and that it was his opinion that Bengel, were he now living, would write nothing more against the Brethren."

full confession of faith, entitled, "Idea fidei Fratrum," or "An abstract of Christian doctrine as taught in the evangelical congregations of the Brethren:" which excellent book has served in a very gratifying manner to prevent any further uncertainty as to their peculiar mode of teaching. How far Bengel himself, and how far other persons of good or bad intentions, contributed by their animadversions to bring about this happy effect, is known only to the Searcher of hearts. Crantz, however, in his History of the Brethren, (p. 161,) remarks that "it may be truly said of some of those writers, that in many and various ways they were serviceable to the Brethren; as, for instance, in showing them wherein they had deviated, though not from the one only ground of salvation, yet from a simple and scriptural mode of teaching; and how they had inconsiderately, in some of their expressions and observances, given occasion of offence to the pure minds of many, who were not accurately informed respecting them. That this had led them deeply to humble themselves before God, and to use more forethought and circumspection in all they say and do."

But though it thus appears that Bengel was one of those who assisted in rectifying the church of the Brethren, at a very critical period of their history, and that hereby he contributed to their attainment of that manifold blessing which has crowned the labours of this church in many parts of the world very remote from each other; still it may be asked, as his opinions had such influence, especially with the religiously disposed, and as that influence, during his life-time, and for many years afterwards, almost excluded from the confines of Würtemberg the beneficial spread of a community, which has promoted so much good wherever it has made its way; whether he did not thus hinder an important blessing from accruing to his country. But, on the other hand, we may ask, whether Bengel and his associates did not abundantly make good any deficiency of this kind, by their procuring for Würtemberg more lenient enactments respecting private meetings, and more liberty of conscience for the exercise of religion in general; hereby effectually thwarting that spirit of separatism which had begun so fearfully to prevail, and obtaining free scope for a more effectual and various development of pure religion than other countries then enjoyed; whether this did not serve to promote there the kingdom of God, far more in respect of solidity, comprehensiveness and result, than if that germ of it which Providence, as it appears, had committed to their own special care, had been consigned over to the charge of the United Brethren. And again, whether Würtemberg, at a season of very general defection in other countries from the ancient doctrine, did not possess such a blessing upon its regular ministry, and in most of its churches such a plenitude of truly vital religion, that abbot * Steinmetz might well say of it as he did, "Würtemberg is the apple of God's eye." Now had settlements of the Brethren been formed in it, and had they drawn into their own community all the friends of true Christianity found amongst us, and moulded them into their own form, especially that imperfect form which then existed, is it so likely that those eminent men of our own church who so excellently defended Christian truth at a time of such peril, would ever have made their appearance? How very many of those active and valuable persons who have helped to the propagation of true Christianity in Germany, and assisted in Bible and Missionary Societies, and in every good that has been effected by the revival of religion during the last twenty or thirty years, have grown up in the church of Würtemberg alone! Neither was it necessary that the kingdom of Christ should be furthered in one particular way, and by one particular instrumentality, in each and every country. Moreover, events have shown, that Bengel rightly observed of his own times, that "the period for concentrating all the good of our various churches was not yet arrived;" and he rightly taught, that to renounce all hope of further spiritual cultivation in the national church, to pluck up the few remaining plants scattered over its general field, and to set them close together in one furrow, would be quite unwarrantable.

* "The church of Würtemberg is ruled by four superintendents, who are styled abbots, and thirty-eight rural deans. A synod is annually held in the autumn. Education, and ecclesiastical studies in particular, are favoured by laudable institutions, not to be found in any other country."—*Pinkerton's Geography.*

CHAPTER XVI.

HIS LESSER WRITINGS.

We conclude our account of Bengel as an author, with observing that, in the year 1724, Mr. Ritter received from him literary contributions for the "Life of Flacius." That in 1722, he composed some hymns for Samuel Urlsperger's "Instructions for the Sick and Dying," at that writer's request. That in 1731 he contributed some annotations on the New Testament, in German, to the editors of the Berlenburg Bible. That he also furnished to the "Pastoral Collections of Fresenius" some notices respecting pastor Gmelin; and began an Essay "On the wisdom of Christ's manner of conversing with his Disciples," the substance of which was afterwards transferred to the second edition of the Gnomon. He was solicited to compose a Gnomon for the *Old* Testament; as also, a System of Divinity; but he declined both, saying, "I rather indulge the hope, that my evening of rest may be at hand; so that I hardly feel competent to undertake works like these, or even a small proportion of them. All I do, appears to me more and more poor and defective; and it becomes the settled disposition and desire of my mind, entirely to sink into the free mercy of my God. Yet I could wish to furnish in my own language an exposition of the prophets, similar to that which Mr. Hedinger has given of the New Testament."

His thoughts on the preparation and arrangement of a Compendium of Divinity, are found in "Burk's Collections for Pastoral Theology," p. 841, &c. The most important of those thoughts are, that "the purest, most complete, and every way best divines, were the apostles and their immediate successors. For they were immediately enlightened in the highest degree (by the Spirit of God). If therefore we would have a correct idea of a true theologian, and of genuine theology, we must abstract all that has incidentally (and non-essentially) been superadded to it in the course of ages, by various modes of teaching, by errors, schisms, &c. That which constitutes a good divine is, to be able to set forth satisfactorily, on every occasion, the ground and order, the plan and method of salvation; as well as to detect and avoid deflections and errors. The Scriptures comprise a compendious system both of history and of doctrine, ready prepared to hand. They are a depository for the church of God from the beginning of the world to the end of it. They treat of the origin, progress, and end of, the world; of the human race, and the church of God; and they show how the living God has, all along, by his doings and testimonies, progressively revealed himself in his omnipotence, justice, and mercy. Examples of a system of doctrine not embodied with the sacred history, may be instanced in the epistle to the Romans, and in that to the Ephesians; or in the first epistle of St. Peter. Each of these may be regarded as a methodical compendium of evangelical truth; in which the benefits we receive by the Father, the Son, and the Holy Ghost, are inferred from the doctrine of the blessed Trinity. Appropriate heads for classification of doctrinal points may be found in many single texts of Scripture, as in John xvi. 8; Acts xx. 21; 1 Tim. iii. 16; Heb. vi. 1, 2. Subordinate subjects may be respectively arranged under those heads, by first bringing together scripture testimonies relating to each. As to the best method of arranging topics or common places, perhaps we should begin with the simple text of Scripture, I mean, without any prolegomena or introductory remarks. For we want first to make out what all the several points of doctrine are; in order to decide which are fundamental, and which not. And then for answering the remainder of our purpose we have every requisite information by barely consulting the text of Holy Writ. See John viii. 24; xvii. 3; Gal. v. 2, &c. 2 Tim. ii. 18, &c. Each common place is to be distributed into theses or chief propositions; in support or illustration of which, select scripture proofs are to be adduced, their force pointed at, and the appropriate application made. It were a good addition, to insert refutations of errors opposite to each doctrine; having respect to whether such errors lie concealed in our moral corruption, or have been openly adopted by older or more recent sects: and in such refutations we might anticipate and remove those objections and shifts which are used for the defence of each special error."

One of his last works was the Preface (dated 20th Oct. 1752) to the Gnomon which his son-in-law, (Ph. D. Burk, M.A.) had composed upon the twelve minor prophets. In this preface he shows the exact harmony prevailing among all the books of the Old and

New Testament; together with the grand comprehensive design in which they unite. He points out at the same time the distinguishing features both of the one and the other, all in his own concise and forcible manner. The last section is remarkably rich in great thoughts. "The Scriptures support the church; the church guards the Scriptures. When the church flourishes, the Scriptures are had in honour; and when the church becomes sickly, the Scriptures suffer by it. Whatever be the condition of the church at any period, the Scriptures are treated accordingly. This treatment has had its various periods ever since the earliest days of the New Testament. First, we have what may be called their *hereditary* or *legitimate* treatment; then, their *moral* treatment; thirdly, the *dry* way of handling them; fourthly, the *revived;* this last was succeeded by the *polemical,* the *doctrinal,* the *demonstrative;* after this, came the *critical,* the *polyglottal* period; the period of *research* into antiquity; the *homiletical;*—but as yet there does not live in the church the *scriptural experience,* and *scriptural knowledge,* which the pure Scripture itself supplies; and this defect is owing to the wanton opinions in doctrine, which have grown out of the several treatments of Scripture above mentioned, and to our own *blindness in the prophetic parts of Scripture.* We are therefore called on to make a further progress yet, that we may arrive at that masculine and royal scripture knowledge, without which we cannot come up to the '*perfection*' wrought in 'the man of God' by means of holy 'Scripture.' But before this will be attained, men will have to be purified through 'tribulation.' Meanwhile, let the present volume be made use of by those who believe that it may help them to acquire a saving knowledge of Scripture; and may the Divine blessing rest upon it, and upon its author!"

We close our chapter with a few subjects upon which Bengel meant to have enlarged, had he had time and opportunity. They are mostly but disputation theses; but, as they are characteristic of himself, so they may serve for useful thoughts to others.

"If I had to make a speech at discretion, I would choose for my subject, *self-knowledge;* a science which learned persons find in some respects more easy, and in others, more difficult, than it appears to the rest of their fellow-men. One of the most direct means of getting knowledge concerning ourselves, is to read what an opponent has written against us.

"A collection of those letters which Roman Catholics at

various times have written to seceders from their communion, would prove one of the best refutations of Popish doctrine. It would be its own evidence what a wretched system of meagre stuff that doctrine is.

" If writing were not now become too laborious for me, I would endeavour to trace out the doctrine of the Hebrew accents. Mr. Boston (of Ettrick) has hit upon the right way of understanding them.*

" It might be made an interesting subject for disputation, 'Whether the polemical heat of many a theologian has not considerably abated by foreign travel;' or

" 'Of Luther's animosity against the canon-lawyers, and of the prejudical influence they had on the Reformation.'

" A whole treatise may be written upon the figurative and tropical language of Scripture; and here it might be shown that many an additional elucidation is obtained by rightly understanding such figures of speech as *Chiasmus*, *Simultaneum*, &c.

" A book is wanted which might be called, 'The Ecclesiastical Year,' showing the origin of Festivals, and of their names; with explanations of the passages of Scripture, selected for such occasions.

" Wherein consists the distinction between an apostate and one who has never been regenerate?

" In what manner may the contrast between possession of the devil, and mystical union with God, be stated with respect to the different degrees of these opposite things?

" The first book of Arndt's 'True Christianity,' bound up with his small devotional work entitled 'The little Paradise,' would form an appropriate manual."

* In his posthumous work, entitled, *Tractatus Stigmologicus Hebræo-biblicus*, printed at Amsterdam in 1738. He was the author of the well-known work entitled, " The Fourfold State."

CHAPTER XVII.

HIS LITERARY CORRESPONDENCE.

I. *On the Criticism of the New Testament.**

G. A. Franke, junior, wrote to a friend of Bengel, (8th Oct. 1723,) as follows:

"As to obtaining Greek MSS. we know not how to advise you; unless Bengel himself will take the trouble to apply to Mr. von Uffenbach; at whose house I remember to have seen some. And really we think it a great loss of time to go further into the criticism of the New Testament; as scarcely one lection of any consequence is likely to be found in MSS. that has not already been noticed in the printed editions."

Bengel replied:

"Let these good men (at Halle) go on cutting out their new channels for the brook of life, to spread fertility in every direction; while I will make it my business to be looking after its hidden chambers and sources among the rocks, in order to clear away all rubbish, that it may run more purely and freely. The latter is a kind of labour little thought of by many, who nevertheless are indebted to it for not a few of the advantages and benefits they at present enjoy. As the nature of what those gentlemen themselves are labouring at, is unknown to the profane, who cannot so much as understand their motives for it, so what I too am engaged in is often not understood even by persons of piety.

"To balance the true and false readings of the sacred text, is but another part of one and the same occupation in the word of God; and the fruit of such labour is, that those who are inclined devoutly to study the Scriptures, are hereby enabled to see many parts and passages of Scripture in a clearer and more important light, and to supply valuable additional communications of their own, something beyond those of dry criticism. One's object is not merely to get readings together, but to collate them for selection; also for confirmation of readings already received as the true ones; for which latter purpose in several

* See above, ch. iii. sect. 2.

instances a sufficient number of MSS. have never yet been cited. Moreover, though the received text, as it is, contains the word of God, on which any soul may rest as safely as on heaven's foundation, still there are many precious gems buried in the great hoard of criticism, by those who have gone before me; and such valuables I feel it my duty to bring out to the sight of all, that no one, if possible, may be ignorant of their real worth. Now this is occupation for which every one has not such leisure and opportunities as are granted to myself. As there are many others, I have no doubt, who are of the same sentiments with our honest friend (Franke) upon this subject, I shall consider his remarks as a call of some importance to insert a few observations upon it in the preface to my work."

II. *To the Missionaries of the Royal Danish Mission at Tranquebar.*

"17 *Nov.* 1751.

"I have watched the progress of the Tranquebar mission from its commencement, and have ever felt an interest in endeavouring to promote its success under the Divine blessing. Some years ago I took an opportunity of sending thither a copy of my edition of the Greek Testament,* and have lately had much pleasure in hearing of its favourable reception and usefulness. From the time that the span of human life became reduced to our three-score years and ten, the Scriptures have been all along, and will continue to be, the standard of instruction in the Divine economy, with respect to the community of God's people at large, as also with respect to individuals. And though much critical erudition as well as common reading has been applied to no better purpose than that of mere head knowledge, still there is no particle of God's word which does not deserve the most careful research, yes, which has not its appropriate and infallible use to those who will give it time and occasions for taking effect. All in it tends to make the man of God perfect, thoroughly furnished for *every good work.* Labourers of your own sort among those converted heathen, to whom Scripture announcements are entirely new, enjoy more frequent opportunities, than we can have, of witnessing the vital operations of Revealed truth. In our christian countries, people become so *formally* familiar with the statements of such truth, that

* See above, ch. iii. sect. 5, of this Third Part.

instead of deriving from it sound nurture and solid satisfaction, they rather seem cloyed, and inclined to loathe it altogether.

"The tidings that reach us respecting the free course of the word of the Lord, with the advancement of his kingdom in distant parts of the East and West, call for gratitude and praise from all who love his salvation; and may well excite us Europeans to a holy jealousy, lest such light as now begins to shine into the darker regions of the earth should at length withdraw from ourselves for having been so little thankful for it, and because we have so little valued it. O that the faithful servants of our common Lord every where, may persevere in prayerful patience, to do with their might whatever the hand of every one in his station may find to do!" &c.

III. *To ——— Müller, M.A., of Dresden.*

"Your communications for my intended edition of the '*Ordo Temporum*' in German, are very acceptable and valuable, and you will find me always ready to impart freely in return whatever my humble ability may permit. As I could get no publisher to undertake the original Latin work, I am publishing it at my own expense, because the subject of it is of importance; though of course I thus incur pecuniary loss, and the Latin edition will go off the slower, when another in German succeeds it. Let me however say, that it will give me real pleasure to promote your valuable design; and if you will have the goodness to send to me your MS., I will adapt it not to the Latin edition, but to my present views, should this equally meet your approbation."

IV. *To Mr. B., a municipal officer at D——.*

This gentleman had written (July 30, 1744,) to Bengel as follows:—

"Reverend Sir,—As your erudition and knowledge of spiritual things may enable you to render many scripture prophecies upon temporal subjects popularly intelligible, and as some information of the kind may, at this changeful and disquieted period, be of great use to a whole community, and even to a particular city, I would ask, with all deference, what you think is likely sooner or later to be the fate and condition of the imperial city of D.? If it is not giving you too much trouble, your communicating to me your sentiments upon this subject will greatly oblige me; and

I would have it to be entirely between ourselves in perfect confidence and secrecy."

Bengel replied: "*Aug.* 12, 1744.

"Honoured Sir,—From the inquiry you put to me, I must conclude that you have heard a very different account of my humble ability from what it really is. I own that scripture intimations, favourable and unfavourable, have afforded me some insight even into futurity, and I bless God for it; but as to the peculiar fate of any single city, or indeed of any single nation, whether of the Roman earth or elsewhere, I certainly can say nothing. Still, as it appears to be no mere chance that a person of political eminence like yourself should thus apply to me, I will frankly communicate to you what I consider to have been imparted to me of God; which may be of more real use than any foreknowledge respecting the issues of peace and war, or of any course of politics.

"We are approaching a time of spiritual, specious, and most extensive seduction; which will be followed up by extraordinary violence. The only true preparative against that seduction is, wisdom from above; and against that violence, to be patient and faithful unto death. Any retaliation that Christians may be provoked to make upon the enemies of the truth, will most certainly recoil upon themselves. Past experience may teach us this, in the instance of many a city and country. Persons therefore who are really concerned to please God, and to promote the public welfare, who sincerely wish to save their own souls and those of others, ought to obtain power from on high against the very severe trials which are likely sooner or later to enter our own borders. They ought to arm themselves with spiritual strength by true repentance and conversion, faith and prayer, steadfastness and hope; and whoever of them are invested with civil or ecclesiastial authority, ought to take care that the Lord's flock be well watched and guarded, against that time, when the Almighty, by wonderful judgments, rebukes, and deliverances, will render his excellent name glorious in the sight of all the world," &c.

V. *To Captain von Franke, upon his inquiring, What we are to think of the comet that appeared in the year* 1744?

"Very opposite opinions prevail respecting comets. The most probable, I think, is, that they are a kind of planets, created originally with the rest of the stars, and having their appropriate positions and courses between the inferior planets. Some reckon upon having nearly ascertained their regular motions, so as to predict the time about which they will reappear. We can hardly imagine them to have no *physical* influence upon our globe with respect to heat, cold, moisture, drought, &c., but that they should forebode any *political* good or evil, is not to be supposed for a moment.

"Faith puts the children of God above comets and all natural phenomena, much as the Creator displays, in such things, his wonderful power and majesty. If we wish, for the strengthening of our faith, to take a look into futurity, the best information about things near to come or more remote in these last times, is to be found in the celestial system of Holy Writ, among the prophecies," &c.

VI. *Correspondence with Marthius, relative to the interpretation of the Apocalypse.*

Bengel having mentioned his apocalyptical discoveries, in a letter to his excellent friend Marthius, of Presburg, (18th April, 1725,) and having observed to him that the massacre which had recently been perpetrated in Thorn, at the instigation of Jesuits, had very much confirmed him in his views, by its happening just at that period, Marthius replied as follows:—

"*Oct.* 18, 1725.

"The MS.* which I think of sending you, contains a variety of painted figures emblazoned with the purest gold, which I must leave you, my dear friend, as a *Greek* cabalist, to decipher and explain. For at the end of your last letter you showed such a predilection for deciphering hieroglyphics of another sort, (prophetico-chronological,) that I may well imagine you will think it neither adventurous nor very difficult to unriddle here what to my poor understanding appears no mystery at all, or much too mysterious for me. You tell me that you hit upon your present views just about the time of that tragical affair at Thorn. By so saying, you furnish me with the key to what would have remained *indeed* a mystery to me, but is now no longer such; so that I think I may regard your discovery as more ingenious than correct. Nay, I am half inclined to reply to you as I lately did to a countryman of mine, who thought he could prove from the Apocalypse that what he called the Philadelphian period is just at hand. I said to him, 'These are but sickly dreams.' And indeed I must tell yourself, that persons who perplex themselves about

* See above, ch. iii. latter part of sect. 2, of this *Third* Part.

fixing the destinies of future ages, appear to me to be going beyond their commission, and to be led by more of credulity, than of faith. (Acts i. 7.) I write this, beloved brother, not from any disposition to be captious, but because I would not have your attention turned away from what we know to be most certain and important, in order to be given to what is less so. Certain and important, I quite concede, it is, that we are living in those last times of the world, of which our Saviour predicted that the love of many would wax cold; and that now more than ever have we to regard those positive admonitions of the Apocalypse and of Revelation in general, 'Remember! Repent! Believe! Press forward into the kingdom of God! Watch! Be zealous!' &c. All our personal Christianity and the success of our ministry are involved in the observance of these and suchlike admonitions."

Bengel replied: "*Nov.* 2, 1725.

"Your last letter, my dear brother, relates to two things: first, a Greek MS., and secondly, research into future times; and I know not whether I am most pleased with your obliging readiness to help me to the former, or with the frankness with which you decline having any thing to do with the latter. In the same manner then will I endeavour to shape my answer upon both matters to yourself. I agree with you in valuing the Scriptures as a whole; and the New Testament as a whole; so as not to muse separately upon the Apocalypse. And as to the Apocalypse itself, I accord with you about treasuring up for personal use those imperative admonitions, 'Watch,' &c. Yes, these are of the last importance. Only as the Scriptures speak to us of something additional, as counting of number, signs of times, years, months, days, hours, and even half hours, and this surely not that such things should be always unknown; are we not to notice and consider them in conjunction with the above practical admonitions? It is true that we cannot arrive at the knowledge of what the Father hath reserved in his own power; but does it not become us to inquire into what he has set before our eyes in the sacred writings, that we may profit withal? What though many have undertaken to discover future events which they promised should transpire before now, thereby exposing their own ignorance; while many others have predicted great things for times still future, (as for about the years 1736, 1739, 1748, 1750,) who will very likely be found as ignorant as the former;

still I think the reason why mistakes of this sort have been made by sanguine and pious minds, will itself be gradually elicited by their very errors; which circumstance will eventually clear the way for the truth to come forth in all its glory and beauty. The massacre at Thorn, it is true, had taken place, when I alighted upon the apocalyptical inference which I expressed to yourself; but not a word had I then heard about that massacre: and I arrived at this inference not by mere reasoning, which often distrusts truth itself; neither by any shrewdness of conjecture, which is as apt to catch at what is untenable; but by yielding in simplicity to a better guidance. If I have any occasion to doubt, when I reflect upon these things, it is not because of the things themselves, but on account of the sense I have of my unworthiness to be favoured with discoveries of the kind. And yet it is possible, that the import of many passages of unfulfilled prophecy, which have been concealed hitherto from the excellent of the earth, may at length be developed by some poor unworthy individual. For lo, while persons, like yourself, have been confining their attention to the substance, but leaving the periods uninquired into, these seem to have been opened to me, as it were, in my very sleep. I would therefore affectionately invite and entreat you, my dear brother, to deem nothing unworthy of research, which the Lord may have thought worthy to be noted in his book; but rather to redouble the vigilance of your wakeful spirit, by turning your attention to the prophetic periods, especially as some trial of your *faith* may come next, even as you have undergone already some trial of your *patience:** (Rev. xiii. 10.) Still, my dear friend, your brotherly and honest advice well deserves my grateful and affectionate acknowledgments; and may it assist me in maintaining all due soberness upon subjects which others have perverted into so many seductions to unholy curiosity, and thus in being mainly concerned about the principal business of my christian calling. I shall be gratified indeed by receiving the MS. you speak of; and assure you, that my curiosity will be not so much about its marginal embellishments, as about the text of the inspired word.

Let both of us, at our posts, do, publicly, as well as privately, just what is right in the eyes of the Lord. A single day spent

* In passing through Prague, he had been informed against as a person connected with covert Hussites. This caused him to be arrested, deprived of his chest of books, and closely cross-examined. But after a few hours' detention he recovered his books and his liberty.

by catechists or ministers in their official engagements, is, in my own account, of more value than the labours of a month spent in mere scholar-like research. Still every man has his work; and the day shall declare it.

Marthius answered:

"*Jan.* 1726.

"My dear Brother,—I have read your two last letters again and again, and my reply to them should be, I think, as follows. In the study of prophecy, and especially of the Apocalypse, we ought certainly to attend to its chronological computations, as well as to the subject-matter. But every attempt to determine its periods before-hand with accurate minuteness, appears to me like a curiousness which is inconsistent with Christian sobriety. You say, God has determined the times before appointed, even to half an hour. True, but his reckoning, and ours, are not the same; (2 Peter iii. 8.) Nay, had you remembered that even human beings of different countries measure time differently, you would never have formed your present conclusions. Certainly every thing will happen at its predicted period; but Christ's first advent teaches us, that in order to know it exactly, we ought to wait till it begins to show its fulfilment by the event. As for what you have alleged by way of proof, I see nothing in it that you can safely rely upon. You say the inquiry is concerning one number which is to be obtained by means of another. But you might just as well have observed that the number to be taken as the standard of reckoning, is called the number of *man*, and stands in the denomination of *six*. Set it then down that it is the number of *man*, because man was created on the *sixth* day. Next see whether the word Λατεῖνος, or its correspondent Hebrew word רומיית, will not give this number. But in like manner did the Huguonots find 666 in the name Ludovicus. What then are we to conclude? Surely either that all computation of this sort is very uncertain; or else, that the words must at present be taken more mysteriously, and not in that clear definition which my dear friend would affix to them. Hence he may easily conclude what I think upon the '*false prophet.*' Grammarians speak of nouns *proper* and *common;* and I am inclined to class the word *pseudo-prophet* with the latter rather than with the former.

"Periods *thus defined* by human conjecture, have no effect to increase my spiritual vigilance; they are either too *obscure* for me, or too *remote.* The cry in Matt. xxv. 6, arouses me more;

and well may it be sounded forth day and night at present. Surely, my dear friend, your own precious time may be far more advantageously applied to what is of greater certainty and of greater importance; at least, let me entreat you not to communicate any of your apocalyptical lucubrations for insertion in your commentary upon the New Testament. If you do this, you will contaminate and spoil the very best part of it. You will also get into unprofitable controversies, and be exposed to many a bitter sarcasm from ungodly men. Should no one else attack you, certainly Kohlreiff, who thinks very highly of his own knowledge of prophecy, will not spare you; and there are plenty of wasps besides, who will not be stirred by you with impunity. Let me likewise beg of you not to give your critical annotations too concisely, under the idea that your readers will take the trouble to *think out* all the meaning which you intend to convey in some two or three words. Your *Prodromus* has been very favourably received in this country: and it was readily agreed to lend you the MS. I requested for you. Let me beg of you one thing more,—that you would get your work finished before I am called away from my frail tabernacle. The more you labour simply to the glory of God in singleness of heart, the more life and strength will he bestow upon you. Think that I embrace you with the tenderest brotherly affection; yes, with a love which constrains me to entreat the Lord to keep as far from you as possible all domestic and bodily suffering, and every spiritual suffering also; especially any feeling of tedium, leanness of soul, scrupulosity, doubt, despondency, &c., or whatever might harass and disquiet, though not oppress and overwhelm you."

Bengel replied:

"*May* 9, 1726.

"O that we could personally converse together about prophetic chronology! You would then, my dear friend, notwithtsanding your sober caution, allow me to be right in some respects, if not in all. It is a subject which I find cannot fairly be discussed between us in writing. How mistaken was I in hoping to despatch it by a few lines to you with my pen; whereas I have but superficially handled it altogether. Still *what I have set down will, I think, partly turn out to be correct; and partly serve to prepare the way for further manifestation of the truth, when every thing in Providence shall by and by be matured for that purpose.* In the mean time, my writings may help to set aside many a *false* notion and interpretation.

"Of course I cannot look for the special signification of 666 in the Hebrew word רומיית, (for the word λατῖνος, as it ought to be written, and not λατεῖνος, expresses only 661;) neither can I seek it in the name LUDOVICUS. All this I should account too puerile and cabalistical.

"I grant we ought not to pursue such inquiries farther than as the written word has furnished us with data; but is it not equally wrong to be satisfied with letting any such data remain unexamined? Certainly the treasures of Deity and Eternity are unsearchable; but in the word of wisdom and in the word of prophecy, bestowed upon sinful man because of his very poverty, there is a Divine condescension purposely adapted to our littleness and ignorance, for the raising of our thoughts and drawing us upwards. Doubtless it is our business to attend to the main matter; yes, and he who does so, knows how to avoid impertinent curiosity, while inquiring into the prophetic periods and their fulfilment. The faithful of old knew how to do this, when they computed the accomplishment of the seventy years in the destruction of Jerusalem, (Dan. ix. 2.) Yes, believers under the Old Testament waited from age to age for the first advent of the Messiah, and gained from time to time increasing conviction that his coming could not be far distant, till at last good old Simeon hit upon the very moment. Why is any event predicted at all? Surely, that the Lord may be magnified upon its arrival. Now, as arrive it must; so will all who love God see it to be the more glorious, the more they shall have been familiarized with it beforehand.

"The only part of your letter which touched me too tenderly, was your saying, I ought to insert nothing of the kind in my commentary. Can you be unaware, my dear brother, what a latitude is always allowed for prophetical and apocalyptical inquiries? Be assured, however, that I shall not venture to commit any thing to print without respectable countenance and advice. Even before your kind admonitions reached me, I had submitted my annotations to the inspection of several who have experience in the words and ways of God; and I am the more ready to avail myself of such help, because hereby many a sentence of mine is erased or softened down; and then, all that is suffered to remain, will be guarded by a preface written with moderation, and with a desire to satisfy pious and considerate persons, though to silence such as are only captious and irreligious. As to yourself, my dear friend, I still indulge the pleasure of thinking that your own wakefulness of spirit, without any reasoning of mine, will bring you at length to the very views I have pointed out as the true ones.

"You desire me to avoid too much brevity in my critical annotations, and I will endeavour to do so. I have to be thankful that the work is briskly proceeding; but I cannot say exactly when it will be out. Whatever may delay it, nothing of the kind shall, I trust, delay either your entrance or mine into the promised rest."

Marthius answered:

"You will be glad to know that the Greek MS. returned safely. I have handed it back to its proper place, with your best thanks to the curators. And I added with it the copy you presented me of your Chrysostom on the Priesthood, that the library may have one memorial of your industry and learning.

"I think I am still bound to add a few more brotherly words of advice, about soberness of inquiry into the prophetic periods. Now because such inquiry proves often as useless as it is laborious, (though I know you too well to fear you will write any thing at random, or publish it without previous careful revisal and consideration,) let each of us, at our retired posts, watch the signs of the times, and we shall certainly see many things coming to pass which a profane worldling never dreams of. For my own part, I think it right to prepare for the worst; and to do so, not by looking at outward things only,—for then we see the most sorrowful times approaching,—but by giving attention to the purposes of God revealed in Scripture; then we see that all things are working together towards the most blessed consummation. Let the flesh suffer and come to nought, so that the spirit but attain to life eternal. Let the outward man perish, if only the inward man be renewed day by day."

Bengel replied:

"I have to thank you, my dear friend, for having replaced the MS. you borrowed for me, as also for what I could not have been bold enough to do myself, your having accompanied it with the copy I gave you of my little work. You shall receive from me another keepsake instead; namely, a copy of my New Testament, should we live to see it published. As to the prophetic periods, I think I have already written enough to you about them; only I will ask you just to consider one thing more. Though we read of 'the times and the seasons, which the Father hath reserved in his own power,' we are to understand by it only that certain things were not to be revealed, till events should become ripe for the purpose. Thus it was intimated to the Apostle St. John, that he should tarry till Jesus Christ should come; and lo, he *did* come. (Compare John xxi. 22, with Rev. i. 7.) Therefore the times which are revealed in Scripture are not kept from us; they are not 'sealed up.' I am fully sensible of my utter unworthiness to be an instrument for disclosing such things; yet I cannot but believe that the commencement of such a disclosure has taken place by means of what I have done in the way of consideration and research; and that more will yet be opened by means of worthier inquirers than myself. O if we were now together, how gladly would I learn from you of things relating to the kingdom of God *within* us; and how ready would you be to allow me to invite you to take a prospect of its *external* borders, which are beginning to brighten upon our view! Believe me, I am not disturbed at seeing evil swelling to its crisis, and strengthening for the great conflict; because, in truth, it is only maturing for final and utter demolition. Therefore I sing new songs upon the hope of Zion; and even if I knew it would be my lot to 'fall asleep' this day, still I should rejoice for my surviving 'brethren and companions' sakes.' In a word, the Apocalypse is preeminently our Lord and Saviour's book. It contains the main substance of all ancient prophecy, from Jerusalem destroyed to Jerusalem renewed, (I mean, the New Jerusalem,) and this with additions concerning the most minute particulars. Here the whole gracious plan of God is presented in the clearest light. This book is, of all others, the most difficult and the most simple.

"I have no dread of Kohlreiff. The doctrine of a Millennium will soon become an article of faith, and people will be ashamed of opposing it. . . . But contemplations on these subjects do not retard my critical work. Indeed it is already in such forwardness, that, if other circumstances shall permit, I may soon send it to the press. What principally holds me back is the delay of Bentley's promised edition of the Greek Testament, a specimen of which was given many months since, in the English 'Library.' Bentley possesses invaluable advantages; but he has prepossessions of his own, which may prove very detrimental to the received text. All dangers, however, of this kind, I hope I have the means of obviating."

Marthius answered:

"While I was contemplating the mystery of the Incarnation,

your letter came to my hand by a Roman Catholic. Before I say any thing else, I am eager to assure you that you are, and must be, the dearest of all my brethren in Christ. My heart longs to be with you. Your kind wish, 'O that we were now together,' is my wish also; and I am sure the hope you have expressed, in which I too join, (respecting the result of our interview,) would not be disappointed; no, you would find me your very attentive scholar in matters of prophetical chronology, though I allow I have hitherto read nothing that has appeared more than probable conjecture on such subjects. Still, my dear friend, we agree in valuing the Apocalypse; it has all its weight with me as an inspired book; though I am not curious to know the times and the seasons of its fulfilment, simply because I consider this knowledge to belong to the Father alone, and that no mortal will ever discover it; for we are permitted to see only its 'back parts,' as is expressed of God concerning himself to Moses, (Exod. xxxiii. 23.) Your connected scripture references please me much; though I still doubt of the meaning of Rev. i. 7, and am inclined to think, that not the coming of a more gifted insight into revelation is here spoken of, but the coming of the glory of CHRIST."

Bengel replied:

"Most certainly it is the coming of the glory of Christ that is meant in Rev. i. 7. But the coming of this glory is gradual. Even as his Resurrection was really the commencement of his Ascension, (for thus we read of it, John xx. 17,) so from the first giving of the Apocalypse is he spoken of as *beginning* to *come*. (Rev. i. 7, 'Behold he *cometh* with clouds,' &c.) All that has been proceeding from that time till now, is no other than a progressive and glorious coming of Christ."

VII.—*To Prelate Oechslin; on the Apocalypse.*

Prelate Joachim Oechlsin, of Würtemberg, wrote to Bengel 15th Sept. 1742, as follows:

"I cannot help thinking that the chief substance of the Apocalypse relates to the destinies of the church and of her enemies; particularly of those intestine enemies, who, under pretext of zeal for Christianity, really oppose and destroy the holy people: and that the destinies of the rest of the world are hardly noticed in this prophecy, except where the concerns of the church have something particular to do with them; as, for instance, those temporal revolutions, which bring to pass some great, unlooked for, and remarkable events. But, with this simplicity of mine, some of your own inferences will not easily harmonize. For example, the persecution against the Jews in Persia, appears too insignificant to be understood as the First Woe; and then, I am obliged to wonder, how the very great change in the condition of the Eastern church could have been unnoticed altogether.

"Neither can I persuade myself that those parts of your system are well balanced which touch so frequently upon the grand total of things in heaven, on earth, and under the earth; or things extending at least beyond this visible world. Witness the view you take of the two last chapters of the Revelation. I am aware that the mind, however intelligent, is put upon a very peculiar kind of exercise, in any attempt to explain such a book as the Apocalypse; and this on account of the highly figurative manner in which most of it is written. Still, if we get into subtilties of interpretation, too remote for common understandings, I think we are departing from the mind of the Spirit, and losing sight of the end and design of revelation itself. This makes me rather afraid of your elaborate system of prophetical chronology, though I cannot but admire its general harmony with itself, and indeed can furnish nothing better in its room. But let the *modulus ingenii mei*, my own poor thoughts and abilities of comprehension, go for nothing; certainly I cannot set up these as the standard of truth, upon the present, or upon any other subject. The numerical periods (in the Apocalypse) certainly conform very much to those of Daniel. But I have always supposed that those in Dan. xii. ought to be taken in their most simple and literal sense, and that they are so far from being mystical, that they refer only to the desolation of the sanctuary under Antiochus Epiphanes. Could we take just the proper stand for considering the prophecies of the Apocalypse, so as to ascertain to what particular event in church history each prediction severally relates, we should probably see their specified dates and periods coinciding so exactly with those historical events, as to leave no room for the idea of *mystical* numbers.

"Hence the following is another of my own perhaps raw ideas, which I cannot bring to accord with your system. I mean, that I am obliged to think that we ought, in determining the periods affixed to subjects even of prophecy, to compute time in the vulgar reckoning, unless the clearest necessity shall compel us to abandon it. Should it ever do so, then we ought, I think, to compute mystical periods after the manner which was common and familiar at the time when the revelation was given. And if so, then I have no evidence that, in St. John's time, the vulgar reckoning was ever made by half years.

"It appears to me, that the *Beast out of the Sea* can symbolize only a common temporal *power;* consequently, by it cannot be meant the pope as an individual, but much more probably the *Germanic* empire. For as to any *Roman* empire existing at present, it is an imaginary notion."

Bengel replied:

"The histories of remote countries and centuries are often far more significant and important in themselves, and in their connexion with the fulfilment of the Divine purposes and decrees, and have often a much more immediate bearing with the affairs of the people of Israel, and of the Christian church, as also with the Divine economy in general, than common consideration of history would lead us to suspect. Historical research has never yet been directed enough to relative bearings and connexions of such a kind. The persecutions carried on against the Jews in Persia have an importance in this very respect. For, had the Jews been free from persecution at that period, they would, humanly speaking, have risen again into power, to the disadvantage of the kingdom of God.

"Neither is the condition of the *Eastern* church omitted to be noticed in the prophecy. It comes into view where we read of the flood which the dragon casts out of his mouth after the woman, as also where the Holy City is spoken of. But the *Western* church is that which is more largely treated of, because it is in the midst of the Western church that *the Beast out of the Sea* stands up.

"To come to any proper interpretation of the Apocalypse, I think it needful to take for granted that it treats of the *invisible,* as well as visible world. For the former is, in chap. vii. 14, 15, and in the fourth and fifth chapters, laid open, as it were, before us. There we find the angels summoned together, with the four heavenly beings and the twenty-four elders, who stand even nearer to God than the angels. All this perfectly agrees with the scope of the Apocalypse, which would set forth the honour and glory of the Lamb, as having received all dominion in heaven and in earth, &c.

"That the *New Jerusalem* extends beyond this life, is evident from the glory and everlasting duration attributed to it, as also from its being set in contrast to the *Lake of Fire*. Not until the arrival of the Last Day is it, that we find the earth and the heavens represented as fleeing away; the new heavens and new earth must therefore be *after* that day, and not *before* it.

"With respect to the three periods called the Woes, I do not show that a day denotes half a natural year, till after I have shown, from the analogy of the prophecy, that a whole natural year would be too long, and a natural day too short. Now, that these apocalyptical periods are entirely mystical, is plainly intimated by that most important expression, '*Here is wisdom!*' In what does this wisdom consist? Surely not in our mere knowledge of the individual Beast, but in our knowledge of God's whole plan and economy throughout this prophecy. Now a comparison of the number 666 with the forty and two lunar months of the Beast, as also with the thousand years, draws our attention to a period in the world's history, wherein we find recorded, facts, exactly coinciding in time and circumstance with the inspired predictions. And though some other method of chronological calculation, different from that I have adopted, may, after all, be the true one, still it must necessarily be found as complex and heterogeneous as my own, because this is the case with the text itself. Besides, do we not find circuitous intricacy and heterogeneous variety in things far less mysterious? For instance, in the revolutions of the planets. Yet in such very complexity we only the more discern the finger of God. Again; how abrupt and intricate is the description of the last things of the world as given in the prophet Ezekiel! *Our* business is only not to lead, but to follow. How intricate is an armillary sphere to an ignorant inspector! How little does he imagine of the regular and scientific plan upon which such an instrument is constructed.

"Lastly, that the '*First Beast*' should denote only a common secular *power*, and that the singularly peculiar establishment of that spiritual-secular monarch, who alone has so near a connexion with the city of Rome, should have no place in the prophecy, are suppositions perfectly inadmissible; especially if we consider that the '*falling away*' began in no part of the world earlier than in the city of Rome itself."

After thus reviewing Bengel's apocalyptical system, it is natural to inquire, how far it is correct; and whether in his bestowing so much time and attention upon it, and in publishing the result, he has done well; as also what good effect has attended its publication.

It cannot be denied that many things in his system do not appear on the face of the sacred text itself. Bengel was quite sensible of this; and therefore referred, upon some points, not to textual showing, but to analogy; maintaining, that isolated portions, interpreted by his general plan and system, give out what is in perfect keeping with the rest. Moreover, we are to recollect his own remarkable observation, "that he would necessarily appear wrong in his conclusions, till about the time of the end. *At* that time, however, the seal of truth would be affixed to his demonstrations in a manner quite unlooked for." From which we may infer, that he expected his correctness, in particular and subordinate matters, to be made out, not so much by any future and better general system of interpretation, as by facts in the world's history, which would by and by transpire. And indeed facts do appear to have suddenly taken quite a new turn in his favour since the year 1830. Be this as it may, we can, on his behalf, allege as follows:

That since the accession of Benedict XIV. in 1740, the papal throne has sustained a variety of successive shocks. That pope was the immediate successor of Clement XII., who embroiled himself in many strange altercations with temporal rulers, but never allayed them. For, soon afterwards, Austria, Spain, France, and several Italian states, began most violently to protest against the papal claims.* Voltaire's declamatory writings kept a multitude of pilgrims from going to Rome and Loretto.† His effusions, congenial as they were with the corrupt dispositions of human nature, and aided by the literary productions of men of his own spirit, produced in the minds of a large mass of the Romish community, that revolution of sentiment which still continues to shake the papal throne. The emperor Joseph enjoined numerous ecclesiastical reforms. The pope himself was at length constrained to abolish the order of Jesuits. Napoleon carried off the pope as his prisoner; deprived him of his temporal sovereignty, by the decree of May 17, 1809; and some years afterwards invested his own son with the title of king of Rome;

* See John Rudolph Schlegel's "Ecclesiastical History of the 18th Century," vol. i. pp. 529, 532, 594, &c.

† And yet Benedict corresponded in friendly terms with Voltaire, and styled him his son in Christ!

indeed, even to the present time, the triple crown has been worn more precariously than it had ever been in former ages.

Upon the peace concluded in 1745, between Frederick II. and Maria Theresa, there succeeded the still more destructive seven years' war, during which Europe witnessed, with amazement, Austria and France, two natural enemies of each other, combined for the overthrow of Frederick II.

The partiality of Frederick II. for Voltaire, and for other free thinkers, occasioned the diffusion of much anti-christian infidelity in Germany; and thus Prussia for a time was one remarkable channel of anti-christian principles.

Bengel's expectation has been confirmed, that, should a course of unusual events not commence so early as between A. D. 1740 and 1750, Europe would remain quiet for a considerable time. And it was not till the breaking out of the French Revolution in 1789, that his other anticipation was fulfilled, namely, that after some such eruption, new scenes would open every quarter of a year; indeed, since the first of July, 1830, some new scene has been disclosing itself almost every month.

The Latin language (as a medium among the learned of different nations) is less and less made use of; and this was preintimated by Bengel, as also by many others. Since the middle of the last century, literature, at least in Germany, has assumed quite a new form; meanwhile how *many* writings upon civil jurisprudence have become obsolete and useless! And how *many more* are likely to become so! Likewise the maps of (European) countries have shared the same fate.

As early as the commencement of the present century, the Germanic Roman empire began to totter, and came to its entire dissolution in the year 1806. Hereupon the German bishoprics and abbeys became secularized. Many states have undergone the most remarkable changes, and are undergoing them even to the present time.

Italy, France, Spain, and Portugal, have suffered most. These are the very nations which have continued insensible of the blessing of gospel grace from the time of their visitation by it in the sixteenth century; and how hard and "strong" have the "bands" been "made," which they chose to retain upon them!

We have lived to see even a *Gallic* emperor, and lo, he was greater and mightier than any of the Germanic Roman emperors his predecessors. But how Bengel, especially according to his system, could prognosticate this by the number 666, is quite inexplicable; yet it was his *system* which obliged him to look for Antichrist in a *French* western emperor. The Turks, since the year 1725, have suffered many a disadvantage; particularly have the Greeks, Russians, and French, reduced them so considerably, that as an independent power they are now at the very point of annihilation.

On the other hand, Russia has grown up to such mighty potency, that the future work which Bengel considered as assigned to that empire, may soon be no longer beyond its ability.

In the very recent "*comings out*" from the Roman Babylon, may perhaps be found one fulfilment of Rev. xviii. 4.

The present condition of Christendom, ecclesiastical, religious, and moral, agrees exactly with the anticipations which Bengel inferred from the small commencements of it discernible in his own times. Scepticism has gradually ended with many, either in avowed infidelity, or in mere deism; or in a sort of philosophic mysticism. Such a change has taken place with relation to old established formularies, that whereas once the Pietists were almost the only party who scrupled about subscription to the protestant symbolical books, they are now almost the only persons who strictly adhere to them. A spirit of defection from the principles of the Reformation, has set itself up in a way of bold counter-protest, and has become almost universally recognised as the life and soul of those churches which are denominated Protestant; indeed, such a latitudinarianism is now asserted for matters of faith and doctrine, that it is impossible to say what may not be openly taught by and by with the sanction of protestant ecclesiastical patronage. All unity upon such matters has so entirely disappeared among Protestants, that it exists only in the vague notion of "*rational* Christianity." The doctrinal system of the great majority among the *improved* and *enlightened* sort, is a meagre circumscription to three ideas: *God; Human Liberty;* and *Immortality*. Their *God*, however, is, in a multitude of instances, a mere metaphysical figment, not the LIVING GOD who can assure life and consolation to the soul; or it is nothing more than the boundless universe, with all their own miserable selfishness included in it. Their *Liberty*, when examined, is found to be a servile dependence on time, circumstance, education, instruction, natural temperament, humour, climate, or, above all, their own lusts and passions. Their *Immortality* is, with many of them, nothing but a final absorption into the mass of the universe; and scarcely any of them believe in a future state of rewards and punishments. On the other hand, by the more philosophical class, the doctrine of the *inward word* is made the fruitful source of manifold mischief. Swedenborg and his followers long since united fanaticism with frigid, independent, and unscriptural reasoning; and later days have exhibited fanatical reasoners of a yet more infidel complexion. The grossest superstition and bigotry are not unfrequently at present seen hand and hand with the most decided infidelity. Nor is the nullifying of Scripture, as a divine record, (with which error we find nevertheless united the belief of a Christ *merely within us*,) confined now to illiterate mystics, but errors of the kind have begun to be abetted even by *divines* themselves; and this has aided in spreading abroad the most extravagant distraction, confusion, and scepticism, upon the fundamental matters of religion. The dogma likewise of predestination has, since the ecclesiastical union between the Reformed and the Lutherans, obtained such an ascendant among the latter, that Bengel's anticipations upon this subject may be considered as realized.

The demoralization of christian countries has kept pace with the increase of infidelity within them: and Bengel was right in expecting that this demoralization would be expressly seen in the multiplication of offences against the Seventh Commandment.

Experience, especially of late years, has clearly evinced how much this alteration in the spirit of the times has been promoted by newspapers and periodical publications; meanwhile, however, there have not been wanting men of "skill and understanding," who have demonstrated that the Scriptures, as a connected whole, are every way worthy of their Divine Author. Hess, Köppen, and others, have been eminent in showing this.

Bengel said, that the emerging of better times would be like vegetation pricking forth from under the dissolving snow. And we may easily observe, in our own day, instances of the kind sufficient to warrant a hope that the real Christian church is gradually emerging to an improved condition.

Missions to the Jews and heathen could effect but little in Bengel's days. But how much has been done in the present century, or at least how much preparation has been made, for the most extensive good! Into how many languages have the Scriptures been translated, and how few discovered nations have not had at least *one* messenger of the gospel sent among them!

As Bengel's anticipations have been thus far fulfilled, can we be surprised that many should regard all this as argument for expecting that the still more important things which he anticipated, and which men are now fearfully "looking for," will, in like manner, come to pass? However, as there is so much of the kind yet remaining unaccomplished, we can hardly think it possible that all will be comprised within the brief space of time now remaining to the expiration of the year 1836; especially as even the preparations for many of such things seem not to have been begun. For at present there is not the remotest appearance of Jerusalem's increasing to a population of seventy thousand; yet Bengel said, that all would go on with comparative smoothness, till something remarkable should happen there.

It is true that in 1830, the spirit of rebellion suddenly and fearfully broke out again. Still we hear nothing as yet of any personal Antichrist fixing his seat at Rome.

Neither has the "false prophet" ever yet clearly discovered himself. For, though the order of Jesuits seem to be zealously prosecuting their craft, no Jesuit has assumed the character of a general agitator.

Many imagined that the mark of the Beast was the tricoloured cockade of the first French Revolution; but this having been only a political and not a religious badge, can be no decisive mark of Antichrist.

The "harvest" and the "vintage," consequently the *seven vials*, are yet future. This is evident from the vast *increase* of population up to the present time.

Thus are many predicted and expected events, and some of the most important of them, not yet arrived. But who shall say that they will not shortly come to pass? Had even nothing already occurred at the periods which Bengel anticipated, nay, had many events taken quite a different turn from what they did, and from what he expected they would, ought we therefore to think he had better have withholden his apocalyptical researches from the world? He has been accused of perplexing some subjects of this prophecy with unprofitable subtilties, and of having added to others his own gratuitous alarms. But, not to mention that the abuse of a thing is no argument that it cannot be rightly used, we surely ought not to overlook the good which Bengel has actually accomplished by means of that very system of apocalyptical interpretation, for the invention and publication of which some have been so ready to censure him. His testimony against the papal domination was, of itself, a word in season; for a dangerous latitudinarianism with respect to popery had, even in his time, begun to show itself within the pale of the protestant church. And in the succeeding period of very general infidelity, the temptation of lapsing to Romanism was strongly felt by many of the more honest and pious Protestants. His views have been likewise a means of preserving very many from schism; and his warnings against infidelity, and against its awful consequences, will be found of use to those who have not yet learnt openly or secretly to abet it. Such warnings, moreover, have proved most efficacious, when drawn from apocalyptical considerations; and Bengel's manner of conceiving and giving them was most unaffected. They were uttered from the convictions of his heart; from convictions impressed upon him by the word of God. And as conscience obliged him to cause his warning voice to be heard, who can condemn him for following that voice himself? Lastly, should what may happen in future years, render such apocalyptical admonitions more necessary for Christendom than ever, will it not appear a peculiar providence, that Bengel was gifted, more than a hundred years ago, with such deep insight into the mysteries of the kingdom of God?

PART IV.

BENGEL'S PRIVATE LIFE.

CHAPTER I.

AS A FAMILY MAN.

SOON after Bengel had become settled in his permanent station at Denkendorf, he looked out for a pious helpmate to share with him the vicissitudes of human life. He was persuaded, he said, that "the heart is so formed by nature, that it cannot easily renounce every kind of recourse to and refuge in 'the creature,'* and that the married state is one of his own wise and gracious ordinances." Such a friend he found in the family of Frederic Seeger, Esq., receiver-general of the provincial estates, whose daughter, Joanna Regina, became endeared to him, as much by her simple piety as by her excellent understanding and disposition. She was engaged to him in April 1714, and they were married in the following June. As, in forming a connexion of this kind, very much depends "on how persons understand each other at first setting out," (which is another of his own remarks,) some passages of his letters to this lady will show how important he considered it, that their mutual alliance should be hallowed by mutual union with Christ.

"Jesus is all in all!

"My beloved and esteemed Friend, "*April* 17, 1714.

"I have continual confidence that what has commenced between us will, by the blessing of the Most High, be the occasion of constantly renewed felicity. May the pure love of Jesus fully occupy us, and keep us in tranquillity and peace!"

* Rom. viii. 19.

"20*th April.*

"Our absence just now from each other may be turned to our spiritual benefit, if we make a proper use of it. Souls that would depend only on God, and live entirely to his glory, have to undergo many self-denials to deliver them from all undue attachment to the creature. Let our mutual absence, therefore, which will be but short, be employed in learning to find our chief delight, more in Him, yes, than in each other. Though we have never seen Christ in the flesh, we cleave to him in spirit; and we know that our love of him, and our desire to enjoy his perfect presence, are to be of far more consequence to us than each other's company. May he therefore dispose our united hearts more and more to himself, and possess them entirely. Thus I remain, now and for ever, my beloved friend's most faithful and attached," &c.

"27*th April.*

"Only let us endeavour more and more unremittingly to exercise lively confidence in God, and to be conscious that we really love him, and we shall never want any manner of thing that is good. This, too, will be the best preparation we can make for our marriage."

"4*th May.*

"No greater joy can I have than to see that my most valued friend is enjoying the grace of God, walking in the love of her Saviour, and thus realizing every true enjoyment at once. This must be the one great concern with us both, and must never, through our alliance with each other, be lost sight of, much less hindered; but promoted. Our heart should be quite as decidedly with the Supreme Lover of our souls, as yours, I am sure, is with me; and we should believe His love towards us to be infinitely greater than we are able to imagine. The best way to experience the truth of this, is to retire into quietness of spirit, into secret communion and childlike converse with him. This is a grace indeed; and as I heartily desire it for us both, I make it a subject of prayer continually. For it is the best foundation for the permanency of our mutual affection, and for the happiness of our union; a union, the comfort and benefit of which are not to be confined to a few early days. And in this way I am, and by God's grace intend to be through life, a life to be spent by us according to his will,

"My highly esteemed and truly dear friend,

"Yours, ———."

"*7th May.*

"The account which my best beloved friend gave of herself, at the conclusion of her letter the day before yesterday, has greatly delighted me. God grant power, grace, and blessing. I am at present, by his great goodness, well and happy both in spirit and bodily health."

"*11th May.*

"Jesus in Heaven,
Jesus in the Heart,
Heaven in the Heart,
The Heart in Heaven!"

"My beloved Friend,—At this moment of my wishing to write to you, the above words occurred to me, and I could not refrain from heading my letter with them, as a salutation and expression of my best wishes to you; and may the power and import of such words be manifested as shed abroad in both our hearts! I continue, through the divine goodness, quite well and happy, and hope to hear the same and more of my beloved friend. The arrangement between our parents respecting the marriage ceremony quite accords with my own feelings, particularly about not inviting too large a company on the occasion."

"*14th May.*

"I must now close my letter; and I do it with sincere prayer to God, that at this pentecostal season, he may fill the heart of my beloved, and my own heart likewise, with the spirit of power, of love, and of a sound mind."

"*18th May.*

"Time will not allow me to add more, or I should most gladly have concluded with a few christian thoughts of a pentecostal kind; but the Spirit of grace can himself teach us all things. To Him let us open and surrender our hearts, that he may sanctify us wholly, and may glorify in us the name of the Lord Jesus."

"*21st May.*

"If my beloved friend has enjoyed through this closing festival season the same spiritual comfort which it has brought by divine grace and goodness to my own unworthy self, I shall have a fresh occasion to rejoice and be thankful."

The following remarks were made by him in reference to his marriage.

"The marriage service in the Würtemberg liturgy is very beautiful, and I have reason to remember to the present hour the deep impression it made upon me. I came to the ceremony quite in a collected frame of spirit; and when that part of the form was read, which relates to the cross, (which no married person can expect entirely to escape,) the whole subject of the cross came into my thoughts; and my heart was inclined, though with much fear and trembling, to resolve entirely to take it up. But when the words, 'O well is thee and happy shalt thou be,' were read, a sweet and cheering composure, with respect to any trials in the married state, came over me, and has never left me to this day."

The choice he had made proved indeed a happy one. He spent the remainder of his life, namely, thirty-eight years, in the married state; and all those years were marked with contentment and the divine blessing. He said, "all along I have been blest with a most valuable helpmate; which has often induced me to pray fervently to God, that, notwithstanding her many critical casualties, he would grant me the mercy of retaining her to the end of my pilgrimage. My petitions have hitherto been answered."

"The married state has been the means of so much benefit to me in the way of christian experience, that even on this one account, I have the highest esteem for it as an ordinance of God. It is only the pride of self-sufficiency that makes some persons disparage and distrust it. What God has ordained for the happiness of his creatures, must surely be ever preferable to what men in their own wisdom prefer."

His following words will tell us how his own marriage became so peculiarly blest. "Real communion with each other in prayer is above all things needful between two married persons: and, next to this, there should be a kind of emulation to outdo each other in mutual forbearance. Patience is at first particularly necessary, till both have learnt how to adapt themselves to each other's dispositions. The greater their mutual esteem, the more tenderly is their love carried on. No other communion, as between brothers, neighbours, friends, &c., is equal to this, in which the parties are always together, and have continual attentions to pay each other. Thus, if they know how to improve their moral and social advantages, they may do it to their daily mutual refreshment. Even when the first charm of novelty is over, the communion between such a christian pair is still incomparably sweet; it is as old wine compared with new.

"We must live always as in the presence of God; this, however, must be done with simplicity, and not with affectation.

"A married man should conduct himself towards the partner of his life, in every respect, as if the thought were always present to him,—Should my wife this day close her eyes in death, how should I then wish I had conducted myself?

"I have learnt by a variety of instances and observations, that marriage is commonly attended with mutual disappointment to those who give way to raillery and repartee, and who, with all their professed knowledge of the truth, indulge a light and trifling spirit. Such disappointments in each other, then come to them as a wholesome rebuke of Providence. Most of those who are in this situation endeavour to conceal it from others, because they hope for no good by talking about it; but their sufferings are pitiable."

God gave him twelve children, half of whom entered the eternal state in their infancy. Of the surviving half, the four eldest were daughters, whom he lived to see happily married; viz. Sophia Elizabeth, born 6th of May, 1717; married 11th of February, 1738, to Dr. Reuss, afterwards physician to the Duke of Würtemberg.—2. Joanna Rosina, born 29th of February, 1720; married 23d of July, 1737, to Christian Gottlieb Williardts, afterwards official counsellor to the Emperor Francis I.—3. Maria Barbara, born 30th of November, 1727; married 23d of June, 1744, to the Rev. Philip David Burk, A.M. afterwards Dean of Kirchheim.—4. Catharine Margaret, born 24th of November, 1730; married 7th of September, 1751, to the Rev. Everard Frederic Helwag, A.M., afterwards Dean of Göppingen. The elder son, Victor, born 16th of August, 1732, was a student in medicine, but survived his father only seven years. The younger, Ernest, born 12th of March, 1735, was a divinity student, and afterwards Dean of Tübingen.

That the early loss of his other children should have occasioned severe sufferings to so affectionate a father, and that he should have found many pleasures and many cares in educating the rest, was to be expected. But the following extracts from his letters will show his remarkably christian state of mind in such circumstances.

"Our joy of late has been considerably moderated by many a concern about our dear children. In endeavouring to cheer myself and others under the cross which continually attends us, I find use enough for what christian knowledge and experience I have acquired.

"Our heavenly Father has again brought my dear wife safely through her sorrows. On the morning of the 29th of August, the same day on which, three years ago, our little Joanna Regina, now reposing in the churchyard, was born, we received in safety a healthy little girl, to whom, as she was born on the same day of the year, we have given a similar name, Anna Regina. We would not choose quite the same name, because we thought it ought to have some distinction from hers whom we still regard as one of the family, though she is fallen asleep."

That child, however, lived only a year. The following very interesting and affecting letter was written by Bengel to his parents immediately after her funeral.

" *Regina's Day, 7th September*, 1722.

"We thank you for the wreaths you sent us to dress the coffin, &c. of our departed and still beloved babe, Anna Regina, and we thank you still more for your affectionate and parental sympathy, as also for your consoling letter. I feel constrained in return to give you some simple account of what God has discovered to us under this visitation of his love.

"When, six weeks before our child's illness, I was suffering by scarlet fever, I endeavoured, as I had done during a former illness, to get my heart into a state of more than ordinary tenderness; but I was unable, this time, to bring my feelings into such entire self-abasement as I wished. I complained of it to a friend who visited me; and expressed to him my expectation, that some severer affliction, which would better answer the purpose, awaited me. It has arrived, and has answered my wishes. While our dear child was lying under so much suffering, and very near its end, I felt the keenest pangs at the thought of losing it; far more so than I had ever felt before, even when I lost our other dear children. Indeed no occasion of the kind ever distressed me so much. Still I was enabled, without feeling the presence of others any interruption, to attend the dear child with prayers, supplications, and tears, till its soul had gained the victory. I was led, during the whole time, to meditate deeply upon two things: 1. The righteousness of God, which had thus disfigured and destroyed such a little tender frame of body, on account of sin inherited from its parents, and through us from the stock of Adam: and 2, That grace of God by which such a transit through death conducts to life everlasting. Hence our little sufferer's pitiable convulsions and labourings for breath no longer aggravated my distress. My spirit became so cheered and strengthened, that notwithstanding this additional affliction at the prospect of another bereavement, I felt in the inward man, more comfort and enjoyment than I had ever realized in the best pleasures of my life. And as I reclined my head upon my dying child's little couch, I thought I could gladly die with it that moment. After its precious soul was departed, I went into the room where it was laid out, and reclined again by the side of it to repose awhile; and again thought how desirable such an exchange must be. David, at his wretched Absalom's death, was urged by his feelings to exclaim, 'O that I might have died *for* thee!' But there was no need for me to use such a lamentation as this for a child that had never lived to enter into the seductions of a wicked world. In my own case it was a satisfaction that I could utter the sweet plaint of a christian parent's love, 'O that I might have died *with* thee!'

"The bills of mortality show that more than half the human race die in infancy and childhood. As God then gave us *five* children and has now taken away *three*, we are not to think ourselves more hardly dealt with than others; especially as these dear little ones have doubtless entered upon a good exchange. There is much in the consideration, that so many immortal human beings are just shown to *this* world, and so quickly removed into *another;* and that the number of the elect is mainly accomplished in this way. They are as those plants which are gathered and housed the moment they are in season; while others, who arrive at maturer age, are as the fewer plants, which, being left for seed, remain longer out in wind and weather. What pains one's natural feelings most is, that we so much miss the delight we have enjoyed in the lovely innocent ways of a thriving child. But even this is made up for by the sure and certain prospect of what is far better. We do not regret the fall of the sweet and delightful blossoms of our plants and trees, though they soon drop off in such multitudes, because the fruit which succeeds is attended with more substantial enjoyment. Had we had no such child born to us a year ago, it is true we should not have been in our present sorrow; but having attended it this day to its grave, we are temporally in the same situation as if we had never possessed it. And yet we can count it gain to be able to reckon one more child of our own in heaven. It therefore was neither 'made for nought,' nor brought into the world in vain, nor has the care we expended on it been thrown away. And now that such care has ceased, and our responsibility with it, we have the more leisure to attend to the one thing needful, and to direct to this great object, in a more undivided manner, the attention of our two surviving children.

" No sooner was its last struggle over, than the little corpse, with ashes put into its hand, was adorned again with clean linen, flowers, citrons, wreaths, &c., which, indeed, could only die and decay with it; and which afforded but a poor and momentary agreeableness to the eye; but how beautiful must that adorning be, with which our heavenly Father clothes the soul in his own presence, in the presence of the Lord Jesus Christ, and of his holy angels!

" Our chief hindrance to entire resignation is, that we are so much addicted to things present and visible, while eternal realities are as yet so foreign to us, and so little known. But could we take one glance at the condition of a spirit thus departed, we should never regret and lament, as we are apt to do, the decease of relatives and friends; but our grief would rather be on account of the dimsightedness of weeping survivors.

" Surely, when the door of paradise is opened to let in any of our departed friends, delicious breezes blow through it upon us from that abode of blessedness. And we ought to avail ourselves of such refreshing influence; we ought to let it quicken us in following after those who have gone before us, rather than wish those friends back again to a world like this. Who could ever think of congratulating any that have been enjoying heavenly rest and security for ten, a hundred, or a thousand years together, upon their having to return back again to the perils and dangers of the present life? Why, then, should we regard it as an affliction that any one of our number has escaped from such perils, and is only entered into perfect peace and security? If a vacancy has been made in the family circle, let it also be remembered, that another vacancy has been filled up in heaven. The nearer we in this world are approaching to the end of all things, the more welcome should be the thought of dying; because every departed Christian finds that the multitude of the blessed is increasingly outnumbering the militant remnant;

and because the whole family of God are thus successively gathering in, that we may all be together for ever with the Lord.

" At the funeral I accepted the condolence and consolations of kind friends, as heartily as if I had possessed no stock of these for myself; and thus God by their mouth sent me many a good word in season, particularly about the communion we still share in the *total* number of our dear children, who are distributed at present between heaven and earth; likewise about the mutual recognition of friends, whom we shall meet in a better world, &c. As we walked from the house behind the corpse, I looked up to the serene heaven, and my mind itself became as serene, as if no such funeral were going on. In the churchyard, after the coffin lid was removed, and the bunches of flowers, which had been fastened to the white pall, were added to the rest inside, I beheld once more the face of our blessed child. The sun was shining with overpowering brightness in the cloudless sky, and I could not forbear saying to the bystanders, as I pointed first to the corpse and then to the sun, 'so will that dear child look, which is now no longer like itself!' Animated as I felt with such a hope, I could easily have taken the shovel out of the sexton's hands, and myself have done the office of closing up the little chamber of rest; although when my firstborn, our dear little Albert Frederic, was buried, the sight of the ceremony at that time made such a sad disturbance in my heart. But on the present occasion, I went from the grave into the church with so much cheerfulness of spirit, that I even wished the remainder of the funeral service could have been reserved for the time of my own departure.

" We are now, once more, outside the burial gate, under our own roof, and returned to the necessary occupations of this vain and shadowy life. But we feel more sensible than ever, that things are rapidly preparing us for the time when these mortal bodies must be borne back through that gate. 'Blessed be the name of the Lord!'"

In the year 1723 his second son, Joseph, was born, but lived only three months. A third, named John William, lived but fourteen days. On this latter occasion, the sorrowing father wrote as follows:—

" Our John William was just shown to us, and its funeral will take place to-morrow morning. I have thought more about its burial than its birth; not because of unbelief, but to be prepared for the occasion.

"The dear babe suffered, during the fourteen days of its little life, by jaundice, cough, and white eruption, with thrush, and died yesterday evening. You have therefore quite as good reason to congratulate us now as you had fourteen days ago. It came into this world to die and go to heaven. I know not whether this rapid succession of bereavements gives us the *greater* pain in one respect, or the *less* in another; the greater, on account of the deeply-wounded state of our hearts, because we lose them so soon: or the less, because we are more accustomed to it. We are willing, however, to abide in the hands of God; let him do with us whatever seemeth him good. Besides, we have not even yet the afflictions of Job; we have not lost all, nor all at once, like him. We have not lost seven, nor any of our grown children, nor any when absent from us; not even two at once, much less seven at once; nor any by a tempest; all which circumstances together, aggravated the affliction of Job. And even had it been our lot to bear all this, still it would have become us to arm ourselves with Job's patience; which we should have found the easier from having his case and example before us, and from our being now nearer than he was to the great consummation.—Amen. The everlasting God be gracious to us, not forsaking us in the time of adversity."

Bengel educated and instructed his children partly himself, and partly by the help of private tutors in his family. These were young clergymen who had not yet been called to a parochial charge. And his choice of them was directed as much by their real piety as by their literary qualifications. The maxims he observed for his children's education were similar to those he had adopted for the education of his seminary pupils.* "That it is not necessary to make many rules for education, the simplest method being the best. That we should avoid whatever looks artificial, education not being one of the arts. That we should contrive to give children favourable opportunities of getting acquainted with the written word of God: if all be not remembered, something of it here and there is remembered. That scripture instruction should commence with the historical parts, not those which are preceptive; because examples awaken interest and stimulate zeal,—precepts do not. That it is not advisable to load young minds with many explanations, neither to

* See above, Part II. ch. i. sect. 1.

demand too much from them; else they get a distaste and aversion for every thing of the kind. Neither, in spiritual matters, should those who are of more tender age desire too eagerly or prematurely the food which belongs to minds of riper growth. Occasionally, in difficult passages and unknown expressions, to show *briefly* the meaning is all the better. He who would form a channel for a running spring, just clears away obstructions, and the water flows on of itself. There are instances in which the powers of memory and reasoning in young persons have been so overcharged, that in coming to a real comprehension of the subject matter of the christian religion, they have been excelled by those who, having known less beforehand, are better prepared to receive such solid food. The mental elasticity of the former has been deadened,—they have been already used to such topics. Hence in after life we often see persons of this sort very indifferent to spiritual subjects, cloyed with them, carnally secure, self-complacent, if not totally irreligious and profane. Children ought not to be absolutely overruled in every respect by the mere will of superintendents. It is better, provided all opportunity for gross excesses be prevented, to leave young persons in general to their own harmless engagements, in any playful amusement to which their lively spirits may be inclined. Some teachers are apt to check them through fear of excessive levity. But here we should not be too strict and particular. Much patience and forbearance are necessary, lest we prune our young nursery trees too closely, which would only injure them." Bengel treated his children as follows:—He is "kind; does not find fault with them upon every occasion, or for every little thing; lets indifferent matters pass; alleges, at proper times and seasons, suitable motives from holy Scripture; does not dress up such motives in too *familiar* or in *false* colouring, as is often done to set children down at once; deters them now and then with a threatening, or even with gentle correction, in case any self-will is discovered. But should matters come to extremities, as when the child has behaved very ill, or has got into a decidedly bad humour, which cannot so easily be recovered from, severity is out of the question. Endeavour must then be made to get at the child's heart by kindness, by talking to him upon other subjects, &c., that he may gradually lose his peevishness or stubbornness; thus, when he is restored to a better frame of feeling, and not before, he is in a state to receive affectionate reproof and admonition. Let children be drawn into a habit of praying every morning and evening at least; and this either by our praying with them, that they may learn how to do it, or by persuading them to pray for themselves. And we should not neglect to pray constantly *for* them, at our own seasons of retirement. Those parents or teachers, who are persons of spiritual communion with God in Christ, are always the most successful in these attempts. Hereby young persons learn in time to retire for private devotion of their own accord. It is reasonable and most desirable that all our intercourse with them should be serene and even-tempered, cheerful, and kind; and as free as possible from every thing like roughness and peevishness. We should be careful to seek, and avail ourselves of, every favourable opportunity which our own frame of mind, or the disposition of theirs, may give us for tendering them suitable advice. Human education, in general, proceeds (' after' one's ' own pleasure,' Heb. xii. 10; or, according to the Lutheran version) ' after' one's ' own thinking,' (*i. e.* upon one's own notions of what is best;*) but in all this, God attains his object. Let our chief aim with young persons be, to bring them to true integrity of heart and simplicity of mind towards Christ. Faith bears with the failings and defects of *children,* as well as with those of riper years; and teaches us to use meekness and gentleness in setting them right. *This* exercise of faith is the only method of properly gaining their confidence and love, and to such a purpose it is marvellously conducive. What immediately tends to secure and increase their love is, their becoming convinced that we are quietly aiming at their improvement, not by any disparaging and setting them down, but by putting up with their defects and failings. Children of the other sex must be guarded against pertness and forwardness, allured to composed reflection, taught to have a real dread of being rudely talkative, and of bringing home all sorts of tittle tattle, strange surprising news, marvellous stories, &c. I have never wished to make my own daughters too knowing about personal appearance, or intellectual talent. They have been all along accustomed to habits of simplicity, much in the patriarchal way; and thus have been fenced out from gallantry, novel-reading, and impertinent curiosity. What is still wanting, can be made good by the husband; who can now form them to his own taste, which he could not so easily have done, had I trained them more decidedly *à-la-mode.* Free and uncontrolled intercourse between unmarried persons of different sexes is always dangerous, even

* Κατὰ τὸ δοκοῦν αὐτοῖς.

with the very best appearance. A reserve, that may look a little like austerity upon that matter, is more becoming, and has its use."

Bengel was able to add:—"As I have always accounted it a thing of importance and conscience to bring up my children in the right way, so I have never yet experienced from them, or from their children, any thing to wound my heart, but much to afford me unmixed joy; and the blessing of a father and grandfather will rest upon them."

In the year 1748, he found it requisite to send his eldest son to the university, and his younger son to the theological seminary of Blaubeuren; but as he still felt the same tender concern for them as when they were at home, the following extracts will show how affectionately he could advise, and how seriously reprove, when necessary. Subjoined to these extracts are a few others, addressed to his married daughters and sons-in-law, which are quite characteristic of his kind sympathy and affection upon every occasion.

From Bengel's Letters to his younger son, Ernest.

"*Nov.* 20, 1748.

"Be diligent in prayer and in study; act prudently, forbearingly, modestly."

"*Nov.* 22, 1748.

"As to parties of entertainment with music and wine, be on your guard against using yourself to take more of the latter than is good for you. There was no need for you to be concerned as to what you should do for money; never have any anxiety on that account. Be economical in every thing, and you may be sure we shall do for you what is necessary. When you go out (for healthful exercise,) beware of venturousness with rash fellow-students.* God bless you. Pray earnestly and constantly; and be ever thinking upon and looking to Jesus."

"*Dec.* 3, 1748.

"You are by this time accustomed in some measure to a student's life, and you find it, I trust, agreeable. Be very attentive to all my advice, particularly about prayer, taking care of your health, benefiting by the lectures, and judiciously conducting

* Literally, "Beware of the *Blau-caldron*," the source of the Blau, (near Blaubeuren) is thus called in Germany, as being round and deep, and the temptation of the younger students was either to bathe in it, or to amuse themselves upon it with small rafts or skiffs.

yourself towards various associates of your own standing. Every thing has its difficulties at first; but you will soon become quite familiar with matters about you. The Lord our Saviour bless and keep you. We all send our love."

"*Dec.* 19, 1748.

"We are pleased at your gaining the fifth place in your class. Be diligent; and though you may find others going to study directly after their meals, or that they sit up late at night, I hope you will keep to the habits you have learnt at home, taking your needful recreation and rest, and thus turning your hours of study to the better account. And may God bless you."

"*Jan.* 2, 1749.

"Your having thought so soon beforehand of the anniversary of my baptism, by writing an ode for the occasion, I take as a token of your love. We hope you have spent the Christmas holidays as days of holy remembrance, in a way that has been profitable to your soul; and that you entered on the new year yesterday in good health. God bless and be with you."

"*June* 8, 1749.

"Be diligent in prayer—and especially for your two married sisters, as they are just now requiring our particular intercessions."

"*Feb.* 13, 1749.

"I have received a sad account from Maulbronn respecting some of the students there; and I understand they have been keeping false keys, by which they have got out at night for bad practices, &c. This reminds me to charge you ever to beware of being led away by others. If we keep ourselves in the fear of God, by using diligent prayer, we are not easily seduced. May He preserve and bless you."

"*March* 12, 1749.

"Endeavour to 'keep thy heart' in continual recollectedness, and in a consciousness of love to your Saviour. May God, who has now upholden you to the return of your fourteenth birthday, continue to bless you."

"*Feb.* 11, 1752.

"God grant you plenteous grace at the holy communion. Δοκιμάζε σεαυτὸν, ('Prove thy own self.')

"Pray diligently; give to no one any just cause to oppose you; learn to yield obligingly to others; but not so as to be a partaker of other men's sins. Never utter any thing which might not be safely repeated after you."

To his elder son, Victor, whose habits at one time, when he was between eighteen and nineteen years of age, seemed to threaten some deviation from rules of order, he wrote (without having occasion thus to write again,) as follows:

"Foolish son! "*Jan.* 18, 1751.

"No sooner had we begun to hear something tolerable about you, than we have been made exceedingly unhappy by the account we have received of your strange and irregular conduct. I positively command you to go every day from the supper table directly to your room; to abstain from all card-playing, tennis-courts, and places where it is not good for you to go or to find acquaintance; to keep out of all unprofitable company; to mind neither to neglect church nor private prayer, especially morning and evening; to keep your room in good order, as the rules enjoin, and to take special care of your fire and candle, so as not to put your neighbours in fear by your carelessness in this respect; to be always in time at lecture, and diligent with your studies in private; to be strict to truth in speaking and writing; to read the Scriptures regularly, and to think upon your temporal and spiritual welfare; and, moreover, to give me information this week, whether you are purposing to follow these admonitions or not.

"So then, after all, you are not going on well. This will never do. All my former misgivings about you are revived. Don't oblige me to consult about you with our friends, so as to act upon a resolution which no entreaties of yours will alter, and which will be to the following effect; that as we are to have no comfort in you, we will incur no scandalous disgrace on your account. Be concerned, I beseech you, once for all, about duty and propriety; and begin truly to care for your real welfare; instead of going on any longer in such an unpromising way, as obliges all your friends to think of nothing for you but warnings and admonitions. Whatever else may give me trouble at present, you are giving me the most. Well; I have fixed a boundary for you in my own mind; and if you pass it, you will have to thank yourself for any change that will be made in your situation and condition. Reflect then at once, whether you intend to value most the love of parents, relatives, and friends, or the good opinion of a parcel of bad fellows; and whether you prefer to be found a useful member of society, or to become a worthless character, an alien from your family, and dependent, for the rest of your life, upon what strangers may please to think of you, and to do for you. God grant you a sound mind, and a better disposition! Troubled as I am upon your account, the good conduct of your brothers and sisters still enables me to subscribe myself,

"Your consoled father."*

LETTERS TO HIS DAUGHTERS AND SONS-IN-LAW.

I.—*On the Death of his first Grandchild (a daughter's son).*

"My dear daughter, "*Aug.* 3, 1740.

"Use every means to get your mind composed; seek your soul's satisfaction in God. Happy is the soul that knows its God. Learn this, my beloved child, and you will have no need of *me;* I at least shall be then as a supernumerary gift to you. We are at best as the clay in the hand of the potter; but He doeth all things well. The longer you seek him, the more I advise you to seek him as a Father, and as having a Father's heart towards yourself. Thus you will possess and increase in patience. May his grace dispose and govern every one of us!"

II.—*To a Daughter who was suffering by Illness.*

"*Nov.* 5, 1741.

"We hear of your sufferings, my dear, with tender sorrow. Though the sad tidings reached us only this afternoon, we had been particularly remembering you of late in our prayers. We take comfort from this circumstance, as hoping that God may have already answered both us and yourselves. Do not suffer your thoughts to be occupied in needless anxieties. Take care rather to spread before the Lord both this trouble and whatever else may be upon your mind; do it with heartfelt humility; entreating him to manifest his Fatherly compassions towards you and towards your expected offspring. He it is 'who quickeneth the dead;' therefore it is an easy thing with him to remedy whatever may seem against you, and to convert it into a benefit and a blessing. Come only to his paternal lovingkindness, with prayer and earnest supplication, till he effectually answer you, and make you perceive and taste of his perfect peace. Meditate upon the hundred and third psalm, applying it to your present

* The good effect of this letter proved that the serious and determined tone of it was well timed.

circumstances. Begin at the sixth verse, and go on to the end; after which take the first five verses; and what you cannot adopt in a way of thanksgiving, turn into prayer; till the divine blessing shall appoint it as thanksgiving for your own mercies. Apart from your immediate sufferings, remember we *all* carry our 'soul continually in' our 'hand,' though this may be more remarkably your own case at the present moment. Well; let it have the effect of leading you to look beyond mere human help and comfort; to commit and surrender yourself entirely into the hands of God, as your Creator, Father, and Redeemer. His we are, and his son Jesus Christ's; to him if we only live and die, all will be well, however we may be at present situated in other respects. Had we the power to choose concerning things future in this world, we ought to be willing to give it back into his own hands; for, even with our eyes shut, we may safely trust Him, that he will do all things well. It is good to be thoroughly convinced what a poor scheme of happiness it must be at the best, which we are eager enough to form, in a variety of ways, out of our earthly allotments. Hereby we shall learn the more ardently to long after our true paternal home, and steadily to hold fast by him, who is the way, the truth, and the life; abiding always in him, be our own strength ever so fluctuating. Whoso cometh unto him, he will in no wise cast out; if it were not so, the many mansions in his Father's house would not be half so replenished with inhabitants as they are already. What then he has actually done for others, exceeding abundantly above all they could ask or think, the same will he do for yourself, insignificant as you may seem; and this shall conduce to his own glory. Let us devoutly pray for one another and *with* one another; waiting patiently for the help of the Lord. Let us pour out all our heart before him, and abide steadfastly upon him, as our strength and our confidence. Farewell, my beloved. Your own faithful father."

III.—*On the Death of a Grand-daughter.*

"The now happy little E. F. J. is registered in our hearts, though the shortness of her stay in this world has prevented us from seeing her. But she was not born in vain. The difference between her own span of life and ours, was merely this, that she was permitted to reach 'the mark' by the shortest way. Let God now rejoice her spirit in the company of her little brother who preceded her; yes, let God comfort her now after the time that he afflicted her, and thus bestow, according to the good pleasure of his will, the more abiding joy upon my dear Maria, their mother. More particularly with respect to thee, my beloved daughter, may he alleviate thy days and nights, till thou art strengthened to quit the sick chamber; and may it please him to grant to all of us, upon this occasion, renewed faith, love, patience, and hope, in measure ever more full and adequate to our necessities!"

IV.—*Upon an Illness of the Mother of one of his Sons-in-law.*

"We doubt not, that under the good hand of God, all is well with yourselves, and with our worthy and suffering friend, Mrs. —— in particular, whom may our great and faithful High Priest mightily superintend! We are very desirous to know how she is. May God manifest his help and salvation, causing his light to arise ever brighter within her, amidst all the feeling she has of her own nothingness. What is man! and yet what cannot the great Creator make of us, if we cast ourselves simply and entirely into his Fatherly hands! Let your beloved mother be assured of our constant and affectionate remembrance, and let her regard us ever more and more as friends who have her in our hearts. Indeed we are mutually quite assured that we are in her heart, and herself in ours. May the Lord our Saviour apprehend her mightily; show the riches of his grace in his care towards her; and, finally, present her faultless in the presence of his Father with exceeding joy!"

V.—*On the Illness of a Grandchild.*

"*Dec.* 27, 1745.

"I would add a few words to thee, my beloved daughter. You say, you are become in some degree resigned about witnessing the continual sufferings of your dear little one; and well may we learn under the Fatherly hand of God. He is doing all things well; but then we must estimate every event, not according to what our nature feels by it now, but according to the end we shall find answered by it when we are got home. Let us plead and fully depend on the name of Jesus, for the little darling and for ourselves; and let that great name be a real comfort and blessing to us. Your dear uncle, my own brother, often suffered by convulsions in his infancy. As long as there is life there is hope, without requiring any special miracle. Let us only serve God, in prayer and supplication, always waiting *upon* him and waiting *for* him. May he lead every one of us, with his own hand, out of the departing year into the new one!"

VI.—*Upon the Death of this Grandchild.*

"*Feb.* 14, 1746.

"I will now add a word of reply to yourself, my beloved daughter. We may safely say that all has been well with the precious child, while it was with us; and we shall go to it by and by. One benefit of its sufferings is, that our remembrance of it is the more dear and tenderly affecting to us. Heretofore thy child depended upon *thee:* now thy soul follows after *it.* This is all right. Our faithful Father in heaven does it out of mere kindness. He may have sent it as a chastening, but he designs it as a benefit. May the consolations of God, which are neither few nor small, be intimately experienced by both of you for permanent benefit! May he cause his face to shine upon yourselves the brighter after this tribulation! Trouble not thyself about the past sufferings of the dear little creature; she is now removed from all suffering, and among the spirits of the just who are made perfect. If the merciful God has commanded man to be merciful to his beast, and even to the bird upon her nest,* how is it possible he can ever gratuitously inflict so many sufferings upon our dear little ones? Doubtless there is a wise, good, and benevolent reason for it."

VII.—*To another Daughter.*

"May the strength of Jesus our Lord be found perfected in thy weakness! Pray; yes, pray and hope. Venture a childlike look towards *your* heavenly Father and *ours;* relying upon the power and privileges he has already granted us in his dear Son: and let me know how that look has sped."

VIII.—*To a Son-in-law, who was going upon a journey of business to Vienna.*

"*Dec.* 1749.

"Heartily do I wish that your journey may be prospered. God grant you daily tokens of his paternal care over you! A Christian's manner of transacting any worldly business, especially in money matters, may be turned to a strong evidence that he is seeking the things which are unseen and eternal. Natural ties

* Deut. xxii. 6, 7.

oblige us to do all affectionate service to relatives and others; but how we are to do it is, for wise and good reasons, left to our own discretion. Yes, 'the ways of the Lord are right,' in this as well as in every thing else; it is only 'the transgressors' who 'fall here,' but 'the just' keep their footing, and 'walk uprightly.' Straightforward faithfulness, prudence, and discretion, will always have the best final issue. It is the faithfulness of God that preserves us, so that surrounding business of the world does not carry away our hearts, but only constrains us to be the more careful to 'keep them' collected 'with all diligence.' When the 'love of God' governs us in things *temporal* as well as spiritual, 'all things *must* necessarily work together for our good.'"

IX.—*To another Son-in-law.*

"*Jan.* 2, 1752.

"Your letter of yesterday serves as a good new year's beginning for another annual course of communion in christian love between us, upon all its most essential matters. The love abiding in your two selves owns and blesses with *us* the goodness of God; and commends us to that goodness in these days (of remembrance), as, indeed, it always does. We also do the same for yourselves. May God bless our beloved friend and son-in-law in his ministerial duties, and in all other concerns engaged in for his glory; may he bless likewise your mutual union, and your dear children with you! We remain assured of your love, even as you continue to be assured of ours.

"Yesterday I attended court as one of the deputation appointed to carry up the new year's address, in company with Counsellor Moser, who *read* it. To-day I have been at the sermon, and heard the court chaplain preach, as I did yesterday the senior preacher to the court. The wishes expressed by them in their sermons (particularly with reference to the new year,) were very energetic and full of meaning."

CHAPTER II.

AS A FRIEND.

THOUGH we have already seen much of Bengel's christian communion with a variety of friends in correspondence, yet, for a clearer view of his private life, it is worth while here to notice further particulars of the kind.

A large part of his early life was spent in pretty much retirement. That disposedness to true religion, that holy seriousness, which characterised even his childhood and youth, necessarily kept him aloof from all circles of worldly frivolity. But his various knowledge, his integrity, and affectionate behaviour, made him kindly regarded everywhere, and drew the hearts of many towards him. Thus even in his younger days at Stuttgart he was not without friends, whose intimacy he retained to the end of life. At Tübingen the number of his particular friends was increased; and a common fellowship of faith, love, and hope bound them for ever together. Bengel, at that period of his life, was remarkable for preferring the friendship of persons much older than himself; but in his later years, as if desiring to repay with interest the benefits he had thus received, he was equally remarkable for his familiar friendship with those who were far his juniors, some of whom were either then, or formerly had been, his own pupils. When he was at Halle, upon his tour for educational and literary information, he had the happiness of commencing the valuable friendship of Matthias Marthius, the well known and accurate editor of the Byzantine MS. We have already noticed him and Bengel frankly and affectionately corresponding upon apocalyptical subjects, (see chap. xvii.) The union between these two friends is further beautifully seen in the following passage of a letter from Marthius, in the year 1720:—

" I am at present so fully occupied, that I should not easily have been persuaded even to sit down and write a letter, were it not, that having been thinking of you, my dear friend, before God, I feel at this moment a strong impulse to express to you my christian love and remembrance. And how can I help loving you, with whom I have so often bowed the knee at the throne of Grace, and thus laid the foundation of a friendship which is to last for ever! May He who, undoubtedly of his special goodness and wisdom, brought us together at Halle, held us so long together under the same roof, and fed us at the same table, sustain us still from the plentiful table of his own grace, and grant us to meet one day in glory as in our Father's house, where the Saviour is preserving many abiding places for them that love him!"

This valuable friendship had extended to the 9th of August, 1734, when Marthius sweetly fell asleep in the faith of his Redeemer. Only a short time before his death, he had given directions that all his sermons should be buried with him in his coffin, and that his funeral should be as private and plain as possible.

Bengel enjoyed a longer term of friendship with prelate Ph. H. Weissensee, whose numerous and most affectionate letters, found among Bengel's papers, fully testify it. We much regret that Bengel's answers to them have not been found, as passages of them, which reappear in those of Weissensee, are of so amiable and delightful a character, that one cannot but wish to peruse the whole. The correspondence of these faithful friends was upon every subject connected with their ministry, the state of their own minds, and their family concerns; and all their communications were evidently seasoned by mutual love to their common Lord. Had we not already somewhat exceeded the prescribed limits of this memoir, we should gladly have inserted many extracts from those interesting letters of Weissensee; but we have only room for the few which follow:—

" *May* 11, 1721.

" During nearly the whole of this vacation our heavenly Father has led me in a different way from that I should have chosen for myself. Thus I am returned home, almost discontented in some respects; especially about the shortness of my hurried visit to yourself. But the Lord is hereby showing me more and more how good and requisite such things are for me; and the more inefficient and unworthy I feel myself to be, the oftener does he grant me moments in which I am overwhelmed by a sense of the glory of Christ, my interest in him, and communion with him; still my unworthiness of such vouchsafements fills me with sacred awe, and makes me almost tremble.—Hallelujah!

"I should like to know how yon worthy tutors at Denkendorf manage respecting the injunction in the statutes, that the students are to converse in Latin. We frequently attempt it here, and it goes on for a while; but every little rise retards the whole team, till at length it stops altogether; and one cannot always be applying stimulants; and as for reproofs, it seems best that they should be reserved for any delinquencies of a more serious nature."

"*Feb.* 14, 1724.

"The work of Marthius which you kindly sent me, shows the well ordered mind of a plain and honest friend, a pious Christian, and a good minister of Jesus Christ; it has arrived most welcomely, for I feel it quite awakens me. Such warm-hearted, savoury, and purifying effusions and utterances of grace, as God still occasionally favours us with, are beneficial in counteracting those chills of despondency with which we are apt to be overtaken in the cold air and iniquity of these Last Times. They dispose us to pause, think of, and anticipate rather what is to be expected of the divine mercy, than what our sins might deservedly bring upon us. Presburg is a good school for practical divinity; yes, the people of God have always thriven best under oppression; and never in general where they have been made much of, and looked up to. God forgive me if it is presumption, to have often wondered that he did not cause his word to have free course everywhere; or at least in our Germany, upon her awakening at the Reformation; instead of which, he has reserved to himself his own prerogative and glory. He best knew what was good for his children, and for his kingdom in general; and how the different medicines for our health required to be mixed. Had the gospel found at first a general acceptance amongst us, its fulness for the harvest would, in my opinion, have long since arrived; as may be seen in some places to have been the case; and if such sights as these are so refreshing, what a joy will arise hereafter at the universal result!

"Take one thought more, which I find in dear Marthius, to God's praise, and my own shame. He says, 'there are some who come to me at my house, to pray with me, and to gain more acquaintance with the Scriptures. Others I visit myself, to inquire after the church which is in their house,' &c. My brother! how is such a poor project-maker as myself to stand, who have poured out sighing supplications before God to the same effect often and often, but have never felt able to break through so many difficulties in my way? Will my *good desires* be of any use to me when I stand before the tribunal of the Lord? will they be any joy to me in that day? Surely they will then be but of little use to me. Jesus must now and ever be my all in all, &c.

"Your industry in the New Testament shows itself in your last letter; and I have only regretted that with all your extensive inquiries after manuscripts, you have had to shake many an empty tree. But in no instance of the kind will the providence of our God be unglorified, neither will your faithful exertions be unblest or unrewarded."

"*June* 4, 1725.

"All the copies of your *Prodromus* which you sent me are 'cast upon the waters,' excepting one, which I reserve for the *pater provincialis* of the Franciscans; for I hope to beat up some game in that bushy quarter. I must beg you to entrust me with a few more for unforeseen occasions," &c.

We close these extracts from Weissensee's letters with part of one he wrote to Bengel's widow on the day of her husband's decease.

"You have done me no more than justice, in considering me as one of those of his friends whose pain at this afflictive bereavement bears the nearest resemblance to what you yourself are suffering. And you show that you thus consider me, in your having transmitted to me, without a moment's delay, the painful tidings of your dearest husband's departure. It is a departure, however, from time into blissful eternity. Still the painful feelings which such a separation occasions me, resemble your own as nearly as any one's feelings well can. For I have now to lament the departure of a friend, whose affectionate intimacy, founded in God, I have enjoyed for more than forty years; which has been tried and strengthened by long and uninterrupted communication upon every occurrence or difficulty that we met with in our ministry or family concerns; and which, up to only a few days since, has been cherished by such frequent interviews and converse between us before the Lord, as surely may promise me the greatest benefit both for time and eternity."

Other intimate friends of Bengel were Samuel Urlsperger, dean of Herrenberg, and afterwards senior Lutheran minister at Augsburg; and Andrew Christian Zeller, who had been Bengel's colleague at Denkendorf, and was afterwards prelate of Anhausen, where he died in 1743. Bengel too had lived upon the best understanding with all his colleagues, and in familiar friendship with many of the most excellent and pious of his country. With his own relatives he carefully maintained a close connexion, and herein exemplified the fidelity of a real Christian. He had also the happy art of turning to good account the favour expressed towards him, on various occasions, by noble and princely personages; so as not to be troublesome to them, and yet not to forget that the advantages of his station, and of his spiritual as well as intellectual endowments, were given him by Divine Providence for the purpose of exciting in such personages a cordial and persevering endeavour to promote the kingdom of God in themselves and others. Striking instances of all this are found in his numerous letters to various friends and relatives; a few more extracts of which we shall here insert, referring our readers to the pastoral letters given above, in Part II. chap. 2, sect. 3.

On the death of Zeller, Bengel wrote to Professor Smalcalder, of Tübingen, one of his younger friends, as follows:—

"*Jan.* 6, 1744.

"The tidings of Zeller's death came to me in a letter from his son. Many years had we been intimate. Communion in official duties and private intercourse had ever knit us closer and closer together. Still I was not overpowered as by any sudden shock at the news; for the bad state of his health had long put me upon preparing to lose him. I always found him a tried friend, and he was equally assured how much I loved him. The loss of him is very painful to me; and I particularly need such friends as yourself, my dearest cousin, to assist me in bearing it. I still love Zeller, even in death; and I have very long had such love for yourself, that I can hardly imagine you likely to be the gainer of more by my appointing you heir to his friendship; but as you will have it so, I do thus appoint you; though I think that I shall be the gainer by it," &c.

Bengel's father-in-law, Mr. Seeger, having, from a presentiment of his approaching departure from this world, distributed several personal articles as memorials to his children, Bengel wrote to him on the occasion as follows:—

"*Nov.* 12, 1738.

"As our beloved and revered father has been pleased to send to his children several personal articles and pieces of furniture,

I write to say, that these little remembrances of parental love, call forth our dutiful and affectionate thanks. And we feel occasion thus given us for some additional thoughts, one or two of which I shall here endeavour to set down. Our natural life in this world makes us to need a variety of things which God of his goodness bestows. But when a pilgrim has reached so near (as you have) to the end of his course, and is just coming up to the mark towards which he has been so long pressing forward, he finds his spirit so much more disencumbered, and on the wing for heaven, that he can easily strike out of his inventory of temporals one thing after another, and regard them *all* as 'the things which are left behind,' that he may the more entirely, purely, and freely 'reach forth,' as he is now better enabled to do, 'after those which are before.' These latter are the things towards which our heavenly calling in Christ Jesus is drawing us, and which the divine power and faithfulness have enabled so many to attain before us. God has tried them, and they have been found faithful.

"Our dear temporal father is conscious of the love he bears towards his relatives, and this puts him upon meditating all sorts of kindnesses. How much more then, and far exceeding, must be the love of our God, the Father everlasting! And if so, let our backward and fearful hearts become emboldened once for all to approach him, by the Spirit of adoption, with the holy familiarity of dear children, that we may in simplicity enjoy and rejoice in his merciful kindness, and in the access which he gives us to himself. Surely this is no more than what the gracious right he has conferred upon us in his only-begotten Son, has put within our own power. As he has made us sensible that for our part we have no title to the smallest favour from him, so let us give him all the glory, by gladly receiving the supply of our every need out of the riches of his glory by Christ Jesus; and most thankfully suffer his Spirit of grace to pervade our whole nature, so as to bear witness with our spirit that we are children of God, and thus to make all within us and about us clear and serene. This also, we can say, is what our soul truly longeth after," &c.

From a letter to his brother, a magistrate at Sulz:—

"Have nothing to do in secret with any unrighteous cause, and in public stand up for the honour of God, and you will be immovable."

Upon the death of this only brother, he wrote to his widow as follows:—

"Most beloved and respected sister! "*July* 26, 1752.

"Let the living and eternal God refresh the spirit of our ever dear and late afflicted brother. He is now set free from all his severe and tedious sufferings, and is entered into his everlasting rest. God had bestowed on him a good preparation for it; and we had been able for some time so to expect the change, as to become daily more familiar with those topics of sorrow and consolation which are often wanted for occasions less foreseen. In such a transitory life as this, seasons of temporary separation from our dearest friends must arrive; but whenever, as in the present case, there is a well-grounded hope concerning the blessedness of the departed, and that we shall soon follow them, we can the more meekly acquiesce in these appointments. I return you, my most beloved and respected sister, in my own name as well as in that of my only and dear departed brother, all imaginable gratitude for the unwearied love and constant faithfulness you have ever shown him during a sacred union of so many years; yes, in all his illnesses, and especially, as we ourselves personally witnessed, during this last distressing one. A large measure of the trials allotted to yourself is thus, we trust, now overcome; and may the consolations of the divine presence alleviate all that our beloved and respected sister still endures! If any or all of us can be of the least service to you, we shall ever prefer showing our faithful affection by more than words. Meanwhile I send you the accompanying small memorial of our love, which may be communicated to friends attending the funeral, and to others who feel an interest in what so tenderly concerns us," &c.

Bengel, by way of recreation in sacred thoughts for himself and friends, occasionally employed himself in metrical composition. The following may serve to give an idea of the piece referred to in the preceding letter:—

Love undivided in Death. (*On the happy Departure of his Brother, Joseph Bengel, Esq., July* 25, 1752.)

My brother dies! that only, truly dear,
  Fraternal spirit, genuine, oft well tried!
Long tedious pain had prov'd his patience here;
  He's gone! and who could wish he had not died?
Yet, who can help but miss him, and exclaim,
'Twas consolation to pronounce his name!

We from our youth were one in mind and heart;
  Still more, when early orphans we were left,
Our thoughts might differ, us they could not part;
  Of mutual love we never were bereft;
In christian mutual love we liv'd as one;
In union that could never be undone.

In this blest union our life-partners shar'd,
  And every branch of my own tender vine,
And wedded scions that with these were pair'd,
  Liv'd as thy children, and their fruit as thine;
All these possess'd thy heart most fatherly;
And joy of mine in them, was joy to thee.

Nor change of place, nor time could us divide,
  Station, nor office with its cares, estrange;
Things that put old remembrances aside,
  And death itself, whose ordinance is change,
Alter'd us not; we lov'd as heretofore,
And heart to heart was but united more.

Nor thy own death divides us, lo! 'tis gain;
  It gives our love more room to rise and flow;
In heaven our treasure and our hearts remain,
  With Him who made us one in heart below;
Death by our love in Christ is overcome;
My love hastes after, thine has reach'd its home.

Thy life was ever an example bright
  Of godly fear, and steadfastness in grace;
To thee was burdensome all vain delight;
  Righteous wast thou in word, and work, and place;
Thy Saviour's glory here was in thine eye;
Thou'rt with him now, and find'st it gain to die.

A spring of life within thee long had flow'd,
  And its bright fulness, at thy latest hour,
Such heavenly peace, and blest assurance show'd,
  In Christ's remember'd words* applied with power,
That all who knew thee in thy walk of faith,
Joy'd at what God had done for thee in death.

* This good man, long before his death, had chosen for his funeral text those words of our Saviour's prayer, in John xvii. 20,—"Neither pray I for these alone, but for them also who shall believe on me through their word," &c.; and on his death-bed he found strong consolation from these words, and was constantly meditating upon them.

Thy parting language would I call to mind:
  "Jesus, my Saviour lives! I find him true!
And O, my long lov'd brother, may'st thou find
  Him thus with thee, and with thy dear ones too!
With me he bids the fear of death to cease;
I only wait to enter into peace.

"Soon, very soon, in him we blest shall be!
  I, in his righteousness complete, but go
Awhile before thee: thou shalt follow me.
  Ready am I; may God support thee so,
That we may meet again, and with the Lord!
We're ever, ever with him! trust his word!"

Amen, amen! Thy happy death awakes
  A wish to die!—whatever dying be,
Thou hast o'ercome it; and thy spirit takes
  Its flight with scarce a sigh:—I'd follow thee!
My heart feels joy at such a thought arise,
And, "O were I too with the Lord!" replies.

For that good part now quite by thee possess'd,
  For peace with God, in pure and endless day,
How must I, dearest brother, hail thee blest,
  From this bad world escap'd so far away;
Rising in praise of HIM, the stars above,
Who drew us to himself, and bade us love!

Yet, gracious Lord! refresh one mourner dear;
  Comfort her thou, as none beside thee can.
God of the widow, Saviour, look on her,
  Who mourns the husband, and the christian man!
O pity her, dissolv'd in nature's tears;
Say to her, "Weep not," and dispel her fears.

Eternal God, our Saviour! thou art HE!
  Eternally abides thy gracious throne:
With heart and mind we jointly cry to thee:
  Thy will is good; and let thy will be done.
Teach us it more and more: so shall we blend
Our lives of mutual love with thine, that knows no end.

To Pastor Hofholz, of Zavelstein.

"*Dec.* 27, 1717.

"Friends who have been personally separated so long as we have been, can easily forget one another, if there are not between them some special occasions to prevent it. We, however, have not forgotten each other. No; your last letter (of the 16th inst.) has made me less liable to it than ever. Your uprightness before God and man had secured my affection all along; but I now discern in you what much enhances its value, namely, a blessed poverty of spirit; and these two qualities united, are the very essence and excellence of every true steward of the mysteries of God.

"All the writings of the beatified Spener supply plentiful suggestions for helping us to this state of mind. His own example breathed it; and the account we have of his great usefulness as a minister and a writer, shows it. On the other hand, it is but too evident, that men in general either have not built at all, or at least not diligently, upon the foundation whereon it is evident that *he* built. The apologies of those three men, Gmelin, Schmoller, and Bauer,* which I have just met with, serve to confirm me in this sentiment.

"My preparation text for the late jubilee of the Reformation had already conducted me to a further conclusion still; for from that text I inferred and stated, that *the Lord Jesus Christ himself is preaching repentance to the fallen protestant church.* From the very beginning of the world human nature has been always disposed to retrograde, especially among those who have been favoured with the outward knowledge of God by preaching and the Scriptures. Thus even our own forefathers, after the Reformation, dealt untruly with their God, though, in comparison with their more degenerate descendants, they may be accounted honest towards him. If we look back to the time of Spener, and further back to the age of Luther, we see the Reformation in the one case, and a revival of religion in the other, each thriving under persecution; then, as we descend the stream of time from either of those periods, we find that, proportionately as our church has been counted unworthy of persecution, in the same proportion has it declined from true Christianity. Yet whoever, even in our own apostate days, is willing to walk in that measure of light which still remains with us, will find it can

* They jointly published a work complaining, in a sectarian spirit, of the corruptions of the church.

yield him saving benefit; and the more he is really in earnest, (I may well add this, for such characters are become very rare,) the more certainly and abundantly will he partake of that benefit." (Is. xl. 29—31.)

To the same.

"May the Most High fill with wisdom, light, holy boldness, and power, the sermons which shall be preached for the edification of the summer visitors at Teinach! * Even in sacred history, as well as in our own times, we see many a preacher finding but little fruit of his ministry among his regular hearers, and yet becoming an instrument of grace to strangers, (Luke iv. 27.) And in the place, my dear friend, where you are at present residing, you will find opportunities of casting the net to advantage; for thither numbers resort, who are not so likely to receive the testimony of their own ministers, (who, knowing their character, have to address them accordingly,) as they are from others, who, being strangers to them, throw the net at a venture among a mixed multitude."

To the same.

"*Dec.* 27, 1718.

"If any thing in my last letter has given occasion to salutary thoughts in the mind of a friend who seeks after God, then the Lord be praised for it, and grant from the riches and fulness of his mighty grace, not only more and more replenishment for ourselves, but seed also for the hearts of others, and fruit in their salvation. Yet when I consider how that same grace has been drawing me these many years in so alluring a manner, and that I am now arrived at the meridian of my temporal course, or rather a little beyond it, so that my time of probation in serving the will of God must be at least more than half expired, I feel I have but too much cause to lament having borne so little fruit, and that of this little, scarcely any is come to perfection. As such backwardness renders me liable to I know not how much merited reproach, this, as well as other considerations, would distress me the more, were it not that I bear about me a continual sense of my poverty, which makes me look away from myself altogether to the unfailing favour of God, as entirely as if I had never offended in a single point; yes, as freely as if I were no sinner at all; nevertheless, as self-abasedly

* A favourite watering place.

as if I had never done a single good action, much less were good in myself. But when any sober testimony of sincere and impartial brethren happens to be given in my favour, as telling me, that by the power of our chief Shepherd, who is the head of the body, some virtue of his saving help has been conveyed to others, even through *me*, I certainly feel encouraged by it; yes, it cheers me only to learn, that such a dim taper as I am, has not been lighted in vain. Still I must tell you, my dear friend, that I cannot allow you to commend me for a humility so perfectly pure as you will have mine to be. Do not pronounce me quite emulation-proof, with regard to other labourers in my own department. It is true I feel my own vast emptiness; (magnum inane:) and yet, if I am not insensible of some gratification when even the ignorant and inexperienced express a breath (auram) of pleasure in my works, surely a laudatory epistle from one on whose opinion I set so much more value, is still more likely to stir in me some feeling of self-complacency; though the feeling is almost sure to be followed by an increase of self-humbling thoughts. Let us then, (for it truly becomes us,) go on dealing with one another in genuine brotherly simplicity, as well in official respects as in every thing else; constantly caring to maintain in ourselves, and in one another, a perpetual sense of *why we are here*, and provoking one another to love and to good works; that by the Divine help, we may build up ourselves, and many more, in the knowledge of our God and of his Christ, and in all that real good which only such knowledge can produce. By intercourse and communion of this sort, whatever would improperly mix with an intimacy like ours, will fly off and disappear."

To the same.

"Beloved Brother, "*Jan.* 4, 1719.

"If the thought of not having written to you till now, could put me upon doubting at all of my love to you, I might allay any such doubt by considering, that at the entrance of this new year, I have been thinking of you as one of my very best friends. My heart's desire is, that the Lord, by whose faithful help those who cleave to Him have been enabled once more to leave behind them the troubles and cares of many a day of the past year, may make this new year a year of great grace to my very worthy and beloved brother; and may favour him with much advantage that even yet may be derived from the experience and trials of the year which is just past. In thus expressing my best wishes, I am not inclined to specify what particular blessings I would heartily desire for others; this I leave to the goodness of that Divine Wisdom which passeth man's understanding. Each person also better knows than I do, what particular blessings he stands in need of; yes, he knows this best at the time when such blessings are immediately wanted. Therefore let my dear brother, with his truly amiable partner in life, be entirely commended by my poor self, both for the present and for all future time, to our own heavenly Father, the merciful disposer of all things. And though, personally, we are far apart one from another, may He, the longer we live, the more closely unite us in communion of spirit, and in its consequent perpetual flow of mutual love!"

To Schmidlin, Dean of Lewisburg.

(Congratulation upon his new appointment.)

"*Oct.* 22, 1720.

"What you have to desire and pray for in your new situation, is better known to yourself than to me in my cloister. The Lord hear your prayer, and fulfil all your desires! May he vouchsafe you light, power, love, wisdom, and holy confidence in himself; and grant that a blessing on your labours may be manifested to men, and before the angels of God! May Christ our Saviour increase his dominion and triumphs, by your instrumentality, among those to whom you are now sent in his name; making you feel the tenderest compassionate care for his own sheep which are scattered abroad, giving you also vigorous and active courage against the wolves, and a good report amongst both! May his Holy Spirit be manifested in you as a spirit of power, love, and a sound mind, that you may deliver your testimony to 'the truth which is after godliness,' so as not to faint nor be discouraged. The Lord be to you and yours a shield and exceeding great reward, and your constant guide in this new path, that you may be found approved in his sight, and in the sight of all his servants. Amen and Amen!"

To Captain von Franke.

"*Dec.* 12, 1747.

"It much affects me to hear of the sad accident your dear and worthy lady has met with. May our faithful God, who in such serious danger has prevented what would have been more distressing, receive our thanks and praise for his providential care and sparing mercy! May he prosper also the means used for her perfect recovery; alleviate the weariness of the sick couch, and give to this affliction a happy issue! Our sufferings in the outward man have their special and essential use for the inner man; therefore may the holy love already so well established, my dear sir, between yourself and your respected lady, only abound more and more, through your mutual unanimity, in enduring affliction together! Days or hours spent in worldly amusements and in the gratifications of the flesh, not unfrequently leave painful stings behind; but if we let our seasons of affliction awaken us to more entire and pure compliance with the holy will of the blessed God, we may have to remember such seasons with constant thankfulness and joy, from having experienced how truly all things work together for good to them that love God. And as his only begotten Son condescended to come into this miserable world for the very purpose of drawing us up to his own heavenly mansions, by making all troubles and disappointments befalling us in the way, even helpful to our advancement thither, how blessed is it to be able to surrender ourselves without reserve to the government and appointments of his grace, and to repose our entire care and dependence on that grace continually! May our God impart to us real and sweet experience of all this, especially for the approaching commemoration of our Saviour's nativity; an event by which the word of truth has so wonderfully manifested to us his kindness and love."

Benigna Maria, born Countess Reuss, sister-in-law of Zinzendorf, having written to Bengel, and informed him of the death of her brother, Count Henry XXIX., Bengel replied as follows:—

"*Dec.* 7, 1747.

"As your ladyship has been so early prepared for the departure of your now happy brother, and so sweetly supported under this severe loss, by having your mind continually directed to the Lord Jesus, there is no harm occasioned by my having been unable to give your letter an earlier reply. When the door opens to admit any pilgrim into the better world, it always permits some escape of the heavenly breezes to refresh and cheer the weeping survivors, and to strengthen them for their own departure. This, I have no doubt, you have experienced; and may God manifest to your ladyship and to your noble relatives, under this trying bereavement, a still larger measure of his grace!

"My thoughts of Count Zinzendorf's system and religious connexion have long led me to conclude, that if these remain confined within our European pale of Protestantism, they will neither spread in Europe much farther than they have done, nor will find, except at a very few stations, any permanent reception. But should they spread forward into Asia, (as the writer of a work, entitled, 'A Portrait of the Kingdom of the Cross,' anticipates) then, if not before, the Christian world will have to open its eyes, and to pay no common attention to this people and to their system.

"Of the tragical events in Lucerne, I have received information from various quarters. The writings of Arndt and Lucius must have produced considerable good effect there. Schmidli was strangled by order of Filippo Acciajole di Fiorenza, the Pope's nuncio; and all protestant books that could be seized were burnt. In France, Hungary, Poland, and Germany, this murderous spirit of popery still continues to show itself. In Poland, within these few years, a decretal was read, Sunday after Sunday in four hundred churches, prohibiting to *heretics* every privilege of fire, bread, commercial and civil intercourse, and the use of the public baths. Persecutions of this sort will not cease till the complete tribulation shall break out under the last great dispensation. Probably, for a time, they will fluctuate much in the same manner as they have done; but by and by they may suddenly break out like a tempest. Let them ebb and flow as they will, only let us continually keep in view, as we ever should, the great banner of grace, mercy, and peace through Jesus Christ our Lord, and be careful, as indeed we must, never to let go from our hearts the all-penetrating and all-prevailing remembrance of his name.

"I remain," &c.

CHAPTER III.

CHARACTERISTIC NOTICES AND GLEANINGS.

THE miscellany we here insert under the above title, may serve to give a further idea of Bengel in his social or private character.

The brief Sermon.

Bengel travelled once in a stage-coach with several gay persons, who being rather heated to merriment by wine, sang drinking songs in chorus together. He kept himself quite aloof: but at last they called upon him to give them a song. He replied,—"If I sing, you must have a sermon afterwards;"—and they were quiet and orderly the rest of the way.

The Friars.

He once had a visit from some Roman Catholic friars of the order which is the most general of all; namely, of that "whose god is their belly." He received them with hospitality, and as they felt themselves perfectly at home, they began to talk in their usually familiar and easy manner, about snug accommodations, good cheer, &c., and by and by got into jestings hardly convenient; seemingly flattering themselves that they were entertainers of the company. Bengel still continued affable and kind, though he said but little, which he took occasion to do at opportunities for any thing solid and serious. He hoped thus to leave upon their minds a deeper impression than if he had directly and pointedly rebuked them.

The reproving Look.

Two young ladies from the country, who had been brought up in a strict religious way, and had been always kept from going to balls, theatres, &c., being on a visit in the metropolis, (Stuttgart,) heard so much there in praise of the amusements of the town, that they felt a wish to go to the opera; and as they were on their way to it, they met in the street a tall reverend-looking person, and knew it was Prelate Bengel, for whom they had heard their parents express such high veneration. His serious eye caught theirs as they passed him, and as they looked behind after him, they found he was doing the same; and his look was to their imagination as if it had taken them by surprise, and as if it seemed to say, "Children, are you going the right way?" So, however, it was, that changing their minds, they turned directly down another street, and went home, ashamed of their worldliness in wishing to go to a play.

The vacant Seats in Heaven.

A lady of rank being once in company with Bengel, addressed him as follows. "I hear, Mr. Provost, that you are a prophet; therefore perhaps you can tell us whether, in the world above, there are any reserved seats for people of quality." He replied, "I certainly, madam, am no prophet, though I acknowledge that God has granted me some acquaintance with his revealed word; and this informs me that reserved seats indeed there are; and that, alas, most of them are sadly in want of occupants. So I read in Matt. xix. 24, and 1 Cor. i. 26."

The poor Sinner.

When he was at Tübingen in 1748, a peasant of the neighbourhood came up to him just as he was leaving the town, and said, how happy he was for once in his life to get a sight of him. He replied, "Well, my good friend, you have only seen one more poor sinner that depends entirely upon the mercy of God."

Provisions for the current Day.

"I act," he said, "like the mistress of a family, who, when a visitor comes in unexpectedly, sets before him the provisions she happens to have at hand. For I always, when any friends call upon me, converse with them just about what my mind is engaged in at the time. As I live by the actual use of my breath, without having to consider what quantity of air I have inhaled in time past, so for my present spiritual life I am not obliged to recur to what I dwelt upon yesterday or the day before, but have only to receive as from God, and to make use of, what he gives me every hour for myself, or for ministering to others. When any person has received a profitable word of mine, so that the little seed in the good ground begins to make its appearance, I have often to admire that power from on high, which has rendered beneficial what did not take its origin from me, but of which I, in much weakness and unprofitableness, was only the medium. It is God who every way worketh all in all. May he work great good by those who have been committed to my charge; may it amount to much more than has ever been accomplished by myself! I am getting into the wane of this life, and it delights me to see any of my younger brethren active, and showing themselves strong, however much they may shame *me*.

Jesus the Standard of our Self-knowledge.

"In trying and proving my own conduct, I endeavour to realize some situation in which our blessed Saviour stood; I think of the variety of characters he had to deal with, and how in every case he judged righteous judgment. Then I inquire of conscience how I should have acted had I been one of those characters, and how the Saviour would have replied or acted by me in return. The answer I thus get from myself, in agreement with the tenor of his written word, is of more value to me than any opinion that can be formed of me by others."

Utility of the Classics.

"If my usual style has any peculiarity, it is that of omitting needless words and things. Here I have somewhat imitated the ancients. Constant reading of the classics has given me quite a liking of their simplicity."

Benefit of Retirement.

"Retirement secures me from what would be too much of this world's din. Thus I get leisure for building up myself in a recollected consciousness of God; without which, we are liable to pass away our term of life we know not how. Very important is it to discern the golden opportunities which God gives us for this purpose, as well as the precious moments of day or night, when he is specially nigh to us. Meditation is sweet to me at all times, but particularly in the night season. Matt. xiv. 13."

Concealment from the World.

"Often have I much wished that I could pass along my appointed way through this world, and be so little noticed as to be no object for the attacks of slander and misrepresentation. This is why I have now heartily declined all learned correspondence with the great doctors of the age, and confined myself principally to correspondence with my former pupils. I feel in this respect like that ancient father,* who desired a disciple of his to bury him directly after his decease, and to raise no monument, not even the mould, over his grave."

Bengel to his Biographers.

"If friends of mine should ever choose to write any memoir of my life, I can only say, with respect to what they may notice of me as a Christian, that I sincerely hope they will spare themselves the trouble of all eulogy; and let God be glorified. I wish no one to think of me beyond what he seeth me to be; and that what he does see in me, may be referred entirely to the divine mercy; for I am but a vessel of that mercy. All I am and have, both in principle and practice, is to be summed up in this one expression—*the Lord's property*. My belonging totally to Christ, as my Saviour, is all my salvation and all my desire. I have no other glory than this, and want no other.

"With respect to my writings, as taken notice of in any such delineation of my character, perhaps it will be difficult entirely to acquit me of over-curiousness. But whatever may be said of me as having laboured conscientiously to communicate what I had learnt, the staple nourishment of my spiritual life has been sought, as my friends well know, in gospel truths of the plainest kind. These have I embraced with sincere simplicity of heart and singleness of mind, apart from all subtile refinement and curious investigation. Faith, hope, love, meekness, and humility, have been my cardinal points."

Bengel's own way of Thinking and Acting.

"To learn thoroughly one's own disposition, requires constant self-observation. My principle has been all along, neither to take any individual Christian for my peculiar model, nor to obtrude myself as such upon others. For in the former case we may incur the error of servile imitation, under the idea that the person whom we regard as our model, has good reasons for every thing he does, while, perhaps, he has no reasons of the kind; and in the latter case, we may do many a thing ourselves from no better motive than to have in it numerous followers and imitators.

"My own personal mode of thinking varies totally from that even of some pious people, who are apt to be mere imitators of

* This some say was St. Anthony; others Hilarion. See the Author's "Acts and Sayings of the Ancient Fathers," p. 479. (Stuttg. published by J. F. Steinkopff.)

another. Our fundamental principles are the same; but we act upon them quite differently. In this respect I am as a loaf baked apart from the batch; or as a Hanse town with its own laws and usages. Still allow me, beloved younger brethren, to press along with you side by side, towards the mark, for the prize of our high calling."

Inward Purification.

" Is it said to me, ' Surely, as one of God's children, you too must have had your share of trial and trouble?' Well, I can reply in the affirmative. But in so doing, I am not particularly thinking of outward trials. It is true I have all my lifetime had a weak constitution; but not many illnesses serious enough to lay me aside from my work. Neither do I here particularly allude to the mournful events which befell me between the years 1716 and 1726, I mean, the sufferings and deaths of six of my children in their infancy; for God blessed these visitations with an abundance of his own vital comforts. Neither do I reckon among my special troubles the undeserved reproach heaped upon me by some of my opponents; for such things are common in mere learned controversy; and as I have always forgiven the persons concerned, and am ready to do them as much service of love as if nothing had happened, so any disagreeables I have suffered in that way are more than compensated by the acceptance which my works have everywhere met with. No, *my* chief suffering was of a spiritual and secret kind. It came on slowly and continued long. More particularly at times an unaccountable pang would surprise me at the thought of an approaching eternity; not that I had any perplexing dread of future misery, though I cannot say I was able cheerfully to look forward to the happiness of a future state. But simple absolute eternity used to overwhelm me with such an awe of its unutterable importance, that I cannot imagine it possible for any of the usual afflictions of life to have given me a spiritual purification so severe as this was. I seemed to be quite in a purgatory of my own.

" In secret exercises of spirit I have often been affectingly impressed with the thought of two remarkable moments in the history of the world; the one, when by one man's disobedience many were made sinners, myself included; the other, when Christ said, ' Father, into thy hands I commend my spirit;' thus virtually bringing me to God."

Bengel, in reference to spiritual temptations which he was

very severely feeling at the time, said, "God's great design is at present, not to delight us with pleasant experiences, but to *exercise* us as his faithful people. Let me, therefore, trust God for the pleasant things, as realities laid up in reversion; for I know they will come in all their fulness by and by, with eternity. As little children give their sweetmeats to their parents to keep for them, so what pleasant things may serve my various needs on the morrow, or the day after, are safer in God's keeping than in my own treacherous heart. Faithful is He that calleth us. One of the Greek versional readings in the first book of Kings, xviii. 15,—'As the Lord God of Hosts liveth, *before whom I stand* THIS DAY,' may at least express my spiritual situation. Forgetting the past, and not taking thought for the morrow, I stand before God to-day as his daily pensioner. I would set my affections, as it were, in a straight direction towards the heart of my heavenly Father, and when there is nothing in the way to divert them from that straight direction, I get on comfortably; but should there be any such obstacle, and is it possible to surmount it, I use every endeavour to do so, until it totally disappears. But if all my endeavours are unavailing, I concern myself about it no further than as a trial and purification, appointed certainly not for my harm, but to work together with all other things certainly for my good. When I look away entirely from self, and dwell upon the wisdom, goodness, and omnipotence of God, I feel in the very element of spiritual delight; I have a joy which invigorates me to go forward. And considering with what wonderful long-suffering he every day bears and carries us as his creatures, if I have a good reason to hope that I am not too burdensome to him, and that it is a small thing for him to deliver me from all evil, this I find a comfort indeed.

"Busy meddling memory often gives me some disquietude. If I have ever uttered an unbefitting word, or taken any step unadvisedly, though many years ago, the thing will frequently recur to me, and gain within me by little and little a burdensome ascendency. Nevertheless, one recollection and another of this kind, about matters which I had hardly noticed at the time, or even not till long afterwards, has a tendency to make me still better acquainted with myself; and thus I have often been humbled into such submission to God, as to be willing that my very least and most secret faults should be published by him in the presence of all his reasonable creatures.

"Every thing I do appears to me so poor; a little obedience, and a willingness to receive what God may be pleased to send; —that is all. Yesterday (Oct., 1748,) at the Lord's supper, I contrived to confront each particular conviction of my own spiritual poverty and unworthiness with its corresponding conviction of the restoring grace of God; and this exercise has yielded me a variety of sweet emotions.

"I feel as if I could still rejoice in the excellent glory of Jesus Christ, in its open manifestation to others, by his word, even though I were incapable of appropriating any 'consolation in Christ' to myself."

In connexion with the above thoughts, we insert the following, as found among Bengel's metrical compositions.

Suffering in Faith and Patience.

I'll think upon the woes,
  Most spotless Lamb of God,
To which thou didst expose,
  Upon th' accursed wood,
Thyself for mine iniquity,
And bless thee still, in chastening me.

Work then within my soul
  True penitence for sin;
My sufferings control,
  Through what thine own have been;
Or give me patience, courage, power,
For every further trying hour.

Why should my will complain,
  When all he means is kind?
Though great my grief and pain,
  To him I'll be resign'd:
Yes, wait and hope, as me behoves;
The Father chastens whom he loves.

Much yet may be t' endure,
  And strength may waste away;
But God, whose word is sure,
  Is working sin's decay;
Therefore I bow beneath his rod;
Pain must be good that leads to God.

Now is the time to bear
  Trial and proof from thee;
Great is my conflict here,
  In this, O strengthen me;
That I, on thee adventuring all,
May wait till soon my Lord shall call.

I cannot take amiss,
  These sufferings as too great;
Thou'rt good, though they increase,
  Still patiently I'll wait;
Ill it becomes me to repine;
Make me in state and spirit thine.

My heart shall envy none,
  Who seem to prosper more;
Only may I be one
  Of thine who so endure,
That here in piety they thrive,
Till heavenly perfectness arrive.

Thou fount of all delight,
  And secret of my joy;
Though many a tearful night
  May still my heart employ;
Yet will I hope one day to see
A blest eternity with thee.

Family Devotion.

Bengel not only read daily in his closet a portion of Scripture for his private edification, but was also a regular maintainer of family worship. For occasions of this sort he made use of Arndt's "True Christianity," Franke's Sermons, Müller's "Hours of Refreshing," and similar works; in reading which, he sometimes added a few remarks of his own. Thus, one day when reading to his family the 149th meditation in Müller's "Hours of Refreshing," he said—"This is worth repeating again and again. But how will it be when God brings us to the full fruition of the things here expressed! How little will it then matter what has been said, either for or against me, in the journals of literature! How delightful will it be in the blessed world above to meet with pious souls that have reached it, one from *this* place, and another from that! What a blessing to arrive in the regions of eternal rest, were it only on account of having escaped out of the confusion of this troublesome world! And what a love of God will glow in the heart of every person thus escaped! Yes, he will feel more of it in a single moment, than can be experienced in the whole term of this earthly pilgrimage."

Prayer, and Answers to it.

Some friends staying at his house being amused to see his tame doves fly so familiarly to the open window, and eat out of his hand, he said—"This exemplifies how easily we may do many a pleasure to others, if they have confidence in us. So if we honour God by putting confidence in Him, he becomes easy of access in prayer, and gives us what we want. Again, as we find our fellow-men communicative proportionately to their confidence in us, so (to compare infinitely great things with small,) all flesh will certainly come and be communicative to the blessed God, in proportion to the confidence they have in him, as a God who heareth and answereth prayer."

He said, "that if he desired the most perfect intimacy with real Christians on one account rather than another, it was for the sake of learning how they manage in secret to keep up their communion with God." His pupil Oetinger had a similar wish, and reckoned upon an excellent opportunity for the purpose when once he happened to take up his abode for the night in the same room with Bengel. But all he could discover was, that the holy man, before he betook himself to rest, went to the window, looked up to heaven, bowed himself a few times, and then in silence and composure laid him down to sleep.

Bengel always made it a matter of prayer that his heavenly Father would enable him to meet his necessities as they should arise; and this, he generally experienced, was done for him. Thus, on Jan. 27, 1740, just when the printer was waiting for a sheet from him, he got such light upon the twelfth chapter of Daniel, as enabled him to complete his observations upon the subject in hand.

When one of his relatives was recovering from a dangerous illness, Bengel said—"I did not regard outward appearances, unfavourable as they were. I prayed, and hoped for a favourable answer, and it has been given. I said nothing about it to any one at the time, but it came to me as a positive assurance, that *God will hear prayer.*"

Once, when a sudden and terrific hailstorm was pouring down

upon the fields, and likely to occasion serious damage, a person rushed into Bengel's room, and exclaimed, " Alas, sir, every thing will be destroyed; we shall lose all!" Bengel went composedly to the window, opened it, lifted up his hands to heaven, and said, " Father, restrain it!" and the tempest actually abated from that moment.

Ejaculation with devout recollectedness.

When one of his children began saying grace while walking up to the table, he said, " My dear, we don't find it written, 'when ye *walk* praying,' but ' when ye *stand* praying.' "

Why we should specially pray for Kings, and for all who are in authority.

" *God will have all men to be saved, and to come to the knowledge of the truth.*" (1 Tim. ii. 1—5.) Oral teaching can seldom be used effectually for instruction of " the mighty upon earth;" this deficiency, therefore, must be supplied by the intercessions of believers for them.

The true Medium in religious Feeling.

How invaluable is it to possess that entire confidence in God, that implicit trust in him, which is balanced by holy fear before him! To be neither too bold, and over confident, but at the same time not too diffident and deficient in holy boldness! He who keeps constant watch over himself, will soon learn how it is with him in this respect.

Implicit reference to Divine Direction.

Bengel having observed, respecting the ways of Providence, how much often depends upon a single minute circumstance; " look, for instance, (he said) how frequently all the events relating to a young clergyman's marriage and future condition in life, and perhaps the destinies of many hundreds of souls, may be traced up to the apparent accident of a vacancy in some pastoral charge." Here a friend replied, " This is what renders it so serious a matter to decide for oneself; that one is perplexed to know whether one ought to proceed according to one's best judgment immediately, or take more time to wait." " This (said Bengel,) is the very thing which makes it so desirable to pray without ceasing."

Reverence at the Name of God the Father.

" It is still a custom with many to bow at the name of Jesus, and of the Holy Spirit. This custom was adopted in ancient times by the orthodox, to distinguish themselves from those heretics who denied the second or the third hypostasis in the Godhead. I use likewise the same outward expression of reverence, why not?—at the name of God the Father. This, I hope, no one will take amiss in me."

Casting Lots.

Bengel had let the business of a letter, which he had written, depend on whether the letter should be called for or not; now it was forgotten to be called for, therefore Bengel resolved to take no further notice of the business of it, but said—" This is my way of casting lots in all doubtful cases. What amounts to lot-drawing with the Herrnhuters, is with me the leaving a matter entirely to the Divine disposal; that while God is ordering every thing, my own will may have no concern in it."

Contentment.

" At any trying occurrence, I represent to myself its worst possibilities; and as many of these as I do not realize, I account as so much gain. In this way contentment is not difficult.

" At the present season of scarcity, one is almost awfully afraid to be receiving from God, not only any superfluities but any conveniences, beyond what are necessary for the support of life. Besides, let me consider that temporal enjoyments, however numerous, at my disposal, are no *essential* part of my portion as a child of God; they are merely appendages to the substance of the promise. As such, however, they show the exuberant goodness of the Lord. Hence it is quite as wrong to be unnaturally abstemious, as to forget self-denial. But temporal good things are certainly placed to men's account as their all, if they seek their happiness in nothing better. They *have their* portion in this life.

" Though, as Würtemberg clergymen, we have many temporal privileges, I desire to use them entirely in a public spirit. They were given to promote, not private interest but pastoral usefulness.

" Our dear Germany is more favoured than many parts of the world. From frequent inundations, earthquakes, pestilence, annoyances of wild beasts, and extreme heat and cold, some of its provinces have been entirely exempt; and the remainder more so than many foreign regions. Surely this is ample compensation for any deficiency of gold mines, precious stones," &c.

Calmness and Equanimity.

A person expressed to Bengel his sympathy for him at being so virulently written against. He replied—"You will not regret this when I tell you, that such very trials teach me only the better how to gather up and strengthen the testimony of my conscience. I have learnt a good method of cheerfully enduring reproach.—I think of the reproaches and revilings which the Son of God has been receiving from the Jews for 1700 years, and of his wonderful long-suffering with them all this while. Thus I learn not to fret at a few relics of the same which may be thrown at *me*."

One of his opponents having dubbed him an enthusiast, he said—"There is a right enthusiasm which surely I would always possess; for without it we are spiritually dead, as living after the flesh. Human nature, without the inspiration of Divine grace, is a root that tends only to rottenness. (On the other hand, the divine and mysterious nature of spiritual religion must ever expose it to the charge of what is falsely called *enthusiasm*. For) Christ ever remains a mystery throughout, even down to the simplest elementary knowledge revealed of him in Scripture." When it was objected, that his endeavouring to interpret the Apocalypse upon so many points still future, might do harm, he replied—"As the kingdom of God cometh not *with observation* (of men in general), what one knows of its coming one ought surely not to conceal; for it will come unobserved enough after all. Though we give warning ever so loudly upon the subject, there will always be multitudes ready enough to drown it. The careless world has acted thus from the beginning; so that the coming of God's kingdom is in general scarcely noticed."

An anonymous publication having appeared in 1742 against his exposition of the Apocalypse, he remarked—"I am not surprised at the variety of conflicting opinions, neither do I regret it for the sake of myself, but only on account of the subject. As for the work of this anonymous writer, it appears more sound where he raises objections, than where he substitutes his own views. I should be glad to be acquainted with him on the score of Christian love; indeed, I have already blessed him in my heart, for I think him an honest lover of the truth."

On another occasion he remarked—"Man's judgment must be a very small thing in the eyes of God, or he would not suffer persons, who really love him, to be assailed with so many revilings and reproaches.

"Let us but keep ourselves from *real guilt*, and we need not be disturbed about any idle reports raised against us. Such reports, whether believed or not believed, are easily forgotten, for the world has always some fresh business in hand. It is right to prevent or correct them, if we can do it becomingly, otherwise it is not worth while to think about them.

"There are occasions when it is very helpful to our composure and equanimity, to look at our *debtor account*, and not merely at the credit side. We may have a real claim to another's deference, and still may be in many respects inferior to him. It is right that the younger should defer to and honour the elder; but it is equally right that the elder should not insist too much upon bare seniority. For others may be in their best bloom and vigour, while we are already in the decline of both. And let us not forget, that with all our eldership, we are but of yesterday."

Bengel was himself quite an example of the equanimity he here recommends; which made some persons of very buoyant spirits regard him as rather grave, or not cheerful enough; whereas, others of sombre temperament or of weak spirits accounted him a very cheerful person.

Charity hopeth all things.

In passing by the place of execution at Stuttgart, Bengel turned to his companion and remarked, with much emotion, "Will it not be said of many a one in the world above, '*all was well with him* HERE?'"

On Palm Sunday, 1741, a gallery broke down in the parish church of Schorndorf, by which several lives were lost. Bengel hearing of it said, "I always hope well of those who are visited with extraordinary trials and calamities. God, I think, thus 'uses sharpness' with them, because he '*has a favour unto*' them."

On another occasion he observed, "Statesmen and rulers are not always actuated by sinister motives upon vitally religious questions that come under their notice. What with their variety of avocations, party entanglements, comprehensive commissions, and so forth, they have often neither time nor opportunity for looking properly into the true bearing of such questions; thus, for want of adequate information to proceed upon, they are sometimes perplexed even to anxiety, at not being able to find the *punctum saliens*, the gist of the matter in hand; and the regret they have expressed at being obliged to refrain from taking any active or preventive part in it, has been perfectly sincere."

Eleemosynary Compensation.

"I neither forget, nor ever mean to forget, that the grace of God is not to be purchased with money, or works of righteousness that we have done. Only as some portion of the unrighteous mammon adheres to all our temporal enjoyments, I am accustomed to give away more than usual whenever any sickness occurs in my family."

False Rumours.

Some hostile troops, in the spring of 1742, having reached the neighbourhood of Herbrechtingen, every one, even Bengel, fled with his movables to a more secure part of the country. This, however, turned out to be needless. A report was afterwards spread that Bengel, *the seer of futurity*, had boasted of knowing beforehand, that the enemy would not advance so far; for that a scrap of paper, inscribed, "Hitherto shalt thou come, and no farther," had been found upon his table. His son-in-law, Williardt, having informed him of this report, he replied, "There is not a word of truth in it. Had it been so, why did we fly? And I am now glad we did so; for it serves to confute the idle rumour. I used to think such ridiculous stories originated from ignorant simplicity; but now I see they are purposely invented and wantonly uttered; for here there is not the shadow of a fact to have occasioned misconception. I should have liked well enough to pass unslandered through the world; but now we are again reminded that it cannot be done. Still it is but a temporal evil. I have long had occasions in plenty for noticing publicly the proverb, 'All men are liars;' and at present, as if to pay me for my trouble, I have a practical proof of it played off upon myself."*

* One of the most flagrant instances of the kind was found in a work published by a person signing himself P. Kepner, which professed to give "*Instruction how a sincere child of God may in special cases ask counsel of the Omniscient, and obtain an answer*;" and which purported to have been "*drawn up according to the system of J. A. Bengel.*" Upon this strange "*Instruction*" Bengel expressly remarked, that he neither held nor taught any thing of the sort.

A Signal from the Finger of God.

On the tenth of June, 1742, a very large oak in the manor wood of the abbey seminary at Herbrechtingen, was struck by lightning, and considerably damaged. A herdsman shortly afterwards passed under it with his drove, and Bengel observed, that "the word of Jesus (with which he cursed the fig-tree) was in its nature more powerful than this thunderbolt; for that the fig-tree instantly withered to the very roots. That all the force of the elements issues from the personal word of God, the LOGOS; and that a tree, thus struck, ought not to be cut down for common use, but to be allowed to stand as a signal to point at the majesty and power of the Almighty."*

The little Martyr.

Hearing the story told of the child who meekly bled under the rod of his unfeeling father, and only said, after he had been so severely used, "He cannot for all this beat the Lord Jesus out of my heart;" Bengel remarked, "I know not how it is, but I feel more delighted at hearing such a story, than in reading Arnold or Taulerus."

A Memento to be Temperate.

"Some well-meaning friends whom I have gone to dine with, have been very apt to press me to eat. I can excuse them; for they only help me to be upon my guard.—Dishes ought not to be so daintily served up as they commonly are; they should contain what is serviceable to refreshment and health, but not be studied for pampering. God's injunctions to the Israelites concerning meats, while they evidently proceeded upon the physical as well as religious condition of that people, had also respect to the constitution of mankind in general. For surely they contain many a good rule for discretion and moderation in diet; and we should make use of them accordingly."

One Consequence of the Fall.

As a labouring person was carrying home upon his shoulders a heavy truss of grass for his cattle, Bengel observed, "See how man is obliged to be servant to the brutes. Surely there is a meaning in this. God intends it for our humility; for it may remind us how the Fall has abased us."

* The oak was accordingly suffered to stand.

Does depravity increase as the world grows older? For men have complained in almost every age, that the world was growing worse instead of better. Are we then to conclude that human nature has really waxed worse and worse from the period of the Fall to the present day?

Bengel observed upon this subject, that the whole human race is in God's eye as one single tree, from which he cuts away at certain times many an injurious branch, while he suffers the good ones to remain. Human wickedness, like such injurious branches, is always on the increase for a season; that is, till God makes havoc upon it by the visitations of his providence. Corruption thus remits a little, but soon returns to its strength; and then another tempest arrives and checks its increase. A stone cast into a pond among a multitude of frogs interrupts their croaking for a while, but the concert soon recommences.

How to account for the increasing Worldliness of those who hear faithful Preachers.

A friend having expressed his surprise that persons quite of a worldly stamp should be found among the regular hearers of a very faithful minister, he replied, "This does not much surprise me; for it is become *fashionable* among worldly people to touch upon religion; and it is even considered a *deficiency in polite education* to be *totally* ignorant of it; indeed it is a kind of accomplishment amongst us to be able to talk correctly about it. Therefore some very worldly persons think it worth the trouble to find out and attend the most *popular* preachers, and sometimes real preachers to the conscience, will, strange to say, be only the *more* popular with them; but for no other reason that I can imagine, except that worldly pleasures are the more decidedly relished for having been, as such hearers think, too warmly attacked. For their consciences having been thus a little disquieted, they run with renewed eagerness into the vanities which they have been hearing *unduly* denounced; and they do so in order to smother the scruples which the preacher has raised in their minds. O what a responsibility awaits such persons; and indeed all professed Christians who are of a worldly character! Though God's pure word is presented to them in ever such a variety of ways, though the provision be ever so daintily served up, none of them really relish it at heart. As well might the preacher have the restless and ungovernable waves of the sea before him, and think to control them with the rod (of Moses), or (at least) with the words (of Christ) "Peace, be still!" All is without effect. Many (at hearing the plain declarations of the gospel,) seem as if they were tormented before the time; and in the midst of their "fearful looking for of judgment," they count it gain to enjoy all the worldly pleasures they can. And though such persons have been certain of dying in an hour's time, they have seldom discovered any inclination to relinquish a single gratification of their lust; for lust is absolutely their free will. Thus to the present day we see how little amendment has been wrought by all the means vouchsafed, and very little more will be wrought while the present Dispensation remains on its ancient footing. "THERE MUST COME AN AWAKENER." When it was here remarked, that "if such shall be the state of things, it would be of little use to enter into the ministry;" Bengel replied, "But the testimony to be borne to the truth, (by public preaching and private admonition,) must still proceed. Our own private design of faithfully executing our commission, is one thing; but our public design, namely, to witness the good effect of our labours, is another. The former of these surely we may always realize."

The Distinction between Converted and Unconverted.

"What is the difference between the faults of the unconverted and the faults of the converted? The former shoot beside the target altogether; and the latter do not hit the middle.

"Children of God are more ready than others to forgive the offences of their fellow-men; and this even when under stronger temptation than others, to lay such offences to heart. As it is the influence of grace that disposes them sincerely to forgive, so they are glad to evince its good effect in their conduct; though what they have to forgive is often more severely felt by them than it could be by unconverted men: for the latter are not so tenderly sensible of good and ill, and they give and take accordingly; whereas a real servant of Christ and child of God becomes, by the grace which prevails within him, more sensible and impressible. He deals gently with his fellow-men; but on this very score it affects him the more painfully, that, in despite of his moderation and kindness, they do not cease to treat him with unfeelingness and asperity."

Why the terms Parson and Preacher are become very unfashionable.*

It may be observed that hardly any minister of Christ, when he publishes a book in these days, ever styles himself parson (of a parish), and in truth there is a reason for it. For properly we are no longer *parsons* (personæ) *of parishes,* since ecclesiastical authority has so dwindled away. And then the force of the scriptural expression *to preach* being lost sight of among our fashionable Christians, the expression itself is very sparingly used (among us) in its serious sense; but the term *pulpit-delivery* is preferred; which indeed is a more proper term, whenever preaching ceases to be, in good truth, *the preaching of Christ.*

The best Form of Government.

"The best system of government, (abstractedly considered,) is the monarchical. The monarch cannot be bribed. Whenever things have proceeded admirably under other systems of government, it has generally been acknowledged as their highest praise, that they 'seemed as if *one mind* controlled them.' What is this but a virtual acknowledgment that the monarchical system is the best?"

The Oldest Nobility.

"It is a great piece of vanity which men indulge about the nobility and antiquity of their families. This vanity virtually splits the human race into two distinct castes, a superior and an inferior one; and those who pride themselves upon their nobility reckon themselves of course in the former. Now the poorest despised Jew is able to trace his noble origin much farther back than any of them; I say is *able* to do it; for he can refer to accurate genealogies which go up to the remotest antiquity."

* The expression, *to preach*, as will be seen in this paragraph, is that which Bengel speaks of as having become disused in Germany; while he complains further on in a line omitted, because not so intelligible to the mere English reader, that the word *preacher* is nevertheless the word commonly substituted in Germany for that of *parson*. (This last expression is adopted by the translator as the nearest equivalent in the acceptation here meant, to the German word, Pfarrer; which is evidently derived from παροικίζω, and in both Protestant and Roman-Catholic Germany denotes the incumbent of a parish.) In England, the expression, *to preach*, is not so out of fashion; but our word, *preacher*, seems to have shared much the same fate as in Germany the expression, *to preach*.—Tr.

The Learned Caste.

"It is rather strange that a person of learning, however competent in talents and acquirements, is not easily looked upon (amongst us) as a licensed man of letters, unless he has been at some university; while others glide into such estimation as a matter of course, if they have run an academical round, though they may owe what little attention they have paid to learning, simply to the constraint of college rules, and have been any thing but studious men.

Nepotism, (or matter-of-course preferment in consideration of family connexions.)

"It is an established rule in W. that whoever expects preferment, must be either a great man's son, or belong by marriage to some family of consequence. The person who gets on without these requisites, is generally a dependent on others who have them; or if no more *eligible* personage stands in his way, preferment may accrue to him by sufferance.

"One great cause of the decline of learning in our universities, is, that it is taken for granted that a professor's son must, by his very birth, &c. be qualified for a professional chair, if he has been educated with that view; he is therefore sent to school and to a university for the purpose. In like manner it is supposed, that a professor's daughter has an hereditary title to be a professor's wife. And yet as such persons do not always prove the best qualified, so God's providence has all along demonstrated how little his appointments have to do with human preferences and classifications."

Truth the Daughter of Time.

"I think it rather unsafe to conclude that such and such events must be true, merely because they are found recorded by a writer who lived when they are said to have happened. Truth is the daughter of time; for time often brings to light what has been enveloped for ages."

A Method of profitably reading the Public Journals.

"If a person has opportunity, let him not only read the journals as they come out, but let him again run over a whole quarter's sequence at one sitting; and it will give him quite another view of things and events. This may serve as a very faint adumbration of things and events as they appear to the eye of an all-seeing God; may intimate at least something of the manner in which men's actions and omissions are regarded by him who knows beforehand the ultimate issue of all."

A Proposal for the Prevention of Duels.

" The following Platonic prescription once occurred to me as good for the prevention of duels. Let a person who has been killed in a duel have a public monument erected to his memory, and let his name be inscribed upon it with *feminine* terminations; thus, 'Here lies Frederic*a* Louis*a* N.'—It would at least have more effect than many *other* prohibitions."

Sweeping Sentiments and Hasty Conclusions.

To a person who used to say he " never went out, without coming home the worse for it," Bengel remarked, " we ought to be careful how we suffer ourselves to form such hasty and sweeping conclusions; for they *must* contain untruth, and may easily be attended with very bad consequences. Suppose the apostles had determined for such a reason as yours never to go out among their fellow-men ; would they have done right ?"

Care for Children.

A person having remarked, that he thought parents must be the prey of much anxiety, if they consider to what temptations their children are exposed: Bengel answered, " What a multitude of children has God in this world; for all and every one of whom he has to care at once; and yet he conducts each of them, step by step, till they come to perfect safety at last. Besides, we may congratulate our children on their being so much nearer the mark than we were in our younger days; as every thing at present is attained by a shorter route than formerly.

Letters written by the Uneducated.

Bengel having received a letter from an illiterate (but pious) person, said, " I know not how it is, but I derive much more pleasure from letters of this sort, than from reading those of Spener, Arnold, and others. Perhaps those worthies themselves felt in the same way."

A Christian is not swallowed up with overmuch Sorrow.

Bengel having (on the 25th of February, 1735,) been apprised of the death of his wife's mother, some friends endeavoured to dissuade him from preaching that morning; but he said, "This is an occasion for testifying how a Christian's mind is disposed; and such an opportunity must not be lost." A child having died suddenly while its mother was from home, and Bengel having to communicate to her the mournful intelligence, upon her inquiring, "How is my child?" replied, "It is engaged in love and praise."

A Temptation of a peculiar kind.

When it was said to Bengel that possibly he might be meant by the third angel in the Apocalypse, he answered, "Supposing your idea to be correct, how can I sufficiently admire the purpose of God as to what he is pleased to make out of such a worm of the dust as I am; and also as to what he may ultimately bring to pass by such a poor weak instrument. But supposing your idea to be false, and I were to think of indulging such a notion, there would hardly have been a more abominable sin committed since the fall of Lucifer."

On another occasion, (in November, 1740,) he gave his sentiments on this subject as follows:—"That a variety of persons had for some time entertained such an opinion, but that he neither did nor could believe it. Still considering all circumstances, he could not utterly dismiss it from his thoughts, but left it entirely to God; and should there be truth in it, his prayer was, that he might be enabled to keep his own heart totally untouched by it. He allowed it was a remarkable fact respecting his 'Exposition of the Apocalypse,' that it had so rapidly gained attention throughout Germany, a success not common to books of the kind. That considering how God had led him all his life long, he could not but praise and magnify to the utmost the grace of God; and might well fall down before him in the dust, and even hide himself in the earth at his presence. That both within himself and without, he found so many occasions for humility, that if any swelling of pride or self-complacency began to show itself, something counteractive to every thing of the kind was soon sent by Providence, which made him sink back into his own proper dimensions. He then spoke affectingly of his own nothingness and unworthiness, &c. and said, that even if God had called him to sustain a character so high as the one in question, he could gain no real advancement by it in the kingdom of God, nor could any such distinction exempt him from liability to 'be disapproved;' from which however he trusted that God would of mere grace preserve him: and that he was very seriously concerned lest he should be made too much of; as this might tempt him considerably to abate in genuine piety." The relater of this adds, "I replied,—and yet the present period appears to be just that of the third angel." "Yes," he answered, "the middle of the period, which commenced with blessed Arndt, and ends in the great term of 1836, with just a hundred and eleven years for its measure, is the year 1725; the very year when light upon these subjects was bestowed upon me." He adds, that "this circumstance had particularly struck him after S. had alleged him to be the third angel, which was even before the publication of Bengel's 'Exposition of the Apocalypse.'" For his own part, however, he had seriously endeavoured to evade such an application of the prophetic symbol as far as he could with a good conscience, that is, without any suppression of the truth. "If," said he, "I am questioned about it, I shall only turn the attention of my inquirers upon themselves." Yet he felt, that such encouragements given him by his friends, were as so many kindnesses on the part of God, which he valued more than he could express; so seasonable had they been to him, just at the time when upon one pretence and another, his name was so contemptuously held up to general notice; which might be only a prelude to still severer treatment. Having afterwards remarked in the same company, how important it is to maintain a constant evenness, meekness, and humility of spirit, and how evidently those who had deviated into errors, had generally done so through irritability of temper, through pride, or too great self-confidence, he added, how very much while revising the Byzantine MS. (of the New Testament,) he had been impressed by those words of our Saviour's sermon on the Mount, "Not every one that saith unto me, Lord, Lord," &c.

He also said, that "should the powerful testimony and warning ascribed to the third angel, have ever been in fact delivered by any preceding writer, or should any such mighty witness be at present or hereafter upon his commission in the world, he (Bengel) would most cheerfully for his own part shrink into the shade."

On the 10th of February, 1742, he expressed himself once

more upon this subject, as follows:—"I can now, with greater certainty than ever, contradict those who have entertained this notion concerning me, in reference to the third angel; and it is much to my own comfort that I can do so. *Could I push myself still further down from the time of Arndt,* I would do it; however, it is quite sufficient for me to say, that as Spener* died just about the period when the Romish missions flourished most, and as at this period the Protestants also began to feel an interest in sending missions to the heathen, it should seem that precisely through these events was the third angel's testimony fulfilled and terminated.

Sarcastic Controversialists.

"A sarcastic manner of writing on theological subjects is not indeed peculiarly edifying: but those who use it, have sometimes been so instrumental to the exposure of errors, that intelligent persons have been made afraid to incur the odium of such errors. In these cases our controversial theologians may be said to have performed the service of light troops in the field."

Salvability of the Pope.

Being asked if he thought any one pope of Rome could ever be saved, he said, "I would not insist that he cannot; but it is likely to go very hard with him: for either he must really think he is what his deluded votaries imagine him, namely, worthy of the profound reverence which is paid him; and that would be a huge abomination; or else he must know that he is not worthy of such reverence; and then he must be an abominable hypocrite."

Registering of Spiritual Experiences.

"To attempt to commit *all* our spiritual experiences to writing, would be like attempting to treasure up in vessels, and lock up in a storehouse the common air we breathe; whereas, such experiences are natural to the life of every Christian, who, in the fear of God maintains a general good state of spiritual health."

Minding one's own Business.

"It was a laudable custom among the Romans to allow none to make the least intrusion upon another's province. When

* Whom Bengel considered as the second angel.

every one punctually discharges his own duty, neither leaving any part of it to persons elsewhere, nor meddling with other people's business, things will go on well, and all the various and busy occupations of a multitude will individually accord in one general harmony."

The characteristic of real Wisdom.

"It belongs to true wisdom to meditate, hit upon, and mind, whatever is to the purpose; at the right time."

Variableness of Theological Winds.

"Whither should we have arrived by now, had we permitted ourselves to be driven by, or carried away with, every wind of doctrine that has risen and made a stir upon spiritual subjects during the last thirty years, (from 1710 to 1740); and yet what favourable winds did these all seem at their first rise! (May we not hence infer that every new spiritual *mode* of our own day should be eyed with suspicion?)"

Military Men's Ideas of a learned Life.

"Military men are apt to entertain a low estimate of a learned life. It is rather from policy or courtesy that they affect to consider honour as acquirable in *that* way. They go off smiling at those who think them to be in earnest. Therefore in the presence of such men we should keep our learning to ourselves till it is called for."

Promotion of young Persons to places of trust.

"When a person is wanted for any service, his being young is no objection, provided he is not to take the lead. We see the appointment of young tutors, &c. answers very well in colleges; for their seniors also reside and superintend. However, it is always best to promote gradually from usefulness in inferior stations to usefulness in superior ones."

How to speed by Orphan Intercessions.

The manual of prayers for the use of the orphan-house having been noticed, Bengel said, "I think that many who desire the intercessions of orphan children, ought to pray more diligently for *themselves;* as Peter directs Simon Magus to do." (Acts viii. 22—24.)

A genuine Government Officer.

"Any official person who, on behalf of government, has to require something of his subordinates, and especially among the people at large, has need to resemble the nut, which is strong and firm on the outside, but tender and mild within."

Influence of the Mind upon bodily Health.

"Moderated feelings of the mind have a kind of physical effect upon us, like that which the gentle stir of the air produces upon vegetation, &c. Many a time have I traced in myself no inconsiderable relief from bodily suffering, to the composure and serenity of my mind."

Jewish Apophthegms.

"The Jews have a pretty but quaint saying: 1. Mine to me, and thine to thee; this is true in strict righteousness. 2. Mine to me, and thine to me; this is robbery and unrighteousness. 3. Mine to thee, and thine to me; this is true love and fairness. 4. Mine to thee, and thine to thee; this is too great liberality.

"The Cross once seen!"

"When the hymn was sung to-day (11th March, 1742,) which begins—

> 'O world, see Him who is thy life,
> Expiring on the cross;'

I thought, this applies to myself, for I am a portion of the 'world,' which is thus addressed. I have need to look *this* way (to the life here set before me;) and he who *does* look this way, is no longer *of the world;* no longer worldly and earthly minded."

Constitutional Self-Diffidence.

"I should have acquired much more mental decision and established firmness of faith by this time, were it not for a sort of constitutional diffidence, which often perplexes me; though I quite believe it is overruled for my benefit; as without it I might have been too much inclined to rigour and harshness."

God's essential love of Truth.

"To be treated ever so uncourteously does not affect me so much as to have my views incorrectly stated by others, who thus spread a false idea of my system. If then *human* estimate of truth can rise so high, how must it be with the Lord God of truth himself. Doubtless the many and great discrepancies which he beholds in our notions of divine things, must appear in His sight as no small abomination, however orderly and decent we may be in our conduct; yea, however distant may be such notions from producing any permanent injury, or condemnation; that is, however much we may live in his faith and fear. For whatever is contrary to truth must, in itself, always be ignoble and base; because the only standard of true honour, glory, and beauty, is TRUTH."

Christian Love's Preferences.

A dignified clergyman, not very piously disposed, happened to be, during a visitation of his deanery, at Bengel's house, when a christian brother of humble rank entered the room. Bengel rose from his chair to meet him at the door, and embraced him in the most friendly manner. Then turning to the dean, he repeated from the 15th Psalm—"but he maketh much of them that fear the Lord;" leaving *him* to think of the former part of the verse.

Titus i. 15.

"Even the least of true believers is a more desirable and wise judge of things in general, than *any* ungodly man can possibly be."

Rage for publications of private Correspondence.

"To catch at every thing uttered by learned men, for instance, at every letter of their correspondence, which, at best, consist generally of common-place subjects, and of the same mere common sense as that of other men, is as if we would enclose common atmospheric air in separate vessels, and lay it up among medical stores, forsooth, because common air is necessary for health. Not to mention, that even great men's thoughts, in their familiar intercourse with friends and acquaintance, are often pitiably dissipated, and too much diverted from the main matter. To be able to deliver good thoughts in a remarkably clear and impressive manner, is always to be regarded as a special vouchsafement of divine guidance; therefore any thing which *is* thus expressed, certainly deserves to be carefully remembered. But then this is the very reason why the present rage for publishing volumes of mere familiar private correspondence cannot be beneficial. Again, what will posterity have to say to us, if we suffer a multitude of published letters to be transmitted to them, without even stating to whom they were addressed?"

The Comprehensiveness of an affirmative Particle.

"I have to-day hit upon a single syllable, which may serve to express faith, hope, love, patience, composure, self-denial, &c. It is the word ναὶ, 'even so,' or 'yea,' as found in Matt. xi. 26. God saith, 'Thou hast sinned.' I answer, 'yea.' He saith, 'I have given thee mine own Son.' I answer, 'yea,' ('even so.') He saith, 'I will save thee for ever.' I answer, 'yea.' He adds, 'Thou hast to suffer here.' I answer, 'yea.' But my answers must all be in the 'spirit,' and not in the (mere) 'letter.' They must not be a lazy indifferent sort of 'yea.' The whole heart must, as it were, be FULL OF 'YEA.'"

Our Saviour's Growth in Wisdom and Stature.

"Wisdom in our blessed Saviour was an innate habit, (habitus innatus); which he needed not first to learn from the word of prophecy; otherwise he could not have replied to the marvelling Jews, as he did in John vii. 15, 16. As his outward man increased in strength, by natural means, so his human spirit increased in wisdom by immediate revelations from his Father. Speaking after the manner of men, we may say, his heavenly Father gave him *collegium privatissimum* (private instruction to himself alone): this instruction having proceeded upon no written book whatever. Our blessed Saviour did, indeed, exercise himself in the written word of prophecy, in the same manner as other men; but this he did not for his own sake, for he needed it not."

As eminent persons often furnish one of the best means of discovering their own character, by what they have expressed respecting others, we will here annex a few of Bengel's sentiments upon some persons and things that have been most prominent in history and literature.

"ARISTOTLE's writings are no longer generally read; for he is looked upon as the father of the Schoolmen: and yet his works contain many excellences. His treatise on ethics describes virtues and vices with great accuracy. Those upon economics, rhetoric, and poetry, are better worth reading than his Metaphysics and Organon. In fixing the peculiar meaning of Greek words he is incomparable."

"In CICERO's first oration against Catiline, there is an impassioned appeal to Jupiter (the primary god of the Romans), which made a deep impression upon me. One cannot, indeed, forget that it is addressed to an idol, which is 'nothing in the world;' otherwise it is most full of devout fervour, and is an instance of the distinction between false or merely natural devotion, and that which is true and divine."

"AUGUSTINE's severity as a writer against the heresies of his time may be traced to his own former entanglement in similar dreadful errors. He had *felt* the mischief of them in his past experience. It is observable that even in his 'Confessions' there are thoughts subtile enough to sound quite *scholastic*, if divested of their devotional form. I think it is his general way to make too much of such fine-spun thoughts."

"The ancient *fathers of the church* often charged heretics with holding much worse opinions than they really did; and this through not understanding their writings, which in their literal meaning frequently appeared absurd; but which also contained a mystical meaning not obvious to every reader."

"I do not think that MAHOMET at first designed a wilful imposture. At his outset he was a merchant of a shrewd and intelligent mind; and having much intercourse at places of travelling resort with Jews, Christians, and pagans, he was free and communicative. Finding the eyes of many opened by his remarks, and that through the sickly and declining state of the Christian church, his ideas gained very ready acceptance, he became encouraged to make bolder pretensions. Being also subject to epilepsy, which was followed by a morbid rapture, he upon occasions of this kind actually did many strange things; and thus learnt to believe his own lie. I think that most of the heresies in the church itself have originated and spread much in the same way. I have long been increasingly disposed to believe that there is an *esoteric* meaning in the Alcorân which Christians have overlooked. Certainly an allegorical manner of teaching prevails in it throughout; and if allegory be really the thing intended, we gain no ground with Mahometans by setting forth its absurdities in the literal meaning."

"LUTHER's character was truly great. All his brother reformers together will not make a Luther. They found it necessary to look to *him*, and he had skill to make use of *them* just where they were wanted. If any of them harboured a different or opposite design to his, they could not disclose it till after his death. This event too was an important epocha; for nothing since it took place has ever been *really* added to the reformation itself. Writers commonly distinguish Luther in his younger days from

Luther in his mature age; but the distinction should rather be, that of his younger days, middle age, and decline of life. The first and last of these were good: but in his middle age, and while engaged in the heat of controversy, he suffered one thing and another to provoke him at times, even to irritation."

" ERASMUS on Free Will, and Luther on the Bondage of the Will, ought to be read *together*. The former skirmishes, like an agile logician, and reproaches the latter with obstinately uttering mere assertions. Luther will not advance a single step without making good his ground; nor is he inferior to Erasmus, even in eloquence: besides which, his reasonings are more convincing. Luther is certainly the happiest of all expositors upon the book of Genesis.

" Luther has a quaint, pretty expression about *beating the* (metal) *mirror into armour;* that is, making use of what we need for godly exercises and defence against evil, so as to look at our own image in it, fall in love with it, stand to admire it, and be quite taken with it, (clothing ourselves as it were with the imagination of our own reflected image;) a thing which people are very apt to do, for when they see any good accomplished in themselves, they presently make too much of it."

" It has been remarked, how little of the active power of the gospel has been put forth in the ANGLICAN CHURCH. But why is this? Its first reformers felt but little of that active power; their *fort* lay rather in speculative divinity."

" CALVIN'S *Institutes*, which had been originally intended to be presented to the king of France, as a confession of faith on the part of the Reformed, is a most excellent work, and well worth reading."

" I am pleased with IGNATIUS LOYOLA for his finding no relish in Erasmus's *Miles Christianus*, because of its loquacity. Hence the Jesuits do not read it, though their way of thinking and acting coincides, in many other respects, with that of Erasmus."

" BELLARMINE has many fine observations. In controversy with the avowed enemies of Christianity he is quite sound. Even in his altercations with the Lutherans he has much mildness and moderation, compared with the raw manner in which controversy is too often handled. A similar remark applies to the COUNCIL OF TRENT. That council contained many well-disposed men, who desired not to have every point so rudely despatched, nor every article drawn up in such crude and general language. Even that of *Justification* is now little more than logomachy; especially when by justification is meant whatever can make us acceptable to God; which, by the way, is the lax meaning adopted in our Symbolical Books. But the gross perversions about *communion in one kind, prohibition of the common people from the free use of the Scriptures*, &c., are altogether inadmissible; for these are evidently dregs from the cup of the Babylonian harlot."

Bengel's high estimation of ARNDT has already been noticed (Part. iii. ch. 6). Speaking of Arndt's contracted means for improving his (theological) education, he remarks, in reference to 1 Cor. i. 25—29, "Arndt, who was a poor clergyman's son, was necessitated, in very early life, to support himself by private tuition, (so that he was less in the way of being formed according to the prevalent academical mould;) and this circumstance, together with his cordial aversion to that spirit of controversy which prevailed in his time, may serve to account for his having struck into a more free way of thinking for himself. But *all* this was so ordered, that it might be the more evident on the one hand, what an efficient character God's special help could make him; and on the other, how poor and weak a creature Arndt would have been without such special help.

"BUXTORF was a man of profound erudition in his way. He sifted to the bottom those matters which had been most neglected, and ought not to have been neglected, by the learned who had preceded him. These he set in so clear a light, that his works will be always valuable."

"I find it really difficult to give a just opinion of JACOB BOEHME's* writings. He says things which clearly do not accord with Scripture; still we find many a passage in him which is exceedingly beautiful. He acknowledges that he cannot always distinguish between what he has derived from the pure fountain of revelation, and what he has added of his own. How then could he expect his readers to do it? His manner is evidently very different from that of the Bible. Multifarious as are the subjects of the sacred volume, and different as were its penmen from one another in such a variety of respects, still, in the Scriptures of the Old and New Testament, we observe one grand idea pervading the whole: and though each single book is a whole of itself, it is only a component part of the entire volume of revelation. Each bears severally its relation to the rest, and contributes its distinct quota to the grand total. And O how

* Generally, but improperly, written *Brehmen* in English works.—TR.

beautiful and captivating is the *simplicity* of Scripture! Christ himself, in each of his temptations, by employing a simple text of Scripture, defeated the sophistry of our great adversary.

"The supposition that some of Boehme's friends published works of their own under his name, is quite improbable. Boehme's writings having so very peculiar a character of their own, it would be more difficult to counterfeit them, than those of any ancient classic. But if he has found, as we may trust he has, his portion in the land of the living, what will his calumniators and revilers have to say for themselves in the last day? Arndt and Boehme lived at the same period; but the instructions of the former have been far more extensively received than the opinions of the latter."

"POIRET, in his little treatise called *Prima Cognita,* has explained the divine greatness and all-sufficiency in a strange manner. The impression one feels in reading it is, 'Had I been God, no other being should have had an existence.'"

"SPINOZA thought that God in his word lowers himself to the physical dispositions of the instruments he makes use of. But this is degrading the proper idea of God; and I am rather disposed to think quite oppositely to such an opinion. All was to go through a process of self-denial; and nature had to bear its portion of it.

"Spinoza's treatise, *De Servitute Humanâ,* is very fine. It savours, indeed, too much of his own peculiar system, but it excellently shows how the various human affections depend, in a natural order, on one another; and that the soul has no independent self-moving principle, any more than a piece of clock-work contains a self-moving spring. This is quite true of our fallen nature, as considered apart from that divine grace to which every one ought to yield, and of which every person ought at once to avail himself. It is grace only that communicates real liberty."

Bengel having, as early as 1713, in his tour through Germany, become acquainted at Halle with AUGUSTUS HERMANN FRANKE, the great disciple of Spener, Franke visited him four years afterwards at Denkendorf. Of this visit, and of Franke's other proceedings in Würtemberg, Bengel gives the following account in a letter to a friend:—

"We have lately had amongst us Professor Franke, a man of noble example; one who appears to live entirely to God, and to depend only upon him. The presence of this excellent man has aided not a little in stirring us all up. Repentance towards

God, and faith towards our Lord Jesus Christ, are every thing with him. He has remarkable talent at conversation, with all sorts of persons, and gains their confidence by his great kindness and affectionate manners. Thus he is powerful in awakening every one to an affectionate regard for the divine word, to earnest prayer, and catechetical instruction; setting all to teach, improve, and save one another. The parting between him and our provost, (Dr. John Frederic Hochstetter,) was really affecting. At Bebenhausen he made himself quite another son to Dr. John Andrew Hochstetter, so well did he supply to him the place of his deceased son, the late Tübingen professor; and such a brother did he prove himself to the rest of that good man's family. I accompanied him in his visit to the Orphan-house at Stuttgart, and could not but admire his humble and beautiful simplicity in conversing with the children. After asking them two or three questions, he would draw them naturally at once upon the most spiritual subjects of our holy religion.

"To my own children, and to my dear wife, who, at my suggestion, put herself with them in his way, to crave his blessing, he affectionately imparted it with imposition of hands.

"On the whole, he left Würtemberg much gratified at what he had seen in our country."

Shortly afterwards, Bengel wrote as follows:—

"Among the christian friends dispersed through the upper, lower, and middle districts of our country, there appears a kindly disposition to become more closely connected with one another; and desirable indeed is it for the honour of faith, hope, and love. Franke, it is quite probable, has contributed in part to stir it up. I know he has eminently done so at Stuttgart. But there are persons alike disposed in other quarters of our land, who, I am equally certain, have had no communication with him. Real Christianity amongst us, if I may compare it with a thing so opposite, reminds me, in one respect at least, of witchcraft; namely, that, with the exception of a single place, it is spreading itself *secretly* and unrecognised among its abettors. But this is not the manner in which it *ought* to spread. Is it right that any two souls who are like-minded, alike seeking the face of God, should never exchange a word with each other upon their mutual fellowship in the One Thing Needful? Is the saints' communion so to be left with God as to be no mutual concern of their own? Surely this is an inconsistency.

"Franke visited Ulm, Augsburg, Anspach, and Nüremberg, on his tour, and by this time, I suppose, has reached home: Various opinions are afloat as to the object of his journey. It may well have been for the sake of his health, but evidently he had an additional object. The dear man has a large heart; and this, I think, prompted him to leave Halle for a time, (especially as that place had no dearth of labourers,) that he might embrace a wider range of usefulness; though his humility would not allow him to declare this. He must have gained much valuable experience on his way; for wherever he came, all sorts of Christians, the tempted and tried, the serious and zealous, the great and little, the learned and the simple, opened their hearts to him, and were forward to communicate their thoughts to his sympathizing spirit. I should like to hear the report he will have to make to his colleagues and friends at his return.

"That his previous good opinion of our beloved country has been increased by his coming amongst us, is not unimportant, especially as he saw more than the outside of things. He had intercourse with many real members of the true church, who repaired to him from all parts, yes, even from remote villages and hamlets. The two pre-eminent endowments of this good man are, love of Scripture and love of prayer; endowments which he wishes to see every one of us likewise cultivate more and more into personal piety, and diligent promotion of one's neighbour's good. This expresses in brief the very tenor of his whole mind; and with such a mind, he is green and flourishing in old age."

Upon his death, which took place in 1727, Bengel wrote as follows:—

"Franke's death has touched the hearts of many in Würtemberg. His life was a continual blessing. It was as if Luther's mighty spirit stirred within him; and a similar spirit has been stirred up in Germany by his instrumentality. May the goodness of Almighty God gather our souls with his among those of just men made perfect in Christ!—Who knows if there can now be brought together in all Christendom three such fellow-labourers as were Breithaupt, Anton, and Franke? Yet these were found in the single town of Halle. Providence had made the cross their medium of union; and the several institutions over which they presided in the same university, were the means of bringing them together for that remarkable usefulness which crowned their harmoniously concerted and diligent exertions. These three were like one family, excluded from all outward intrusion."

"I have not for some time met with any new publication which has pleased me so much as STEINHOFER's 'Discourses on the Epistle to the Hebrews.' It is just such an exposition as was wanted. But why did he not put his name to it?"

"Count ZINZENDORF's *Jeremiah* I consider as one of his best works; I often think upon the proverb,

Οὐκ ἐν τῷ μεγαλῳ τὸ εὐ,
'Αλλ' ἐν τῷ ἐυ τὸ μέγα κεῖται.

('Goodness does not consist in greatness, but greatness in goodness.'")

In 1725, the well known *Frederic Rock*, one of the leaders of the *Inspirati* (as they were called) came to Tübingen, and solemnly deposited a copy of his *prophetic* effusions in the collegiate church of that city. Ten years afterwards (12th Sept. 1735) he came to Bengel at Denkendorf, accompanied by his associates, Wickmark, Metz, and Karr. Just before they arrived, Bengel happened to have been reading Sleidan's "Account of the disturbances raised by Münster and his party at the time of the Reformation." Possibly this had contributed to put him on his guard; however, he was more reserved to them than they had expected; but they made themselves quite affable and agreeable, though in truth they were greatly disappointed in him. Rock, therefore, a few days after this interview, sent him an *inspired* effusion (dated Sept. 17,) upbraiding him with monstrous pride of heart, and menacing divine judgments upon him. He also distributed written copies of this extraordinary document in various parts of Würtemberg, taking care to send one to the Rev. Andrew Bardili, the pastor of Heiningen, who was one of Bengel's particular friends. Bengel expressed himself upon the subject as follows:—"It is true that in my conversation with Rock I kept myself pretty high, that is, I was becomingly reserved; for I was not at all disposed to coincide with him. He addressed me as a chief preceptor; an appellation which, for very good reasons, I was inclined rather not to hear than to censure. Whether my guardedness was among the incidents that moved him to draw up the 'judgment' he has since pronounced upon me, I know not; Rock perhaps himself does not know, and the Searcher of hearts alone can decide. On the 17th of September, (the date of the 'judgment,') I felt, to the best of my recollection, a tolerable serenity of spirit; and preached shortly afterwards from the text, 'Every one that exalteth himself shall be abased,' &c., without any self-accusation on the subject; indeed, I felt particular comfort and encouragement in meditating upon the words of the Psalmist, 'Lord! my heart is not haughty, nor mine eyes lofty.' As far as I know any thing of my own state, I should have expected reproach for almost any thing rather than haughtiness of demeanour, or high thoughts of myself. But even were it an admonition of the Lord's sending, I cannot exculpate those by whom it is sent, from having gone beyond their commission, as they were not satisfied with conveying it to me only, but have thought it necessary to circulate written copies of it elsewhere; and this supererogation of zeal may prevent not a few from benefiting by my humble efforts; for many, who disagree with Rock in every thing else, appear ready enough to hear any thing he may have to say against *me*. As to whether they are acting with God's approval, the day will declare it.—My belief is, that God will yet raise up other and better witnesses than such as these. The longer I live, the more strictly do I adhere to and depend on his (written) *word*, which is 'tried unto the uttermost;' neither shall I have to repent of so doing at the last moment of my life, though it should come to-day."

In 1745, a person of the name of *Streib*, of M., imagined himself to be one of *the* "*two witnesses*" in the Apocalypse. He even came to Bengel, who, after kindly and patiently hearing all he had to say, frankly told him what part of his views he considered untenable, and endeavoured to show him how easily corrupt notions of every sort may intermix with what in the main is excellent and scriptural. All Bengel's remarks being accompanied with much love and mildness, were kindly received; but Streib, persisting in his own notions, Bengel wrote of him as follows:—"Even what flows from the truth itself, may become strangely mingled with fallen nature's impurities; this too may happen to sincere and honest persons, and the mixture be so inconceivably subtile, that whoever is not aware of the variety of its strange results, can have but little suspicion of such a thing. In conversing with Streib, I was quite prepared to regard him as a pious person of some spiritual experience. But as to his *prophetic* qualifications, I was not able in so short a time to give him sufficient attention; and chronology is not the only disputed point upon which I advised him to be prudent for his own sake, and moderate in what he uttered upon such subjects to others. I observed to him how particularly desirable it was that he should refrain from declaring himself one of the 'two witnesses;' that he should not thus speak of himself, even in the most private manner; no, nor allow his heart to suggest such a thought. The human heart, unless restrained and regulated by the word of God, proves 'deceitful above all things;' and though it may be drawn off from worldly cares and lusts, still it will seek *its own*, even in spiritual things themselves, (so as to become wonderfully inflated with spiritual pride.) He ought, therefore, to take seasonable warning, lest his own heart should easily become so inflated, as to be very injurious to his welfare, both temporally and spiritually. I am perfectly willing that this warning, and the remarks which have occasioned it, should be communicated to him; indeed, I request that it may be done, with my kind regards. I am still in the same mind as when I conversed with him, both with respect to every kind feeling towards him, and not less with respect to that careful discrimination which is so indispensable upon all subjects of this nature."

CHAPTER IV.

HIS LAST ILLNESS AND DEATH.

BENGEL inherited a weakly constitution, and was always of delicate health. But, by the divine blessing, upon careful attention to it, he reached the age of sixty-five. He sometimes had dangerous illnesses, and felt more and more the frailty of his earthly tabernacle, especially in his later years. To a feeling of this sort we may ascribe a remark he made long before his last illness, that " the life of man is a constant tendency to death," (*perpetua tendentia ad mortem;*) but he gave full scope to his religious convictions, not wishing to hide from himself the thought of dying, but endeavouring to become familiar with it. And " as he did not consider theology to be a mere knowledge of the art of dying, so he held it to be the Christian's most important business to emerge from a state of sin to a confirmed state of grace; and herein to wait, not for death, but for the appearing of our Lord Jesus Christ. For he regarded death as only a thing by the way, and not properly a part of God's arrangement for man, because not originally such." Accordingly his whole spiritual life was so occupied with the consideration of our mortality, that it would be giving a very imperfect account of him not to notice how he endeavoured for years together to become familiar with the business of departure. Here then we may properly insert some extracts from his correspondence, in which may be discerned all along, from an early period of his life, the same feelings which he expressed at his last illness and death.

Writing to Marthius, as far back as in the year 1725, he says, " What if I should go before you, my dear friend, into the eternal world! When I was travelling last summer on a very windy day, upon a visit to my friend Weissensee, I experienced such a weakness in the head and stomach, as to have been in great danger of apoplexy. Having reached Boll, I was confined to bed, without any human adviser or any medical person near me that I could put confidence in; so that you may well imagine I must have had many a painful hour there. But it was a time for seeking the face of God. This I did; and he sent help from above. For immediately after I had been praying to him, it occurred to me that I ought to be satisfied with the nearest medical assistance I could procure, and that he could show his favour towards me just as well by a person of ordinary skill, as by one of the greatest repute. I therefore sent for one who lived close by; and as I had believed, so was it done unto me. I am now quite recovered, and at my work again, but longing and praying for the *rest* which remaineth to the people of God, whether I am to enter into it earlier or later. Indeed I have a foretaste of it already, in my daily employment."

"*Jan.* 2, 1727.

"Last Thursday I suffered violently from cholic and gravel. Some of the paroxysms were unusually severe; but at present I am without pain, and even indulge a hope that I shall continue so for a while. I am thankful to God for such chastenings, as well as for his previous and subsequent sparing mercy and help."

In November 1735, a serious epidemic prevailed; and Bengel himself began to suffer by it on the fourth of that month. But even after this disease had gained considerably upon him, he could not think it right to remain within doors, but continued to preach till after the sixth, when having delivered a sermon upon Matt. xviii. 20—35, "On the three sorts of reckoning which God makes with men," he became, as soon as the service was over, considerably worse. He had felt weaker while preaching; but had gone on with his sermon, because he was experiencing such spiritual joy, that he could gladly have died in the pulpit. During the fever he had strong delirium; but at intervals "endeavoured to collect his thoughts, that he might be in readiness for whatever his heavenly Father should appoint." His cousin, the Rev. Mr. Schmidlin, stood at his bedside, and heard him express himself as follows:—

"In my inward man, things go on by sudden impressions (celeres puncturas.) It often happens that all joy is denied me. I have frequently a deep and awful sense of eternity, unaccompanied by any immediate pleasure or pain. Neither bliss nor perdition are at the time in my thoughts, and yet the impression grows so awful that my mind is at length pained by it. A charming state of thought gleams at intervals, but soon leaves me. However, I try in quietness and composure to improve my small gifts (minutiæ); for I know that even with these I must be faithful. My mother has often given me a gentle rebuke for over-scrupulousness; saying, that if the main matter be attended to, all will be well. But I retreat behind some such arguments as the following. There are vegetables which would satisfy our absolute wants, just as they are gathered; but good housewives do not suffer them to come to table without a careful picking and cleansing. When a garment has ever so small a rent in it, neat persons will always get it repaired, though for its main use it might answer the purpose as it is."

On November 10, his remarks were continually upon the subject of death. He was cheerfully preparing himself by prayer for joining the church triumphant, and for being numbered with God's saints in glory everlasting. He was frequently breathing the words of the psalmist, "As the hart panteth after the water-brooks, so panteth my soul after thee, O God." Ps. xlii. "I have nothing," he said, "to detain me here; God only vouchsafe to open my eyes, reveal every thing to me, and make me perfectly humble and submissive to his will."

"I commit myself," he said, "to my faithful Creator, my intimate Redeemer, my tried and approved Comforter. I know not where to find any thing comparable to my Saviour. Only let *me* be made no account of, especially when I am gone. I wish my spiritual experience to be no more obtruded upon the world after my death, than it has been during my life. As 'man's judgment' can neither benefit nor hurt me, so things will appear in quite a different light at the great day. 'Judge nothing before the time.' Is it not better that it should be said to me in that day, 'Art *thou* also here?' than that it should be said, 'Where is such and such a renowned saint?' Much human infirmity still adheres in this life even to gracious characters. Let nothing be made of any expressions that I may happen to utter upon my death-bed. Jesus, with his apostles and martyrs, is light sufficient for all that survive me. I am no light. The example of a dying Christian in the present day, is for the benefit of his family in private; not for the gaze of the world. Human beings are often made too much of by one another, and things are cried up about them which turn out to be nothing at last. I can fully confide in pious persons, as such, however the world may despise them. But still they are creatures, and they are human; so that it seems impossible to confide to any one of them implicitly one's whole *self.* I delight to think of young and active disciples now engaged in the heat of the battle, many of whom were not born when I was in my vigour. I look upon myself as a tree decaying with age. My work on the Holy Scriptures, (Criticism of the New Testament,) it gives me pleasure to think of before the Lord, harsh as are the human judgments which it brings upon me from the good as well as the bad. The dawn of its future usefulness already rejoices my heart; posterity will have more light still, and will profit by it. Yet though my own mind were now full of the most important discoveries, it would not keep me a moment from wishing to go home."

He then mentioned his library, and said that "in the event of his death, he did not desire it to be reserved for the use of his children, but to be immediately arranged and disposed of; as there would soon be a great change in the state of literature, and that books of a quite different kind would make their appearance."

He again solemnly and affectingly expressed his lively confidence in the grace of Christ, and how he desired to depart and to be with Him. He prayed that God would not permit him to continue in the world *out of season,* but that, if a short time still remained to him for further usefulness, he might yet be spared, even should it be to outlive his family, and to see all his children pass over before him. Gen. xxxii. 23. But if the present were the best opportunity for his departure, he prayed that God would not permit it to go by."

On the 17th of November his friends thought his last moment arrived, and Schmidlin begged his parting blessing. But he replied, "It is not come to that yet, my dear cousin. I see clearly that I am at some distance from the haven, and shall be driven for a while out to sea again. I only pray God that my remaining days may not be useless, how little soever I may be able to do. But I will take courage; for little drops form abundant showers; single stones make up a fortification; and a stone itself is composed of small sand-grains, &c. The most important transactions of justice are not brought about by skill in jurisprudence, nor are the most heroic achievements wrought by the prowess of warriors, nor the most valuable remedies discovered by the genius of physicians; neither are the still more valuable healings of souls devised by the talents and acquirements of christian ministers. No; let every one do what he can, however little it may be. A gardener sows his little seed, or plants his little slip, &c. without knowing what it may come to, or whether it will come to any thing. So it is with all other human works. Only let every one faithfully, cheerfully, and without anxiety for the event, do whatsoever his hand findeth to do."

About the same time his friend Oetinger visited him; to whom he said, " Illnesses serve to quicken and enlarge us in spirit, after we have been dwindling (*quasi in flore interno*) like a bud that is slow in bursting into blossom and fragrance. When our spiritual lamp burns dimly, it is often because its wick needs retrenching; by which I mean those retrenchments that are made from time to time upon the outward man, by sickness and affliction. Thus our carnal encumbrances get removed by little and little, till they are totally and deservedly consumed. O what noble elevation, liberty, and ease do we experience, when we yield our hearts entirely to those gracious influences by which our heavenly Father of his own good pleasure draws us to Jesus Christ his Son; and which are always so exactly suited to the condition of each individual, that they may be readily and cheerfully complied with, and followed in preference to all human teaching and example, however good and excellent! With what safety and security are we guided by his eye, when we lay all our concerns before him, and submit them cordially and implicitly to him! How singly does that all-seeing eye aim at, and with what admirable simplicity does it direct us unto, whatever is good and profitable, not only to ourselves, but to many others at the same time with us! Holy Paul had not a more endeared associate than Timothy; and it is natural enough to ask, what was the favourite subject of communication between two such men of God. That apostle himself informs us what it was, when he sums up all at the close of his glorious course; and it is found to consist of faith, love, and hope. I own, that a congeniality of taste with the whole family of God has, by the simple use of Scripture, insensibly grown upon me; which saves me much troublesome inquiry and casuistry, and leads me off from many an elaborate definition upon a variety of very important subjects. I have now no need of these artificial processes. Set aside Divine revelation, and I have nothing left but natural elements, (theories originating in the reason of fallen *man*,) whereas, (I as a fallen man want help and information from *God*;) I want elements of information which are spiritual, influential, and practical. And very little of this kind is ever gained by all our human considerations and reasonings. It is a spirit of affectionate obedience actuating our every movement, that is the safeguard against error, and the immediate guide to truth."

"*Jan.* 1, 1741.

"I find myself awakened to circumspection much more by considering that I may have a little longer to live, than by thinking I may be just going to have done with this life. For what have I to do in the latter case except to fall at once into the arms of the divine mercy, in which I am constantly trusting that it will bring me through at last? But in the former case, I have still the duties of a steward to attend to; and, as 'it is required of a steward that he be found faithful,' I thus feel more impressively, while it lasts, the weight of my commission."

During one of his illnesses, Bengel, desiring consolation from some spiritual brother, and no one being at hand except a student of the Institution, he sent for such an one, and requested him to impart a word of consolation. The youth replied, "Sir, I am but a pupil, a mere learner; I don't know what to say to a teacher like *you*." "What!" said Bengel, "a divinity student, and not able to communicate a word of scriptural comfort!" The student, quite abashed and confused, then contrived to utter the following text, "The blood of Jesus Christ, the Son of God, cleanseth us from all sin." "That is the very word I want," said Bengel, "it is quite enough;" and, taking him affectionately by the hand, he dismissed him.

"*April* 14, 1742.

"How weary am I of the mere *letter*, as contradistinct to the *spirit* of what is good. Yes, how insipid and poor do I find every device and agency which originates in fallen man! Well; there is a particular pleasure in thinking we have advanced so far out of this mortal life, as to be subject to very few more of its changes and chances."

"*June* 25, 1742.

"How near do I seem to the time of putting off this frail tabernacle! In how many things was I busily engaged but a little while ago, and they are now gone by and done with for ever! The Lord bring us at length unto himself!"

"*March* 25, 1744.

"What a happiness should I think it to be allowed by my Redeemer soon to go home! There is nothing new in this world for me to live to see. I am quite tired of the works of men. I seek only to be found upright in heart before God. I have had enough of the world's honour and of the world's reproach."

"1745.

"Were it left to myself, I should choose Tübingen or Stuttgart for the place of my interment."

"*Aug.* 4, 1746.

"I feel in a manner satiated of this life. O, if my faithful God grant me only with this feeling a spirit of entire self-renunciation, all will be well. Probably I shall soon be ripe."

"1749.

"I am so weary of the mere learned world, that it is hardly with willingness that I do what is necessary in connexion with it; and which, after all, is but vanity. The nearer my advancing years bring me to the gate of eternity, the more gladly do I turn away from the exterior to the central matter, and look off from the means to the end and its enjoyment. At the same time, the more I retire from human celebrity, the more sweet do I experience the presence of God alone. Yes, he is to me more than all the learned world. But I discover that even yet I want more prudence and skill for eluding the praise of men. For while it flies from some who are so eager to pursue it, a light gale of it still overtakes myself, though it brings with it many an aspersion."

"*March* 6, 1749.

"Three times last year at Herbrechtingen, I was obliged to take to my couch; first about Easter; then on St. James's day; and lastly after the vintage. In the second of these illnesses, I was, to all human appearance, very near death; and, with my weak constitution and declining years, I still suffer many a shock. But under God's paternal care and direction, I am going on as usual, till he at length bring me to himself."

"*March* 4, 1752.

"During the first fortnight of February I was very ill with catarrhal fever, cholic, calculous hemorrhage, and other bad symptoms. But God has raised me up again, and, meanwhile, has given me a gentle intimation of going home; together with some anticipation of that right moment which, perhaps, will be rather sudden when it does arrive. Should he permit me to live a little longer, may he direct me to employ the interval to his glory, and in glorifying his Son Jesus Christ, our Lord, whose we are, whether living or dying!"

Bengel's final illness, says one of his cotemporaries, may be considered as having commenced with his sixty-sixth year, (June 24, 1752,) when he began to complain of loss of appetite, languor, pains in the body, and more evident waste of strength and animal spirits, occasioned by calculous disease, with frequent and violent perspirations. Early in October his debility and failure of appetite increased, without particular pain. But he all along endeavoured to rally for business in the consistory and synod, though, upon returning home, he became each time very drowsy, and spent most of the intermediate days in bed; till at length, sixteen days before his happy departure, a continual decrease of vital energy, with total loss of appetite, and other serious symptoms, confined him to his bed entirely. On the 26th of October, however, he said, "I do not think I shall have to close my eyes just immediately." But on the evening of Saturday the 28th, an abdominal inflammation commenced, which soon reached the chest; and, though he seemed relieved at intervals, the pulmonary oppression increased, attended by much suspense of circulation, and by general prostration of his remaining strength. But the more all bodily powers failed him, the more collected appeared those of his mind and spirit. This was manifest upon every occasion he had for showing it. His dying moments were now a faithful recapitulation of his whole life. He said but few words, but they were full of power and unction. Calm, serene, and silent, his soul reposed on God, that it might gather renewed strength for itself, and for strengthening even the souls of others who might need it. Carefully avoiding all distraction, his thoughts and feelings were perpetually rising and collecting in God. His countenance showed him engaged in continual prayer. Though he felt bound, he said, to utter from his heart whatever might occur to it, as likely to be of service to his friends around him, yet he must use brevity, that there might be less room for any objectionable thing to mingle with that quietness of spirit, which is, in the sight of God, of great price. And yet it seemed as if he had laid up a good treasure in his heart purposely to communicate it to his friends at his decease; for on this solemn occasion he addressed them with so many observations and such great power of spirit, that they felt the remembrance of it as long as they lived.

He had intended to partake of the Lord's Supper once more with his family in the collegiate church, but his illness increased too rapidly to allow him that gratification. He mentioned this the day before his death, and said he wished he could enjoy that ordinance once more with his family, should it please God to grant him the strength for it. It was suggested that it could easily be done in the sick chamber; and then twelve of his nearest relatives who were present, his children, grandchildren, and sons-in-law, with the venerable father and mother of his excellent wife, signified their readiness to solemnize such a holy communion with this dying father of the family. The proposal appeared much to delight and enliven him; and the following day (his last) was, by his own wish, appointed for the purpose. When the family were assembled on the occasion, Bengel, who at other times could hardly utter a few words connectedly, now, to the surprise of all present, poured forth such a full confession of his faith, accompanied with expressions of humiliation and prayer, as occupied quite half an hour; and such was its coherence and power of language, that it seemed quite extraordinary, nor could it seem any thing less. Every one in the room was touched by it to the heart in no common degree; and the recollection of it will be a comfort to them as long as they live. They only regretted their inability at the time to note down, for their own and others' benefit, those last words of this heavenly-minded man; such precious things were they which he then uttered, as one who had become very ripe in acquaintance with God. He seemed to forget nothing that was worth remembering. The prince, with his illustrious house, and then all the various departments of the government, were severally and affectionately commended by him to God, with thanksgiving for the blessings enjoyed by their means. Next, he prayed for the church; then, for his beloved country, and the provincial estates of the realm; then, descending to more private matters, he mentioned first the faithful partner of his life, then his children, grandchildren, sons-in-law, and all other relatives; then, those who were in union of spirit with him;

then all mankind. These were thankfully, tenderly, paternally and affectionately commended by him to the grace and blessing of God. Nor did he forget the minister who officially attended him; and into whose heart he trusted God had put some word of life which should benefit him in his last moments. When he had thus delivered the pious thoughts and wishes of his soul, he was responded to by all with a hearty Amen. Then some verses were sung from the hymn which begins, "O Jesu Christ, my purest light," &c. (from the Old Würtemberg Church Hymn-book, No. 161.) The confessions of the other communicants were next heard, and consolations administered from the word of God. Then the consecrated elements were delivered first to the dying father, to his almost heart-broken wife, to their sons, daughters, and other relatives, in succession. After this, two appropriate verses were sung from the hymn, "Who knows how near my end may be!" (No. 324,)—and so the solemn service was concluded. The whole scene was composing and yet most affecting; it appeared also very seasonably providential. A few hours afterwards the fever returned to its height, with much oppression of breath, and his spirit was forced back into its former stillness. In this state he remained supported by the word of God to the last moment; enjoying the prayers uttered beside him by his beloved sons-in-law and by his own children. On one occasion, however, he made the following remark: "We have not earned a stock of grace, but it is given out for our use as we want it. (Non mancipio gratia, sed usui data.) As for those who think they earn it, God is able to make them often feel very empty; and he means them no harm by it."

At the point of his departure, the following words were pronounced over him. "Lord Jesus, to Thee I live; to Thee I suffer; to Thee I die; THINE I AM, in death and in life; save and bless me, O Saviour, for ever and ever: Amen." Upon hearing the words, "*Thine I am*," he laid his right hand upon his heart; evidently signifying his full assent; and so he fell asleep in Jesus, on Thursday, the 2d of November, 1752, between the hours of one and two in the morning; having lived in this world sixty-five years four months and eighteen days.

The following remarks of Oetinger are worth inserting.

"Bengel departed agreeably to his own idea of prescribing no formal rules for the art of dying. He was occupied in the correction of his proof-sheets just as much at his dying season as he had ever been.* He did not wish to die in spiritual parade, but in the ordinary way; like a person called out to the street-door from the midst of his business. Hence we have no imposing particulars to relate concerning him. He received the Lord's Supper with his family, but took no formal leave of them. One remarkable thing he said was, that *he should for a while be forgotten, but afterwards come into remembrance.* And why should he not? Würtemberg has not yet produced another such a worthy; of course I mean just of *his* description. The Lord knoweth all them that are his; and it is he who appoints, and not we, the range which his saints shall severally occupy."

"His remains were deposited at Stuttgart, according to his own wish; and at his funeral, which was on Sunday, November 5, a sermon was preached in the hospital church, by Dr. W. G. Tafinger, collegiate minister, and counsellor of Consistory, from Heb. vii. 24, 25. 'Christ, who abideth for ever, hath an imperishable priesthood: wherefore also he is able to save to the uttermost (end of time), those who come unto God by him; seeing he ever liveth to make intercession for them.' This text was selected for the occasion, because the departed saint had said upon his death-bed, 'The ground I feel under me is this; that by the power of the Holy Ghost, I confide in Jesus as our everlasting High Priest, in whom I have all and abound.'"

The interest and sympathy excited every where by Bengel's departure, may be seen to this day from the number of elegiac pieces that were written on the occasion. Those which were printed, with the funeral discourse,† amount to no less than twenty-five. As a specimen of the feeling expressed by them all, we select that of Dr. John Philip Fresenius, senior minister of Frankfort, particularly as it contains such a true and striking outline of Bengel's real character.

* His German version of the New Testament, and the preface he wrote for the Old Testament Gnomon of his son-in-law, were then in the press.

† Printed at Stuttgart by John David Hallberger.

A PILLAR FALLS!

A LIGHT EXPIRES!

A STAR OF THE FIRST MAGNITUDE

WHICH

IN THE VISIBLE HEAVEN OF THE CHURCH

SHONE BRIGHTLY,

STOPS ITS COURSE,

WITHDRAWS,

AND MINGLES WITH THE SUPERIOR GLORY

OF THE SPIRITS MADE PERFECT.

BENGEL DIES!

AN ANGEL OF PEACE!

WHO WAS

AS PIOUS AS HE WAS INDUSTRIOUS,

AS CHILDLIKE AS HE WAS LEARNED,

AS RICH IN SPIRIT AS HE WAS ACUTE IN MIND,

AS HUMBLE AS HE WAS GREAT,

AS MODEST AS HE WAS CIRCUMSPECT

IN HIS WALK

AND BUSINESS

OF LIFE.

A FRIEND OF GOD EXPIRES!

WHOM THE ETERNAL WISDOM

HAD LED INTO

HER CHAMBERS.

TO HIM WERE OPENED

THE OUTGOINGS OF THAT LIGHT

WHICH ENLIGHTENS HUMAN MINDS;

THE POWERS OF THAT WORD

WHICH QUICKENS SOULS;

THE TREASURES OF THAT GRACE

WHICH ALLURES, LEADS, AND SAVES US.

THESE WERE OPENED TO HIM

MORE

THAN TO A THOUSAND OTHER SERVANTS OF THE LORD.

A GREAT SPIRIT LEAVES THE EARTH,

WHO,

WHETHER HE MEASURED THE HEIGHTS,

OR SOUNDED THE DEPTHS,

SHOWED HIMSELF EQUALLY GREAT.

THE MOST SACRED OF ALL BOOKS

WAS HIS INVALUABLE TREASURE.

HE NUMBERED AND PROVED

WORDS AND POINTS;

AND THE MOST ACUTE AND INTELLIGENT ADMIRED HIM.

HE VENTURED

INTO THE OBSCURER DEPTHS OF PROPHECY;

AND POSTERITY WILL BE ABLE TO JUDGE

TO WHAT EXTENT HE FOUND

FIRM FOOTING.

WHAT TO OTHERS SEEMED BUT DRY,

TO HIM WAS VERDURE:

WHAT APPEARS DESPISED BY THE MANY,

WAS TO HIM THE SOURCE OF LIGHT AND POWER,

SPIRIT AND LIFE.

HE WAS

EYES TO THE BLIND,

COUNSEL TO THE SEEING,

A LEADER TO THE WEAK,

A PATTERN TO THE STRONG,

A LUMINARY TO THE LEARNED,

AN ORNAMENT TO THE CHURCH.

A TREASURY IS CLOSED,

IN WHICH

THE LORD OF ALL THE TREASURES OF GRACE

HAD DEPOSITED

WONDROUS WEALTH

OF KNOWLEDGE AND WISDOM.

ONE STORE AFTER ANOTHER

WAS COMMUNICATED

BY HIM

FOR THE BENEFIT OF THE NEEDY,

AND OF THOSE WHO WISHED TO LEARN;

YEA, EVEN OFFERED TO A THANKLESS WORLD.

BUT NOW

ITS DOORS ARE SHUT!

ALAS! THAT THEY NO LONGER STAND OPEN!

WHY WAS IT NOT EMPTIED BEFORE?

WHY ARE SO MANY PRECIOUS THINGS CLOSED UP WITH IT?

WHY CLOSED UP,

WHEN THE FAITHFUL STEWARD

EVER STRETCHED OUT HIS READY HAND

TO BRING FORTH SOMETHING NEW OUT OF HIS TREASURE?

A TEACHER MIGHTY IN THE SCRIPTURES DEPARTS!

SIGH, YE INFANT CHILDREN,

YOUR FATHERS FALL ASLEEP,

AND THE CHILDREN ARE NOT ARRIVED AT MATURITY.

THE WORD ACCOMPANIED WITH POWER, WITHDRAWS,

AND FALSELY NAMED PHILOSOPHY SPREADS ABROAD!

THE KERNEL IS GONE,

AND THE HUSKS REMAIN BEHIND!

LORD! STOP THE PLAGUE

IN CHURCHES AND IN SCHOOLS!

LET WEISMANN'S SPIRIT,

LET BENGEL'S POWER,

SOON

AND IN DOUBLE PORTION

RETURN!

DEAR DEPARTED BENGEL!

THIS IS

MY OWN MEMORIAL OF LOVE,

AND

THE LAMENTATION OF THE CHURCH,

AND

THE WISH OF THE PIOUS.

THY PECULIAR DESERT

WILL THE COUNTRY THAT GAVE THEE BIRTH

FOR HER PART

MOURNFULLY REGRET

AND

EVER ADMIRE!

THE END.

Breinigsville, PA USA
05 November 2009
227132BV00003B/16/P

9 781597 521994